"Rich in resources and thorough in content, *The State of New Testament Studies* offers a vital resource for the new millennium. From sage established scholars and rising stars of the next generation readers learn the recent history of the field. These new vistas in methodology create fresh insights into and applications of the text. I will certainly put this into the hands of my students and keep it easily accessible for myself."

—**Amy Peeler**, Wheaton College

"What a remarkable achievement and welcome contribution! When I was finishing my PhD and applying for jobs, I devoured Osborne and McKnight's *The Face of New Testament Studies* to make sure I would have a general, up-to-date understanding of the parts of the New Testament that my own narrow research had inevitably missed. With that book as the original inspiration, McKnight and Gupta have gathered a thoughtful range of scholars to provide a needed, current 'state of the art' discussion of the New Testament. This will be a valuable resource for years to come."

—**Jonathan T. Pennington**, Southern Baptist Theological Seminary

"Sketching a generalized picture of the journey of New Testament scholarship to date is initially a daunting and precarious task. Yet these essays, by drawing on a breadth and depth of scholarship, by asking the right questions, and by curating new ones, have accomplished it superbly! This collection not only reminds Bible students of the need to rehearse, rethink, and re-evaluate the landscape of scholarly discourse in the field but also offers excellent critical resources to do so. Readers at all levels who value the importance of situating New Testament research on the historical bedrock of scholarly insight will find this compendium deeply satisfying."

—**Andrew Boakye**, University of Manchester

The State of New Testament Studies

The State of New Testament Studies

A Survey of Recent Research

Edited by
Scot McKnight
and Nijay K. Gupta

© 2019 by Scot McKnight and Nijay K. Gupta

Published by Baker Academic
a division of Baker Publishing Group
PO Box 6287, Grand Rapids, MI 49516-6287
www.bakeracademic.com

Printed in the United States of America

All rights reserved. No part of this publication may be reproduced, stored in a retrieval system, or transmitted in any form or by any means—for example, electronic, photocopy, recording—without the prior written permission of the publisher. The only exception is brief quotations in printed reviews.

Library of Congress Cataloging-in-Publication Data

Names: McKnight, Scot, editor.
Title: The state of New Testament studies : a survey of recent research / edited by Scot McKnight and Nijay K. Gupta.
Description: Grand Rapids : Baker Academic, a division of Baker Publishing Group, 2019. | Includes index.
Identifiers: LCCN 2019019621 | ISBN 9780801098796 (pbk.)
Subjects: LCSH: Bible. New Testament—Criticism, interpretation, etc.
Classification: LCC BS2361.3 .S73 2019 | DDC 225.6—dc23
LC record available at https://lccn.loc.gov/2019019621

ISBN 978-1-5409-6240-9 (casebound)

Scripture quotations labeled NRSV are from the New Revised Standard Version of the Bible, copyright © 1989 National Council of the Churches of Christ in the United States of America. Used by permission. All rights reserved.

Scripture quotations labeled CSB are from The Christian Standard Bible. Copyright © 2017 by Holman Bible Publishers. Used by permission. Christian Standard Bible®, and CSB® are federally registered trademarks of Holman Bible Publishers, all rights reserved.

Scripture quotations labeled ESV are from The Holy Bible, English Standard Version® (ESV®), copyright © 2001 by Crossway, a publishing ministry of Good News Publishers. Used by permission. All rights reserved. ESV Text Edition: 2016

Scripture quotations labeled NIV are from the Holy Bible, New International Version®. NIV®. Copyright © 1973, 1978, 1984, 2011 by Biblica, Inc.™ Used by permission of Zondervan. All rights reserved worldwide. www.zondervan.com. The "NIV" and "New International Version" are trademarks registered in the United States Patent and Trademark Office by Biblica, Inc.™

Scripture quotations labeled RSV are from the Revised Standard Version of the Bible, copyright 1946, 1952 [2nd edition, 1971] National Council of the Churches of Christ in the United States of America. Used by permission. All rights reserved worldwide.

In keeping with biblical principles of creation stewardship, Baker Publishing Group advocates the responsible use of our natural resources. As a member of the Green Press Initiative, our company uses recycled paper when possible. The text paper of this book is composed in part of post-consumer waste.

19 20 21 22 23 24 25   7 6 5 4 3 2 1

Contents

Acknowledgments x
Abbreviations xi

Introduction 1
Nijay K. Gupta and Scot McKnight

Part 1: Ancient Context

1. Early Christianity and the Roman Empire 9
   Greg Carey

2. Women in the Jewish, Greco-Roman, and Early Christian World 35
   Lynn H. Cohick

Part 2: Interpretation

3. Hermeneutics and Exegesis 63
   Dennis R. Edwards

4. The Old Testament in the New Testament 83
   Matthew W. Bates

5. The Genre of the Gospels 103
   Wes Olmstead

6. The Study of the Greek Language   120
   Dana M. Harris

Part 3: Jesus, Paul, and New Testament Theology

7. Jesus of Nazareth   139
   Rebekah Eklund
8. New Testament Christology   161
   David B. Capes
9. Paul, a Jew among Jews, Greeks, and Romans   182
   Michael F. Bird
10. Pauline Theology: *Perspectives, Perennial Topics, and Prospects*   197
    Michael J. Gorman
11. New Testament Eschatologies   224
    Patrick Mitchel
12. New Testament Ethics   253
    Nijay K. Gupta

Part 4: New Testament Texts

13. The Gospel of Matthew   275
    Rodney Reeves
14. The Gospel of Mark   297
    Jin Young Choi
15. The Gospel of Luke   315
    Drew J. Strait
16. The Gospel of John   334
    Alicia D. Myers
17. The Acts of the Apostles   350
    Joshua W. Jipp
18. Paul and Romans   368
    Scot McKnight

19. The Epistle to the Hebrews   389
    David M. Moffitt
20. The Epistle of James   407
    Mariam Kamell Kovalishyn
21. The Petrine Letters   425
    Abson Joseph
22. The Epistles of John   444
    Toan Do
23. The Book of Revelation   459
    Michael C. Thompson

Contributors   477

Scripture and Ancient Writings Index   479

Author Index   487

Select Subject Index   495

Acknowledgments

The inspiration for this book originally came from the 2004 Baker title *The Face of New Testament Studies*, edited by Grant Osborne and Scot McKnight. When I (Nijay) was in seminary, *The Face of New Testament Studies* helped me gain a better understanding of the landscape of New Testament studies. When I approached Scot with the idea of producing a similar volume for a new era of scholarship, he was eager to coedit this project with me. We are thankful for the support and feedback from editor extraordinaire Bryan Dyer and the rest of the Baker team. We also appreciate the almost two dozen contributors, New Testament scholars who lent their time and expertise to this project with commitment and enthusiasm.

Scot and I wish to dedicate this book to Grant Osborne, whom Scot knew personally as a teacher, colleague, and friend, and whom I knew through his enriching scholarship. We celebrate with this volume both the life and the scholarship of Grant.

Nijay K. Gupta and Scot McKnight

Abbreviations

General

b.	born	NPP	New Perspective on Paul
ca.	circa/about	NRSV	New Revised Standard Version
chap(s).	chapter(s)	NT	New Testament
esp.	especially	NTE	New Testament ethics
ESV	English Standard Version	OT	Old Testament
ET	English translation	par.	paragraph
Gk.	Greek	p(p).	page(s)
JT	Justification Theory	RSV	Revised Standard Version
LXX	Septuagint (Greek version of the Jewish Scriptures)	SBL	Society of Biblical Literature
NA^{28}	*Novum Testamentum Graece*, Nestle-Aland, 28th ed.	UBS^5	*The Greek New Testament*, United Bible Societies, 5th ed.
NIV	New International Version	v(v).	verse(s)

Deuterocanonical Works

1–4 Macc.	1–4 Maccabees	Sir.	Sirach
Jdt.	Judith	Tob.	Tobit

Old Testament Pseudepigrapha

Asc. Isa.	Martyrdom and Ascension of Isaiah 6–11	Let. Aris.	Letter of Aristeas
		Pss. Sol.	Psalms of Solomon
En.	Enoch	Sib. Or.	Sibylline Oracles
Jub.	Jubilees		

Dead Sea Scrolls and Related Texts

CD	Damascus Document	1QSa	Rule of the Congregation
DSS	Dead Sea Scrolls	4Q159	Ordinances
1QS	Rule of the Community		

Other Ancient Sources

Ag. Ap.	Josephus, *Against Apion*	Hist.	*Historiae*, various authors
Ant.	Josephus, *Antiquities of the Jews*	Hist. eccl.	Eusebius, *Ecclesiastical History*
Apol.	Aristides, *Apology of Aristides*	Inst.	Quintilian, *Institutio oratoria*
1 Apol.	Justin, *First Apology*	J.W.	Josephus, *Jewish War*
Haer.	Irenaeus, *Against Heresies*	Strom.	Clement of Alexandria, *Miscellanies*
Herm.	Shepherd of Hermas		

Secondary Sources

AB	Anchor Bible	BHTP	*Bibliotheca Historico-Philologico-Theologica*
ABRL	Anchor Bible Reference Library		
AGJU	Arbeiten zur Geschichte des antiken Judentums und des Urchristentums	BibInt	*Biblical Interpretation*
		BICS	*Bulletin of the Institute of Classical Studies*
AJEC	Ancient Judaism and Early Christianity	BIS	Biblical Interpretation Series
		BJS	Brown Judaic Studies
AJP	*American Journal of Philology*	BK	*Bibel und Kirche*
AnBib	Analecta Biblica	BSac	*Bibliotheca Sacra*
ANRW	*Aufstieg und Niedergang der römischen Welt: Geschichte und Kultur Roms im Spiegel der neuren Forschung*. Edited by Hildegard Temporini and Wolfgang Haase. Berlin: de Gruyter, 1972–	BTB	*Biblical Theology Bulletin*
		BTC	Brazos Theological Commentary
		BTCP	Biblical Theology for Christian Proclamation
		BWANT	Beiträge zur Wissenschaft vom Alten und Neuen Testament
		BZNW	Beihefte zur Zeitschrift für die neutestamentliche Wissenschaft
ANTC	Abingdon New Testament Commentaries		
AYB	Anchor Yale Bible Commentaries	CBET	Contributions to Biblical Exegesis and Theology
AYBRL	Anchor Yale Bible Reference Library	CBQ	*Catholic Biblical Quarterly*
		CBQMS	Catholic Biblical Quarterly Monograph Series
BBR	*Bulletin for Biblical Research*		
BDF	Friedrich Blass, Albert Debrunner, and Robert W. Funk. *A Greek Grammar of the New Testament and Other Early Christian Literature*. Chicago: University of Chicago Press, 1961	CBR	*Currents in Biblical Research*
		CC	*Corpus Christianorum*
		CCSS	Catholic Commentary on Sacred Scripture
		CH	*Church History*
		CIJ	*Corpus Inscriptionum Judaicarum*. Edited by Jean-Baptiste Frey. 2 vols. Rome: Pontifical Biblical Institute, 1936–52
BECNT	Baker Exegetical Commentary on the New Testament		
BETL	Bibliotheca Ephemeridum Theologicarum Lovaniensium		
		ConBNT	Coniectanea Biblica New Testament Series
BFCT	Beiträge zur Förderung christlicher Theologie	ConcC	Concordia Commentary

Abbreviations

DBSJ	*Detroit Baptist Seminary Journal*	JPTSup	*Journal of Pentecostal Theology Supplement Series*
DSE	*Dictionary of Scripture and Ethics*. Edited by Joel Green, Jacqueline Lapsley, Rebekah Miles, and Allen Verhey. Grand Rapids: Baker Academic, 2011	JR	*Journal of Religion*
		JRS	*Journal of Roman Studies*
		JSJ	*Journal for the Study of Judaism*
		JSJSup	*Journal for the Study of Judaism Supplement Series*
EBC	Expositor's Bible Commentary	JSNT	*Journal for the Study of the New Testament*
ECC	Eerdmans Critical Commentary	JSNTSup	*Journal for the Study of the New Testament Supplement Series*
ECIL	Early Christianity and Its Literature		
EDSS	*Encyclopedia of the Dead Sea Scrolls*. Edited by Lawrence H. Schiffman and James C. VanderKam. 2 vols. New York: Oxford University Press, 2000	JSPL	*Journal for the Study of Paul and His Letters*
		JSP	*Journal for the Study of the Pseudepigrapha*
		JTI	*Journal for Theological Interpretation*
EGGNT	Exegetical Guide to the Greek New Testament	JTS	*Journal of Theological Studies*
EJIL	Early Judaism and Its Literature	JVG	N. T. Wright, *Jesus and the Victory of God*
ETL	*Ephemerides Theologicae Lovanienses*	KEK	Kritisch-exegetischer Kommentar über das Neue Testament (Meyer-Kommentar)
EQ	*Encyclopaedia of the Qurʾān*. Edited by Jane Dammen McAuliffe. 6 vols. Leiden: Brill, 2001–6	LBS	Linguistic Biblical Studies
		LCL	Loeb Classical Library
		LEC	Library of Early Christology
ExpTim	*Expository Times*	LHBOTS	The Library of Hebrew Bible / Old Testament Studies
FBP	Fortress Bible Preaching Commentary	LNTS	The Library of New Testament Studies
FN	*Filologia Neotestamentaria*		
FRLANT	Forschungen zur Religion und Literatur des Alten und Neuen Testaments	*MdB*	*Le Monde de la Bible*
		NABPRSS	National Association of Baptist Professors of Religion Special Studies
HTR	Harvard Theological Review		
ICC	International Critical Commentary	NAC	New American Commentary
		NACSBT	New American Commentary Studies in Bible and Theology
Int	*Interpretation*		
JBL	*Journal of Biblical Literature*	NCBC	New Cambridge Bible Commentary
JBRec	*Journal of the Bible and Its Reception*	*Neot*	*Neotestamentica*
JECH	*Journal of Early Christian History*	NICNT	New International Commentary on the New Testament
JETS	*Journal of the Evangelical Theological Society*	NIGTC	New International Greek Testament Commentary
JFSR	*Journal of Feminist Studies in Religion*	NIVAC	NIV Application Commentary

NovT	*Novum Testamentum*	ScrHier	Scripta Hierosolymitana
NovTSup	Supplements to Novum Testamentum	SGBC	Story of God Bible Commentary
NSBT	New Studies in Biblical Theology	SHBC	Smyth & Helwys Bible Commentary
NTL	New Testament Library	SJ	Studia Judaica
NTM	New Testament Monographs	*SJT*	*Scottish Journal of Theology*
NTOA	Novum Testamentum et Orbis Antiquus	SNTSMS	Society for New Testament Studies Monograph Series
NTPG	N. T. Wright, *The New Testament and the People of God*	SP	Sacra Pagina
		StABH	Studies in American Biblical Hermeneutics
NTS	*New Testament Studies*	StBibLit	Studies in Biblical Literature
NTT	New Testament Theology	STDJ	Studies on the Texts of the Desert of Judah
ÖTK	Ökumenischer Taschenbuch-Kommentar		
PFG	N. T. Wright, *Paul and the Faithfulness of God*	*StudBT*	*Studia Biblica et Theologica*
		SubBi	Subsidia Biblica
PCNT	Paideia Commentaries on the New Testament	TBN	Themes in Biblical Narrative
		THNTC	Two Horizons New Testament Commentary
PNTC	Pillar New Testament Commentary		
		TJ	*Trinity Journal*
PRS	*Perspectives in Religious Studies*	*TS*	*Theological Studies*
		TTC	Teach the Text Commentary Series
RBL	*Review of Biblical Literature*		
RBS	Resources for Biblical Study	*TynBul*	*Tyndale Bulletin*
REC	Reformed Expository Commentary	*VC*	*Vigiliae Christianae*
		VIOTh	Veröffentlichungen des Instituts für Orthodoxe Theologie
RevQ	*Revue de Qumrân*		
RSG	N. T. Wright, *The Resurrection of the Son of God*	WATSA	What Are They Saying About Series
SANt	Studia Aarhusiana Neotestamentica	WBC	Word Biblical Commentary
		WMANT	Wissenschaftliche Monographien zum Alten und Neuen Testament
SBG	Studies in Biblical Greek		
SBLDS	Society of Biblical Literature Dissertation Series		
		WUNT	Wissenschaftliche Untersuchungen zum Neuen Testament
SBLMS	Society of Biblical Literature Monograph Series		
		WW	*Word and World*
SBLRBS	Society of Biblical Literature Resources for Biblical Study	ZECNT	Zondervan Exegetical Commentary on the New Testament
SBLSS	Society of Biblical Literature Semeia Studies		
SBLSymS	Society of Biblical Literature Symposium Series	*ZNW*	*Zeitschrift für die neutestamentliche Wissenschaft*
SBT	Studies in Biblical Theology		

Introduction

Nijay K. Gupta and Scot McKnight

I (Nijay) first encountered the book *The Face of New Testament Studies*, this book's predecessor, when I was in graduate school. I went to seminary primarily because I wanted to learn how to study the Bible in depth for personal and ministry formation. I had not studied the Bible in an academic setting prior to that. The "world" of biblical studies for this neophyte seminary student was intriguing but mystifying—so many technical terms, multiple differing perspectives, views, and ideas proposed and presented, and all of this was in flux as scholarship moved forward decade after decade. Thankfully, *The Face of New Testament Studies* (2004) gave me insight into the landscape of NT studies, provided some counsel on the key questions and issues under debate and showed me how different views go in different directions and why. Now, about fifteen years later, the landscape inevitably has changed. Not completely, of course. To play a bit more with the geographical metaphor, we can say that certain landmarks, oceans, and mountains will probably always be there, but some parts of this "world" have grown, others have eroded, and some have gone through a life cycle of destruction and renewal. This new volume, *The State of New Testament Studies*, has a similar objective for a new landscape of scholarship: to orient readers to the field of NT studies today. We have retained the basic structure of the earlier book, but all essays are freshly written by current experts, and we have expanded the scope of the project.

At the risk of oversimplification, we can trace at least six major trends in the current state of NT scholarship, tendencies and patterns noticeably demonstrated in many of the essays in this book.

Proliferation of Tools and Methods

The end of the last century saw a major increase of academic methods. Literary criticism, social-scientific criticism, rhetorical criticism, and sociopragmatics all added to the dominant historical-critical method. Now, in the late first quarter of the twenty-first century, we have even further proliferation of tools, methods, and perspectives. In many ways, this is salutary as biblical scholars learn from other disciplines. But it can also lead to microspecialization and minute fragmentation in the guild. Some of the program units at the annual meeting of the Society of Biblical Literature, for example, are very specific, and it is easy for scholars to focus on the "trees" without stepping back and getting a sense for the whole "forest." The PhD often forces scholars to become experts in a very narrow area, while teaching duties pull them out into broader topics in Bible and theology. Scholars have always performed this balancing act, but now they must travel further to "exit the forest," as it were. Thankfully, books such as this one serve as a handy map for eager and inevitably overwhelmed explorers![1]

Global and Diverse Perspectives

One of the major developments in biblical scholarship over the last fifteen years has been a move toward attention to and appreciation of global and diverse perspectives.[2] The facile notion of "objective reading" has been roundly refuted. Marginalized voices in reading and interpretation have been welcomed in the attempt to "triangulate" meaning (to borrow a helpful idea from my friend David deSilva). And one can easily see that this book has attempted to capture this value with our own group of contributors. And no doubt this value will continue to pervade biblical studies, especially as guild leadership becomes more diverse and global. Yet clearly some fields have not been penetrated as deeply by global and diverse scholarship.

Tending to Neglected NT Texts

One of the most obvious recent trends in NT studies is increased attention to historically neglected NT texts. It is obvious that Paul and the Gospels have received the lion's share of academic interest for several centuries, especially

---

1. On biblical studies methods and perspectives, see especially the essay by Dennis R. Edwards, chap. 3 of this volume.
2. See, e.g., Craig Keener and M. Daniel Carroll R., eds., *Global Voices: Reading the Bible in the Majority World* (Peabody, MA: Hendrickson, 2012).

since the Reformation and in Western Christianity. There are probably more academic books on Romans than on all the other NT books combined! But that tide is turning. Of course scholars are still fascinated with the theology of Paul and the life of Jesus, but Acts, Revelation, and the Catholic Epistles are now being studied much more.

Sophisticated Historical Contextualization

Biblical scholars are also much more attentive to reading NT books in their ancient context—that is, their Jewish, Greek, and Roman worlds. In the second half of the twentieth century, the study of early Judaism became a bona fide discipline. This has significantly expanded in the last several decades. We benefit today from expansive study of the Dead Sea Scrolls, critical Greek editions of almost all relevant Hellenistic Jewish literature, and fresh English translations of all of these texts—a privilege that would have been unimaginable a generation ago.[3]

Also, in the last few decades there has been a surging interest in reading the NT and understanding early Christian life within the Roman Empire—especially under imperial authority.[4] This has led to a brand-new subdiscipline in biblical studies called "empire studies."[5] Once upon a time, scholars tried to press Jesus or Paul into a Hellenistic or Jewish identity—because they were primarily focused on religious and philosophical influences, "Roman" was seemingly not an option. Now, scholars commonly see Jesus and the early church as part of a complex, pluricultural world with many influences—hence the Jew Paul writing in Greek to Jesus-followers in Rome. Again, now more than ever, NT scholars find themselves especially concerned with what archaeological news comes out of not only Jordan and Jerusalem but also Pompeii and Herculaneum, Ostia Antica, Ephesus, and Colossae.[6] They are learning from and partnering with departments of ancient Judaism, classics,

---

3. I (Nijay) remember an era when I had to use a Greek concordance of the OT Pseudepigrapha that was only in print (no digital, searchable version was widely available) and only in French (no English!). Now I have instant, searchable access in Greek and English through multiple software programs. I (Scot) remember when the OT Pseudepigrapha was available only to one who either had lots of money or easy access to a library, and I also remember the excitement of the steady publication of DSS.

4. See the essay by Greg Carey in chap. 1 of this book.

5. See Scot McKnight and Joseph Modica, eds., *Jesus Is Lord, Caesar Is Not: Evaluating Empire in New Testament Studies* (Downers Grove, IL: IVP Academic, 2013).

6. See, for example, Peter Oakes, *Reading Romans in Pompeii: Paul's Letter at Ground Level* (Waco: Baylor University Press, 2013); Michael Trainor, "Colossae: The State of Forthcoming Excavations," *JSPL* 1, no. 1 (2011): 133–35; Alan H. Cadwallader and Michael Trainor, eds., *Colossae in Space and Time: Linking to an Ancient City* (Göttingen: Vandenhoeck & Ruprecht, 2011).

and history. These are exciting times as we are able to piece together daily life in the first-century Roman world (education, religious experiences, politics, entertainment, etc.) better than ever, not only with attention to adult men but also to women and children.

Alongside this attention to historical context is an intense examination of Greek grammar and syntax, not to ignore the computer-generated tools now accessible, with regular publications and challenges to age-old paradigms.[7] Thinking of the developments in our understanding of the Greek language leads also to the recognition today of how the texts we read in the NT were performed to their original audiences, and performance criticism highlights the surge of interest in rhetorical criticism of the Pauline letters.[8]

Theological Interpretation of Scripture

Another major trend worth mentioning is the emergence of theological readings of Scripture.[9] Of course, over the last two thousand years some people have always been interested in reading the Bible for its theological messages and meaning. But particularly within the *academy*, for far too long the guild was divided between those who read it from a confessional perspective (i.e., Christians and Jews) and those whose interests were more cultural, ideological, and historical. Though it is hard to trace the origins of "theological interpretation of Scripture," it is now a major interest among many scholars, creating guild space for questions about the theological meaning and importance of the NT texts. This has obviously opened up fresh conversations between confessional and nonconfessional scholars; it has also turned attention to "precritical" literature on Scripture and prompted interest in the works of Catholic, Orthodox, Reformation, and Anabaptist theologians.

Looking to the Past

That brings us to a final trend in modern scholarship—special interest in reception history and history of interpretation of Scripture. Virtually all biblical scholars today readily admit that we read the NT not just off a page, but through lenses and traditions we have received from those who came before us. This helps modern readers better recognize our cultural biases and

---

7. See the essay by Dana M. Harris in chap. 6 of this book.
8. See, e.g., Ben Witherington III, *New Testament Rhetoric: An Introductory Guide to the Art of Persuasion in and of the New Testament* (Eugene, OR: Wipf & Stock, 2009).
9. See Kevin J. Vanhoozer, *Dictionary of Theological Interpretation of the Bible* (Grand Rapids: Baker Academic, 2005).

tendencies—not to erase them, but to appreciate this hermeneutical agency. This has brought new, or rather *old*, worlds to life so we can examine carefully how they read and interpreted Scripture. Obviously the global impact of the Bible over the last two millennia has been massive, but reception scholarship is interested not just in theologians and books but also in the Bible's impact on music, art, politics, and popular culture.[10]

In twenty-three chapters, the contributors to this book, all experts in their respective fields, survey the state of academic discussion with respect to their text or topic. Each chapter breaks the conversations into a few key headings with guidance on the most important contributions, controversies, and questions. At the end of each chapter you will find a set of reflections that sum up in brief the "state of New Testament studies" today.

---

10. A good example of this is David Gowler, *The Parables after Jesus: Their Imaginative Receptions across Two Millennia* (Grand Rapids: Baker Academic, 2017). European publisher de Gruyter is producing a nineteen-volume *Encyclopedia of the Bible and Its Reception* (2009–) with a projected total of thirty thousand entries.

PART 1

Ancient Context

1

Early Christianity and the Roman Empire

Greg Carey

Introduction

Jesus was "crucified for us under Pontius Pilate," according to the Nicene Creed, itself a product of Roman imperial politics. Facing intractable divisions among his Eastern churches, Emperor Constantine convened the first great ecumenical council in an attempt to restore unity to the church. The council produced this confession—a confession that identifies Rome with Jesus's public execution—with the emperor personally present during the deliberations.

The phrase "crucified for us under Pontius Pilate" embodies the ambiguity that marks early Christianity's relationship with Rome. Early Christians venerated a Jewish messiah who suffered execution at the hands of Roman authorities, a brutal fact that complicated all their attempts to establish public identity. The NT's three references to *Christianoi* (Acts 11:26; 26:28; 1 Pet. 4:16) do not indicate a new world religion populated by "Christians," as many of us might imagine. We might better translate *Christianoi* as "seditionists," or more precisely "messianists," for each occurrence indicates the suspicion with which others regarded the movement.[1]

---

1. See Craig S. Keener, *Acts: An Exegetical Commentary* (Grand Rapids: Baker Academic, 2013), 2:1847–50; David Horrell, "The Label *Christianos*: 1 Pet 4.16 and the Formation of Christian Identity," *JBL* 126 (2007): 361–81.

Jesus and his first generations of followers lived within the Roman Empire and faced the pressing question of allegiance. The three Synoptic Gospels all record a scene in which Jesus confronts the question of paying taxes to Caesar, and the Gospel passion narratives all raise the problem of Jesus's identity as king—or seditionist. Writing to Rome itself, Paul enjoins believers to submit to the ruling authorities in a passage that agitates Christian ethicists to this day (Rom. 13:1–7), but he also derides "the rulers of this age," who, had they grasped divine wisdom, "would not have crucified the Lord of glory" (1 Cor. 2:8). Addressing its readers as diasporic exiles (1:1) and foreigners (2:11), 1 Peter refers to Rome as "Babylon" (5:13). This usage emerges in Jewish literature only after Rome's sack of Jerusalem in 70 CE, and it appears in Revelation as well, most notably in chapters 17–18. Without question, Rome and its empire were on the minds of early Christian writers, not least in the NT. Yet it appears the first generations who worshiped Jesus developed complex and diverse—we might say, ambivalent—ways of relating to Rome and its institutions. Moreover, many interpreters have a great deal at stake in the question of how early Christians related to their imperial context.

The Stakes

We biblical scholars, who frequently cloak our passions in the language of academic objectivity, often reveal our commitments in assessing how early Christians negotiated their relationship to Rome. Those who are critical of American military, cultural, and economic adventurism—I would include myself among them—rely on Scripture as an essential resource for articulating our critiques.[2] In a classic essay on Paul and slavery, Richard A. Horsley gives voice to this point of view.

> [Paul] was evidently attempting to establish communities of what was, in effect, an international counter-imperial (alternative) society. It was international (and multicultural) insofar as assemblies were established in a number of cities and peoples, and as the assemblies in particular cities involved people of various and/or hybrid ethnic and cultural background. It was counter-imperial insofar as it owed its loyalty to Christ, who was enthroned in heaven as the true emperor or *kyrios* [Lord] of the assemblies, indeed of the world. . . . And it was an alternative society insofar as the assemblies were to conduct their own affairs, without interacting with the civil and other aspects of the dominant society

---

2. To cite one example, consider the title and subtitle of Richard A. Horsley, ed., *In the Shadow of Empire: Reclaiming the Bible as a History of Faithful Resistance* (Louisville: Westminster John Knox, 2008), to which I contributed an essay on Revelation.

while recruiting and expanding their movement . . . during the time remaining before the parousia of their Lord.[3]

Horsley foregrounds Paul's ministry in terms not of theology but of cultural formation. In contrast to Rome's lord, Caesar, Pauline assemblies proclaim the crucified messiah Jesus as the one true Lord. The movement expresses itself through diverse assemblies that scatter around the empire and practice "alternative" lifestyles as they await the culmination of Jesus's rule.

Interpreters of the historical Jesus have also maximized the ways in which Jesus's ministry amounted to countercultural resistance. Although many scholars produced important work in the 1990s, public attention focused on debates between John Dominic Crossan and N. T. Wright. Suspicious of the portrayal of Jesus in the canonical Gospels, Crossan argued that Jesus rejected apocalyptic theology, the expectation of God's violent intervention to remove Israel's enemies and establish justice in the world. Wright trusted the Gospel accounts and placed apocalyptic expectation at the center of Jesus's ministry. Crossan begins his account of Jesus with a study of Roman imperial culture, while Wright places Jesus in the context of anti-Roman sentiment in first-century Judaism. Theological liberals gravitated to Crossan's work, while conservatives rallied around Wright. Yet both authors agreed, and still agree, on the notion of Jesus's ministry as a form of critique and resistance against Rome. Both Crossan and Wright identify Jesus as a counterimperial revolutionary.[4]

Crossan, who is Irish-American, and Wright, who is English, were writing at a particular point in American adventurism. With the Cold War drawing to a close, a congressional investigation had just unraveled Reagan administration interventions in Central American civil wars, and US forces had successfully invaded both Panama and Grenada. Francis Fukuyama authored his classic essay "The End of History?," arguing that the Soviet Union's dissolution would open the path for universal democracy and the end of large-scale conflict.[5] The same year that Crossan and Wright published their first major monographs on the historical Jesus, President George H. W. Bush declared "a new world order" in his State of the Union address. Theorists rushed to redefine the concept of empire from a nation-state model to more abstruse networks of commercial and diplomatic

3. Richard A. Horsley, "Paul and Slavery: A Critical Alternative to Recent Readings," *Semeia* 83/84 (1998): 176.
4. John Dominic Crossan, *The Historical Jesus: The Life of a Mediterranean Jewish Peasant* (San Francisco: HarperSanFrancisco, 1991); N. T. Wright, *Jesus and the Victory of God* (Minneapolis: Fortress, 1991).
5. Francis Fukuyama, "The End of History?," *The National Interest* 16, no. 3 (1989): 3–18.

hegemony.⁶ If ever the United States looked like an empire, this was the moment.

Before launching into an investigation of Christian identity in the context of empire, we do well to consider some unanticipated implications.⁷ For example, a predisposition to identify with early Christianity as a counter-imperial movement can foster a peculiar exceptionalism. As assemblies who sometimes considered themselves at odds with the larger society—"aliens and exiles," as 1 Peter would have it (2:11), and a "third race," in the words of Aristides (*Apol.* 2.1), Clement of Alexandria (*Strom.* 6.5.41), and others—Christians defined themselves as neither Jews nor Greeks nor anything else.⁸ We Christians already have a long habit of labeling our origins as exceptional or unique.⁹ Assessing appropriations of early Christian identity in the context of queer theory, Maia Kotrosits observes, "The queer 'early Christian' is positioned—almost by definition—as out of alignment with and even in opposition to the Roman Empire in some way."¹⁰ Appeals to Christian uniqueness have a way of turning ugly. To take one particularly dangerous example, Christian anti-Judaism often expresses itself in critiques of ancient Judaism as exclusionary, formulaic, legalistic, misogynist, and lacking in grace. What if, instead of emphasizing uniqueness, we also called attention to the ways in which Christians imbricated themselves into their cultural contexts just as their neighbors did—and just as we all do?¹¹

Practicing Empire

Appreciation for Jewish history is essential for understanding early Christian engagement with Roman hegemony.¹² Ancient Israel and Judah encountered several ancient empires. The four beasts of Daniel 7:1–8 characterize four

---

6. Michael Hardt and Antonio Negri, *Empire* (Cambridge: Harvard University Press, 2000).

7. As we have seen, the term *Christian* applies to the Pauline assemblies and other circles of Jesus devotees only anachronistically. I use it pragmatically as convenient shorthand for those groups. Within the NT, *Christian* is not a self-designation but an accusation on the part of outsiders. We do see traces of *Christian* identity in Matthean references to "their synagogues" (esp. 10:17), the language of churches (*ekklēsiai*), and in Paul's language of being "in Christ."

8. Judith Lieu, *Neither Jew Nor Greek? Constructing Early Christianity*, 2nd ed. (London: Bloomsbury T&T Clark, 2016), 72.

9. Maia Kotrosits, *Rethinking Early Christian Identity: Affect, Violence, and Belonging* (Minneapolis: Fortress, 2015), 51–53.

10. Kotrosits, *Rethinking Early Christian Identity*, 51.

11. See Douglas Boin, *Coming Out Christian in the Roman World: How the Followers of Jesus Made a Place in Caesar's Empire* (New York: Bloomsbury T&T Clark, 2014); Greg Carey, *Sinners: Jesus and His Earliest Followers* (Waco: Baylor University Press, 2009), 125–50.

12. As with *Christian* and *Christianity*, many interpreters regard *Jewish* and *Judaism* as anachronistic. I do not.

empires as monstrous predators: Babylon, Media, Persia, and the Hellenistic Seleucid Empire. Revelation later draws on these same beasts, rolling them all into a single monster in its characterization of Rome (13:1–2).

This Seleucid Empire, particularly under the reign of Antiochus IV (Epiphanes), proves a crucial antecedent to the Roman Empire. The Seleucid dynasty inherited a major portion of the empire established by Alexander the Great. It is all but impossible to reconstruct Antiochus's motives and behaviors,[13] but for our purposes what matters more is how Jews—both contemporaneous and in later generations—interpreted his reign and the conflicts it engendered. As our sources remember it, Antiochus embarked on a project of Hellenization in Judea and Galilee, promoting Greek language and cultural institutions as a means of unifying his empire. He established a cult of Zeus in the Jerusalem temple. When some Judeans rejected Antiochus's reforms in 167 BCE, Antiochus responded with repression. Jewish tradition has it that Antiochus banned Jewish practices, forbidding circumcision and forcing Jews to eat pork. Such religious oppression would have been highly unusual—if not unique—in the ancient world, and historians rightly question whether our primary sources fairly characterize Antiochus.[14] Nevertheless, the ensuing revolt led to Antiochus's expulsion from Judea in 164 BCE and a more decisive overthrow of Seleucid power in 142 BCE. The following eighty years witnesses waxing and waning levels of Judean independence, including rule by indigenous priest-kings. We should note that while some Judeans resisted Antiochus, others took a more accommodationist stance. These "renegades" function as villains in Jewish memory.

Far clearer than the history is how the conflict with Antiochus stamped itself on Jewish modes of self-understanding and of the relationships between Judaism and empire. For one thing, the Maccabean Revolt had been successful, encouraging hopes of resistance among later generations. Moreover, three pillars of Jewish identity—diet, Sabbath, and circumcision—acquired even greater weight. The tradition links faithfulness to these identity markers as a cause for martyrdom. Thus we should not be surprised by the degree to which Paul's letters reflect concerns over precisely these three items. As gentiles entered the churches, conflicts regarding these issues marked much of his ministry (see Rom. 13–15; 1 Cor. 8:1–13; 10:1–22; all of Galatians; Phil. 3:2–4:1). The Antiochene crisis set up cultural

---

13. As one example of a historian sifting through the problems, see David A. deSilva, *Introducing the Apocrypha*, 2nd ed. (Grand Rapids: Baker Academic, 2018), 271–86. Taking a more trusting attitude toward the Jewish primary sources is Anathea Portier-Young, *Apocalypse against Empire: Theologies of Resistance in Early Judaism* (Grand Rapids: Eerdmans, 2011), 176–216.

14. Steven Weitzman, "Plotting Antiochus' Persecution," *JBL* 123 (2004): 219–34.

behavior, what we moderns might call religious faithfulness, as a life-and-death issue.

Rome played a prominent role in the conflicts attending Antiochus's reign, but Judea experienced Roman power most directly in 63 BCE. Invited to intervene by both parties of a Judean civil war, the Roman administrator/general Pompey captured Jerusalem and subjected it to direct Roman rule. Roman rule over Judea, Samaria, Galilee, Idumea, Perea, and other areas continued with notable interruptions throughout the early Christian period.

The NT introduces us to a small cast of Roman authorities and to Judeans who hold various kinds of power under Roman hegemony. Herod the Great appears in Matthew's Gospel. Herod was appointed "King of the Jews" by the Roman Senate, having driven Parthian forces from the land, and he administered the region from 37 BCE until 4 CE. Herod is noted for his monumental building projects, most notably a glorious refurbishing and expansion of the Jerusalem temple, and for his ability to sustain peace in the land and a flow of tribute to Rome. After his death the Romans divided the region into smaller administrative districts. In the Gospels we meet Herod's son Herod Antipas, who governed Galilee and Perea until 39 CE, and Pontius Pilate, the Roman prefect of Judea from 26 to 37 CE. Acts introduces us to Herod Agrippa I (called simply "Herod")—who first governed Galilee (37–41 CE), then came to rule over all of Palestine (41–44 CE)—and Herod Agrippa II ("Agrippa" in Acts), who reigned over various parts of Palestine over a long period of time (48–93 CE). We meet Antonius Felix, Roman procurator of Judea from 52 to 58 CE, who is characterized as corrupt (Acts 24:24–27), and his successor, Porcius Festus (59–62 CE). We also encounter the high priests Annas and Caiaphas, who administered Jerusalem and the temple under Roman supervision during the career of Jesus, and Ananias, who confronts the apostle Paul.

Classic empires projected force in order to extract resources from their territories and to enforce their will within their spheres of influence. The Romans did so as well. Social historian and theorist Michael Mann describes Rome as the first successful territorial empire, exerting control through its military and by enlisting the cooperation of indigenous elites through its class culture.[15] When Revelation presents Rome as a fearsome monster, the whole earth cries out in wonder, "Who is like the beast, and who can fight against it?" (13:4). But Revelation also points out Rome's acquisitiveness. A Prostitute rides the Beast, and she conducts commerce with kings, merchants, and sailors. The merchants grieve Rome's destruction because it puts an end to their commercial

---

15. Michael Mann, *The Sources of Social Power*, vol. 1, *The History of Power from the Beginning to AD 1760* (New York: Cambridge University Press, 1986), 250.

system. "And the merchants of the earth weep and mourn for her, since no one buys their cargo anymore, cargo of gold, silver, jewels and pearls, fine linen, purple, silk and scarlet, all kinds of scented wood, all articles of ivory, all articles of costly wood, bronze, iron, and marble, cinnamon, spice, incense, myrrh, frankincense, wine, olive oil, choice flour and wheat, cattle and sheep, horses and chariots, slaves—and human lives" (18:11–13). Luxury items come first and foremost in this list of commodities, along with implements of war[16] and slaves. The Greeks and Romans transformed the ubiquitous practice of slavery into the basis of their economies.[17] Perhaps 20 percent of the empire's population was enslaved,[18] maybe as many as half the people in major cities. In his treatise *On Clemency* the Roman politician and philosopher Seneca recalls how the Senate considered a proposal to require slaves in the city to wear clothing that indicated their status. Once the Senate realized that the measure might reveal how many slaves lived in the city, perhaps inspiring revolt, it was dismissed as imprudent (1.24.1).

Various forms of taxation sent revenue from ordinary people to local elites and then to Rome. Indeed, the Romans did find it necessary to calculate just how much they could extract from subjected peoples without either exhausting their resources or provoking rebellion. "I want my sheep shorn, not shaved," Tiberius reportedly scolded one prefect.[19] Juvenal, perhaps not so satirically, advises new governors to curb their greed, rather than sucking dry the marrow of their client kings.[20]

The Romans themselves understood how deeply their underlings resented them. The historian Tacitus depicts a speech, albeit fictional, by the British general Calgacus against the Romans: "To plunder, butcher, steal, these things they misname empire. They make a desolation and call it peace."[21] Likewise Sallust imagines a letter from Mithridates of Pontus to the Persian emperor. The Romans make war only for the sake of dominion and self-enrichment (*Hist.* 4.69.5). Are you not aware, Mithridates asks, "that from the beginning they have possessed nothing but what they have stolen: their homes, wives,

---

16. Horses and chariots primarily served military purposes in the ancient world.

17. S. Scott Bartchy, "Slaves and Slavery in the Roman World," in *The World of the New Testament: Cultural, Social, and Historical Contexts*, ed. Joel B. Green and Lee Martin McDonald (Grand Rapids: Baker Academic, 2013), 169.

18. Bartchy, "Slaves and Slavery," 170.

19. Dio Cassius, *History of Rome* 57.10, cited in Neil Elliott, *The Arrogance of Nations: Reading Romans in the Shadow of Empire* (Minneapolis: Fortress, 2008), 31.

20. Following Elliott, *Arrogance of Nations*, 31, who quotes Juvenal, *Satire* 8.87–90 (LCL). I am drawing from the language of A. S. Kline, *Juvenal: The Satires*, http://www.poetryintranslation.com/klineasjuvenal.php.

21. Tacitus, *Agricola* 30.4, quoted in Bruce W. Longenecker, "Peace, Prosperity, and Propaganda: Advertisement and Reality in the Early Roman Empire," in *An Introduction to Empire in the New Testament*, ed. Adam Winn (Atlanta: SBL Press, 2016), 41.

land, and dominion?" (*Hist.* 4.69.17 LCL).[22] One imagines the Romans found amusement in such fictional characterizations of themselves.

Nevertheless, living standards rose when empire flourished: even in the provinces, standards of living seem to have increased.[23] Former generations of scholars argued that taxation from Rome and Jerusalem impoverished ordinary people in Judea and Galilee, displacing many from their homes, but that view has not withstood scrutiny.[24] Economic grievances indeed contributed to the First Jewish Revolt of 66–70 CE.[25] But many scholars would also argue that societies flourished under Roman domination. People of my generation recall the "What Have the Romans Ever Done for Us?" scene in the 1979 Monty Python film, *Life of Brian*. Inciting rebellion, Reg declaims: "They've bled us white, the bastards. They've taken everything we had, and not just from us, from our fathers, and from our fathers' fathers. And what have they ever given us in return?" Things begin to go downhill, as characters recite the benefits of empire: "The aqueduct." "And the sanitation." "And the roads."

"Well, yeah. Obviously the roads. I mean, the roads go without saying, don't they? But apart from the sanitation, the aqueduct, and the roads. . . ."

"Irrigation."

"Medicine."

"Education."

"And the wine."

"And it's safe to walk in the streets at night now, Reg."

"Yeah, they certainly know how to keep order. Let's face it. They're the only ones who could in a place like this."[26]

Whatever its marks for historical accuracy, the scene depicts the dilemma that Rome's subjects faced. At the price of subjugation and exploitation, Rome promised peace, development, and even a measure of freedom. Revelation is the NT's most unambiguous anti-Roman voice, but it also reveals the loyalty of local elites to Roman beneficence. Roman Asia enjoyed a strong reputation for its demonstrations of loyalty, particularly by petitioning the Senate for the right to build temples and hold festivals in honor of the empire and the emperor. Revelation 13 depicts this reality: a Second Beast from the

---

22. Quoted in Longenecker, "Peace, Prosperity, and Propaganda," 42.

23. Mann, *Sources of Social Power*, 1:265–67.

24. David J. Downs, "Economics, Taxes, and Tithes," in Green and McDonald, *World of the New Testament*, 160–66.

25. Samuel L. Adams, *Social and Economic Life in Second Temple Judea* (Louisville: Westminster John Knox, 2014), 180–81; Eric M. Meyers and Mark A. Chancey, *Alexander to Constantine: Archaeology of the Land of the Bible*, AYBRL (New Haven: Yale University Press, 2012), 140.

26. *Monty Python's Life of Brian*, directed by Terry Jones (London: HandMade Films / Warner Bros. Pictures, 1979).

land encourages the inhabitants of the earth to worship the Beast, Rome—a likely indication of indigenous appreciation for Rome's benefits and loyalty to its emperor.[27] Such devotion was neither required nor directly rewarded; rather, it was characterized by "spontaneity and autonomy."[28]

Not everyone celebrated Rome's provision of stability and commerce. Rome devoted a great deal of attention to the threat of rebellion. Indeed, the great Jewish Revolt was one of four simultaneous rebellions within the empire. And some rebellions were successful.[29] Roman provincial administrators found themselves tugged between their duty to provide stability and revenue on behalf of Rome and the necessity to maintain decent relationships with their subjects. Judea and Galilee are especially important to early Christian interaction with Rome, largely because Jesus's crucifixion occurred under Roman authority and because the catastrophic First Jewish Revolt casts a strong shadow on the Gospels and other parts of the NT. Ordered by Emperor Caligula to set up a statue to the emperor in the Jerusalem temple, the governor of Syria, Publius Petronius, pleaded to the populace: "I, too, am bound to obey the law of my master. . . . I myself, just like you, must submit to orders" (Josephus, *Ant.* 18.265 LCL). When Petronius delayed in executing this command, legend has it that Caligula ordered him to commit suicide, but in January 41 CE Caligula himself was assassinated while the order was en route (*J.W.* 2.184–203).[30] Numerous NT scenes allude to this same tension. Most notable are the Gospel portrayals of Pontius Pilate trying to placate the crowds rather than crucify Jesus. We might also consider the numerous trial scenes in Acts, especially the ones involving Roman officials like Gallio (Acts 18:12–17), Felix (24:1–27), Festus (25:1–12), and Agrippa (25:13–26:32).[31] The Gospels mention *sicarii* and zealots, and of course the catastrophic First Jewish Revolt (66–70 CE) shadows how the Gospels, Acts, and some other NT books look on the empire.

Resistance to Rome occurred for cultural and religious as well as economic reasons. The Jewish rebel/historian Josephus records several outbreaks of resistance prior to the First Jewish Revolt, many of which involved what we

---

27. J. Nelson Kraybill, *Apocalypse and Allegiance: Worship, Politics, and Devotion in the Book of Revelation* (Grand Rapids: Brazos, 2010), 139–55; Steven J. Friesen, *Imperial Cults and the Apocalypse of John: Reading Revelation in the Ruins* (New York: Oxford University Press, 2001).

28. Karl Galinsky, *Augustan Culture* (Princeton: Princeton University Press, 1996), 325.

29. Martin Goodman, "Enemies of Rome," in *The Roman Empire: Economy, Society and Culture*, ed. Peter Garnsey and Richard Saller, 2nd ed. (Berkeley: University of California Press, 2015), 56–57.

30. Christopher J. Fuhrmann, *Policing the Roman Empire: Soldiers, Administration, and the Public Order* (New York: Oxford University Press, 2011), 171.

31. Matthew L. Skinner, *The Trial Narratives: Conflict, Power, and Identity in the New Testament* (Louisville: Westminster John Knox, 2011).

might call cultural, even religious, grievances as well as responses to perceived Roman provocations. Apart from Jesus, several other would-be messiahs, acclaimed or self-proclaimed, emerged during the first century. Nor was cultural resistance to Rome unique to Galilee and Judea, being especially prominent in the East, where hellenization had taken root. But widespread, unified, anti-Roman sentiment apparently did not emerge.[32] Rebellion did not extend beyond the local and the ethnic.

Proving Empire

The maintenance of empire demands significant energy, and not just commercial, administrative, and military. Empires generally find it necessary to justify their existence and promote their benefits. Certainly Rome did. We know this legitimation process as imperial propaganda.[33]

Historiography, the kind that blurs the mythological with the legendary, provided a key vehicle for Roman legitimation. *The History of Rome* by Titus Livius traces Rome back to the Trojan Aeneas and identifies its founder as Aeneas's descendant Romulus. So does Virgil's *Aeneid*, also composed under Augustus's reign. Details vary from one source to another. Nevertheless, the larger picture clusters around (1) Aeneas's military prowess and his destiny to found a great nation and (2) Romulus's violent rise to power, along with (3) rumors that Romulus was the son of Mars, the god of war. Romulus kills his own brother in a dispute concerning where to establish the new city, shouting, "So perish anyone else who shall leap over my walls."[34] In the *Aeneid* Jupiter speaks of the Romans what they already believe about themselves: "I have no fixed boundaries to the dominions, no fixed term to their rule. I have given them empire without end. [The gods will show] favor to the Romans, masters of the world, the people of the toga. This has been decreed" (1.278–83).[35] To build, fight, conquer, and dominate: that is Roman Manifest Destiny.[36]

The Romans likely produced their foundation narratives to form their own sense of identity, not to persuade others. But they also relied heavily on imperial propaganda promoted by those they had conquered. The massive

---

32. Jesper Majbom Madsen, "Intellectual Resistance to Rome and Its Hegemony," in *Rome and the Black Sea Region*, ed. Tonnes Bekker-Nielsen (Aarhus, DK: Aarhus Universitetsforlag, 2006), 63–82.

33. For concise introductions to Roman propaganda, see Longenecker, "Peace, Prosperity, and Propaganda"; John Dominic Crossan, "Roman Imperial Theology," in Horsley, *In the Shadow of Empire*, 59–73.

34. Mary Beard, *SPQR: A History of Ancient Rome* (New York: Norton, 2015), 56–59.

35. Translation by Longenecker, "Peace, Prosperity, and Propaganda," 20–21.

36. Davina C. Lopez, *Apostle to the Conquered: Reimagining Paul's Mission* (Minneapolis: Fortress, 2008), 56–118.

building projects of Herod the Great, all sorts of projects—including a spectacular renovation of the temple—reflected Roman architectural models.[37] Herod named his greatest city Caesarea and his Jerusalem fortress Antonia.[38] As Eric Meyers and Mark Chancey put it, "Anyone who saw [Caesarea] from sea or land would associate it with Caesar and witness the visual grandeur of the Roman Empire as well as the loyalty of one of its most prominent client kings."[39]

Rome happily installed self-congratulatory propaganda throughout its empire, and indigenous elites reinforced the message. Copies of Augustus's "Deeds of the Divine Augustus" (*Res gestae divi Augusti*) have been identified all over the empire, often inscribed in monumental buildings in both Greek and Latin. In preparation for his own death, Augustus praises both his conquests and his beneficence. If modern standards of modesty do not apply to ancient emperors, Augustus could also rely on local support. In 29 CE the province of Asia promised a crown "for the person who devised the greatest honors for the god" Augustus.[40] One Greek inscription notes that Augustus, "son of God," "has by his benefaction to all people outdone even the Olympian Gods" (I. Olympia 53). Better known is the Priene Inscription, which proclaims Augustus's birthday as the new New Year's Day, attributes Augustus's accomplishments to providence, and identifies Augustus as the savior who fulfills prophecy and brings peace.[41] Christians will recognize in the inscription the Greek terms *epiphanēs* (epiphany), *sōtēr* (savior), and *euangelion* (often translated "gospel"). Indeed, Rome promoted its own eschatology, contemporaneously naming Augustus's reign a "golden age."[42] As we have seen, Greek cities literally competed for the privilege of expressing their devotion to emperor and empire through the dedication of temples and festivals.

Rome extended its marketing campaign in images as well as words—and in the combination of the two. Early coins in Roman Corinth blend Roman and Greek motifs, placing an image of Julius Caesar on one side and Bellerophon riding Pegasus on the other.[43] Roman coins frequently depict the deities Mars and Victoria, war and victory, together.[44] After vanquishing the First Jewish

---

37. Meyers and Chancey, *Alexander to Constantine*, 51–52.
38. Meyers and Chancey, *Alexander to Constantine*, 54.
39. Meyers and Chancey, *Alexander to Constantine*, 63.
40. Galinsky, *Augustan Culture*, 324.
41. For discussion of these oft-cited primary sources, see Longenecker, "Peace, Prosperity, and Propaganda," 17–19; Elliott, *Arrogance of Nations*, 29.
42. Galinsky, *Augustan Culture*, 90–121.
43. Carla Swafford Works, *The Church in the Wilderness: Paul's Use of Exodus Traditions in 1 Corinthians*, WUNT 2/379 (Tübingen: Mohr Siebeck, 2014), 22.
44. Wes Howard-Brook and Anthony Gwyther, *Unveiling Empire: Reading Revelation Then and Now* (Maryknoll, NY: Orbis, 1999), 228–29.

Revolt, the Romans issued an "extensive" series of *Judaea Capta* coins, all attesting to Roman domination over the Jewish people.[45] Roman sculpture and coinage frequently show powerful Roman men physically threatening partially (or totally) exposed foreign women, an artistic interpretation of conquest as rape. Davina C. Lopez captures the pattern: the women as "embattled, disheveled, captured and subdued, and shown in deferent line."[46] The Altar of Peace (*Ara Pacis*) shows the goddess Roma holding a sword and sitting on the weapons of Rome's vanquished enemies.[47] Roman peace proceeds from conquest.

The Persecution Question

Every significant layer of the NT, along with a great deal of other early Christian literature, features a preoccupation with the likelihood of persecution. Paul identifies himself as both a persecutor (1 Cor. 15:9; Gal. 1:13, 23; Phil. 3:6) and a victim of persecution (1 Cor. 4:12; 2 Cor. 4:9; 11:23–26; 12:10; Gal. 5:11). He also shows awareness that early Christian communities were vulnerable to persecution (Rom. 12:14; Gal. 6:12; 1 Thess. 2:14–16; 3:4, 7). We must assume that Paul's references to imprisonment, or "chains," also indicate persecution (Rom. 16:7; 2 Cor. 6:5; 11:23; Phil. 1:7, 13–17; Philem. 1, 9, 23). A brief review of allusions to persecution in Paul's undisputed letters alone reveals his intense awareness of the persecution he faces along with his colleagues. Unfortunately, we cannot know the actual reasons Paul persecuted Christian believers, who were almost assuredly other Jews, or why he and others experienced persecution.[48] He alludes to persecution both from fellow Jews and from gentiles (2 Cor. 11:26). Unfortunately, he never discloses the exact nature of the persecution he describes or the authority under which it occurred. This omission leaves open the question of whether Roman authorities were involved.

The canonical Gospels include diverse warnings regarding the likelihood of persecution. While Paul identifies specific forms of persecution, such as flogging and imprisonment, attended by the possibility of execution, the Greek word *thlipsis* can indicate simple hardship. Yet the Synoptic Jesus identifies such hardship as a condition of discipleship and warns his followers that they will face a fate like his (Matt. 10:17–18; 24:9; Mark 13:9–11; Luke 21:12–19). The Synoptic "little apocalypses" (Matt. 24; Mark 13; Luke 21) alert readers

---

45. See the discussion in Lopez, *Apostle to the Conquered*, 35–38.
46. Lopez, *Apostle to the Conquered*, 50.
47. Kraybill, *Apocalypse and Allegiance*, 59.
48. Calvin Roetzel, *Paul: The Man and the Myth* (Minneapolis: Fortress, 1999), 38–42.

to the inevitability of end-time persecution. As for John's Gospel, following Jesus leads to expulsion from the synagogue (9:22; 12:42; 16:2): because such an action is implausible within the context of Jesus's own ministry, scholars have expended enormous energy in attempting to explain it.[49] Near John's conclusion, Jesus informs Peter as to the manner of the apostle's death (21:18–19), a passage cryptic to modern readers but perhaps crystal clear to John's audience. In their own ways, all four Gospels identify the suffering of believers with that of Jesus (e.g., Mark 8:34–38; Matt. 16:24–27; Luke 9:23–26; John 15:18–25).

Space does not allow a deep survey, but the trend continues throughout the NT. In Acts Jesus's followers meet persecution from Jewish authorities in Jerusalem, from Herod, and from Jewish and gentile adversaries alike as the gospel progresses around the Mediterranean. Basically, they are accused of subverting public order in one way or another, but there's also a sense that their Jewish persecutors are trying to quash the proclamation of Jesus. For Acts, however, persecution leads to the church's expansion. Hebrews, James, and 1 Peter all attempt to engage persecution and suffering as a theological question, with 1 Peter most acutely aware of persecution throughout the epistle. Revelation identifies its author as a victim of persecution in some sense (1:9), names one actual martyr (2:13), and envisions a crowd of martyrs (6:9–11). Among the earliest Christian apocalypses, persecution amounts to a primary concern for the Shepherd of Hermas and as a real concern in the Apocalypse of Peter and the Ascension of Isaiah. The letters of Ignatius emerge from the bishop's journey toward martyrdom in Rome (110 CE).

Clearly persecution was on the minds of early Christians, including persecution at the hands of local and (sometimes) imperial officials. Apart from early Christian sources, however, indications of official persecution against Christians are few. We receive the impression that no Roman policy proscribed Christianity; instead, early Christians encountered various kinds of resistance at diverse times and locations. The Romans were suspicious of all kinds of associations as potential hotbeds for sedition, and Christian assemblies probably looked very much like other associations.[50] The emperors Tiberius and Claudius expelled Jews from Rome, presumably for the same reasons other groups were occasionally expelled: to protect public order. (Acts 18:2 alludes

---

49. Adele Reinhartz, "The Johannine Community and Its Jewish Neighbors: A Reappraisal," in *What Is John?*, vol. 2, *Readers and Readings of the Fourth Gospel*, ed. Fernando F. Segovia (Atlanta: Scholars Press, 1998), 111–38.

50. For a balanced assessment of Roman attitudes toward associations and for an overview of synagogues and Christian assemblies in the ancient Mediterranean world, see Philip A. Harland, *Associations, Synagogues, and Congregations: Claiming a Place in Ancient Mediterranean Society* (Minneapolis: Fortress, 2003); cf. Ramsay MacMullen, *Enemies of the Roman Order* (1966; repr., London: Routledge, 1992).

to one of these occasions.) It is possible, perhaps likely, that the second expulsion involved a conflict among Jews regarding Christianity.[51] But official persecution of Christians *as Christians* is hard to identify.[52] The combination of widespread Christian concern over persecution and the lack of external evidence leaves historians in a quandary.

Three potential episodes of persecution attract high levels of interest. A massive fire devastated most of Rome in 64 CE, under the emperor Nero. Writing more than fifty years later, the historian Tacitus claims that Nero blamed the fire on Christians and subjected multitudes of them to all sorts of horrible deaths (*Annales* 15.44). Tacitus clearly does not like Christians, but neither does he like Nero: many historians suspect his account is exaggerated or even fictional.[53] A Christian tradition that Nero would return from the dead (or that he never really died) to persecute believers emerged fairly quickly, lending plausibility to the notion that Nero did execute Christians in Rome.[54]

A second possible instance of persecution involves the emperor Domitian. Church tradition traces the book of Revelation to Domitian's reign and traces Revelation's several allusions to persecution to Domitian's policies. This narrative suffers from a total lack of confirmation from Roman sources, and no remotely contemporaneous Christian sources link Domitian with persecution. Revelation may well reflect various kinds of persecution in Roman Asia, but official imperial persecution is highly unlikely.[55]

More intriguing is a third instance, reflected in correspondence between the Roman governor Pliny the Younger and the emperor Trajan (Pliny, *Epistles* 10.96–97). Writing from Bithynia, adjacent to Roman Asia, around 110 CE,

---

51. Leonard Victor Rutgers, "Roman Policy toward the Jews: Expulsions from the City of Rome during the First Century CE," in *Judaism and Christianity in First-Century Rome*, ed. Karl P. Donfried and Peter Richardson (1998; repr., Eugene, OR: Wipf & Stock, 2003), 93–116.

52. For a popular introduction to the problem, see Candida Moss, *The Myth of Persecution: How Early Christians Invented a Story of Martyrdom* (New York: HarperOne, 2013).

53. See the debate between Brent D. Shaw and Christopher P. Jones: Shaw, "The Myth of the Neronian Persecution," *JRS* 105 (2015): 1–28; Shaw, "Response to Christopher Jones: The Historicity of Neronian Persecution," *NTS* 64 (2018): 231–42; Jones, "The Historicity of the Neronian Persecution: A Response to Brent Shaw," *NTS* 63 (2017): 146–52. It is my impression that historians of ancient Rome generally accept Nero's persecution of Christians, as in John Pollini, "Burning Rome, Burning Christians," in *The Cambridge Companion to the Age of Nero*, ed. Shadi Bartsch, Kirk Freudenburg, and Cedrick Littlewood (New York: Cambridge University Press, 2017), 213–36.

54. See Rev. 13:3; 17:8–11; Asc. Isa. 4:2–8; Sib. Or. 3:63–74; 4:119–24, 138–39; 5:361–96. Roman historians describe three individuals who claimed to be Nero (see Craig R. Koester, *Revelation*, AYB 38A [New Haven: Yale University Press, 2014], 571). Here I disagree with Jan Willem van Henten, who in "*Nero Redivivus* Demolished: The Coherence of the Nero Traditions in the *Sibylline Oracles*," *JSP* 21 (2000): 3–17, discusses the relevant primary sources but focuses on Sibylline Oracles.

55. Harland, *Associations, Synagogues, and Congregations*, 184–89; see Michael Naylor, "The Roman Imperial Cult and Revelation," *CBR* 8, no. 2 (2010): 225–27.

Pliny seeks Trajan's advice: anonymous accusations have arisen against Christians. Pliny does not seek out these Christians, and he knows no policy for dealing with them. But he does examine the accused, offering them clemency if they curse Jesus and offer sacrifices to the imperial deities. Remarkably, Pliny mentions there are "many" such Christians in his region, and that his intervention has led to a revival of commerce at local temples. Trajan essentially approves of Pliny's practice.

The historical problems with these three episodes are formidable. In my view, the all-but-ubiquitous fascination with persecution among early Christians, combined with the admittedly sketchy information we receive from Roman sources, suggests a historical dimension to the concern. For the NT period, it appears there was no official, widespread, or programmatic persecution of Christians by Rome. Yet Christians found it both difficult and occasionally dangerous to negotiate life within the empire. Several factors may explain this danger: a general (and official) suspicion of mysterious associations and possible pressure to participate in festivals and other occasions that demanded public expressions of loyalty to Rome[56] stand first among them.

Diverse Testimonies

With respect to early Christianity's relationship to the Roman Empire, we might begin with the obvious. Devotees of Jesus established communities of worship around the Mediterranean world, very rapidly and especially in cities. By the time the apostle Paul reaches Damascus, in southern Syria, a church is already present. So also for Antioch, a metropolis in northern Syria, and Ephesus, another metropolis in Roman Asia (now southwestern Turkey). When Paul writes a letter to the Romans, multiple congregations have already formed in that city. Moreover, these assemblies demonstrate a remarkable desire to stay in touch with one another by means of travel, letter writing, and the sharing of documents. One scholar characterizes their close bonds as a "holy internet."[57]

That these assemblies should establish themselves over such a vast territory, inhabiting diverse, albeit cosmopolitan, cultural centers, and enduring over a long period of time, invites reflection. We should intuit that their experiences, contexts, and challenges were diverse—and that the ways in which they inhabited their imperial situation were likewise diverse. We should

---

56. Friesen, *Imperial Cults*.
57. Michael B. Thompson, "The Holy Internet: Communication between Churches in the First Christian Generation," in *The Gospels for All Christians: Rethinking the Gospel Audiences*, ed. Richard Bauckham (Grand Rapids: Eerdmans, 1998), 49–70.

avoid discussing how they "related" or "responded" to the empire, as if they stood apart from their contexts. They no more stood apart from Rome than contemporary North American readers do from Washington, Ottawa, or Mexico City. If Paul finds no offense in food that's been offered to the gods (see esp. 1 Cor. 8:1–13), and John of Revelation condemns eating such food as idolatry (Rev. 2:14, 20), we may attribute their apparent disagreement to diverse contexts. Alternatively, they may have disagreed on principle, although one cannot separate context from conviction so neatly.

If ancient Christian traditions were diverse, so are the opinions of their interpreters. We may only begin to tease out the diverse options according to which Christians may have expressed resistance or accommodation.[58] Consider these options:

- The Romans claimed to administer true justice. Does Paul's emphasis on justification by grace, in a letter specifically addressed to Rome, amount to a sophisticated form of sub-tweeting? Some interpreters see Paul's language as a kind of "hidden transcript," a coded form of cultural subversion.[59] But if resistance happens only in hiding, does it make a sound?
- Roman society is often characterized in terms of competition for status: Should we call it "counterimperial" that Jesus advises people not to promote themselves at banquets (Luke 14:7–11) or that Paul exhorts believers to bear one another's burdens (Gal. 6:2)?
- Romans addressed their emperors as Son of God, savior, and lord, celebrating the peace they brought to the world. Early Christians referred to Jesus in precisely the same terms. What would Caesar say about that?

Nowhere do we encounter early Christians calling for armed revolt. We can identify clear instances of resistance when we see literary criticism of Rome, and we can probably agree that the refusal to comply with Roman law and to show loyalty to the empire both constitute resistance. The following case studies are far too brief, and their interpretation is often controversial, but they suggest the diverse ways in which early Christians related to the realities of empire.

58. Adam Winn, "Striking Back at the Empire: Empire Theory and Responses to Empire in the New Testament," in Winn, *Introduction to Empire in the New Testament*, 1–14.
59. On this point interpreters draw from the cultural anthropology of James C. Scott, esp. *Weapons of the Weak: Everyday Forms of Peasant Resistance* (New Haven: Yale University Press, 1985); Scott, *Domination and the Arts of Resistance* (New Haven: Yale University Press, 1990). See Richard A. Horsley, ed., *Hidden Transcripts and the Arts of Resistance: Applying the Work of James C. Scott to Jesus and Paul*, SBLSS 48 (Atlanta: SBL Press, 2004); Elliott, *Arrogance of Nations*.

Memories of Jesus

The Synoptic Gospels reflect how early generations of Christians remembered Jesus, activating those memories in their own contexts.[60] Matthew, Mark, and Luke often differ in how they present these traditions, and we should not assume they share a common view of Rome and its representatives. That said, we may remember that they hold in common key elements of a basic story line.

The Synoptics present John, the baptizer of Jesus, in the context of Isaiah 40:3, a call for the remnant of Israel to return from exile. John's baptism of repentance prepares a people—in the symbolic Jordan River, no less—for a messianic age in which they reclaim their land. They also portray Herod Antipas as a fickle and unstable local tyrant who executes John. Luke chooses not to narrate John's execution but later informs us that Herod is seeking to kill Jesus. Jesus's reply to hearing of this plan—"Go and tell that fox" (13:31–32)—suggests neither admiration nor allegiance, and (only in Luke) Herod later mocks Jesus during his trial (23:1–12). Interpreters debate whether Jesus shares John's message, but there is no question that John and Jesus alike meet death at the hands of the ruling authorities.[61]

In all three Synoptics Jesus encounters a man tormented by many demons. The demons identify themselves as "Legion," a word that within Rome's empire points directly to a basic Roman military unit. The story plays out as an anti-imperial fantasy. Jesus drives Legion into a herd of pigs, who drown themselves in the sea. Pigs are unclean animals, and Jewish anti-imperial literature commonly depicts Greek and Roman oppressors as coming from the sea. The drowning pigs remind us what happens to Pharaoh's soldiers in Exodus 14–15 and what many Jews fantasized would happen to Roman armies. The passage is replete with military imagery: the pigs form a military unit (*agelē*), Jesus "dismisses" them (*epetrepsen*), and they charge (*ōrmēsen*) into the sea.[62]

Jesus faces opposition throughout the Gospels, but things reach a new level when he enters Jerusalem at Passover season. Passover is a liberationist as well as a patriotic festival. Celebrating Israel's liberation from Egyptian bondage, the festival provided the occasion for notable outbreaks of sedition. Roman governors, like Pontius Pilate, typically allowed the temple authorities to manage affairs in Jerusalem, and it is precisely those temple authorities whom Jesus antagonizes—and who initially arrest Jesus. We may read

---

60. Anthony Le Donne, *Historical Jesus: What Can We Know and How Can We Know It?* (Grand Rapids: Eerdmans, 2011).

61. I have omitted Matthew's portrayal of Herod the Great, at once fearful and murderous (2:1–11).

62. For a classic reading of this passage in Mark, see Ched Myers, *Binding the Strong Man: A Political Reading of Mark's Story of Jesus* (Maryknoll, NY: Orbis, 1988), 190–92.

Jesus's entry into the city and his initial confrontation in the temple as public demonstrations. Though the three Synoptics present the moment differently, the crowd responds to Jesus's tiny parade with royal acclamation. Whether they understand Jesus correctly is open to debate. But the temple authorities directly appreciate the provocation of Jesus's temple occupation. As tensions escalate, the temple authorities deliver Jesus over to Pontius Pilate, who holds ultimate authority in Judea. All four Gospels reflect the political dimensions of Jesus's execution by indicating the inscription affixed to Jesus's cross: "The King of the Jews." Indeed, the choice of crucifixion as a means of execution likewise indicates that Pilate treated Jesus as a seditionist.[63]

According to the Synoptics, Jesus endured a series of public controversies in those final days. Two of them, commonly misinterpreted in popular understanding, identify Jesus as a critic of both Rome's underlings, the temple authorities, and Rome itself. In the first controversy, Jesus faces a hostile question: Is it legal for Jews to pay taxes to Caesar? Much of Christian tradition has understood Jesus's answer—"Give to the emperor the things that are the emperor's, and to God the things that are God's" (Mark 12:17)—as an affirmation of allegiance to God and of duty to the state. However, details within the story suggest a more provocative interpretation. First, Jesus demonstrates that his interrogators hold the coin necessary for paying the tax, one that features the emperor's image and likely blasphemous material as well. Jesus apparently does not carry such a coin, but his observant critics do. Second, readers should ponder what it means to give Caesar what is Caesar's. What does Caesar require, after all? And what belongs to God? Both Caesar and the God of Israel claim authority over the entire world and everything in it. Jesus's reply posits a direct conflict between the interests of God and those of Caesar.

The taxation controversy demonstrates Jesus's disregard of Roman claims. The story of the widow's mite voices Jesus's criticism of Rome's local agents, the temple authorities. Read alone, the story appears to show Jesus advancing the widow as a model of generosity, and that is how she is generally understood. Mark and Luke, however, place her story immediately after Jesus's critique of the scribes, who "devour *widows'* houses" (Mark 12:40; Luke 20:47).[64] In this context, a widow sacrificing her final resources looks more like a case study in institutional exploitation than an example of generosity.

The Synoptics consistently portray Rome and its administrative underlings in an unflattering light. They identify Jesus with John, who leads a national

---

63. I pursue this reading of Jesus's final days in *Sinners*, 79–124.
64. That Matthew omits both this particular criticism of the scribes and the widow's case study is a problem worthy of investigation.

movement of renewal and possibly resistance. Jesus initiates conflict with the temple authorities, to whom Rome delegated a great deal of authority, during a volatile national festival. He rejects Rome's right to extract taxation. As the Synoptics remember things, no wonder the authorities arrest Jesus, and no wonder the Romans crucify him.

That Slippery Paul

Jesus's crucifixion leads us directly to Paul, who has a great deal to say about it. Yet anyone who browses the Paul collection in a seminary library will recognize that Paul is a slippery character, whose legacy scholars and theologians would appropriate if only they could keep him under control. The complications attending the interpretation of Paul's Letters involve active debates concerning which letters, even which passages, Paul actually wrote and how much we should rely on Acts for details concerning Paul's background, ministry, and outlook. Even if we could agree on these matters, we'd still face the difficulties posed by the letters themselves.

When it comes to Paul's outlook regarding Rome and its empire, one passage stands out as particularly vexing: Romans 13:1–7. A surface reading, which may well be correct, suggests that Paul believed Christians should be good, submissive citizens. Paul enjoins the Roman believers to "be subject to the governing authorities." He rests this position on theological grounds that seem universal: God appoints the authorities, authorizing them to employ violence against wrongdoers. Since the authorities ultimately serve God, believers are to pay taxes and give honor to those authorities. Around this passage have many theologies of church-state relations revolved.[65]

Paul never argues the opposite point, that followers of Jesus should actively resist Rome. But other aspects of his letters lead many interpreters to attribute a counterimperial outlook to the apostle. In Richard A. Horsley's words, quoted near the beginning of this essay, the Pauline assemblies constituted "an international counter-imperial (alternative) society."[66] We might recall that Paul collaborated with already-established churches too. These gatherings called themselves assemblies (*ekklēsiai*), language that suggests a democratic process.[67] Paul proclaimed a messiah, an anointed ruler or judge who will deliver Israel, to whose reign history pointed—a messiah crucified

---

65. Mark Reasoner, *Romans in Full Circle: A History of Interpretation* (Louisville: Westminster John Knox, 2005), 129–42.
66. Horsley, "Paul and Slavery," 176.
67. Elisabeth Schüssler Fiorenza, *The Power of the Word: Scripture and the Rhetoric of Empire* (Minneapolis: Fortress, 2007), 69–109.

under Roman authority. In contrast, "the rulers of this age" are "doomed to perish"; had they known God's ways, "they would not have crucified the Lord of glory" (1 Cor. 2:6–8). Paul commonly identified Jesus as "Lord" but also as "Savior," acclamations also addressed to the emperor. It is Jesus who demonstrates divine righteousness (*dikaiosynē*) and faithfulness (*pistis*), and Jesus who bestows righteousness, faithfulness, and peace to his followers. All of Paul's letters begin by extending grace and peace, Rome's prerogatives, to the churches.[68]

Interpreters struggle to reconcile Romans 13:1–7 with the insinuations laced throughout Paul's letters. Some remind us that all of Paul's letters are "occasional"; that is, they constitute direct communication with particular groups of people in response to particular circumstances. As such, they may not provide Paul's abstract or general theological positions. Quite a few interpreters apply this framework to Romans 13:1–7. We know that the emperor Claudius had expelled Jews from Rome, perhaps due to unrest regarding Jesus. In Romans Paul seems preoccupied with relations between Jewish and gentile believers, especially as Jewish believers may have been subject to particular scrutiny after their return. On these grounds some argue that Paul intends to protect Jewish believers who face such a precarious situation.[69] The theological rationale Paul provides in Romans 13:1–7 poses the greatest obstacle to such counterimperial readings.

Apologetic or Revolutionary?

The book of Acts seems the perfect laboratory for exploring how early Christians related to Rome. Acts offers an exquisite case study in how highly skilled interpreters can arrive at contradictory conclusions.

Some interpreters see Acts as largely apologetic toward Rome. The book repeatedly depicts mobs bringing believers before local Roman authorities. According to Acts' general pattern, people instigate a mob reaction against the missionaries, but local Roman officials do not enact judgment against the preachers.[70] Indeed, the believers routinely defend themselves against charges

---

68. For counterimperial readings of Paul, see Neil Elliott, *Liberating Paul: The Justice of God and the Politics of the Apostle*, Bible and Liberation (Maryknoll, NY: Orbis, 1994); Richard A. Horsley, ed., *Paul and Empire: Religion and Power in Roman Imperial Society* (Harrisburg, PA: Trinity Press International, 1997).

69. Elliott, *Liberating Paul*, 217–26; A. Katherine Grieb, *The Story of Romans: A Narrative Defense of God's Righteousness* (Louisville: Westminster John Knox, 2002), 122–26.

70. Although Roman authorities do not seek out the believers as objects of persecution in Acts, their motives and behavior are hardly spotless; see Drew W. Strait, "Proclaiming Another King Named Jesus? The Acts of the Apostles and the Roman Imperial Cult(s)," in *Jesus Is Lord,*

of disruption. As Agrippa says to Festus, Paul "could have been set free if he had not appealed to the emperor" (Acts 26:32). Acts' divinely driven plot does undermine imperial authority, as ultimately the fate of the gospel and its proponents rests in God's hands.[71] But the gospel message itself, many argue, does not directly challenge Roman authority.[72] When a centurion like Cornelius accepts the gospel, he does not relinquish his military service (see Luke 3:14). Thus Shelly Matthews argues that Acts highlights "compatibility between its concerns and values and those of the Roman Empire."[73]

Others find Acts implicitly counterimperial. C. Kavin Rowe considers the charges against Paul and Silas in Thessalonica—"These people who have been turning the world upside down have come here also" (17:6)—and presents several cases in which the proclamation of the gospel undermines conventional imperial culture. For example, the citizens of Philippi (16:11–12, 16–24) and Ephesus (19:23–41) correctly grasp that Paul's proclamation threatens the tie between local commerce and religion. They also apprehend what it means when the believers proclaim Jesus as king (17:7).[74] Brigitte Kahl maintains that the expansion of the gospel, with its conquest of territories and inclusion of peoples, reverses Rome's imperial script, showing that "God, not Caesar" rules the world.[75]

Acts' disposition toward Jews and Judaism complicates the picture. Although it welcomes gentiles into the church apart from the law, Acts insists that Jesus's Jewish followers are Torah observant. In Jerusalem they worship in the temple, and they go to great lengths to demonstrate that even Paul remains faithful to the Torah (21:17–26; 28:17). Yet Acts frequently blames Jews, not Romans, for killing Jesus (2:23; 3:13; 4:10; 7:52; 10:39; 13:27–29) and for instigating persecution against the new movement (9:23–24; 13:50; 14:2–6, 19–20; 17:5–7; 18:12–17; 20:19; 23:12; 24:19; 26:11). At the book's end Paul all but implies that due to Jewish rejection "this salvation" is moving along to gentiles (28:25–29). This mixed picture, a Torah-observant Jewish movement largely persecuted by other Jews, led Lloyd Gaston to conclude,

---

Caesar Is Not: Evaluating Empire in New Testament Studies, ed. Scot McKnight and Joseph B. Modica (Downers Grove, IL: IVP Academic, 2013), 130–45.

71. Skinner, *Trial Narratives*.

72. Christopher Bryan, *Render to Caesar: Jesus, the Early Church, and the Roman Superpower* (New York: Oxford University Press, 2005), 104.

73. Shelly Matthews, *The Acts of the Apostles: Taming the Tongues of Fire* (2013; repr., New York: Bloomsbury T&T Clark, 2017), 45.

74. C. Kavin Rowe, *World Upside Down: Reading Acts in the Graeco-Roman Age* (New York: Oxford University Press, 2011).

75. Brigitte Kahl, "Acts of the Apostles: Pro(to)-Imperial Script and Hidden Transcript," in Horsley, *In the Shadow of Empire*, 149. Kahl's interpretation is ambivalent in that she sees Acts as communicating a double message, one that would seem safe to Roman imperial readers but subversive to believers in Jesus.

"Luke-Acts is one of the most pro-Jewish and one of the most anti-Jewish writings in the New Testament."[76] Some judge that this scheme allowed Luke to characterize early Christianity as harmless to Roman authority. As Matthew L. Skinner observes, "No one in Acts openly advocates or declares the upending of the imperial system."[77] After all, Roman authorities generally find Paul and his colleagues innocent, expressing annoyance toward the Jews who oppose the missionary movement.

Exiles and Aliens

A good deal of early Christian literature voices tension with the larger world. In John's Gospel Jesus admonishes his disciples to expect animosity: "If the world hates you, be aware that it hated me before it hated you." After all, "you do not belong to the world" (15:18–19). First Peter stands out in this respect, addressing its audience as "exiles of the Diaspora" (1:1, author's translation). As "aliens and exiles," they are to "conduct [themselves] honorably among the Gentiles" (2:11–12). The appeal to a diasporic identity, combined with sensitivity toward gentiles, leads some interpreters to assign 1 Peter to an audience of Jewish followers of Jesus. The letter's later indication that it is written from "Babylon" (5:13) further suggests a Jewish audience, for only in Jewish literature after the temple's destruction in 70 CE do we encounter references to Rome as Babylon, the first empire to destroy the Holy City and its temple. However, the letter's reminder "Once you were not a people" (2:10) strongly points to a gentile audience, who receive references to diaspora, exile, and Babylon as invitations to identify themselves with the story of Judah.

The epistle reinforces the marginal identity it assigns to its readers by advising them not to be surprised by coming persecutions (1 Pet. 4:12). Here the question of empire comes to the fore. For like Ephesians, Colossians, and 1 Timothy, 1 Peter calls slaves and wives to submit to the authority of their masters and husbands, respectively (2:18–3:8). Immediately before doing so, 1 Peter also calls the audience to "accept the authority of every human institution," including emperors and governors, an instruction that concludes, "Honor the emperor" (2:13–17).

We can understand this block of material—submit to authorities, masters, and husbands—in two very different ways. All three subunits include

---

76. Lloyd Gaston, "Anti-Judaism and the Passion Narrative in Luke and Acts," in *Anti-Judaism and Early Christianity*, vol. 1, *Paul and the Gospels*, ed. Peter Richardson and Paul Granskou (Waterloo, ON: Wilfrid Laurier University Press, 1986), 153.

77. Skinner, *Trial Narratives*, 153, though Skinner does not perceive a purely apologetic approach to Rome.

a theological rationale: subordinate believers are to obey because it is the right thing to do. However, it's also possible to interpret these commands as responses to the threat of persecution. First Peter identifies Babylon as its sending address and invites believers to take on a diasporic identity. Furthermore, the letter repeatedly encourages believers to submit to unjust persecution (2:12, 18–20; 3:14–22; 4:14–16), even to glorify God on such occasions (4:16). Indeed, these references to unjust persecution immediately precede (2:12) and follow (3:8–22) the calls to submission (2:13–3:7). Considered along these lines, 1 Peter places emperors and governors first among the list of those who behave unjustly toward believers and calls believers to respond by leading lives of innocence and reverence. This hardly constitutes a call for resistance, but neither is it flattering toward ~~Babylon~~ Rome.[78]

Apocalyptic Anxieties

Our final set of case studies involves the earliest Christian literary apocalypses: Revelation, the Shepherd of Hermas, the Ascension of Isaiah, and the Apocalypse of Peter. These texts participate in the literary tradition of the great Jewish apocalypses. Daniel and much of 1 Enoch respond to the Seleucid Empire of Antiochus IV, while 2 Baruch, 3 Baruch, 4 Ezra, and the Apocalypse of Abraham all react to the devastation of Jerusalem by the Romans. Their responses vary, but these early Jewish apocalypses all deal deeply with the problem of empire.[79]

All four of the early Christian apocalypses deal with the question of persecution. Revelation characterizes Rome through two key images: the Beast who makes war against the saints and conquers them (13:7) and the Prostitute who imbibes their blood (17:6). Hermas opens with Hermas's vision of a woman who confronts him with his inconsistent faithfulness, concluding, "Be manly, Hermas" (Herm. 4.2, author's translation). Hermas encounters the woman again in a second vision, and she encourages those who do righteousness and are not "double-minded": "Blessed are you who endure the coming great persecution" (Herm. 6.7). In his fourth vision, Hermas encounters a Beast. Terrified, he hears the woman again: "Do not be double-minded, Hermas" (Herm. 22.7). Hermas summons his courage, surrenders himself to the Beast,

---

78. Carey, *Sinners*, 141–44.
79. For a survey of ancient Jewish and Christian apocalypses, see Greg Carey, *Ultimate Things: An Introduction to Jewish and Christian Apocalyptic Literature* (St. Louis: Chalice, 2005). The standard introduction to Jewish apocalyptic literature is John J. Collins, *The Apocalyptic Imagination: An Introduction to Jewish Apocalyptic Literature*, 3rd ed. (Grand Rapids: Eerdmans, 2016). We might identify many more texts as "apocalyptic," but these are the earliest literary apocalypses.

and the Beast just lies down, sticks out its tongue, and lets him pass by (Herm. 22.8–9). Hermas's manly single-mindedness subdues the monster.

Hermas shows no particular antipathy toward Rome, but Revelation does. Many interpreters see a broad critique of imperial culture as Revelation's driving concern. Revelation acknowledges that people worship the Beast, whether the empire or its emperor (13:8–18), and it requires its audience to abstain from the imperial cults and from eating idol food (2:14, 20). It enjoins believers to keep their clothes clean (3:4) and to remove themselves from association with the Prostitute (18:4). In addition to the problems of idolatry and persecution, Revelation condemns the exploitative nature of imperial commerce (18:11–17).[80]

Persecution figures less prominently in the Ascension of Isaiah and the Apocalypse of Peter, but it does appear. The Apocalypse of Peter is best known for its tour of hell, where sinners suffer eternal punishments that fit their crimes. Among many offenders, Peter's tour includes those who persecute and betray the righteous, those who speak evil of the righteous path, and those who bear false witness (27–29). Hell also includes those who have fallen away from the faith, perhaps under threat of persecution (23). All these punishments likely indicate a concern with persecution, but no counterimperial language figures directly in this apocalypse. The Ascension of Isaiah, however, appeals to the *Nero redivivus* myth: the devil Beliar sends a man resembling a lawless king who has murdered his own mother, a reference to Nero. This tyrant will gather followers, persecute the church, and establish a cult in his own honor. This crisis provokes the Beloved One, Jesus, to bring about a final judgment (Asc. Isa. 4:2–19). Beyond the subtle echo of Nero and the imperial cult, however, the Ascension never identifies or criticizes Rome directly.

Revelation's canonical status brings it far more critical attention than the other early Christian apocalypses receive. The emergence of postcolonial criticism has complicated the conversation a great deal. Interpreters have long debated whether Revelation is too violent, too misogynistic, or too escapist to contribute to Christian imagination. Postcolonial theory adds another layer: to some degree every act of resistance undermines itself by relying on the very imperial culture it resists. Rome promises peace by threatening to annihilate its foes; Revelation offers peace through Rome's annihilation. Rome promises prosperity in return for submission; Revelation's New Jerusalem arrives resplendent in precious stones and metals. Roman iconography relies on images of women, with Rome victorious and those who resist stripped and humiliated; Revelation offers the radiant woman clothed with the sun

---

80. Richard Bauckham, "The Economic Critique of Rome in Revelation 18," in *The Climax of Prophecy: Studies on the Book of Revelation* (Edinburgh: T&T Clark, 1993), 338–83.

and the New Jerusalem, on the one hand, and the sexually debased Jezebel and Prostitute, on the other hand. It appears to many interpreters, including me, that Revelation has not transcended imperial discourse.[81]

The earliest Christian apocalypses all indicate concern with persecution. But while Revelation (especially) and the Ascension of Isaiah (obliquely) also critique Rome, Hermas and the Apocalypse of Peter do not. We might attribute this difference to the nature of these apocalypses: some apocalypses show a concern for the workings of history, while others are more involved with heavenly and hellish regions and the fate of individuals. Revelation and Hermas belong to the "historical apocalypse" subcategory. This literary distinction, while helpful, is not sufficient for explaining *why* some authors would choose the historical route while others would not. That question remains unexplained.

Reflections

Early Christianity emerged as a movement within the Roman Empire. It is a mistake to characterize early Christians as "responding" to the empire, since they lived their entire lives within that imperial reality and contributed to it. We might, however, discuss the diverse ways in which early Christians lived out their identities within an imperial context.[82]

How early Christians related to empire matters to many interpreters. According to a traditional view, early Christianity was largely apolitical: Christians acknowledged the legitimacy of government, and they sought to obey the authorities in so far as that was possible. They recognized the possibility of unjust persecution and abstained from the imperial cult, but they did not advocate active resistance to Rome. Over the past few decades, perhaps in response to the wave of liberationist movements in the 1960s and 1970s, empire-critical research has flourished. Increasingly interpreters have appreciated early Christianity's view toward the larger world, debating the diverse ways in which the movement may or may not have resisted or undermined Roman hegemony.

---

81. For a sample of this conversation, see Robert M. Royalty, *The Streets of Heaven: The Ideology of Wealth in the Apocalypse of John* (Macon, GA: Mercer University Press, 1998); Greg Carey, *Elusive Apocalypse: Reading Authority in the Revelation to John*, StABH 15 (Macon, GA: Mercer University Press, 1999); Shanell T. Smith, *The Woman Babylon and the Marks of Empire: Reading Revelation with a Postcolonial Womanist Hermeneutics of Ambiveilence* (Minneapolis: Fortress, 2014); Lynne St. Clair Darden, *Scripturalizing Revelation: An African Postcolonial Reading of Empire*, SBLSS 80 (Atlanta: SBL Press, 2015).

82. Cynthia Long Westfall, "Running the Gamut: The Varied Responses to Empire in Jewish Christianity," in *Empire in the New Testament*, ed. Stanley E. Porter and Cynthia Long Westfall (Eugene, OR: Pickwick, 2011), 230–58.

Rome created the first successful territorial empire by exploiting its military and commercial power and by enlisting indigenous elites as both beneficiaries and enablers of its rule. The Romans developed sophisticated means of promoting their version of history: Rome was fated to attain dominion, its efforts brought peace and prosperity to those who would partner with it, and destruction awaited those who would resist. Epic poetry, architecture, civil engineering, sculpture, and coinage all reinforced this message. This is not to deny the presence of cultural and economic resistance. Although revolt broke out from time to time, the Romans managed to sustain hegemony over a remarkably long period. The First Jewish revolt figured especially prominently in the formation of early Christian discourse.

Interpretation of early Christianity demands an appreciation for the movement's diversity. By the end of the first century Christian assemblies established themselves over vast areas, engaged diverse social contexts, and in many cases endured over a significant time. A topic like "early Christianity and the Roman Empire" opens a wide range of options. Perhaps Roman hegemony is merely a contextual issue, a matter taken for granted by the first Christians but hardly problematized. Alternatively, some believers may have accommodated themselves to empire, even hoping for favor or protection from the authorities. Still other circles may have challenged widespread cultural values and symbols; without confronting Rome directly, they could have developed practices that countered those promoted by Rome. Some of those practices and discourses may have been covert, the resistance of the oppressed. Yet some believers may have condemned Rome outright, refused to collaborate with the authorities in any significant way, and awaited a final judgment. Our selected case studies show that while interpreters may hold conflicting views regarding individual texts, these options are all possible. Indeed, it is likely that we encounter them all.

2

Women in the Jewish, Greco-Roman, and Early Christian World

Lynn H. Cohick

Introduction

In the first century CE, Valerius Maximus praised Hortensia, the daughter of the famous Roman orator Quintus Hortensius (114–50 BCE). He records that Hortensia "pleaded the case before the triumvirs, both firmly and successfully. For by bringing back her father's eloquence, she brought about the remission of the greater part of the tax. Quintus Hortensius lived again in the female line and breathed through his daughter's words."[1] Valerius's remarks remind us of the presence of women in public life during the late Roman Republic. More than that, he testifies to a woman's eloquence, education, and decorum, suitable for a leading rhetorician. In this chapter, I hope to add to Valerius's observations, rendering a more detailed sketch of women in the Greco-Roman world. Before we dive into our topic, several assumptions about this area of study must be laid out.

---

1. Valerius Maximus, *Memorable Deeds and Sayings* 8.3, in Mary R. Lefkowitz and Maureen B. Fant, eds., *Women's Life in Greece and Rome: A Source Book in Translation*, 2nd ed. (Baltimore: Johns Hopkins University Press, 1992), 152. The tax was levied on wealthy Roman matrons.

Assumptions Reflected in the Chapter's Title

The title "Women in the Jewish, Greco-Roman, and Early Christian World" includes key assumptions that make such a study interesting and challenging. The fact that this book does not have a parallel chapter on "Men in the Jewish, Greco-Roman, and Early Christian World" acknowledges the normativity of the male experience and the simple reality that men wrote most of history, preserved most literary works, and had the most power and influence in the ancient cultures. The title supposes that woman *qua* woman is a useful category, but we will find that women's cultural, economic, social, religious, and class context can be equally determinative, such that any given group of women might have more in common with a particular group of men than with another group of women.

Second, the title speaks of "women," which suggests that attention will focus on historical women or the lives of women, rather than on ideological and philosophical positions about the categories of gender and female. Most scholars today, however, propose that gender realities affect women's lives, and so gender will be part of our conversation. Gender can be defined as "culturally constructed meanings assigned to or associated with biological sex that vary considerably from one cultural context to another."[2] Another key category used in discussing women is "feminism," defined by Phyllis Trible as "a critique of culture in light of misogyny."[3] Claims that evidence of ancient women's authority and influence is but modern wishful thinking are now justly challenged as driven more by apologetic and confessional convictions than by proper historical methodology.[4]

Third, the chapter title could be read as implying the Jewish world is separate from the Greco-Roman world; however, this view has few adherents in today's academy. Greco-Roman culture dominated our period, Greek was the lingua franca, and the all-encompassing Hellenism was paired with imperial Roman ideology. Within this overarching culture, Jews practiced their traditions and followed their laws in their homeland and in cities across the Roman Empire (and further east in the Parthian Empire). In one sense, then, all Jews at this time were Hellenistic Jews, for they expressed their ancestral rites and beliefs within a context vastly changed from that of their Israelite forebears who were part of the ancient Near East cultures. And all women who were Christ-followers negotiated the imperial context, whether they were ethnic Jews or gentiles.

---

2. Ross Shepard Kraemer, *Unreliable Witnesses: Religion, Gender, and History in the Greco-Roman Mediterranean* (Oxford: Oxford University Press, 2011), 15.

3. Phyllis Trible, *God and the Rhetoric of Sexuality* (Philadelphia: Fortress, 1978), 7.

4. Shelly Matthews, "Thinking of Thecla: Issues in Feminist Historiography," *JFSR* 17 (2001): 42–43, examines some scholars' negative reactions to interpretations of the Acts of Paul and Thecla that stress women as subjects with agency and influence in the development of Christianity.

Fourth, the insertion of "Christian" in the title reflects a religious dimension to our discussion of women in this chapter. From a historical perspective, first-century Christians were gentiles or Jews who now identified as followers of a Jewish messiah. For a Jewish woman, that claim might mean being ostracized from her synagogue;[5] for a gentile woman, condemnation by her family for abandoning paganism. Religious beliefs and practices will separate women into groups, but these same women might be reconfigured into different groupings if the category was wealth, social location, an urban/rural divide, or the like. This reflects the social landscape of the highly stratified Roman world, as Celia Schultz explains: "In many cases rituals open to women were not open to *all* women, or at least not to all women equally."[6]

Fifth, the focus on religious activities has the potential to shift the conversation from historical description to prescriptions about women's appropriate behaviors, roles, and attitudes. This is especially true for women mentioned in the biblical text and theological claims made about women or gender within its pages. The vast range of opinions about female biblical characters and theological injunctions concerning women prevents us from exploring NT texts or characters specifically. However, the same questions of method that pertain to the study of women generally in our sources can be employed to one degree or another in works addressing biblical texts.

Despite these caveats, the title of this chapter serves a useful purpose by highlighting an area of NT studies that sprang onto the scene about half a century ago. The study of women, and later gender, in the biblical text and context promises to grow as scholars place more emphasis on ancient minority and marginal voices and connect their studies with our contemporary world, in which women play increasingly more public, powerful, and authoritative roles.

Assumptions about the Context of the Greco-Roman World

Several assumptions about Greco-Roman women and their cultural context have governed scholars' discussions. These include a rather homogeneous,

---

5. The "parting of the ways" between Judaism and Christianity, or between Christians and Jews, is a hotly debated subject. See James D. G. Dunn, ed., *Jews and Christians: The Parting of the Ways, AD 70 to 135*, WUNT 66 (Tübingen: Mohr Siebeck, 1992); A. H. Becker and Annette Yoshiko Reed, eds., *The Ways That Never Parted: Jews and Christians in Late Antiquity and the Early Middle Ages* (Minneapolis: Fortress, 2007).

6. Celia E. Schultz, *Women's Religious Activity in the Roman Republic* (Chapel Hill: University of North Carolina Press, 2006), 139. She adds, "Not all aspects of Roman religious praxis were open to all Romans: gender, social, and marital status often dictated what opportunities were available to an individual."

highly patriarchal, honor/shame cultural milieu. Underlying these suppositions is an analysis of culture that postulates a seamless structure that is internally consistent. Moreover, deprivation theory hypothesizes that women felt dispossessed of autonomy or self-actualization in some way and that religious groups offered compensation or freedom. For example, the theory argues that a gentile woman might join a Christian congregation because she would experience freedom from marriage by embracing a celibate life.[7] Most of the research on women presupposes that personal autonomy is a good thing and that women benefit from having more authority over their decisions. Structures that limit individual autonomy, including religious institutions and practices, are critiqued, while practices such as celibacy and belief in charismatic authority, for example, are understood to benefit women.

Additionally, most earlier studies on ancient women assumed a strongly gendered dichotomy between private and public spaces, with women located in the former and men in the latter. These assumptions lead some scholars to suggest that a woman speaking in public, holding an office, or exerting authority must be (1) an exception that proves the rule, (2) an example of resisting social norms and the status quo, or (3) representative of competing social subgroups within a larger group. Scholars point to tensions between early Christians, based on perceived competing positions in each group's texts. They postulate rival groups who produced 1 Timothy and the Acts of Paul and Thecla, surmising each sought to influence the wider Christian community and enforce their position on women's authority.

Some of these assumptions are now called into question. The most significant challenge is a shift within anthropological views of culture. Pierre Bourdieu's views of *habitus*, or "disposition," have reshaped the landscape.[8] Bourdieu rejects methodological objectivism in favor of a theory of practice. He argues that people negotiate cultural rules and expectations as they apply commonly held values to given situations.[9] *Habitus* reflects Bourdieu's theory

---

7. Kraemer, *Unreliable Witnesses*, 266–67, assesses deprivation theory's strengths and weaknesses.

8. Pierre Bourdieu writes, "The structures constitutive of a particular type of environment . . . produce *habitus*, systems of durable, transposable *dispositions*, structured structures redisposed to function as structuring structures, that is, as principles of the generation and structuring of practices and representations which can be objectively 'regulated' and 'regular' without in any way being the product of obedience to rules . . . and, being all this, collectively orchestrated without being the product of the orchestrating action of a conductor." Bourdieu, *Outline of a Theory of Practice*, trans. R. Nice (Cambridge: Cambridge University Press, 1977), 72.

9. Bourdieu, *Outline of a Theory of Practice*, 73. Bourdieu explains, "It is necessary to abandon all theories which explicitly or implicitly treat practice as a mechanical reaction, directly determined by the antecedent conditions and entirely reducible to the mechanical functioning of pre-established assemblies, 'models' or 'roles.'"

that individuals engage their culture's rules and express its values by privileging one virtue over another in one situation, only to reverse the order in another setting. The individual as an agent applies the virtues and is part of a community that guides and reinforces specific values. The dynamic mixing of virtues in decision-making does not suggest a cultural free-for-all, but rather the benign tensions inherent in social life. Susan Hylen remarks that cultures "allow for multiple expressions of the same values," adding that texts could express "complex and even conflicting values."[10] Applying Bourdieu's theory to the highly stratified Roman world, we find elite women's religious practices reflecting and reinforcing their high status and wealth. These elite women had limited autonomy relative to elite men in their religious expressions, but they also benefited from the social structure that provided greater autonomy and elevated them above non-elite men.[11]

Methodology and Sources

There are two major ways of approaching the topic of women in the ancient world. One avenue seeks to discover something of real women's lives, using historical, archaeological, and social sciences to explore the terrain. The other path winds through literary theory as it examines cultural and ideological constructs of woman, female, and notions of the feminine. At times, these two approaches are at odds, as when a scholar despairs of the historical project altogether, concluding that texts are unable to shed reliable light on the past. In other cases, the two perspectives offer responsible correctives to each other, warning the eager reader not to take a description of women at face value or to dismiss all hope of ascertaining reliable information about historical women. Feminist hermeneutics analyzes women and the category of female in the text and material remnants by attending to the patriarchy of the ancient world and the resulting oppressive social structures that limit and repress women. The hermeneutics of suspicion is one way scholars read "against the grain" of a text so as to discover a more accurate picture of ancient life and to discern male-dominated prescriptions that hinder women's full flourishing. This approach mistrusts the text to provide a straightforward explanation of women's lives, and it challenges patriarchal bias.

    10. Susan E. Hylen, *A Modest Apostle: Thecla and the History of Women in the Early Church* (Oxford: Oxford University Press, 2015), 10. See also Susan E. Hylen, "Modest, Industrious, and Loyal: Reinterpreting Conflicting Evidence for Women's Roles," *BTB* 44 (2014): 3–12.
    11. Schultz concludes that parameters placed on elite women's religious expression by elite men reflect the Roman social fabric. "The importance of ritual in simultaneously strengthening social distinctions and integrating different groups into society as a whole was not limited to women but applied to all Romans." Schultz, *Women's Religious Activity*, 146.

Sources available for the study of women (and gender) are predominantly textual, usually literary works penned by politically connected, elite males. Few and far between are the texts written by women.[12] Our literary sources, in other words, have been selected and even interpreted for us based on the male author's interests and biases. For example, we know some features of the major public festivals of the Bona Dea, or the duties of the Vestal Virgins, but precious little about household religious activities. Additionally, as Celia Schultz indicates, ancient historians often presented events so as to teach virtues and to warn against vices. Schultz adds, "Thus, we have a host of stories, like that of Claudia Quinta and the Magna Mater, in which a woman's virtue is tested within a religious context."[13] This reality makes it all the more important that studies about ancient women include epigraphic and archaeological evidence, some of which is from women themselves. For example, inscriptions reveal women office holders and religious practices about which our literary sources are silent, while terra-cotta votive offerings molded in the shape of body parts reveal the average person's interaction with the gods.[14]

Challenges in writing this chapter include choosing representative authors. With few exceptions, all scholars included here are women. The lack of male representation does not imply that only women can speak about women's history or theology. Nor is it to say that female biblical scholars and historians tend to focus on women or issues of feminism within Scripture. Rather it is to showcase the breadth of female scholars' opinions and approaches to this study. Women authors in biblical and theological studies bring their lived experience of being a woman in a "man's" world of academic studies. Their experiences shape the questions they ask of the material. This is of course true of male scholars; however, because their experience is often equated with normative scholarship, their particular perspective (bias?) has not always been acknowledged.

In the Beginning . . .

In the fall of 1984, my first semester of graduate school at the University of Pennsylvania, I took a class on feminism and Christianity. Of the approximately

---

12. I. M. Plant, ed., *Women Writers of Ancient Greece and Rome: An Anthology* (Norman: University of Oklahoma Press, 2004). As an example of scholars' debate over female authorship, see the discussion concerning the Martyrdom of Perpetua and Felicitas in Lynn H. Cohick and Amy Brown Hughes, *Christian Women in the Patristic World: Their Influence, Authority, and Legacy in the Second through Fifth Centuries* (Grand Rapids: Baker Academic, 2017), 34–36.

13. Schultz, *Women's Religious Activity*, 8. She concludes that most ancient accounts are not "manufactured wholesale" but do include "some manipulation and distortion, including anachronism."

14. Schultz, *Women's Religious Activity*, 10–12, provides a brief description of this evidence's importance. See also pp. 47–120 for a detailed analysis of the material related to Roman women.

twenty students (all female), most identified as "post-Christian." Significant events outside the classroom influenced our discussions. Incumbent president Ronald Reagan and George H. W. Bush trounced Walter Mondale and his running mate, Geraldine Ferraro, the first woman in the United States to be a major-party nominee. The landslide victory was viewed as a crushing defeat for women by many of the students, who redoubled their intensity in discovering women of the past.

The 1970s and '80s were decades of great upheaval as female scholars and women's studies shook the academy. The call went out to repopulate the ancient landscape with women. Scholars raised theological concerns and offered a range of positions about the relationship between the church, the God of the Bible, and women. Several deserve special mention, including Mary Daly, Phyllis Trible, Elisabeth Schüssler Fiorenza, and Rosemary Radford Ruether.

At the far left of the early movement stood Mary Daly, who argued that Christianity is irredeemably misogynistic.[15] She made headlines by refusing to admit men to her class on feminist ethics at Boston College (but allowed men in her other classes). She identified herself as a radical lesbian feminist and invented new terms to deconstruct patriarchal language, evidenced by the title of her book *Gyn/Ecology: The Metaethics of Radical Feminism*.[16]

Instead of rejecting the biblical text as irretrievably patriarchal, Phyllis Trible concludes that the Bible is a pilgrim through time, containing different, even contradictory positions. Trible broke exegetical ground using rhetorical criticism to study women of the OT / Hebrew Bible. *God and the Rhetoric of Sexuality*, published in 1978, was followed in 1984 by *Texts of Terror*; both works address sexism in the Bible through literary criticism and a strong emphasis on the reader's opportunity to challenge the patriarchy within the text.[17] The Bible invites readers to be pilgrims as well, drawing on their own context and the counter voices within the biblical text as ways to spotlight affirming images of women and the female made in God's image.[18]

In 1983, Elisabeth Schüssler Fiorenza published *In Memory of Her: A Feminist Theological Reconstruction of Christian Origins*, and she launched the modern study of NT women.[19] In this work, Schüssler Fiorenza reconstructs earliest Christianity as egalitarian in its practices. She speaks of a "discipleship of equals" within the earliest Christian community that allowed women to

---

15. Mary Daly, *Beyond God the Father: Toward a Philosophy of Women's Liberation* (Boston: Beacon, 1973); Daly, *Pure Lust: Elemental Feminist Philosophy* (Boston: Beacon, 1984).
16. Mary Daly, *Gyn/Ecology: The Metaethics of Radical Feminism* (Boston: Beacon, 1978).
17. Trible, *God and the Rhetoric of Sexuality*; Phyllis Trible, *Texts of Terror: Literary-Feminist Readings of Biblical Narratives* (Philadelphia: Fortress, 1984).
18. Trible, *God and the Rhetoric of Sexuality*, 200–202.
19. Elisabeth Schüssler Fiorenza, *In Memory of Her: A Feminist Theological Reconstruction of Christian Origins* (1983; repr., New York: Crossroad, 1994).

inhabit leadership roles and participate as teachers and preachers. Schüssler Fiorenza concludes that this egalitarian moment was short lived and that the church developed misogynistic patterns and structures.

Also in 1983, Rosemary Radford Ruether published her influential book *Sexism and God-Talk*.[20] Ruether presumes that whatever in the biblical text affirms "the full humanity of women" should be taken as representative of "the Holy . . . the authentic message of redemption and the mission of redemptive community."[21] She places her judgment of sexism and androcentrism alongside other critiques, including norming the white Western wealthy expression of humanity and privileging humans to the detriment of other creatures.[22]

These pioneers blazed a trail for further exploration into the world of ancient women. As the discipline grew, new methods questioned the conclusions of older research. The desire to engage modern conversations about women's roles continues, sometimes implicitly, as the study of ancient women informs today's expectations and prescriptions about women's authority and power.

Historical Women in Judaism, Paganism, and Christianity

In 1982, Bernadette Brooten published her Harvard dissertation, *Women Leaders in the Ancient Synagogue: Inscriptional Evidence and Background Issues*.[23] She presents a rereading of nineteen inscriptions from the Roman and Byzantine periods that include Jewish women with titles such as "head of the synagogue" and "mother of the synagogue." Brooten alleges the inscriptions were misinterpreted as honorific titles based on scholars' a priori assumptions that women could not be leaders in Jewish communities. She challenges the uncritical use of rabbinic sources for a historical reconstruction of women's lives, and her critique remains relevant for current scholarship thirty-five years later. Moreover, her emphasis on material culture and inscriptional evidence has continued with impressive results today. Depictions of women in catacombs and artwork in synagogues, funerary and honorary

20. Rosemary Radford Ruether, *Sexism and God-Talk: Toward a Feminist Theology*, 2nd ed. (1983; repr., Boston: Beacon, 1993).
21. Ruether, *Sexism and God-Talk*, 19.
22. Ruether, *Sexism and God-Talk*, 20. Ruether continues to write on these topics, including *Gaia and God: An Ecofeminist Theology of Earth Healing* (San Francisco: HarperSanFrancisco, 1992); *Goddesses and the Divine Feminine: A Western Religious History* (Berkeley: University of California Press, 2005); and *Integrating Ecofeminism, Globalization, and World Religions* (London: Rowman & Littlefield, 2005). See also her *My Quests for Hope and Meaning: An Autobiography* (Eugene, OR: Cascade, 2013).
23. Bernadette J. Brooten, *Women Leaders in the Ancient Synagogue: Inscriptional Evidence and Background Issues*, BJS 36 (Atlanta: Scholars Press, 1982).

monuments, marriage contracts, and business receipts all provide evidence to help us better imagine historical women's lives.[24]

Tal Ilan's in-depth analysis of Jewish women in Palestine recognizes that Jewish women living in the diaspora, some of whom we know about through the apostle Paul's letters and the book of Acts, would have different experiences than those who lived in Judea and Galilee. She carefully distinguishes the attitude of the text's author toward women from the actual history of women.[25] Ilan's project locates women within the wider, heterogeneous environment of Palestinian Judaism and points out that the majority of literary sources reflect elite authors' perspectives. This means, for example, that injunctions that women remain secluded in specific areas of their homes presumes a large home—a luxury few could afford. Again, Ilan found that while *Tannaitic* writings presume all women at this time practiced the Pharisaic approach to *niddah* (menstrual purity laws), we learn from our sources that the Sadducees did not.[26] She summarizes the problems with rabbinic texts as possible sources for women's historical lives, but nevertheless argues that some history can be ascertained from this extensive corpus with its numerous redactions.[27] Reconstructions of Jewish women's lives in Roman Palestine aid in reconstructing the earliest communities of Jesus-followers in Judea and Galilee and often undergird analysis of specific Gospel passages.

In 1988, Ross Kraemer published *Maenads, Martyrs, Matrons, Monastics: A Sourcebook on Women's Religions in the Greco-Roman World* (the second edition was published in 2004 with the title *Women's Religions in the Greco-Roman World: A Sourcebook*).[28] Kraemer includes numerous epitaphs, contracts, and women's personal papers, such as those of Babatha, a second-century Jewish woman who likely perished during the Bar Kokhba

---

24. Lynn H. Cohick, *Women in the World of the Earliest Christians: Illuminating Ancient Ways of Life* (Grand Rapids: Baker Academic, 2009).

25. Tal Ilan, *Jewish Women in Greco-Roman Palestine* (Tübingen: Mohr Siebeck, 1995; repr., Peabody, MA: Hendrickson, 1996), 41. Ilan published a collection of essays, *Integrating Women into Second Temple History* (Tübingen: Mohr Siebeck, 1999). She continues to write in this area; see Ilan, "Jewish Women's Studies," in *The Oxford Handbook of Jewish Studies*, ed. Martin Goodman (Oxford: Oxford University Press, 2002), 770–96.

26. Ilan, *Jewish Women*, 227.

27. Tal Ilan, *Mine and Yours Are Hers: Retrieving Women's History from Rabbinic Literature* (Leiden: Brill, 1997), 37. Ilan explains her methodology as literary and "'post-literary': It applies to the sources a full literary analysis, which reveals legendary, folklorist and other elements of fiction found in them, and only after extracting these is a search for the historical kernel within the traditions initiated." Ilan, *Mine and Yours Are Hers*, 37.

28. Ross Shepard Kraemer, ed., *Maenads, Martyrs, Matrons, Monastics: A Sourcebook on Women's Religions in the Greco-Roman World* (Philadelphia: Fortress, 1988); Kraemer, *Women's Religions in the Greco-Roman World: A Sourcebook* (Oxford: Oxford University Press, 2004).

revolt. In the second edition, Kraemer reflects on the changes that occurred between 1988 and 2004 in feminist scholarship. She admits to being "much less sanguine about the assumptions that undergirded their [the categories'] initial formulation."[29] Now she has concerns about the social construction of texts that renders it much harder to glean historical information. Additionally, "variable ideas about gender—about what it means to be female and male—permeate ancient thought, culture, and experience so extensively that sources that appear to be about women may often instead be devices by which ancient authors . . . wrote about all sorts of other concerns."[30]

I will return below to the methodological shift represented by Kraemer's second edition of *Women's Religions in the Greco-Roman World* and her 2011 book, *Unreliable Witnesses: Religion, Gender, and History in the Greco-Roman Mediterranean*. At this point, we must attend to the charge of anti-Semitism raised by Kraemer and others, leveled at some historical reconstructions of women in early Christianity. The simple question "Was Jesus good for women?" often is answered by portraying Judaism as highly patriarchal and demeaning to Jewish women and contrasting it with Jesus's message, which liberated them.[31] Some scholars portray Jewish men as retrograde, such that any interaction Jesus had with women looks progressive by comparison.[32] For example, Jewish menstrual purity laws are presumed onerous and shameful, although we have no idea if ancient women understood them as such. Gender segregation in the synagogue is assumed, yet no reliable, material, contemporary evidence exists to support this. Again, the Dead Sea Scrolls have been understood to exclude and marginalize women, with the purity codes typically being understood as severely ostracizing women in the group.[33] Often such negative conclusions rely on reading later mishnaic or talmudic texts selectively and without distinguishing the internal debate evident in the text or whether such texts are descriptive or proscriptive.[34] Amy-Jill Levine points out that scholars who see Jesus as "pro-women" must still explain why no women were part of his inner circle of disciples and why none were mentioned at the Last Supper. Levine highlights the many social opportunities afforded to Jewish

---

29. Kraemer, *Women's Religions*, 5.
30. Kraemer, *Women's Religions*, 5.
31. Ross Shepard Kraemer, "Jewish Women and Christian Origins: Some Caveats," in *Women and Christian Origins*, ed. Ross Shepard Kraemer and Mary Rose D'Angelo (Oxford: Oxford University Press, 1999), 35–38.
32. Amy-Jill Levine, "Bearing False Witness: Common Errors Made about Early Judaism," in *The Jewish Annotated New Testament*, ed. Amy-Jill Levine and Marc Zvi Brettler (Oxford: Oxford University Press, 2011), 502–3.
33. Cecilia Wassen, *Women in the Damascus Document* (Atlanta: SBL Press, 2005), 11.
34. Kraemer, "Jewish Women and Christian Origins," 35–49.

women as indicated by the ancient texts and material remains, thereby calling into question the reconstruction of Second Temple Judaism as uniformly problematic for women.[35]

Turning to Christian communities in the wider Greco-Roman world, Carolyn Osiek and Margaret Y. MacDonald explore the house church as a venue to understand the lives of earliest Christian women.[36] Their research relies on the evidence of gentile Roman women, both literary and nonliterary, which they believe can offer a historical reconstruction. What they find is that Roman women had more social freedom than their sisters centuries earlier in the classical Greek period. For example, a woman in the imperial period typically married *sine manu*—that is, the wife was not under the husband's authority but remained under the control or authority of her father's family.[37] Osiek and MacDonald conclude that Christianity followed the path already marked out by Roman legal and social codes, such that "early Christian women did not exercise unique or more advanced leadership roles in early church groups in comparison to other women of their times."[38]

Cautioning against stretching the dichotomy of "public versus private" too far, Osiek and MacDonald observe that business was conducted in the ancient house, unlike the modern Western notion of house as private space. It would be incorrect, therefore, either to suggest that women had more freedom in a house church because it was private space or to assume that women were absent from the public arena.[39] Osiek and MacDonald also point out the leadership roles of married women, correcting a common misperception that only celibate women served in roles of authority. Osiek and MacDonald take advantage of recent research on (1) meals in the Greco-Roman world, (2) patronage and benefaction, and (3) honor/shame cultures. They remind us that honor/shame cultures vary, and thus we do well not to generalize over time or geography. They conclude that women contributed in all levels of the house church, including its functions as *"the center for worship, hospitality, patronage, education, communication, social services, evangelization, and mission."*[40]

---

35. Levine, "Bearing False Witness," 503. See also Amy-Jill Levine, ed., *"Women Like This": New Perspectives on Jewish Women in the Greco-Roman World* (Atlanta: SBL Press, 1991). Rosemary R. Ruether likewise addresses the issue of anti-Semitism in Christianity but does not link it particularly to the study of women; see Ruether, *Faith and Fratricide: The Theological Roots of Anti-Semitism* (Eugene, OR: Wipf & Stock, 1997).

36. Carolyn Osiek and Margaret Y. MacDonald, with Janet H. Tulloch, *A Woman's Place: House Churches in Earliest Christianity* (Minneapolis: Augsburg Fortress, 2006).

37. Cohick, *Women in the World of the Earliest Christians*, 99–112.

38. Osiek and MacDonald, *Woman's Place*, 249.

39. Osiek and MacDonald, *Woman's Place*, 3.

40. Osiek and MacDonald, *Woman's Place*, 9.

Widening the lens further to include pagan communities, Kraemer explores women's devotion to pagan gods and goddesses as well as Jewish and Christian women's experiences. In *Her Share of the Blessings*, Kraemer highlights the Roman propensity for categorizing and classifying.[41] Literary sources on women's religious activities do not escape this tendency to label women as freeborn, freed, or slave; citizen or noncitizen; plebeian or patrician. Moreover, Kraemer is rightly cautious about assuming that a priestess would necessarily have social power outside her religious role, and in fact, it might be that a woman with existing social authority was more likely to function as a priestess.[42] Schultz observes that the literary and epigraphic material on priesthood reveals that while both men and women were chosen based on lineage and personal virtue, "the standards of priestly behavior [for women] were much more stringent and personal."[43] In general, women were responsible for maintaining the propitiation of the household gods, and they participated in festivals and offered prayers for health and good fortune.[44] In many ways, women's religious activities mirrored men's religious devotion; however, our literary sources, written by men, underscore proper feminine decorum and chastity.[45]

Historical surveys of women's religious activities in the Greco-Roman world paint a landscape populated with women at all levels of society engaged in religious activities.[46] Spotlighting women's activities counters the prevailing notion that women were absent from public life and had little involvement in the development of their respective religious traditions. Most reconstructions argue that women could hold religious offices that carried some measure of authority or influence in their religious communities. Yet alongside the continuing exploration of historical women, a trajectory of scholarship has questioned whether texts (or material remains) really provide the historical data necessary for such a reconstruction.

---

41. Ross Shepard Kraemer, *Her Share of the Blessings: Women's Religions among Pagans, Jews, and Christians in the Greco-Roman World* (Oxford: Oxford University Press, 1992), 84–89. See also Kraemer, "Women and Gender," in *The Oxford Handbook of Early Christian Studies*, ed. Susan Ashbrook Harvey and David G. Hunter (Oxford: Oxford University Press, 2008), 466.

42. Kraemer, *Her Share of the Blessings*, 90–92. Kraemer uses Mary Douglas's theory that examines a group's cohesion and the level of rule enforcement and individual freedom. Douglas challenged aspects of deprivation theory that argued that women joined religious groups to compensate for deficiencies in other areas of their lives.

43. Schultz, *Women's Religious Activity*, 141.

44. Cohick, *Women in the World of the Earliest Christians*, 159–93.

45. Cohick, *Women in the World of the Earliest Christians*, 180–83.

46. Eve D'Ambra, *Roman Women*, Cambridge Introduction to Roman Civilization (Cambridge: Cambridge University Press, 2007). See also Maryline Parca and Angeliki Tzanetou, eds., *Finding Persephone: Women's Rituals in the Ancient Mediterranean* (Bloomington: Indiana University Press, 2007).

Construction of Women and Gender

In 1998, Elizabeth A. Clark wrote of the new dilemma facing scholars of women in history—namely, the struggle to ascertain the lives of real women from texts shaped by often highly misogynistic gender constructs.[47] Clark notes the shift in feminist studies that occurred as poststructuralism reshaped ideas about linguistics and epistemology. With language now at the center, and not the subjective experience of women, the subject was removed. Clark observes, "Decentering the male subject eventually annihilated the female subject as well."[48] Clark concludes that narratives about women, such as those found in the Acts of Paul and Thecla, do not reveal real women, but expose the theological and ideological leanings of the author. She advocates for further work on gender and on the construction of gender in social structures. Clark argues that "texts are seen as engaged in contests, contests constituted in and through language, but also by events and interests within the broader discursive and social field."[49]

Construction of Gender and the Acts of Paul and Thecla

Kraemer's extensive work over several decades on women in the ancient world presents a useful guide to chart the methodological questions that emerged within feminist studies about ancient women and gender.[50] A convenient way to trace this development is by examining writings on the apocryphal Acts, specifically on the Acts of Paul and Thecla, to which we now turn.[51] In her earlier work, Kraemer states that while the specific story of Paul and Thecla is a fabrication, "there must have been women just like Thecla, who did deny marriage and childbearing, authority and hierarchy, who taught and baptized."[52] Her recent book *Unreliable Witnesses* is more cautious. Although Kraemer still holds that women baptized, traveled, and taught, she does so not because we see it in the Acts of Paul and Thecla, but because various Christian texts reveal extensive debate about these practices. She emphasizes the role of gender construction in such stories, concluding, "Paul's fictive

---

47. Elizabeth A. Clark, "The Lady Vanishes: Dilemmas of a Feminist Historian after the Linguistic Turn," *CH* 67, no. 1 (1998): 1–31. Clark works primarily in the late antiquity period, but her observations are pertinent to our period.
48. Clark, "Lady Vanishes," 3.
49. Clark, "Lady Vanishes," 31.
50. Kraemer reflects that "in the intervening years [from 1992], it has become much clearer to me that interwoven problems of data and theory attend any attempt at the accurate reconstruction and subsequent redescription and explanation of women's religious behaviors and beliefs in Greco-Roman antiquity encounters." Kraemer, *Unreliable Witnesses*, 6.
51. Cohick and Hughes, *Christian Women in the Patristic World*, 1–25.
52. Kraemer, *Her Share of the Blessings*, 154.

disciple Thecla, from the *Acts of (Paul and) Thecla*, offers a narrative of Christians as the ultimate exemplars of ascetic and philosophical virtues."[53] The emphasis on celibacy holds verisimilitude because debates about it and asceticism occurred among Christians.

Kraemer suggests that 1 Timothy reflects a counterargument to the teaching represented by Thecla and that the Acts of Paul and Thecla serves to subvert both the social and familial framework of second-century Christians raised within the imperial milieu. The text promotes Christian morals as superior to those of pagans. The female heroine reinforces the point, as Thecla defies the common assumptions that women were more gullible and immoral than men. Kraemer also highlights the text's emphasis on mother/daughter relationships, suggesting that they display the early Christian communities' reshaping of familial structures away from natal loyalties.[54] Moreover, the positive presentation of almost all the women in the story and the negative presentation of most men suggest to Kraemer "the use of gender inversion to express Christian critique and challenge of Greco-Roman culture and power."[55] Kraemer points to Thecla's demonstration of masculine virtues, such as self-control and public speech, at the end of her story and concludes that the gender reversal promotes Christian women as "the ultimate exemplars of masculine morality and piety."[56]

A second influential voice in the discussion of Thecla is Kate Cooper, who argues that the Acts of Paul and Thecla (along with other narratives among the apocryphal Acts) is best understood alongside the ancient romance novel, which served to reinforce the Roman male author's civic views.[57] She emphasizes the public/private social division, suggesting that Roman male civic virtue was linked to private sexual morality, specifically self-mastery and marital concord. Cooper claims that elite males competed for public honor and political dominance using rhetoric of the family to establish their superiority over rivals. A harmonious home indicated a solid civic leader, and marital concord was highly esteemed as men produced legitimate children for imperial Rome. The romance novel served a male population, and the stories reinforced elite Roman political and moral virtues. The women in the story were merely rhetorical devices with little connection to a historical

---

53. Kraemer, *Unreliable Witnesses*, 244.
54. Kraemer, *Unreliable Witnesses*, 134–35.
55. Kraemer, *Unreliable Witnesses*, 136. See also Lynn H. Cohick, "Mothers, Martyrs, and Manly Courage: The Female Martyr in 2 Maccabees, 4 Maccabees, and *The Acts of Paul and Thecla*," in *A Most Reliable Witness: Essays in Honor of Ross Shepard Kraemer*, ed. Susan Ashbrook Harvey et al., BJS 358 (Providence: Brown University, 2015), 123–32.
56. Kraemer, *Unreliable Witnesses*, 147.
57. Kate Cooper, *The Virgin and the Bride: Idealized Womanhood in Late Antiquity* (Cambridge: Harvard University Press, 1996).

social context outside the text. Cooper assumes that "whenever a woman is mentioned a man's character is being judged" and thus explains the female protagonist's presence in this literature.[58]

Cooper concludes that the Acts of Paul and Thecla is driven by a desire to promote Paul, the hero, with Thecla cast as the faithful listener. Paul's antagonist is Thecla's jilted fiancé, Thamyris, who competes with Paul for a pure virgin but fails to win his prize. Cooper reckons that "the challenge posed here by Christianity is not really about women, or even about sexual continence, but about authority and the social order."[59] Christian men subverted the romance novel's aim by elevating the female virgin and substituting the family of God for biological (or adopted) kin, all in hopes of supplanting elite pagan influence in cities.[60] Rather than focus on self-mastery and a chaste marriage, Christians focused on asceticism and continence.

To help interpret the Acts of Paul and Thecla, Cooper focuses on a brief comment from Tertullian wherein the church father laments that some women have used the story of Thecla to support their own practice of women baptizing and teaching, activities Tertullian strongly opposes.[61] Cooper suggests that a "lack of cultural sophistication or a deliberate, self-interested blind eye" led these women to misinterpret the text's intentions. She points to Tertullian's comment that the Acts of Paul and Thecla were composed by a presbyter who was disciplined for his inappropriate (if well meaning) composition.

Cooper's intriguing reading is not without its critics. Shelly Matthews suggests that Cooper overstates her case and neglects to take full account of the fact that the early church included women alongside men in its communities. Matthews concludes that Thecla's story as it was used by the early church "had quite a lot to do with women," even as it may also have reflected wider debates about social order.[62] Kraemer adds that Cooper relies too heavily both on a presumption of authorial intent being accessible to modern scholars and on her assessment of the female-only readership that allegedly misread Thecla's story.[63] In an ironic

---

58. Cooper, *Virgin and the Bride*, 19.
59. Cooper, *Virgin and the Bride*, 55.
60. Cooper writes that the "rivalry between two men over the allegiance of a woman formed the central narrative outline" of the Christian Acts, and she concludes, "The rejection of the romance's ideal of passionate marriage was also a response to the romance's call for renewal of the city." Cooper, *Virgin and the Bride*, 52.
61. Cooper, *Virgin and the Bride*, 64–65; see Tertullian, *On Baptism* 1.17 (CC 1.291).
62. Matthews, "Thinking of Thecla," 53.
63. Kraemer writes, "Cooper then argues that function [male power struggles] points to authorial intention, yet denies that their one historically attested function, the legitimation of women's agency with regard to baptism and teaching, is related to their authorial intention." Kraemer, *Unreliable Witnesses*, 131.

twist, Cooper sees historical women in a text, but only those whom Tertullian chastises as misinformed readers.

A third scholar who has recently weighed in on Thecla is Susan Hylen, who is more confident in the possibility of ascertaining historical information about women's lives from ancient texts. Hylen studies the topic of modesty and its various manifestations in the ancient church and context, specifically focusing on the Acts of Paul and Thecla and 1 Timothy.[64] She addresses the apparent contradiction between women's public leadership or authority and the widespread conviction that women must be private and modest. The inconsistency is only apparent, Hylen argues, for it is rooted in our inadequate understanding of how culture works. Using Pierre Bourdieu's theory (noted above), she suggests that perceived differences between texts need not represent boundary-making, but rather represent cultural negotiation of shared values performed in different ways in a given narrative setting. Hylen focuses on a woman's agency in expressing her culture's virtues, which might seem to readers today as at one point resisting and at another point affirming of the community's values.

Hylen challenges the dominant view that 1 Timothy and the Acts of Paul and Thecla represent two Christian communities at odds with each other over women's authority.[65] She does so in part by suggesting that married women had leadership opportunities based on social influence, increased social status, and access to their husband's financial resources as they managed their households. Thus 1 Timothy's call for young women to marry was not a roadblock to authority, but "might be an avenue towards leadership."[66]

Thecla's story continues to intrigue, and her impact for studies of women in antiquity will likely endure. The Acts' narrative form invites new interpretations, and Thecla's activities of baptizing (herself) and teaching and preaching (to women only?) offer interesting trajectories in studying women in the early Roman imperial period. Descriptions of other women in the story—their wealth and social position, their friendships, their roles as mothers and daughters—provide rich resources as more material and epigraphic evidence emerge and new theories of cultural interpretation provide methods for further study.

---

64. Hylen, *Modest Apostle*, 7–11.

65. Margaret M. Mitchell writes, "Recent research has suggested a link between the Christians whom this author opposes and those who held to traditions found in the later apocryphal *Acts of Paul and Thecla*, which validates women's ministries and claimed Paul as the champion of an ascetic and celibate lifestyle. In this view, 1 Timothy is a kind of 'corrective composition' whose author is seeking to 'fix' Paul's authentic legacy for an early second-century audience." Mitchell, "1 Timothy," in *The New Oxford Annotated Bible*, 4th ed. (Oxford: Oxford University Press, 2010), 2085.

66. Hylen, *Modest Apostle*, 69. See 1 Tim. 5:11–15.

Reflections

The study of ancient women in their daily lives, including religious expression, will continue to generate new views and insights, and the study of gender will broaden and deepen our appreciation for these Jewish, pagan, and Christian women and perhaps raise awareness of our own gendered context. Below I suggest six areas where scholarship on ancient women will continue to grow.

Women and the Dead Sea Scrolls

New Testament studies experienced seismic shifts with the rise of the New Perspective on Paul and its reevaluation of Second Temple Judaism, and with the publication of the DSS corpus. Both movements made an impact on the study of Jewish women in the Greco-Roman world. With a chastened attitude toward the historical reliability of early rabbinic writings came a new appreciation for the variety of Jewish perspectives, including on women's participation in daily life and religious events. Again, the widespread availability of the DSS allowed greater study of this collection's views on gender and the assumptions about women's activities in the group. As with other textual evidence for groups of women, so too with the scrolls: we cannot simply lift the presentation of women off the page and present it as historical fact.

Eileen Schuller, an editor of the DSS in the Discoveries in the Judaean Desert series, was one of the earliest scholars to explore the DSS from a feminist perspective. In 1994, she broke ground in a conference paper (later published) that drew on a reconstruction of women's roles in the sect by using the Damascus Document (CD) and Rule of the Congregation (1QSa).[67] She acknowledges that the texts reflect an androcentric bias, but she suggests that at least some of the codes, expressed in the masculine, would apply equally to women. Following the feminist assumption that women were full members of the community unless explicitly stated otherwise, she concludes that 1QSa does not specifically list women as excluded, even as it itemizes those who are impure or have a physical deformity.[68] Again, she argues that "if women had designated titles 'mothers,' 'sisters,' 'elders,' this too suggests full membership within the community."[69]

At the fiftieth anniversary of the scrolls' discovery (1997), Schuller noted that little had been written on women and the scrolls, but this state of affairs

---

67. Eileen M. Schuller, "Women in the Dead Sea Scrolls," in *Methods of Investigation of the Dead Sea Scrolls and the Khirbet Qumran Site*, ed. Michael Wise et al., Annals of the New York Academy of Sciences 722 (New York: New York Academy of Sciences, 1994), 114–32.
68. Schuller, "Women in the Dead Sea Scrolls," 124.
69. Schuller, "Women in the Dead Sea Scrolls," 122–23.

changed quickly.⁷⁰ Cecilia Wassen examines the Damascus Document (CD), challenging the consensus that the Essenes elevated celibacy more highly than marriage.⁷¹ She suggests that both pursuits were equally valued and that women could be considered as ones who walk in perfect holiness, even as were the male members of the group.⁷² She also points out that both the CD and 1QSa (Rule of the Congregation) take the presence of women and children for granted; this in distinction to 1QS (Rule of the Community), which does not mention women. Wassen draws a picture of Essene women as belonging to the community, probably as full members, and as having intimate knowledge of the sect's laws and practices: "Thus it makes sense that women at least attended meetings in which legal issues were discussed and judgements were made, as attested in 1QSa I 11."⁷³

Maxine Grossman explores the sectarian works found among the scrolls' corpus, specifically examining the gender assumptions that inform views on women.⁷⁴ She reads "against the grain" and focuses on spaces of tension within the texts, places where there seems to be disagreement over women's practices, the scope of their authority, or their standing in the sectarian community. She postulates that sexual intimacy in marriage is an area of greater responsibility for women, but general teachings of the sect might offer women less authority.

Grossman explores passages about marriage in CD and 4Q159 (4QOrdinances) that speak of knowledgeable and trustworthy women who inspect or examine a virgin whose bad reputation could prevent a suitable marriage. These women determine the virgin's respectability or religious maturity, and Grossman adds, "There is real social impact in the role these women would have played, with significant importance for group stability."⁷⁵ In a similar vein, 1QSa insists that the wife bear witness to the leaders of the community about her husband concerning the Torah's ordinances. Most likely the

---

70. Eileen Schuller, "Women in the Dead Sea Scrolls: Some Observations from a Dictionary," *RevQ* 24 (2009): 49–59. See also Eileen Schuller and Cecilia Wassen, "Women: Daily Life," *EDSS* 2:981–84; Sidnie White Crawford, "Not according to Rule: Women, the Dead Sea Scrolls and Qumran," in *Emanuel: Studies in Hebrew Bible, Septuagint, and Dead Sea Scrolls in Honor of Emanuel Tov*, ed. Shalom M. Paul et al. (Leiden: Brill, 2003), 127–50.

71. Wassen, *Women in the Damascus Document*, 127–29. See CD VII, 4b–10a.

72. Wassen says she "presents a highly complex picture in which women in some cases are depicted as inferior to men and in other cases as their equals. Thus . . . my study challenges the common assumption that the Essene women were extensively marginalized in communal life." Wassen, *Women in the Damascus Document*, 12.

73. Wassen, *Women in the Damascus Document*, 201.

74. Maxine Grossman, "The World of Qumran and the Sectarian Dead Sea Scrolls in Gendered Perspective," in *Early Jewish Writings*, ed. Eileen Schuller and Marie-Theres Wacker (Atlanta: SBL Press, 2017), 225–46.

75. Grossman, "World of Qumran," 239.

ordinances in view relate to the constrained sexual norms of the group.[76] How then does one explain the statement from 4Q270 (Damascus Document fragment) that distinguishes punishments for one who complains against a Father of the community versus one who complains against a Mother?[77] Offending a Father results in permanent expulsion, but doing the same to a Mother results in merely a ten-day suspension. The text clarifies the difference by noting that the Mother has no authoritative status. Grossman explores the tension point further, suggesting that the definitive statement about Mothers having no authoritative status indicates that a debate simmered in the community over women's influence and agency.[78]

The exploration of women's participation in the community reflected in the scrolls, including the possibility of making oaths, affects our understanding of Jewish women in Jesus's group (or John the Baptist's band of followers, or any other Jewish sect).[79] What sort of expectations did Jewish women in Roman Palestine hold about expressing their religious convictions? And what issues were uppermost as they practiced their beliefs? The menstrual purity codes seem prominent in the scrolls and are basically absent from discussion in the Gospels.[80] Was this a topic of discussion among Jewish women? The picture of women testifying about matters critical to the purity of the community should influence views about the value of NT women's testimony, including their claims about Jesus's resurrection (Matt. 28:8–10; Luke 24:9–12; John 20:18). Investigation results from studying the sectarian scrolls offer more texture to the historical fabric of the Jewish woman's religious possibilities in Roman Palestine.

Gnosticism, Gnostic Texts, and Women

In 1979, Elaine Pagels of Princeton University shaped the national conversation about Christianity with the publication of *The Gnostic Gospels*.[81] Hal Taussig remarks, "It is probably not an overstatement to say that Pagels has influenced religion in America more directly than any New Testament scholar in the past fifty years."[82] Her award-winning book presents an early Christian

---

76. Grossman, "World of Qumran," 239–40. See also Wassen, *Women in the Damascus Document*, 87–88.
77. 4Q270 7 i 13–15.
78. Grossman, "World of Qumran," 241–42. Wassen suggests that the term translated as "authority" could refer to an embroidered garment, perhaps similar to a priestly garment, worn only by the Fathers. Wassen, *Women in the Damascus Document*, 191–93.
79. Wassen, *Women in the Damascus Document*, 136–38.
80. Cohick, *Women in the World of the Earliest Christians*, 208.
81. Elaine Pagels, *The Gnostic Gospels* (New York: Random House, 1979). See also Pagels, *Adam, Eve, and the Serpent* (New York: Random House, 1988).
82. Hal Taussig, ed., *A New New Testament: A Bible for the 21st Century Combining Traditional and Newly Discovered Texts* (New York: Houghton Mifflin Harcourt, 2013), 534.

group that wrote texts with positive, sympathetic female imagery, which, Pagels suggests, likely translated into women occupying leadership roles within their communities.[83] Pagels drew on the recently discovered manuscripts from Nag Hammadi, Egypt, which included works hitherto known only by the descriptions of their antagonists, the church heresiologists such as Irenaeus.

In a chapter published in 1999, Ann McGuire suggests a more complex reading that takes account of both divine and human gender in mythic narrative.[84] She argues against the earlier assessments of Gnostic material that assumed "a direct correlation between gnostic images of the female and the social status of women in gnostic communities. . . . In addition, . . . [such assessments] . . . reflect a generalizing conception of 'gnosticism' as a single religious movement with a fairly unified body of imagery, thought, and practice."[85] McGuire brings epigraphic evidence to bear in the discussion. For example, she points to the Flavia Sophē inscription and remarks, "This inscription provides invaluable evidence for the spirituality and hopes of a third-century Christian woman in Rome and suggests some of the reasons why such a woman would be attracted to the religious rituals and claims of gnostic traditions."[86] McGuire wonders whether this woman, Sophē, was preparing for a visionary experience, having been baptized and anointed. McGuire also points out the male language used to describe the divine figures, except perhaps the aeons, who might include both male and female.

The stele's inscription reads in part:

> Longing for the Father's light, my sister and spouse, Sophe,
> Anointed in the bath of Christ with ointment imperishable, holy,
> You were eager to see the divine faces of the Aeons,
> The great angel of the Great Council, the true Son.
> Entering the bridal chamber and ascending, incorruptible, to the bridal
> Bed of the Father . . . you were crowned . . .[87]

This little-known figure still captures scholars' imaginations, but with distinct foci that represent the shifts in scholarship concerning women. H. Gregory Snyder locates the poem within the wider social and literary context of mid-

---

83. Schüssler Fiorenza drew the opposite conclusion—namely, that when "male" and "female" categories were used, they did not reference actual men and women, but spoke of archetypes and cosmic realities. Schüssler Fiorenza, *In Memory of Her*, 274.

84. Ann McGuire, "Women, Gender, and Gnosis in Gnostic Texts and Traditions," in Kraemer and D'Angelo, *Women and Christian Origins*, 257–99.

85. McGuire, "Women, Gender, and Gnosis in Gnostic Texts and Traditions," 259.

86. McGuire, "Women, Gender, and Gnosis in Gnostic Texts and Traditions," 267.

87. Translation in H. Gregory Snyder, "The Discovery and Interpretation of the Flavia Sophe Inscription: New Results," *VC* 68, no. 1 (2014): 27.

to-late-second-century pagan culture in Rome.[88] Snyder compares the inscription's content and poetic form to the poetic tradition of the Greco-Roman culture, specifically funerary epigrams. He argues that, while the Flavia poem reflects Valentinian theology and terminology familiar to funeral epigrams, the poem uses such language subversively as it builds an alternative picture of death and life after death. He points out that the poem speaks of yearning, a common sentiment in Christian and pagan funeral settings. The difference is that Flavia, the deceased, yearns for the divine, while pagans yearn for their deceased to return to them.

Some recent works on Gnosticism, such as Karen King's *What Is Gnosticism?*, published in 2003, have very little on women or gender.[89] Yet King's work on the *Gospel of Mary*, also published in 2003, highlights issues of gender as well as the similarities between canonical and noncanonical texts in the areas of ethics, ritual, and theology.[90] She suggests that the *Gospel of Mary* and other noncanonical texts provide historical texture to the early centuries of Christianity, which was a time of heated debates and variant practices. She encourages readers to judge for themselves whether the message found in the *Gospel of Mary* is one they should embrace.[91]

A similar sentiment undergirds *A New New Testament*, which is a collection of NT books and ten additional works, including several from the Nag Hammadi corpus.[92] The editor, Hal Taussig, includes a chapter titled "Giving Birth to *A New New Testament* and Retiring the Idea of Gnosticism," which explains this volume's view on Gnosticism. Following King, Taussig argues for the inadequacy of labeling certain ancient texts as representative of a coherent group called Gnostics; instead, he suggests that the Nag Hammadi documents demonstrate the extensive diversity among early Christians.[93] Reading these texts together with other Christian texts provides the public additional spiritual resources.

The committee that assembled *A New New Testament* not only looked at material from Nag Hammadi but also considered texts such as the Acts of Paul and Thecla and the Martyrdom of Perpetua and Felicitas. They chose to include Thecla's story because it showed a Christian woman making successful, independent choices to teach and lead and to stand against government

---

88. Snyder writes, "At the very least, we may confidently assert that Flavia Sophe and her circle were structuring their rituals with reference to Valentinian theological principles." Snyder, "Discovery and Interpretation of the Flavia Sophe Inscription," 52.
89. Karen L. King, *What Is Gnosticism?* (Cambridge: Harvard University Press, 2003).
90. Karen L. King, *The Gospel of Mary of Magdala: Jesus and the First Woman Apostle* (Santa Rosa, CA: Polebridge, 2003).
91. King, *Gospel of Mary of Magdala*, 7.
92. Taussig, *New New Testament*.
93. Taussig, *New New Testament*, 529–31, 535–36.

and cultural authorities that sought to deny her those decisions. By including Thecla's narrative, plus the Gospel of Mary and The Thunder: Perfect Mind, the committee hopes to change "the commonly held picture of gender and power in the first centuries of Christianity." Specifically, they wish to "provide much more support for a tradition of gender mutuality and allow twenty-first-century women to see themselves as powerful spiritual leaders."[94] I suspect the use of ancient sources that feature women will continue to provide popular resources for those who see such stories as malleable means to create a new, personal version of spirituality.

Wisdom and Sophia in Scripture

The figure of Sophia/Wisdom has been a part of feminist study of the Bible for decades.[95] Reflection on Lady Wisdom of Proverbs and the feminine noun *sophia*, the Greek term for wisdom, have prompted discussion about the feminine qualities of God and the spiritual capacity of women. For example, in 2017, Schüssler Fiorenza published a commentary on Ephesians for the Wisdom Commentary.[96] In her commentary's foreword, she argues that the Bible is written in "kyriocentric" language, having come from patri-kyriarchal cultures that generate misogyny and oppression. Yet she is convinced that because the Bible is sacred text, it can "inspire and authorize wo/men in our struggles against dehumanizing oppression"; the way forward is through the hermeneutic of "wisdom/Wisdom."[97] Her approach, which she has followed throughout her career, is to read "against the grain of the letter's androcentric language."[98] She emphasizes both lowercase "wisdom"—as that which is discerning, creative knowledge—and capitalized "Wisdom," which is a divine figure.[99] Barbara E. Reid, the series' general editor, explains that the Wisdom Commentary does not focus on feminism alone, but also includes discussion of "intersecting issues of power, authority, ethnicity, race, class, and religious belief and practice."[100]

---

94. Taussig, *New New Testament*, 335.
95. For example, see Carol P. Christ and Judith Plaskow, eds., *Womanspirit Rising: A Feminist Reader in Religion* (1979; repr., San Francisco: HarperSanFrancisco, 1992).
96. Elisabeth Schüssler Fiorenza, *Ephesians*, Wisdom Commentary (Collegeville, MN: Liturgical Press, 2017).
97. Schüssler Fiorenza, *Ephesians*, xxii.
98. Schüssler Fiorenza, *Ephesians*, lviii.
99. Schüssler Fiorenza describes the Wisdom commentary series as "the spiraling circle dance of wisdom/Wisdom, as a Spirit/spiritual intellectual movement in the open space of wisdom/Wisdom who calls readers to critically analyze, debate, and reimagine biblical texts and their commentaries as wisdom/Wisdom texts inspired by visions of justice and well-being for everyone and everything." Schüssler Fiorenza, *Ephesians*, xxiii.
100. Barbara E. Reid, ed., "Editor's Introduction," in Schüssler Fiorenza, *Ephesians*, xxv.

Similarly, in 2014, Schüssler Fiorenza edited a volume in the *Bible and Women* encyclopedia, titled *Feminist Biblical Studies in the Twentieth Century: Scholarship and Movement*.[101] Chapters address feminist biblical studies from scholars across the globe and from Jewish, Christian, and Muslim perspectives. The volume also attends to hermeneutical, political, and ethical issues arising within the discussion. Schüssler Fiorenza writes in her introduction that "identity is not only constituted by gender but also by immigrant status, class, education, nationality, sexuality, ability, race, religion, and more," adding that identity is "multiplex and shaped by intersecting structures of dominations."[102]

Intersectionality and Global Female Voices

The term *intersectionality* was first used in 1989 when Kimberlé Williams Crenshaw, a legal scholar, developed the theory of intersectionality in an attempt to explain effects of various forms of discrimination—racism, sexism, classism—especially as they related to black women's experiences of the legal system in the United States.[103] She observed that racism was often defined from the experience of black men, and feminism from the experiences of white women. The black woman experienced racism and sexism differently in the work place, and the antidiscrimination laws did not support her. Crenshaw's observations are reflected in Womanist and Latina theologies, which highlight the ways in which black and Hispanic women struggle against racism and sexism in interconnected ways. As more global minority voices explore ancient texts about women, including canonical works, we should expect a greater discussion about the intersection of race, class, and gender on ancient women's lives. And as studies on gender and constructions of femininity grow, a new trajectory of study has emerged that focuses on masculinity. This should not be surprising, as ideal feminine values and virtues are typically developed in tandem with or opposition to ideals of masculinity.[104]

---

101. Elisabeth Schüssler Fiorenza, ed., *Feminist Biblical Studies in the Twentieth Century: Scholarship and Movement*, vol. 9.1 of *The Bible and Women: An Encyclopedia of Exegesis and Cultural History*, ed. Jorunn Økland et al. (Atlanta: SBL Press, 2014). This series is published in German, Italian, Spanish, and English.

102. Elisabeth Schüssler Fiorenza, "Between Movement and Academy: Feminist Biblical Studies in the Twentieth Century," in *Feminist Biblical Studies in the Twentieth Century*, 10.

103. Kimberlé Williams Crenshaw, "Demarginalizing the Intersection of Race and Sex: A Black Feminist Critique of Antidiscrimination Doctrine, Feminist Theory and Antiracist Politics," *University of Chicago Legal Forum* 1 (1989): 139–67.

104. L. Stephanie Cobb, *Dying to Be Men: Gender and Language in Early Christian Martyr Texts* (New York: Columbia University Press, 2008); Colleen M. Conway, *Behold the Man: Jesus and Greco-Roman Masculinity* (New York: Oxford University Press, 2008); Kelly Olson, *Masculinity and Dress in Roman Antiquity* (New York: Routledge, 2017); Brittany E. Wilson,

Methodologies for the Mid-Twenty-First Century

In the 1970s, scholars sought out historical women's stories as a way to empower contemporary women in their goals for political, educational, and economic equality. Yet the descriptive task of the historian, coupled with the epistemological positivism that undergirded the research, hindered scholars from critiquing the patriarchal milieu that bound women's experiences. The influence of poststructuralism on literary criticism and philosophy played a large part in refocusing discussions around gender construction as well as, or instead of, *real* women, for the discussions about gender construction and historical women's stories are understood to be inseparable. As texts and history were deconstructed, scholars grew increasingly uncertain that material available offered a plausible picture of women in the ancient world.[105] Dale Martin labels the new attention to theories and methods of poststructuralism (discourse analysis, ideology criticism, etc.) as the "cultural turn," a movement in scholarship that reflects the linguistic and philosophical changes under the umbrella of poststructuralism.[106] More work is still to be done on the cultural background and social status that construct gender and inform women's lives.

Additionally, performance theory will likely be used more extensively. This approach focuses on ritual and linguistic actions done before an audience. Performance communicates the subject's intentions to others and includes the audience in evaluating the communication. This approach focuses on individual actors as grammatical, philosophical, or historical subjects. In the study of ancient women, this approach asserts women's ownership of their identities, even as they (and men) experienced the restrictions of culture within their communities. Performance theory explores women as subjects or agents who live into their cultural norms or resist them. In general, ancient women are credited with agency when they reject cultural norms and act subversively, but performance theory challenges such insistence on subversive action as the marker of authenticity. Susan Hylen focuses on the apparent contradiction that characterizes Thecla, who both speaks and is silent, who seems to "inhabit" and "break free" from her patriarchal context.[107] Hylen looks for agency not only in acts of resistance to cultural norms but in behavior or

---

Unmanly Men: Refigurations of Masculinity in Luke-Acts (New York: Oxford University Press, 2015).

105. Kraemer, *Unreliable Witnesses*, 273. Kraemer draws on Pierre Bourdieu, crediting him with the insight that "masculine domination, indeed all domination, is embedded in *habitus*, even the very thought structures with which we attempt to think about all this."

106. Dale B. Martin, introduction to *The Cultural Turn in Late Ancient Studies: Gender, Asceticism, and Historiography*, ed. Dale B. Martin and Patricia Cox Miller (Durham, NC: Duke University Press, 2005), 7–9.

107. Hylen, *Modest Apostle*, 1.

speech that "is shaped by and embedded within social relationships" of a given cultural framework.[108]

The use of performance theory coincides with a new interest in the topic of modesty, a shift from the study of asceticism and virginity that dominated earlier scholarship. Hylen explores modesty not as a restricting set of norms, but as a complex set of options available for women to exert their influence and power in both civic and familial settings. Kate Wilkinson argues that "modesty is reflexive. It is an opportunity for active self-formation and self-representation in a community."[109] She contrasts her argument with those of others who see modesty as simply the result of sexual self-discipline or a public cover-up for a lack of sexual restraint. Wilkinson suggests that "modest dress and domesticity are not entirely unusual places to look for women's agency," because women employed these avenues for "self-representation and creative being."[110] She pursues what will likely be a growing area of exploration—namely, clothing and its rhetorical and real connections with wealth, status, and gender.[111] For example, she explores the use of the veil, suggesting that ancient discussions about the practice of veiling reveal that the matter required the modest woman to make choices that served to establish and maintain her identity.[112]

Role of Women in Church and Synagogue Today

It is no coincidence that the study of women in the Greco-Roman world sprouted at the same time as the second wave of feminism swept across Western Europe and the United States. Exploration of Jewish and Christian women at the start of Christianity and rabbinic Judaism was not only interesting in its own right but also historians, social scientists, and literary theorists often drew conclusions about present-day organizational structures from past examples of women leaders exercising authority. For example, Brooten's work on synagogue inscriptions postulated that (male) scholars read modern rabbinic teachings on gender back onto ancient sources, thus failing to see that ancient Jewish women held positions of authority and influence in their synagogues.[113]

---

108. Hylen, *Modest Apostle*, 12.
109. Hylen, *Modest Apostle*, 17. See also p. 104, where she argues that "the subject of modesty was not cut off from her voice; she was responsible for it, held accountable for it by a discriminating audience who considered much more than simply whether or not she spoke."
110. Kate Wilkinson, *Women and Modesty in Late Antiquity* (Cambridge: Cambridge University Press, 2015), 89–90.
111. Wilkinson, *Women and Modesty in Late Antiquity*, 33–49.
112. Wilkinson, *Women and Modesty in Late Antiquity*, 51–56.
113. Kraemer observes that Brooten's interpretation of ancient inscriptions about Jewish women, which distinguished between honorary and functional, was part of the modern

Scholars of Judaism continue to analyze women in the biblical and rabbinic texts, often with gender questions at the forefront.[114]

Looking at the early church, Schüssler Fiorenza suggests a brief period of egalitarian relationships that soon shifted to hierarchical arrangements that pushed women out of positions of authority. More recently, Cooper critiques such articulations of a radical, ascetic, charismatic church that folded under a developing hierarchy, claiming that such theories miss the rhetorical thrusts of early texts against established Roman civic virtues and sexual morality.[115] Osiek and MacDonald, in contrast to Cooper's position, submit that Christianity reflected the broadening opportunities for social freedom found in the Roman Empire and that Christian women contributed to the new movement in ways "whose effects are still with us today."[116] Kraemer observes that NT studies about women have been shaped by modern questions of women's ordination, with the result that historical questions become theological minefields.[117] Said another way, scholars evaluate whether the limited participation by ancient women in leadership relates only to social and historical context of Greco-Roman patriarchy or whether it reflects an essential aspect of Christian theological teaching. I think it is fair to conclude that, in most cases, scholars find examples of Christian women exerting positive, authoritative influence in their communities, and many point to this as evidence for women's leadership today.

The recent interest in the study of women in the Jewish, Greco-Roman, and early Christian world coincides with the rise of women's rights around the globe. Historians face questions of method as they sift through the inadequate and often patriarchal textual and material remains concerning women of the Greco-Roman world. Poststructuralism, with its attending "cultural turn," addresses the question of whether we can even know ancient women's historical lives based on the textual evidence. The study of ancient women is therefore not only a historical pursuit but also an inherently political and ethical endeavor, even if at times only implicitly so. Conversations about women of the ancient world do not occur between disinterested parties, for scholars' findings about women's power and influence, or lack thereof, play into modern debates about women's roles in the workplace, in the family, and in religious institutions. Given our current climate, the dialogue is far from finished.

---

discussion about women's roles in the modern synagogue and church. Kraemer, *Unreliable Witnesses*, 233.

114. Frederick E. Greenspahn, ed., *Women and Judaism: New Insights and Scholarship* (New York: New York University Press, 2009).

115. Cooper, *Virgin and the Bride*, 57.

116. Osiek and MacDonald, *Woman's Place*, 16.

117. Kraemer, "Women and Gender," 475.

PART 2

Interpretation

3

Hermeneutics and Exegesis

Dennis R. Edwards

Introduction

"Interpreting the Bible is an act of power."[1] Indeed. Barbara E. Reid asserts that feminist interpreters have long understood that axiom, but we may well conclude that all Bible readers whose voices have been muted over eons know the power that comes from being able to interpret the Bible. Over the last fifteen years or so, we have witnessed exponential growth in the volume of literature offering biblical interpretation from a wide-ranging and ever-growing perspective. As these interpretative perspectives grow so does the realization that "all biblical interpretation is an art, not a formula that can be followed exactly so as to produce the correct meaning for all time."[2]

This chapter highlights the development and trajectory of what could be called postmodern biblical interpretation. The cornerstone of modern approaches to the Bible is historical criticism. Other modern approaches include form criticism, source criticism, redaction criticism, and social-scientific criticism. However, these modern approaches are being eclipsed by newer strategies. Postmodern biblical interpretation consists of virtually unlimited approaches that employ the terms *criticism*, *hermeneutics*, and

---

1. Barbara E. Reid, "Editor's Introduction to Wisdom Commentary," in Annette Bourland Huizenga, *1 and 2 Timothy, Titus* (Collegeville, MN: Michael Glazier, 2016), xxxiii.
2. Barbara E. Reid, *Wisdom's Feast: An Invitation to Feminist Interpretation of the Scriptures* (Grand Rapids: Eerdmans, 2016), 11.

biblical interpretation interchangeably, such as "feminist criticism," "feminist hermeneutics," or "feminist biblical interpretation." These postmodern approaches are a result of traditionally marginalized people (e.g., women, ethnic minorities in the United States, and Bible readers outside of the Western Hemisphere) reading the Bible from their perspective and place in the world. Having grappled with the fact that the Bible has been used to oppress people in the United States as well as other places, interpreters continually explore how the Bible might speak to those who formerly did not have the power to interpret it. With that reality in mind, this chapter strives to describe the landscape of African American, womanist and feminist, Latinx, and postcolonial biblical interpretation. Practical concerns prevent the discussion of more disciplines, such as African biblical interpretation, Asian American biblical interpretation, LGBTQ hermeneutics, and other socially located approaches to Scripture, but some of the resources in my footnotes may be helpful for exploring those areas.

There has also been a growing appreciation of the reality that people also read the Bible from a particular theological perspective. There are scholars whose faith brings them to the biblical text, and they do not approach it clinically or merely as ancient literature. Theological interpretation of Scripture is a flourishing enterprise despite the difficulty of defining it and the lack of any evident methodology for its practice.

I wish to acknowledge at the outset one resource that I cite frequently in this chapter: *Scripture and Its Interpretation: A Global, Ecumenical Introduction to the Bible*, edited by Michael J. Gorman.[3] This excellent collection of essays is written by experts and offers all those interested in the Bible—not just scholars—helpful introductions to a variety of topics related to the Bible and the study of it. Readers will find the book's glossary to be an indispensable resource while navigating the terrain surrounding the study of the Bible.

Modern versus Postmodern Biblical Interpretation

When I naively started my doctoral studies at Fordham University in New York City many years ago, I wondered how Roman Catholic faculty and students would receive me—a Protestant—at that Jesuit university.[4] During a new student orientation, I confessed my nervousness to a prominent scholar who was also a Roman Catholic priest. His response was, in part, "A Hebrew verb

---

3. Michael J. Gorman, ed., *Scripture and Its Interpretation: A Global, Ecumenical Introduction to the Bible* (Grand Rapids: Baker Academic, 2017).

4. Because I moved to Washington, DC, to serve a church there, I completed my studies at the Catholic University of America, but I appreciated my time at Fordham.

is a Hebrew verb." That answer encouraged me, as it communicates that no one person or group has a lock on serious study of the Bible. However, some of my Protestant acquaintances feared that I might abandon Protestantism by studying alongside Roman Catholics. I did not share that fear, but I began to wonder whether my church background was a hindrance or help in my academic studies. Looking back on those days, I view the response of the scholar along with the apprehension that my acquaintances sparked in me as representing a degree of one of the tensions in biblical studies—a tension between modern and postmodern approaches to the Bible.

The professor's quick remark that "a Hebrew verb is a Hebrew verb" may reflect the way many viewed historical-critical study of the Bible, taking it to be a clinical enterprise, performed by individuals and detached from one's faith, gender, or cultural background. Such study was governed by a set of rules and could, theoretically, lead to the one correct meaning of a Scripture passage. Joel Green notes that, with regard to modern approaches to the Bible, "interpreters must operate autonomously, or independently—independent of the interpreter's own faith (or lack of faith), independent of the church's theology, and independent of the church's (or any other) authority and influence."[5] In contrast to this autonomous approach to the Bible are postmodern approaches:

> Postmodern approaches to biblical interpretation are held together less by a common commitment to a certain method or even constellation of methods, and more by their critical sensibilities. On the one hand, in contrast to modernist, Enlightenment thinking, postmodern interpreters urge that we have no objectively determined ledge of truth on which to stand in order to make value-free judgments in the work of making meaning. Interpreters cannot hide behind the veil of presumed ideological neutrality. For many postmoderns, on the other hand, "truth" does not exist as an abstract reality apart from human knowing. Thus, for students of the Bible, "meaning" is not simply a property of the text that the reader must discover or excavate but is somehow the product of the interaction of readers with texts.[6]

It is this tension between modern and postmodern biblical interpretation that is partly behind the emergence and growth of what has been called *theological interpretation* (or *exegesis*) of Scripture, a practice that has witnessed an explosion of interest over the last two decades or so. Kevin J. Vanhoozer observes, "The 'theological interpretation of the Bible' has become something

---

5. Joel B. Green, "Modern and Postmodern Methods of Biblical Interpretation," in Gorman, *Scripture and Its Interpretation*, 188.
6. Green, "Modern and Postmodern Methods," 196–97.

of a growth industry of late, spawning new journals, academic conferences, and commentary series."[7]

The Eclipse of Historical-Critical Biblical Interpretation

A prominent voice in the practice of theological interpretation is Stephen Fowl, who asserts that "the demise of the conceptual apparatus that allowed for the dominance of historical-critical interpretation of the Bible has not led to the elimination of historical criticism, nor should it. It has, however, opened the door to critical approaches to the Bible that do not grant historical concerns priority over all others. In theory this means that there is now room for theological concerns to reenter the scholarly realm."[8] That conceptual apparatus, according to Fowl, is the result of the convergence of "scientific, cultural, political, and philosophical movements" that allowed for historical criticism's methodological hegemony within academic biblical study. However, societal changes over the last century impacting science, culture, politics, and philosophy worked to subvert historical criticism's dominance. "Recall that historical concerns took precedence over theological concerns only when people assumed they could comprehend the world and its past in more or less immediate or direct ways, apart from the lenses provided by Scripture read theologically."[9] Yet our understanding of history is colored by our place in the world—"we never perceive or comprehend the world and its past without our own set of lenses."[10]

The trenchant observations of Richard B. Hays in his essay "Reading the Bible with Eyes of Faith: The Practice of Theological Exegesis" attempt to account for the downfall of historical criticism.[11] Hays cites examples—from the Society of Biblical Literature website as well as scholarly addresses—suggesting an antifaith bias within the field of biblical studies: "Whereas a generation ago it was widely accepted that there would be a fruitful synthesis of historical and theological inquiry in biblical studies, this claim is

---

7. Kevin J. Vanhoozer, Daniel Treier, and N. T. Wright, eds., *Theological Interpretation of the New Testament: A Book-by-Book Survey* (Grand Rapids: Baker Academic, 2008), 13.

8. Stephen Fowl, "Theological Interpretation of the Bible," in Gorman, *Scripture and Its Interpretation*, 211. Fowl, a Roman Catholic, acknowledges that historical-critical methodology still plays a role in biblical interpretation. Another Roman Catholic and giant of biblical scholarship, Joseph A. Fitzmyer, in his defense of the historical-critical method, admitted that some postmodern approaches (e.g., liberation theology and feminism) "have been . . . and can continue to be, valuable refinements of that basic method [historical-critical], even offering at times useful correctives." Fitzmyer, *The Interpretation of Scripture: In Defense of the Historical-Critical Method* (Mahwah, NJ: Paulist Press, 2008), 82–83.

9. Fowl, "Theological Interpretation," 209.

10. Fowl, "Theological Interpretation," 210.

11. Richard B. Hays, "Reading the Bible with Eyes of Faith: The Practice of Theological Exegesis," *JTI* 1, no. 1 (2007): 5–21.

increasingly challenged by some insistent voices that seek to exclude any sort of explicitly religious or theological perspective from a place at the table in scholarly study of the Bible."[12]

As the heyday of historical-critical study of the Bible wanes, Hays is one of an ever-increasing number of scholars who are proponents and practitioners of theological interpretation of Scripture. Such interpretation, however, is difficult to quantify, as "it is not a set of discrete procedures that could be set alongside, say, textual criticism or redaction criticism. Rather, theological exegesis is a complex *practice*, a way of approaching Scripture with eyes of faith and seeking to understand it within the community of faith."[13] Fowl concurs, noting, "Rather than being a precise method of interpretation, theological interpretation is more like the exercise of a type of wisdom."[14] This lack of concrete methodology is behind some of the criticism of theological interpretation. D. A. Carson avers that "Theological Interpretation of Scripture (TIS) is partly disparate movement, partly a call to reformation in biblical interpretation, partly a disorganized array of methodological commitments in hermeneutics, partly a serious enterprise and partly (I suspect) a fad."[15]

Toward the Practice of Theological Interpretation of Scripture

Since many have undertaken to draw up an account of what makes for theological interpretation of Scripture, it is difficult to arrive at a single description.[16] However, the compact definition offered in *Scripture and Its Interpretation* is helpful: "theological interpretation: The interpretive approach that emphasizes (a) the interpreters' ecclesial location; (b) commitment to the church's confessions, traditions, and liturgical life; and (c) the prioritizing

---

12. Hays, "Reading the Bible with Eyes of Faith," 8.
13. Hays, "Reading the Bible with Eyes of Faith," 11.
14. Fowl, "Theological Interpretation," 217.
15. D. A. Carson, "Theological Interpretation of Scripture: Yes, But . . . ," in *Theological Commentary: Evangelical Perspectives*, ed. R. Michael Allen (New York: T&T Clark, 2011), 187.
16. Hays, in the aforementioned "Reading the Bible with Eyes of Faith," proposes twelve "identifying marks" of theological interpretation. Even more recent is Kevin J. Vanhoozer, "Ten Theses on the Theological Interpretation of Scripture," *Modern Reformation* 19, no. 4 (July/August 20l0): 17–18. Carson, in "Theological Interpretation of Scripture," evaluates six "propositions" of theological interpretation using a "yes, but" format. See also Stephen E. Fowl, *Theological Interpretation of Scripture* (Eugene, OR: Cascade, 2009); Joel B. Green, *Practicing Theological Interpretation: Engaging Biblical Texts for Faith and Formation* (Grand Rapids: Baker Academic, 2012); Daniel J. Treier, *Introducing Theological Interpretation of Scripture: Recovering a Christian Practice* (Grand Rapids: Baker Academic, 2008); and Thorsten Moritz, "Scripture and Theological Exegesis," in *The Sacred Text: Excavating the Texts, Exploring the Interpretations, and Engaging the Theologies of the Christian Scriptures*, ed. Michael F. Bird and Michael W. Pahl (Piscataway, NJ: Gorgias, 2010), 119–40.

of theological concerns over other concerns—all with the goal of enhancing faithful living and worshiping before God by bringing theological concerns to bear on scriptural interpretation, and vice versa."[17]

Theological interpreters attempt to engage in a type of catholicity, where interpreting Scripture means departing from the autonomy of modern interpretation (noted above) and engaging the broader Christian community. That Christian community includes interpreters from the past as well as the present. Theological interpretation consistently claims to be recovering an ancient practice; consequently, it embraces precritical readings of Scripture, including allegorical and other figurative readings. Furthermore, "theological exegesis must always be done from a posture of prayer and humility before the word."[18] The goal of such a posture is "to discern how the Holy Spirit leads members of the Christian community to discover the meaning of Scripture, and in particular how different parts of the body of Christ connect with each other in that process."[19]

Carson offers this assessment of theological interpretation: "At this moment, however, I am inclined to think that what is most valuable in TIS (and much is), is not new; what is new in TIS varies from ambiguous to mistaken, depending in part on the theological location of the interpreter."[20] I suspect that all interpretation, even that employing historical-critical methodology, can be ambiguous and mistaken, depending on the theological location of the interpreter. Therefore, theological interpretation—like all interpretation—must be an ongoing practice, always being reformed. Stanley E. Porter offers a more recent critique of theological interpretation. After a thorough treatment of books by Joel B. Green, Daniel J. Treier, Stephen Fowl, and J. Todd Billings, Porter concludes:

> I asked two questions in the title of this paper—what is theological interpretation of Scripture, and is it hermeneutically robust enough for the task to which it has been appointed? The answer to the first question is—it depends upon whom you ask.... The answer to the second question regarding its hermeneutical robustness is—no, it is not, at least as it has so far been defined. For some, theological hermeneutics remains simply an ancillary form of modern criticism. Even for those who wish to distinguish it especially from historical criticism, it is often heavily dependent upon other forms of modern critical interpretation. In all cases, it lacks a hermeneutical robustness that is appropriate for its self-proclaimed task of providing a means of theologically interpreting Scripture.[21]

17. Gorman, *Scripture and Its Interpretation*, 423.
18. Hays, "Reading the Bible with Eyes of Faith," 15.
19. Treier, *Introducing Theological Interpretation*, 80.
20. Carson, "Theological Interpretation of Scripture," 207.
21. Stanley E. Porter, "What Exactly Is Theological Interpretation of Scripture, and Is It Hermeneutically Robust Enough for the Task to Which It Has Been Appointed?," in *Horizons*

The future of theological interpretation may require works that bring more clarity to the question of how aspects of historical-critical methodology work in concert with theological readings of Scripture. Theological interpreters seek to bridge the divide between biblical scholarship and theology; yet it is not always clear what such a bridge looks like. Carson claims that the Brazos Theological Commentary on the Bible (a series devoted to theological interpretation) "has, in several of its volumes, proved so unsatisfying."[22] Carson explains, "Because readers could not forge the actual connections between text and theology ostensibly derived from a *commentary* on the text, they balked—and rightly so."[23]

Despite the criticism of theological interpretation of Scripture, including its methodological ambiguity, the number of vehicles for the practice and development of the field continues to grow and now includes the following journals: *Pro Ecclesia*, *Journal for Theological Interpretation*, *Ex Auditu*, and *Horizons in Biblical Theology*. As for commentaries, in addition to the Brazos Theological Commentary on the Bible, there are Studies in Theological Interpretation (Baker), the Two Horizons Commentary (Eerdmans), The Story of God Bible Commentary (Zondervan), and Belief—A Theological Commentary on the Bible (Westminster John Knox).

Related to theological interpretation is the practice of missional hermeneutics, which "locates the Bible and its interpretation within the arc of God's mission (the *missio Dei*) as this is articulated in Scripture; it also inquires into how the Bible might shape the church's contemporary identity and mission."[24] Missional hermeneutics is an example of a postmodern approach to Scripture that pays attention to broader, global Christian perspectives. Such perspectives are growing and too numerous to discuss in this chapter. However, the following discussion will hopefully provide some signposts along the road of socially located biblical interpretation.

Reader-Response Hermeneutics

Anthony C. Thiselton explains that "reader-response theory places an emphasis on the active role of the reader in interpreting texts. At its simplest, it depends on the axiom that a reader, or community of readers, 'completes' the meaning of a text. It rests on the assumption that even if it may speak

---

in *Hermeneutics: A Festschrift in Honor of Anthony C. Thiselton*, ed. Anthony C. Thiselton, Stanley E. Porter, and Matthew R. Malcolm (Grand Rapids: Eerdmans, 2013), 267.
22. Carson, "Theological Interpretation of Scripture," 207.
23. Carson, "Theological Interpretation of Scripture," 207.
24. Green, "Modern and Postmodern Methods," 201. To map more of the discussions around missional hermeneutics, consult The Gospel and Our Culture Network (www.gocn.org).

legitimately of an author's intention, that intention is not fulfilled until a reader (or readers) appropriates the text."[25] In light of such a definition, it becomes obvious that the meanings of biblical texts are connected to the lens (which is a function of social location) through which readers encounter the text. Green explains that meaning "is what happens at the intersection of textual interests and readerly interests."[26] Reader-response criticism is a fruit of postmodernism, and "postmodern approaches recognize that readers come in all shapes and sizes, from many different cultural backgrounds. . . . Postmodern methods take for granted that we always read from 'a place' with 'place' or 'social location' capable of being explained in numerous ways—for example, in terms of gender or racial-ethnic identity, ecclesial tradition or socioeconomic status, and so on."[27]

As we might imagine, such observations suggest a virtually limitless list of approaches to biblical interpretation. For practical reasons the following discussion has been confined to what might be considered some of the most prominent reader-response approaches to biblical interpretation: African American, womanist and feminist, Latinx, and more generally, postcolonial biblical interpretation.

African American Biblical Interpretation

In his 1998 *Washington Post* article "Black Scholars Find Their Way," journalist Brian Lewis noted that at the time, "Of the thousands of biblical scholars with PhDs, there are only an estimated 35 to 50 African Americans."[28] As black scholars have been finding their way, so has the entire field of African American biblical interpretation, which was a relatively new enterprise even toward the end of the twentieth century. One of the scholars featured in the aforementioned *Washington Post* article was Cain Hope Felder, whose *Troubling Biblical Waters: Race, Class, and Family*, published in 1990, proved to be a landmark work in African American biblical

---

25. Anthony C. Thiselton, *Hermeneutics: An Introduction* (Grand Rapids: Eerdmans, 2009), 306.
26. Green, "Modern and Postmodern Methods," 199.
27. Green, "Modern and Postmodern Methods," 199–200.
28. Brian Lewis, "Black Scholars Find Their Way," *Washington Post*, July 11, 1998, https://www.washingtonpost.com/archive/local/1998/07/11/black-scholars-find-their-way/22b20230-f899-4fb8-8bc7-3013d5c0f0ec/?utm_term=.3d9409d9ac20. I was in the thick of my own PhD studies at the Catholic University of America (CUA) in Washington, DC, when this article appeared, and it helped to shed light on the reasons why I had trouble finding an African American scholarly mentor. I sought out Cain Hope Felder at nearby Howard University for his advice. In the moments after I defended my PhD thesis, the dean of CUA's school of religion remarked that I was the first African American to earn a PhD in biblical studies from CUA.

interpretation.[29] It was twenty years prior to Felder's book, under the influence of liberation theology, that James Cone produced his groundbreaking contribution. Cone's *A Black Theology of Liberation* lit a torch that allowed increasing numbers of African American theologians and biblical scholars to find their way.[30] Liberation has always been a key theme in African American hermeneutics, with the exodus story of the OT providing inspiration and affirmation. African American Christians, since the time of slavery, have seen themselves in the exodus narrative, and thereby have been prompted to worship a God who executes judgment on oppressive powers while rescuing people from bondage and helping them to find their way.[31]

As one might imagine, as more African American scholars found their way to and from the library stacks, while simultaneously being involved in local churches, African American hermeneutics began to grow. One prominent fruit of such growth is the work produced in 2007 by a cadre of African American scholars. These scholars, under the editorial eyes of Brian K. Blount, Cain Hope Felder, Clarice J. Martin, and Emerson B. Powery, open their work with this proposition: "'What if the reading of and thinking about the Bible . . . were read through African American experience?' That is precicely the question the commentary intends to answer."[32] *True to Our Native Land: An African American New Testament Commentary* is a compendium of research on each NT writing as well as on issues of particular interest to African Americans, such as slavery, Pauline theology and ethics, and preaching.

Of particular note in *True to Our Native Land* is the contribution by Vincent L. Wimbush, which he calls a "trenchant anti-commentary essay."[33]

---

29. Cain Hope Felder, *Troubling Biblical Waters: Race, Class, and Family* (Maryknoll, NY: Orbis, 1990).

30. In 2010 a fortieth anniversary edition of Cone's work was published: James H. Cone, *A Black Theology of Liberation* (Maryknoll, NY: Orbis, 2010).

31. For a brief history, see C. Anthony Hunt, "African American Biblical Interpretation," in Gorman, *Scripture and Its Interpretation*, 298–310.

32. Brian K. Blount et al., eds., *True to Our Native Land: An African American New Testament Commentary* (Minneapolis: Fortress, 2007), 1. I hasten to note the influence that the Black National Anthem, "Lift Ev'ry Voice and Sing" (James Weldon Johnson), has had on the titles of works by African American biblical scholars. In 1991, Cain Hope Felder published a list of essays taken from the second stanza of "Lift Ev'ry Voice and Sing" (*Stony the Road We Trod: African American Biblical Interpretation* [Minneapolis: Augsburg Fortress, 1991]). In 2003 biblical scholar Randall Bailey published a collection of essays also from the second stanza (*Yet with a Steady Beat: The African American Struggle for Recognition in the Episcopal Church* [Norcross, GA: Trinity Press International, 1996]). The most recent work, *True to Our Native Land*, is taken from the final stanza of this classic song.

33. Vincent L. Wimbush, "'We Will Make Our Own Future Text': An Alternative Orientation to Interpretation," in Blount et al., *True to Our Native Land*, 43–53. Part of the title, "we will make our own future text," is a quotation from the novel by African American author Ishmael Reed, *Mumbo Jumbo* (New York: Scribner, 1972).

Wimbush questions the validity of commentaries, which he says force "the interpreter to begin not in his or her own time, not in or with his or her own world situation, but in another one—that (one that is imagined or assumed to be) of the text."[34] After a brief consideration of the writings of W. E. B. DuBois and Toni Morrison, Wimbush concludes, "For black and subaltern critical consciousness there is no meaning in any Western-translated narrative, script, text, and tradition unless such is first ripped, broken, and then 'entranced,' blackened, made usable for weaving meaning."[35]

Wimbush earlier explored the way African Americans have read the Bible in *The Bible and African Americans: A Brief History*.[36] Allen Dwight Callahan probed similar themes in *The Talking Book: African Americans and the Bible*.[37] Blount applies his expertise in NT studies to investigate NT ethics in *Then the Whisper Put On Flesh: New Testament Ethics in an African American Context*.[38] Blount also has written commentaries on the book of Revelation, with one that explicitly keeps the African American experience in view.[39] Similarly, my commentary on 1 Peter is replete with illustrations flowing out of African American history and experiences.[40] The Acts commentary by African American theologian Willie Jennings resonates with allusions familiar to many African Americans.[41] More and more African Americans, following the lead of their forebears, are writing works that appeal to themes of liberation, justice, and forgiveness.

While African American biblical interpretation unquestionably has the experience of slavery as a backdrop, such interpretation is practiced with a constant gaze directed toward the homeland, Africa.[42] *The Africana Bible: Reading Israel's Scriptures from Africa and the African Diaspora* makes explicit the connection between African American and African biblical interpretation.[43]

---

34. Wimbush, "'We Will Make Our Own Future Text,'" 44.

35. Wimbush, "'We Will Make Our Own Future Text,'" 51.

36. Vincent L. Wimbush, *The Bible and African Americans: A Brief History* (Minneapolis: Fortress, 2003).

37. Allen Dwight Callahan, *The Talking Book: African Americans and the Bible* (New Haven: Yale University Press, 2008).

38. Brian K. Blount, *Then the Whisper Put On Flesh: New Testament Ethics in an African American Context* (Nashville: Abingdon, 2001).

39. Brian K. Blount, *Revelation* (Louisville: Westminster John Knox, 2009); Blount, *Can I Get a Witness? Reading Revelation through African American Culture* (Louisville: Westminster John Knox, 2005).

40. Dennis R. Edwards, *1 Peter*, SGBC (Grand Rapids: Zondervan, 2017).

41. Willie James Jennings, *Acts: A Theological Commentary on the Bible* (Louisville: Westminster John Knox Press, 2017).

42. For example, see Rodney S. Sadler Jr., "The Place and Role of Africa and African Imagery in the Bible," in Blount et al., *True to Our Native Land*, 23–30.

43. Hugh R. Page Jr. et al., eds., *The Africana Bible: Reading Israel's Scriptures from Africa and the African Diaspora* (Minneapolis: Fortress, 2009).

African biblical interpretation is part of what may be more broadly called postcolonial biblical interpretation. African biblical interpretation seeks to respect the ancient context of the biblical writings and, similar to most modern readings, contextualize the Bible in order to have its words resonate with contemporary African life.[44]

The glossary in *Scripture and Its Interpretation* helpfully defines African American criticism as "an interpretive approach that (a) highlights the presence of Africa and Africans in the Bible, (b) resists racist and oppressive interpretations, (c) stresses themes such as exodus and liberation, and (d) draws on traditional and contemporary African American resources in interpretation for the preservation and progress of African American churches and communities."[45] Certainly, "there is, of course, no single African American perspective."[46] Yet despite the denominational, social, economic, and political differences among African American Christians, their particular history and culture contributes uniquely to the overall work of biblical interpretation.

Womanist and Feminist Biblical Interpretation

Although initially controversial, womanist hermeneutics continues to grow, and it functions as a link of sorts between African American biblical interpretation and feminist hermeneutics. Feminist biblical interpretation may be defined as "interpretative strategies that include (a) conducting historical and literary investigations into the portrayal of women and other marginalized groups in biblical texts as well as (b) bringing contemporary concerns of and about women and other marginalized groups into the practice of biblical interpretation."[47] The author Alice Walker is credited with coining the term *womanist*, a word "that would revolutionize the theological landscape," according to Raquel St. Clair.[48] Gay L. Byron and Vanessa Lovelace chronicle how, in 1979, Walker initially introduced the term *womanist* as a variant of *womanish*, "a word our mothers used to describe, and attempt to

---

44. See Bungishabaku Katho, "African Biblical Interpretation," in Gorman, *Scripture and Its Interpretation*, 284–97.
45. Gorman, *Scripture and Its Interpretation*, 401.
46. Blount, *True to Our Native Land*, xiv.
47. See Gorman, *Scripture and Its Interpretation*, 409.
48. Raquel St. Clair, "Womanist Biblical Interpretation," in Blount et al., *True to Our Native Land*, 54. St. Clair elaborates a bit on the initial controversy over womanist theology, quoting Cheryl J. Sanders: "The fact is that womanist is essentially a secular category whose theological and ecclesial significations are rather tenuous. Theological content too easily gets 'read into' the womanist concept, whose central emphasis remains the self-assertion and struggle of black women for freedom, with or without the aid of God or Jesus or anybody else." St. Clair, "Womanist Biblical Interpretation," 60n5. See Cheryl J. Sanders, "Roundtable: Christian Ethics and Theology in Womanist Perspective," *JFSR* 5 (1989): 83–112.

inhibit, strong, outrageous, or outspoken behavior when we were children."[49] Walker went on to refine the term in her 1973 prose collection, *In Search of Our Mothers' Gardens*, noting that a "womanist" is "a black feminist or feminist of color."[50]

Womanist Interpretations of the Bible: Expanding the Discourse is a collection of essays, primarily focusing on select OT and NT texts, sorted into the following four categories that "reflect some of the overarching themes of womanist biblical interpretation": (1) gender and sexuality, (2) agency and advocacy, (3) foregrounding women on the margins, and (4) illuminating biblical children/childhood.[51] A stated goal of this collection of essays is for "readers to come away with a new understanding of womanist readings of sacred texts that highlight the myriad perspectives that black and other women of color bring to interpreting these texts."[52] St. Clair's essay in *True to Our Native Land*, "Womanist Biblical Interpretation," advances a "hermeneutic of wholeness," which must "promote the wholeness of African American women without prohibiting the wholeness of others."[53]

I Found God in Me: A Womanist Biblical Hermeneutics Reader is a recent collection of essays by seasoned as well as newer womanist scholars that seeks to demonstrate the diverse methodologies involved in womanist biblical interpretation.[54] The body of writings produced by womanist scholars continues to grow and is not confined to articles in particular journals (such as *Journal of Feminist Studies in Religion*) or essays within a collection. The recent work by Wil Gafney, *Womanist Midrash: A Reintroduction to the Women of the Torah and the Throne*, is an example of an entire book employing womanist and feminist approaches to biblical interpretation.[55] Nyasha Junior's con-

---

49. Gay L. Byron and Vanessa Lovelace, "Introduction: Methods and the Making of Womanist Biblical Hermeneutics," in *Womanist Interpretations of the Bible: Expanding the Discourse*, ed. Gay L. Byron and Vanessa Lovelace, Semeia 47 (Atlanta: Scholars Press, 1989), 1–2. Byron and Lovelace offer a history of womanist biblical interpretation as does St. Clair (see prior note).

50. Alice Walker, *In Search of Our Mothers' Gardens: Womanist Prose* (New York: Harcourt Brace Jovanovich, 1973). Cited in Byron and Lovelace, "Introduction: Methods and the Making," 2, and also in St. Clair, "Womanist Biblical Interpretation," 54–55.

51. Byron and Lovelace, "Methods and the Making," 9–14.

52. Byron and Lovelace, "Methods and the Making," 15. A particularly helpful essay for ongoing research is Gay L. Byron, "Black Collectors and Keepers of Tradition: Resources for a Womanist Biblical Ethic of (Re)Interpretation," in Byron and Lovelace, *Womanist Interpretations of the Bible*, 187–208. Byron identifies various collectors and Africana collections that relate to the Bible and early Christianity.

53. St. Clair, "Womanist Biblical Interpretation," 59.

54. Mitzi J. Smith, ed., *I Found God in Me: A Womanist Biblical Hermeneutics Reader* (Eugene, OR: Cascade, 2015); see also Smith, *Insights from African American Interpretation* (Minneapolis: Fortress, 2017).

55. Wilda C. Gafney, *Womanist Midrash: A Reintroduction to the Women of the Torah and the Throne* (Louisville: Westminster John Knox, 2017).

tribution, *An Introduction to Womanist Biblical Interpretation*, is another book-length study devoted to exploring the development of womanist biblical interpretation, its connection to African American biblical interpretation, and its distinction from feminist biblical interpretation.[56] The author, however, offers this interesting disclaimer: "To some, it may seem strange that I should write a book about womanist biblical interpretation since I do not identify myself as a womanist."[57] Even so, Junior's book is a helpful resource for understanding the field of womanist biblical interpretation and where it may be going.

Barbara E. Reid, in *Wisdom's Feast: An Invitation to Feminist Interpretation of the Scriptures*, mentions that developing alongside womanist biblical interpretation is Latina feminist, or *mujerista*, interpretation.[58] Womanist and *mujerista* approaches to biblical study are in some ways the daughters of feminist biblical interpretation, a practice that has a relatively long history. In *Wisdom's Feast*, Reid gives a brief history of feminist theological studies as well as a basic outline of how the practice takes shape, before offering studies on the creation narratives of Genesis as well as essays treating some NT passages that focus on women. Reid's section "How to Interpret the Bible from a Feminist Liberationist Perspective" proposes seven steps.[59] Briefly, those steps are as follows:

1. Begin with women's experience.
2. Identify the interpreter's social location.
3. Ask, "Who says?"[60]
4. Evaluate by asking, What does the text do? (E.g., Does the text "reinforce domination and oppression? Or does it liberate for full life?")
5. Unleash creative imagination. "It is necessary to engage all the powers of creative imagination to dream of a world in which equality and dignity of women is a fact."
6. Re-member and reconstruct.[61]

---

56. Nyasha Junior, *An Introduction to Womanist Biblical Interpretation* (Louisville: Westminster John Knox, 2015).
57. Junior, *Introduction to Womanist Biblical Interpretation*, 129.
58. Reid, *Wisdom's Feast*, 6.
59. Reid, *Wisdom's Feast*, 8–12.
60. On the surface this third step appears to employ historical-critical methodology, as Reid explains: "Question who wrote the text, for whom, in what circumstances, and with what purpose" (*Wisdom's Feast*, 9). Yet she continues, "Here it is important to acknowledge that the books of the Bible have been written, for the most part, by men, for men, about men, and to serve men's purposes. . . . We should not regard as 'the Word of God' any text that denies, diminishes, or distorts the full humanity of women" (9–10).
61. Reid explains, "The use of the hyphen in 're-member' is intended to evoke the importance of realizing that women were among the members of disciples, missionaries, apostles, teachers,

7. Take action for transformative change. After analyzing a text, "the process must culminate in deliberate action aimed at transformation."[62]

Reid has also contributed to a significant recent development in feminist biblical interpretation, the Wisdom Commentary series from Liturgical Press. Each volume in the series contains a foreword by Elisabeth Schüssler Fiorenza and an editor's introduction by Reid. The introduction gives a brief history of feminist biblical interpretation and also explains that a continually updated bibliography can be found at www.wisdomcommentary.org. Schüssler Fiorenza, perhaps the most prominent voice in feminist biblical criticism, continues to shape and outline the future of the practice. She counsels that feminist hermeneutics is not a "finished research product" but rather "an ongoing process within the context of women's societal and ecclesial struggles for justice and liberation."[63] Although men are welcome to engage in feminist biblical interpretation, the voice of women needs to be prominent. My notes includes several recent works by women, notably those by Frances Taylor Gench, Marion Ann Taylor, and Heather Weir.

Latinx Biblical Interpretation

Fernando F. Segovia, a leading voice in Latinx biblical interpretation, ponders the role of identity in Latinx biblical interpretation as well as the related question of "praxis or agenda"; that is, to what extent does the work of the Latinx scholar focus on social location?[64] Segovia concludes that simply being a Latinx biblical scholar does not automatically equate to being a scholar who engages in Latinx biblical interpretation. Also, a scholar who is not Latinx, yet strives to be an ally with Latinx scholars, does not engage in Latinx biblical interpretation. For Sevogia, being a Latinx biblical interpreter requires membership in the Latinx community and also a "conscientization, of praxis and agenda, from within" the community. As with African American, womanist, and feminist interpretation, the ethnic and gender identity of the interpreter is an integral part of the practice of Latinx biblical interpretation, something that interpreters from the dominant culture in the United States have not always acknowledged.

---

teachers, preachers, and so forth in the past and are still full members today" (*Wisdom's Feast*, 11n21).

62. Reid, *Wisdom's Feast*, 12.

63. Elisabeth Schüssler Fiorenza, *Changing Horizons: Explorations in Feminist Interpretation* (Minneapolis: Fortress, 2013), 101.

64. Fernando F. Segovia, "Toward Latino/a American Biblical Criticism: Latin(o/a)ness as Problematic," in *They Were All Together in One Place: Toward Minority Biblical Criticism*, ed. Randall C. Bailey, Tat-siong Benny Liew, and Fernando F. Segovia (Boston: Brill, 2009).

Considering identity, M. Daniel Carroll R. explains that "the label Latino/Latina can be controversial. The US government created the label 'Hispanic' for the 1980 census to refer to all peoples of Iberian descent, which includes those from the countries south of the US border and most of the Caribbean. This tag, however, put populations of different national histories and of diverse languages and cultures under a single rubric."[65] Consequently, "Within the larger culture, the term 'Hispanic' is now common parlance, but it is resisted by many of these communities."[66] As with African American biblical interpretation, Latinx biblical interpretation is a practice encompassing the experiences of a diaspora people and has been shaped by Latin American liberation theology. Carroll R. asserts that "textual techniques among Latinx biblical scholars and theologians might vary, but—whatever the method chosen—this orientation offers new insights into the text."[67] While Carroll R. does not elaborate on the varying methods of Latinx scholars and theologians, Segovia does touch on the topic. Segovia traces what he sees as five major proposals in the trajectory of Latinx biblical interpretation; he compares and contrasts the work of Luis Rivera Rodriguez, Efrain Agosto, Justo González, Jean-Pierre Ruiz, and M. Daniel Carroll R.[68] The reality of having different approaches suggests a development of the practice of biblical interpretation, as more Latinx scholars emerge and contribute.[69] Yet despite the word *Latinx* being part of the analysis, Segovia discusses only the work of male scholars.

There are, however, Latina feminist interpreters, as noted above, and Cristina García-Alfonso is a Latina scholar of Hebrew Bible who also addresses the role of identity in Latinx biblical interpretation. García-Alfonso rehearses some of her personal story while exploring the notion of "survival hermeneutics," which is "deeply shaped by the context of survival, *resolviendo*,

---

65. M. Daniel Carroll R., "Latino/a Biblical Interpretation," in Gorman, *Scripture and Its Interpretation*, 311–12.
66. Carroll R., "Latino/a Biblical Interpretation," 312.
67. Carroll R., "Latino/a Biblical Interpretation," 316.
68. Fernando F. Segovia, "Introduction: Approaching Latino/a Biblical Criticism: A Trajectory of Visions and Missions," in *Latino/a Biblical Hermeneutics: Problematics, Objectives, Strategies*, ed. Francisco Lozada Jr. and Fernando F. Segovia (Atlanta: SBL Press, 2014), 1–39.
69. While Carroll R. contends that "Latino/a biblical approaches to the Bible are in their infancy" ("Latino/a Biblical Interpretation," 321), Segovia points out that the reality of varying approaches in the field "is a sign of growth in numbers within the movement, as more and more Latino/as join the circle of biblical criticism. It is also a sign of growth in sophistication, as more and more attempts at self-reflection take place." Segovia, "Introduction: Approaching Latino/a Biblical Criticism," 4.

which is still very much present in Cuba."⁷⁰ She then offers a study of the biblical character Rahab. García-Alfonso concludes, "Being a Latina biblical scholar means embracing all that I am as a Cuban feminist living at this particular time in history in the United States (geographical and academic location). Embracing all that I am means embracing my Cuban identity: an identity that is corporal, feminist, and deeply shaped by a sense of survival, family survival. This location, not defined by the mass of water that separates the United States and Cuba, is what I call a socioemotional and existential location."⁷¹

In *Taking Up the Cross: New Testament Interpretations through Latina and Feminist Eyes*, Barbara Reid explains, "Being conscious of my own privileged position as a white, middle-class, well-educated North American woman, I have attempted to listen to the voices of women whose experiences with poverty, oppression, and violence give a different perspective on making meaning of the cross and the resurrection."⁷² Consequently, in light of the aforementioned writings of Segovia and García-Alfonso, one might question if Reid engages in the practice of Latina biblical criticism. Even so, Reid respects Latina voices as she interprets several NT texts from the Gospels, employing her feminist liberationist perspective, which includes historical-critical methodology.

Latinx biblical scholars share concerns regarding the marginal status of their people, social justice, the centrality of family, solidarity, and liberation. They see their discipline growing in its ability to critique itself and also in engaging the broader scholarly community, particularly in the areas of Latin American studies and postcolonial studies. And, as with all biblical interpretation from marginalized people, some scholars, such as M. Daniel Carroll R., express concern that scholarship will become increasingly removed from the grassroots. Carroll R. describes the "two possible dangers"—namely, confining conversations to scholarly circles and having Latinx prophetic voices "domesticated by inclusion."⁷³

Postcolonial Biblical Interpretation

"Since the Bible has been used to justify untold acts of government sanctioned violence and silencing the voices of women throughout the ages, we as responsible biblical scholars would do well to face head on the life-stealing

---

70. Cristina García-Alfonso, "Latino/a Biblical Hermeneutics: Problematics, Objectives, Strategies," in Lozada and Segovia, *Latino/a Biblical Hermeneutics*, 152.
71. García-Alfonso, "Latino/a Biblical Hermeneutics," 163.
72. Barbara E. Reid, *Taking Up the Cross: New Testament Interpretations through Latina and Feminist Eyes* (Minneapolis: Fortress, 2007), 3.
73. Carroll R., "Latino/a Biblical Interpretation," 321.

aspects of the Bible in order to have the life-giving words speak unencumbered for themselves."[74] Jennifer G. Bird acknowledges that the Bible has been used to oppress people throughout the world and that reality rests behind postcolonial biblical interpretation.[75] Perhaps the most prominent proponent of postcolonial biblical interpretation is Rasiah S. Sugirtharajah. Sugirtharajah asserts that when it comes to the attitude of the colonizing nations, "there is a willful amnesia and a moral blindness" regarding the negative impact colonialism has had on countless numbers of people around the world.[76]

Scripture and Its Interpretation defines postcolonial criticism (or hermeneutics) as "An interpretive approach that attempts (a) to expose and critique colonialism and power structures more generally, as well as (b) to identify and critique the use of the Bible to support or challenge imperial power and other forms of abusive power."[77] Sugirtharajah further explains that "postcolonial biblical criticism is basically about posing its questions differently to the biblical narratives and to the manner in which they have been interpreted."[78] All critical study of the Bible asks questions of a text related to delimiting that text, to understanding its authorship, and attempting to discern its impact upon readers. However, postcolonial biblical critics, rather than approaching such questions with a perspective shaped by Western cultural norms, come to the biblical text as people seeking to reveal the impact of empires—ancient and modern. "Essentially, postcolonial biblical criticism is about exploring who is entitled to tell stories and who has the authority to interpret them."[79] As noted at the start of this chapter, it is an act of power to interpret the Bible, and that power has, until relatively recently, rested in the hands of white people who descend from the colonizers.

---

74. Jennifer G. Bird, "Scripture and New Interpretive Approaches: Feminist and Post-Colonial," in Bird and Pahl, *Sacred*, 173.

75. Postcolonial biblical interpretation is a global enterprise, but, as noted throughout my essay, unique American experiences contribute to this approach. For example, see Bailey, Liew, and Segovia, *They Were All Together in One Place*. The editors express their purpose as wanting "to explore how racial-ethnic minority scholars of the Bible within the United States may cross the 'color line' to form a coalition or an alliance to transform the discipline of biblical studies" (4). They also point out that Native Americans are not represented in their work because of the woefully small number of Native American scholars, but also because they, the editors, consider "minority" to be "an inappropriate term for Native Americans because 'minority' does not communicate the fact that their rights, including their land claims, existed prior to and independent of the U.S. government" (4n2).

76. R. S. Sugirtharajah, *Exploring Postcolonial Biblical Criticism: History, Method, Practice* (Malden, MA: Wiley-Blackwell, 2012), 8. Note also an earlier work, R. S. Sugirtharajah, ed., *The Postcolonial Biblical Reader* (Malden, MA: Blackwell, 2006).

77. Gorman, *Scripture and Its Interpretation*, 419.

78. Sugirtharajah, *Exploring Postcolonial Biblical Criticism*, 2.

79. Sugirtharajah, *Exploring Postcolonial Biblical Criticism*, 3.

Postcolonial biblical interpretation impacts how one views the history of Christian missionary activity. Scholars continue to wrestle with repercussions of having had the gospel of Jesus Christ delivered through the voice and actions of colonizers. Gregory Lee Cuéllar and Randy S. Woodley quote Sugirtharajah, who, in commenting on Spanish missionary activity, asserts, "The voice of God blended with the voice of the invader."[80] The work of Christian missionaries is but one place where postcolonial biblical interpretation intersects with other areas. Stephen D. Moore and Fernando F. Segovia offer a history of postcolonial biblical studies, explore ways the discipline intersects with other fields of study, and describe the trajectory of the discipline.[81] Among other things, Moore and Segovia warn against postcolonial biblical interpretation becoming faddish or neglecting self-criticism.

Postcolonial Biblical Criticism: Interdisciplinary Intersections is part of a series published by Bloomsbury T&T Clark (series editor R. S. Sugirtharajah). Other works in the series include *A Postcolonial Commentary on the New Testament Writings, The Postcolonial Bible, Vernacular Hermeneutics, Interpreting beyond Borders, Last Stop before Antarctica: The Bible and Postcolonialism in Australia,* and *John and Postcolonialism: Travel, Space and Power*. There is much to explore in postcolonial readings of Scripture. However, regarding the future of postcolonial biblical interpretation, Sugirtharajah avers, "The constant challenge a postcolonial critic faces is how to maintain marginal status. How to be on the edge. How to remain an outsider. There is danger awaiting those who are located in the academies. Universities are increasingly becoming collaborators with corporate capitalism rather than being its critics."[82] As additional marginal voices become part of the mainstream, will they continue to challenge the powerful status quo?

Reflections

Many years ago I came across a cartoon whose caption made me burst out laughing. The cartoon pictured three people sitting in a semicircle, dressed in what appeared to be first-century attire. One, his mouth open to speak,

---

80. Rasiah S. Sugirtharajah, *Bible and Empire:Postcolonial Explorations* (New York: Cambridge University Press, 2005), 89, quoted in Gregory Lee Cuéllar and Randy S. Woodley, "North American Mission and Motives: Following the Markers," in *Evangelical Postcolonial Conversations: Global Awakenings in Theology and Praxis*, ed. Kay Higuera Smith (Downers Grove, IL: InterVarsity, 2014), 64–65.

81. Stephen D. Moore and Fernando F. Segovia, "Postcolonial Biblical Criticism: Beginnings, Trajectories, Intersections," in *Postcolonial Biblical Criticism: Interdisciplinary Intersections*, ed. Stephen D. Moore and Fernando F. Segovia (New York: T&T Clark, 2007), 1–22.

82. Sugirtharajah, *Exploring Postcolonial Biblical Criticism*, 185.

held a scroll with the heading "Bible Study, AD 75." The caption consisted of the words from the one holding the scroll: "I believe Paul wants us all to go around and say what this verse means to you." I laughed because that format described virtually every Bible study group in which I had been for years of my life. But having been a pastor as well as instructor of Bible for many years, as I describe that cartoon to church laity or to divinity school students early in their studies, I observe that the reaction has evolved over time. Early on, many would laugh as I did (and even now, most of the laughter comes from older students). Those more familiar with historical-critical methodology find the cartoon humorous, partly because they see the approach of that small group Bible study as subjective; they understand that meaning is not determined by the group but belongs to Paul, the author of the letter. Also, those who laugh do not think of the apostle Paul as someone who would invite others to bring their meaning to his writing. However, in more recent years students do not laugh as much, but they find the cartoon welcoming. Lay Bible readers and newer divinity school students typically expect to exercise the power of biblical interpretation. As one of my students said regarding the cartoon, "I like that people are invited to discuss the text." That student had come from a church background where congregants were not encouraged to engage the biblical text but merely to receive authoritative teaching from the priest or pastor.

Postmodern approaches to the Bible bring power to the people. The expression "biblical interpretation" without any additional adjectives has meant white, Eurocentric, typically male, biblical interpretation, despite the hope that historical-critical methodology would yield objective, unbiased interpretations of Scripture. Such biblical interpretation often fortified the structures of oppression, including colonialism around the world and slavery in the United States. As a growing number of marginalized people became educated, and as those from the dominant cultures became more sensitive to the plight of others, approaches to the Bible became more diversified. This chapter has explored a few of those postmodern approaches—those that bring adjectives before the word "biblical" in "biblical interpretation." These approaches, likely to be accompanied by many more, will long be part of the landscape of biblical interpretation. Yet care must be taken not to throw out the historical-critical baby with the modern biblical interpretation bathwater. Many postmodern interpreters agree that we will always need to employ elements of historical-critical methodology.

As is evident with historical critics, postmodern interpreters differ on their view of biblical authority. There will continue to be a range of views on what it means to call the Bible the Word of God. Even with a variety of understandings about biblical authority, postmodern interpreters will maintain their exploration into what the Bible suggests about the nature of God and how

God relates to human beings. These interpreters will also shed light on the lived experiences of people around the world and how these people understand Jesus. For example, numerous studies have focused on the people who came in contact with Jesus, according to the Gospels, paying close attention to the social location of the people in the story and relating it to people in contemporary times with analogous situations.

Even though the practice of theological interpretation has grown tremendously during the last fifteen years or so, the future of the practice remains uncertain. The absence of a clear methodology may explain some of the growth, as various practitioners strive to illustrate the practice. However, younger interpreters of Scripture, formed in the postmodern milieu, seem less troubled by the ambiguity that results from a lack of a clear methodology. Also, while, on the one hand, theological interpreters bring their ecclesial backgrounds more openly to the task of interpretation, on the other hand, increasing numbers of people are willfully ignorant of denominational distinctions. It will be interesting to see how theological interpretation fares in what might be viewed as a postdenominational culture.

One concern that emerges from several voices relates to the future of postmodern biblical studies as more people from previously underrepresented groups become increasingly established in the academy. As people from minority groups try to find their way in academic circles without losing touch with the people whose causes they champion, they will face all sorts of challenges—professional and personal. Hopefully the edgy prophetic voices will not be blunted as minority scholars move into the mainstream.

As we strive to learn from the vast array of thinkers and writers who study the Bible, perhaps the hopeful approach of Tom Greggs may be a fitting final word. Greggs proposes a "hermeneutics of *agape*" and explains,

> Reading face to face with another, indeed with a member of another faith community, reading lovingly, confronts us with the need to engage texts with sensitivity when we read by ourselves. It challenges us to contemplate where we locate ourselves in texts, and crucially has the effect of deassuring us theologically of our insider status, our hubris and our self-created binary exclusivisms. The process of reading with religious others is not just a process which *displays* a loving reading, but is one which *engenders* in a far more reaching way a reading which critically challenges the preoccupation with the self and the text, and points us towards the other, aiding us perhaps to understand something more of the ultimate otherness of God.[83]

---

83. Tom Greggs, "Reading Scripture in a Pluralistic World: A Path to Discovering the Hermeneutics of *Agape*," in Thiselton, Porter, and Malcolm, *Horizons in Hermeneutics*, 215.

4

The Old Testament in the New Testament

Matthew W. Bates

Introduction

It is intimidating. As we attempt to heighten our appreciation for how NT authors made use of the OT, the conversation rapidly turns technical: Did Matthew engage the OT in Hebrew, Aramaic, Syriac, or Greek? In what dialectical variation? Did he reuse Mark's OT citations, or did he engage the OT on its own terms—and how consistently? Was Matthew aware of the broader OT context? If so, which dimensions of the context? To what degree did he appreciate OT theologies, genre differences, sources, redaction, literary art, and historical claims? And in assessing all these matters, what's the ancient evidence? How certain are the conclusions we can draw?

Moreover, in weighing the use of the OT in the NT, we must ask all such questions not merely for Matthew but for Paul, Luke, John, the author of Hebrews, and so forth. And answering one question ripples outward so that a host of new ones emerge. For example, if it is determined (correctly) that Paul preferred to cite the OT in Greek, does Paul's text correspond to ancient manuscript families that represent translations of the OT that we might broadly classify as Septuagintal, or does it compare better with those produced by Aquila, Theodotion, or Symmachus? And if related to the Septuagint (LXX), what of the evidence that, contrary to ancient legend, the so-called Septuagint itself was not a uniform product, but involved multiple translators, revisions, and recensions produced over a long time?[1] Furthermore, why does Paul leave words out, add words, and change words when quoting the OT? Can specific patterns of behavior in this regard be detected and described? And even more troubling, if we determine (correctly!) that sometimes Paul's modifications to the exact wording are intentional and ideological, what does this mean for overall theories about the doctrine of Scripture?

Even if the blitzkrieg of technical details leaves us bewildered, we should also acknowledge that it is exceedingly important that specialists control them—especially because all aren't called to this peculiar specialization. It is only in dealing with such fine-grained details that we can move from vague impressions about the use of the OT in the NT, indeed about Scripture as a whole, to the actual truth. It might be easy to make doctrinaire assertions about the nature of Scripture using impressive-sounding terms like *inerrancy*, *infallibility*, *inspiration*, and *perspicuity* when flying thirty thousand feet above ancient compositional practices; it is quite another thing to figure out what such terms could allowably mean in light of the ground-level realia of ancient exegeses, manuscripts, and scribal techniques. This is not to say that terms like *inspiration* are untrue or unhelpful, but it is to say that it is easy for pastors, teachers, and scholars who are committed Christians (myself included) to give convenient, prepackaged answers that grossly oversimplify.

The State of the Field

Ready to feel disappointed and relieved simultaneously? As undeniably important as such technical details are for arriving at the full truth, our task here is to summarize the most recent trends in the study of the use of the OT in the NT. And scholarship has by and large not been advancing quickly on these specialized fronts, but rather confirming and modestly refining well-established results. It would be impossible in any case to summarize a fraction of these more specialized questions in this short chapter—although other chapters in this book can help jump-start interested readers, and I will mention several additional resources. Meanwhile the opportunity to look at broader themes should be welcomed by all.

---

1. See Timothy Michael Law, *When God Spoke Greek: The Septuagint and the Making of the Christian Bible* (Oxford: Oxford University Press, 2013).

One-Stop Resources and Comprehensive Projects

As the study of the OT in the NT has matured, it is unsurprising that helpful resources have been produced that seek to serve as a one-stop launching point for students, pastors, and scholars approaching this technical area of inquiry. Four deserve special mention.

Greg K. Beale's *Handbook on the New Testament Use of the Old Testament* is a valuable how-to manual for those doing detailed scholarly research or writing exegetical papers.[2] The book does many things well. It surveys key points of continued scholarly debate. It considers distinctive issues pertaining to various modes of OT-in-the-NT engagement (quotation, allusion, echo). Need a sensible step-by-step research procedure for a paper or sermon? You'll find it here. Furthermore the book analyzes ancient interpretative techniques, introduces relevant noncanonical sources, and illustrates how to apply all that has been learned via a case study. All this is accompanied by generous bibliographical aids.

Greg K. Beale and D. A. Carson's *Commentary on the New Testament Use of the Old Testament* is even more indispensable than the handbook, for it comprehensively surveys the use of the OT separately for each NT book in a verse-by-verse style.[3] The commentary is written by multiple scholars, many of whom are already acknowledged experts on how the particular NT book uses the OT. Each author was compelled to use the same six-part method throughout by analyzing the NT context, OT context, use of the OT text in Second Temple and rabbinic Judaism, text-critical matters, the hermeneutic employed, and theological usage. This six-part method ensures that each instance of the OT in the NT is discussed with uniform depth and rigor. Yet lamentably there are a couple of methodological oversights. For instance, the commentary does not systematically assess how any particular use of the OT was carried out elsewhere in the NT. Moreover it only rarely shows awareness that the use of the OT in the post-NT church could help us more accurately recover NT usage.[4] Despite these shortcomings, it brings a tremendous amount of trustworthy scholarship together and gives helpful bibliographic information. It remains the single best resource with which to begin and undertake the study of the OT in the NT.

---

2. Greg K. Beale, *Handbook on the New Testament Use of the Old Testament: Exegesis and Interpretation* (Grand Rapids: Baker Academic, 2012).
3. Greg K. Beale and D. A. Carson, *Commentary on the New Testament Use of the Old Testament* (Grand Rapids: Baker Academic, 2007).
4. For these criticisms, see Matthew W. Bates, *The Hermeneutics of the Apostolic Proclamation: The Center of Paul's Method of Scriptural Interpretation* (Waco: Baylor University Press, 2012), 51–53.

Ben Witherington III's ongoing "Old and New" series seeks to treat NT use of the OT in a fairly comprehensive fashion. Three volumes in the series have appeared thus far: Ben Witherington III, *Isaiah Old and New: Exegesis, Intertextuality, and Hermeneutics* (Minneapolis: Fortress, 2017); Witherington, *Psalms Old and New: Exegesis, Intertextuality, and Hermeneutics* (Minneapolis: Fortress, 2017); and Witherington, *Torah Old and New: Exegesis, Intertextuality, and Hermeneutics* (Minneapolis: Fortress, 2018).

Steve Moyise's series of studies surveys NT texts comprehensively, with students and pastors primarily in view as the audience. For a primer in this series, see Steve Moyise, *The Old Testament in the New: An Introduction*, 2nd ed. (New York: Bloomsbury T&T Clark, 2015). For expanded treatment, see Moyise, *Jesus and Scripture: Studying the New Testament Use of the Old Testament* (Grand Rapids: Baker Academic, 2011); Moyise, *Paul and Scripture: Studying the New Testament Use of the Old Testament* (Grand Rapids: Baker Academic, 2010); Moyise, *The Later New Testament Writings and Scripture: The Old Testament in Acts, Hebrews, the Catholic Epistles, and Revelation* (Grand Rapids: Baker Academic, 2012).

These attempts to consolidate the field are indispensable for those seeking orientation.[5] Nevertheless the most striking advances in the last decades in the study of the OT in the NT—and arguably the most interesting too—have involved a movement away from considering it a self-contained subfield or a specialized problem and toward an increased appreciation of its continuity with ancient Jewish, Christian, and pagan textual production. It has long been recognized that certain pagan and Jewish exegetical techniques overlap with those of our NT authors. Yet we're now more aware of the ways in which these exegetical techniques participate in worldview-level "storied" assumptions about the shape of reality.

We can now speak with greater confidence about an ongoing exegetical conversation or competition between ancient socioreligious communities about what constitutes a proper reading or continuation of the OT story—with scholars seeing the use of the OT in the NT as a manifestation of this phenomenon. The NT authors evidence diversity in seeing precisely what constitutes a convincing reading and deployment of the OT, but they are united in the conviction that the events surrounding Jesus of Nazareth are central. These observations have been coupled with a rising appreciation among scholars for how strategies for textual production relate to rhetoric, reading, and education in the Hellenistic world of the NT and early Christianity, broadly conceived.

---

5. Although it largely reflects older conversations related to hermeneutical theory and doctrine of Scripture rather than recent advances, students may appreciate the lively dialogical format of Kenneth Berding and Jonathan Lunde, eds., *Three Views on the New Testament Use of the Old Testament* (Grand Rapids: Zondervan, 2008).

Narrative and Intra-Jewish Competition

Narrative Approaches

The rise of narrative approaches should be regarded as one of the most important trends in the study of the OT in the NT. Originally much of the energy for this approach was siphoned from structuralism. Building on the linguistics of Ferdinand de Saussure and cultural anthropology of Claude Lévi-Strauss, structuralists hoped to uncover a universal pattern of storytelling and meaning-making through analyzing binary oppositions, stereotyped roles, and substitution. Thus, Vladimir Propp and A. J. Greimas sought to distill folktales into a storied grammar, so that the underlying narrative logic could be exposed through an "actantial" model.

Through the work of scholars such as Edmund R. Leach, Mary Douglas, John D. Crossan, Robert Funk, Dan Via, and Daniel Patte, structuralist analysis entered into the mainstream of biblical studies.[6] Yet the potential of narrative analysis for the specific problem of how the NT uses the OT was initially unrealized. Richard Hays in his published dissertation, *The Faith of Jesus Christ*, showed the degree to which Paul uses submerged OT stories in his argumentative logic.[7] Hays used Greimas's actantial model to show that Paul's surface argument depends on a more primal logic that has been informed by certain OT narratives.

Hays's dissertation has proven enormously influential. Not only did it reopen the *pistis christou* debate ("faith" or "faithfulness" of Christ) in NT scholarship; it also alerted other biblical scholars to the possibility that analysis of submerged OT narratives might cast light on the NT. The effect on the study of Paul was immediate and has been pronounced.[8] It has also colored the study of the Gospels and the remainder of the NT corpus—to such a degree that I can mention only a couple of representative studies.[9] Meanwhile,

---

6. For an overview, see David Jobling, "Structuralism and Deconstruction," in *Dictionary of Biblical Interpretation*, ed. John H. Hayes, 2 vols. (Nashville: Abingdon, 1999), 2:509–14.

7. Richard B. Hays, *The Faith of Jesus Christ: An Investigation of the Narrative Substructure of Galatians 3:1–4:11*, SBLDS 56 (Atlanta: SBL Press, 1983).

8. N. T. Wright, *The Climax of the Covenant: Christ and the Law in Pauline Theology* (Minneapolis: Fortress, 1992), 193–219; Ben Witherington III, *Paul's Narrative Thought World: The Tapestry of Tragedy and Triumph* (Louisville: Westminster John Knox, 1994); Sylvia C. Keesmaat, *Paul and His Story: (Re)Interpreting the Exodus Tradition*, JSNTSup 181 (Sheffield: Sheffield Academic, 1999); Bruce W. Longenecker, ed., *Narrative Dynamics in Paul: A Critical Assessment* (Louisville: Westminster John Knox, 2002).

9. N. T. Wright, *The New Testament and the People of God* (Minneapolis: Fortress, 1991), 69–77, 216–23, 369–417; Wright, *Jesus and the Victory of God* (Minneapolis: Fortress, 1996), 244, 310, 461; Rikki E. Watts, *Isaiah's New Exodus in Mark*, WUNT 2/88 (Tübingen: Mohr Siebeck, 1997); David W. Pao, *Acts and the Isaianic New Exodus*, WUNT 2/130 (Tübingen:

shedding the formalism of structuralism, studies that rely heavily on an analysis of submerged OT narratives continue to multiply fruitfully.[10]

Intra-Jewish Competition

While prior scholarship had certainly been cognizant of the need to situate the use of the OT in the NT within the matrix of Judaism, the discovery of the DSS and the explosive scholarly expansion into Second Temple Judaism has significantly altered approaches and results. For example, prior to the discovery of the DSS, when scholars sought to position the use of the OT in the NT against its Jewish background, the primary points of comparison were rabbinic Judaism on the one hand (primarily the Mishnah, Talmudim, and midrashic literature) and philosophical Judaism on the other (especially Philo).[11] Scholarship has not given up on comparing the use of the OT in the NT to rabbinic practices—one will still frequently find discussion in handbooks of the (so-called) seven rules (*middot*) of exegesis attributed to Rabbi Hillel, mention of the thirteen of Rabbi Ishmael, or reference to the thirty-two associated with Rabbi Eliezer ben Jose ha-Galili.[12] Moreover, scholars frequently (and usually correctly) note that select uses of the OT in the NT manifest a *qal wahomer* (light to heavy) interpretive principle.[13]

Yet, at the same time, scholars are increasingly reluctant to offer such rabbinic interpretive rules as *the definitive* interpretive explanation. For example, Richard Hays remarks about the limitations regarding the explanatory power of such rabbinic rules: "Apart from the considerable difficulty of interpreting and dating the *middot*, they do not in any case actually provide rules for the interpretation of Scripture. They are not rules or limiting guidelines, but an inventory of *tropes*: the *middot* provide a descriptive account of a repertoire of possible imaginative operations that can be performed on the text in the act of interpretation. They do not tell the interpreter how to find out what a text means; instead, they suggest ways to make the text mean more than it says."[14] Hays's point is that the *middot* are tropes, or figures that allow an interpreter

---

Mohr Siebeck, 2000); Brant Pitre, *Jesus, the Tribulation, and the End of the Exile: Restoration Eschatology and the Origin of the Atonement*, WUNT 2/204 (Tübingen: Mohr Siebeck, 2005).

10. E.g., Rodrigo J. Morales, *The Spirit and the Restoration of Israel: New Exodus and New Creation Motifs in Galatians*, WUNT 2/282 (Tübingen: Mohr Siebeck, 2010); N. T. Wright, *Paul and the Faithfulness of God* (Minneapolis: Fortress, 2013), esp. 456–537.

11. Otto Michel, *Paulus und Seine Bibel*, BFCT 2.18 (Gütersloh: Bertelsmann, 1929); Joseph Bonsirven, *Exégèse rabbinique et exégèse paulinienne* (Paris: Beauchesne et ses fils, 1938).

12. E.g., Richard N. Longenecker, *Biblical Exegesis in the Apostolic Period*, 2nd ed. (Grand Rapids: Eerdmans, 1999), 18–24.

13. E.g., Matt. 12:12; Rom. 5:15; 1 Cor. 9:9–10; 1 Tim. 5:18; 1 Pet. 3:6.

14. Richard B. Hays, *Echoes of Scripture in the Letters of Paul* (New Haven: Yale University Press, 1989), 12.

to extend the text—for example, to make an application by bridging between the ancient and the contemporary context.

Jesus, for instance, says, "Which one of you who has a sheep, if it falls into a pit on the Sabbath, will not seize it and lift it out? How much more valuable is a man than a sheep. So it is lawful to do good on the Sabbath" (Matt. 12:11–12, author's translation). Here Jesus is portrayed as using *qal wahomer* in two different ways. First, he tacitly appeals to the OT command that it is necessary to help your brother or neighbor if livestock falls into a pit (Deut. 22:4)—with the assumption that if this is true with regard to your *neighbor's* animal, then *how much more* should you help your *own* animal. Then he applies the text to the human situation; if helping a troubled *animal* is to be welcomed on the Sabbath, *how much more* healing a *person* with a deformed hand.

In line with Hays's observation that the *middot* are not interpretive principles but tropes that allow the interpreter to make a text "mean more than it says," notice that in both *how much more* inferences, Jesus does not use *qal wahomer* to exegete the text (i.e., to draw out its "plain sense" or "literal" meaning), but instead to relate the text's meaning to new contexts.[15] Jesus's opponents, of course, were not impressed with Jesus's interpretive application. They promptly began plotting how they might kill him (Matt. 12:14).

And they were not alone in opposing Jesus's interpretation. The Qumran community would not permit animals that fell in a pit to be rescued on the Sabbath: "No one should help an animal give birth on the Sabbath; and if it falls into a well or a pit, he may not lift it out on the Sabbath" (CD A 11.13–14).[16]

Meanwhile Jesus's argument presupposes that the Pharisees permitted such activities. Jesus agrees with the Pharisees over against the Qumran community in the application of the first *qal wahomer*—if your neighbor's animal, how much more your own. But Jesus thinks that the Pharisees are tragically shortsighted in their failure to apply the second *qal wahomer*—that is, the Pharisees have failed to see that this OT law about animals shows that God welcomes Sabbath-day healings for people even more. So Jesus agrees with the "literal" exegesis and ruling of the Pharisees, but profoundly disagrees with how this exegesis should be applied beyond the case of animals.

It is evidence like this from the DSS and the Gospels that has heightened scholarly awareness of the degree to which OT interpretation by the NT authors involved an intra-Jewish competition pertaining to the proper

---

15. What is meant by the "literal" or "plain sense" is not obvious. See also the section "Reading Norms" below.

16. This translation is from Michael O. Wise, Martin G. Abegg Jr., and Edward M. Cook, trans. and comm., *The Dead Sea Scrolls: A New Translation* (San Francisco: HarperOne, 2005).

boundaries that were felt to delineate God's covenant community.[17] The DSS opened up new horizons of inquiry, allowing scholars to compare scribal practices at Qumran with those of earliest Christianity.[18] Vague early attempts to describe the creative scribal practices as "midrash" or "midrash pesher" have largely now given way to more sophisticated analyses. N. T. Wright and Francis Watson exemplify two current approaches.

COMPETING STORIES-ABOUT-THE-STORY

Drawing on the narrative approach (and its structuralist foundations), N. T. Wright's sprawling multivolume project, *Christian Origins and the Question of God*, examines the way in which specific Second Temple groups were grafting themselves into the OT story and its continuation differently. This OT story was conceived as ongoing and moving toward a definite conclusion: YHWH would judge the world and vindicate those who had "read" the story properly so as to live that story out through fitting practices.

Wright argues that a foundational Jewish story is articulated in the OT. When I call Wright's approach the competing-stories-about-the-story model, this is what is meant by "the story." The Creator God desires to send the gift of his wise rule to the whole world. The agent through whom this wise rule will be brought about is Israel. To assist Israel in fulfilling its mission, God has given the Torah and the temple. Meanwhile paganism, worship of idols rather than YHWH, is the threat to Israel. Idolatrous paganism is the opponent that might prevent Israel from successfully delivering the wise rule of God to the world.

Wright suggests, however, that this primal Jewish story had subtly morphed in the NT era. So this deviation is also in a sense "the story," because Wright contends that it was widely held in the late Second Temple period. This new story is that Israel is unable to accomplish its mission because it has been disobedient to the covenant. Roman occupation of the Holy Land indicates, for Wright, that Israel is still in exile (exile the ultimate curse for covenant disobedience) even though Israel is technically living in the promised land. Thus a "return from exile" is necessary, and this return can be (and was) further conceptualized as a "new exodus."

---

17. To speak of intra-"Jewish" competition and to compare and contrast it with the label "Christian" is problematic since the labels and boundaries between these communities were fluid and under intense negotiation in the first century. Yet we have no agreed-on accurate (nonanachronistic) labels, so this imperfect shorthand will need to suffice for our present purposes.

18. Krister Stendahl, *The School of St. Matthew and Its Use of the Old Testament*, 2nd ed. (Philadelphia: Fortress, 1968); E. Earle Ellis, *Paul's Use of the Old Testament* (Grand Rapids: Eerdmans, 1957); Yigael Yadin, "The Dead Sea Scrolls and the Epistle to the Hebrews," in *Aspects of the Dead Sea Scrolls*, ed. Chaim Rabin and Yigael Yadin, ScrHier 4 (Jerusalem: Hebrew University, 1958), 36–55.

The upshot of this new (deviant) story is that God first desires to send "rescue" to Israel prior to sending his wise rule to the whole world—and this first goal has become the only goal for many late Second Temple Jews. The subsequent goal, the blessing for all nations, has faded from view entirely. The agent through which this new rescue will be achieved is torah (rather than torah being Israel's helper as in the original sequence). Torah enshrines God's covenant purposes, and it will rescue Israel. Torah is assisted in its ability to do this by God's promises and by God's prior deliverances. Meanwhile pagans—and unfaithful Israelites (those who are misreading the OT and its extension into the present)—oppose the torah and God's covenant purposes, making the outcome of this rescue operation uncertain.[19]

For an Israelite living during the NT era, what is necessary in this new (deviant) sequence? One must be able to show that one's group is faithful Israel, the group that has best "read" the OT story and its continuation into the present—and in so doing to prove that one has remained faithful to God's covenant intentions for his people. Wright shows that the OT interpretations and practices of the major Jewish groups active in the NT era—the Pharisees, Sadducees, Essenes, Zealots, *and the earliest Christians*—can be fruitfully understood as different ways of reading and responding to the singular OT story. Meanwhile, the stories—the diverse interpretations and retellings of that singular story—that are on offer during the NT era create, reinforce, and seek to vindicate the validity of sociopolitical boundaries between various sects.

Ultimately Wright argues that the historical Jesus successfully recovered the most primal OT story in crafting an agenda for Israel while bringing that story to its God-ordained climax. The creator God has given the gift of his wise rule to the world through the kingship of Jesus. And indeed this has been accomplished through Israel—but not through Israel on its own steam—rather through God's own action in sending his Son as a true Israelite, the messiah, to rescue Israel through a new covenant. The Son has taken his fitting position at the right hand of God as the Lord of heaven and earth.[20] In the Gospels, the earliest Christian interpreters of Jesus were able to offer this reconfigured story of the victory of God through Jesus the messiah as a counterpoint to popular Jewish tellings.[21] Moreover, the apostle Paul, as the first extant Christian author, was deliberately doing theology as he rethought the story of Israel. Paul discovered through his rereading of Scripture in light of the resurrection and the experience of the Holy Spirit the proper position of the Mosaic covenant in God's economy of salvation—and in so doing became

19. Wright, *NTPG*, 221–23.
20. Wright, *JVG*, 244–46, 472–74.
21. Wright, *NTPG*, 371–417.

convinced that Jesus had fulfilled the true purpose of Israel by bringing the blessing to the nations, so that the nations could join Israel as the one people of God under the banner of Jesus the king.[22]

Although Wright's vast project continues to receive scrutiny in the academy, criticism has been sharpest regarding his notion of ongoing exile, his views regarding salvation-historical continuity versus apocalyptic disruption, his tendency to slide complex metaphors together when offering explanations (e.g., Spirit implies new exodus, which evokes temple and implies Shekinah glory, and so forth), and concern that his large-scale controlling narratives might cause him to trample the details.[23] But nobody should doubt the invigorating brilliance and importance to the field of Wright's contribution. Wright's work will endure because it has enormous explanatory power. His competing-stories-about-the-story model continues to set the research agenda or appear as a primary sparring partner for nearly everyone working on the use of the OT in the NT.

Three-Way Conversation

In *Paul and the Hermeneutics of Faith*, Francis Watson offers a model for the use of the OT in the NT that is just as interested in narrative analysis and intra-Jewish competition as N. T. Wright's. Yet its theoretical underpinnings are different, and this causes him to ask different questions of the texts. Fresh vistas result. Watson suggests that the study of the OT in the NT is best considered not as a monologue (as if the OT alone speaks when probed by an NT author), or even a two-way conversation (as if the dialogue between the OT and the NT takes place in a social vacuum), but a three-way conversation.

What are these three conversation partners? They are (1) the specific NT document in question, (2) the OT passage engaged, and (3) the non-Christian literature of Second Temple Judaism that engages the same OT passage. So, for Watson, when studying Romans 1:17, since Paul cites Habakkuk 2:4, one must undertake a close reading not only of Romans but also of Habakkuk in its diverse OT historical, literary, and canonical contexts. And one must *additionally* explore the use of Habakkuk 2:4 in the so-called Habakkuk Pesher in the DSS and so on.

Watson laments that these bodies of literature are all too often studied in isolation. But his model seeks to do the opposite: "The intention here is to

---

22. Wright, *PFG*, 456–537, esp. 521.
23. For a critical assessment of Wright, see Samuel V. Adams, *The Reality of God and Historical Method: Apocalyptic Theology in Conversation with N. T. Wright* (Downers Grove, IL: IVP Academic, 2015); James M. Scott, ed., *Exile: A Conversation with N. T. Wright* (Downers Grove, IL: IVP Academic, 2017).

get these texts talking to each other—or rather, to show how they are as they are by virtue of an ongoing conversation in which they already participate."[24] That is, Watson is not merely trying to bring these texts into dialogue with one another; he shows that a close reading of each shows that they are *already* mutually informing: that we cannot fully appreciate what each text uniquely "is" without identifying the way a text responds to or generates a response from its dialogue partners. In other words, Watson contends that his three-way model is a genuine interpretative conversation in which each text involved is able to act back on the others, changing what each means.

But surely this is nonsense—a reader of Watson might object—as Habakkuk 2:4 (within Habakkuk, the Book of the Twelve, the Prophets, and the OT more broadly) has its own meaning quite apart from how Paul interpreted it. Meanwhile, Habakkuk was written prior to Paul's letters— and Habakkuk intended to communicate effectively to a real pre-Pauline audience. So it is impossible for Paul to act back on Habakkuk or the Book of the Twelve, changing what they mean. If we allow the suggestion that Paul's interpretation changes the actual meaning of Habakkuk, we have illegitimately bent the arrow of time backward. We've tied ourselves into a hermeneutical knot that eviscerates the ability of the OT to speak on its own as God's Word independently from the NT.[25] The author of Habakkuk quite simply could not have been impacted by Paul, and when our exegesis suggests otherwise, we've gone dreadfully off the rails (so an objector might argue).

Watson's claim, however, is that we do not have access (nor would we benefit if it were otherwise) to OT texts such as Habakkuk, or the Pentateuch, in the uninterpreted raw. We as interpreters are located within the time stream of the Pentateuch's reception history, as is Paul. As Watson puts it, it is no longer possible "to justify an approach to the scriptural text that abstracts it from its own history of interpretation—as if the only proper object of study were a text that remained unread. Text and interpretation lie on a continuum. To analyze early Jewish readings of the Pentateuch as interactions with the text is to contribute to the study of the Pentateuch itself."[26] Watson is quick to clarify that this does not mean that the OT texts are devoid of their own unique semantic potential; rather, it is to affirm that

---

24. Francis Watson, *Paul and the Hermeneutics of Faith*, 2nd ed. (London: Bloomsbury T&T Clark, 2016), 2.

25. This is a portion of the objection to Watson's project raised by Christopher R. Seitz, *The Character of Christian Scripture: The Significance of a Two-Testament Bible* (Grand Rapids: Baker Academic, 2011), 53–62, esp. 57. For Watson's response, see *Paul and the Hermeneutics*, lvi–lxi.

26. Watson, *Paul and the Hermeneutics*, 4.

we do not have access to their semantic potential apart from the fact that these texts have a reception history (in which we are located too), as if we could somehow transcend that limitation. We should be suspicious of any contemporary interpreters who naively think otherwise. So it is impossible to get access to an OT text's meaning as divorced from its reception history. Whether we like it or not, both the NT texts that respond to the OT and our own contemporary interpretive efforts belong within that reception history.

In this way Watson suggests that the use of the OT in the NT is best regarded as a three-way dialogue between (1) specific OT texts, (2) their reception in the NT, and (3) their reception in Second Temple Judaism. The "meaning" that the contemporary biblical scholar will find in each depends on the dialogical contribution of the other conversation partners. In this way, the intertextual field does not move simply from the OT to the NT or vice versa, but there is a give and take between each one and the others, and they are not alone, for each is changed by the Second Temple literature. So Watson is wary of contemporary interpretations of the NT that suggest that the OT spoke into the NT era in a monochromatic fashion, as if there was not an intense negotiation—a competition—transpiring in late Second Temple Judaism over the meaning of specific OT passages.

Although I've devoted most of my space to a discussion of Watson's three-way method, regarding recent trends in the study of the OT in the NT, his results with respect to Paul's letters are also noteworthy for the entire subfield. Watson argues that Paul was a *sequential* reader of *the entire* Pentateuch, not just a reader of isolated passages or select textual blocks—and this was determinative for Paul's overall hermeneutical posture in approaching the OT.

More specifically, for Watson, Paul read the Pentateuch as a consecutive story and in so doing discovered a progression. God promises to bless all the nations unconditionally through Abraham and his seed (Gen. 12:3; 15:5). Abraham responds with faith, on the basis of which God credits Abraham with righteousness (15:6). Yet the subsequent giving of the law (Exod. 19–20) places the promises in jeopardy, because they now appear to be conditioned on proper human obedience. The law appears to hold out life for covenant performance (Lev. 18:5), but the failure of the Israelites in the wilderness (Numbers) shows that the covenant cannot actually be maintained by the unfaithful Israelites. All transgressors are under a curse (Deut. 27:26), including exile and death. However, God will bring Israel through exile and initialize a new covenant that will allow the Israelites to be obedient from the heart (Deut. 30–32). Watson believes that it was Paul's sequential reading of the whole Pentateuch that showed him that the unconditional promissory strand of the story eventually triumphs in God's plan over the conditional legal-performance strand.[27]

The result is that for Watson's Paul, the Christ event is of secondary significance in generating Paul's hermeneutical framework. Rather, it was Paul's reading of the Pentateuch largely independent from his christological convictions that led to Paul's overall theory of how to interpret the OT. Watson's construct is plausible on first blush, but other scholars, myself included, remain unconvinced, seeing Paul's kerygmatic convictions about Jesus as far more generative for Paul's hermeneutic than Watson has allowed. For example, evidence that countermands Watson's proposal can be found in passages where Paul identifies the Messiah as speaking in the OT—a phenomenon that Richard Hays has explained along the lines of a *Davidic typology*,[28] but that I've identified as a different ancient reading strategy altogether, a little-known strategy (but broadly evidenced) that is best termed *prosopological exegesis*.[29] Paul's use of prosopological exegesis is one of several pieces of evidence that suggest Paul's hermeneutic was not christologically reticent (contra Watson) or ecclesiocentric (contra Hays), but *kerygmacentric* and *missioncentric* as he applied and extended christological protocreeds in interpreting the OT.[30]

In the previous subsection we chronicled Wright's contribution. In this section we've looked at Watson's model and results. Watson's sequential approach and three-way-conversation model is also a narrative approach that pertains to intra-Jewish textual competition—even if his method and results are distinct from Wright's. Watson's claim that Paul is best understood as a sequential reader of the whole Pentateuch will doubtless continue to generate studies testing that claim with regard to Paul, while also stimulating related studies regarding other NT authors. Furthermore, Watson's three-way-conversation model is sophisticated and commendably helps us better take into account Second Temple Jewish texts contemporaneous with the NT when studying the use of the OT in the NT. Yet one wonders why Watson has limited the intertextual field to a three-way conversation. Why not four- or

---

27. See Watson, *Paul and the Hermeneutics*, 514–19.

28. Richard B. Hays, "Christ Prays the Psalms: Paul's Use of Early Christian Exegetical Convention," in *The Conversion of the Imagination: Paul as Interpreter of Israel's Scripture* (Grand Rapids: Eerdmans, 2005), 101–18. Hays's methodology is largely followed by Matthew Scott, *The Hermeneutics of Christological Psalmody in Paul: An Intertextual Enquiry*, SNTSMS 158 (Cambridge: Cambridge University Press, 2014).

29. Bates, *Hermeneutics of the Apostolic Proclamation*, 183–328, 350–52; Matthew W. Bates, *The Birth of the Trinity: Jesus, God, and Spirit in New Testament and Early Christian Interpretations of the Old Testament* (Oxford: Oxford University Press, 2015), 27–36.

30. Watson, *Paul and the Hermeneutics*, 21; Hays, *Echoes of Scripture in the Letters of Paul*, xiii; Bates, *Hermeneutics of the Apostolic Proclamation*, 329–35, 344–45.

five-way, or more? Does a model that merely treats the OT in the NT as an intra-Jewish dialogue leave out crucial conversation partners?

Early Christian and Greco-Roman Literary Contexts

Continuity with the Early Patristic Era

Let's say that we want to understand Matthew's interpretation of the OT—his techniques, principles of selection, and his overarching hermeneutical principles. Are the best comparative data to be found in the DSS, the Jewish pseudepigrapha, and Philo of Alexandria? Would it not be better to compare Matthew's interpretation of the OT with the interpretations of those who shared his basic convictions about Jesus as the Messiah—that is, with Paul, Luke, the author of Hebrews, Pseudo-Barnabas, Clement of Rome, and Justin Martyr? A number of scholars have produced studies showing that the use of the OT in the NT can be profitably studied not only as an intra-Jewish debate but also through an intra-Christian framework informed by Greco-Roman rhetoric and educational norms.[31]

Although numerous studies deserve further consideration, I will mention two in particular. These two are especially pertinent because they demonstrate that analysis of the use of the OT by subsequent Christians can help us better understand what the NT authors were doing in theory and in practice—and they do so by drawing connections to the wider Greco-Roman interpretative context. In short, this is an important approach because the hermeneutical posture, interpretive methods, and even the specific exegetical decisions of the NT authors were largely continuous with their immediate successors. The two studies can be considered together: Frances M. Young, *Biblical Exegesis and the Formation of Christian Culture*, and John J. O'Keefe and R. R. Reno, *Sanctified Vision*.[32]

---

31. The seminal work of R. M. Grant, *The Letter and the Spirit* (New York: Macmillan, 1957), still repays careful study. More recently, consider Manlio Simonetti, *Biblical Interpretation in the Early Church: An Historical Introduction to Patristic Exegesis* (Edinburgh: T&T Clark, 1994); Christopher A. Hall, *Reading Scripture with the Church Fathers* (Downers Grove, IL: InterVarsity, 1998); Ronald E. Heine, *Reading the Old Testament with the Ancient Church: Exploring the Formation of Early Christian Thought* (Grand Rapids: Baker Academic, 2007); Michael Graves, *The Inspiration and Interpretation of Scripture: What the Early Church Can Teach Us* (Grand Rapids: Eerdmans, 2014); Hans Boersma, *Scripture as Real Presence: Sacramental Exegesis in the Early Church* (Grand Rapids: Baker Academic, 2017); Sean A. Adams and Seth M. Ehorn, eds., *Composite Citations in Antiquity: Jewish, Graeco-Roman, and Early Christian Uses*, 2 vols., LNTS (London: Bloomsbury T&T Clark, 2015–18).

32. Frances M. Young, *Biblical Exegesis and the Formation of Christian Culture* (Cambridge: Cambridge University Press, 1997); John J. O'Keefe and R. R. Reno, *Sanctified Vision:*

Reference within the Divine Economy

For O'Keefe and Reno, contemporary scriptural interpretation in the academy and the church is predominantly concerned with external references in its construction of the meaning and truth value of the biblical text. This method of interpretation is convinced that the truly real is some "x" outside the text or behind the text. The truth is out there in some other form, and the Bible must conform to it if the Bible is to be regarded as a bearer of truth. Most of the time the "x" is felt to be "what really happened," and this is equated with "history." Secondarily the "x" is regarded as "what the laws of nature can show to be true" and is equated with "science." Of course, such judgments are loaded with philosophical commitments (often operating as background assumptions and never made explicit) about what language, history, and science are and how each connects meaning to truth. Regardless, for most moderns the true importance of the words in the text is found in their ability to point at (refer to) something external to the text: "this passage describes what really happened in the world" or "this Scripture can be proven by archaeological records" or "the Bbible says God created the universe, and background radiation proves that the universe came into existence about fourteen billion years ago"[33]—thus, the dominance of the historical-critical method in contemporary scholarship.

For ancient Christian interpreters the situation was quite different. The Scriptures were felt to be true not because they referred successfully to the external world beyond the text—as if the outside world is the deepest reality, and the Bible's truth depends on it—but rather because the Bible was like a mirror that disclosed the pattern of all reality. In other words, the world within the text reflects the divine economy, God's arrangement and orchestration of all affairs from creation to new creation, and truth resides there.[34] Meanwhile, Frances Young makes the equally important point that patristic exegesis did in fact distinguish between the lexical signs (the verbal dress) and the mental "idea" embodied by the signs. The linguistic sign represented the reality of the idea to which it referred, and in this sense, patristic exegesis is very interested in the "x" to which the language refers. The important point is that for early Christian interpreters, the "x" refers to an idea as located within the divine economy, not translated outside the divine economy. Thus for Young, *hermeneia* (or interpretation) in the early church "'translates' the symbols by pointing out their real reference," and this is to be located primarily within

---

An Introduction to Early Christian Interpretation of the Bible (Baltimore: Johns Hopkins University Press, 2005).

33. See O'Keefe and Reno, *Sanctified Vision*, 8–10; the examples placed in quotation marks are my own.

34. O'Keefe and Reno, *Sanctified Vision*, 11–13.

the divine economy.³⁵ The truth of Scripture and of the world are mutually informing in a dialectical fashion. The Scripture discloses the latent pattern that explains all reality; meanwhile created reality precisely imitates Scripture because both are authored by God.

Thus O'Keefe and Reno and Young are in agreement that creation and Scripture are sacramental, pointing beyond themselves to the self-same reference: God and his divine economy. In order to exemplify how this works, O'Keefe and Reno invite us to consider Gregory of Nyssa's *The Life of Moses*. In *The Life of Moses* the *historia* (narrative sequence about Moses) is not focused on determining "what really happened" but on providing moral exhortation by emphasizing certain details in the scriptural text as part of the retelling—intensifying the text as a key to its own meaning. The second part of *The Life of Moses* is the *theōria* ("contemplation"). The *theōria*, while offering a spiritual interpretation of the life of Moses in terms of the soul's ascent, is nonetheless thoroughly grounded in the nitty-gritty details of the text. "Gregory is moving across the text of the Bible, not past it."³⁶ So the created order speaks beyond itself, and its collective speech mirrors the economy disclosed in Scripture. The Scripture, however, is the crystallized revelation of God, so it takes the lead in showing what all of God's reality is like.

Reading Norms

Beyond these fundamental matters regarding how our early Christian interpreters located truth within a divine economy, more is offered by Young and by O'Keefe and Reno that is informative for the study of the OT in the NT. For instance, both treat the manner in which early Christian hermeneutical norms were impacted by the "canon of truth" or "rule of faith" as this interfaced with Greco-Roman compositional strategies (e.g., involving *hypothesis*, *oikonomia*, and *anakephalaiōsis*).³⁷ That is, early Christian interpreters did not approach the OT from neutral ground, but traditions about Jesus's incarnation, life, death, resurrection, and ascension impacted biblical exegesis. This is true for our NT authors in their use of the OT as well—as, for example, Paul (e.g., Rom. 1:2–4; 1 Cor. 15:3–5), Luke (e.g., 24:25–27, 44–47; Acts 17:2–3), John (e.g., 2:22; 12:16), and others all indicate that the Scriptures were retrospectively correlated with Christ events, so that these Christ events served as hermeneutical guideposts.³⁸

---

35. Young, *Biblical Exegesis*, 122.
36. O'Keefe and Reno, *Sanctified Vision*, 16.
37. Young, *Biblical Exegesis*, 17–45; O'Keefe and Reno, *Sanctified Vision*, 24–44, 119–28.
38. On retrospective reading, see esp. Richard B. Hays, *Reading Backward: Figural Christology and the Fourfold Gospel Witness* (Waco: Baylor University Press, 2014). Other statements include J. Ross Wagner, *Heralds of the Good News: Isaiah and Paul in Concert in the Letter to*

Those interested in hermeneutical method will also appreciate Young's and O'Keefe and Reno's nuanced discussions of allegory and so-called typology—especially as these interfaced with the rule of faith and Greco-Roman rhetoric and composition.[39] An emerging trend in the study of the OT in the NT, indeed of the Bible as a whole, is an increased sophistication in articulating what is meant by the "literal" sense of Scripture as informed by *inventio*, *dispositio*, and *elocutio* in Greco-Roman composition, and how this might relate to interpretative strategies such as *allēgoria*, the *typos* metaphor ("typology"), *historia*, *theōria*, moral exhortation, and the like.[40]

Seeking New Models

After surveying models that stress narrative and intra-Jewish debate (Wright and Watson) and exploring two studies that suggest hermeneutical continuity between the NT and the early patristic era (Young, O'Keefe, and Reno), the question becomes, Are there theoretical models and methods of study that can hold these approaches together?

Diachronic Intertextuality

Diachronic intertextuality has been proposed as one possible way forward. Diachronic intertextuality seeks to recover the fundamental insight of Julia Kristeva with regard to intertextuality: the idea that any specific "text" is informed by all the sociohistorical discourse that precedes, envelops, and comes after it.[41] Meanwhile diachronic intertextuality seeks to do away with Kristeva's problematic disdain for the role of genetic influence in creating

---

the Romans, NovTSup 101 (Leiden: Brill, 2003), 307–28, 356–59; Bates, *Hermeneutics of the Apostolic Proclamation*, 329–35; Richard B. Hays, *Echoes of Scripture in the Gospels* (Waco: Baylor University Press, 2016), 347–66; David I. Starling, *Hermeneutics as Apprenticeship: How the Bible Shapes Our Interpretative Habits and Practices* (Grand Rapids: Baker Academic, 2016), 105–17.

39. Young, *Biblical Exegesis*, 152–85, 189–201; O'Keefe and Reno, *Sanctified Vision*, 69–113.

40. Seminal studies include Brevard Childs, "The Sensus Literalis of Scripture: An Ancient and Modern Problem," in *Beiträge zur Alttestamentlichen Theologie: Festschrift für Walther Zimmerli zum 70. Geburtstag*, ed. Herbert Donner, Robert Hanhart, and Rudolf Smend (Göttingen: Vandenhoeck & Ruprecht, 1977), 80–93; Paul R. Noble, "The 'Sensus Literalis': Jowett, Childs, and Barr," *JTS* 44 (1993): 1–23. For a recent reflection, see Iain Provan, *The Reformation and the Right Reading of Scripture* (Waco: Baylor University Press, 2017), chap. 4. For specifics pertaining to the OT in the NT, see Bates, *Hermeneutics of the Apostolic Proclamation*, 109–17 (invention and expression), 133–48 (types), 149–60 (allegory), and 160–81 (literal versus spiritual reading); Starling, *Hermeneutics as Apprenticeship*, 147–62 (allegory), 163–74 (exhortation).

41. See Julia Kristeva, *Desire in Language: A Semiotic Approach to Literature and Art*, ed. Leon S. Roudiez, trans. Thomas Gora, Alice Jardin, and Leon S. Roudiez (New York: Columbia University Press, 1980).

textual meaning. Toward that end I have proposed that the meaning of any specific NT "text" needs to take into account more than just the "pre-text" (the specific OT passage involved) and more than just Jewish "co-texts" (Second Temple Jewish passages that use the same "pre-text"). Rather, explicitly Christian "co-texts" and "post-texts" must be included when appraising use of the OT in the NT. Co-texts are early Christian texts that use the same OT "pre-text" independently.[42] For example, if the "text" is Romans 1:17 in its citation of Habakkuk 2:4, then a "co-text" is Hebrews 10:38, since this cites Habakkuk 2:4 with no obvious influence from Romans 1:17. Meanwhile, an early Christian "post-text" does show a relationship of dependence on the NT "text" that uses the OT. For example, Irenaeus gives us information about the meaning of the use of Habakkuk 2:4 in Romans 1:17, because he cites Romans 1:17 and in so doing offers an interpretive take on the meaning of Habakkuk 2:4 in Romans 1:17. My claim is that if a specific use of the OT in the NT is a "text," we must make use of all the relevant pre-texts, co-texts, and post-texts at our disposal, whether Jewish, Christian, pagan, or otherwise. I've spelled the details of a diachronic intertextual model out in much fuller detail elsewhere.[43]

Intertextual Encyclopedia

Meanwhile, others have articulated similar ideas using Umberto Eco's concept of an intertextual encyclopedia.[44] Eco moves the question of word meaning beyond a dictionary approach to that of an encyclopedia, for in the end, "a dictionary is a disguised encyclopedia."[45] The basic idea in semiotics is that meaning in language is created through differentiation. But with regard to universals and labels, differentiation must be carried out with regard to the local, or else meaning disintegrates because it can remain only a regulative idea. For Eco, larger categories (e.g., universal labels) such as we find in a dictionary are metatheoretical constructs that ultimately dissolve when we try to interpret them according to the dictionary apart from specific local settings, because a "given text requires a background encyclopedic knowledge in order

---

42. On the problematic nature of the labels "Jewish" and "Christian," see my note 17 above.

43. Bates, *Hermeneutics of the Apostolic Proclamation*, 44–56; Matthew W. Bates, "Beyond Hays's Echoes of Scripture in the Letters of Paul: A Proposed Diachronic Intertextuality with Romans 10:16 as a Test-Case," in *Paul and Scripture: Extending the Conversation*, ed. Christopher D. Stanley (Atlanta: SBL Press, 2012), 263–92.

44. E.g., Richard B. Hays, "Paul and the Hermeneutics of Truth," *Pro Ecclesia* 16 (2007): 126–40, esp. 131; Leroy A. Huizenga, *The New Isaac: Tradition and Intertextuality in the Gospel of Matthew*, NovTSup 131 (Leiden: Brill, 2009), 21–28, 265; Justin Langford, *Defending Hope: Semiotics and Intertextuality in 1 Peter* (Eugene, OR: Wipf & Stock, 2013).

45. Umberto Eco, *Semiotics and the Philosophy of Language* (Bloomington: Indiana University Press, 1986), 68.

to be interpreted."⁴⁶ That is, dictionaries work only because they assume a shared cultural encyclopedia. So in order to disambiguate the meaning of any word in context, one must bring a sufficiently shared cultural encyclopedia of linguistic and nonlinguistic knowledge to bear on the word and sentence in context. Going beyond Eco and updating the discussion, the point as this applies to the OT in the NT is this: meaning is created through the shared cultural encyclopedia of the author, the texts, and their readers as each is locally manifested.

In seeking interpretative meaning, diachronic intertextuality and intertextual encyclopedia are models that seek to take into account all cultural discourse that precedes, surrounds, and follows a textual event. For theists committed to God's sovereignty, another way of speaking about this is that textual meaning is informed by the entire divine economy—God's superintendence of all affairs, including his own purposes as these are manifested in the human cultural production, reception, and interpretation of Scripture in church and world. Thus appreciation of the divine economy can serve as a point of unity between ancient and modern hermeneutics.

The strength of such models is that they take ancient horizons of textual production, intention, and initial reception seriously, and they also show why subsequent reception history and communal interpretation are bound up with textual meaning. We cannot simply search for what, for example, Matthew *meant* when in 8:17 he cited Isaiah 53:4, "He received our weaknesses and bore our diseases," apart from how both Matthew and Isaiah are informed not just by what was happening "back then" but also how "back then" created a cultural-interpretative history and communities in which we as modern exegetes now find ourselves. There is no method by which we can entirely separate our own meaning-making from the text's meaning, but instead we must spiral toward the truth by becoming acquainted with all relevant past and present culture, so that we can allow it to reshape our present horizons of understanding. We genuinely can approach the full truth encapsulated in a specific use of the OT in the NT as we seek to decode it in ever more exacting and refined ways, but it is hard historical, social, and cultural work.

Reflections

The survey of recent trends in the study of the OT in the NT conducted in this chapter suggests a certain irony. Emerging scholarship indicates that the subdiscipline of the OT in the NT is achieving the largest strides when it intentionally breaches the boundaries that make it a distinct subdiscipline. The

---

46. Eco, *Semiotics*, 68.

models provided by Wright and Watson indicate that progress continues to be made when we take the storied dimension of the OT seriously and when we treat the use of the OT in the NT as an intra-Jewish competition. Meanwhile a greater appreciation for the continuity between the use of the OT in the NT and the early patristic era has produced new insights, as numerous studies attest. The contributions of Young and O'Keefe and Reno show that early patristic writers demonstrated a commitment to a divine economy in their engagement with the OT, as they sought to mobilize the use of the OT through moral exhortation and the use of suitable rhetorical tropes, much as in the NT era.

Scholarship is currently seeking models that can hold these insights together. The models of diachronic intertextuality and of an intertextual encyclopedia are two such proposals. Although I haven't discussed it here, promising work in cognitive linguistics, the study of the physical processes by which the brain makes meaning and how this relates to language, may ultimately allow such models to be refined or replaced.[47] Meanwhile, it is clear that studies pertaining to what is meant by "literal" in relationship to purportedly nonliteral modes of interpretation ("figuration") will continue to attract conversation. Scholars who ground their results thoroughly in the Jewish and Greco-Roman realia of compositional practices and reading norms are likely to make a lasting impact.

47. See Vyvyan Evans and Melanie Green, *Cognitive Linguistics: An Introduction* (London: Routledge, 2006).

5

The Genre of the Gospels

Wes Olmstead

Introduction

That scholars think about the genre of the Gospels in dramatically different terms than they did twenty-five years ago is to be attributed above all to the singular impact of Richard Burridge's 1992 Cambridge monograph (2nd ed., 2004), *What Are the Gospels?*[1] Not everyone agrees with Burridge, of course, but all subsequent discussion responds, in one way or another, to his thesis. In this chapter, I summarize Burridge's argument, consider critiques it has elicited, and discuss two important alternative proposals. Each of these three major proposals makes an important contribution to our understanding of the genre of the canonical Gospels.[2] In short, the Gospels are *bioi*, but *bioi* of a particular type: they are *kerygmatic bioi* richly informed by, and drawing to climax, Israel's scriptural narratives.

Richard Burridge: The Gospels as *Bioi*

Antecedent Discussions

Burridge's chief contention is that the Gospels are ancient biographies (*bioi*). He is not the first to argue this, so there is a story to be told about

---

1. Richard A. Burridge, *What Are the Gospels? A Comparison with Graeco-Roman Biography*, SNTSMS (Cambridge: Cambridge University Press, 1992; 2nd ed., Grand Rapids: Eerdmans, 2004).
2. The important question of the genre of the other early Christian "Gospels" lies outside the purview of this chapter.

103

why his thesis has proved seminal.[3] It appears that throughout most of the church's history, ordinary readers and scholars alike took the Gospels to be, in some sense, narratives of the life of Jesus.[4] The eighteenth and nineteenth centuries featured a series of *Lives of Jesus*[5] that proceeded on the same assumption—even if they insisted that the Gospels must be critically sifted to reveal Jesus as he was.[6]

If Albert Schweitzer offered a devastating exposé of these *Lives*, the remainder of the twentieth century would not be kinder to their working assumption that the Gospels were to be understood as biographies of Jesus. It was the form critics, above all, who were responsible for the turning of the tide. For Karl Ludwig Schmidt, the Gospels were "not *Hochliteratur*, but *Kleinliteratur*, not the product of an individual author, but a folk-book, not biography but cult legend."[7] Rudolf Bultmann concurred: "There is no historical-biographical interest in the Gospels, and that is why they have nothing to say about Jesus' human personality, his appearance and character, his origin, education and development; quite apart from the fact that they do not command the cultivated techniques of composition necessary for grand literature, nor let the personalities of their author appear."[8] We need, Bultmann thought, analogies for the components of the Gospels (miracle stories, similitudes, etc.) but not for the Gospels as complete works. Indeed, "the analogies that are to hand serve only to throw the uniqueness of the Gospel into still stronger relief."[9] The Gospels are sui generis (without parallel), "an original creation of Christianity."[10]

---

3. For useful reviews of earlier scholarship, see, e.g., Robert Guelich, "The Gospel Genre," in *The Gospel and the Gospels*, ed. Peter Stuhlmacher (Grand Rapids: Eerdmans, 1991), 173–208; Robert H. Gundry, *The Old Is Better: New Testament Essays in Support of Traditional Interpretations* (Tübingen: Mohr Siebeck, 2005), 18–48; Judith Diehl, "What Is a 'Gospel'? Recent Studies in the Gospel Genre," *CBR* 9, no. 2 (2011): 171–99.

4. Albrecht Dihle notes that even though every first-semester theological student is warned *not* to interpret the Gospels as biographies, this posture "runs counter to an understanding that prevailed for more than 1500 years . . . and the life-of-Jesus research of the nineteenth century, which steadily distanced itself from the doctrinal tradition of the Church, still shared this understanding of the Gospels." Dihle, "The Gospels and Greek Biography," in Stuhlmacher, *Gospel and the Gospels*, 361.

5. Famously chronicled by Albert Schweitzer in *Von Reimarus zu Wrede: Geschichte der Leben-Jesu-Forschung* (Tübingen: Mohr Siebeck, 1906; translated as *The Quest of the Historical Jesus*, ed. John Bowden [Minneapolis: Fortress, 2001]).

6. Cf., e.g., Ernest Renan, *Life of Jesus* (New York: Grosset & Dunlap, 1923), 67 (trans. from the 23rd French ed.).

7. Karl Ludwig Schmidt, *The Place of the Gospels in the General History of Literature*, trans. Byron R. McCane (Columbia: University of South Carolina Press, 2002), 27, quoted in Burridge, *What Are the Gospels?*, 8–9.

8. Rudolf Bultmann, *The History of the Synoptic Tradition*, trans. John Marsh, rev. ed. (New York: Harper & Row, 1963), 372.

9. Bultmann, *History of the Synoptic Tradition*, 373.

10. Bultmann, *History of the Synoptic Tradition*, 374.

This conclusion, that the Gospels were without literary antecedent, quickly established itself as the consensus among NT specialists.[11]

Burridge was not the first to challenge the consensus,[12] but he was the first to shake it.[13] The impact of his challenge is probably to be explained by a convergence of several factors,[14] but chief among them is the care with which he makes his case.

The Gospels as Bioi: *Burridge's Argument*

GENRE ITSELF

Burridge begins with a consideration of genre itself. Without suggesting that writers and speakers, readers and listeners are always *consciously* making generic distinctions, he argues for the centrality of genre in all verbal communication. This was no less the case for the ancients than it is for moderns (or indeed, postmoderns).[15] Following literary critic Heather Dubrow, he suggests that genre forms a kind of *contract* between author and reader, setting expectations and establishing ground rules.[16] Generic expectations exert an influence on both parties, but, since genre is dynamic and flexible, these expectations can be modified as a text unfolds. Thus we should understand genre neither in prescriptive terms (think conventions, not rules) nor in merely descriptive terms (think expectations, not after-the-fact explications). Basic to Burridge's case is the notion that "all work is dependent on what precedes it; anything completely new would be incommunicable."[17] Still, most genres can be subdivided. Whereas genres are marked out by a series of family traits related to *both* form and content, subgenres tend to be distinguished by

---

11. To cite but two examples, cf. C. F. D. Moule, *The Birth of the New Testament* (London: Adam & Charles Black, 1962), 4–5; W. G. Kümmel, *Introduction to the New Testament* (London: SCM, 1975), 37.

12. Cf., e.g., Charles H. Talbert, *What Is a Gospel? The Genre of the Canonical Gospels* (Philadelphia: Fortress, 1977); Philip L. Shuler, *A Genre for the Gospels: The Biographical Character of Matthew* (Philadelphia: Fortress, 1982). David Aune concludes that the Gospels are "a type of ancient biography." Aune, *The New Testament in Its Literary Environment* (Philadelphia: Fortress, 1987), 17–76, here 46.

13. Steve Walton, "What Are the Gospels? Richard Burridge's Impact on Scholarly Understanding of the Genre of the Gospels," *CBR* 14, no. 1 (2015): 81–93.

14. As Burridge himself observes, "Once redaction critics had demonstrated that the evangelists were not mindless recorders of the oral tradition, but had creative, *theological* purposes in writing their gospels, then questions about their creative *literary* intentions, including genre, could not be far behind." Burridge, *What Are the Gospels?*, 15.

15. Burridge points, e.g., to Quintilian, *Inst.* 10.2.21 ("Each genre has its own rules and proprieties") and suggests that Aristotelian genre theory continued to be important into the early years of the twentieth century. See Burridge, *What Are the Gospels?*, 27–28.

16. Heather Dubrow, *Genre* (London: Methuen, 1982), 31.

17. Burridge, *What Are the Gospels?*, 45. Cf. René Wellek and Austin Warren, *Theory of Literature*, 3rd ed. (Harmondsworth: Penguin, 1982), 235, to which he appeals here.

content alone. All of this leads Burridge to two primary conclusions: (1) it is nonsense to speak of the Gospels as being unique generically, and (2) they must be compared with works from their own era.[18]

The Generic Features of *Bioi*

Like other genres, *bioi* are marked by a cluster of family traits. Burridge's analysis of ten *bioi* ranging from the fifth century BCE to the third century CE (five preceding[19] and five postdating[20] the Gospels) reveals generic features of four basic types.

First, like other works of the period, *bioi* are distinguished by their beginnings—that is, by their titles (whether assigned by the author or added subsequently) and by their opening lines: "History, epideictic oratory, philosophical dialogue, political treatise or whatever, your first sentence had to announce what you were writing."[21] All the *bioi* that Burridge examines announce the name of the subject either at their very outset or immediately following a prologue.

Second, *bioi* are marked by a "strong concentration . . . on *one* person"[22] that may even be observed at the syntactical level. Turning to statistical analysis, Burridge documents a "skewing effect" that demonstrates that one person dominates as the subject of the narrative's verbs. But he also shows that *bioi* exhibit considerable diversity in the way they depict their subjects' lives: some devote relatively even coverage to the main periods of their subjects' lives, while others concentrate heavily on one or two periods to the relative neglect of others.[23]

Third, with respect to "external features" (mode of representation, meter, size and length, etc.), "βίοι are works mostly in prose narrative and of medium length; their structure is a bare chronological framework of birth/arrival and death with topical material inserted; the scale is always limited to the subject; a mixture of literary units, notably anecdotes, stories, speeches, and sayings, selected from a wide range of oral and written sources, displays the subject's character indirectly through words and deeds rather than by direct analysis."[24]

---

18. Burridge, *What Are the Gospels?*, 51.
19. Isocrates's *Evagoras*, Xenophon's *Agesilaus*, Satyrus's *Euripides*, Nepos's *Atticus*, and Philo's *Moses*.
20. Tacitus's *Agricola*, Plutarch's *Cato Minor*, Suetonius's *Lives of the Caesars*, Lucian's *Demonax*, and Philostratus's *Apollonius of Tyana*.
21. Donald Earl, "Prologue-Form in Ancient Historiography," *ANRW*, part 1, *Von den Anfängen Roms bis zum Ausgang der Republik*, 2:856, quoted in Burridge, *What Are the Gospels?*, 109.
22. Burridge, *What Are the Gospels?*, 131. Cf. Justin Marc Smith, *Why βίος? On the Relationship between Gospel Genre and Implied Audience*, LNTS 518 (London: Bloomsbury T&T Clark, 2015), 203: "The emphasis on the words and deeds of a particular individual is the hallmark of this literature."
23. Burridge, *What Are the Gospels?*, 133.
24. Burridge, *What Are the Gospels?*, 140.

Bioi also display a predictable set of "internal features" (setting, motifs, tone, quality of characterization, etc.). Those *bioi* that have survived are typically "fairly literary," but there is evidence for more popular works, no longer extant. Although *bioi* focus on one person, the topics addressed vary within a range of typical options. The tone is generally serious. *Bioi* appear to be written with a wide range of often overlapping rhetorical purposes (entertainment, exemplification, apologetic, polemic, instruction, etc.).[25]

If it is true that *bioi* are marked by a discernible set of generic family traits, individual *bioi* incorporate and adapt these traits freely. Moreover, none of these traits are unique to *bioi*. Unsurprisingly, then, *bioi* share generic traits with a number of *genera proxima* (neighboring genres): "Plutarch's βίοι [*bioi*] exemplify the flexible nature of the genre, nestling between history, rhetoric, and moral philosophy, with a variety of literary and artistic purposes."[26] It is, therefore, precisely the *clustering* of generic traits that sets a work off as a *bios* as opposed to something else.

The Gospels as *Bioi*

The final step in Burridge's argument is to demonstrate that first the Synoptics, and then John, share this same family resemblance.[27] They too are of medium length; they each introduce their subject either in the opening lines or immediately after the prologue; they feature a persistent focus on one person; and so on. Set alongside these ancient *lives*, despite their obvious differences in content, the genre of the Gospels becomes obvious: they too are *bioi*.

Hermeneutical Implications

Burridge's critics have sometimes charged that *bioi* are diverse enough that, even if we accept his thesis, the hermeneutical payoff is meager. But if the Gospels are *bioi*, one important interpretive conclusion (with at least a couple of corollaries) probably does follow.[28] If the Gospels are *bioi*, they are *about Jesus* and are to be read as christological narratives.[29]

To the extent that the Gospels are *bioi*, and thus about a person, they are not about (or probably for) specific communities.[30] In an essay in *The*

---

25. Burridge, *What Are the Gospels?*, 140–48.
26. Burridge, *What Are the Gospels?*, 170.
27. Regarding Synoptics, see Burridge, *What Are the Gospels?*, 185–212. Regarding John, see Burridge, *What Are the Gospels?*, 213–32.
28. For Burridge's own response to this critique, see *What Are the Gospels?*, 252–307.
29. Burridge, *What Are the Gospels?*, 288–94, 338.
30. To say that the Gospels are about Jesus raises important questions about historicity. The question is complicated, not least because of distinctions between ancient and contemporary historiographical practice. Generic discussions are useful here but also limited. Richard

Gospels for All Christians,³¹ which was designed to challenge the (then current) consensus that the Gospels were written for specific churches, Burridge explores the question of Gospel audiences from the vantage of Gospel genre. His most important observation is that, while we may speak of *target audiences* or *market niches* for extant *bioi*, in no case can we identify a *bios* written for a specific community.³² Justin Smith's recent monograph proposes a typology that addresses the relationships between authors of *bioi* and their subjects, on the one hand, and authors and their audiences, on the other. He concludes that "the evangelists chose the genre of biography because it was the genre best suited to present the words and deeds of Jesus to the largest possible audience."³³ If we accept Burridge's and Smith's arguments, a serious question mark must be placed over the project of reconstructing hypothetical communities that form the lens through which the Gospels are read.

Similarly, inasmuch as the Gospels are *bioi*, they grant their subject (Jesus) a paradigmatic role. David Capes offers an article-length defense of this conclusion in four steps.³⁴ First, in both the Greco-Roman and the Jewish literature of this era, an ethos exists "in which writers, moralists, and theologians held notable figures as models to be imitated."³⁵ Second, in the NT outside the Gospels, early Christian writers regularly exhorted their readers to imitate the life of Jesus.³⁶ Third, the Gospels themselves are punctuated

---

Bauckham, *The Testimony of the Beloved Disciple: Narrative, History, and Theology in the Gospel of John* (Grand Rapids: Baker Academic, 2007), 16–21, argues that the generic clues in John's Gospel place it at the end of the spectrum where *bios* overlapped with historiography. But he also observes that this generic argument does not tell us whether the Gospel actually meets the expectations it suggests to its (ancient) readers. For a recent attempt to explore what can be learned about the nature of the evangelists' historical claims by comparing their compositional techniques with those employed by the biographer Plutarch, see Michael R. Licona, *Why Are There Differences in the Gospels? What We Can Learn from Ancient Biography* (Oxford: Oxford University Press, 2017).

31. Richard A. Burridge, "About People, by People, for People: Gospel Genre and Audiences," in *The Gospels for All Christians: Rethinking the Gospel Audiences*, ed. Richard Bauckham (Grand Rapids: Eerdmans, 1998), 113–45. See now Burridge, "Who Writes, Why, and for Whom?," in *The Written Gospel*, ed. Markus Bockmuehl and Donald A. Hagner (Cambridge: Cambridge University Press, 2005), 110–15.

32. This should not be taken to mean that the authors of *bioi* were not influenced by local circumstances.

33. Smith, *Why βίος?*, 202.

34. David B. Capes, "*Imitatio Christi* and the Gospel Genre," *BBR* 13, no. 1 (2003): 1–19. Cf. Adela Yarbro Collins, *Mark: A Commentary*, Hermeneia (Minneapolis: Fortress, 2007), 18. Although she doubts that Mark is a *bios*, Collins observes matter-of-factly, "The conclusion that Mark is a life of Jesus or a biography implies that it is a record of an individual who serves as a model for others."

35. Capes, "*Imitatio Christi*," 3; see also 3–10. Among Greco-Roman writers, he appeals to Seneca, Quintilian, Dio Chrysostom, Isocrates, Plutarch, and Lucian.

36. Capes, "*Imitatio Christi*," 10–13.

by such exhortations.³⁷ Finally, in the post-NT era, this is precisely how Christian readers read, and were urged to read, the Gospels.³⁸ Capes points to the well-known text from Justin's *First Apology* as evidence: "And on the day called Sunday, all who live in cites [*sic*] or in the country gather together to one place, and the memoirs of the apostles or the writings of the prophets are read, as long as time permits; then, when the reader has ceased, the president verbally instructs, and exhorts to the imitation of these good things."³⁹ That the Gospels function this way and were designed to function this way seems secure. Jesus's role is of course not only exemplary, as many have observed:⁴⁰ in the Gospels Jesus is more, but not less, than a model for his followers.

Critiques of the Biographical Hypothesis

Adela Yarbro Collins has leveled one of the most substantive critiques of Burridge's argument. First, she observes that Burridge never actually defines the genre *bios*.⁴¹ His emphasis on flexible generic boundaries and overlapping circles formed by *genera proxima* offers a necessary corrective to unduly rigid notions of genre but must be complemented by a clear articulation of what distinguishes these genres. This, however, is precisely what Burridge fails to provide. Second, among the generic features that Burridge highlights, subject and purpose are among the most promising. But, although Burridge begins by referring to *subject matter*, his investigation actually centers on grammatical subjects (so shifting the discussion from literary motif to syntax), and his discussion of the *purposes* of *bioi* is so general as to be unhelpful. Third, Burridge's argument fails to discuss seriously the alternatives; historical monograph, in particular, deserves careful consideration. Fourth, the Gospels are deeply influenced by antecedent biblical literature, but it is not clear that we can speak of biography as a pre-Hellenistic biblical genre (we can of course speak of biographical elements). Fifth, none of the evangelists describes his work as a *bios*.⁴²

---

37. Capes, "*Imitatio Christi*," 3–16.
38. Capes, "*Imitatio Christi*," 6–19.
39. *1 Apol.* 67, quoted in Capes, "*Imitatio Christi*," 18.
40. Cf., e.g., Larry Hurtado, *Lord Jesus Christ: Devotion to Jesus in Earliest Christianity* (Grand Rapids: Eerdmans, 2003), 282, 277, 279; Collins, *Mark*, 28; Jonathan T. Pennington, *Reading the Gospels Wisely: A Narrative and Theological Introduction* (Grand Rapids: Baker Academic, 2012), 27.
41. Adela Yarbro Collins, "Genre and the Gospels," *JR* 75, no. 2 (1995): 239–46. The following paragraph draws on this review.
42. So too Joel Marcus, *Mark 1–8: A New Translation with Introduction and Commentary*, AB 27 (New York: Doubleday, 2000), 65; Gundry, *Old Is Better*, 39.

Sixth, and vitally for Collins, in the Gospels the story of Jesus is not told for its own sake, but as part of a larger story of the outworking of God's purposes.[43]

Like Collins, Joel Marcus thinks that the Gospel of Mark shares more in common with ancient history, especially ancient biblical history, than with ancient biography.[44] And while there are undeniably biographical elements in the Gospels, Mark's Gospel might more accurately be described as the biography of a *movement* than of an individual.[45] Finally, in stark contrast to the typical *bios*, which recounts "the story of the completed life of a revered (or reviled) figure of the past," Mark's Jesus is *not* a figure of the past, nor can his story ever be completed.[46]

John Riches insists that Schmidt rightly distinguished the Gospels from ancient biographies on the basis of the absence, in the Gospels, of any concern for portraiture and, especially, any sense of authorial personality.[47] The latter distinction may be observed in particular in the treatment of sources: unlike the biographers, the evangelists display no critical distance from their sources. Thus "whatever else the evangelists were, they were not ancient biographers."[48]

Though quibbles could of course be multiplied, perhaps the most important criticisms of Burridge's biographical thesis are that it remains too general (What kind of *bios* is a Gospel?), that it fails to account for the uniqueness of the Gospels over against Greco-Roman *bioi*, and that it fails to give sufficient weight to the influence of Israel's Scriptures on the shape of the Gospels. The most important alternative generic proposals for the Gospels aim to grapple with these precise issues.

Alternative Proposals

There is no shortage of novel proposals about the genre of the Gospels. Lawrence Wills, for example, argues that Mark and John comprise aretalogical biographies that depend on a common source, which bears the stamp of both

43. So too, e.g., Guelich, "Gospel Genre," 181; Marcus, *Mark 1–8*, 66.
44. Marcus, *Mark 1–8*, 65.
45. Marcus, *Mark 1–8*, 66.
46. Marcus, *Mark 1–8*, 66–67.
47. John Riches, "Introduction: Karl Ludwig Schmidt's *The Place of the Gospels in the General History of Literature*," in Schmidt, *Place of the Gospels*, xv.
48. Riches, "Introduction," xxi. Gundry also finds Schmidt's dismantling of the biographical hypothesis decisive (Gundry, *Old Is Better*, 18–48). Although Schmidt was responding to C. W. Votaw, *The Gospels and Contemporary Biographies in the Greco-Roman World* (repr., Philadelphia: Fortress, 1970), Gundry sees nothing in Burridge sufficiently distinct from Votaw to warrant further discussion.

Jewish and Hellenistic influences, a cult narrative for a dead hero.[49] Dennis MacDonald thinks that Mark's Gospel imitates the *Iliad* and the *Odyssey*.[50] Michael Vines, drawing on the work of Mikhail Bakhtin, insists that Mark most closely resembles an ancient Jewish novel.[51] Kasper Bro Larsen edits a series of essays[52] that probe the insights of Harold Attridge's presidential address at the 2001 annual meeting of the Society of Biblical Literature,[53] which argues that John's Gospel bends historical and biographical generic expectations by including dramatic and novelistic features. As I see it, however, the two most serious current alternatives to Burridge's biographical hypothesis actually revive older hypotheses: the Gospels are, on one view, historical monographs and, on the other, generically unique.

The Gospels as Historical Monographs

Collins thinks that the Gospels have strong affinities to the historical biographies of the Greco-Roman tradition. But she is also convinced that they share much in common with historical monographs. Indeed, deciding between the two closely related genres depends on whether one thinks their accent falls on the activity of Jesus or on the accomplishment of God's purposes through Jesus.[54] Since, for Collins, Mark is an account of what *God* was doing in history through Jesus, the Gospel is finally to be located alongside other ancient historical monographs.[55] In support of this conclusion, Collins appeals to several lines of evidence.

First, the earliest readers of Mark appear to have received it as history. Collins observes that Justin referred to the Gospels both as *euangelia* (Gospels) and as *apomnēmoneumata* (memoirs or notes), and Origen could refer to them, or their contents, as *historiai* (histories or investigations)—that is, both associated them with historical writing.[56] The ancients, as Quintilian

---

49. Lawrence M. Wills, *The Quest of the Historical Gospel: Mark, John, and the Origins of the Gospel Genre* (London: Routledge, 1997).
50. Dennis R. MacDonald, *The Homeric Epics and the Gospel of Mark* (New Haven: Yale University Press, 2000).
51. Michael E. Vines, *The Problem of the Markan Genre: The Gospel of Mark and the Jewish Novel* (Atlanta: SBL Press, 2002).
52. Kasper Bro Larsen, ed., *The Gospel of John as Genre Mosaic*, SANt 3 (Göttingen: Vandenhoeck & Ruprecht, 2015).
53. Harold Attridge, "Genre Bending in the Fourth Gospel," *JBL* 121, no. 1 (2002): 3–21.
54. Collins, *Mark*, 33.
55. Collins, *Mark*, 34, 36. Collins observes that Eve-Marie Becker thinks that, like the canonical Gospels, Mark is sui generis; Becker also thinks that Mark can be situated "in the context of ancient historiography"; see Collins, *Mark*, 34; Eve-Marie Becker, *Das Markus-Evangelium im Rahmen antiker Historiographie*, WUNT 194 (Tübingen: Mohr Siebeck, 2006), 50, 52.
56. Collins, *Mark*, 16–17, 33.

demonstrates, were quite at home distinguishing between historical and other types of narrative.[57]

Second, although historical writing had traditionally focused on large-scale events in the worlds of politics and war, we can already see in the fourth-century-BCE historian Theopompus an increased focus on individuals, a tendency that becomes "explicit and marked" in works dealing with Alexander.[58] Charles William Fornara could thus speak of "a sort of biographical history."[59] The Gospels' consistent focus on Jesus, then, need not distinguish them, generically, from ancient history.

Third, the Gospels are at home in the world of *biblical* history. Like the biblical historians, Mark (and, by extension, the other evangelists) is concerned with the *significance* of the story he tells for Israel. Moreover, instead of disqualifying him as an author, Mark's editorial procedures locate him within the biblical tradition.[60] That Mark does not introduce himself and state his purposes in the manner of the Greco-Roman historians may be explained similarly: he follows the precedent set by the biblical historians. More generally, Mark's style (parataxis, blocks of independent material set in a rough chronological framework, use of editorial comment, etc.), which is often thought to distinguish his work from literature proper, actually links him both to the biblical historians, on the one hand, and to Herodotus, on the other.[61]

Fourth, Mark's Gospel does signal the dawn of a new era, generically speaking, but not something unrelated to prior works. Instead, it is a historical monograph of a particular sort, as Mark 1:1–3 suggests. For Collins, "the first word, 'beginning' (ἀρχή [*archē*]), reflects the historian's decision about the proper starting point for the descriptive and explanatory narrative,"[62] while what follows ("of the gospel . . . just as it is written") indicates what sort of history the evangelist intends to write: it is an *eschatological*, historical monograph that narrates the fulfilment of the divine purposes. Mark 1:14–15 offers confirmation: the gospel that Jesus proclaims concerns the time of fulfilment, the time of the dawn of God's kingdom.[63] There are important parallels between Jesus and earlier leaders in Israel,

---

57. Quintilian, *Inst*. 2.4.2, cited in Collins, *Mark*, 35. Unlike fictitious and realistic narratives, respectively, historical narrative "is an exposition of something done."
58. Collins, *Mark*, 37.
59. Charles William Fornara, *The Nature of History in Ancient Greece and Rome* (Berkeley: University of California Press, 1983), 35, cited in Collins, *Mark*, 37.
60. Collins, *Mark*, 37–38.
61. Collins, *Mark*, 41.
62. Collins, *Mark*, 42.
63. Collins, *Mark*, 42.

but Mark's narrative is marked by an eschatology that is absent from the biblical histories.[64]

Fifth, although Jesus remains front and center throughout the Gospel as the one through whom God's eschatological purposes find fulfilment, Mark's narrative is finally about the achievement of those purposes. "Mark's interest," therefore, "was not so much in what sort of man Jesus was, in general, as it was in what sort of messiah, prophet, or divine mediator he was."[65] In the end, then, Mark is not to be considered a *bios* but a historical monograph.

The Gospels as Unique

The second major alternative to the biographical hypothesis is the persistent notion, variously nuanced, that the Gospels are unique generically. Readers rightly hear echoes, sometimes clear and sometimes faint, of the classic form-critical insistence that the Gospels are sui generis.

In a very brief but typically provocative discussion, Francis Watson insists that the evangelists were responsible for the creation of a new genre. Watson thinks not of creation ex nihilo—the evangelists happily employed many of the conventions of the Hellenistic *bios*—but of a generic creation nonetheless.[66] Most of his discussion focuses on Mark. While recognizing that the point is disputed, Watson finds in Mark 1:1 ("The beginning of the gospel . . .") a clear reference to the written narrative that Mark composed.[67] The title assigned to his narrative offers important evidence that this is in fact how Mark's *Gospel* was received: "While it may be that the original manuscript of the 'Gospel according to Mark' did not bear this title, the fact remains that for all its known readers its genre was that of gospel (*euangelion kata . . .*). They may or may not have been aware of connections with other, secular genres—the Graeco-Roman *bios* or *vita*, for example—but they do not assign to this text any such title as *peri tou biou Iēsou*; they can think of it only as *euangelion*."[68] It was as Gospels, then, that the church received these texts. Watson appeals to Irenaeus, who, in brief compass, refers both to the (singular) gospel and to the (plural) Gospels: "God 'has given us the gospel under four aspects, but

---

64. Collins, *Mark*, 42; Collins follows John Van Seters, *In Search of History: Historiography in the Ancient World and the Origins of Biblical History* (Winona Lake, IN: Eisenbrauns, 1997), 8–9.

65. Collins, *Mark*, 43.

66. Francis Watson, *Text and Truth: Redefining Biblical Theology* (Grand Rapids: Eerdmans, 1997), 89n7. Strangely, apart from a very brief discussion of Luke's prologue, Watson's major recent work on the Gospels, *Gospel Writing: A Canonical Perspective* (Grand Rapids: Eerdmans, 2013), passes over the question of the genre of the canonical Gospels in silence. He does discuss the genre of the Gospel of Thomas.

67. Watson, *Text and Truth*, 75.

68. Watson, *Text and Truth*, 74–75.

bound together by one Spirit,' and he has done so in the form of 'gospels' which 'cannot be either more or fewer in number than they actually are.'"[69] "This plural form," Watson observes, "develops naturally out of the earlier singular usage."[70] The Gospels announce the gospel.

Like Watson, Martin Hengel concludes that a new literary genre comes to birth with Mark's Gospel.[71] But, unlike Watson, Hengel displays a certain ambivalence in his discussion of the relationship of the Gospels to ancient *bioi*. On the one hand, he refers readers interested in the question of the literary genre of the Gospels to "the informative work of R. A. Burridge," adds that "by the standards of antiquity they are βίοι [*bioi*],"[72] speaks of Luke's Gospel as "a real 'Jesus biography,'"[73] observes that Matthew and Luke have "a stronger 'biographical' character,"[74] and continues to refer to the Gospels as biographies. On the other hand—and this is where the accent falls—the Gospels represent something dramatically new. *Bioi* they may be by ancient standards, "but as 'saving event' they have a unique, one might almost say incomparable, character. Ordinary biographies do not contain a message of faith which is decisive for eternal life and the last judgment. That is what is completely new about the 'genre' Gospel."[75] Hengel's preferred designation for this "new literary 'genre'" is "'kerygmatic' biography."[76] This emphasis on the kerygma naturally recalls the common form-critical conviction about the Gospels, but, against Bultmann, Hengel argues that Mark's Gospel serves not merely to illustrate the kerygma. Instead, as a narrative, it *is* the saving message itself.[77]

Also like Watson, Hengel thinks that the opening words of Mark's narrative ("the beginning of the gospel" [Mark 1:1]) designate the evangelist's work a "Gospel." Whereas in Paul, *euangelion* (gospel) refers to the oral, christologically stamped proclamation of "the living 'message of salvation,'"[78] in Mark it comes to refer also to the narrative expression of that same message.[79] The whole Gospel "contains the *whole* offer of the message of salvation."[80] Hengel finds Mark's final use of the term *euangelion* equally illuminating. At

69. Irenaeus, *Haer.* 3.11.8, quoted in Watson, *Text and Truth*, 74.
70. Watson, *Text and Truth*, 74.
71. Martin Hengel, *The Four Gospels and the One Gospel of Jesus Christ: An Investigation of the Collection and Origin of the Canonical Gospels* (London: SCM, 2000), 49.
72. Hengel, *Four Gospels*, 266n368.
73. Hengel, *Four Gospels*, 80, 99.
74. Hengel, *Four Gospels*, 105–6.
75. Hengel, *Four Gospels*, 266n368.
76. Hengel, *Four Gospels*, 49. See also Hengel, *Four Gospels*, 97, 98, 108–9, 111.
77. Hengel, *Four Gospels*, 86–87.
78. Hengel, *Four Gospels*, 61.
79. Hengel, *Four Gospels*, 93–94.
80. Hengel, *Four Gospels*, 90.

Mark 14:9, in defense of the unnamed woman who has anointed him, Jesus declares, "Wherever the gospel is proclaimed in the whole world, what she has done will also be spoken in memory of her" (NIV alt.). "Here," Hengel observes, "the preaching of the Gospel is fused directly with the telling of a unique story. The unprecedented, offensive action of the woman is part of the Gospel."[81]

Mark's decision to call his kerygmatic biography a Gospel left its mark on the whole Gospel tradition; even later imitators necessarily took up the compulsory title.[82] But it is easy to overstate the difference between Pauline and Markan uses of *euangelion*. Even in Paul, *gospel* necessarily implies a narrative framework:[83] "Before it could be believed in and confessed in the Pauline mission communities, this saving event had to be narrated and interpreted so that it could be understood by the communities which had been newly founded by the apostle."[84] Thus, for Hengel, the Gospels, formally *bioi*, are more fundamentally something new. They are kerygmatic biographies.

Gospel also features centrally in Joel Marcus's distinctive understanding of the genre of Mark. Our best clue, Marcus suggests, as to how Mark would answer a question put to him about the kind of work he had written is the word by which he designates it, *euangelion*.[85] But in spite of the structural similarity between Mark's Gospel and, for example, Peter's missionary proclamation in Acts 10:36–43,[86] Mark's Gospel was probably not aimed at outsiders. Informed by his conclusion that Mark wrote for a very specific audience,[87] and taking an important cue from Justin ("the memoirs of the apostles [= Gospels] or the writings of the prophets are read *for as long as time permits*"),[88] Marcus proposes that "Mark may very well be a dramatization of the good news that was originally staged in the context of a Christian worship service."[89] No doubt Mark borrows from other genres, but in the end the genre is new: "It is *euangelion*, a proclamation of good news: a redemptive story reeanacted and reexperienced" in worship in Mark's community.[90]

81. Hengel, *Four Gospels*, 92–93.
82. Hengel, *Four Gospels*, 104–5.
83. Hengel, *Four Gospels*, 146–53.
84. Hengel, *Four Gospels*, 147. Cf. Hengel, "Eye-Witness Memory and the Writing of the Gospels," in *The Written Gospel*, ed. Markus Bockmuehl and Donald A. Hagner (Cambridge: Cambridge University Press, 2005), 75–76: "*Without the narration of Jesus tradition the stereotyped 'kerygma' would have been incomprehensible to the church from the beginning.*"
85. Marcus, *Mark 1–8*, 67, cf. 65.
86. Cf. C. H. Dodd, *The Apostolic Preaching and Its Developments* (New York: Harper & Row, 1964), 46–52.
87. See Marcus, *Mark 1–8*, 24–39.
88. *1 Apol.* 67; quoted, with the gloss ([= Gospel]) and italics, by Marcus, *Mark 1–8*, 68.
89. Marcus, *Mark 1–8*, 69.
90. Marcus, *Mark 1–8*, 69.

Robert Gundry agrees that the Gospels carve out new space generically, but not as "Gospels."[91] One can, of course, identify general parallels between the Gospels and other forms of literature, but unless there is at least "a modicum of specificity," generic distinctions become meaningless.[92] When we press beyond the general parallels, it is the uniqueness of the Gospels that becomes apparent, presumably because "the configuration and particulars of Jesus' career shattered some literary conventions."[93] Moreover, it is a mistake to think of "Gospel" as a genre, both because that would imply "a literary tradition of that kind *prior* to our Gospels"[94] and because the literary features that unite the Gospels may arise from documentary relationships (their dependence on each other and on common tradition) rather than on a set of generic expectations.[95] We should be content to regard the Gospels as unique.

Reflections

Discussions of the genre of the Gospels are of course always theological, sometimes explicitly so, as William Franke's recent essay illustrates.[96] Franke argues that the Gospels are neither biography nor history but unique, ostensibly because "[their] purpose is not to recount the facts of Jesus' life per se, but to show what he meant for his disciples. . . . [Gospel] proclaims a message of salvation rather than simply telling a story or a history for its own sake."[97] There is much to affirm in Franke's essay, but his argument strangely assumes that biographies and histories aim *only* to record the past. To say that the Gospels set prophetic demands before their readers does not yet say *how* (i.e., by what manner of communication) they do so. That is a question of genre. Discussions that stress the uniqueness of the Gospels sometimes tend in Franke's direction. It is possible, as we have seen, to highlight either the distinctiveness of the Gospels or their similarities to other ancient texts. But one wonders, when pondering the uniqueness of the Gospels, whether it is not Jesus himself who, in the view of the evangelists, is sui generis?[98] Do the startling christological and theological claims in Paul's letters signal the launch of a new genre there? Is it not rather that old wineskins are filled with new wine?

91. Gundry, *Old Is Better*, 18–48.
92. Gundry, *Old Is Better*, 38.
93. Gundry, *Old Is Better*, 36.
94. Gundry, *Old Is Better*, 38.
95. Gundry, *Old Is Better*, 36–39.
96. William Franke, "Gospel as Personal Knowing: Theological Reflections on Not Just a Literary Genre," *Theology Today* 68, no. 4 (2012): 413–23.
97. Franke, "Gospel as Personal Knowing," 414.
98. Cf. Loveday Alexander, "What Is a Gospel?," in *The Cambridge Companion to the Gospels*, ed. Stephen C. Barton (Cambridge: Cambridge University Press, 2006), 21.

Nevertheless, each of the three major proposals considered above (the Gospels as *bioi*, as historical monographs, and as generically unique) brings something important to the table in the discussion about Gospel genre. David Aune wisely aims to bring the first and last of these worlds together: "The most convincing solution is to regard the Gospels as a recognizable subtype of Hellenistic biography, distinctive because of their content . . . , while in form and function they are primarily Hellenistic."[99] They are distinctive in content because of the singularity of the events they narrate and (as Collins correctly stresses) because of the formative influence of the Jewish Scriptures.[100]

I suspect that Watson, Hengel, Marcus, and others are right to find in *euangelion* (gospel; Mark 1:1) Mark's designation of his narrative.[101] But if we think the reference is to the content of his narrative, then the *euangelion* is the story that Mark's Gospel tells. Thus Mark either calls his text a Gospel or calls the story that his text preserves the gospel. Either way, Mark secures a narrative understanding of *euangelion*. Something similar can be said of the use of the term at Mark 14:9. The unnamed woman's story becomes part of the larger gospel story. This makes very good sense if the gospel to which Mark refers is the one he is writing, but even if *euangelion* refers here more generally to the gospel story, it is that story that his Gospel tells. Mark's Gospel proclaims the gospel.

In Matthew's Gospel, the word *euangelion* appears only four times, each time in conjunction with the verb *kēryssō* (to proclaim) and, in the first three instances, as part of a distinctive Matthean construction, either "the gospel of the kingdom" (4:23; 9:35) or "this gospel of the kingdom" (24:14). But, as in Mark, the final occurrence of the word intrigues: Matthew's parallel to Mark 14:9 reads, "Wherever *this gospel* is preached in the whole world, what she has done will also be spoken in memory of her" (Matt. 26:13 RSV alt.). Mark's "the gospel" has become "this gospel." We should ask why. We should also ask why, when Matthew edits Mark's account here, he does not

---

99. David E. Aune, "Gospel, Literary Genre Of," in *The Westminster Dictionary of New Testament and Early Christian Rhetoric* (Louisville: Westminster John Knox, 2003), 204–5; cf. 81. For the conviction that the Gospels are *bioi*, but *bioi* of a distinctive sort, see also, e.g., Hurtado, *Lord Jesus Christ*, 278; Scot McKnight, "Matthew as Gospel," in *Jesus, Matthew's Gospel and Early Christianity*, ed. Daniel M. Gurtner, Joel Willits, and Richard A. Burridge, LNTS 435 (London: T&T Clark, 2011), 59–75; Pennington, *Reading the Gospels Wisely*, 25, 31, 35; Michael F. Bird, *The Gospel of the Lord: How the Early Church Wrote the Story of Jesus* (Grand Rapids: Eerdmans, 2014), 271.

100. Alexander nudges us in the right direction. In the Gospels, she writes, we meet "a form whose external shape is strongly reminiscent of the Greek *bios* but whose narrative mode and theological framework (connectives, narrative structure, use of direct speech, intertextuality) owe much to the Bible" (Alexander, "What Is a Gospel?," 29). This debt to Israel's Scriptures explains the anomalies that, for Riches, set the Gospels outside of the category of *bioi*.

101. So too, earlier, Guelich, "Gospel Genre," 195.

opt for his preferred collocation, "the gospel of the kingdom." It is possible, as Jonathan Pennington has suggested, that "this gospel" is designed simply to refer readers back to the earlier references to "the gospel of the kingdom" in Matthew 4:23 and 9:35.[102] But it is not obvious why Matthew, preferring the fuller designation elsewhere (including 24:14), should opt for an abbreviated form here. More probably, the expression is distinctive because Matthew's purpose is distinctive: like Mark before him—but even more clearly—he refers to his own *written* account.[103]

In their use of *euangelion*, however, the evangelists are probably not radical innovators. We have noted Hengel's observation that a narrative is implied already in Paul's references to the *euangelion*. Scot McKnight rightly pushes further in this direction. McKnight agrees with Burridge that the Gospels are *bioi*, but adds that "the apostolic catholic gospel tradition clarifies what kind of βίος we are talking about."[104] When Mark and Matthew use the word *gospel*, "they are standing on established tradition."[105] For both Paul and the tradition on which he depends, "the gospel is the declaration that Jesus is the Messiah and Lord and Savior and that he fulfills Israel's Story in the compass of his entire story."[106] A Gospel is thus a *bios* that "gospels"—that tells the saving story of Israel's Messiah.[107] But this leads to one final observation: as kerygmatic *bioi* proclaiming the gospel of Israel's Messiah, the Gospels necessarily take up the story of Israel.

Mark's opening verses explicitly link his narrative account of the gospel to Israel's Scriptures. Against the large majority of English translations,[108] it is highly unlikely that Mark 1:2 introduces a new sentence. Elsewhere in Mark, *kathōs* (just as), the first word in verse 2, appears seven times,[109] but never introducing a new sentence. Moreover, although it occurs more than fifty times in the NT, the phrase *kathōs gegraptai* (just as it is written) "simply does not begin a thought."[110] But if a comma rather than a full stop is to be place at the end of verse 1, Mark begins his narrative of the gospel *just as it was written* in Isaiah. Mark's kerygmatic *bios* is explicitly set against the

---

102. Pennington, *Reading the Gospels Wisely*, 9–10n22.
103. So also, e.g., Graham N. Stanton, *A Gospel for a New People: Studies in Matthew* (Edinburgh: T&T Clark, 1992), 13–18, although he thinks that Matthew is the first to use the term this way. Contrast, however, W. D. Davies and Dale C. Allison Jr., *The Gospel according to Saint Matthew*, 3 vols. (Edinburgh: T&T Clark, 1988–97), 3:448.
104. McKnight, "Matthew as Gospel," 67. Cf. Hurtado, *Lord Jesus Christ*, 272, 281.
105. McKnight, "Matthew as Gospel," 62.
106. McKnight, "Matthew as Gospel," 67.
107. McKnight, "Matthew as Gospel," 67–75.
108. But see NIV 2011's translation of Mark 1:1–2: "The beginning of the good news about Jesus the Messiah, the Son of God, as it is written in Isaiah the prophet . . ."
109. Mark 4:33; 9:13; 11:6; 14:16, 21; 15:8; 16:7.
110. Guelich, "Gospel Genre," 194; cf. Hengel, *Four Gospels*, 267n374.

backdrop of Israel's Scripture, since the kerygma announces the climax of Israel's story.

This understanding of the genre of the Gospels owes something to each of the three major proposals considered above: The Gospels are *bioi*, but of a particular type: by subgenre, they are Gospels, narrative depictions of the gospel richly informed by, and drawing to a climax, Israel's scriptural narratives.

6

The Study of the Greek Language

Dana M. Harris

Introduction

When seminary students begin to learn Koine Greek, many assume that they are learning a "dead" language and that little has changed in our understanding of this language since the writing of the NT. Nothing could be further from the truth! The past several decades have seen several significant and exciting developments in current understanding of Koine Greek in general and of the Greek of the NT in particular. Much of this is the result of increasing appropriation of linguistic advances by biblical scholars. This chapter will focus on three major issues in recent Greek language studies: verbal aspect, discourse analysis, and verbal voice.

Greek Verbs and Verbal Aspect

Verbal Aspect: An Overview and Recent Contributions

The complex relationship between Greek verb forms, tense (temporal reference), aspect (the viewpoint from which an action is presented), and *Aktionsart* (kind/type of action) has been variously understood in biblical studies. "Traditional" views claim that Greek indicative tense forms indicate both time and *Aktionsart*.[1] For example, the aorist tense form indicates a past punctiliar action, whereas the present tense form indicates a present durative or progressive action.[2] Some approaches distinguish three *Aktionsarten*, which are aligned with the three main tense stems: punctiliar (aorist stem), durative (present stem), and perfective/resultative (perfect stem)[3]—the last of which presents a "condition or state as the result of a past action."[4] Additional *Aktionsarten* may be presented for a given tense form, such as the ingressive aorist, the conative present, or even the aoristic present.[5]

About thirty years ago, however, the nearly simultaneous publication of two monographs, one by Stanley Porter and the other by Buist Fanning, challenged many long-held convictions concerning tense, aspect, and *Aktionsart*.[6] These works showed that aspect was a (the?) major feature of Greek verbs and challenged the importance (or even existence) of time in Greek indicative verbs. Their approaches, however, were quite different and have been extensively debated.[7]

Stanley E. Porter applies systemic linguistics to the study of verbal aspect in NT Greek.[8] Key for Porter is the distinction between semantics (an uncancelable, morphological verbal feature) and pragmatics (verbal form usage). He

---

1. It is generally agreed that temporal values (if they exist) are restricted to the indicative. For further discussion see Constantine R. Campbell, *Advances in the Study of Greek: New Insights for Reading the New Testament* (Grand Rapids: Zondervan, 2015), 31, 110.

2. See BDF §318. Although BDF initially distinguishes between "*Aktionsarten* (kinds of actions)" and "aspects (points of view)," the ensuing discussion focuses on *Aktionsarten* and does not clearly distinguish *Aktionsarten* from aspect. The history of aspect and *Aktionsart* in Greek grammars is surveyed extensively in Stanley E. Porter, *Verbal Aspect in the Greek of the New Testament with Reference to Tense and Mood*, SBG 1 (New York: Peter Lang, 1989), 22–65. See also Buist M. Fanning, *Verbal Aspect in New Testament Greek*, Oxford Theological Monographs (Oxford: Clarendon, 1990), 8–42.

3. For example, BDF §318. Cf. A. T. Robertson, *A Grammar of the Greek New Testament in the Light of Historical Research* (Nashville: Broadman, 1914; 4th ed., 1934), 823. See also the discussion in Francis G. H. Pang, *Revisiting Aspect and* Aktionsart: *A Corpus Approach to Koine Greek Event Typology*, LBS 14 (Leiden: Brill, 2016), 45–47.

4. BDF §318 (4).

5. BDF §331, 319, 320, respectively.

6. Porter, *Verbal Aspect in the Greek of the New Testament*; and Fanning, *Verbal Aspect in New Testament Greek*.

7. See, for example, D. A. Carson, "An Introduction to the Porter/Fanning Debate," in *Biblical Greek Language and Linguistics: Open Questions in Current Research*, ed. Stanley E. Porter and D. A. Carson, JSNTSup 80 (Sheffield: JSOT Press, 1993), 18–25. In the same volume, see also Daryl D. Schmidt, "Verbal Aspect in Greek: Two Approaches," 63–73, and Moisés Silva, "A Response to Fanning and Porter on Verbal Aspect," 74–82. The volume also includes responses by Fanning and Porter. Also helpful are the following articles: Stanley E. Porter and Andrew W. Pitts, "New Testament Greek Languages and Linguistics in Recent Research," *CBR* 6, no. 2 (2008): 214–55; Andrew David Naselli, "A Brief Introduction to Verbal Aspect in New Testament Greek," *DBSJ* 12, no. 1 (2007): 17–28.

8. Porter, *Verbal Aspect*.

argues that "Greek verbal aspect is a synthetic semantic category (realized in the forms of verbs) used of meaningful oppositions in a network of tense systems to grammaticalize the author's reasoned subjective choice of conception of a process."[9] For Porter, Greek verbal forms indicate aspect only—they do not indicate any temporal reference.[10] Porter identifies three aspects in Koine Greek linked to three tense forms: perfective aspect (aorist tense form), in which "the action is conceived of by the language user as a complete and undifferentiated process"; imperfective aspect (present, imperfect tense forms), in which "the action is conceived of by the language user as being in progress"; and stative aspect (perfect, pluperfect tense forms), in which "the action is conceived of by the language user as reflecting a given (often complex) state of affairs."[11] The future tense is considered nonaspectual.[12]

Buist M. Fanning defines verbal aspect as "the focus or viewpoint of the speaker in regard to the action or condition which the verb describes"[13]—"the action can be viewed from a reference-point *within* the action, without reference to the beginning or end-point of the action . . . or the action can be viewed from a vantage-point *outside* the action, with focus on the whole action from beginning to end."[14] He calls the former "present" aspect (which aligns with the spatial value of proximity), and the latter "aorist" aspect (which aspect aligns with distance).[15] Although Fanning argues that verbal aspect is a verb's main component, aspect alone cannot be determinative for verbal meaning.[16] Instead, aspect must be understood in conjunction with a

---

9. Porter, *Verbal Aspect*, 88.

10. Porter draws on the earlier work of Kenneth L. McKay, who argued that aspect was more important than time in Greek verbs ("On the Perfect and Other Aspects in New Testament Greek," *NovT* 23 [1981]: 289–329). McKay also posited three aspects: imperfective, aorist, and perfect. The future, understood as an aspect, constitutes "a fourth aspect of intention" (*A New Syntax of the Verb in New Testament Greek: An Aspectual Approach*, SBG 5 [New York: Peter Lang, 1994], 27). McKay also noted the impact of lexical types on aspect (*New Syntax*, 28–29). Significantly, McKay argued that Greek verb tenses did not signal time, but rather time references were implied from the larger context (*New Syntax*, 39–40). These earlier views are summarized and expanded on in *New Syntax*. See also McKay, "The Use of the Ancient Greek Perfect Down to the End of the Second Century AD," *BICS* 12 (1965): 1–21; McKay, "Syntax in Exegesis," *TynBul* 23 (1972): 39–57; McKay, "Time and Aspect in New Testament Greek," *NovT* 34 (1992): 209–28. Also significant is McKay's "recognition of the subjective nature of aspectual choice, [and] its close relationship to context." McKay, "On the Perfect," 329.

11. Stanley E. Porter, *Idioms of the Greek New Testament*, 2nd ed. (Sheffield: Sheffield Academic, 1994), 221–22.

12. Porter, *Verbal Aspect*, 403.

13. Fanning, *Verbal Aspect*, 84.

14. Fanning, *Verbal Aspect*, 85 (italics original).

15. Fanning, *Verbal Aspect*, 86–103. This can also be understood as contemporaneous or antecedent time (Fanning, *Verbal Aspect*, 27).

16. Fanning, *Verbal Aspect*, vi.

temporal element, *Aktionsart*, and lexis.[17] This complex interaction is key for Fanning: "Aspect interacts so closely with such features and is so significantly affected by them that no analysis of aspect can be fully meaningful without attention to these interactions."[18]

Since the publication of Porter's *Verbal Aspect* and Fanning's *Verbal Aspect*, the importance of aspect for understanding Koine Greek verbs (and especially in the NT) has been increasingly recognized. Several important works have extended the understanding of verbal aspect in Koine Greek.[19] The most recent major contributor to this study is Constantine R. Campbell. Like Porter, Campbell clearly distinguishes semantics (an uncancelable feature of a tense form) and pragmatics (the function of a tense form in a given context). For Campbell, aspect is a semantic feature of Greek verbs and *Aktionsart* is a pragmatic one. Like Fanning, Campbell argues that there are only two aspects in Greek: perfective and imperfective. Campbell also understands aspect in conjunction with the spatial values of remoteness and proximity.[20] Campbell thus explains why the majority of aorists occur in past-referring contexts. The aorist form itself does not grammaticalize past time, but rather expresses a perfective aspect and the spatial value of remoteness at the semantic level, although this is often expressed as temporal remoteness (e.g., past time) at the pragmatic level. Similarly, "the spatial value of proximity will most often express temporal proximity—present time."[21] Campbell also takes seriously *Aktionsart*, which he views as resulting on the level of pragmatics from the combination of aspect (including spatial value), the type of lexeme involved

---

17. Fanning relies heavily on the lexical taxonomies of verbal actions set forth in Zeno Vendler, "Verbs and Times," *Philosophical Review* 66 (1957): 43–60; Anthony Kenny, *Action, Emotion and Will* (London: Routledge and Kegan Paul, 1963).

18. Fanning, *Verbal Aspect*, 85.

19. Several important works can only be briefly mentioned. Mari Broman Olsen's doctoral dissertation offers a sophisticated cross-linguistic approach that focuses on both lexical and grammatical aspect (*A Semantic and Pragmatic Model of Lexical and Grammatical Aspect*, Outstanding Dissertations in Linguistics [New York: Garland, 1997]). Three studies have applied Porter's model to specific NT documents: Rodney J. Decker, *Temporal Deixis of the Greek Verb in the Gospel of Mark with Reference to Verbal Aspect*, SBG 10 (New York: Peter Lang, 2001); David L. Mathewson, *Verbal Aspect in the Book of Revelation: The Function of Greek Verb Tenses in John's Apocalypse*, LBS 4 (Leiden: Brill, 2010); Wally V. Cirafesi, *Verbal Aspect in Synoptic Parallels: On the Method and Meaning of Divergent Tense-Form Usage in the Synoptic Passion Narratives*, LBS 7 (Leiden: Brill, 2013). Other specialized works include Trevor V. Evans, *Verbal Syntax in the Greek Pentateuch: Natural Greek Usage and Hebrew Interference* (Oxford: Oxford University Press, 2001); Douglas S. Huffman, *Verbal Aspect and the Prohibitions in the Greek New Testament*, SBG 16 (New York: Peter Lang, 2014).

20. Constantine R. Campbell, *Verbal Aspect, the Indicative Mood, and Narrative: Soundings in the Greek of the New Testament*, SBG 13 (New York: Peter Lang, 2007), 14–16.

21. Campbell, *Advances in the Study*, 115; cf. Campbell, *Basics of Verbal Aspect in Biblical Greek* (Grand Rapids: Zondervan, 2008), 129–30.

(e.g., punctiliar, transitive), and the larger context in which the verb occurs (e.g., past-referring narrative).

One of the helpful elements in Campbell's approach is his sensitivity to genre, especially narrative.[22] He distinguishes between narrative proper ("event-based story") and discourse proper (e.g., reported speech and thought).[23] Narrative proper may be further divided between mainline ("the skeletal structure of the entire narrative") and offline ("supplemental information that comments on, explains, and fills out the mainline action") strands.[24] Campbell further distinguishes three types of discourse: direct discourse (speech within the narrative), indirect (or reported) discourse, and authorial ("direct communication of the author to the reader") discourse. Patterns of indicative tense-form distribution align with each of these narrative elements: mainline events (aorist), offline information (imperfect, pluperfect), direct discourse (present, perfect, future), indirect discourse (present, perfect), and authorial discourse (present, perfect).[25]

Trying to summarize something as complex as verbal aspect in NT Greek is not easy. As Campbell notes, "Verbal aspect has been the most controversial issue within Greek studies in the last twenty-five years."[26] There is, however, emerging consensus that aspect is a significant (if not the most significant) element of the Greek verb. There is agreement that aspect represents the author/speaker's viewpoint. Consensus has been reached that there are at least two aspects in Greek: the imperfective and perfective.[27] Yet areas of disagreement clearly exist. Aspect proponents do not agree on basic issues of terminology or even the number of aspects in the Koine Greek verbal system. Also debated is the relationship between aspect (indicated morphologically) and *Aktionsart* (lexically conditioned).[28] Finally, the question of whether the Greek verb tenses

---

22. E.g., Campbell, *Verbal Aspect, the Indicative Mood, and Narrative*.

23. Summarized from Campbell, *Basics of Verbal Aspect*, 38–39; *Advances in the Study*, 124; cf. *Verbal Aspect, the Indicative Mood, and Narrative*, 3–4.

24. Campbell, *Advances in the Study*, 124; Campbell, *Basics of Verbal Aspect*, 43–44.

25. Campbell, *Advances in the Study*, 125. He notes: "The various aspectual values are seen to be associated with certain strands of discourse, and as such form predictable patterns of distribution" (4).

26. Campbell, *Advances in the Study*, 105.

27. Cf. Buist Fanning, "Porter and Fanning on New Testament Greek Verbal Aspect," in *The Greek Verb Revisited: A Fresh Approach for Biblical Exegesis; Proceedings of the Lingistics and the Greek Verb Conference, Cambridge University, 2015*, ed. Steven E. Runge and Christopher J. Fresch (Bellingham, WA: Lexham, 2016), 11. See also Stanley E. Porter, "The Perfect Tense-Form and Stative Aspect: The Meaning of the Greek Perfect Tense-Form in the Greek Verbal System," in *Linguistic Analysis of the Greek New Testament: Studies in Tools, Methods, and Practice* (Grand Rapids: Baker Academic, 2015), 198.

28. See esp. Pang, *Revisiting Aspect and* Aktionsart. See also his discussion on the various ways that the terms "aspect" and *Aktionsart* are used by biblical scholars versus linguists (pp. 9–12). See the discussion in Porter, "Perfect Tense-Form," 200–203.

encode temporal values is not resolved.[29] Several recent works have challenged nontemporal, aspectual-only approaches to the Greek verb.[30]

Recent Issues in Verbal Aspect

In addition to these core questions, there are numerous questions pertaining to individual tense forms. The next section focuses on two such areas with particular significance for NT exegesis.

THE PERFECT INDICATIVE

One of the most contested issues within the already controversial study of verbal aspect is the function of the perfect tense form. A traditional understanding of the perfect is that it depicts a past action with ongoing results in the present and is thus a combination of the aorist and the present.[31] Yet obviously challenges to a temporal semantic understanding of Greek verbs also question this understanding of the perfect tense. As with other areas of aspect studies, no consensus has emerged regarding the perfect. Debated is whether the perfect encodes a third aspect (e.g., stative) and, if not, whether it grammaticalizes imperfective or perfective aspect.

An aspectual understanding of the perfect is a significant feature of Kenneth McKay's work. He claims that "the perfect tense expresses the state or condition of the subject of the verb, as a result of an action (logically a prior action), but most often with comparably little reference to the action itself."[32] He adds that the perfect occurs "mostly in present-time contexts and those without specific time reference, and in some circumstances [see below] it has an added strong reference to an event which is already past."[33] Moreover, McKay argues that "the state signaled by the perfect aspect is properly and always that of the subject."[34]

For Fanning, the perfect is "a complex verbal category denoting, in its basic sense, a state which results from a prior occurrence."[35] He argues that the perfect reflects the combination of three elements: past tense (internal time-value of

---

29. For the argument that aspect itself is actually a temporal concept, see Christopher J. Thomson, "What Is Aspect? Contrasting Definitions in General Linguistics and New Testament Studies," in Runge and Fresch, *Greek Verb Revisited*, 13–80.

30. See, for example, Christopher J. Fresch, "Typology, Polysemy, and Prototypes: Situating Nonpast Aorist Indicatives," in Runge and Fresch, *Greek Verb Revisited*, 379–415. Although Fresch argues that perfective aspect is the primary semantic component of the aorist indicative, he also maintains that past-temporal reference is a secondary component.

31. E.g., BDF §340; Robertson, *Grammar*, 894–96.

32. McKay, *New Syntax*, 31; cf. the nearly identical definition in his 1981 article, "On the Perfect," 296.

33. McKay, *New Syntax*, 49.

34. McKay, "On the Perfect," 310.

35. Fanning, *Verbal Aspect*, 119.

anteriority), stative *Aktionsart* (the perfect consistently denotes existing condition), and aorist aspect (summary, external).[36] Fanning argues that nearly all perfects juxtapose two situations: an occurrence and a consequence of that occurrence; this also includes a temporal expression with a dual time-reference, past and present together.[37] Taken together, these features "result in a sense usually described as denoting 'a condition resulting from an anterior occurrence.'"[38]

Like Fanning, Porter aligns the perfect with stativity, but not as an *Aktionsart*. Instead, he claims that the perfect tense form grammaticalizes stative *aspect*. As noted, Porter aligns three aspects with three main verbal stems in Greek (perfective with the aorist stem, imperfective with the present stem, and stative with the perfect stem). The perfect indicates "the state or condition of the grammatical subject as conceived by the speaker. Whether a previous event is alluded to or exists at all is a matter of lexis in context and not part of aspectual semantics."[39] He adds: "The perfect and pluperfect tense-forms occur in contexts where the user of Greek wishes to depict the action as reflecting a given (often complex) state of affairs."[40] Moreover, the three aspects can be understood in terms of planes of discourse: the aorist presents background information, the present (and imperfect) present foreground information, and the perfect (and pluperfect) present frontground information. Porter concludes this in part based on the concept of markedness: the perfect and pluperfect are the least common tense forms (distributionally marked) and have the "most morphological bulk" (materially marked).[41]

As noted, Campbell posits two aspects: imperfective and perfective. He claims that the perfect encodes imperfective aspect and the spatial value of heightened proximity (heightened proximity distinguishes the perfect tense form from the proximity of the present tense form). Similarly, the pluperfect encodes imperfective aspect and the spatial value of heightened remoteness (distinguishing it from the remoteness of the imperfect). Campbell reaches this conclusion by noticing how the perfect parallels the present in many patterns of usage in narratives, both within discourse and in narrative proper.[42] Like Fanning, he understands stativity as an *Aktionsart*. Moreover, stativity best aligns with imperfective aspect. The fact that many stative lexemes occur in the perfect tense further supports this claim.[43]

---

36. Fanning, *Verbal Aspect*, 112; cf. 290–91. Campbell refers to Fanning's approach as "an aspectually-modified version of the traditional understanding of the perfect" (*Advances in the Study*, 118). For Porter's assessment, see Porter, "Perfect Tense-Form," 203–5.
37. Fanning, *Verbal Aspect*, 112.
38. Fanning, *Verbal Aspect*, 291.
39. Porter, *Verbal Aspect*, 259.
40. Porter, *Idioms*, 39. See also Porter, "Perfect Tense-Form," 209–15.
41. Porter, *Verbal Aspect*, 246–47.
42. Campbell, *Basics of Verbal Aspect*, 50.
43. Campbell, *Basics of Verbal Aspect*, 50.

The differing approaches of Porter, Fanning, and Campbell were the focal point of a session at the 2013 annual meeting of the Society of Biblical Literature aptly named "The Perfect Storm."[64] In addition to these three scholars, a recent work is worth noting. Robert Crellin's doctoral dissertation surveys a large corpus of nonbiblical Greek covering several centuries before and after the NT era.[45] His work focuses on lexical aspect—"the aspectual contribution made by the semantics of individual lexical items."[46] He proposes that "the perfect stem presents an event as a property of the subject as a function of the event described by the verb having run to some terminal point." If a state is in view, then the perfect does not imply a prior event or situation, whereas if no state is in view, "the perfect simply presents the event as completed at a point prior to reference time." The perfect contrasts with the aorist and present (which are event oriented) by being "subject focused and static."

The So-Called Historical Present

A frequent phenomenon of NT Greek (especially Mark's Gospel) is the occurrence of a present indicative (in lieu of an expected aorist indicative) in the context of a (past-referring) narrative. Traditional approaches typically refer to these present indicatives as "historical presents" and maintain that they are used to add vividness, dramatically portraying the action as if it were currently taking place.[47] On a "tense = time" view of Greek verbs, such usage represents a "deviation" from "standard" usage.[48]

---

64. See D. A. Carson, ed., *The Perfect Volume: Critical Discussion of the Semantics of the Greek Perfect Tense under Aspect Theory* (New York: Peter Lang, forthcoming). For Porter's critique of Campbell's approach, see Stanley E. Porter, "Greek Linguistics and Lexicography," in *Understanding the Times: New Testament Studies in the 21st Century: Essays in Honor of D. A. Carson on the Occasion of His 65th Birthday*, ed. Andreas J. Köstenberger and Robert W. Yarbrough (Wheaton: Crossway, 2011), 46–54. For Campbell's reply, see *Advances in the Study*, 118–19.

45. Robert Crellin, "The Greek Perfect Active System, 200 BC–AD 150" (PhD diss., University of Cambridge, Faculty of Classics, 2011). See also Crellin, "The Semantics of the Perfect in the Greek of the New Testament," in Runge and Fresch, *Greek Verb Revisited*, 430–57. Another recent work is Alexander Andrason and Christian Locatell, "The Perfect Wave: A Cognitive Approach to the Greek Verbal System," *Biblical and Ancient Greek Linguistics* 5 (2016): 7–121.

46. This summary of Crellin's dissertation is taken from Robert Crellin, "The Greek Perfect Active System, 200 BC–AD 150," *TynBul* 64 (2013): 157–60, esp. 159.

47. Consider BDF §321: "The historical present can replace the aorist indicative in a vivid narrative at the events of which the narrator imagines himself to be present; the *Aktionsart* usually remains punctiliar in spite of the present tense form." An alternative explanation is that the tense of the historical present has been reduced to zero (e.g., Paul Kiparsky, "Tense and Mood in Indo-European Syntax," *Foundations of Language* 4 [1968]: 30–57).

48. BDF §321: "This usage is common among NT authors, especially Mk . . . only Lk uses it less frequently, but probably because he regarded it as a vulgarism."

The element of vividness also factors in Fanning's approach, in which he argues that the historical present is used with "vivid or dramatic narration."[49] Furthermore, "the key feature which prompts the use of the present is the *temporal* transfer, not some sort of *aspectual* effect."[50] This temporal transfer "neutralizes" the aspectual force of the present. Fanning also, however, notes that the historical present functions as a discourse marker to begin a paragraph, to introduce new participants, and so on.[51] Porter argues that the historical present "is used at those places where the author feels that he wishes to draw attention to an event or series of events."[52]

Stephen H. Levinsohn claims that the historical present has a discourse function that "most often has the effect of highlighting what follows."[53] This highlighting concerns "not so much the speech or act to which it refers but the event(s) that follow."[54]

Campbell notes that the historical present in Mark and John is associated with two classes of verbs. First, when historical presents occur with verbs of propulsion (e.g., ἔρχομαι [*erchomai*]), they "heighten the sense of transition inherent in these verbs."[55] Second, historical presents occur with verbs that introduce discourse. In these cases, "the proximate-imperfective nature of discourse 'spills over' to the verb that introduces it."[56]

Steven Runge challenges explanations for the historical present that involve vividness, tense reduction, or a transition to a new scene or character. Instead the historical present marks prominence: "The present form is the most viable option for marking prominence in a past-time setting."[57] This prominence is signaled because both the tense (present) and aspect (imperfective) are unexpected in a context where an aorist with perfective aspect is expected, indicating mainline information in a narrative context. He continues: "Writers use markers such as the HP [historical present] to make sure that the reader does not miss changes or transitions in the discourse. They have the effect

---

49. Fanning, *Verbal Aspect*, 226.
50. Fanning, *Verbal Aspect*, 227.
51. Fanning, *Verbal Aspect*, 232.
52. Porter, *Verbal Aspect*, 196.
53. Stephen H. Levinsohn, *Discourse Features of New Testament Greek: A Coursebook on the Information Structure of New Testament Greek*, 2nd ed. (Dallas: SIL International, 2000), 197.
54. Levinsohn, *Discourse Features*, 200.
55. Campbell, *Verbal Aspect, the Indicative Mood, and Narrative*, 76.
56. Campbell, *Basics of Verbal Aspect*, 66. More specifically, he writes, "the imperfective-proximity of the present indicative attracts it to the imperfective nature of discourse, as both an introducer of discourse and a major discourse verbal form." Campbell, *Verbal Aspect, the Indicative Mood, and Narrative*, 76.
57. Runge, *Discourse Grammar*, 130. See also Elizabeth Robar, "The Historical Present in NT Greek: An Exercise in Interpreting Matthew," in Runge and Fresch, *Greek Verb Revisited*, 329–52.

of slowing down the pace and attracting the reader's attention."[58] Following Levinsohn, Steven Runge argues that the historical present calls attention to what follows it ("forward-pointing").[59]

Discourse Analysis

Many have lamented that advances from general linguistics are not readily appropriated into biblical studies, which is unfortunate since such advances often offer significant benefits for biblical studies. One example of this concerns the study of discourse analysis, although the term itself often means different things according to its various proponents.[60] Campbell helpfully defines discourse analysis as "an interdisciplinary approach to understanding how units of text relate to one another in order to create the theme, message, and structure of a text."[61]

Certain core assumptions guide most approaches to discourse analysis.[62] Perhaps foremost is that "choice implies meaning"—a speaker/writer's choice between various options is a significant insight into the meaning of a given text. Second, discourse analysis focuses on the linguistic level larger than the sentence, such as a paragraph, a pericope, or even an entire epistle. Another core concern for discourse analysis is *cohesion*, or those factors that bind a text into a meaningful whole.[63] Jeffrey Reed defines linguistic cohesiveness as "the means by which an immediate linguistic context meaningfully relates to a preceding context and/or context of situation (i.e., meaningful relationships between text, co-text and context)."[64] By "co-text," Reed means the

---

58. Runge, *Discourse Grammar*, 134.
59. Runge, *Discourse Grammar*, 137.
60. In 1995, Stanley E. Porter identified four major approaches to discourse analysis (with overlap between approaches): the Summer Institute of Linguistics/North American school (Eugene Nida, Kathleen Callow, Stephen Levinsohn); the Hallidayan school (M. A. K. Halliday; followed by J. R. Firth, Stanley E. Porter); a continental European school (R. D. Beaugrande); and a South African school (J. P. Louw) (Stanley E. Porter, "Discourse Analysis and New Testament Studies: An Introductory Survey," in *Discourse Analysis and Other Topics*, ed. Stanley E. Porter and D. A. Carson, JSNTSup 113 [Sheffield: Sheffield Academic, 1995], 24). The first two approaches have been most widely appropriated into biblical studies. See also Campbell, *Advances in the Study*, 148–91.
61. Campbell, *Advances in the Study*, 148–49.
62. Summary based on Jeffrey T. Reed, "Modern Linguistics in the New Testament: A Basic Guide to Theory, Terminology, and Literature," in *Approaches to New Testament Study*, ed. Stanley E. Porter and David Tombs, JSNTSup 120 (Sheffield: Sheffield Academic, 1995), 222–65; Campbell, *Advances in the Study*, 148–51.
63. Assumed here is that discourse presents a *"cohesive* piece of communication rather than a jumble of unrelated words and sentences." Reed, "Modern Linguistics," 239 (italics original).
64. Jeffrey T. Reed, "The Cohesiveness of Discourse: Towards a Model of Linguistics Criteria for Analyzing New Testament Discourse," in *Discourse Analysis and the New Testament:*

surrounding linguistic context (e.g., words, phrases, clauses). The context of situation refers to the immediate situation in which a discourse occurs. Other important factors include the context of culture (e.g., historical backgrounds), the genre of given discourse, and the speaker/writer's idiolect (the way that a particular individual uses a language).

Some elements that signal cohesion include conjunctions, which provide cohesion between clauses and paragraphs and set boundaries between pericopes. A pronoun and its antecedent also signal cohesion. Additionally, one can speak of lexical cohesion, such as the use of repetition or synonymy, where multiple words with overlapping meaning are employed.[65]

An additional major focus of discourse analysis is prominence (also called emphasis, grounding, relevance, or salience). Kathleen Callow defines prominence as "any device whatsoever which gives certain events, participants, or objects more significance than others in the same context."[66] One can also speak of levels of prominence, such as *background*, *theme* ("information central to author's message"; what is being talked about), and *focus* (like a spotlight on one actor on stage).[67] One factor that indicates prominence is constituent order (such as a word placed at the beginning of a clause or sentence).[68] Other factors include verbal aspect, genitive absolutes, and the use of τότε (*tote*) and ἰδού (*idou*).[69]

Discourse analysis studies often present the nonspecialist with unfamiliar terminology and highly technical discussions. One recent work that makes many features of discourse analysis more accessible to biblical scholars is Steven E. Runge, *Discourse Grammar of the Greek New Testament*.[70] Runge

---

Approaches and Results, ed. Stanley E. Porter and Jeffrey T. Reed, LNTS 170 (Sheffield: Sheffield Academic, 1999), 29.

65. Campbell, *Advances in the Study*, 156.

66. Kathleen Callow, *Discourse Considerations in Translating the Word of God* (Grand Rapids: Zondervan, 1974), 50. The often-quoted comment by Robert Longacre is helpful here: "If all parts of a discourse are equally prominent, total unintelligibility results. The result is like being presented with a piece of black paper and being told, 'This is a picture of black camels crossing black sands at midnight.'" Robert Longacre, "Sentence Structure as a Statement Calculus," *Language* 46 (1970): 10.

67. Jeffery T. Reed and Ruth A. Reese, "Verbal Aspect, Discourse Prominence, and the Letter of Jude," *FN* 9 (1996): 187.

68. See, for example, Stephen H. Levinsohn, "A Discourse Study of Constituent Order and the Article in Philippians," in Porter and Carson, *Discourse Analysis and Other Topics*, 60–74.

69. Levinsohn, *Discourse Features*, 173, 197.

70. In the preface to Runge's *Discourse Grammar*, Daniel B. Wallace (xv) rightly notes the need for an accessible guide to discourse analysis: "The esoteric vocabulary, minimal illustrations (especially of any substantial exegetical significance), and conflicting linguistic models have all contributed to massive inertia on the part of exegetes to dive into the material." See also Steven E. Runge, ed., *The Lexham Discourse New Testament* (Bellingham, WA: Logos Research Systems, 2008), in which Runge's approach is applied to the entire Greek NT.

sets out to present a "function-based approach to language using discourse grammar."[71] Key to Runge's approach are "three core principles."[72] First, "choice implies meaning," which is a core tenet of discourse analysis. For example, if a writer can use either a participle or an indicative to express an action, then the choice of either "implies that there is some meaning associated with this decision."[73] Second, "semantic or inherent meaning should be differentiated from pragmatic effect." For example, the historical present has the pragmatic effect of "attract[ing] extra attention to the speech or event that follows," even though "the present tense does not have the inherent meaning of 'highlighting.'"[74] Third, "default patterns of usage should be distinguished from marked ones." By this, Runge draws on markedness theory, in which a given category, such as perfective aspect in narrative (e.g., the aorist), is the "default" and the choice to use imperfective aspect (e.g., the present) is thus marked. Also key for Runge is prominence (making something stand out) and contrast (with expected patterns).[75]

The first part of Runge's grammar considers how propositions are connected. He notes that traditional approaches (such as that of Daniel B. Wallace) often associate the same Greek connective with multiple functions. For example, Wallace ascribes the following functions and corresponding translations to δέ (*de*): connective/copulative (coordinate, with the meaning "and"; adjunctive, with the meaning "also"), contrastive/adversative, ascensive ("even"), emphatic ("certainly," "indeed"), explanatory/causal ("for," "that is," "namely"), and transitional ("now," "then").[76] Such an array makes it difficult to understand what δέ is actually doing at the discourse level. Instead, Runge proposes that connectives "play the role of specifying what kind of relationship the writer intended" between two adjacent elements.[77] This can be mapped in terms of what type of constraint the connective adds to the discourse. Thus, although both καί (*kai*) and δέ are coordinating conjunctions, δέ "includes the added constraint of signaling a new development" in the discourse.[78]

The rest of Runge's work surveys two major discourse categories. The first concerns forward-pointing devices, which are "a number of conventions

---

71. Runge, *Discourse Grammar*, 3.
72. Summarized from Runge, *Discourse Grammar*, 3–16.
73. Runge, *Discourse Grammar*, 6.
74. Runge, *Discourse Grammar*, 9.
75. Runge, *Discourse Grammar*, 13–16.
76. Daniel B. Wallace, *Greek Grammar beyond the Basics: An Exegetical Syntax of the New Testament* (Grand Rapids: Zondervan, 1996), 761, as summarized in Runge, *Discourse Grammar*, 18.
77. Runge, *Discourse Grammar*, 19.
78. Runge, *Discourse Grammar*, 31. For another recent article, see Christopher J. Fresch, "Is There an Emphatic μέν? A Consideration of the Particle's Development and Its Function in Koine," *NTS* 63 (2017): 261–79.

used to attract attention to something significant in the discourse." They are "prominence-marking devices."⁷⁹ Examples include "point/counterpoint sets" that use μέν (*men*), εἰ μή (*ei mē*), πλήν (*plēn*), or ἀλλά (*alla*) "to explicitly link two things together that otherwise might not have been connected" and "to slow down the flow of the text in order to attract attention to [a] significant proposition that follows."⁸⁰ Other examples include the historical present, previously discussed,⁸¹ and "redundant quotative frames," such as the common usage of ἀποκριθεὶς εἶπεν (*apokritheis eipen*; e.g., Matt. 21:24).⁸² The second major discourse category involves "information structuring devices," which focus especially on variations in word or constituent order to structure discourse in Greek. One such example is a "framing device," such as a temporal preposition phrase placed at the beginning of a clause to frame a discourse within a particular time frame.⁸³ Perhaps one of the most helpful aspects of Runge's work is that every discourse device is amply illustrated with numerous examples from the Greek NT.

Deponency and Voice Polarity

An area of NT Greek that has received increasing attention is that of grammatical voice. Traditionally, this has been understood in terms of three discrete voices: active, middle, and passive. The middle voice, however, is frequently misunderstood, in part because there is no direct English counterpart. Additionally, traditional approaches (1) identify (middle) "deponent" verbs as verbs without active forms in Koine Greek and whose middle forms are thus active in meaning (e.g., ἔρχομαι, πορεύομαι [*poreuomai*]) and (2) identify "passive deponent" verbs as verbs with a passive form but an active meaning (e.g., ἐγενήθην [*egenēthēn*] and ἀπεκρίθην [*apekrithēn*]). Standard Greek grammars often present deponency as an undisputed category. Its legitimacy, however, has been challenged by several recent studies, which also suggest that voice is best understood as a semantic range rather than three discrete categories.

The Death of Deponency?

In *Advances in the Study of Greek*, Campbell surveys doubts about and challenges to deponency in the Greek grammars, beginning with James Hope

79. Runge, *Discourse Grammar*, 59.
80. Runge, *Discourse Grammar*, 386.
81. See Runge, *Discourse Grammar*, 125–43.
82. Runge, *Discourse Grammar*, 153; see also 145–62.
83. Runge, *Discourse Grammar*, 216. He also discusses topical and spatial framing devices; see 207–25.

Moulton[84] and A. T. Robertson[85] in the early twentieth century. At the beginning of this century, Neva F. Miller showed that "deponents," rather than functioning as active voice verbs, were actually functioning as true middles, properly understood.[86] Her work was followed by Bernard A. Taylor, who challenged both the term and the concept of deponency.[87] In 2002, Carl W. Conrad declared deponency to be "detrimental" to understanding Greek and argued that voice in Greek should be understood as an active-middle polarity, not an active-passive one.[88] In his 2002 dissertation, Rutger J. Allan argued that there is no historical evidence that "middle-only" verbs ever "laid aside" an active form.[89] Instead, the middle voice is marked for "subject-affectedness."[90]

Drawing on these studies, Jonathan T. Pennington notes that the passive voice was a later development in Greek, arising from an original active-middle polarity. The passive voice then encroached on, and eventually replaced, the middle voice.[91] He surveys problems that the middle voice poses for English speakers and concludes that even the term *middle* is misleading, since it does not indicate something between the active and passive voices. He also considers verbs with present actives and future middles (sometimes called "mixed

---

84. James Hope Moulton, *A Grammar of New Testament Greek: Prolegomena* (Edinburgh: T&T Clark, 1908), 153, referenced in Campbell, *Advances in the Study*, 92.

85. Robertson, *Grammar*, 332–33, referenced in Campbell, *Advances in the Study*, 92.

86. Neva F. Miller, "A Theory of Deponent Verbs," appendix 2, in *Analytical Lexicon of the Greek New Testament*, ed. Timothy Friberg, Barbara Friberg, and Neva F. Miller (Grand Rapids: Baker Books, 2000), 423–30, referenced in Campbell, *Advances in the Study*, 93. To demonstrate the range of middle-voice functions, Miller offers an extensive survey of NT middle-only verbs presented under seven classifications: "reciprocity," "reflexivity," "self-involvement," "self-interest," "receptivity," "passivity," and "state, condition" (Miller, "Theory of Deponent Verbs," 427–29).

87. Bernard A. Taylor, "Deponency and Greek Lexicography," in *Biblical Greek Language and Lexicography: Essays in Honor of Frederick W. Danker*, ed. Bernard A. Taylor et al. (Grand Rapids: Eerdmans, 2004), drawing on an earlier, 2001 work; also referenced in Campbell, *Advances in the Study*, 93–94.

88. Carl W. Conrad, "New Observations on Voice in the Ancient Greek Verb" (self-published paper, 2002, available through the website of Washington University in St. Louis, https://pages.wustl.edu/files/pages/imce/cwconrad/newobsancgrkvc.pdf), 3; also referenced in Campbell, *Advances in the Study*, 94–95.

89. Rutger J. Allan, "The Middle Voice in Ancient Greek: A Study in Polysemy" (PhD diss., University of Amsterdam, 2002), http://dare.uva.nl/record/108538. Jonathan T. Pennington similarly challenges this assumption: "Middle-only verbs are not 'defective' verbs that have at some point lost or laid aside their active forms." Jonathan T. Pennington, "Setting Aside 'Deponency': Rediscovering the Greek Middle Voice in New Testament Studies," in *The Linguistic as Pedagogue: Trends in the Teaching and Linguistic Analysis of the Greek New Testament*, ed. Stanley E. Porter and Matthew Brook O'Donnell, NTM 11 (Sheffield: Sheffield Phoenix, 2009), 181–203, here 189.

90. Allen, "Middle Voice," 185 (italics removed), cited in Campbell, *Advances in the Study*, 95–96.

91. Pennington, "Setting Aside 'Deponency,'" 182.

deponents"; e.g., γινώσκω [ginōskō], γνώσομαι [gnōsomai]) and so-called passive deponents (e.g., ἀπεκρίθην [apekrithēn]). Like previous studies, Pennington demonstrates that a true middle sense is evident in both cases. Specifically, the use of the middle in verbs with present active forms but future middles likely reflects the "the mental disposition or intention" inherent in the future tense.[92] The occurrence of "passive deponents" is best explained as evidence of the gradual erosion of the middle voice and its replacement by the passive.[93] Thus appeal to deponency is unnecessary;[94] indeed, "the category of deponency should be eliminated from our reconstruction of Greek grammar."[95]

What unifies all these studies is that the concept and category of deponency becomes unnecessary when the full range of functions for the middle voice is correctly understood. Papers presented at the Biblical Greek Language and Linguistics Unit session at the 2010 annual meeting of SBL were unified in challenging the legitimacy of deponency and arguing for its demise.[96] This is not the end of the discussion, however. Further study is needed to clarify the function of the middle voice more fully, to explain "passive deponents" and "mixed deponents," and to explore connections between voice and specific lexemes (i.e., why middle-only verb forms often describe mental or emotional states).[97]

Which Polarity: Active-Passive or Active-Middle?

As noted, Carl Conrad questions whether the often-assumed polarity in Greek is actually active-passive. Instead he argues that it is active-middle, noting that the distinction between the middle and the passive did not always require different morphology (e.g., the shared middle and passive forms in the present and perfect). He also argues that passivity was not an essential element of the -θη (-thē) ending, but rather passivity was determined from context.[98]

---

92. Pennington, "Setting Aside 'Deponency,'" 194. He adds that "there is a close semantic connection in many languages between the middle voice and the future tense."

93. Pennington, "Setting Aside 'Deponency,'" 195. He (196) refers to this phenomenon as a "slipping of register."

94. Jonathan T. Pennington, "Deponency in Koine Greek: The Grammatical Question and the Lexicographical Dilemma," *TJ* 24 (2003): 56.

95. Pennington, "Setting Aside 'Deponency,'" 182.

96. This trend is reflected in several recent grammars: e.g., Stanley E. Porter, Jeffrey T. Reed, and Matthew Brook O'Donnell, *Fundamentals of New Testament Greek* (Grand Rapids: Eerdmans, 2010), 125; Rodney J. Decker, *Reading Koine Greek: An Introduction and Integrated Workbook* (Grand Rapids: Baker Academic, 2014), 226–28, 252–53; Dana M. Harris, *An Introduction to Biblical Greek Grammar: Elementary Syntax and Linguistics* (Grand Rapids: Zondervan, forthcoming).

97. Cf. Campbell, *Advances in the Study*, 100–104.

98. Conrad, "New Observations on Voice," 5, 7–9.

These ideas are pressed further by Rachel Aubrey.⁹⁹ Her work draws upon cross-linguistic studies of voice functions.¹⁰⁰ With regard to Greek, she notes that the -θη ending shows greater diversity than is often understood; it encodes both voice (middle-passive) *and* aspect (perfective). She argues for moving beyond a simple pairing of the -θη ending with passivity, since deviations from this expectation (e.g., the subject performs rather than receives the action) are treated as exceptions (e.g., Luke 24:8) and labeled as "passive deponents."¹⁰¹ Instead she shows that the multiple functions of -θη are all encompassed within the middle domain.¹⁰²

Aubrey draws on a prototype model of categorization for language, in which voice categories are understood as to how similar they are to several prototypes. Thus a single morpheme (θη) can have multiple functions that can be classified together. Diachronically, although morphemes may have originated with a primary semantic function, they typically acquired other, related functions. Thus the -θη ending originally indicated a "change of state" from a spontaneous event (e.g., "broke," "learned").¹⁰³ This likely explains why the -θη ending integrated with the aorist stem and not the present one, since the former was already associated with spontaneous changes of state. In time, the morpheme added more functions, specifically ones that focused on the change of the state *of the object* by an external force; in this way, the -θη ending became associated with passivity.

Based on conceptual prototypes in other Indo-European languages, Aubrey further argues that verbal voice concerns two factors: a flow of energy from an agent to a patient (object) and a focus of attention. In the active voice, the energy flows from an agent to a patient (object), and the focus is on the agent. In the passive voice, the focus is on the patient (object) such that focus on the agent is greatly diminished. Although originally associated with spontaneous events (e.g., ἐπικράνθη [*epikranthē*] in Rev. 10:10), the -θη ending eventually acquired a wider semantic range that focused more on the patient (object).¹⁰⁴ At the same time, the -θη ending acquired functions that focused more on the agent, such as reflexive/grooming (e.g., ἐβαπτίσθη [*ebaptisthē*]

---

99. Rachel Aubrey, "Motivated Categories, Middle Voice, and Passive Morphology," in Runge and Fresch, *Greek Verb Revisited*, 563–625.

100. Specifically, Aubrey says she employs a "cognitive linguistic approach [that] brings to bear the human conceptual and experiential motivations that help to identify a semantic basis for -θη morphology." Aubrey, "Motivated Categories," 564–65.

101. Aubrey, "Motivated Categories," 566–67.

102. Aubrey, "Motivated Categories," 565.

103. Aubrey, "Motivated Categories," 571.

104. E.g., including motion (e.g., ἐστράφη [*estraphē*] in John 20:14), collective motion (e.g., συνήχθη [*synēchthē*] in Mark 5:21), and (spontaneous) mental process (e.g., συνεχύθη [*synechythē*] in Acts 2:6). Examples taken from Aubrey, "Motivated Categories," 598, 600, 601.

in Luke 11:38), reciprocal events (e.g., διελέχθησαν [*dielechthēsan*] in Mark 9:34), mental activity (e.g., μεταμεληθήσεται [*metamelēthēsetai*] in Heb. 7:21), speech acts (e.g., δεήθητε [*deēthēte*] in Matt. 9:38), and perception (e.g., ὠσφράνθη [*ōsphranthē*] in Gen. 27:27).[105] These are all functions of the "middle domain," but they also shift the focus from the agent to the patient (object) in various ways.[106]

The implications of Aubrey's work for understanding the middle voice and the -θη ending have significant potential for helping to better understand the Greek middle and so-called deponent verbs: "Changing our categorization of -(θ)η from the analogous English counterpart (passive) to a typologically attested middle form alters our view of Greek voice. Instead of seeing it as a passive marker with defective active outliers in an active-passive system, -(θ)η is rightly treated as marking the less-transitive middle events—including passives—within a larger transitivity continuum in an active-middle system."[107]

Reflections

While verbal aspect, discourse analysis, and verbal voice are three significant developments in the study of Greek in the past few years, many other studies have also contributed to our understanding of Koine Greek, and especially the Greek of the NT.[108] Many of these studies have yet to be applied to the entire NT corpus or incorporated by Greek grammars or NT commentaries. The study of the Greek of the NT, its exegesis, and application will only be enhanced as biblical scholars continue to appropriate and develop recent advances in linguistics and related disciplines. A "dead" language indeed! Many exciting studies and trends keep the study of the Greek language very much alive.

---

105. For extensive discussion of each of these (and additional) examples, see Aubrey, "Motivated Categories," 594–612.

106. See the helpful semantic map that summarizes these functions in Aubrey, "Motivated Categories," 615.

107. Aubrey, "Motivated Categories," 620.

108. The following significant monographs can only be mentioned: Daniel B. Wallace, *Granville Sharp's Canon and Its Kin: Semantics and Significance* (New York: Peter Lang, 2009); Margaret S. Sim, *Marking Thought and Talk in New Testament Greek: New Light from Linguistics on the Particles* ἵνα *and* ὅτι (Eugene, OR: Pickwick, 2010); Murray J. Harris, *Prepositions and Theology in the Greek New Testament: An Essential Reference Resource for Exegesis* (Grand Rapids: Zondervan, 2012); Douglas Estes, *Questions and Rhetoric in the Greek New Testament: A Essential Reference Resource for Exegesis* (Grand Rapids: Zondervan, 2017).

PART 3

Jesus, Paul, and New Testament Theology

7

Jesus of Nazareth

REBEKAH EKLUND

Introduction

Historical Jesus research relies on a gap. For some it is wide; for others, narrow. For all, it is the distance between the Jesus of history and the Jesus of the extant written sources. Some view the gap as unbridgeable yet unimportant; the real Jesus, and the only Jesus to whom we have any access, is the Jesus of the canonical Gospels. For other scholars, the gap is a chasm they long to cross; the authentic Jesus of history is obscured not only by the passage of time but also by the very sources that purport to reveal him to us.

Most of the scholars discussed in this chapter acknowledge the real distance between the Jesus of history, the Jesus of the canonical Gospels, and the historical Jesus (the Jesus constructed through the use of historical methods), yet they do not despair of our abilities to seek out and find the Jesus of history using the sources available to us. By and large, they reject the pessimism of Rudolf Bultmann, who affirmed that Jesus existed but doubted whether we could know anything beyond that bare fact (a fact that continues to be disputed by a small but vocal chorus of voices).[1] Yet many scholars are also

---

1. Skepticism over the existence of Jesus flowered in the early 1970s, notably in John Marco Allegro's *The Sacred Mushroom and the Cross* (London: Hodder and Stoughton, 1970), but has had a recent renaissance in writings of the so-called mythicists; e.g., Frank R. Zindler and Robert M. Price, eds., *Bart Ehrman and the Quest of the Historical Jesus of Nazareth: An Evaluation of Erhman's "Did Jesus Exist?"* (Cranford, NJ: American Atheist Press, 2013);

increasingly convinced that we have been using the wrong methods to try to gain access to the Jesus of history.

The Decline and Fall of the Criteria for Authenticity

The aptly titled *Jesus, Criteria, and the Demise of Authenticity*, edited by Chris Keith and Anthony Le Donne, thoroughly maps out this first trend.[2] Keith represents the most disillusioned, writing that the criteria approach is "irreparably broken and invalid as a historical method."[3] Others make more tempered appeals for the modification and cautious ongoing use of (some of) the criteria.

The criteria rose to dominance in the mid-twentieth century and quickly gained widespread acceptance. Scholars have long used the criteria to determine whether a saying or event attributed to Jesus is authentic—that is, whether it originated with the Jesus of history or was added to the tradition later. It is common to use the criteria both negatively (to rule out events and sayings) and positively (to rule them in). Although lists vary, frequently cited criteria include the following:

- double dissimilarity (material that has no foundation in or similarity to either early Judaism or the teachings of the early church)
- embarrassment (something that would have caused embarrassment to the early church and therefore that the church was unlikely to create)
- multiple attestation (material found in independent traditions or in different literary forms within the same sources)
- Semitic language (material that demonstrates a background in Semitic or Aramaic language patterns)
- coherence or consistency (material that fits or coheres with material already established by one of the other criteria)

Criticism of the criteria is not new. Arguments against them appeared in print as early as 1970 and 1972, in essays by Morna Hooker and Robin Barbour.[4]

Thomas L. Thompson and Thomas S. Verenna, eds., *'Is This Not the Carpenter?' The Question of the Historicity of the Figure of Jesus* (Sheffield: Equinox, 2012).

2. Chris Keith and Anthony Le Donne, eds., *Jesus, Criteria, and the Demise of Authenticity* (New York: T&T Clark, 2012). The volume includes essays by Keith, Jens Schröter, Loren T. Stuckenbruck, Le Donne, Dagmar Winter, Rafael Rodríguez, Mark Goodacre, Scot McKnight, and Dale C. Allison Jr.

3. Chris Keith, *Jesus against the Scribal Elite: The Origins of the Conflict* (Grand Rapids: Baker Academic, 2014), 81.

4. Morna Hooker, "Christology and Methodology," *NTS* 17 (1970): 480–87; Robin S. Barbour, *Traditio-Historical Criticism of the Gospels* (London: SPCK, 1972). See Hooker's foreword in Keith and Le Donne, *Jesus, Criteria*, xiii.

But discomfort with them has been steadily growing in the twenty-first century, among the very scholars who once employed these tools. Dale Allison is representative. He offers a personal account of his decision to part ways with the traditional criteria, writing, "The means that most scholars have employed and continue to employ for constructing the historical Jesus are too flimsy to endure, or at least too flimsy for me to countenance any longer."[5]

The disillusionment is due in part to the conflicting and idiosyncratic results of historical Jesus research. Of course, some variety is to be expected but perhaps not the contradictory portraits of the last century.[6] Along the same lines, scholars have become increasingly—and rightly—discomfited at the non-Jewish Jesus often produced by the criteria. But dissatisfaction with the criteria has also resulted from scrutinizing their methodological underpinnings. Allison, for example, uses the example of the words of institution at the Last Supper to demonstrate that the criteria are often in direct conflict with one another.[7] Loren Stuckenbruck thoroughly catalogs the many methodological difficulties with using one particular criterion—Semitic language background—as a reliable guide to authenticity.[8]

Geza Vermes points out that several of the criteria, especially dissimilarity, tend to be weighted in favor of inauthenticity.[9] Thus some scholars, such as Craig Evans, call for using the criteria only positively rather than negatively—that is, only to argue *for* rather than *against* authenticity.[10] Vermes himself does not abandon the criteria altogether, and in the same essay makes use of the criterion of embarrassment (without naming it as such) to argue for Jesus's belief in the imminent arrival of the kingdom of God: "Nobody would have

---

5. Dale C. Allison Jr., *Constructing Jesus: Memory, Imagination, and History* (Grand Rapids: Baker Academic, 2010), x. See also Allison, "It Don't Come Easy: A History of Disillusionment," in Keith and Le Donne, *Jesus, Criteria*, 186–99.

6. Michael Licona argues that scholars shouldn't jettison the criteria simply because they don't produce consensus, since all historians have "conflicting horizons" that tend to thwart consensus. Licona, "Is the Sky Falling in the World of Historical Jesus Research?," *BBR* 26, no. 3 (2016): 353–67.

7. Dale C. Allison Jr., "How to Marginalize the Traditional Criteria of Authenticity," in *Handbook for the Study of the Historical Jesus*, 4 vols., ed. Tom Holmén and Stanley E. Porter (Leiden: Brill, 2011), 1:12–13.

8. Loren T. Stuckenbruck, "'Semitic Influence on Greek': An Authenticating Criterion in Jesus Research?," in Keith and Le Donne, *Jesus, Criteria*, 73–94. See also Stanley E. Porter, "How Do We Know What We Think We Know? Methodological Reflections on Jesus Research," in *Jesus Research: New Methodologies and Perceptions*, ed. James H. Charlesworth (Grand Rapids: Eerdmans, 2014), 95.

9. Geza Vermes, "Reflections on Improving Methodology in Jesus Research," in Charlesworth, *Jesus Research: New Methodologies*, 22.

10. Craig A. Evans, *Fabricating Jesus: How Modern Scholars Distort the Gospels* (Downers Grove, IL: InterVarsity Press, 2006), 51.

invented it later when it was, and could be seen to be, patently untrue."[11] Other scholars have pointed out that what is embarrassing to us may not have fazed a first-century Christian; still others have noted that the criterion of embarrassment assumes that the church was in the business of creating or inventing material about Jesus that has no basis at all in history. Finally, Rafael Rodríguez points out that the embarrassment criterion tends to lead to the same material as dissimilarity, a criterion that has fallen on especially hard times.[12]

Thus some scholars find the criteria too flawed to be of any further use. For many of them, their abandonment of the criteria overlaps with growing skepticism over form criticism, especially the traditional form-critical construal of the relationship between oral and written traditions. Keith, for example, argues that the criteria approach continues to depend on "a form-critical methodological framework."[13] For other scholars like Le Donne, the primary problem is the criteria's entanglement with positivist historiography.[14] When the criteria seek to establish what is "authentic" to Jesus—that is, what really happened in history—postmodern critics argue that this betrays the assumptions of positivism, a historical approach grounded in empiricism, or the conviction that the natural world presents us with self-evident, fully knowable phenomena. Positivism grants the status of positive knowledge only to assertions that are based on such phenomena.[15] Postmodern historiography, or what Jens Schröter refers to as a "construction" approach, seeks to incorporate the insights of contemporary linguistics and argues instead for the subjectivity

---

11. Vermes, "Reflections on Improving," 26.

12. Rafael Rodríguez, "The Embarrassing Truth about Jesus: The Criterion of Embarrassment and the Failure of Historical Authenticity," in Keith and Le Donne, *Jesus, Criteria*, 138, 141. See also Tom Holmén, "Doubts about Double Dissimilarity: Restructuring the Main Criterion on Jesus-of-History Research," in *Authenticating the Words of Jesus*, ed. Bruce Chilton and Craig A. Evans (Leiden: Brill, 1999), 75.

13. Chris Keith, "The Indebtedness of the Criteria Approach to Form Criticism and Recent Attempts to Rehabilitate the Search for an Authentic Jesus," in Keith and Le Donne, *Jesus, Criteria*, 29, 31. See also Rodríguez, "Embarrassing Truth," 132–51.

14. Anthony Le Donne, "The Rise of the Quest for an Authentic Jesus: An Introduction to the Crumbling Foundations of Jesus Research," in Keith and Le Donne, *Jesus, Criteria*, 3. See also Le Donne, *The Historiographical Jesus: Memory, Typology, and the Son of David* (Waco: Baylor University Press, 2009). Likewise Daniel Marguerat writes, "Positivism is an epistemological error" (Marguerat, "Historical Jesus and Christ of Faith: A Relevant Dichotomy?," in *Jesus—Gestalt und Gestaltungen: Rezeptionen des Galiläers in Wissenschaft, Kirche und Gesellschaft; Festschrift für Gerd Theißen zum 70. Geburtstag*, ed. Petra von Gemünden, David G. Horrell, and Max Küchler [Göttingen: Vandenhoeck & Ruprecht, 2013], 434). Stanley Porter critiques the criteria as both too positivist and too tied to form criticism, in Porter, "How Do We Know What We Think We Know?," 82–99.

15. See Stanley E. Porter, "Criteria of Authenticity," in *Dictionary of Jesus and the Gospels*, 2nd ed., ed. Joel B. Green, Jeannine K. Brown, and Nicholas Perrin (Downers Grove, IL: IVP Academic, 2013), 161; Samuel Byrskog, "The Historicity of Jesus: How Do We Know That Jesus Existed?," in Holmén and Porter, *Handbook*, 3:2184–85.

of knowledge (or, perhaps more precisely, the subjectivity of the historian). More extreme versions of this view are associated with a coherence notion of truth, or the view that the truth of a matter is evaluated by whether it fits with other established truths.[16] More modest versions propose that "history exists as a relation between the past and the present."[17]

Not all scholars are convinced that positivism is the problem, or that accepting a coherence notion of truth is a promising path. Michael Licona, for one, argues that Keith and Le Donne (et al.) are both too pessimistic about the criteria and too postmodernist in their approach to history.[18] But Licona agrees that the criteria need adjusting or modifying and that scholars have often been too confident in their results.[19] Craig Keener likewise continues to use many of the criteria, but with caution.[20]

Others suggest that one or two of the criteria might have a limited sort of usefulness. Gerd Theissen and Annette Merz make a case for the criterion of coherence to be applied independently of questions about dissimilarity and to be paired with the criterion of contextual plausibility (see below).[21] For Le Donne, coherence is of no use in determining authenticity, "but it might help us chart the development of memory in a limited way."[22] Similarly, Mark Goodacre concedes that multiple attestation has some usefulness for beginning students, but beyond the introductory level "it becomes problematic, misleading and ultimately unusable."[23] For Goodacre this is true in part because of the criterion's dependence on the Q hypothesis and on use of the Gospel of Thomas as a source, which not all scholars find equally troublesome.[24]

16. See Moisés Mayordomo and Peter-Ben Smit, "The Quest for the Historical Jesus in Postmodern Perspective: A Hypothetical Argument," in Holmén and Porter, *Handbook*, 2:1377–409; Jens Schröter, *From Jesus to the New Testament: Early Christian Theology and the Origin of the New Testament Canon*, trans. Wayne Coppins (Waco: Baylor University Press, 2013), 1, 33–48, 98 (originally published as *Von Jesus zum Neuen Testament* [Tübingen: Mohr Siebeck, 2007]).
17. Byrskog, "Historicity of Jesus," 2185.
18. Licona, "Is the Sky Falling?," 353.
19. Licona, "Is the Sky Falling?," 353–65.
20. Craig S. Keener, *The Historical Jesus of the Gospels* (Grand Rapids: Eerdmans, 2009), 155–59.
21. Gerd Theissen and Annette Merz, "The Delay of the Parousia as a Test Case for the Criterion of Coherence," *Louvain Studies* 32 (2007): 49–66. Their application of the criterion ends up functioning more like multiple attestation and bears some similarity to what Allison calls recurrent attestation. See also Gerd Theissen and Dagmar Winter, *Die Kriterienfrage in der Jesusforschung: Vom Differenzkriterium zum Plausibilitätskriterium*, NTOA 34 (Göttingen: Vandenhoeck & Ruprecht, 1997).
22. Anthony Le Donne, "The Criterion of Coherence: Its Development, Inevitability, and Historiographical Limitations," in Keith and Le Donne, *Jesus, Criteria*, 113.
23. Mark Goodacre, "Criticizing the Criterion of Multiple Attestation: The Historical Jesus and the Question of Sources," in Keith and Le Donne, *Jesus, Criteria*, 154.
24. Goodacre, "Criticizing the Criterion of Multiple Attestation," 154–64. Porter also criticizes multiple attestation for being dependent on prior assumptions regarding the development

This chastened confidence has led to a tentative and emerging consensus around two approaches: a move from double dissimilarity to contextual plausibility, and from multiple to recurrent attestation.

Contextual Plausibility

A criterion—or perhaps a theme—that has endured and garners ever more research is contextual plausibility, or efforts to locate Jesus within his social, political, cultural, and historical contexts.[25] Contributors to the two recent *Jesus Research* volumes (subtitled, respectively, *New Methodologies and Perceptions* and *An International Perspective*) frequently draw on other disciplines, including "sociology, anthropology, archaeology, rhetoric, and psychobiography," pointing to a growing interest in inter- and cross-disciplinary research skills, sources, and methods.[26] In one sense, more thorough understanding of Jesus's historical context is simply an interpretive tool used to understand the force and meaning of Jesus's teachings and actions. Yet scholars also use contextual studies to argue that actions and events in the Gospels that cohere with what we know of Second Temple Judaism (and, sometimes, Christian origins) are more likely to be authentic to the Jesus of history.

Contributing to this approach is the special ire aimed at double dissimilarity for producing a Jesus who is detached from his Jewish roots. Tom Holmén builds on claims made by Ben Meyer (in *The Aims of Jesus*) to argue for single

---

of the Gospels, such as a particular solution to the Synoptic Problem. Porter, "How Do We Know What We Think We Know?," 95.

25. Some examples are Amy-Jill Levine, Dale C. Allison Jr., and John Dominic Crossan, eds., *The Historical Jesus in Context*, Princeton Readings in Religions (Princeton: Princeton University Press, 2006); Carsten Claussen and Jörg Frey, eds., *Jesus und die Archäologie Galiläas* (Neukirchen-Vluyn: Neukirchener Verlag, 2008); James H. Charlesworth and Mordechai Aviam, "Reconstructing First-Century Galilee: Reflections on Ten Major Problems," in Charlesworth, *Jesus Research: New Methodologies*, 103–37; David A. Fiensy and Ralph K. Hawkins, *The Galilean Economy in the Time of Jesus* (Atlanta: SBL Press, 2013); Seán Freyne, "Reimagining Jesus in His Culture: Reflections on Some Recent Scholarly Byways," in Charlesworth, *Jesus Research: New Methodologies*, 138–48; Jens Schröter, "Jesus of Galilee: The Role of Location in Understanding Jesus," in *Jesus Research: An International Perspective*, ed. James H. Charlesworth and Petr Pokorný (Grand Rapids: Eerdmans, 2009), 36–55; Craig A. Evans, *Jesus and the Remains of His Day: Studies in Jesus and the Evidence of Material Culture* (Peabody, MA: Hendrickson, 2015).

26. *Jesus Research: An International Perspective* (ed. Charlesworth and Pokorný) emerged from the First Princeton-Prague Symposium on Jesus Research, Prague, 2005; *Jesus Research: New Methodologies* (ed. Charlesworth) emerged from the Second Princeton-Prague Symposium on Jesus Research, Princeton 2007. For the list of disciplines, see the introduction to Charlesworth, *Jesus Research: New Methodologies*, 2. See also István Czachesz, "Jesus' Religious Experience in the Gospels: Toward a Cognitive Neuroscience Approach," in von Gemünden, Horrell, and Küchler, *Jesus—Gestalt*, 569–96.

rather than double dissimilarity, defending the view that dissimilarity from the views of the early church can indicate an authentic tradition.[27] But this approach remains open to charges that even single dissimilarity produces a Jesus whose identity and views fail to account for the development of early Christian thought. Several scholars distance themselves further from double dissimilarity by advocating for "double similarity," reversing the original criterion to focus instead on a Jesus who cohered with his setting in Second Temple Judaism and makes sense of Christian origins.[28] Even scholars who otherwise continue to use the criteria have sometimes reversed the criterion of double dissimilarity in order to place Jesus "in the Judaism-Christianity continuum" rather than outside of it.[29]

For other scholars, contextual plausibility breaks with the criteria approach altogether by refusing to judge the authenticity of any *individual* saying or action. Instead, placing Jesus within his sociopolitical, historical context illuminates the larger themes and patterns that are attributable to the Jesus of history.

Recurrent Attestation: Big-Picture Themes

The second major approach emerging from the rejection of the authenticity criteria is a search for big-picture themes, or patterns that recur repeatedly across the Gospel traditions. In James Dunn's book *A New Perspective on Jesus* (2005), he critiques the criteria, especially dissimilarity, for their anti-Jewish assumptions, and he calls for the adoption of one broad criterion, the "characteristic Jesus." He suggests that scholars have performed too much "atomistic exegesis" and have failed to pay sufficient attention to the consistent themes and emphases of the Gospels, especially the Synoptics. His effort to look for themes that are "characteristic within the Jesus tradition" echoes a suggestion also made by Allison.[30]

27. Holmén, "Doubts about Double Dissimilarity," 47–80.
28. For N. T. Wright's "double similarity," see his *Jesus and the Victory of God*, vol. 2 of *Christian Origins and the Question of God* (Minneapolis: Fortress, 1996), 132; Keith, "Indebtedness," 41. Theissen and Winter call it the "criterion of plausibility" (Theissen and Winter, *Die Kriterienfrage*, 175, 192–94). See also Winter, "Saving the Quest for Authenticity from the Criterion of Dissimilarity: History and Plausibility," in Keith and Le Donne, *Jesus, Criteria*, 115–31; Brant Pitre, *Jesus and the Last Supper* (Grand Rapids: Eerdmans, 2015), 41.
29. So Robert L. Webb, "The Historical Enterprise and Historical Jesus Research," in *Key Events in the Life of the Historical Jesus*, ed. Darrell L. Bock and Robert L. Webb (Tübingen: Mohr Siebeck, 2009), 67.
30. James D. G. Dunn, *A New Perspective on Jesus: What the Quest for the Historical Jesus Missed* (Grand Rapids: Baker Academic, 2005), 69, 70. In Dunn's *Jesus Remembered*, he frequently uses several criteria, especially multiple attestation and embarrassment, even while criticizing them for depending too much on a literary rather than oral model; see Dunn, *Jesus Remembered*, vol. 1 of *Christianity in the Making* (Grand Rapids: Eerdmans, 2003), 336.

Allison proposes that we should concentrate less on determining the authenticity of individual sayings or actions and instead hope that the primary sources provide us with "substantial and substantially reliable broad impressions."[31] While we might not be able to nail down the particulars, "what matters is the larger pattern," or the themes and motifs that repeatedly appear across the Jesus traditions. He terms these larger patterns "recurrent attestation."[32]

Darrell Bock takes a similar approach by looking for recurring big-picture themes in the Gospels and—perhaps not surprisingly—finds a portrait not unlike Allison's when he claims that Jesus is best placed in a Jewish prophetic/apocalyptic environment.[33] Brant Pitre's work shows marks of a related approach when he writes that he pursues neither the *ipsissima verba Jesu* (the exact words of Jesus) nor the *ipsissima vox Jesu* (the exact voice of Jesus) but the *substantia verba Jesu* (the substance of the words of Jesus).[34] So also Gerhard Lohfink, commenting on John 14:9–10: "Jesus certainly never talked like that. . . . And yet the language of the Johannine Jesus touches precisely what Jesus was."[35] This approach, of course, tends to work well at a general level but is of less help in evaluating the particular.

Social Memory and Oral Traditions

A second major trend is attention to the role of memory in the Gospel accounts. Allison, Eric Eve, and Keith represent scholars who bridge the first and second trends by using memory theory to argue against use of the criteria. As Eve writes (and Keith approvingly quotes), "The project of trying to separate authentic from inauthentic material in the Jesus tradition is fundamentally misconceived. The workings of memory and oral tradition simply do not allow such a neat separation."[36]

Orality studies are certainly not new. Early form critics like Hermann Gunkel relied on understandings of the oral transmission of tradition that have now been widely discredited or nuanced.[37] Contemporary Jesus researchers

---

31. Allison, *Constructing Jesus*, 17; Allison, "How to Marginalize," 22–30.
32. Allison, *Constructing Jesus*, 18–19, 20.
33. Darrell L. Bock, "Key Events in the Life of the Historical Jesus: A Summary," in Bock and Webb, *Key Events*, 826.
34. Pitre, *Jesus and the Last Supper*, 47.
35. Gerhard Lohfink, *Jesus of Nazareth: What He Wanted, Who He Was*, trans. Linda M. Maloney (Collegeville, MN: Liturgical Press, 2012, 2015), 22–23.
36. Eric Eve, *Behind the Gospels: Understanding the Oral Tradition* (London: SCM, 2013), 181; Keith, *Jesus against the Scribal Elite*, 69, 81.
37. See Alan Kirk, "Memory Theory and Jesus Research," in Holmén and Porter, *Handbook*, 1:809–42. Gunkel developed his theory of form criticism in several works, especially in

increasingly interact with the social memory theory of Maurice Halbwachs (et al.), as well as studies of how oral tradition functions in other contexts and cultures. For example, Milman Parry and Albert Lord's study of the singers of epic ballads in the Balkans applied explicitly to the development of the Homeric epics, but was adapted by NT scholars to correct what many saw as the deficiencies of the early form-critical model.[38] The writings of Birger Gerhardsson and Kenneth Bailey, which originally appeared in 1961 and 1980, respectively, remain especially influential, although both have been sharply critiqued.[39]

Gerhardsson modeled his theory of the transmission of the oral tradition on rabbinic Judaism, a move sometimes decried as anachronistic. Bailey derived his views from thirty years of living in the Middle East. (Bailey anticipates our final theme through his insistence on reading Jesus and the Gospels through a Middle Eastern rather than a Western lens.) Bailey locates his understanding of oral tradition in between Bultmann's and Gerhardsson's theories, describing Bultmann's view of transmission as "informal uncontrolled," Gerhardsson's as "formal controlled," and his own as "informal controlled," wherein the community exercised certain flexible controls over the transmission of tradition but without a set teacher or rigidity concerning the details.[40] Critics also charge that Bailey's model is anachronistic, relying too much on analogies between his anecdotal observations of contemporary Middle Eastern Arab culture and first-century Jewish Palestine.[41] But others have found his observations useful, alongside the Parry-Lord study, for illuminating the typical patterns of oral cultures. Parallels remain inexact, not least because far more was presumably

---

his commentary on Genesis: Hermann Gunkel, *Genesis*, trans. Mark E. Biddle (Macon, GA: Mercer University Press, 1997).

38. Maurice Halbwachs's study on collective memory was first published in French in 1950; it is now available as *On Collective Memory*, ed. and trans. Lewis A. Coser (Chicago: University of Chicago Press, 2008). For the Parry-Lord study, see Albert B. Lord, *The Singer of Tales*, ed. Stephen Mitchell and Gregory Nagy, 2nd ed. (Cambridge: Harvard University Press, 2003; first edition published in 1960). See Daniel J. Castellano, "The Priority of Matthew's Gospel," Repository of Arcane Knowledge, 2014, http://www.arcaneknowledge.org/catholic/matthew3.htm#sec3_2_2.

39. Birger Gerhardsson, *Memory and Manuscript: Oral Tradition and Written Transmission in Rabbinic Judaism and Early Christianity* (Uppsala: Gleerup, 1961), republished in 1998 as *Tradition and Transmission in Early Christianity* (Peabody, MA: Hendrickson, 2001); and Kenneth E. Bailey, *Jesus through Middle Eastern Eyes: Cultural Studies in the Gospels* (Downers Grove, IL: IVP Academic, 2008). For interaction with the work of both scholars, see Werner H. Kelber and Samuel Byrskog, eds., *Jesus in Memory: Traditions in Oral and Scribal Perspectives* (Waco: Baylor University Press, 2009).

40. Kenneth E. Bailey, "Informal Controlled Oral Tradition and the Synoptic Gospels," *Themelios* 20, no. 2 (1995): 4–6. See the discussion of Bailey's approach in Terence C. Mournet, "The Jesus Tradition as Oral Tradition," in Kelber and Byrskog, *Jesus in Memory*, 52.

41. Mournet, "Jesus Tradition as Oral Tradition," 54–56.

at stake for the first Jesus-followers in the preservation and transmission of the Jesus tradition than in the retelling of epic songs or ballads.

The Gist of It

Gerhardsson once wrote that his studies in orality had convinced him "that we can hear the voice of Jesus himself in the Gospels."[42] Today fewer scholars adopt this view, at least as it relates to recovering the *ipsissima verba Jesu*. Instead, in line with the recurrent attestation motif described above, it is becoming more common for scholars today to focus on the broader themes and larger patterns of Jesus's teaching and actions, drawing on social memory theory to account for what Terence Mournet calls "the 'fixity' and 'flexibility' inherent in the tradition."[43] Paul Rhodes Eddy and Gregory Boyd likewise argue that the Synoptic Gospels contain the "fixed-yet-flexible" style that tends to characterize oral traditions.[44]

The motif of flexibility appears in Le Donne's work as a discussion of the distortions of memory, especially narrativization ("the tendency for memories to be conventionalized through the constraints of story telling") and articulation ("the tendency for memories to conform to language conventions").[45] Memory is *always* selective and distorted. Allison likewise begins *Constructing Jesus* with a sober assessment of the frailty of human memory.[46] For Bart Ehrman, this frailty—the unreliability of memory and of eyewitness testimony—points to the fundamental unreliability of the Gospel accounts.[47] Yet for Le Donne (and Allison), "distortion" need not indicate nonhistoricity. Instead, there is also fixity, in the form of "diachronic continuity," an essential component of collective memory. This continuity ensures that "wholesale fiction" was almost certainly not added to the Jesus tradition "within a generation of the historical events."[48]

Distortion does not necessarily imply theological obscuration either. Instead, Le Donne argues that the presence of interpretative agendas is no argu-

---

42. Birger Gerhardsson, *The Reliability of the Gospel Tradition* (Peabody, MA: Hendrickson, 2001), xxiv.
43. Mournet, "Jesus Tradition as Oral Tradition," 53.
44. Paul Rhodes Eddy and Gregory A. Boyd, *The Jesus Legend: A Case for the Historical Reliability of the Synoptic Jesus Tradition* (Grand Rapids: Baker Academic, 2007), 427–37, here 437.
45. Anthony Le Donne, "Theological Memory Distortion in the Jesus Tradition: A Study in Social Memory Theory," in *Memory in the Bible and Antiquity: The Fifth Durham-Tübingen Research Symposium*, ed. Stephen C. Barton, Loren T. Stuckenbruck, and Benjamin G. Wold (Tübingen: Mohr Siebeck, 2007), 168.
46. Allison, *Constructing Jesus*, 1–10.
47. Bart D. Ehrman, *Jesus before the Gospels: How the Earliest Christians Remembered, Changed, and Invented Their Stories of the Savior* (New York: HarperOne, 2016).
48. Le Donne, "Theological Memory Distortion," 175, 176.

ment against primitivity or authenticity, since we should expect theological interpretation at the earliest stages of the Jesus traditions.[49] Keener likewise concludes that literacy studies and memory theory indicate that Jesus's teachings would have been adapted but passed along "substantially accurately."[50] Alan Kirk suggests that memory always "infuses past events with *meaning*."[51] On one level, this is a rather straightforward observation that people interpret events as they remember and retell them; that is, there is no such thing as uninterpreted data. But it can also be understood as a challenge to Enlightenment attempts to disentangle pure history from theological reflection.

Robert McIver applies the memory studies of experimental psychology to the Synoptic Gospels and offers similarly measured conclusions based on his exploration of different kinds of memories (individual autobiographic, collective, eyewitness). He suggests that "flashbulb" or "personal event" memories are more long-lived and reliable than other types of memories, "even if some of the details might be lost or even wrong."[52] Suggestibility and hindsight bias can account for inaccurate details but generally do not alter "the gist of the situations described."[53] Despite the frailties of memory, McIver concludes, the Gospels are "generally reliable."[54] Allison concurs in his discussion of the passion narrative, in a characteristically cautious statement: if Jesus's followers responded in the usual ways to the death of a friend (i.e., by telling stories about it), "then doubtless some of the traditions behind the passion narratives had their genesis very early on, which surely ups the odds of their containing some true-to-life memory."[55] Similarly, but more optimistically, Eddy and Boyd's *The Jesus Legend* (2007) summarizes studies of orality, literacy, and memory to make a case for the historical reliability of the Gospels.[56]

Eyewitness Testimony

One of Dunn's central claims in *Jesus Remembered* is that the Synoptics preserve "the memories of the first disciples," which were transmitted in oral form before eventually being written down. "In other words, what we today are confronted with in the Gospels is not the top layer (last edition) of a series of

---

49. Le Donne, "Theological Memory Distortion," 163. See also Licona, "Is the Sky Falling?," 353–61.
50. Keener, *Historical Jesus*, 151.
51. Kirk, "Memory Theory," 835.
52. Robert McIver, *Memory, Jesus, and the Synoptic Gospels* (Atlanta: SBL Press, 2011), 58.
53. McIver, *Memory, Jesus, and the Synoptic Gospels*, 80.
54. McIver, *Memory, Jesus, and the Synoptic Gospels*, 187.
55. Allison, *Constructing Jesus*, 424.
56. Eddy and Boyd, *Jesus Legend*, 235–306.

increasingly impenetrable layers, but the living tradition of Christian celebration which takes us with surprising immediacy to the heart of the first memories of Jesus."[57] As with other scholars making use of memory theory, Dunn is interested in "the impression made by Jesus on his disciples" rather than precision in the details.[58] Allison takes a similar approach, proposing that the Gospels indeed contain memories of Jesus and that we will find those memories by looking for recurrent themes, motifs, and rhetorical strategies, especially those that recur across the Synoptic Gospels, rather than those that seem particular to one evangelist (echoing some aspects of the criterion of multiple attestation).[59] John's Gospel, as always, remains set apart; even the most ardent defenders of memory theory tend to shy away from finding memories in John.

Richard Bauckham is an exception to this rule. He goes one step further by arguing that all four canonical Gospels contain eyewitness testimony and even concludes that an eyewitness to the life of Jesus composed the Gospel of John. For Bauckham, the Gospels give us a more direct kind of access to the memories of the first followers of Jesus than theories of oral tradition typically suggest.[60] In this, Bauckham picks up on the work of Swedish scholar Samuel Byrskog, whose 2000 book *Story as History—History as Story* studies the role of living memory and testimony in Greco-Roman history and concludes that ancient historians valued eyewitness testimony as an essential means of understanding and reporting the past.[61] While many scholars remain unconvinced of Bauckham's theses, they have influenced all subsequent studies of the role of memory in the Gospels.

Allison, for one, rejects Bauckham's view that eyewitnesses or companions of eyewitnesses composed the canonical Gospels.[62] But he agrees with Bauckham that the Gospels have a closer link to the memories of the disciples than is often assumed in historical-critical scholarship. For example, he challenges John Dominic Crossan's proposal that the passion narratives, because they connect Jesus to various OT prophecies, are "prophecy historicized" rather than "history remembered."[63] Allison argues instead that "memory can be told in many languages, including the language of Scripture."[64] He invokes

---

57. Dunn, *Jesus Remembered*, 130–31, 254. For responses to criticisms of *Jesus Remembered*, see Dunn, *The Oral Gospel Tradition* (Grand Rapids: Eerdmans, 2013).

58. Dunn, *Jesus Remembered*, 382.

59. Allison, *Constructing Jesus*, 15.

60. Richard Bauckham, *Jesus and the Eyewitnesses: The Gospels as Eyewitness Testimony*, 2nd ed. (Grand Rapids: Eerdmans, 2017).

61. Samuel Byrskog, *Story as History—History as Story* (Tübingen: Mohr Siebeck, 2000); see Bauckham, *Jesus and the Eyewitnesses*, 8–11.

62. Allison, *Constructing Jesus*, 1.

63. John Dominic Crossan, *Who Killed Jesus? Exposing the Roots of Anti-Semitism in the Gospel Story of the Death of Jesus* (San Francisco: HarperSanFrancisco, 1996).

64. Allison, *Constructing Jesus*, 389.

Goodacre's category of "history scripturalized" to suggest that "to biblicize is not necessarily to invent."[65] Goodacre himself appreciates the move to orality but cautions his fellow scholars not to let the pendulum swing too far away from the importance of texts. Scholars like Dunn, he writes, might underestimate "the importance of literacy among early Christian authors and tradents, whose world we should reconstruct as one characterized by a lively interaction between text and tradition."[66]

Which Sources?

In terms of the interaction between text and tradition, two specific cases are worth noting briefly here: the persistence of the Q theory and debates over noncanonical material, especially the Gospel of Thomas. Goodacre links the Q theory to orality studies by suggesting that an unfortunate by-product of scholarly commitment to Q is a "reduction of the variety and richness of oral tradition to the level of the reconstruction of the precise wording of a hypothetical document."[67] Indeed, scholarly works often treat Q as a written document capable of precise reconstruction (one recent book, simply titled *Q*, has the somewhat astonishing subtitle *The First Writing about Jesus*[68]). Goodacre's 2002 book *The Case against Q* lays out a thorough argument against the Q hypothesis, following Austin Farrer and Michael Goulder's proposal that Luke's use of Matthew and Mark is a more plausible explanation for the so-called Synoptic Problem.[69]

Most scholars, however, continue to use Q. While Dunn accepts Goodacre's criticism that the Q model often relies too heavily on an exclusively literary framework, without attention to the role of oral tradition, he accepts the two-source theory (Mark and Q). Helen Bond's clear introductory-level text *The Historical Jesus: A Guide for the Perplexed* devotes one paragraph to explaining that Q is a theory (not an extant written source) that most scholars think best explains the relationship between the Synoptic Gospels, but the rest of the

---

65. Mark Goodacre, "Scripturalization in Mark's Crucifixion Narrative," in *The Trial and Death of Jesus: Essays on the Passion Narrative in Mark*, ed. Geert Van Oyen and Tom Shepherd (Leuven: Peeters, 2006), 33–47.

66. Mark Goodacre, *Thomas and the Gospels: The Case for Thomas's Familiarity with the Synoptics* (Grand Rapids: Eerdmans, 2012), 130.

67. Mark Goodacre, *The Case against Q: Studies in Markan Priority and the Synoptic Problem* (Harrisburg, PA: Trinity Press International, 2002), 188. Alan Kirk uses orality and memory theories to argue for Matthew's use of Q, in *Q in Matthew: Ancient Media, Memory, and Early Scribal Transmission of the Jesus Tradition*, LNTS 564 (New York: Bloomsbury T&T Clark, 2016).

68. Yoseop Ra, *Q, the First Writing about Jesus* (Eugene, OR: Wipf & Stock, 2016).

69. Goodacre, *Case against Q*.

book typically refers to Q as a document on par with other written sources like the Gospel of Thomas or even Mark.[70] An even more striking example is Larry Hurtado, who refers in one place to Q as "a carefully designed text" and "a very successful literary product." (He concludes, against the grain of much Q-scholarship, that it reflects a devotion to Jesus consistent with other texts, including the Synoptics.[71])

Beginning in the later decades of the twentieth century, a wave of scholarly research has defended the reliability of several noncanonical texts, including the Gospel of Peter and the Gospel of Thomas, on the grounds that they contain early traditions, sometimes even traditions that predate the canonical Gospels.[72] Other scholars have pushed back against these arguments. Evans, for one, suggests that many scholars take a "hypercritical" approach to the canonical Gospels and a "surprisingly uncritical" approach to the extracanonicals.[73]

Perhaps the most controversial noncanonical text is the Gospel of Thomas, and here, as with the case of Q, Goodacre is at the forefront. He suggests that some arguments about the primitivity of the Gospel of Thomas rest on erroneous form-critical assumptions (e.g., that shorter is more primitive, rather than its shortness being evidence of its redactional tendencies).[74] Goodacre concludes that the Gospel of Thomas is familiar with and dependent on the Synoptics. While not all scholars have been persuaded by Goodacre, the optimism about the Gospel of Thomas's independence has not remained as strong as ongoing commitment to the Q theory.

Early Jesus-Devotion

Debates over the dating of the sources often correlate to quarrels over how the earliest Jesus-followers understood Jesus in terms of his identity and mission—and often to assumptions that original views about Jesus traveled a historical trajectory from low (Jesus as a human being) to high (Jesus as

---

70. Helen K. Bond, *The Historical Jesus: A Guide for the Perplexed* (London: T&T Clark, 2012).

71. Larry W. Hurtado, *Lord Jesus Christ: Devotion to Jesus in Earliest Christianity* (Grand Rapids: Eerdmans, 2003), 257.

72. E.g., Elaine Pagels, *The Gnostic Gospels* (New York: Random House, 1979); Ron Cameron, ed., *The Other Gospels: Non-Canonical Gospel Texts* (Philadelphia: Westminster, 1982); Bart D. Ehrman and Zlatko Pleše, *The Other Gospels: Accounts of Jesus from outside the New Testament* (Oxford: Oxford University Press, 2013).

73. Craig A. Evans, "Jesus and the Extracanonical Works," in Charlesworth, *Jesus Research: New Methodologies*, 662. See also Pheme Perkins, "Apocryphal Gospels and the Historical Jesus," in Charlesworth, *Jesus Research: New Methodologies*, 690.

74. Goodacre, *Thomas and the Gospels*, 145–49.

fully divine). This, of course, assigns a certain historicity to the "low" view. In the last few decades, Hurtado and Bauckham have been the most vigorous defenders of the alternative view that "Jesus-devotion" or worship of Jesus emerged very early after Jesus's death. This area of study typically focuses its energies not on Jesus himself but on the beliefs and practices of the first generation or two of Jesus-followers, especially as those beliefs relate to Jewish monotheism. Yet studies of early Christology step into historical-Jesus territory regarding criteria of similarity (to early church teachings) and contextual plausibility (in relation to Jewish monotheism), and considerations of what Jesus taught about himself, his mission, and his identity in relation to the God of Israel.

For example, Allison uses elements of two themes already explored in this chapter (recurrent attestation and memory theory) to advance the claim that the Jesus of history had an "exalted" view of himself, although he stops short of spelling this out in concrete terms or titles: Messiah? Maybe. King? Perhaps. Danielic Son of Man? Likely. (Scholars remain especially interested in Jesus's self-understanding as the Son of Man; for instance, Adela Yarbro Collins and John Collins agree with Allison that Jesus likely identified himself as the Danielic Son of Man.[75]) Allison concludes firmly, "We should hold a funeral for the view that Jesus entertained no exalted thoughts about himself."[76] Others, like Hurtado, decline to make claims about Jesus's self-understanding and focus instead on the beliefs and practices of the first Jesus-followers.[77] For the most part, those investigations fall outside the purview of historical-Jesus studies (see David B. Capes's essay in this volume on the Christology of early Christianity).

Also at issue is the question of whether the Jesus of history was merely human or was indeed the divine Son of God, worthy of worship alongside and with the God of Israel. Many scholars have shied away from making the latter claim on historical grounds, ascribing it (understandably) to the realm of faith rather than academics. Yet there are certainly scholars who have argued vigorously, and on *historical* grounds, that Jesus was demonstrably not divine, and that the divinity ascribed to him was an invention of the later church. This likewise brings some studies on early high Christology into the territory of historical-Jesus research, largely through the work of scholars

---

75. Adela Yarbro Collins and John J. Collins, *King and Messiah as Son of God: Divine, Human, and Angelic Messianic Figures in Biblical and Related Literature* (Grand Rapids: Eerdmans, 2008), 170–73. Other recent studies interested in Jesus as the Son of Man include essays in Dieter Sänger, ed., *Gottessohn und Menschensohn* (Göttingen: Vandenhoeck & Ruprecht, 2004); Larry W. Hurtado and Paul L. Owen, eds., *'Who Is This Son of Man?'* (London: T&T Clark, 2011).

76. Allison, *Constructing Jesus*, 304.

77. See, e.g., Hurtado, *Lord Jesus Christ*, 31, 55.

who seek to demonstrate that the Jesus of history was neither divine nor worshiped as such.[78]

The Eastern Jesus

The vast majority of the scholars discussed so far are white, Western, and male; the preponderance of scholars in this section are not. The overriding concern within this trend is to examine Jesus from non-Western or nonwhite perspectives, whether they be minority perspectives within the United States (e.g., Kelly Brown Douglas and Delbert Burkett's "The Black Christ"), views of Jesus from the majority or two-thirds world (especially Africa and Asia), or investigations of Jesus through the lens of other religions (especially Islam).[79]

One strand within this trend examines the intertwining of Western historical-Jesus research with nationalism, whether German, British, or American. In *Jesus and the Rise of Nationalism* (2012), Halvor Moxnes analyzes the "lives of Jesus" of Ernest Renan in France, Friedrich Schleiermacher and David Friedrich Strauss in Germany, and George Adam Smith in England, for their entanglements with nineteenth-century European nationalisms.[80] James Crossley is more blunt and controversial about the present: in his estimation, some contemporary NT scholarship "is grounded in outdated, nationalist, imperialist and, at times, plain racist social-sciences, some of which directly relate to Anglo-American foreign policy interests in the Middle East and beyond."[81] Crossley's book is largely a polemic against the Context Group, members of which aim to apply the social sciences to the study of the NT, but other scholars (including Gerd Theissen and N. T. Wright) draw his fire for making Jesus "Jewish . . . but not that Jewish," because they stress both Jesus's Jewishness and his differences from certain features of first-century Judaism (which, of course, the canonical Gospels themselves tend to affirm).[82]

For many scholars in this area, whether from Africa, Asia, or the Middle East, the Jesus produced by historical-Jesus research is a "privileged, westernized Jesus," whose Eastern roots must be reclaimed.[83] The edited volume *Faces*

---

78. E.g., Bart D. Ehrman, *How Jesus Became God: The Exaltation of a Jewish Preacher from Galilee* (New York: HarperOne, 2014).

79. Kelly Brown Douglas with Delbert Burkett, "The Black Christ," in *The Blackwell Companion to Jesus*, ed. Delbert Burkett (Malden, MA: Wiley-Blackwell, 2011), 410–26.

80. Halvor Moxnes, *Jesus and the Rise of Nationalism: A New Quest for the Nineteenth-Century Historical Jesus* (London: Tauris, 2012).

81. James G. Crossley, *Jesus in an Age of Terror: Scholarly Projects for a New American Century* (Oakville, CT: Equinox, 2008), xiv.

82. Crossley, *Jesus in an Age of Terror*, 173–94.

83. Teresa Okure, "Historical Jesus Research in Global Cultural Context," in Holmén and Porter, *Handbook*, 2:981.

of Jesus in Africa seeks the Jesus of the Gospels before his Europeanization, explaining, "African values and customs are often closer to the Semitic values that pervade the Scriptures and the story of Jesus than the European Christian values that have been imposed upon them."[84] A chapter of Paul-Gordon Chandler's *Pilgrims of Christ on the Muslim Road* is titled "Resurrecting the Eastern Christ: Embracing the Semitic Face of Jesus"; in it Chandler explores Christianity's shift from East to West: "Christianity is indeed a Middle Eastern faith in origin, not a Western faith. . . . Christ was a Middle Easterner."[85]

Likewise Sri Lankan scholar R. S. Sugirtharajah writes, "Images of Jesus imported to Asia are so wrapped up in various christological configurations that one often overlooks the fact that Jesus came from Asia, or to be precise, west Asia. . . . These discourses [in *Asian Faces of Jesus*] try to re-Asianize and refashion Jesus on Asian terms to meet the contextual needs of Asian peoples."[86] Meeting the contextual needs of people is another important theme of non-Western scholarship, as it involves reclaiming the Jesus of history as poor and oppressed—and therefore a figure who shares the socioeconomic status of large swaths of the population in the countries where these scholars live and work.

This emphasis, of course, has always been present in liberation theology. Veli-Matti Kärkkäinen notes that "Liberationists begin with the historical Jesus . . . who lived a real life under real human conditions." But Kärkkäinen distinguishes this from the quests for the historical Jesus, which he identifies with classical liberalism: "Whereas for Liberals, the historical *facts* of the life of Jesus were the main focus in their desire to reconstruct the life of Jesus, for Liberationists the key is the need to understand the *relevance* of the history of Jesus to the struggles of Latin America."[87] Jesus's relevance for the struggles of the poor and oppressed in Latin America, Africa, and elsewhere arises from his solidarity with and life among the poor, and also from his advocacy for them through his confrontations with the systems that dominated and excluded them. For Teresa Okure, "the Jesus movement in the gospel itself was basically a grassroots movement whereby the poor and marginalized of

---

84. Robert J. Schreiter, "Jesus Christ in Africa Today," in *Faces of Jesus in Africa*, ed. Robert J. Schreiter (Maryknoll, NY: Orbis, 1991), viii.

85. Paul-Gordon Chandler, *Pilgrims of Christ on the Muslim Road: Exploring a New Path between Two Faiths* (Lanham, MD: Cowley, 2007), 128. See also Andrew Thompson, *Jesus of Arabia: Christ through Middle Eastern Eyes* (Lanham, MD: Rowman & Littlefield, 2014).

86. R. S. Sugirtharajah, ed., *Asian Faces of Jesus* (Maryknoll, NY: Orbis, 1993), viii. See also Gene L. Green, Stephen T. Pardue, and K. K. Yeo, eds., *Jesus without Borders: Christology in the Majority World* (Grand Rapids: Eerdmans, 2014).

87. Veli-Matti Kärkkäinen, "Christology in Africa, Asia, and Latin America," in Burkett, *Blackwell Companion*, 378.

society found in him a champion and advocate for their cause."[88] Likewise Zablon Nthamburi focuses on Jesus's solidarity with the suffering, hungry, and weak. And John Waliggo points to a Jesus who was rejected and therefore identifies with the contemporary African struggle.[89]

To be sure, these emphases are found in Western scholarship too, in the work of scholars like Seán Freyne and Richard Horsley.[90] The difference tends to be in application: the African scholars are interested less in reconstructing Jesus in his original context and more in examining what he means for the African church and for the lives of the African poor today. Pablo Richard describes Jesus research in Latin America as a "fourth quest," which is characterized by seeking Jesus from the perspective of the poor and marginalized in the two-thirds world; reconstructing the historical character of the Jesus movement in its earliest, postresurrection days (i.e., a concomitant quest "for the historical apostolic churches" prior to the establishment of hierarchical power structures); and recapturing the historical Jesus for the reformation of the contemporary church.[91]

Another emerging strand in this larger trend investigates Jesus through the lens of other religions. The 2011 *Blackwell Companion to Jesus* includes essays on Jewish, Hindu, Islamic, and Buddhist perspectives on Jesus.[92] Recent scholarship from a Muslim perspective draws its energy from the necessity for interfaith dialogue between Christians and Muslims, especially post-9/11. Mona Siddiqui, for example, explores with clarity and grace "the views, doctrines and conversations Christians and Muslims have held on the figure of Jesus Christ."[93]

Zeki Saritoprak seeks to do what Reza Aslan's popular 2013 book *Zealot* did not: explain what Muslims think about Jesus and how those views might differ (or not) from Christian views. (Despite misconceptions that *Zealot* was a portrayal of Jesus from an Islamic perspective, Aslan's book retreads

88. Okure, "Historical Jesus Research," in Holmén and Porter, *Handbook*, 2:973.
89. Zablon Nthamburi, "Christ as Seen by an African: A Christological Quest," in Schreiter, *Faces of Jesus in Africa*, 65–69. John M. Waliggo, "African Christology in a Situation of Suffering," in Schreiter, *Faces of Jesus in Africa*, 164–80.
90. Seán Freyne, *The Jesus Movement and Its Expansion: Meaning and Mission* (Grand Rapids: Eerdmans, 2014); Richard A. Horsley, *Jesus and the Powers: Conflict, Covenant, and the Hope of the Poor* (Minneapolis: Fortress, 2011).
91. Pablo Richard, "Jesus: A Latin American Perspective," in *Global Bible Commentary*, ed. Daniel Patte (Nashville: Abingdon, 2004), 338–40.
92. See the following in Burkett, *Blackwell Companion*: Michael J. Cook, "Jewish Perspectives on Jesus," 215–31; Reem A. Meshal and M. Reza Pirbhai, "Islamic Perspectives on Jesus," 232–49; Sandy Bharat, "Hindu Perspectives on Jesus," 250–66; Peggy Morgan, "Buddhist Perspectives on Jesus," 267–82.
93. Mona Siddiqui, *Christians, Muslims, and Jesus* (New Haven: Yale University Press, 2013), 2.

territory laid down as early as the eighteenth century by Hermann Samuel Reimarus.[94]) Saritoprak aims to demonstrate that the Jesus seen through Muslim eyes is "not at all dissimilar from Christianity's Jesus."[95]

Mustafa Akyol's *Islamic Jesus* has a similar goal: to introduce readers to "the Islamic view of Jesus."[96] His book has a second and more primary aim: to demonstrate the close connections between "Jewish Christianity" and Muslim teachings about Jesus—and thereby to claim the historicity of both over against mainstream Christianity, which Akyol sees as originating from Paul rather than Jesus. Akyol is a journalist and newspaper columnist rather than a scholar, and he relies on some NT scholarship that is widely disputed (e.g., that which asserts a sharp difference between Jewish and Pauline/gentile Christianity). Not everyone will accept his assumptions about the nature of Jewish Christianity—for example, his claim that the Infancy Gospel of Thomas originated (very early) from Jewish Christianity, not from later, Gnostic Christianity.[97]

Mahmoud Ayoub's *A Muslim View of Christianity* aims to educate Christians otherwise unfamiliar with Muslims views; one part of the book walks through key components of Muslim teachings about Jesus—perhaps most centrally, that he did not die but was taken up into heaven by God—and includes some helpful discussion of the role of the Gospel of Barnabas and the reliability of the canonical Gospels from a Muslim perspective.[98]

Comparatively greater openness to questions of faith is a notable feature of much of this non-Western research, especially in Africa and Asia. Okure is representative when she insists that historical-Jesus research must include two dimensions of faith: (1) the faith of the evangelists and the first Christian communities and (2) the faith of committed believers today. "Outside this life-centered, faith-based optic and orbit, the discourse or research on the historical Jesus, especially from a global perspective, risks losing much of its relevance and significance."[99] For Okure (and others), this means that Jesus research must also include investigation of the reception of the historical Jesus in various cultures, especially from the perspective of the poor and marginalized. Okure says it more decisively: "While the North or West seems

---

94. Reza Aslan, *Zealot: The Life and Times of Jesus of Nazareth* (New York: Random House, 2013).
95. Zeki Saritoprak, *Islam's Jesus* (Gainesville: University Press of Florida, 2014), xi.
96. Akyo Mustafa Akyol, *The Islamic Jesus: How the King of the Jews Became a Prophet of the Muslims* (New York: St. Martin's Press, 2017), l, 8.
97. Akyol, *Islamic Jesus*, 141.
98. Mahmoud Ayoub, *A Muslim View of Christianity*, ed. Irfan A. Omar (Maryknoll, NY: Orbis, 2007), 173–74, 223–27. See also Suleiman A. Mourad, "Jesus in the Qur'an and Other Early Islamic Texts," in Charlesworth, *Jesus Research: New Methodologies*, 753–65.
99. Okure, "Historical Jesus Research," in Holmén and Porter, *Handbook*, 2:956, 957.

bent on and committed to endless 'quests' or 'research' into the historical Jesus, the South prefers to devote its psychic, intellectual and spiritual energy and resources to the 'reception' of this same historical Jesus."[100]

The contributors to *Asian Faces of Jesus* similarly "show little interest in an academic reconstruction of biographical details. . . . For [Asian interpreters], the artificial dichotomy imposed by Western academics between historical exegesis and theology—between the brute historical facts and faith formulations—does not exist. The crucial hermeneutical question is not what the historical Jesus looked like but what he means for Asia today."[101] There may be a bit of slippage in terminology here, since Okure and the contributors to *Asian Faces of Jesus* seem largely interested in what this essay has called the Jesus of history, rather than the reconstructed historical Jesus. Nonetheless the shift in focus away from detailed historical reconstruction and toward the relevance of Jesus for present-day suffering—in all his historical particularity as one who also suffered—holds true.

Reflections

The preceding survey of global approaches highlights a persistent undercurrent of Jesus research: the contentious role of theology and faith. Recent scholarship splits sharply over their place in Jesus research. James Charlesworth expresses confidence that modern Jesus research has successfully divorced history from theology: "The life and mind of Jesus of Nazareth is no longer lost in the fog of theological pronouncements."[102] Scot McKnight argues instead that the task of reconstructing the historical Jesus is "both possible and theologically useless (for the church)."[103] Somewhere in between Charlesworth and McKnight we find Allison. In *The Historical Christ and the Theological Jesus*—a title that deliberately reverses the usual pairing—Allison considers the "religious implications" of the quest for the historical Jesus and wonders, "How much history does theology require?" (Answer: some.)[104]

---

100. Okure, "Historical Jesus Research," in Holmén and Porter, *Handbook*, 2:984.

101. Sugirtharajah, *Asian Faces of Jesus*, x.

102. Charlesworth and Pokorný, editors' introduction to *Jesus Research: An International Perspective*, 14. See also Charlesworth, *Jesus Research: New Methodologies*, 9; Bruce D. Chilton, "Method in a Critical Study of Jesus," in Holmén and Porter, *Handbook*, 1:129.

103. Scot McKnight, "Why the Authentic Jesus Is of No Use for the Church," in Keith and Le Donne, *Jesus, Criteria*, 175.

104. Dale C. Allison Jr., *The Historical Christ and the Theological Jesus* (Grand Rapids: Eerdmans, 2009), 3, 32. Cf. Lohfink writes, "Historical criticism is indispensable to research on Jesus," but at the same time "the real 'historical Jesus' cannot be grasped independently of faith in him"—that is, apart from the faith "of the first witnesses and those who handed on

Dunn and McKnight's collection *The Historical Jesus in Recent Research* notes that their project is at least amenable to a quest that springs from faith rather than skepticism: "The desire to see and hear Jesus as he was seen and heard by the fishermen and villagers of first-century Galilee is not in itself antithetical to faith."[105] In another recent collected volume, *Key Events in the Life of the Historical Jesus* (edited by Darrell Bock and Robert Webb), all the essayists have a declared commitment to the Christian faith.[106] Holmén and Porter's ambitious four-volume *Handbook for the Study of the Historical Jesus* stakes out no claim one way or the other, opting instead to collect Jesus research in all its abundance and diversity ("a worthy expression of the range of viable thought currently available in historical Jesus studies").[107]

Particularly as multiple fields abandon the myth of pure scholarly objectivity, it makes little sense to tar so-called confessional scholars as more biased than nonconfessional scholars. As Clive Marsh writes, "The Quest of the Historical Jesus has never only been about the quest for Jesus."[108] When Marsh surveys the various "agendas" of Jesus questers, it is a long and sometimes overlapping list of lenses: theological, anti-ecclesial (one could add anti-Catholic here), ethical, political, cultural-religious, psychological.

At the least, the abandonment of Enlightenment naturalism (à la David Hume) in relation to Jesus research seems long overdue, and some recent research provides resources along those lines. Webb's opening essay in *Key Events in the Life of the Historical Jesus* includes a helpful discussion of how to handle divine causality from a historical perspective.[109] Keener periodically takes up questions of divine causation in *The Historical Jesus of the Gospels*.[110] In a chapter titled "Miracles and Method," Eddy and Boyd opt for what they call "an open historical-critical method" over against a naturalistic one.[111]

It remains to be seen how many of the trends named here will endure. So far the application of memory studies has produced mixed results, with scholars using memory theory to argue both for and against the canonical Gospels'

---

the story" (Lohfink, *Jesus of Nazareth*, xi); see also Marguerat, "Historical Jesus and Christ of Faith," 442.

105. James D. G. Dunn and Scot McKnight, eds., *The Historical Jesus in Recent Research* (Winona Lake, IN: Eisenbrauns, 2005), xii. "Recent" here is a broad term; the volume is a survey of classical voices (Schweitzer, Bultmann, Jeremias, Kümmel, et al.) and key players over the last several decades (Wright, Meyer, Dunn, Sanders, et al.).

106. Bock and Webb, *Key Events*, 7.

107. Holmén and Porter, editors' introduction to *Handbook for the Study of the Historical Jesus*, 1:xvii.

108. Clive Marsh, "Diverse Agendas at Work in the Jesus Quest," in Holmén and Porter, *Handbook*, 2:985.

109. Webb, "Historical Enterprise," in Bock and Webb, *Key Events*, 39–54.

110. Keener, *Historical Jesus*, 347–8, 379–88.

111. Eddy and Boyd, *Jesus Legend*, 85. See also Lohfink, *Jesus of Nazareth*, 128–52.

reliability. While use of the criteria for authenticity is still deeply rooted in Gospels research, evidence suggests that this stubborn soil may finally be giving way; who knows what will yet flower out of such newly fertile ground?

As Goodacre suggests, contemporary NT scholarship can be, and has been, invigorated by newer methods such as narrative criticism and literary and film studies (see, for example, Goodacre's creative use of Jesus films to illustrate aspects of the Synoptic problem).[112] It seems clear that Jesus research is becoming increasingly interdisciplinary in approach and method.

Finally, especially as the church's center of gravity shifts increasingly to the global south, Jesus research in the West must attend to the work being done in other parts of the world. Where Jesus matters most, in the end, is in communities of faith, wherever they are found. While the Jesus of history may be of interest to the nonreligious, he is of supreme and pressing importance to those around the world—in both West and East—who claim him also as the risen Lord.

---

112. Goodacre, *Case against Q*, 105–6, 121. For Jesus films and the Synoptic Problem, see Goodacre, *Case against Q*, 121–32; Goodacre, "The Synoptic Jesus and the Celluloid Christ: Solving the Synoptic Problem through Film," *JSNT* 80 (2000): 31–43.

8

New Testament Christology

David B. Capes

Introduction

In 1979 Larry Hurtado published an article titled "New Testament Christology: A Critique of Bousset's Influence."[1] Hurtado ends the article suggesting some fruitful ways forward for understanding how early Christians wrestled with Jesus and his significance. In particular, he makes two recommendations. First, he says that important new lines of research will lie in "the influence of the OT on early Christology." Earlier generations of scholars had paid little attention to the ways early Christian readings of the OT had generated fresh assessments of Jesus's significance. Hurtado was convinced that new insights into the history and theology of early Christianity were available to those who took up this question. But what we call the OT is not a single book under a black leather cover. It is scrolls meticulously hand copied and handed down for generations. This is why scholars are drawn to the Dead Sea Scrolls (DSS), Pseudepigrapha, and other Second Temple literature. These Jewish texts reflect the state of the OT and the Jewish religion at the time of Jesus, Paul, and other NT writers. They show how the early Jesus-followers might have read, interpreted, applied, and updated these texts.

---

1. Larry W. Hurtado, "New Testament Christology: A Critique of Bousset's Influence," *TS* 40 (1979): 306–17.

Second, Hurtado proposes that a promising way forward might involve recognition that Jesus's life and earthly ministry held significance for early Christians in the formation of their Christologies. For decades, scholars have placed the weight of christological development on what happened after stories of Jesus's resurrection began to circulate among his disciples. A good example of this is the climactic statement in Peter's Pentecost sermon (Acts 2:36): "Therefore let the entire house of Israel know with certainty that God has made him both Lord and Messiah, this Jesus whom you crucified." Hurtado suggests that scholars ought to consider the ways Jesus's followers remembered him to gain greater insights into the NT era and its developments. Indeed, christological studies over the last twenty to thirty years have been influenced by reassessments of Jesus's life and influence on his followers and on Christian readings of the OT.

Key Questions

The conversation about NT Christology has changed, but scholars are still grappling with many of the same questions that held the attention of earlier interpreters.

Early Christian backgrounds. What data do we use in understanding early Christian claims about Jesus? Are there patterns of language or behavior that we should take into account? What philosophical or religious backgrounds served as the rich soil where Christology grew? Did early Christians import pagan practices and beliefs into their communities in order to claim Jesus as "divine"?

Perhaps an even more fundamental set of questions is the following.

Early Christology. What does it mean to call Jesus "divine"? How early did a divine Christology emerge? Did early Christians worship Jesus? If so, when and where did it start? What role did Jesus himself play in shaping his followers' perceptions of him? What role did belief in the resurrection play? Did early Christians' readings of their Scriptures generate novel ideas about who Jesus was/is and what role he plays in the redemption of the world? By emphasizing a fully divine Christology do we run the risk of denying or neglecting the humanity of Jesus?

Monotheism. Did monotheism preclude Jewish Christians from worshiping Jesus or seeing him as one with God? What is monotheism in an ancient context?

Other ancient texts. Are there antecedent texts and traditions that might explain the kind of claims made of Jesus? Does reference to divine agents (e.g., Wisdom, Melchizedek, Enoch, Michael) help us understand the kinds of things early Christians said and did in regard to Jesus?

Other Christian texts. Are claims made by later NT writers (e.g., the author of Hebrews and John's Gospel) consistent with earlier claims?

Other questions are asked, of course, but these have been some of the principal questions posed by scholars investigating NT Christology in the past twenty years. Our goal here is not to examine each question. That would require a book-length monograph. Our goal is to see how the main contours of the discussion over the last twenty to thirty years have dealt with some of these questions.

Throughout much of the twentieth century scholars investigated NT Christology primarily by analyzing the various christological titles used in the NT to describe Jesus. They focused their research on understanding and unpacking the meaning of christological titles such as Son of God, Son of Man, Lord, Christ, Prophet, Teacher/Rabbi, Image of God, Second Adam.[2] Some scholars have devoted entire books to examining christological titles, often through their Greco-Roman and Jewish backgrounds.

Scholars today build on those studies and yet realize that titles alone are not sufficient for grasping the significance of Jesus for earliest Christians. Messianic exegesis, patterns of nontitular language, patterns of behavior, historical studies, and various narrative strategies form other data which scholars mine to reconstruct the Christology of early Christianity. Titles inform those discussions, often serving as gateways to further explorations over against the Jewish or Roman milieu.[3]

Finally, while NT Christology properly has to do with the entire corpus known as "the New Testament," a great deal of effort has been spent on understanding the Christology prior to the written record. In other words, many of the questions asked by scholars have been historical questions about Christian origins. While it is extremely messy—and unwise—to try to order the NT books chronologically and then attempt to track development of ideas, influences, and so on, few doubt that embedded within the NT are bits of earlier traditions (e.g., hymns, creeds, phrases) that are christologically rich. Furthermore, there is broad agreement that Paul's letters represent the earliest literary activity that gave rise to the collection we call the NT. So the letters of Paul have been a particular focus for understanding the origins and significance of christological claims made about Jesus within the early Jesus movement.[4]

---

2. E.g., Oscar Cullmann, *The Christology of the New Testament*, trans. Shirley Guthrie and Charles A. M. Hall (Philadelphia: Westminster, 1959); Werner G. Kramer, *Christ, Lord, Son of God*, trans. Brian Hardy (London: SCM, 1966).

3. Martin Hengel, *The Son of God: The Origin of Christology and the History of Jewish-Hellenistic Religion*, trans. John Bowden (Philadelphia: Fortress; London: SCM, 1974); C. Kavin Rowe, *Early Narrative Christology: The Lord in the Gospel of Luke* (Grand Rapids: Baker Academic, 2009).

4. The most thorough investigation of Paul's Christology of late is Gordon Fee, *Pauline Christology: An Exegetical-Theological Study* (Grand Rapids: Baker Academic, 2013). A more

Jewish Background

Martin Hengel catalyzed a good deal of christological discussion in the last few decades. His mammoth work *Judaism and Hellenism* asserts—persuasively for most scholars—that Judaism had been Hellenized for centuries before the birth of Jesus and that the Judaisms of late antiquity, not pagan religions, provided the rich soils into which the movement founded by and on Jesus had been planted and thrived.[5] Furthermore, his brief but insightful book *The Son of God* makes a startling case for how quickly a divine Christology could have emerged.[6] Hengel famously noted that more happened in the first twenty years after the execution of Jesus toward the development of Christology than in the next seven hundred.[7] The man executed as a state criminal was in short order depicted as a preexistent, divine figure who became man. To account for this explosive development, Hengel urged colleagues to turn to the texts and language of Second Temple Judaism.

Hengel's work reflects a sea change that was taking place in NT studies. If we wish to understand what has happened in Christology in recent years, we have to grasp the enduring influence of Hengel's work. Prior generations of scholars, from Wilhelm Bousset (1865–1920) to Rudolf Bultmann (1884–1976), proposed that the best way to explain Christianity in historical terms was through the polytheistic, pagan influences that crept inside the church from the outside culture. Where there were "gods-a-plenty," Jesus could simply be identified as another. This was the prevailing view among the educated. But is that truly what happened?

After World War II ended and the horrors of the Holocaust were exposed, Hengel and other scholars began to challenge the scholarly orthodoxy that assumed Second Temple Judaism had degenerated beyond recovery in the postprophetic period. With the discovery of the DSS and the publication of more Jewish documents from the era (from the 1950s to 1990s), many more data became available to scholars. A new perspective, a more generous perspective, on Judaism at the time of Jesus was emerging among a new generation of interpreters who refused to accept the prevailing anti-Semitism in the academy. Scholars steeped in Jewish texts and traditions turned their eye to how early Christians regarded Jesus.

---

concise version is his *Jesus the Lord according to Paul the Apostle: A Concise Introduction* (Grand Rapids: Baker Academic, 2018).

5. Martin Hengel, *Judaism and Hellenism: Studies in Their Encounter in Palestine during the Early Hellenistic Period* (London: SCM, 1974).

6. Martin Hengel, *The Son of God: The Origin of Christology and the History of Jewish-Hellenistic Religion*, trans. John Bowden (Philadelphia: Fortress, 1976).

7. Martin Hengel, "Christology and New Testament Chronology: A Problem in the History of Earliest Christianity," in *Between Jesus and Paul: Studies in the Earliest History of Christianity* (Philadelphia: Fortress, 1983), 30–47.

Antecedent Traditions

One important impulse over the last quarter-century of NT christological studies has been to go in search of the antecedent traditions that early Christians drew on in order to describe the origins and development of Christology. Because of Hengel, much of the focus has been on Jewish categories as potential sources for early Christology.

Angelomorphic Traditions

Certain themes and concepts found in the NT have been traced to Jewish angel traditions.[8] Charles Gieschen describes this approach as "Angelomorphic" Christology—that is, the early Christian tendency to use Jewish angel motifs (reflected in the Hebrew Bible, Pseudepigrapha, DSS) to describe the significance of Jesus. This did not mean that early Christians perceived Jesus to have been an angel; it means only that they used the same kind of language found in angelic texts to express their understanding of him. Gieschen draws heavily on a variety of texts and images: Angel of the Lord traditions, principal angel traditions (e.g., Michael, Yahoel, Metatron, Gabriel), personified attributes (the Name, the Glory, Word and Wisdom), and exalted humans. The Angel of YHWH traditions that depict God in human form likely had a significant impact on early expressions of Christology. They provided early Christians with the proper categories for linking the crucified, resurrected, ascended Jesus to the name and dignity of God.

Messianic Traditions

Given the significance and predominance of the claim that "Jesus is the Messiah" (that is, "the Christ"), scholars have returned to that title and its abundant associations in assessing Jesus's significance. William Horbury makes the case that a majority of christological expressions found in the NT owe their substance to Jewish messianism.[9] Horbury moves against the grain of previous biblical scholarship, because other scholars had concluded that messianic hopes were not mainstream and belonged to the margins. While everyone else emphasizes the Judaisms (plural) of late antiquity, Horbury argues that a strain of royal messianism ran through the Jewish biblical canon and underwrites even those Jewish texts where the notion of the messianic hope is not expressed (e.g., 1 and 2 Macc., Tob., Jdt.). Horbury defines the concept of messiah broadly as "the expectation of a coming pre-eminent

---

8. Charles Gieschen, *Angelomorphic Christology: Antecedents and Early Evidence*, AGJU 42 (Leiden: Brill, 1998).
9. William Horbury, *Jewish Messianism and the Cult of Christ* (London: SCM, 1998).

ruler,"[10] an ideal rooted in the Hebrew Bible but developed further in later Jewish texts. Horbury admits that Jewish texts betray a variety of messianic images and hopes, but he finds that sitting beneath the surface is a coherence rooted in a royal ideology. He does admit that gentile ruler cults influenced early Christology, but by and large it is messianic expectation, especially that of an angelic or spiritual messiah, that accounts for the kinds of expressions and actions directed toward the risen Jesus. According to Horbury, language that appears to describe the worship of Christ is typical of the praise of kings. Horbury considers Jewish messianism so central that it accounts for most of the christological titles, including Christ, Lord, Son of God, Son of Man, High Priest, and Savior. Even the claim that Jesus is "God" can be handled under the broad stroke of messianism.

Although not everyone has accepted Horbury's opinions, most today regard messianism as a catalytic, not an obsolete, category. But was it as mainstream as Horbury imagines? John J. Collins, an influential interpreter of Jewish messianism in the Second Temple period, thinks not. Take, for instance, Qumran messianism; it is a messy business that defies systemization. In other words, messianism was not a stock Jewish hope ready to be applied to Jesus. Rather than restricting his investigation to passages that use the Hebrew for word "anointing," Collins draws together those texts that speak of "figures who have important roles in the future hope of the people."[11] Collins identifies four paradigms: king, priest, prophet, and heavenly messiah. According to Collins, royal ideology waxes and wanes in the Second Temple period; but when it reemerges, it fixates on a human king who will destroy the wicked, restore the fortunes of God's people, and reinstate the Davidic dynasty. What is most pronounced among the DSS is the expectation of two messiahs: the Davidic "Prince of the Congregation" and the messianic priest. For Collins, anyone interested in understanding messianic claims made about Jesus must grapple with the fluidity of messianic hopes in the period.

Matthew Novenson is another scholar who has worked to reclaim Jewish messianism as a fundamental christological category.[12] Earlier generations of scholars had dismissed Jewish messianic ideals as sources for the emerging faith. F. C. Baur, to cite one example, thought that even though Paul referred to Jesus as *Christos* (the Greek translation of *Messiah*), this habit had nothing to do with Jewish messianic expectations since the apostle to the gentiles freed Christianity from the constraints of Judaism. Likewise,

---

10. Horbury, *Jewish Messianism and the Cult of Christ*, 7.
11. John J. Collins, *The Scepter and the Star: The Messiahs of the Dead Sea Scrolls and Other Ancient Literature*, ABRL (New York: Doubleday, 1995), 12.
12. Matthew V. Novenson, *Christ among the Messiahs: Christ Language in Paul and Messiah Language in Ancient Judaism* (Oxford: Oxford University Press, 2012).

Bousset recognized that wave after wave of gentile converts shifted the focus from Jewish to Hellenistic claims that Jesus is "Lord." In the end, for many scholars "Christ" was merely a second name for Jesus in Paul and other early Christian circles. Novenson carefully deconstructs that position, arguing that "Christ" was neither a proper name (such as "Jesus") nor a title (e.g., "Son of God"); it was an "honorific" that could stand for the proper name and be used in combination with other titles (e.g., the phrase "Lord Jesus Christ"). In this way, Novenson likens "Christ" in Paul to the honorific "Augustus" for Octavian or "Maccabee" for Judah ben Mattathias. Yet the word *Christ* (with its root meaning of "anointed") belonged to a community that shared common language and ideals to describe their longings for a new age, ideas rooted in the Hebrew Scriptures. For Novenson, though messianic hopes were not uniform, there were nevertheless stock language and shared resources. Not every use of "Christ" in Paul comes with deep messianic resonances, yet there were places in his letters where he employed messianic language intentionally in recognizable and predictable patterns (e.g., Rom. 9:4–5; 15:7–12; 1 Cor. 15:20–28; Gal. 3:16).

Scholars continue to build on recent work on Jewish messianism and extend it in important new directions. Joshua Jipp investigates the Christ language in Paul, which, he argues, is sourced in Greco-Roman and Jewish notions of the ideal king.[13] Paul reworks this tradition as creatively "activated through the fate of Jesus and the early Christians' continued experience of him."[14] According to Jipp, "the Christ" is more than the ideal ruler; he is the "living enactment of the law."[15] In the Gospel of Matthew, the portrayal of Jesus is informed in large measure by the idealized king of the Davidic tradition. When narrating the Gospel story, the writer links that tradition to Jesus and reworks David's Son into a humble king and healing shepherd.[16] Daniel Boyarin thinks Christology develops when the Jewish Jesus fits pre-Christian Jewish expectations of a suffering and divine Messiah: "The job description—Required: one Christ, will be divine, will be Son of Man, will be sovereign and savior of the Jews and the world—was there already."[17] Like many scholars today, Boyarin regards Daniel 7 as the genesis of the Son of Man tradition reflected in the Gospels. In Daniel, the Son of Man is a second divine figure, the residue of older "binitarian" views, not just a symbol of the people of Israel.

13. Joshua W. Jipp, *Christ Is King: Paul's Royal Ideology* (Minneapolis: Fortress, 2015).
14. Jipp, *Christ Is King*, 9.
15. Jipp, *Christ Is King*, 75.
16. H. Daniel Zacharias, *Matthew's Presentation of the Son of David* (Edinburgh: Bloomsbury T&T Clark, 2016).
17. Daniel Boyarin, *The Jewish Gospels: The Story of the Jewish Christ* (New York: New Press, 2012), 73.

Divine Agents

In addition to angelomorphic language and messianic hopes, scholars search for the antecedents of an early, divine Christology in other places. Pointing out that passages like 1 Corinthians 8:6 depict the "binitarian shape" to early Christian devotion, Hurtado appeals to the category of divine agency in Second Temple Judaism as central. Many Jewish texts from the era describe God as having a chief agent, second to him only in rank. These divine agents carry out divine functions such as creating, sustaining, and administering the world under God's hand. Hurtado classifies those agents as (a) divine attributes (e.g., Wisdom and Logos), (b) exalted patriarchs (e.g., Enoch and Moses), and (c) principal angels (e.g., Michael, Melchizedek, and Yahoel). Although these agents are close to God and exercise what appear to be divine powers, these agents never pose a threat to God's oneness because they are never the recipients of worship.[18] Cultic devotion to Christ distinguishes early Christian faith and practice from Judaism's category of divine agency. Ultimately, the worship of Jesus provided a unique challenge to monotheism and resulted in a "mutation" of Jewish monotheism that allowed for God's agent, Jesus, to be worshiped alongside God.

A similar line of argument is posited by James McGrath.[19] For him, Paul's Christianized Shema (1 Cor. 8:6) does not feature a divine Christ as much as it features a Christ who is God's unique agent. The key issue for him is the flexible nature of Jewish monotheism in the era. Rather than reflecting a fixed, strict category, beliefs and practices by Jews in the NT era demonstrate a fluid approach to God's oneness. Nothing in early Christianity, including its Christology, marks a definitive break with Judaism, and the parting of the ways happens "significantly later than the period in which the texts now incorporated in the New Testament were produced."[20]

Divine Identity

Not all scholars are convinced that semidivine, intermediary figures provided the relevant antecedents in Judaism to account for an early high Christology. Richard Bauckham proposes instead that "early Christians included Jesus, precisely and unambiguously, within the unique identity of the one

---

18. Larry W. Hurtado, *One God, One Lord: Early Christian Devotion and Ancient Jewish Monotheism* (Philadelphia: Fortress, 1988; 2nd ed., Edinburgh: T&T Clark, 1998), 1–39 (1988 edition). Hurtado develops his arguments further in *Lord Jesus Christ: Devotion to Jesus in Earliest Christianity* (Grand Rapids: Eerdmans, 2003).

19. James F. McGrath, *The Only True God: Early Christian Monotheism in Its Jewish Context* (Urbana: University of Illinois Press, 2009).

20. McGrath, *Only True God*, 2.

God of Israel."[21] For Bauckham, the most significant factor in the emergence of a fully divine Christology—given the Jewish commitment to God's oneness—is "divine identity." Divine identity, according to Bauckham, provides a better handle for the evidence found in contemporary Jewish literature. Divine identity has to do with God as a person who acts, speaks, knows, and is known. It distinguishes God from everything that is not God. In particular, it is God in relationship that explains early Christology. For Israel, God reveals himself as a covenant partner, making himself known through acts in history. For the rest of creation, God relates as Creator, Sustainer, and Ruler of all things. So there are two sides to the reality ledger: (a) the God side and (b) the creation side. Where did early Christians place Jesus?

When Bauckham comes to the NT itself, he concludes that early Christians included Jesus on God's side of the ledger, effectively including him within the identity of Israel's God. They acknowledge Christ as Creator and Sovereign Lord (e.g., Col. 1:15–20). They view him as bearing the divine name and without hesitation worship him. Before the first books of the NT are written, a fully divine Christology was the common property of the church. Bauckham acknowledges that this "christological monotheism" was an innovation, yet he considers it consistent with Jewish monotheism. The very nature of Jewish beliefs in and practices toward God provided room for this development. Generally, Bauckham believes that Christology developed through creative readings of biblical texts such as Psalm 110:1 and the Shema. Early Christians mined every resource available in Scripture to sculpt a theology that includes Jesus within the unique identity of Israel's One, True God.

Like Bauckham, N. T. Wright does not think early Christology developed out of some modification of the Jewish category of divine agency. Instead, he argues, it was a robust concretizing of hopes concentrated on the one, true God and his promise to return one day to Zion.[22] Scholars who appeal to mediation traditions, Wright thinks, have started in the wrong place. If it is true that early Christians regarded Jesus as divine and worshiped him in ways previously thought to be appropriate only to God, why not begin with God rather than some exalted patriarchs, principal angels, or divine attributes? Wright notes that many Second Temple Jews held on to the conviction that Israel's God, having abandoned Jerusalem and the temple prior to its destruction (586 BCE), had promised to return to his people one day. He would return in person and in glory. He would return as judge and redeemer, specifically, to bring about a new exodus, overthrowing the enemies of Israel

---

21. Richard Bauckham, *God Crucified: Monotheism and Christology in the New Testament* (Grand Rapids: Eerdmans, 1998), vii.

22. N. T. Wright, *Paul and the Faithfulness of God* (Minneapolis: Fortress, 2013), 633.

and releasing God's people from exile. In short, God would return to be king. The origin of Christology, according to Wright, is "the long-awaited return of YHWH to Zion."[23] Israel's God had promised to return, and return he did in the person of Jesus the Christ.

British scholar Crispin Fletcher-Louis finds himself in broad agreement with aspects of what he calls the "emerging consensus" that has developed in NT christological studies thanks to the work of Hurtado and Bauckham.[24] The consensus holds that a fully divine Christology is early and located historically within a Jewish milieu; it did not arise late in the first century only after gentiles had streamed in and overtaken the Jesus movement. In the end, however, Fletcher-Louis does not think that divine identity or divine agency offers a satisfactory account of christological origins.

Although the worship of Jesus alongside God and beliefs in his divine identity are new and surprising, they could have been anticipated by anyone attuned to certain movements and ideas within Second Temple Judaism. To cite one example, the Similitudes of Enoch (1 En. 37–70) and Daniel 7:13 offer evidence that many Jews expected the arrival of a divine Messiah (likely of priestly significance). More controversially, the Life of Adam and Eve demonstrates that Jews before Christ would have been familiar with the worship of Adam, who served as an icon through which heavenly creatures worshiped God. While not the direct cause of what effectively becomes a reoriented Jesus-monotheism, such antecedent traditions provided the hook on which Jesus-followers could reasonably hang their way of thinking of Jesus as a new Adam.

Fletcher-Louis situates the causative factor not in powerful religious experiences in the aftermath of the resurrection but in Jesus's own self-consciousness. He claims that the historical Jesus had an incarnational self-consciousness that was expressed in his words and actions and remembered by his disciples. The resurrection, of course, is a key event, for the crucifixion appears to deny Jesus's messianic and divine claims. In the resurrection something happened to reverse the negating elements of Jesus's death and to confirm not only that Jesus is Israel's Messiah but also that he is the incarnation of a divine being. So Fletcher-Louis goes beyond scholarly predecessors in attempting to locate the belief in a divine Messiah in the self-awareness of Jesus.

Similarly, Andrew Ter Ern Loke makes the case that the teachings of Jesus provided the impetus needed for Jesus-followers to make divine claims about

---

23. Wright, *PFG*, 654. See Ezek. 1; Isa. 40–66; Zec.; Mal.; Sir. 24. In Sir. 24 YHWH returns to the temple in terms of divine Wisdom, codified in the Torah.

24. See Crispin Fletcher-Louis, *Jesus Monotheism: Christological Origins; The Emerging Consensus and Beyond* (Eugene, OR: Cascade, 2015).

him.²⁵ Jesus taught in such a way and claimed such things about himself as to, on reflection, demonstrate that he was divine and deserved to be reverenced along with God. Essentially, the resurrection prompted their memories of his teachings and served to validate those divine claims and actions. Unless Jesus had declared himself divine, Loke argues, his followers would have rejected any move to make him such.

As we have seen, scholars account for the phenomenon of Christology in various ways. They appeal to various forces and factors, including Jesus's own teachings, powerful religious experiences, angelic and other forms of divine mediation, categories of meaning and associations related to Jewish messianism, hopes and aspirations about the return of YHWH to Zion, and the notion of divine identity. In the end, a high Christology and the early worship of Jesus in the opening decades of the Christian movement was likely due not to a single factor but to the interplay of complex religious, social, and historical factors.

The Divine Christ

Discussions of the divinity of Christ have characterized NT christological studies the last twenty to thirty years. In addition to the areas already mentioned, scholars have attempted to explain NT Christology via patterns of exegesis and parallels between the OT and NT. The letters of Paul have been of particular interest.

In *Paul and the Faithfulness of God* (PFG), Wright notes that it has become "commonplace" for scholars to point out that Paul regularly referred to Jesus using scriptural quotations where the Greek word *kyrios* stands for the tetragrammaton.²⁶ Exactly how and when it became commonplace Wright does not say. This was a feature I discussed at length in an earlier book that investigated Paul's use of YHWH texts in reference to Jesus.²⁷

For an earlier generation of scholars, it was "commonplace" to say that in Paul's letters *kyrios* (Lord) refers to Jesus everywhere except in those passages where he is quoting an OT passage containing the divine name. In those verses, Paul refers to God the Father, not Jesus, by the *kyrios* predicate nominative. Scholars provided no reasons for this conclusion, nor did they offer any contextual analysis of these passages. It was merely a working assumption.

---

25. Andrew Ter Ern Loke, *The Origin of Divine Christology*, SNTSMS (Cambridge: Cambridge University Press, 2017).
26. Wright, *PFG*, 701.
27. David B. Capes, *Old Testament Yahweh Texts in Paul's Christology*, WUNT 2/47 (1992; repr., Waco: Baylor University Press, 2017); Capes, *The Divine Christ: Paul, the Lord Jesus, and the Scriptures of Israel* (Grand Rapids: Baker Academic, 2018).

A YHWH text refers to a quotation of or an allusion to an OT text that refers directly to the divine name. Since Paul writes to his churches in Greek, the interest has been in OT quotations and allusions containing the *kyrios* predicate nominative in which *kyrios* translates or renders the divine name. On a number of occasions Paul quotes from or alludes to an OT YHWH text and applies that Scripture to Jesus (e.g., Rom. 10:13 [Joel 2:32]; Rom. 14:11[Isa. 45:23]; Phil. 2:10–11 [Isa. 45:23]; 1 Thess. 3:13 [Zech. 14:5]). Many scholars today recognize the significance of this exegetical move; they note that Paul consciously and unambiguously applies to Jesus sacred words and texts originally reserved for YHWH, the unspeakable name of God. This has significant meaning for Jewish Christians like Paul; it means among other things that he included Jesus within the name, dignity, and identity of God. This practice, along with other patterns of religious devotion, points to a high Christology in the first extant documents of the Christian movement.

Working from another angle, Chris Tilling posed the questions of whether Paul's Christology can properly be described as "divine," in what sense, and how it came to be.[28] Tilling answers the first of these questions in the affirmative: Paul's Christology is indeed a divine Christology. While building on the work of others (Fee, Hurtado, Bauckham), Tilling mines another aspect of Paul's letters to add another level to the superstructure of an early high Christology.

The phrase that summarizes Tilling's approach is this: "The Christ-relation is Paul's divine-Christology expressed as relationship."[29] The Christ-relation language is significant in Paul, so significant that some scholars regard the center of Paul's theology to be "participation in Christ," a shorthand way of describing the many ways in which the Christ-believers stand in relationship to and participate in the life of Christ. Tilling notes that Christ's relation to his people stands in direct continuity with YHWH's relation to his people Israel. To put it another way, when Paul speaks about the relation between Christ-believers and the risen Jesus, he uses the same language and themes found in Second Temple Jewish texts to speak of Israel's relation to YHWH. Tilling consistently says the data form a pattern that Paul himself would have recognized. In Tilling's own words, "It will be maintained that this pattern of Christ-relation language in Paul is only that which a Jew used to express the relation between Israel/the individual Jew and YHWH. No other figure of any kind, apart from YHWH, was related to in the same way, with the same pattern of language, not even the various exalted human and angelic intermediary figures in the literature of Second Temple Judaism that

---

28. Chris Tilling, *Paul's Divine Christology*, WUNT 2/323 (Tübingen: Mohr Siebeck, 2012).
29. Tilling, *Paul's Divine Christology*, 3.

occasionally receive worship and are described in very exalted terms."[30] Tilling's work moves beyond quotations and allusions applied to Jesus from OT Scripture and highlights various patterns of language and relational categories that exist between God and Israel. This is a promising way ahead for future christological investigations.

The Worship of Jesus and Jewish Monotheism

In June 1998 St. Mary's College of the University of St. Andrews (Scotland) held the International Conference on the Origins of the Worship of Jesus. The thrust of the conference was to examine the phenomenon of Christ-devotion in early Christianity within the context of Jewish monotheism. Many of the scholars who attended agreed that early Christians did worship Jesus, but they disagreed on how this came about. Some focused on trying to understand the nature of pre-Christian monotheism. Others went in search of any antecedent practices that might explain how early Christians could worship Jesus within a monotheistic faith. Still others questioned whether the first generations of Christians, constrained by their monotheistic heritage, worshiped Jesus at all.

One of the scholars leading these discussions is Hurtado. Through dozens of published articles, conference papers, and a number of important books,[31] Hurtado continues to address some of the more salient questions about NT Christology:[32] How and when did the followers of Jesus begin to worship him and regard him as divine? How did Jewish monotheism contribute to or detract from how early Christians came to think of Jesus? What role did religious experience play in creating this new movement?

Hurtado is one of the founding members of the "Early High Christology Club,"[33] an informal fellowship of scholars from various continents, backgrounds, and institutional affiliations. Since its founding in the mid-1990s, many scholars have joined the ranks. All "members" make the case, in one way or another through published works, that a divine Christology emerges early among Jewish-Christians; it is not the result of centuries or even decades

---

30. Tilling, *Paul's Divine Christology*, 73.
31. Chief among these are Hurtado, *One God, One Lord*; Hurtado, *Lord Jesus Christ*; Hurtado, *How on Earth Did Jesus Become a God? Historical Questions about Earliest Devotion to Jesus* (Grand Rapids: Eerdmans, 2005).
32. Many of these articles have been gathered and published in an anchor volume as part of LEC by Baylor University Press. See Larry W. Hurtado, *Ancient Jewish Monotheism and Early Christian Jesus-Devotion: The Context and Character of Christological Faith*, LEC (Waco: Baylor University Press, 2017).
33. The original members are Larry Hurtado, Alan F. Segal, Carey Newman, and David Capes.

of assimilation with Greek and Roman ideas. Hurtado has been a pioneer in those discussions.[34]

At the core of Hurtado's project has been a consistent claim that practices, not beliefs, defined Roman-era religions including Christianity. Rather than thinking of "religion" primarily as system of beliefs—as most moderns do—Hurtado makes a cogent case that Roman-era society considered "religion" a set of practices; and no practice was more central to Roman religions than worship. Hurtado has argued routinely that the worship of Jesus constituted the single most remarkable development in early Christianity.

For Hurtado, early Christianity was distinguished from other religions by a constellation of devotional practices that featured Jesus as the rightful recipient. It was distinct from Judaism because it included the risen Jesus as a recipient of worship along with God. It was distinct from other Roman-era religions because it excluded the worship of all gods except the one, true God of Israel and the man seated at his right hand. If we wish to understand Christology, Hurtado insists that we focus on worship, not beliefs or doctrines.

Various practices and habits provide evidence that early Christians worshiped Jesus. First, they addressed him in prayer and prayed to God through him (Rom. 1:8; 1 Cor. 1:3; 16:22; 1 Thess. 3:11–13). Second, they invoked him and confessed him to be "Lord" (Acts 9:14, 21; Rom. 10:9–13; 1 Cor. 1:2). Third, they baptized new believers in Jesus's name (Acts 2:38; Rom. 6:3–4). Fourth, they routinely celebrated the Lord's Supper (1 Cor. 10:14–22; 11:17–34). Fifth, they composed and sang hymns, psalms, and spiritual songs in which Jesus features significantly (John 1:1–18; Eph. 5:18–20; Phil. 2:6–11; Col. 1:15–20; 3:16–17). Finally, they regarded prophecy uttered through Spirit inspiration to be the words of Jesus (1 Cor. 12:4–11; Rev. 1:9–16).

Put simply, the first followers of Jesus were convinced that God required them to revere Jesus. Those convictions were based on several factors: (a) how they remembered the earthly Jesus, (b) the conviction that God raised Jesus and exalted him to his right hand, (c) post-Easter prophecies and religious experience, and (d) a phenomenon known as "charismatic exegesis." The confluence of these forces and factors led to something completely new within a Jewish framework—that is, Jesus occupying a place of divine honor. How believers read and reread their Scriptures (roughly equivalent to our OT) in light of the life, death, burial, and resurrection of Jesus proved to be an important factor in Christology. Through charismatic exegesis OT stories are replotted on a new-covenant and new-creation grid so that Jesus takes on a remarkable role in Israel's story and has the divine name and status bestowed on him.

---

34. Hurtado, *Ancient Jewish Monotheism and Early Christian Jesus-Devotion*.

Hurtado has made the case that powerful religious experiences postresurrection caused these early Jewish followers to consider Jesus divine and to worship him. Apparently, through visions and prophetic utterances early Christians "saw" Jesus enthroned at God's right hand and came to "see" that worshiping Jesus was the will of God. While Fletcher-Louis applauds Hurtado's sense that we need to take seriously the role of religious experience, he does not consider it enough to account for what happened so quickly after Jesus's execution. The problem, as he sees it, is that with no precedent for the worship of a divine person or Messiah in pre-Christian Judaism or without taking seriously the possibility that Jesus's himself had a sense of his own divine identity, it is hard to account for the speed with which Christ-devotion developed and the exact shape it took in the first decades after Jesus's execution. It is more believable, according to Fletcher-Louis, that Jesus had a divine self-consciousness.[35]

Not all, of course, have agreed with Hurtado's findings. Some conclude the evidence cited does not add up to the kinds of innovations Hurtado describes. Most famously, James D. G. Dunn responded to Hurtado's claims in his 2010 book *Did the First Christians Worship Jesus?*[36] While affirming Hurtado's conclusions in the long run, Dunn analyzes the NT evidence and comes to a different conclusion. At first he appears to answer the title's question with a qualified yes; still, he comes finally to a qualified no: "No, *by and large* the first Christians did not worship Jesus *as such*."[37] Dunn's ambivalence is evident throughout the book. He often remarks that the early Christians' language and disposition toward Jesus is striking, remarkable, and without precedent in Judaism. He finds that the reverence addressed to Jesus is of a different order than reverence addressed to God. Early Christians may have adored Jesus, but they did not worship him.[38]

For many scholars, the question whether early Christians like Paul—or even before him—worshiped Jesus is settled, and the answer is yes. But others, like Dunn and Maurice Casey,[39] are not so sure. They know it happened eventually, but it was a later development that unfolded slowly, perhaps two

---

35. Fletcher-Louis, *Jesus Monotheism*.
36. James D. G. Dunn, *Did the First Christians Worship Jesus? The New Testament Evidence* (Louisville: Westminster John Knox Press, 2010).
37. Dunn, *Did the First Christians Worship Jesus?*, 150 (italics added).
38. In private conversation Dunn expressed to me that early Christians "adored" Jesus much as modern Christians "adore" the Virgin Mary. They would have understood worship as directed uniquely to God.
39. Maurice Casey, *From Jewish Prophet to Gentile God: The Origins and Development of New Testament Christology* (Louisville: Westminster John Knox, 1991). As the title suggests, Casey thinks Jesus was regarded among the first Jewish followers as a prophet of God; only later did gentiles exalt him and regard him as a God.

to three generations following the execution of Jesus. This continues to be a live question. More clarity will be needed on the patterns of language, dispositions, and actions that constitute worship and related claims of divine identity.

Issues in the Christology of the Synoptic Gospels

While the last few decades have witnessed a good deal of interest in Paul's Christology, some scholars have turned their attention to the Christology of the Synoptic Gospels. Simon Gathercole, for example, has argued that the preexistence of Jesus is not a perspective confined to the last Gospel written—that is, John's Gospel (e.g., John 1:1–18); he thinks a proper reading of the Synoptics demonstrates that it is implied there as well.[40] Historically, he notes, this would have been possible because a Christology of a preexistent Christ predated the writing the Synoptics by twenty to thirty years. While he considers a variety of texts within the Gospels, his major point is to show that many of the "I have come" statements imply that Jesus has come from somewhere to do something. And where would he have come from? From heaven. Gathercole goes in search of anything in Judaism that might help explain these kinds of sayings; he finds it in similar texts where angels are said to have come in order to accomplish a particular purpose. The angel clearly existed prior to its coming into the world, and so we ought to think of Jesus similarly. There are other sayings as well where Jesus describes himself as "sent," various Son of Man sayings (e.g., Luke 19:10: "For the Son of man came to seek out and to save the lost"), and other *logia* that describe Jesus in one way or another transcending a normal human life (Matt. 23:37). Although many scholars link the preexistence of Jesus with the notion of preexistent Wisdom (Prov. 8; Sir. 24; 1 En. 42), Gathercole plays down the explanatory value of that identification.

Another approach to Synoptic Christology comes from the discipline of narrative criticism.[41] At the heart of C. Kavin Rowe's project is what it meant to call Jesus *kyrios* (Lord) in Luke's Gospel. Since the narrative identity of any figure is not situated in this or that text, one must consider the book as a whole. The accumulation of qualities, features, images, sayings, and actions forms the narrative identity of Jesus in the Gospel of Luke. Rowe proposes that the infancy narratives (Luke 1–2) set the tone for the rest of the story. In the

---

40. Simon Gathercole, *The Preexistent Son: Recovering the Christologies of Matthew, Mark, and Luke* (Grand Rapids: Eerdmans, 2006).

41. C. Kavin Rowe, *Early Narrative Christology: The Lord in the Gospel of Luke*, BZNW 139 (Berlin: de Gruyter, 2006; Grand Rapids: Baker Academic, 2009).

infancy narratives not only is YHWH, the God of Israel, called *kyrios*, but so is Jesus. The identification of Jesus as *kyrios* along with Israel's one true God makes an essential claim about his unity with God. We should not overlook the fact that in Luke Jesus is *kyrios* from his birth, not from the resurrection.

More recently, Rowe's teacher, Richard Hays, has ventured into christological readings of the Gospels through figural interpretation.[42] Figural interpretation involves connecting two texts so that a past person (or event) signifies that person as well as another in the future. The interplay between those two texts brings greater insight to both texts. Each sheds light on the other. It is a way of "reading backward." This has nothing to do with past predictions that are "fulfilled" in the future, although there are places where Gospel writers appear to make those kinds of connections as well. At the heart of figural interpretation is the notion that a text might mean more than a human author ever intended. Once a writer has released his or her text, later audiences are able to read backward through significant events/persons in order to see connections.

Hays works carefully through the Gospel texts, listening for the echoes and helping his readers see and experience these in fresh and exciting ways. One example is the episode when Jesus walks on the Sea of Galilee (Mark 6:47–52). Although Mark does not make any explicit biblical allusions, the way he tells the story conjures up certain images from the Hebrew Bible. In particular, Hays notes how Mark says Jesus appears to intend to pass his disciples by (v. 48). Why does Mark include this unusual detail? Hays claims that the strange remark "He intended to pass them by" (v. 48) recalls Job 9, particularly the Greek version of Job 9:11 (LXX). Hays thinks there is a not-so-subtle identification of Jesus with the God who created the land and seas in the first place. In the end, Hays contends that the Gospel writers portray Jesus as the embodiment of the God of Israel.

How Jesus Became God

The question of how Jesus "became God" has come up from time to time. In 2014 Bart Ehrman, a popular historian and interpreter of early Christianity, dealt with the question in a book of the same title: *How Jesus Became*

---

42. Richard B. Hays's book *Echoes of Scripture in the Gospels* (Waco: Baylor University Press, 2016) extends an earlier project, *Reading Backwards: Figural Christology and the Fourfold Gospel Witness* (Waco: Baylor University Press, 2014). It echoes an even earlier work, *Echoes of Scripture in the Letters of Paul* (New Haven: Yale University Press, 1993). Hays's primary influence is the work of Eric Auerbach, *Mimesis: The Representation of Reality in Western Literature* (1953; repr., Princeton: Princeton University Press, 2013).

God.[43] The book was published by HarperOne the same year another group of scholars responded to Ehrman in a Zondervan publication: *How God Became Jesus.*[44] Ehrman's approach is familiar. Jesus did not claim to be God or divine. His earliest followers did not regard him as such, nor did they worship him during his earthly career. But shortly after his execution, some followers assigned to him divine status and began to worship him. Ehrman thinks that the conferral of divinity on Jesus comes about in part because Greco-Roman culture was awash in gods and divine humans (especially deified rulers); these cultural phenomena paved the road nicely for those who ended up claiming Jesus had "become" God.

Early witnesses that Jesus had conquered death and appeared to some of his followers catalyzed the claim (e.g., 1 Cor. 15:3–8). Ehrman likens these visions of Jesus to the kinds of hallucinations people have when they are bereaved. He distinguishes two types of divine Christology. Exaltation Christology is based on the conviction that God had bestowed on the man Jesus an exalted status in the resurrection. Somewhat later incarnational Christology develops, which claims that Jesus was a preexistent, divine being who came into the world. Both versions of Christology emerge relatively early and are assumed by Paul when he begins writing his letters in the 50s. So when Paul shares the christological hymn in Philippians 2:6–11, it contains elements of both (a) a preexistent one who becomes man and humbles himself to death on the cross and (b) a man whom God (super)exalts and grants the very name of God (YHWH-*kyrios*). As a result, the preexistent, exalted Jesus who bears God's name is rightly worshiped by heavenly, earthly, and under-earthly creatures.

Scholars have criticized Ehrman's reconstruction in the whole and in the details. For example, Ehrman claims on the basis of a single text (Gal. 4:14) that Paul considered Jesus an angel: "[You] welcomed me as an angel of God, as Christ Jesus."[45] Most interpreters read this in an ascending pattern, not as an identifying one.[46] Ehrman asserts that it is unlikely the crucified Jesus was ever buried, so there could not have been an empty tomb as the Gospels attest. But he fails to take into account the Jewish commitment to bury the dead, including those (wrongly) condemned as criminals (e.g., Tob. 1; Josephus, J.W. 4.317).[47] Another problem is that Ehrman characterizes NT texts rather

---

43. Bart D. Ehrman, *How Jesus Became God: The Exaltation of a Jewish Preacher from Galilee* (New York: HarperOne, 2014).

44. Michael F. Bird, Craig A. Evans, Simon J. Gathercole, Charles E. Hill, and Chris Tilling, *How God Became Jesus: The Real Origins of Beliefs in Jesus' Divine Nature* (Grand Rapids: Zondervan, 2014). Interestingly, Zondervan is a part of HarperCollins.

45. Ehrman, *How Jesus Became God*, 252.

46. E.g., Douglas Moo, *Galatians*, BECNT (Grand Rapids: Baker Academic, 2013), 285; Ronald Y. K. Fung, *The Epistle to the Galatians*, NICNT (Grand Rapids: Eerdmans, 1988), 198.

47. The essay by Craig A. Evans in Michael F. Bird et al., *How God Became Jesus* (Grand Rapids: Zondervan, 2014) (see esp. pp. 73–91), effectively challenges most of Ehrman's claims.

than engaging in close, contextual readings of them. Finally, Ehrman does not engage the significant published works of other scholars in the field (e.g., Bauckham, Tilling, Wright). When he does, he often mischaracterizes their work or misses their points altogether.

Hurtado also addresses the question in *How on Earth Did Jesus Become a God?* This brief volume summarizes and epitomizes his full-length study *Lord Jesus Christ*. Hurtado has spent a good part of his academic career arguing for what can be known in historical terms about the rise of religious devotion to Jesus in early Christianity. For Hurtado it is the most remarkable feature of early Christianity. But this remarkable feature did not evolve over a long time; it burst on the scene, in historical terms, quickly, not long after the execution of Jesus. The fact of Jesus-devotion can be seen primarily in the practices that characterize the churches' gatherings: hymns composed and sung about Jesus in worship; prayers addressed to and through Jesus, and in his name; the ritual invocation of Jesus's name in baptism, exorcism, and excommunications; participation in the "Lord's Supper"; prophecy uttered in Jesus's name. Yet apparently such lofty views of Jesus and the worship practices that flowed from it did not break the back of the Jewish commitment to the one God of Israel. Somehow, the worship of Jesus is accommodated without detracting from the honor due the one true God. On the contrary, to hymn his story, bow the knee to him, and confess him as *Kyrios* is the will of God (Phil. 2:9–11). Such was the nature of early Christian devotion, and this devotion set Jesus-followers on a collision course with powerful spiritual and political leaders. Like their Maccabean ancestors in the faith, they would not give in despite the heartache and trouble that followed. In the end Hurtado relies on the NT accounts and the social sciences to get at the nature and power of religious experience. Early Christians report experiencing potent visions and revelations of the risen Jesus that reframed their thinking about Scripture and the God of Israel. As they read and reread these texts, they made fantastic, innovative connections that many regarded as the work of the Spirit among them.

The Humanity of Jesus

In recent days there has been renewed interest in the humanity of Jesus. Some scholars feel that the emphasis on Jesus's divinity the last thirty years has misread the evidence and discounted those clear texts where the humanity of Jesus appears to be on display. Daniel Kirk, in particular, challenges those who believe the divinity of Jesus is evident in the Synoptic Gospels.[48] He attempts

---

48. J. R. Daniel Kirk, *A Man Attested by God: The Human Jesus of the Synoptic Gospels* (Grand Rapids: Eerdmans, 2016).

to reclaim the idealized humanity of Jesus that sits at the center of the first three Gospels. The tendency to read Matthew, Mark, and Luke through the lens of the Fourth Gospel or of Paul's divine Christology is misguided and ignores the clear sense of what the Gospels were intending to do. For the Gospel writers Jesus was an extraordinary figure not because of his deity but because of his humanity. The grand scheme of the Bible presents the God of Israel as one who does not give up on humanity. From the beginning God had a plan and vision for what humanity was supposed to be. So Kirk proposes that the Synoptics offer a "high human Christology"—that is, a fully realized humanity. In other words, the Synoptics present a Jesus who is everything humanity was created and supposed to be.

Now Kirk does not deny that the divinity of Christ is a feature of NT Christology. He just thinks the Synoptics tell a different sort of story, a story that can easily be lost in accentuating Jesus's divinity. As long as the stress is on Jesus's divinity, followers do not have to take seriously what it means to walk as he walked, forgive as he forgave, and love as he loved. In other words "following Jesus" can be subsumed in simply worshiping him.

With some similar interests, Brandon Crowe regards all the Gospels as presenting Jesus implicitly and explicitly as the last Adam.[49] Therefore, the Gospels read the life of Jesus over against the disobedient Adam of Genesis. If Adam is the type, then Jesus is the antitype. Crowe emphasizes Jesus's life of obedience to God and argues that his life, not just his death and resurrection, is critical to his work in salvation.

Reflections

Given the state of NT Christology, it will be appropriate for scholars in the future to consider how NT Christology contributed to what later becomes trinitarian doctrine. To do so, interpreters will need to lean heavily on second- and third-century data. In a recent book Matthew Bates argues that the NT and other early Christian writings employ a technique of "prosopological" exegesis that, along with other factors, contributed to defining and describing the doctrine of the Trinity. In prosopological exegesis, readers overhear the "persons" of the Trinity speaking to one another; they are let in on the relationship between Father, Son, and Spirit, which can only be "characterized by relentless affection and concern for one another."[50] The NT books

---

49. Brandon Crowe, *The Last Adam: A Theology of the Obedient Life of Jesus in the Gospels* (Grand Rapids: Baker Academic, 2017).

50. Matthew W. Bates, *The Birth of the Trinity: Jesus, God, and Spirit in New Testament and Early Christian Interpretations of the Old Testament* (Oxford: Oxford University Press, 2015), 7.

contain a variety of conversations at key junctures in the career of Jesus: preexistence, incarnation, earthly mission, death on the cross, the resurrection, and enthronement. One of the best-known examples is Psalm 2:7—"You are my son; today I have begotten you"—spoken by the Father to the Son at the baptism and transfiguration (Mark 1:11 and parallels; Mark 9:2–8 and parallels; Acts 13:32–35; Heb. 5:5). Jesus's identity is thereafter wrapped up "with this scripturally informed 'You are my Son' conviction."[51] Another important example is the dialogue between Father and Son at the incarnation (Heb. 10:5–7, quoting Ps. 40:6–8 [LXX]). Bates's approach is sure to provoke discussion around the question of how Christians may have overheard the voice of Father, Son, and Spirit in their Scriptures and how this hermeneutic might have contributed to NT and post-NT Christologies.

Another fruitful avenue already being explored is the intersection of the divinity and humanity of Jesus. What sort of humanity does Jesus represent? If early Christians believed in the divinity of Christ and reverenced him as or alongside God, then how did they think about his humanity? From all accounts, the physical body of Jesus mattered, but why and in what way? And how does that address human embodiment generally? The field of theological anthropology can help us think through some of these issues.

If, as some scholars hold, Jesus represents the ideal of humanity—what humans are and are supposed to be—then what is that ideal, and how are Christ-followers to imitate it? Do early Christian perspectives on Jesus's humanity and embodiment reframe how dearly Christians think about their own humanity in light of this? The field of theological anthropology can help us think through some of these issues.

Finally, scholars need to continue to explore how the life, teachings, and actions of Jesus informed the Christology of early believers. Did what Jesus said and did during his earthly ministry influence what his disciples came to think of him? If so, how? Immediately, we are thrown into the questions related to the historical Jesus and how his disciples remembered him. Over the past twenty years a good deal of work has been done to apply social and cultural memory theory to the Jesus tradition. These studies will continue to be important as we continue to assess the significance of Jesus in the opening decades of the common era.[52]

---

51. Bates, *Birth of the Trinity*, 65–66.
52. Bart D. Ehrman, *Jesus before the Gospels: How the Earliest Christians Remembered, Changed, and Invented Their Stories of the Savior* (New York: HarperOne, 2016); Richard Bauckham, *Jesus and the Eyewitnesses: The Gospels as Eyewitness Testimony*, 2nd ed. (Grand Rapids: Eerdmans, 2017; first published 2006); Alan Kirk, *Memory and the Jesus Tradition* (London: Bloomsbury T&T Clark, 2018).

9

Paul, a Jew among Jews, Greeks, and Romans

MICHAEL F. BIRD

Introduction

One of the few undisputed things in Pauline scholarship is that the apostle Paul was a man who inhabited three worlds: the Jewish, the Greek, and the Roman.[1] Of course, it would be a grievous mistake to regard those worlds as insulated and siloed from one another, as if to say that Paul was *religiously* Jewish, *culturally* Greek, and *politically* Roman. The reality is that Paul's beliefs and worldview were not so neatly compartmentalized, so it is more fitting to say that Paul's Jewishness, Greekness, and Romanness made themselves felt in his religious, cultural, and political expressions. Paul was, after all, a Jewish Messiah-believer, reared in the Hellenistic diaspora, and operating largely within Roman city-states and provinces. Paul was, just like others of his time, a complex and synthetic person, shaped by a confluence of contexts, while appropriating and interacting with those contexts in different ways. Accordingly, a more contested matter is how Paul related to the Jewish, Greek, and Roman worlds in terms of absorbing their frames, resisting their norms, and negotiating their complexities. So it is more fitting to ask, *How*

---

1. See Richard Wallace and Wynne Williams, *The Three Worlds of Paul of Tarsus* (London: Routledge, 1998).

is Paul Jewish, *how* is Paul Greek, and *how* is Paul Roman? In fact, much of Pauline scholarship has vigorously argued over these very issues, to the point that a survey of Paul in relation to these tripartite worlds is a good entrée into Pauline scholarship and a helpful way of trying to understand Paul in his own setting. Therefore, this chapter aims to describe Paul as a figure among Jews, Greeks, and Romans with a view to acquiring firsthand familiarity with Pauline scholarship on the matters.

Paul among the Jews

Paul, as a direct result of his Damascus Road experience, became a Jewish "Messiah-believer."[2] In addition, Paul continued to self-identify as a Jew[3] even as he undertook his missiological vocation as an apostle of Messiah Jesus to the gentiles (Rom. 9:3–4; 2 Cor. 11:22; Gal. 2:15; Phil. 3:5; cf. Acts 21:39; 22:3). Even though Paul strenuously resisted any attempt by Jewish messianic competitors to compel his gentile converts to judaize to the point of circumcision (e.g., Gal. 2:1–21; 5:1–13; 6:12–13; Phil. 3:1–11), nonetheless, Paul deliberately moved his mostly gentile assemblies within the orbit of Jewish belief and practice by insisting on the theological tenets of monotheism (e.g., Rom. 3:30; 1 Cor. 8:4–6; Gal. 3:20), proclaiming an overt messianism (e.g., 1 Cor. 1:18–2:5; 15:1–5; Gal. 3:1), prohibiting idolatry (e.g., Rom. 1:18–32; 1 Cor. 6:9; 10:7, 14; 12:2; 2 Cor. 6:16; 1 Thess. 1:9), forbidding sexual immorality and intermarriage with unbelievers (e.g., 1 Cor. 5:1–13; 7:1–2; 10:8; 2 Cor. 6:14–15; 12:21; Gal. 5:19; 1 Thess. 4:3), setting forth the normative nature of Jewish sacred texts (e.g., Rom. 15:4; 1 Cor. 4:6; 6:16), and identifying his assemblies as standing in continuity with "Israel" as God's historical covenant people (e.g., Rom. 4:23–25; 9:6, 24–26; 1 Cor. 10:11; Gal. 6:16). Viewed this way, Paul's converts did in fact judaize by abandoning the religious beliefs

---

2. I say "Messiah-believer" in order to avoid the anachronistic problems of calling Paul a "Christian."

3. Debates revolve around how to define Jewishness, being *Ioudaios*, whether it is ethnic, religious, or territorial, or a mix of these (see Daniel R. Schwartz, "'Judaean' or 'Jew'? How Should We Translate *Ioudaios* in Josephus?," in *Jewish Identity in the Greco-Roman World*, ed. Jörg Frey, Daniel R. Schwartz, and Stephanie Gripentrog, AJEC 71 [Leiden: Brill, 2007], 3–27); on Judaism as an ethno-religious classification, note the definition of Joshua Ezra Burns: "I propose to define ancient Judaism as a dynamic objective connoting different characteristics in different contexts. Nevertheless I maintain that the idea of Jewish identity guiding that objective was predicated on certain fixed assumptions as to its subject's cultic, ethical, and intellectual orientation. In other words, while ancient Jews were not subject to a monolithic standard of cultural identification, they generally perceived their collective as one bound by a set of practices and beliefs unique to their nation, if not always to the exclusion of practices or beliefs learned from other nations." Burns, *The Christian Schism in Jewish History and Jewish Memory* (Cambridge: Cambridge University Press, 2016), 67.

and practices of Greco-Roman cities and joining a Jewish messianic sect open to the admission of gentiles, albeit without circumcision, observing Jewish dietary laws, or celebrating Jewish holy days.[4]

We observe an example of Paul's "creative fidelity"[5] to Judaism in a close reading of Romans 4 and Galatians 3–4, where Paul effectively dissolved the social position of "God-fearer," a gentile guest or partial adherent who did not have the same insider status as Jews.[6] Paul claimed that through faith and allegiance to Jesus as the crucified and risen Messiah, the way was now open for gentiles to know and worship the God of Israel *as* gentiles. Gentiles could be equal with Jews in social settings, by *pistis* (faith, trust, allegiance), because they were *dikaios* (righteous) before God without observing the Jewish cultus and customs and without assimilating to the Jewish ethos and *ethnos*.[7] Paul brought his largely gentile assemblies into the theological, ethical, and social orbit of Judaism, and thus Paul was arguably the most successful evangelist of the Jewish religion in its history.

But that is only one side of the ledger; we also have to countenance how Paul's thought and practice caused a rupture with his fellow Jewish Messiah-believers and with other Jews as well.

First, concerning his own position vis-à-vis Jews and Judaism, Paul can list his inherited privileges as a Jewish-born Pharisee and then crassly claim that he now considers those privileges as "refuse" or "crap" compared to knowing the Messiah (Phil. 3:4–8). In postconversion hindsight, Paul reconfigures the memory of his former "way of life in Judaism," with stress on its Pharisaic expression, which is now removed from his current way of life *en Christō* (Gal. 1:13–16 CSB). Elsewhere Paul regards Jewishness as something he plays, puts on, or acts out in order to recruit Jews to the messianic assemblies; while this might be hypocrisy, it cannot be explained away as hyperbole (1 Cor. 9:20).[8] Paul also located his identity and that of other Messiah-believers from other ethnic groups in a position that is "in Messiah," where ethnic, social, and gender distinctions are *in some sense* nullified (Gal. 3:28; Col. 3:11). While Paul no longer saw himself "in Judaism," at least its Pharisaic Judean expression (Gal. 1:13), he did not consider his gentile converts any longer in "paganism"

---

4. See Paula Fredriksen, "Judaizing the Nations: The Ritual Demands of Paul's Gospel," *NTS* 56 (2010): 232–52.

5. Patrick Gray, *Paul as a Problem in History and Culture: The Apostle Paul and His Critics through the Centuries* (Grand Rapids: Baker Academic, 2016), 209.

6. See Michael F. Bird, *Crossing over Sea and Land: Jewish Missionary Activity in the Second Temple Period* (Peabody, MA: Hendrickson, 2010), 134–40.

7. For more on these issues see Michael F. Bird, *The Saving Righteousness of God* (Eugene, OR: Wipf & Stock, 2007).

8. Contra E. P. Sanders, *Paul: The Apostle's Life, Letters, and Thought* (Minneapolis: Fortress, 2015), 110–11.

(1 Cor. 12:2; 1 Thess. 1:9; 4:5). They had entered into a new social horizon and occupied an ambiguous socioreligious space (Gal. 3:28; Col. 3:11). We might say that they constituted a "third race,"[9] since Paul divided humanity into the classes of "Jews . . . Greeks [and] the church of God" (1 Cor. 10:32). It would be a mistake to infer from this that Paul founded or invented Christianity; more properly, Paul introduced a "forged mutational Jewish identity" that included gentiles within it.[10]

Second, in regard to the Torah, Paul is brutally confronting in his pronouncements. To begin with, Paul asserts that a Messiah-believing Jew like himself (Gal. 2:19) and Messiah-believing gentiles (Rom. 7:4) have died to the Torah by dying with the Messiah (Rom 6:1–14; Gal. 2:20). Paul considers himself not under Torah but instead under God's torah which is the Messiah's torah (1 Cor. 9:20–21). Obeying the Torah is not an instrument of divine deliverance for Jews or gentiles; instead, the Torah brings knowledge of sin (Rom. 3:20), brings divine wrath (4:15), and amplifies evil rather than rectifies persons (5:20). In a jarring statement, Paul declares, "All who rely on the works of the Torah are under a curse" (Gal. 3:10 NRSV alt.), which implies that all Jews who endeavor to please God by living a faithful life under Torah are merely rearranging the furniture on a sinking ship. Furthermore, Paul locates the Torah within a triumvirate of evil powers comprising Torah-Sin-Death, from which humanity needed deliverance (Rom. 8:2; 1 Cor. 15:56). Paul comes within a bee's whisker of saying that the Torah was from angels and not from God (Gal. 3:19–20) and that for gentiles to obey the Torah is tantamount to becoming enslaved again to pagan deities (4:8–9). Paul believed that there was a problem with humanity that Israel's Torah and covenants could not fix.[11] This yields a number of discontinuities from common Judaism in regard to the divine agency and instrument of human appropriation for salvation.[12]

Third, the social practices that Paul prescribes clearly pushed the boundaries of common Judaism. Paul can advocate Jews and gentiles eating together (Gal. 2:11–14) and eating food sacrificed to idols (1 Cor. 8:1–10; 10:25–30). This is significant given how many other Messiah-believing Jews regarded eating with gentiles or consuming impure food as clearly disloyal to God (Acts 11:1–3; Gal. 2:12; Rev. 2:14, 20) and given that many Jews regarded some form of separation/abstention from eating with gentiles as paramount (e.g.,

---

9. Aristides, *Apol.* 15; see N. T. Wright, *Paul and the Faithfulness of God* (London: SPCK, 2013), 1444–49; E. P. Sanders, *Paul, the Law, and the Jewish People* (Minneapolis: Fortress, 1983), 171–79.

10. Ellis Rivkin, "Paul's Jewish Odyssey," *Judaism* 38 (1989): 233.

11. Bruce Longenecker, *The Triumph of Abraham's God: The Transformation of Christian Identity in Galatians* (Nashville: Abingdon, 1998), 77–79.

12. Michael F. Bird, *An Anomalous Jew: Paul among Jews, Greeks, and Romans* (Grand Rapids: Eerdmans, 2017), 31–69.

Let. Aris. 139; Jub. 22:16; Josephus, *Ag. Ap.* 2.174; Tacitus, *Hist.* 5.5.1, 2). Paul can do this because in a blatantly blasé manner he voids the entire suite of scriptural regulations pertaining to *kashrut*, Jewish dietary regulations about impure food (Rom. 14:14). Certainly there was a range of options for how and to what degree diaspora Jews and gentiles could interact in social spaces and share meals.[13] Even so, we have to remember that diaspora Jews largely observed Jewish dietary customs,[14] and disregard for food laws was a surefire way to get oneself accused of apostasy in diaspora communities (see 4 Macc. 4:26).[15]

Despite Paul's explicit negative statements about the Torah and his practice of infringing Jew-gentile boundaries as some Jews constructed them, it would be mistaken to conceive of Paul as rejecting the Torah outright and in toto. More properly, Paul engaged in repudiation of the Torah for certain ends (i.e., consummated salvation and community boundaries), the relativization of the Torah for personal practice (see esp. Rom. 14), and a retooling of the Torah as prophecy and wisdom in light of the revelation of the end of ages (see, e.g., Rom. 3:21; 1 Cor. 9:9).[16] That said, no matter how concerted one's apology for Paul as a Jewish thinker, this is all very difficult to square with common Jewish beliefs about living a faithful life under the aegis of the Torah.

Fourth, Paul received a violent and hostile response from his fellow Jews both in the diaspora and in Judea. Just as Paul once persecuted the Judean churches, so too he was persecuted by his fellow Jews for his faith in the Messiah and his service to Syrian, Asian, and Aegean churches (2 Cor. 11:24–26; Gal. 5:11; 1 Thess. 3:3–4, 7). Paul was persecuted by Jewish groups most probably because he was perceived as fomenting "a rogue cult" that was "damaging Judaism and misleading gentiles by telling them that they could worship the God of Israel without becoming Jewish."[17] Or else, he was allegedly a bad influence on diaspora Jews, purportedly telling them that the Torah no longer mattered for them (see Acts 21:21; Rom. 3:7–8). In which case, as Jewish as Paul was, he provoked ire, umbrage, and violence from his fellow Jews. He conceived of his own identity and vocation as indelibly connected to Israel's sacred history but determined more properly by his connection to Israel's Messiah. He paradoxically regarded the Torah as both repudiated and

---

13. See Markus Bockmuehl, *Jewish Law in Gentile Churches* (Grand Rapids: Baker Academic, 2000), 57–59.

14. E. P. Sanders, *Jewish Law from Jesus to the Mishnah: Five Studies* (Minneapolis: Fortress, 2016), 37.

15. John M. G. Barclay, "Who Was Considered an Apostate in the Jewish Diaspora?," in *Pauline Churches and Diaspora Jews: Beyond the New Perspective*, WUNT 275 (Tübingen: Mohr Siebeck, 2011), 141–55 (esp. 151–54).

16. Brian R. Rosner, *Paul and the Law*, NSBT (Downers Grove, IL: InterVarsity Press, 2013).

17. Sanders, *Paul: The Apostle's Life*, 194–95, 494.

reappropriated in the new age that had dawned in Messiah Jesus. He described Messiah-believers as sharing in Israel's blessings without the symbols of their covenantal belonging and as incipiently experiencing the new creation ahead of the nation of Israel.

Viewed this way, Paul arguably initiated the gradual gentilization of the church and unconsciously contributed to the eventual "parting of the ways" between Christianity and Judaism.[18] Indeed, in the post-70 CE and post-135 CE era, Paul's messianic wine would eventually burst the old wine skins of Judaism. However, such a parting was never Paul's intention. In Paul's mind, as far as we can surmise, he was bringing Judaism to its eschatological climax in the Messiah by recasting Jewish identity and hope in light of the Messiah's death, resurrection, and future return. If anyone was responsible for founding Christianity, declares Patrick Gray, it was perhaps those Jewish leaders who determined that the teachings of Paul and other like-minded Messiah-believers threatened to stretch Judaism to a breaking point and that those teachings therefore warranted ostracism.[19]

Quite clearly Paul's relationship to Judaism was deeply complex. We've observed how Paul can affirm, recast, and repudiate various aspects of Jewish identity, practices, and beliefs. The challenge in scholarship has been over how we best describe this phenomenon.

One section of scholarship sees Paul as fully fitted within Judaism and varyingly tries to understand Paul's reasoning and rhetoric, his proclamation and practices, and the social location of his gentile converts as part of in-house Jewish debates about gentiles and messianic faith in relation to Jewish communities.[20] Others accentuate discontinuity and regard Paul as a former Jew who was in the process of breaking out, theologically and socially, from Judaism. Barthian interpreters see Paul leaving behind Israel's religion in light of the rupture caused by the Christ event.[21] Or else Paul was a catalyst in transitioning certain Messiah-believing communities from a reform movement within Judaism to a new social entity that was independent of and insulated from Jewish synagogue communities.[22] In addition,

---

18. See Alan Segal, *Paul the Convert: The Apostolate and Apostasy of Saul the Pharisee* (New Haven: Yale University Press, 1990), 267; James D. G. Dunn, *The Parting of the Ways: Between Christianity and Judaism and Their Significance for the Character of Christianity* (London: SCM, 1990), 139; Sanders, *Paul, the Law*, 207–10.

19. Gray, *Paul as a Problem*, 132.

20. See Mark D. Nanos and Magnus Zetterholm, eds., *Paul within Judaism: Restoring the First-Century Context to the Apostle* (Minneapolis: Fortress, 2015).

21. I'm thinking here of J. Louis Martyn, *Galatians*, AB (New Haven: Yale University Press, 1997).

22. Francis Watson, *Paul, Judaism, and the Gentiles: Beyond the New Perspective*, rev. ed. (Grand Rapids: Eerdmans, 2007).

given Paul's jolting statements in Galatians 3:28 and 1 Corinthians 9:19–23, some scholars conceive of Paul as locating himself and his converts away from Judaism and placing them in a new ethnoracial category based on being in Christ.[23] Then there is another band of scholars, largely associated with the New Perspective on Paul, who emphasize how Paul in essence was a transformed Jew. Paul was enmeshed in Jewish sectarian debates about gentiles, purity, and Torah, and resourced messianic faith and the experience of the Holy Spirit to engage such debates. In effect, Paul does not repudiate Judaism but redraws the Jewish worldview, symbols, and story around Jesus as the Lord and Messiah.[24]

One approach I find helpful is to describe Paul as an "anomalous Jew."[25] The designation is indebted to John Barclay, who originally identified Paul as anomalous in the sense that Paul was strongly antagonistic toward Hellenistic religion and culture, even while he radically defined traditional Jewish categories and adopted a lifestyle and a theology that questioned the normativity of his ancestral customs.[26] Paul was confronting the same issues as other Jews in the diaspora, much like Philo of Alexandria or Josephus, on how to be faithful under Greco-Roman hegemony and what to do with gentile adherents to Jewish ways. But Paul was distinctive in the sense of having a particular view of God's revelation of himself in Israel's crucified and risen Messiah and holding to a particular belief that the end of ages was now already a burgeoning reality. So Paul stood out because, as Ronald Charles says, "Paul was a diasporic male Judean of low social status negotiating different spaces; he was a devotee and interpreter of Christ among the nations; he was socially deviant, with little of an economic or political power base, and in the process of signifying a new empire under the authority of Christ in the first-century Mediterranean world."[27]

That said, I do not see the essence of the Pauline anomaly to be the paradoxes involved in Paul's attempt to negotiate his way within the Jewish diaspora. Instead, Paul's anomaly was the social praxes that followed from his messianic eschatology—namely, his attempt to create a social space for a unified body of Jewish and gentile Messiah-believers worshiping God. For Paul, this anomaly was known to him as the "revelation of Jesus Christ"

---

23. Love L. Sechrest, *A Former Jew: Paul and the Dialectics of Race*, LNTS 410 (London: T&T Clark, 2009).

24. See esp. Wright, *PFG*; James D. G. Dunn, *The New Perspective on Paul*, rev. ed. (Grand Rapids: Eerdmans, 2008).

25. See Bird, *Anomalous Jew*, 25–27.

26. John Barclay, *Jews in the Mediterranean Diaspora, from Alexander to Trajan* (London: T&T Clark, 1996), 381–95; Barclay, "Paul among Diaspora Jews: Anomaly or Apostate?," *JSNT* 60 (1995): 89–120.

27. Ronald Charles, *Paul and the Politics of Diaspora* (Minneapolis: Fortress, 2014), 248.

(Gal. 1:12), which disclosed how faith in the Messiah without Torah was the instrument that brought Jews and gentiles into reconciliation with God and into the renewal of all things. In my estimation, the anomalous nature of Paul's thought consists of his apocalyptic interpretation of the Messiah's death and resurrection, which forced him into a rereading of Jewish Scripture and into a praxis that yielded a transformation of "common Judaism," whereby the story and symbols of Judaism were now redrawn around Jesus the Messiah and his followers, who constituted the renewed Israel of an inaugurated eschaton.[28]

Paul among the Greeks

The world that Paul inhabited was Hellenistic. Since the conquests of Alexander the Great, the eastern Mediterranean had been colonized by and acculturated to Greek culture in varying degrees. While "Judaism" (*Ioudaismos*) was first couched as a form of resistance against "Hellenism" (*Hellēnismos*), particularly during the Maccabean period, by the time of Paul's day, all Judaism, in Palestine and in the diaspora, had been touched by Hellenism.[29]

Paul clearly traversed Jewish and Hellenistic cultures. Due to his family upbringing, education, and travels to Palestine, Paul was undoubtedly familiar with the challenges of diasporan communities, Judean social life, Pharisaic halakah, protorabbinic scriptural interpretation, and the Jerusalem cultus, yet his mother tongue and intellectual orientation were thoroughly Hellenistic. Paul grew up in Tarsus in Cilicia (Acts 22:3), a city known for its philosophers and schools, where he was very probably exposed to Hellenistic philosophy, literature, and rhetoric.[30] Paul wrote in Greek, and one can find various resonances or parallels between his letters and motifs in Hellenistic philosophy.[31] At one point, Paul quotes a popular proverb of Euripides extant in Menander's comedy *Thais* (1 Cor. 15:33), and Luke portrays Paul as quoting the Cilician Stoic poet Aratus (Acts 17:28). Paul was an itinerant speaker and knew he was in danger of being

---

28. Bird, *Anomalous Jew*, 25–27.
29. See Martin Hengel, *Judaism and Hellenism: Studies in Their Encounter in Palestine during the Hellenistic Period*, trans. J. Bowden, 2 vols. (Philadelphia: Fortress, 1974); Anders Gerdmar, *Rethinking the Judaism-Hellenism Dichotomy: A Historiographical Case Study of Second Peter and Jude*, ConBNT 36 (Stockholm: Almqvist & Wiksell, 2001); Troels Engberg-Pedersen, ed., *Paul beyond the Judaism/Hellenism Divide* (Louisville: Westminster John Knox, 2001).
30. For a sketch of Paul's early life see N. T. Wright, *Paul: A Biography* (San Francisco: HarperOne, 2018), 27–102.
31. Abraham Malherbe, *Paul and the Popular Philosophers* (Minneapolis: Fortress, 1989); M. Eugene Boring, Klaus Berger, and Carsten Colpe, *Hellenistic Commentary to the New Testament* (Nashville: Abingdon, 1995).

mistaken for a charlatan philosopher for hire (1 Cor. 9:1–19; 2 Cor. 2:17; 1 Thess. 2:1–12). When hitting his argumentative stride, Paul was able to express opinions on divinity, virtue, natural law, sexual desire, friendship, marriage, and the body politic with the same high-caliber discourse as any of his learned contemporaries.[32] Paul could express pessimism about philosophy (Rom. 2:1–11; 1 Cor. 1:18–2:8; 2 Cor. 10:5; Col. 2:8) even while exemplifying rhetorical verve and demonstrating remarkable philosophical fluency, meaning he probably engaged in a mixture of confrontation and adaptation of Greco-Roman philosophy.[33] In fact, it is no stretch of the imagination to conceive of Paul as a Greek intellectual, like Philo of Alexandria or Plutarch, and his thought has left an indelible imprint on Western philosophy and civilization.[34]

One particular debate has been the extent to which Paul is indebted to Stoic philosophy. The Stoics were a school of Hellenistic philosophy derived from Zeno (ca. 333–264 BCE), concerned with logic, physics, and ethics. Stoic philosophy subsequently developed and was diversely expressed by many of Zeno's subsequent followers, not least by Epictetus and Seneca in the first century. The name *Stoics* derived from the Athenian "painted porch" (*Stoa Poikilē*) where Zeno taught. Stoicism is a classic form of pantheism that sees divinity in everything. The Greek gods, Zeus and company, were all manifestations of the one divinity who permeated all things. Stoics viewed world history as based on a repetitious cycle, though one day a great cosmic conflagration would purify the world and bring it to a time of peace and stillness. The chief goal of Stoic philosophy was moral enlightenment, cultivating virtue and pruning vice, with the hope of becoming wise and virtuous, attaining self-mastery, and living in accordance with nature.[35]

There are various points of contact between Stoic tradition and the NT in general and Paul in particular.[36] Troels Engberg-Pedersen has used the Stoic tradition to engage in a philosophical exegesis of Paul in order to illuminate much of Paul's thought in regard to conversion, cosmology, moral citizenship and fellowship, the church as an ideal society, exhortation and ethics, and the

---

32. See Joseph R. Dodson and David E. Briones, *Paul and the Giants of Philosophy: Reading the Apostle in Greco-Roman Context* (Downers Grove, IL: InterVarsity, 2019).

33. Wright, *PFG*, 201.

34. See Stanislas Breton, *The Radical Philosophy of Saint Paul* (New York: Columbia University Press, 2011).

35. For a short summary of Stoicism see Wright, *PFG*, 211–29; for a fuller discussion, John Sellars, *Stoicism* (Berkeley: University of California, 2006).

36. On Stoicism and the NT, see Howard Clark Kee, *The Beginnings of Christianity: An Introduction to the New Testament* (New York: T&T Clark, 2005), 451–62; Troels Engberg-Pedersen, "Stoicism in Early Christianity," in *The Routledge Handbook on the Stoic Tradition*, ed. John Sellars (London: Routledge, 2015), 29–43.

nature of the Spirit.³⁷ This approach has some traction given Paul's claim in Philippians 4:11 to having learned "self-mastery" (*autarkēs*), which is quintessentially Stoic; his fictional soliloquy in Romans 7:7–25 rehearses the problem of a "weakness of the will" (*akrasia*) known to Stoics; his description of a cosmic renovation in Romans 8:18–25 resembles Stoic accounts of "cosmic flagration" (*ekpyrōsis*) and re-creation (*palingenesis*); and his exhortations about love, goodness, and virtue in Philippians 4:8 and Romans 12:9–21 all play well in a Stoic key. Paul certainly can sound Stoic in his ethics and ability to put up with hardship.

However, Paul's faith and fortitude are resourced in a very different reality—new creation in the Messiah—and his quest for moral improvement has a different goal: conformity to the Messiah rather than the untroubled life or indifference to suffering. If Paul seeks to live in accord with nature, it will be the new nature, the new person, the new creation, embodied in the Messiah and life in the Spirit. Stoics principally wanted to form the individual, whereas Paul was about forming communities.³⁸ Paul was not a first-century moralizing philosopher of the Stoic variety with a few daft ideas about Jesus, Torah, and the end of the world. Nor was Paul a messianic fanatic who had memorized a few good Stoic aphorisms. Rather, Paul knew and could speak the moral language of the agora and Areopagus, but he did so out of a Jewish narrative that was retold in a messianic and pneumatic key. In addition, C. Kavin Rowe wonders if Christianity and Stoicism, for all their similarities, remain deeply rival traditions over the very nature of God, goodness, and cosmos that result in living very different kinds of lives. He states, "The Christians and the Stoics are not, in the profoundest and most difficult philosophical sense, saying the same thing. They face each other with different and competing stories about all that is. . . . They are, permanently and irreducibly, traditions in conflict."³⁹

Paul could no doubt hold his own in a philosophical symposium, and some Christians even tried to imagine what Paul would say to Seneca in the fourth-century pseudepigraphical Letters of Paul and Seneca. For all of Paul's warnings about pagan pageantry and philosophy, he clearly resources Hellenistic ideas and tropes as part of his effort to "take every thought captive to obey

---

37. Troels Engberg-Pedersen, "Stoicism in Philippians," in *Paul in His Hellenistic Context*, ed. Troels Engberg-Pedersen (Edinburgh: T&T Clark, 1994), 256–90; Engberg-Pedersen, *Paul and the Stoics* (Edinburgh: T&T Clark, 2000); Engberg-Pedersen, *Cosmology and Self in Paul: The Material Spirit* (Oxford: Oxford University Press, 2011); Engberg-Pedersen, "Stoicism in Early Christianity," 29–43; Tuomas Rasimus, Troels Engberg-Pedersen, and Ismo Dunderberg, eds., *Stoicism in Early Christianity* (Grand Rapids: Baker Academic, 2010).

38. Wright, *PFG*, 1359–407.

39. C. Kavin Rowe, *One True Life: The Stoics and Early Christians as Rival Traditions* (New Haven: Yale University Press, 2016), 235.

Christ" (2 Cor. 10:5), even if his overall framework is radically different. Paul can indeed be placed among the Greek and Roman philosophers.

Paul among the Romans

Paul's relationship with the Roman Empire and with its provincial officials, media, and footprint in cities in the eastern Mediterranean is a scintillating topic.[40] The Roman Empire was an impinging sociopolitical reality, everywhere felt even if not always visible, known in relation to everything from taxes to games to religion to laws to commerce and political appointments. Of course, Roman power was expressed and experienced differently, whether through client rulers like Herod the Great and Herod Antipas, through direct rule over a province like Achaia or Judea, or in free cities that were granted special privileges like exemption from taxation, as in the case of Philippi. Moreover, as many have noted, the Roman Empire, with its networks of roads and sea channels, relative peace and security, urbanization, religious pluralism, economic opportunities, literary culture, common languages, and smelting pot of peoples, is what largely facilitated the expansion and rise of Christianity in the ancient world.[41] The questions are, What did Paul think of the Roman Empire? Did he think it was a good thing to be Christianized or a bad thing to be overthrown? Was Paul a Constantinian Catholic or a radical Anabaptist? Would Paul rather hang out with the Jewish apostate and imperial apparatchik Tiberius Alexander, or would he find more in common with the Qumran sectarians, who wanted an angelic army to annihilate the Romans? Would Paul rather have been Nero's chaplain or Nero's assassin?[42]

The argument is intriguing and involves asking questions for which we do not have explicit answers in Paul. On the one hand, Paul regarded the empire as a benign entity or perhaps even a nonentity. Judging from Paul's letters, he was hardly engaged in political activism, as he nowhere tries to organize a cabal for the Judean People's Front, nor does he signal agendas analogous to #OccupyRome or #SlaveLivesMatter. Plus, Jewish responses to Roman power were remarkably diverse, depending upon one's social position

---

40. See Michael Bird, "Rome, Roman Empire," in *The Baker Illustrated Bible Dictionary*, ed. Tremper Longman III (Grand Rapids: Baker Books, 2013), 1446–51.

41. Eckhard J. Schnabel, *Early Christian Mission*, 2 vols. (Downers Grove, IL: InterVarsity, 2004), 1:557–652.

42. For a survey of these issues see Scot McKnight and Joseph B. Modica, eds., *Jesus Is Lord, Caesar Is Not: Evaluating Empire Criticism in New Testament Studies* (Downers Grove, IL: IVP Academic, 2013); Stanley E. Porter and Cynthia L. Westfall, eds., *Empire in the New Testament* (Eugene, OR: Wipf & Stock, 2011); Christoph Heilig, *Hidden Criticism? The Methodology and Plausibility of the Search for a Counter-Imperial Subtext in Paul* (Minneapolis: Fortress, 2017); Bird, *Anomalous Jew*, 205–55.

and regional setting, from Tiberius Alexander to Qumran, and everyone in between. Unsurprisingly, many synagogues were quite content to live under imperial jurisdiction, and some even sought benefaction from local elites to help with the building of synagogues and engaged in charitable projects with those elites.[43] Those persons in churches from prominent Roman households (Rom. 16:10–11), even Caesar's household (Phil. 4:22), or who held public offices like "director of public works" (Rom. 16:23) were probably not praying every night for the fall of Rome. In addition, Paul's clearest statement about Roman power, written to churches in Rome while anti-Roman sentiment was concurrently festering in Judea, requires Messiah-believers to submit to governing authorities as servants appointed by God (13:1–17).[44] Barclay infers from evidence of this order that Paul regarded Rome not as the great enemy of God's people but as just another insignificant expression of human idolatry.[45]

On the other hand, it is possible to picture Paul as tacitly subversive toward Roman power and its various manifestations. First, Paul's theological register implies a tacit resistance to imperial ideology. Paul's terms for Jesus, such as "Lord," "Savior," and "Son of God," are appropriated from the Septuagint (LXX) and reflect a Jewish grammar for his messianism. However, this same terminology overlapped with claims made by and about the Roman emperor, who could also be lauded as "Lord," "Savior," and "Son of God." The imperial cults of the ancient world as well as the propaganda and media of the empire made grandiose claims for the emperor as a god, master, benefactor, and deliverer of the people of the Mediterranean basin. Therefore, some scholars detect in Paul's writings a type of parody and polemic against claims associated with the Roman emperor. Scholars surmise that Paul's language issues a challenge to the superlative claims made about the emperor by postulating Jesus as Caesar's rival. Consequently, the true "Lord" of the world was not a Roman Son of Augustus, not the self-titled *Sebastos* (i.e., venerable one); rather, it was the Jewish Son of David, the *Christos*, who was truly in charge.[46]

Second, one cannot help but notice that in the history of the reception of Paul, he was remembered as a counterimperial figure. We see this initially

---

43. A well-known inscription from Acmonia in the first century CE refers to Julia Severa donating a building to the Jewish community even while she was a high priestess in the imperial cult during the time of Nero (see *CIJ* §766). An inscription at Aphrodisias in the third century CE records a number of "God-fearers" who helped establish what appears to be the ancient equivalent of a soup kitchen or burial society (see J. Reynolds and R. Tannenbaum, *Jews and Godfearers at Aphrodisias* [Cambridge: Philological Society, 1987]).

44. See discussion in Michael F. Bird, *Romans*, SGBC (Grand Rapids: Zondervan, 2016), 441–50.

45. John Barclay, *Pauline Churches and Diaspora Jew* (Grand Rapids: Eerdmans, 2016), 345–87.

46. See on *kyrios* (Lord) language, Joseph D. Fantin, *Lord of the Entire World: Lord Jesus, a Challenge to Lord Caesar?*, NTM 31 (Sheffield: Sheffield Phoenix, 2011).

in the writing of Luke in the late first century (see esp. Acts 17:6–7) and elsewhere in works such as the Acts of Paul in the late second century (Acts of Paul 11:2). The memory of Paul's martyrdom would facilitate Christians understanding themselves as living on the margins of the empire and in some cases resisting the empire's malevolent intentions toward them for being treasonous atheists.[47]

Third, a counterimperial thrust to Pauline theology should be expected when Christians inherited a set of scriptures with a particular narrative that posited a contest between YHWH and pagan deities. This scriptural narrative was freshly recast with apocalyptic and messianic themes, resulting in a picture of God the Father appointing Jesus as his agent of judgment and salvation over all peoples and powers (see Rom. 15:12 = Isa. 11:10). Paul's conviction was that God in the Messiah already had defeated and would yet defeat the "powers," whether the Roman pantheon or the Roman legions, and establish his reign over all things (see Rom. 8:38; 13:11–14; 1 Cor. 2:8; 15:24; Eph. 6:12; Col. 2:15). In which case, opposition to the imperial cult and Roman power was simply an extension of the Jewishness of the early churches.

When it came to Rome, Paul, like most Jews of his day, hovered between accommodation and resistance. The pragmatic reality was that Paul would not be comfortable singing *Ave imperii* (hail the empire), but neither was he likely to lead a mob charging up the Palatine Hill toward the emperor's residence chanting *Sic semper tyrannis* (always to the tyrant). The kingdom of Paul's Messiah did not constitute an overt military threat to the Roman Empire; there was, after all, no point in swapping one malevolent regime just for another one to rise after it. However, Paul's churches, who regarded Rome's religious tradition as blasphemous and dehumanizing, certainly saw themselves as offering a social alternative to Roman culture by establishing rival modes of patronage and devotion as well as expressions of family and kinship that competed with existing hierarchies.[48] Ultimately Paul defies the categories of pro- or anti-Rome. He urges his congregations to ensure that their public behavior matches the gospel (Rom. 12:14–18; Gal. 6:10; Eph. 4:1, 28; Phil. 1:17; Col. 1:10; 1 Thess. 2:12; 5:15), because he knows that God is already leading his people in a victory over the powers of this age, while Rome's injustice, brutality, and pretentions to divinity will receive their just deserts (Rom. 2:16; 8:37; 13:11–14; 15:12; 1 Cor. 2:8; 2 Cor. 2:14; Phil. 1:18; Col. 2:15).[49]

---

47. On Paul as martyr, see David Eastman, *Paul the Martyr: The Cult of the Apostle Paul in the Latin West* (Atlanta: SBL Press, 2014).

48. Bird, *Anomalous Jew*, 250–53.

49. Wright, *PFG*, 1298–99.

Reflections

Study of Paul in his Jewish, Greek, and Roman contexts is not merely an academic exercise, but has contemporary relevance.

First, study of Paul's Jewishness cannot be done in isolation from the question of how Christians and Jews should relate to each other. The topic is particularly confronting given the history of Christian anti-Semitism that lead to the Holocaust and given contemporary issues concerning how Christians relate to the state of Israel and its place in Middle Eastern politics. What would Paul say to a Jewish audience in a guest lecture to be delivered at the Holocaust memorial Yad Vasham in Israel, or what would Paul say in a sermon delivered to Christian Arabs living in Bethlehem? Would Paul write what he did in 1 Thessalonians 2:14–16 and Romans 9–11 if he knew the history we know? Modern Jewish authors have long viewed Paul with suspicion, regarding him as an apostate, the father of Jewish pogroms, the quintessential self-hating Jew.[50] Alternatively, a Jewish reclamation of Paul has been undertaken in recent decades, trying to recapture Paul as a Jewish figure who simply believed that Jesus brokered gentiles into Jewish communal life.[51] In any case, it is worth remembering that Paul is simultaneously a stumbling block and also a resource in interfaith relations between Christians and Jews.

Second, since the 1990s Paul has been the subject of several philosophical inquiries by philosophers of diverse persuasions.[52] One might be wondering why European Marxist atheist philosophers would have any interest in Paul. What does Tarsus have to do with Stalingrad? Well, as it turns out, Paul is interesting on many fronts, in regard to pluralism, socialism, the separation of religion from ethnicity, and the invention of the individual—Paul can be linked to all these notions. Paul was no philosopher, but he has bequeathed to us particular claims, reasons, questions, and problems that we can wrestle with as we contemplate what it means to be a human being and how to contribute to human flourishing.

Third, Paul is a stimulus toward thinking about empire. Now I do have to wonder if the whole industry of postulating Paul as an anti-imperial agent provocateur owes more to liberal college professors and their gripe with American foreign policy than it does to anything that Paul was actually talking about. I cannot help but notice that some Pauline scholars can gravitate toward

---

50. See Gray, *Paul as a Problem*, 117–42.
51. See Michael F. Bird and Preston Sprinkle, "Jewish Interpretation of Paul in the Last Thirty Years," *CBR* 6, no. 3 (2008): 355–76; Daniel R. Langton, *Apostle Paul in Jewish Imagination: A Study in Modern Jewish-Christian Relations* (New York: Cambridge University Press, 2014).
52. See John D. Caputo and Linda Alcoff, eds., *St. Paul among the Philosophers* (Bloomington: Indiana University Press, 2003); Ward Blanton and Hent de Vries, *Paul and the Philosophers* (New York: Fordham University Press, 2013).

anti-imperial readings of Paul when America has a Republican in the White House, but the mood suddenly turns Niebuhrian and almost Constantinian when a Democrat is the commander-in-chief. Fair comment?

Still, Paul does write as a socioreligious dissident on the margins, facing the threat of mob violence and death penalty by the state. Paul speaks to Christians who live under the threat of empire, whether that is Greek Orthodox in Turkey, Baptists in Russia, or Pentecostals in China. Paul is an informative teacher on how to be faithful to Christ in dangerous and adversarial settings. Dictators and demagogues might like to not-so-subtly remind the church that Christians like Paul got beheaded by Nero. The church might like to respond by pointing out that people today name their sons Paul and their dogs Nero.

10

Pauline Theology

Perspectives, Perennial Topics, and Prospects

MICHAEL J. GORMAN

Introduction

Paul was a controversial figure, and his letters were contested, even misused, because they contained "some things in them hard to understand" (2 Pet. 3:15–16). This interpretive challenge remains today.[1] Accordingly, this chapter will first provide an overview of several major perspectives on Paul's theology in what is, generally speaking, a post–New Perspective era. Next it will consider several recent theologies of Paul as well as developments in certain perennial issues in Pauline theology. It will then look at aspects of Paul the "practical" theologian. The chapter will conclude with a brief consideration of the directions Pauline theology may be going.[2]

---

1. The discussion here will focus on the "undisputed" letters: Romans, 1–2 Corinthians, Galatians, Philippians, 1 Thessalonians, and Philemon.
2. Fully covering the immense field of Pauline theology is impossible in this chapter. For longer treatments, see N. T. Wright, *Paul and His Recent Interpreters* (Minneapolis: Fortress, 2015); Magnus Zetterholm, *Approaches to Paul: A Student's Guide to Recent Scholarship* (Minneapolis: Fortress, 2009).

Perspectives on Paul

There is no perfect way to catalog the various approaches to or perspectives on Paul and his theology.[3] Any such effort is undertaken primarily for heuristic purposes and will be imperfect. Thus I offer three caveats: there is variety within each perspective; there is overlap among the perspectives; and some interpreters defy categorization. Furthermore, it is important to recognize that most students of Paul's theology bring their own hermeneutical (interpretive) concerns to the task, concerns that may be more or less explicit.

The Traditional/Reformational/Lutheran/Old Perspective

In the beginning, so to speak, was the traditional (or Reformational, or Lutheran, or old) perspective on Paul. At least that's what most interpreters would say about the last half-century of Pauline interpretation. But what precisely is this traditional (largely Protestant) interpretation? In its simplest formulation, we may say it means that because of Christ's substitutionary death for sinners, God graciously declares those who have faith in Christ to be righteous, apart from any effort or works on their part. Justification is a juridical, or forensic, act, and Christ's righteousness is often said to be "imputed" to believers in this verdict. Of course, there are various historical and contemporary nuances of this perspective as well as various critiques and defenses of it.

Perhaps the most thoroughgoing defense of the "old" perspective, with rejoinders to the New Perspective on Paul, which arose in response to it (NPP, described below), comes from Stephen Westerholm.[4] Westerholm reviews Augustine, Luther, Calvin, and Wesley on Paul before responding to critics of the traditional view and presenting his own interpretation of Paul on righteousness, the law, grace, and justification. Westerholm concludes that Paul is an advocate of grace abounding to sinners (traditional emphasis) *and* of erasing ethnic boundaries (NPP emphasis). This is a nuanced view that is, or should be, acceptable to many interpreters.

Similarly, one finds in certain practitioners of this more traditional approach, such as Douglas Moo, an openness to engaging fundamentally different perspectives, including the NPP and the apocalyptic and participationist

---

3. For books that consider several perspectives in a single volume, see Michael F. Bird, ed., *Four Views on the Apostle Paul* (Grand Rapids: Zondervan, 2012), with essays by Thomas Schreiner (Reformed), Luke Johnson (Roman Catholic), Douglas Campbell (post–New Perspective), and Mark Nanos (Jewish), each responding to the others; also, Scot McKnight and Joseph B. Modica, eds., *Preaching Romans: Four Perspectives* (Grand Rapids: Eerdmans, 2019), with perspectives from Stephen Westerholm (Reformational), Scot McKnight (new), Douglas Campbell (apocalyptic), and Michael Gorman (participationist).

4. Stephen Westerholm, *Perspectives Old and New on Paul: The "Lutheran" Paul and His Critics* (Grand Rapids: Eerdmans, 2004).

approaches.⁵ Moreover, Simon Gathercole's monographs on boasting and salvation, and on substitutionary atonement, are examples of rigorous, nuanced examinations of contested issues.⁶

Additional proponents of the traditional perspective include A. Andrew Das, Thomas Schreiner, and John Piper. Piper is best known for his critique of N. T. Wright on justification.⁷ Schreiner's contribution includes several commentaries, biblical theologies, and theological works in which Pauline theology is prominent.⁸

Recent studies of the Reformers have stressed that their theologies of justification cannot be separated from their theologies of union with Christ. The most significant work on this connection with respect to interpreting Paul is Stephen Chester's *Reading Paul with the Reformers*, which has been hailed as a landmark volume by scholars from various perspectives.⁹ Chester seeks to reconcile old and newer perspectives by arguing that the Reformers' "incorporated righteousness" addresses the concerns expressed by the new, apocalyptic, and participationist perspectives.

The New Perspective(s)

The origin of the New Perspective on Paul (NPP)—which should really be called the New Perspectives (plural)—is generally traced back to Krister Stendahl. Paul, said Stendahl, did not have a Luther-like or modern introspective guilt complex, and he was not converted but called.¹⁰ The fundamental goal of the NPP, led by its three major architects—E. P. Sanders, James D. G. Dunn, and N. T. Wright—is to situate Paul more firmly in his Jewish context.¹¹ Their position is sometimes summarized as having two major claims: Paul was concerned about "ethnocentrism," and he understood justification as a social, horizontal, or ecclesial reality. That is, Paul's main concern in dismissing "works of the law" for justification was not legalism or "works

---

5. E.g., Douglas Moo, *Galatians*, BECNT (Grand Rapids: Baker Academic, 2013).

6. Simon J. Gathercole, *Where Is Boasting? Early Jewish Soteriology and Paul's Response in Romans 1–5* (Grand Rapids: Eerdmans, 2002); Gathercole, *Defending Substitution: An Essay on Atonement in Paul* (Grand Rapids: Baker Academic, 2015).

7. John Piper, *The Future of Justification: A Response to N. T. Wright* (Wheaton: Crossway, 2007).

8. E.g., Thomas R. Schreiner, *Paul, Apostle of God's Glory in Christ: A Pauline Theology* (Downers Grove, IL: InterVarsity, 2001); Schreiner, *Galatians*, ZECNT (Grand Rapids: Zondervan, 2010); Schreiner, *Faith Alone: The Doctrine of Justification—What the Reformers Taught . . . and Why It Still Matters* (Grand Rapids: Zondervan, 2015).

9. Stephen J. Chester, *Reading Paul with the Reformers: Reconciling Old and New Perspectives* (Grand Rapids: Eerdmans, 2017).

10. Krister Stendahl, *Paul among Jews and Gentiles* (Philadelphia: Fortress, 1976).

11. For a survey, see Kent L. Yinger, *The New Perspective on Paul: An Introduction* (Eugene, OR: Cascade, 2011).

righteousness" (as associated, rightly or wrongly, with the old perspective) but the misuse of boundary markers like circumcision and food and calendar practices to exclude gentiles.

E. P. Sanders's highly influential *Paul and Palestinian Judaism* (1977) had revolutionized Pauline studies by critiquing the common view of Second Temple Judaism as a religion of works righteousness, replacing that construct with what he called "covenantal nomism," and by proposing participation in Christ, rather than justification, as the center of Paul's theology. Of course, Sanders's arguments would not go unchallenged, but the revolution had begun.[12]

Unfortunately, in his 2015 capstone treatment of Paul, Sanders does not interact with those who have critiqued his work—or with most other recent interpreters of Paul.[13] He does, however, re-present many of his original claims while introducing new emphases: the distinction between unnecessary "works of law" (like circumcision) and necessary "good deeds," the essentially synonymous character of justification and participation, and the likelihood that Paul's thinking evolved.

In 2005, James Dunn published a collection of essays written over the course of a quarter-century. In the preface to that volume, Dunn says both that he believes the new perspective has made significant contributions and that it is not intended to *replace* but to *complement* other perspectives, including the old.[14] As for the third major architect of the NPP, N. T. Wright, we will consider his work separately below.

In many ways, as noted earlier, we live in the post–New Perspective era, though many or some—depending on one's perspective!—of the NPP insights and emphases remain with us.

The Narrative Perspective

Is Paul a narrative theologian? Does a story, or do stories, lie within or as the foundation of his letters? These sorts of questions began to surface at about the same time as the NPP was in high gear. The early work of Richard Hays on narrative "substructures," the contributions of Wright on worldviews expressed in stories, and Ben Witherington's claims about Paul's

---

12. E. P. Sanders, *Paul and Palestinian Judaism* (Philadelphia: Fortress, 1977). For challenges to the NPP, see, e.g., Westerholm, *Perspectives*; Donald Carson, Peter T. O'Brien, and Mark A. Seifrid, eds., *Justification and Variegated Nomism*, vol. 1, *The Complexities of Second Temple Judaism* (Grand Rapids: Baker Academic, 2001); Carson, O'Brien, and Seifrid, eds., *Justification and Variegated Nomism*, vol. 2, *The Paradoxes of Paul* (Grand Rapids: Baker Academic, 2004).

13. E. P. Sanders, *Paul: The Apostle's Life, Letters, and Thought* (Minneapolis: Fortress, 2015).

14. James D. G. Dunn, *The New Perspective on Paul*, rev. ed. (Grand Rapids: Eerdmans, 2008). See esp. p. xi of the preface.

"narrative thought world" put an affirmative answer to such questions on the table.[15]

A collection of essays on the various stories within Romans and Galatians (e.g., creation, Abraham, Israel, Jesus), edited by Bruce Longenecker, provided a good sense of the issues and positions in 2002, but it is probably time for an updated assessment.[16] Seeing a connection between narrative and apocalyptic (see further below), Longenecker and Todd Still display a hybrid understanding of Paul's theological discourse as an "apocalyptic narrative." They compare Paul's "grand" narrative with contemporary Jewish and Roman "macro-narratives" and show how Paul wants to shape the embodied "micro-narratives" of early Christian communities.[17]

My own work on Paul has also stressed narrative, particularly in describing Paul's spirituality of cruciformity (cross-shaped existence) and his soteriology.[18] J. Paul Sampley, among others, finds a "Big Story" in Paul, from creation to its final restoration, that is centered on Christ's death and resurrection and that helps provide moral resources for believers, or "new creation beings."[19] With respect to specific letters, Hays's work on Galatians remains influential, while both Katherine Grieb and Wright have produced influential narrative readings of Romans.[20]

At the same time, A. Andrew Das has issued a significant warning after examining various proposals for the alleged narratives underlying Galatians as a whole (e.g., covenant, exodus, or the imperial cult).[21] Das urges caution and the need for careful argument when scholars claim to find narratives, especially grand narratives, in Paul's letters.

---

15. Richard B. Hays, *The Faith of Jesus Christ: The Narrative Substructure of Gal 3:1–4:11*, 2nd ed. (Grand Rapids: Eerdmans, 2002; first published 1983); N. T. Wright, *The New Testament and the People of God* (Minneapolis: Fortress, 1992); Ben Witherington III, *Paul's Narrative Thought World* (Louisville: Westminster John Knox, 1994).

16. Bruce W. Longenecker, ed., *Narrative Dynamics in Paul* (Louisville: Westminster John Knox, 2002). Contributors include Longenecker, Douglas Campbell, John Barclay, Andrew Lincoln, James Dunn, and Francis Watson.

17. Bruce W. Longenecker and Todd D. Still, *Thinking through Paul: An Introduction to His Life, Letters, and Theology* (Grand Rapids: Zondervan, 2014), 295–377.

18. Michael J. Gorman, *Cruciformity: Paul's Narrative Spirituality of the Cross* (Grand Rapids: Eerdmans, 2001); Gorman, *Inhabiting the Cruciform God: Kenosis, Justification, and Theosis in Paul's Narrative Soteriology* (Grand Rapids: Eerdmans, 2009).

19. J. Paul Sampley, *Walking in Love: Moral Progress and Spiritual Growth with the Apostle Paul* (Minneapolis: Fortress, 2016).

20. A. Katherine Grieb, *The Story of Romans: A Narrative Defense of God's Righteousness* (Louisville: Westminster John Knox, 2002); N. T. Wright, "The Letter to the Romans: Introduction, Commentary, and Reflections," in *The New Interpreter's Bible*, vol. 10, ed. Leander E. Keck et al. (Nashville: Abingdon, 2002), 393–770.

21. A. Andrew Das, *Paul and the Stories of Israel: Grand Thematic Narratives in Galatians* (Minneapolis: Fortress, 2016).

The Apocalyptic Perspective

The apocalyptic perspective stresses that God's apocalypse (revelation, unveiling) in Christ is God's unexpected incursion into human history to rescue people, and eventually the entire cosmos, from the cosmic powers of Sin and Death. Thus traditional lawcourt imagery for justification and salvation is deemed insufficient, and any language that suggests a continuous salvation history (which can be associated with certain forms of both old and new perspectives) needs to be replaced, or at least radically modified. The foundations of this approach were laid in the last century by Ernst Käsemann, J. Christiaan Beker, and J. Louis Martyn, and they have been especially developed by Martyn's formal and informal students. A comment by Martyn about Galatians is representative of this approach: "Galatians is a particularly clear witness to one of Paul's basic convictions: the gospel is about the divine invasion of the cosmos (theology), not about human movement into blessedness (religion)."[22]

Continuing the tradition of interpreting Galatians in this way is the commentary of Martinus de Boer, as well as some of the work of Susan Eastman (who also emphasizes participation, discussed below).[23] Another leading voice within the apocalyptic school is Beverly Gaventa, whose recent focus has been Romans: a short introduction, a commentary (in preparation), and, as editor, a significant collection of essays on Romans 5–8.[24] Contributors to that volume include Gaventa herself, de Boer, Eastman, Martyn, and theologian Philip Ziegler from the apocalyptic school, but also scholars from other perspectives, including Stephen Westerholm, John Barclay, and Neil Elliott.

No one has made Romans 5–8 and the apocalyptic interpretation of Paul more central to his work than Douglas Campbell, especially in his magnum opus, *The Deliverance of God*.[25] Campbell seeks to rediscover Paul's theology of justification in Romans and elsewhere. He hopes simultaneously to rescue church and academy from the deleterious theological error (as he sees it) of justification theory (JT; i.e., the old perspective) and to resolve "the Romans debate"—the quest for the letter's occasion and message. Campbell calls JT an individualist, prospective, conditional, contractual, and possibly even idolatrous pseudogospel of divine retributive justice and soteriological desert; its

---

22. J. Louis Martyn, *Galatians*, AYB 33A (New York: Doubleday, 1998), 349. Martyn's debt to Karl Barth is apparent.

23. Martinus C. de Boer, *Galatians*, NTL (Louisville: Westminster John Knox, 2011); Susan Grove Eastman, *Recovering Paul's Mother Tongue: Language and Theology in Galatians* (Grand Rapids: Eerdmans, 2007).

24. Beverly Roberts Gaventa, *When in Romans: An Invitation to Linger with the Gospel according to Paul* (Grand Rapids: Baker Academic, 2016); Beverly Roberts Gaventa, ed., *Apocalyptic Paul: Cosmos and Anthropos in Romans 5–8* (Waco: Baylor University Press, 2013).

25. Douglas A. Campbell, *The Deliverance of God: An Apocalyptic Rereading of Justification in Paul* (Grand Rapids: Eerdmans, 2009).

"textual citadel" is Romans 1–4. Campbell argues that much of these chapters (especially 1:18–3:20) reflects the misguided view of the Teacher(s) at Rome, which view Paul corrects especially in Romans 5–8. For Paul, argues Campbell, justification is liberative, participatory, transformative, trinitarian, and communal. Paul's gospel is noncontractual and can be discerned only retrospectively (in light of Christ), not prospectively (from plight to solution, sin to salvation).[26] Campbell calls this not a new *perspective* (which he says did not change much), but a new *paradigm*. As with Martyn, Barth's influence is palpable.

Reaction to Campbell has been strong and mixed. Advocates of the traditional perspective have found both his polemic unfair and his substance unconvincing. Even supporters of his overall interpretation may find the polemic inappropriate and the treatment of 1:18–3:20 misguided.[27]

Following Martyn's lead, proponents of the apocalyptic view generally see apocalyptic (focusing on disruption) and covenant (focusing on fulfillment) as antithetical to each other. Some therefore minimize or discredit the notion of salvation-historical continuities between the story of Israel and the Christ event. However, there is a wide diversity of understanding about what apocalypse and apocalyptic mean in Paul, as a collection of essays titled *Paul and the Apocalyptic Imagination* demonstrates.[28] It contains essays by leading scholars, with varying (and at times nearly antithetical) views: de Boer, Campbell, Gaventa, and Ziegler from the apocalyptic school; Wright, his student J. P. Davies, and the present author looking for covenant, promise, and salvation history *as well as* sudden incursion; and other important voices. Some of the essays, then, represent a growing chorus of scholars who say that it is erroneous to pit apocalyptic and covenant (or salvation history) against each other. These themes, according to such scholars, are complementary aspects of Paul's theology.[29]

The Participationist/Transformational Perspective

The themes of participation and transformation in Christ are aspects of Paul's letters that all interpreters of Paul note. Some interpreters, however,

---

26. In an earlier work, Campbell abbreviates Paul's gospel as PPME: "pneumatologically participatory martyrological eschatology." Campbell, *The Quest for Paul's Gospel: A Suggested Strategy* (New York: T&T Clark, 2005).

27. In addition to numerous reviews of the book, see Chris Tilling, ed., *Beyond Old and New Perspectives on Paul: Reflections on the Work of Douglas Campbell* (Eugene, OR: Cascade, 2014).

28. Ben C. Blackwell, John K. Goodrich, and Jason Maston, eds., *Paul and the Apocalyptic Imagination* (Minneapolis: Fortress, 2016).

29. See also, e.g., Jamie P. Davies, *Paul among the Apocalypses? An Evaluation of the "Apocalyptic Paul" in the Context of Jewish and Christian Apocalyptic Literature*, LNTS 562 (London: Bloomsbury T&T Clark, 2016); D. A. B. Shaw, "Apocalyptic and Covenant: Perspectives on Paul or Antinomies at War?," *JSNT* 36 (2013): 155–71.

following the claims of early twentieth-century scholars such as Albert Schweitzer and Adolf Deissmann, and later E. P. Sanders, find participation to be at the center of Paul's theology and experience. Two key linguistic elements express participation in Paul's letters: the phrase "in Christ" (and similar phrases) and the preposition and prefix *syn/sym-*, meaning *with* or *co-*.[30] In addition to *participation* itself and *(being) in Christ*, terms that have been used to designate Paul's theology of participation (or aspects of it) include *incorporation, identification, union, (mutual) indwelling*, and even *(Christ-) mysticism*.

A recent collection of essays on the topic, coedited by theologian Kevin Vanhoozer, includes Vanhoozer's own helpful survey of developments in the study of this topic.[31] Contributors include apocalyptic interpreters Douglas Campbell, who argues that "faith" in Paul is participatory, and Susan Eastman, who focuses on participation and the Spirit. Their presence reflects the frequent overlap between apocalyptic and participationist approaches to Paul. Constantine Campbell, Joshua Jipp, and Grant Macaskill, each of whom has contributed a monograph to the discussion, have essays in the book.[32] My own contribution connects the theme of participation (theosis) to that of mission.

Although Sanders claimed participation was central to Paul, he also said he did not know exactly what participation means. Richard Hays took a stab at an answer, offering four "models" of participation in Paul: belonging to a family, being in political or military solidarity with Christ, participating in the *ekklēsia*, and (especially, for Hays) living within the Christ-story.[33] Others have followed suit in various ways.

Prompted in part by Morna Hooker's analysis of Pauline "interchange" texts (such as Rom. 8:3–4; 2 Cor. 5:21; Gal. 3:13), which resemble the patristic notion that "Christ became what we are so that we could become what he is," and also by Richard Hays's suggestion that scholars "look East" (i.e.,

---

30. For a comprehensive exegetical and theological analysis, see Constantine R. Campbell, *Paul and Union with Christ: An Exegetical and Theological Study* (Grand Rapids: Zondervan, 2012); for an insightful approach using cognitive linguistics, see Frederick S. Tappenden, *Resurrection in Paul: Cognition, Metaphor, and Transformation*, ECIL 19 (Atlanta: SBL Press, 2016).

31. Michael J. Thate, Kevin J. Vanhoozer, and Constantine R. Campbell, eds., *"In Christ" in Paul: Explorations in Paul's Theology of Union and Participation* (Grand Rapids: Eerdmans, 2018). For an overview, see also Haley Goranson Jacob, *Conformed to the Image of His Son: Reconsidering Paul's Theology of Glory in Romans* (Downers Grove, IL: InterVarsity, 2018), 123–40.

32. See also C. Campbell, *Paul and Union with Christ*; Joshua W. Jipp, *Christ Is King: Paul's Royal Ideology* (Minneapolis: Fortress, 2015); Grant Macaskill, *Union with Christ in the New Testament* (New York: Oxford University Press, 2013).

33. Richard B. Hays, "What Is 'Real Participation in Christ'? A Dialogue with E. P. Sanders on Pauline Soteriology," in *Redefining First-Century Jewish and Christian Identities: Essays in Honor of Ed Parish Sanders*, ed. Fabian E. Udoh et al. (Notre Dame, IN: University of Notre Dame Press, 2008), 335–51.

to the fathers and Eastern Orthodoxy) to understand Paul's participatory idiom,[34] several scholars have argued that because Paul's language of participation includes transformation, other terms may be needed to describe his theology. This has led to historical and literary/theological investigations that use words such as *Christification* or *Christosis* (e.g., Ben Blackwell) and even *deification* or *theosis* (e.g., David Litwa, Gorman) to characterize Paul's theology of participation and transformation.[35] *Cruci*formity, one might say, is actually *theo*formity. Blackwell has led the way among Western scholars in reading Paul with the help of the church fathers, especially Irenaeus and Cyril of Alexandria. Litwa, however, has situated Paul's notion of deification within Paul's contemporary religious environment.

The suggestion to "look East" has come to fruition in additional ways. Athanasios Despotis, an Orthodox scholar working in Germany, has both published a monograph and edited a collection of essays that bring into conversation Orthodox perspectives and other approaches to Paul, especially the old and the new perspectives.[36] The collection includes contributions from Orthodox scholars such as Despotis himself, Edith Humphrey, Konstantinos Nikolakopoulos, and James Buchanan Wallace, as well as from non-Orthodox scholars such as Michael Wolter, Jacobus (Kobus) Kok, John Anthony Dunne, and the present author. Somewhat similarly, some recent Roman Catholic contributions, especially on justification, have been in critical dialogue with newer perspectives and have contended for a transformative understanding of justification.[37]

The theme of participation has occasionally been linked as well with specific hermeneutical concerns. For instance, Pathipati Victor Paul in India argues for an "inclusive liberative ecclesiology" in his study of Paul's "in Christ" language.[38]

---

34. Morna D. Hooker, *From Adam to Christ: Essays on Paul* (Cambridge: Cambridge University Press, 1990); Hays, "What Is 'Real Participation'?," xxxii.

35. Ben C. Blackwell, *Christosis: Engaging Paul's Soteriology with His Patristic Interpreters* (Grand Rapids: Eerdmans, 2016); M. David Litwa, *We Are Being Transformed: Deification in Paul's Soteriology*, BZNW 187 (Berlin: de Gruyter, 2012); Gorman, *Inhabiting the Cruciform God*.

36. Athanasios Despotis, *Die "New Perspective on Paul" und die griechisch-orthodoxe Paulusinterpretation*, VIOTh 11 (St. Ottilien: EOS-Verlag, 2014); Athanasios Despotis, ed., *Participation, Justification, and Conversion: Eastern Orthodox Interpretation of Paul and the Debate between "Old and New Perspectives on Paul*," WUNT 2/442 (Tübingen: Mohr Siebeck, 2017).

37. E.g., Jean-Noël Aletti, *Justification by Faith in the Letters of Saint Paul: Keys to Interpretation*, trans. Peggy Manning Meyer (Rome: Gregorian & Biblical Press, 2015); Thomas D. Stegman, "Paul's Use of *dikaio-* Terminology: Moving beyond N. T. Wright's Forensic Interpretation," *TS* 72 (2011): 496–524. Stegman is appreciative of Hays and Gorman.

38. Pathipati Victor Paul, *Exploring Socio-Cultural Aspects of Pauline Ecclesiology: A Study of Paul's Term "in Christ,"* Biblical Hermeneutics Rediscovered 13 (New Delhi, India: Christian World Imprints, 2018).

Political Perspectives (Anti-imperial, Liberationist, Postcolonial)

We come now to a cluster of closely related political perspectives. The anti-imperial perspective on Paul—once labeled by N. T. Wright as the "fresh perspective"[39]—contends that Paul's gospel was implicitly or explicitly a critique of, and an alternative to, Rome: its lords and gods, especially the emperor; its underlying "gospel," or ideology; its values of honor, piety, fidelity, and justice. Proponents of this perspective contend that Paul presents Jesus rather than Caesar as the true lord, and the in-Christ community as an alternative politic to the oppressive empire. In Wright's oft-quoted words, "If Jesus is Lord, Caesar is not."

An early version of this perspective was Dieter Georgi's *Theocracy in Paul's Praxis and Theology*.[40] One of its leading architects has been Richard Horsley, whose pioneering work included the editing of several volumes of essays by various advocates.[41] Major proponents besides Horsley and Wright include Neil Elliott, Sylvia Keesmaat, and Gordon Zerbe.[42]

The anti-imperial reading of Paul originated in and, for most proponents, implicitly or explicitly addresses perceived contemporary political and economic imperialism. That is, it offers both a historical and a hermeneutical perspective on Paul. Accordingly, critics of this perspective have leveled charges against both aspects. Among the critics from a historical, exegetical perspective have been John Barclay (in a famous exchange with Wright at the 2007 annual meeting of the Society of Biblical Literature) and Seyoon Kim.[43]

Similarly, an increasing number of studies of Pauline theology have interpreted Paul from a liberationist or postcolonial perspective. Although some of these have come from scholars in the developed world, it is majority-world

---

39. N. T. Wright, *Paul: In Fresh Perspective* (Minneapolis: Fortress, 2005), 40, 59–79.

40. Dieter Georgi, *Theocracy in Paul's Praxis and Theology*, trans. David E. Green (Minneapolis: Fortress, 1991).

41. Horsley's edited volumes include *Paul and Empire: Religion and Power in Roman Imperial Society* (Harrisburg, PA: Trinity Press International, 1997), and *Paul and Politics: Ekklesia, Israel, Imperium, Interpretation: Essays in Honor of Krister Stendahl* (Harrisburg, PA: Trinity Press International, 2000).

42. E.g., Neil Elliott, *The Arrogance of Nations: Reading Romans in the Context of Empire* (Minneapolis: Fortress, 2008); Brian J. Walsh and Sylvia C. Keesmaat, *Colossians Remixed: Subverting the Empire* (Downers Grove, IL: InterVarsity, 2004); Keesmaat and Walsh, *Romans Disarmed: Resisting Empire, Demanding Justice* (Grand Rapids: Brazos, 2019); Gordon Mark Zerbe, *Citizenship: Paul on Peace and Politics* (Winnipeg: CMU Press, 2012). See also John Dominic Crossan and Jonathan Reed, *In Search of Paul: How Jesus' Apostle Opposed Rome's Empire with God's Kingdom* (New York: HarperCollins, 2004).

43. See John M. G. Barclay, "Why the Roman Empire Was Significant to Paul," in *Pauline Churches and Diaspora Jews* (Grand Rapids: Eerdmans, 2016), 363–87; Seyoon Kim, *Christ and Caesar: The Gospel and the Roman Empire in the Writings of Paul and Luke* (Grand Rapids: Eerdmans, 2008). Cf. Scot McKnight and Joseph B. Modica, eds., *Jesus Is Lord, Caesar Is Not: Evaluating Empire in New Testament Studies* (Downers Grove, IL: IVP Academic, 2013).

scholars who are leading the way. Liberationist and postcolonial approaches to Paul share the general concerns of such ideological commitments: (1) to identify and oppose the forces of oppression and colonialism that are expressed in texts and in interpreters of those texts; and (2) to identify texts and interpreters that can assist in dismantling oppression and colonialism. Many works from the majority world pay particular attention to interpreting Paul within an interreligious context and with sensitivity to global Christianity.

A convenient compendium of various approaches to Paul and colonialism is *The Colonized Apostle*, edited by Christopher Stanley.[44] Contributors are mostly North American academics, though several come from, or have lived in, places outside North America that have experienced forms of oppression and colonialism. One proponent of this perspective, Elsa Tamez, wrote an early work on justification from a Latin American liberationist perspective; more recently, she has published essays and a liberationist, feminist commentary on Philippians.[45] Similarly, Nestor Míguez has interpreted 1 Thessalonians as a message of hope in Latin American perspective.[46] From an Asian and Asian American viewpoint, Yung Suk Kim interprets the body metaphor in 1 Corinthians in terms of diversity more than unity, attention to the marginalized, and critique of power as he focuses on the *crucified* body of Christ.[47]

Other sorts of liberationist readings of Paul also continue. For example, recent feminist interpretations of Paul may be found in some of the work of apocalyptic interpreter Beverly Gaventa in North America and that of Kathy Ehrensperger in Britain and Europe.[48]

Related to this cluster of perspectives, and to the globalization of Pauline studies, is the question of understanding and interpreting Paul cross-culturally. Ehrensperger, for instance, sees Paul as theologizing about Christ in the "space between" Jewish and gentile peoples.[49] Other scholars have attempted to put

44. Christopher Stanley, ed. *The Colonized Apostle: Paul in Postcolonial Eyes*, Paul in Critical Contexts (Minneapolis: Fortress, 2011).
45. Elsa Tamez, *The Amnesty of Grace: Justification by Faith from a Latin American Perspective*, trans. Sharon H. Ringe (Nashville: Abingdon, 1993); Tamez, "Philippians," in *Philippians, Colossians, Philemon*, ed. Elsa Tamez et al., Wisdom Commentary (Collegeville, MN: Liturgical Press, 2017).
46. Nestor O. Míguez, *The Practice of Hope: Ideology and Intention in 1 Thessalonians*, trans. Aquíles Martínez, Paul in Critical Contexts (Minneapolis: Fortress, 2012).
47. Yung Suk Kim, *Christ's Body in Corinth: The Politics of a Metaphor*, Paul in Critical Contexts (Minneapolis: Fortress, 2008).
48. Beverly Roberts Gaventa, *Our Mother Saint Paul* (Louisville: Westminster John Knox, 2007); Kathy Ehrensperger, *That We May Be Mutually Encouraged: Feminism and the New Perspective in Pauline Studies* (New York: T&T Clark, 2004).
49. Kathy Ehrensperger, *Paul at the Crossroads of Cultures: Theologizing in the Space Between*, LNTS 456 (London: Bloomsbury T&T Clark, 2013).

Paul in dialogue with contemporary cultures across the globe, from North American to Asian and African.[50]

The Paul-within-Judaism Perspective

One prominent recent reaction to both old and new perspectives is the Paul-within-Judaism perspective (sometimes called the "radical perspective," or "radical new perspective"). This approach grows out of the work done toward the end of the last century by Stanley Stowers, Lloyd Gaston, and John Gager, who found two ways of salvation in Paul: Christ for gentiles, Torah observance for Jews. Advocates find both the old charge of legalism and the new charge of ethnocentrism that Paul allegedly found problematic in the Judaism of his day to be mischaracterizations of both ancient Judaism and Paul. They also find that the traditional and even the new perspectives are too influenced by their proponents' own Christian beliefs, thus failing to understand Paul and his communities adequately. Advocates contend that Paul remained firmly within Judaism as a Torah-observant Jew, even as an apostle of the Messiah. Among the Christian as well as Jewish scholars who take this approach to Paul are Pamela Eisenbaum, Neil Elliott, Paula Fredriksen, Mark Nanos, Matthew Thiessen, and Magnus Zetterholm. Nanos and Zetterholm have edited a collection of essays by such scholars.[51]

Two examples of this perspective, one by a Jewish scholar and one by a Christian, are Eisenbaum's *Paul Was Not a Christian* and Thiessen's *Paul and the Gentile Problem*.[52] Eisenbaum claims, uncontroversially, that Paul lived and died a Jew. She is therefore somewhat appreciative of the new perspective, but she is highly critical of the old. Ultimately, however, she parts company with the NPP in arguing that Jews are already justified and thus do not need Christ. Similarly, though perhaps a bit more appreciative of aspects of the traditional perspective, Thiessen contends Paul did not in any way oppose Jews, the law, or Jewish practice of the law; he only opposed requiring gentiles to practice the law. Thiessen further maintains that gentiles become related to Abraham not by circumcision but by receiving the *pneuma* (spirit) of the Messiah Jesus.

Proponents of the radical new perspective have been affirmed in their insistence on Paul's Jewishness. But questions remain about how Torah-observant

---

50. See, e.g., Charles H. Cosgrove, Herold D. Weiss, and K. K. (Khiok-Khng) Yeo, *Cross-Cultural Paul: Journeys to Others, Journeys to Ourselves* (Grand Rapids: Eerdmans, 2005).

51. Mark D. Nanos and Magnus Zetterholm, eds., *Paul within Judaism: Restoring the First-Century Context to the Apostle* (Minneapolis: Fortress, 2015).

52. Pamela Eisenbaum, *Paul Was Not a Christian: The Original Message of a Misunderstood Apostle* (New York: HarperOne, 2009); Matthew Thiessen, *Paul and the Gentile Problem* (New York: Oxford University Press, 2016).

Paul was, and especially about the claim that he did not see Christ as the way of salvation for Jews.

The "Wrightian" Perspective (N. T. Wright and His Students)

N. T. Wright is arguably the most influential interpreter of Paul of the last four decades. Even his strongest critics must engage his work. Here we consider just two of his books.[53]

Paul: In Fresh Perspective is Wright's revision of the Hulsean Lectures, given at Cambridge. The book's two parts deal, respectively, with "themes" and "structures." The themes include subjects such as Paul's three worlds, creation and covenant, messiah and apocalyptic, and empire, while the structures comprise rethinking God, God's people, and God's future. The first part interacts with certain issues in Pauline studies, while the second presents Wright's understanding of Paul's theological task: to rework the main motifs of Second Temple Jewish theology in light of Christ and the Spirit.

Paul and the Faithfulness of God (*PFG*), Wright's magnum opus, is his full outworking of the theses found in *Fresh Perspective*: Paul's reconfiguring of Jewish monotheism, election, and eschatology around Jesus and the Spirit, all simultaneously in conversation with Greek philosophy and religion as well as the realities of the Roman Empire. Arguing for narrative and theological coherence in Paul's thought, Wright seeks to overcome numerous dichotomies that have characterized recent Pauline scholarship, such as juridical versus participationist and apocalyptic versus covenantal/salvation-historical. Wright begins with Paul's worldview, or mind-set, which he claims led inevitably to theology so that the worldview could be sustained. The *ekklēsia* is the central symbol of the new worldview and, in its unity and holiness, a "microcosmos" of God's future.

Wright finds in Paul an early, "high" Christology and pneumatology that are at the heart of his reinterpretation of Paul's soteriological narrative about YHWH and Israel. This narrative framework has three main components: (1) the return of YHWH in and as Jesus, which effects the new exodus and ends Israel's continuing exile; (2) God's putting the world to rights not through Israel, which failed at its assigned task, but through the Messiah Jesus as Israel's faithful representative; and (3) the stark contrast between YHWH's activity in Jesus and the salvation narrative of the Roman Empire. The prophetically promised restoration of Israel and new covenant have begun, shockingly (i.e., "apocalyptically") in and through the death and resurrection of the Messiah, creating a new temple (the *ekklēsia*) for the dwelling of God's Spirit.

---

53. See also, among others, Wright's *Pauline Perspectives: Essays on Paul, 1978–2013* (Minneapolis: Fortress, 2013).

Wright's work has received both praise and criticism at every turn. Criticisms have included charges of misunderstanding justification (as divine declaration of who is in the covenant), lacking evidence for the sense of continuing exile of Israel in Second Temple Judaism, and embracing supersessionism. In addition to the many reviews of his main books, there is an entire collection of essays engaging *PFG*.[54]

Among Wright's doctoral students, both from earlier periods and more recently, we see some of his themes carried on in new directions.[55] No less important, however, have been Wright's informal students from afar, including fellow scholars, who have developed some of his work as well.

The Social-Science Perspective

Social-scientific approaches to Paul interpret him in light of first-century social realities and/or models derived from the social sciences. In what is surprising to some, Wright has found this approach, exemplified especially in the work of Wayne Meeks and David Horrell, quite congenial.[56] Meeks's older, groundbreaking work (1983) is a social description of Paul's churches and their practices, with special attention to Corinth. As social history, it has implicit, though not explicit, implications for contemporary ecclesiology. Horrell's volume, however, is explicitly hermeneutical, as he frames the Pauline problem of difference and solidarity within contemporary liberal and communitarian ethical perspectives. Horrell's theses about the *ekklēsia*'s purity and distinctiveness from the surrounding culture, as well as its internal solidarity combined with Christlike other-regard that permits the expression of certain cultural differences, resonates with much recent work both in Pauline studies (including Wright's) and in Christian ethics.

Others within this general sort of approach include Francis Watson and Peter Oakes. Oakes's work on reading Romans as an address to a house church of craftworkers "on the ground" of a first-century city might be characterized as implicitly stressing the "incarnational" reality of living the gospel

---

54. Christoph Heilig, J. Thomas Hewitt, and Michael F. Bird, eds., *God and the Faithfulness of Paul: A Critical Examination of the Pauline Theology of N. T. Wright*, WUNT 2/413 (Tübingen: Mohr Siebeck, 2016), contains thirty essays and a sixty-page response from Wright. See also James M. Scott, *Exile: A Conversation with N. T. Wright* (Downers Grove, IL: InterVarsity, 2017).

55. See, e.g., Sylvia C. Keesmaat, *Paul and His Story: (Re)Interpreting the Exodus Tradition*, JSNTSup 181 (Sheffield: Sheffield Academic, 1999); Davies, *Paul among the Apocalypses?*; Jacob, *Conformed to the Image of His Son*.

56. See Wayne A. Meeks, *The First Urban Christians: The Social World of the Apostle Paul*, 2nd ed. (New Haven: Yale University Press, 2003; 1st ed., 1983); David G. Horrell, *Solidarity and Difference: A Contemporary Reading of Paul's Ethics*, 2nd ed. (London: Bloomsbury T&T Clark, 2016; 1st ed., 2005).

in concrete circumstances.⁵⁷ Watson is more explicitly theological—and more complicated.⁵⁸ The first edition of his *Paul, Judaism, and the Gentiles* (1986) is a strong critique of the "Lutheran"/Bultmannian perspective in favor of something closer to the NPP, all done from a sociological approach that stressed the sectarian character of Pauline communities. The second edition, however, is subtitled *Beyond the New Perspective*; it maintains the sectarian thesis but finds a wider separation between the Pauline communities and "Judaism," meaning basically Pharisaism. Paul's strong emphasis on grace and the transforming Spirit, versus the law, is critical. Watson's view of Paul is obviously quite different from those of the Paul-within-Judaism school, but, contrary to some critics, his is not a return to a simply "traditional" Protestant reading.

John Barclay's work has most fully highlighted the theological consequences of reading Paul with attention to his social world. His magnum opus, *Paul and the Gift*, has been compared in significance to Sanders's *Paul and Palestinian Judaism*, though of course that sort of judgment will not be final for some time.⁵⁹

Barclay situates his study of grace/divine gift (Gk. *charis*) in Paul (Galatians and Romans) within the context of ancient gift-giving, Second Temple Judaism, the reception of Paul from Marcion to the NPP and beyond, modern anthropological theory, and contemporary gift-giving. For Paul, the Christ-gift is above all incongruous: it is God's love for the unlovely, eliminating all prior systems of worth and available to all, Jew and gentile. Furthermore, within the context of ancient gift-giving, the event of Christ's life, death, and resurrection as incongruous divine gift is *unconditioned* but not *unconditional*; grace requires the obedience of faith. When received, the gift must in some sense be returned. Furthermore, it creates a new community, the fitting result of the gift, in which a Christian *habitus* is constructed. It too, like God in Christ, is characterized by countercultural graciousness.

This brief summary hardly does Barclay's book justice.⁶⁰ Its claims, however, have wide and deep implications for understanding grace both historically and theologically, for understanding the nature and scope of Paul's gospel, and for the self-understanding of Christian communities.

---

57. Peter Oakes, *Reading Romans in Pompeii: Paul's Letter at Ground Level* (Minneapolis: Fortress, 2009).
58. We will consider only Francis Watson, *Paul, Judaism, and the Gentiles: Beyond the New Perspective*, rev. ed. (Grand Rapids: Eerdmans, 2007; first published 1986).
59. John M. G. Barclay, *Paul and the Gift* (Grand Rapids: Eerdmans, 2015), with a helpful summary on 562–74.
60. I have not, for instance, discussed his treatment of the six "perfections" of grace, which would require much more space.

Pauline Theologies: Beyond Wright, Campbell, and Barclay

The issue of addressing Pauline theology as a whole has been a rather contentious one (even apart from the controversial nature of some of its recent practitioners). For a time there was a trend to consider Paul's theology letter by letter; this was the basic approach of the Society of Biblical Literature's Pauline theology unit, which published four volumes in the 1990s. James Dunn's 1998 synthetic theology of Paul, which reflected a somewhat chastened new perspective with a participationist bent, was deliberately modeled on Paul's most systematic letter, Romans.[61] But Dunn is sometimes criticized for allowing Romans to serve as the outline of Paul's theology, even though Dunn is fond of stressing that Paul is as much a theologizer as a theologian.

It may be the case today that one person cannot do all the "heavy lifting" required for a Pauline theology. A sort of combined effort in 2004 included some of the best international scholars to write about Paul's theology as a work in progress (his and theirs).[62] Among the contributors were Jean-Noël Aletti, Giuseppe Barbaglio, James Dunn, Neil Elliott, Daniel Marguerat, Romano Penna, and Udo Schnelle.

Schnelle is one of two significant German scholars who have recently written theologies of Paul that are translated into English. Schnelle takes a developmental, contextualized approach, from Paul's pre-Christian life and thought through his seven undisputed letters in sequence (1 Thessalonians to Romans), before offering a synthesis of the basic structures (theology proper, Christology, etc.) of Paul's theology.[63] For Schnelle, the center of that theology is the presence of salvation, which includes a strong emphasis on participation and transformation ("life within the sphere of Christ"), and on righteousness. Schnelle also emphasizes Paul as one who engaged in historical-meaning formation (interpreting events) and the formation of Christian identity for action in the world.

Like Schnelle's volume, Michael Wolter's work on Paul is also concerned with identity formation.[64] Unlike Schnelle, Wolter does not deal with individual letters but sees them as a theological whole. Wolter's contribution is also distinctive in several other respects, not least that he finds Paul to be an ecumenical figure: the Antioch incident, narrated in Galatians, was almost as

---

61. James D. G. Dunn, *The Theology of Paul the Apostle* (Grand Rapids: Eerdmans, 1998).

62. Andreas Dettwiler, Jean-Daniel Kaestli, and Daniel Marguerat, eds., *Paul, une Théologie en Construction* (Geneva: Labor et Fides, 2004). See also Stanley E. Porter, ed., *Paul and His Theology*, Pauline Studies 3 (Boston: Brill, 2006).

63. Udo Schnelle, *Apostle Paul: His Life and Theology*, trans. M. Eugene Boring (Grand Rapids: Baker Academic, 2005).

64. Michael Wolter, *Paul: An Outline of His Theology*, trans. Robert L. Brawley (Waco: Baylor University Press, 2015).

critical for Paul's theology as his conversion. What unites diverse believers then and now is "Christ-faith," the interpretation of all things (e.g., social relations) in light of the new creation that exists in Christ. Justification is about both soteriology and ecclesiology, both declaration and transformation. Wolter's own ecumenical conversations have clearly shaped his approach to Paul.

Frank Matera's theology of Paul is unique in a different way: it engages all thirteen letters. It is centered, like Barclay's magnum opus, on the uncontroversial but highly significant theme of "God's saving grace," which is, Matera also emphasizes, transformative.[65] Matera seeks to demonstrate the theological coherence within, and the theological interrelationships among, all thirteen letters without engaging in harmonization of the diverse texts. Colossians, Ephesians, and the Pastorals are essentially faithful to Paul, argues Matera. Among other contributions, this book shows the inseparability of justification and sanctification, and it argues that "works of the law" include both boundary markers like circumcision and all attempts at law keeping.

Something of a union of Schnelle and Matera, Garwood Anderson's monograph takes a developmental approach to Paul's theology through all thirteen letters, arguing that participation is the "red thread" that runs throughout the corpus.[66] He contends that the NPP gets the early Paul right, while the old perspective gets the later letters (which contain Paul's own "new perspective"!) right.

My own theology of Paul and his letters has much in common with the work of Dunn, Schnelle, Anderson, and Matera in stressing participation and transformation. Some of its distinctive emphases include the centrality of cruciformity (without neglecting the resurrection) and the prophetic character of Paul as an advocate of biblical shalom (peace and justice).[67]

Perennial Topics: Some Developments

We turn now from the big picture to a few specific issues. In the following brief reviews of recent trends, there is perhaps one important theme that emerges: the importance of *relationship* in Paul's theology.

---

65. Frank J. Matera, *God's Saving Grace: A Pauline Theology* (Grand Rapids: Eerdmans, 2012). A similar emphasis on both divine grace and human transformation appears in Brant Pitre, Michael P. Barber, and John A. Kincaid, *Paul, a New Covenant Jew: Rethinking Pauline Theology* (Grand Rapids: Eerdmans, 2019). The authors, who are Roman Catholics like Matera, aim to synthesize some of the competing approaches to Paul.

66. Garwood P. Anderson, *Paul's New Perspective: A Soteriological Itinerary* (Downers Grove, IL: InterVarsity Press, 2016).

67. Michael J. Gorman, *Apostle of the Crucified Lord: A Theological Introduction to Paul and His Letters*, 2nd ed. (Grand Rapids: Eerdmans, 2017).

Christology: Cross, Resurrection, Identity

Christology has remained a critical issue in Pauline theology, with special attention in recent years focused on the significance of Jesus's death and resurrection as well as his identity as the Messiah and, perhaps, as God—what is sometimes referred to as Paul's contribution to an "early high Christology."

Regarding the cross we may mention two influential books, though neither is only about Paul or solely academic in focus. From the apocalyptic side, there is Fleming Rutledge's *The Crucifixion*, while N. T. Wright offers a more narrative, salvation-historical interpretation.[68] For Wright, the death of Jesus in Paul is primarily a new Passover/exodus, in which the great narratives of Scripture have reached their goal. But this goal is "revolutionary," indeed a "revolutionary rescue" that issues from divine love and creates a new, missional people; Wright finds truth in both substitutionary and apocalyptic/ Christus victor understandings of the atonement.[69]

Several recent studies have demonstrated renewed interest in the resurrection to balance, so to speak, attention to the cross in Paul. Wright's massive tome on Jesus's resurrection deals in depth with multiple Pauline texts.[70] Daniel Kirk argues that resurrection is the key to Romans; that the theme confirms God's fidelity to Israel and inclusion of gentiles, vindicating/justifying both God and humanity; and that it includes, for believers, present resurrection (to new life), not simply eschatological resurrection.[71] Andrew Boakye finds the theology of resurrection and revivification to be central to Galatians, indebted to the biblical prophets and essential to rectification, new life, and a new cosmos.[72]

The identity of the crucified and resurrected Jesus continues to be explored. Matthew Novenson's influential work on messianism argues that for Paul "Christ" is neither a name nor a title, but an "honorific," similar to "Augustus" or "Epiphanes" in secular political contexts, yet fully Jewish and messianic in significance.[73] Joshua Jipp argues that Paul's "Christ" language reveals his creative adaptation of ancient ideologies about good kingship, and that this

---

68. Fleming Rutledge, *The Crucifixion: Understanding the Death of Jesus Christ* (Grand Rapids: Eerdmans, 2015); N. T. Wright, *The Day the Revolution Began: Reconsidering the Meaning of Jesus's Crucifixion* (New York: HarperCollins, 2016), esp. 227–351.

69. On the cross, see also Gorman, *Cruciformity*; Gorman, *The Death of the Messiah and the Birth of the New Covenant: A (Not So) New Model of the Atonement* (Eugene, OR: Cascade, 2014).

70. N. T. Wright, *The Resurrection of the Son of God*, vol. 3 of *Christian Origins and the Question of God* (Minneapolis: Fortress, 2003).

71. J. R. Daniel Kirk, *Unlocking Romans: Resurrection and the Justification of God* (Grand Rapids: Eerdmans, 2008). On present resurrection, see also Tappenden, *Resurrection in Paul*.

72. Andrew K. Boakye, *Death and Life: Jesus' Resurrection, Israel's Restoration, and Humanity's Rectification in Paul's Letter to the Galatians* (Eugene, OR: Pickwick, 2017).

73. Matthew V. Novenson, *Christ among the Messiahs: Christ Language in Paul and Messiah Language in Ancient Judaism* (Oxford: Oxford University Press, 2012).

innovation permeates significant aspects of Paul's Christocentric theology: law, ethics, righteousness/justice, worship, and participation (i.e., in the messiah's royal rule).[74] Jipp also finds royal ideology—in which both God and the messiah possess kingly rights and responsibilities—to be the key to Jesus's "divine identity" in Paul.

Regarding that question of divine identity, Gordon Fee's massive survey of all thirteen letters, before providing a synthesis of them, focuses especially on the "person" of Christ, which is indicated by divine titles and prerogatives attributed to him. Fee concludes that Paul remains monotheistic but includes Christ (and the Spirit) within the divine identity.[75] David Capes also argues vigorously for Paul's early high Christology: Paul rereads Israel's Scripture, assigning YHWH texts to Jesus. Capes's recent book, *The Divine Christ*, takes up his earlier work on the same subject, in conversation with the intervening years of scholarship.[76]

Similar conclusions are found in the highly influential contributions of Richard Bauckham.[77] Bauckham's preferred term is "christological monotheism." Like Fee, Capes, and others, Bauckham looks at the numerous "YHWH texts" throughout Paul, with special attention to Romans 10:13, 1 Corinthians 8:5–6, and Philippians 2:6–11. Bauckham largely dismisses the relevance of Jewish intermediary figures, which some have proposed as precedents for Paul's Christology. This then raises the question of how Jesus came to be included in the divine identity.

Paul's Christology has recently been especially examined with respect to believers' relationship to the resurrected Lord. Larry Hurtado's comprehensive study of early Christian devotion to Jesus includes an in-depth treatment of "early Pauline Christianity" that explores six major christological themes: Jesus as Christ, Son of God, Lord, preexistent one, redeemer through death and resurrection, and example. Hurtado finds in Paul (and indeed before him) a "binitarian" understanding of the one God of Israel that includes Jesus the Son within cultic devotion to the one God, while giving "primacy" to the Father.[78] Chris Tilling finds the work of Fee, Bauckham, and Hurtado

---

74. Jipp, *Christ Is King*.

75. Gordon D. Fee, *Pauline Christology: An Exegetical-Theological Study* (Peabody, MA: Hendrickson, 2007).

76. David B. Capes, *The Divine Christ: Paul, the Lord Jesus, and the Scriptures of Israel* (Grand Rapids: Baker Academic, 2018); Capes, *Old Testament Yahweh Texts in Paul's Christology*, WUNT 2/47 (Tübingen: Mohr Siebeck, 1992).

77. Richard Bauckham, *Jesus and the God of Israel: God Crucified and Other Studies on the New Testament's Christology of Divine Identity* (Grand Rapids: Eerdmans, 2008), which includes and expands his earlier *God Crucified: Monotheism and Christology in the New Testament* (Grand Rapids: Eerdmans, 1998).

78. Larry W. Hurtado, *Lord Jesus Christ: Devotion to Jesus in Earliest Christianity* (Grand Rapids: Eerdmans, 2003), 79–153.

"vulnerable." He therefore argues for parallels between texts about Jewish and early Christian relations with *God* and Pauline texts about relations with the risen Lord *Jesus* as the basis for speaking about Christ's divine identity in Paul.[79]

Pneumatology and the Trinity

Paul's theology of the Holy Spirit, often neglected in the past, was given a boost with the 1994 publication of Gordon Fee's *God's Empowering Presence*.[80] More recently, Volker Rabens has published numerous articles and a monograph on the relational and transformational role of the Spirit.[81] Still, the Spirit remains a relatively neglected aspect of Pauline theology.

In his treatments of Paul's Christology and pneumatology, Fee refers to Paul as "proto-trinitarian" and "functionally Trinitarian."[82] Two important monographs make extensive arguments for the presence of trinitarian theology in Paul: Wesley Hill's *Paul and the Trinity* and Matthew Bates's *The Birth of the Trinity*.[83]

Hill brings systematic theology and critical biblical studies into conversation in an exploration of what he calls the neglected relationships present in Paul's "God-talk." He then proceeds to look at God (i.e., the Father) in relation to Jesus, Jesus in relation to God, and the Spirit in relation to both. For Paul, the identity of both God and Jesus is inseparable from their mutual relationship. But Hill also argues against binitarianism, contending that the Spirit is theologically and christologically determined, and also that the Spirit is critical in determining the identity of both the Father and the Son. Hence trinitarian theology is the appropriate consequence of Paul's own understanding and experience of God.

Bates's work, though not exclusively about Paul, further develops his contention that Paul (and other early Christians) read Scripture prosopologically, or theodramatically.[84] That is, Paul attributes various voices in the scriptural (OT) texts to specific characters, especially Christ or God the Father. For

---

79. Chris Tilling, *Paul's Divine Christology* (Grand Rapids: Eerdmans, 2015).
80. Gordon D. Fee, *God's Empowering Presence: The Holy Spirit in the Letters of Paul* (Peabody, MA: Hendrickson, 1994).
81. Volker Rabens, *The Holy Spirit and Ethics in Paul: Transformation and Empowering for Religious-Ethical Life*, 2nd rev. ed. (Minneapolis: Fortress, 2014).
82. Fee, *Pauline Christology*, 586–93; Fee, *God's Empowering Presence*, 839–42.
83. Wesley Hill, *Paul and the Trinity: Persons, Relations, and the Pauline Letters* (Grand Rapids: Eerdmans, 2015); Matthew W. Bates, *The Birth of the Trinity: Jesus, God, and Spirit in New Testament and Early Christian Interpretations of the Old Testament* (New York: Oxford University Press, 2015).
84. See Matthew Bates, *The Hermeneutics of the Apostolic Proclamation: The Center of Paul's Method of Scriptural Interpretation* (Waco: Baylor University Press, 2012).

Paul, then, Scripture bears witness to relations and even conversations among Father, Son, and Spirit prior to the Father's sending of the Son and the Spirit.

Justification and Faith

We have already encountered the issue of justification in earlier discussions. Here we first simply note the obvious: the subject remains contested. Is justification about "vertical" relations or "horizontal"? About the individual or the community? Is it only declarative or also inherently transformative? What is its relationship to participation? Andy Johnson has published a concise overview of some of the major voices,[85] but of course an entire chapter could be devoted to this subject.

At the same time and for various reasons there is—in some circles—greater agreement on basic exegetical and theological questions than there was in earlier generations.[86] The *Joint Declaration on the Doctrine of Justification*, issued in 1999 by Roman Catholics and Lutherans (and later accepted by Methodist, Reformed, and Anglican bodies), may be a factor in this convergence, together with ongoing scholarly and ecclesial dialogues. One promising word (literally) is Peter Leithart's neologism "deliverdict," which summarizes his claim that justification is both a verdict and an act of divine deliverance.[87]

Also still contested among interpreters is the Greek phrase *pistis Christou* (and similar phrases). Does Paul connect justification only to human faith, "faith in Christ" (the so-called objective reading of the genitive construction), or also to "the faith (faithfulness) of Christ" (the so-called subjective interpretation)?[88] Some have proposed that *pistis Christou* implies both, sometimes called "Christ-faith."

A significant development in the discussion of (human) faith in Paul has been the expansion of faith beyond "assent" to include relationship: trust, participation, and fidelity.[89] As with other theological topics in Paul, old debates

---

85. Andy Johnson, "Navigating Justification: Conversing with Paul," Catalyst: Contemporary Evangelical Perspectives for United Methodist Seminarians, November 1, 2010, http://www.catalystresources.org/navigating-justification-conversing-with-paul.

86. For one attempt to steer a middle course between old and new perspectives, see Michael F. Bird, *The Saving Righteousness of God: Studies on Paul, Justification, and the New Perspective* (Eugene, OR: Wipf & Stock, 2007).

87. Peter J. Leithart, *Delivered from the Elements of the World: Atonement, Justification, Mission* (Downers Grove, IL: InterVarsity, 2016).

88. See Michael F. Bird and Preston M. Sprinkle, eds., *The Faith of Jesus Christ: Exegetical, Biblical, and Theological Studies* (Peabody, MA: Hendrickson, 2009).

89. See, e.g., Gorman, *Cruciformity*, 95–154; Teresa Morgan, *Roman Faith and Christian Faith: Pistis and Fides in the Early Roman Empire and Early Churches* (New York: Oxford University Press, 2015), esp. 262–306; Matthew W. Bates, *Salvation by Allegiance Alone: Rethinking Faith, Works, and the Gospel of Jesus the King* (Grand Rapids: Baker Academic, 2017); Nijay K. Gupta, *Paul and the Language of Faith* (Grand Rapids: Eerdmans, forthcoming).

about faith have encountered "new perspectives" related to participation and relationships.

Paul the "Practical" Theologian

The question of the meaning of "faith" reminds us that Paul is understood rightly when perceived as something other than an "armchair theologian." The moral, missional, and spiritual dimensions of Paul's theology indicate that he is a "practical theologian." *Practicing with Paul*, edited by Presian Burroughs, is a good example of this concern for Paul in his context—and for his voice as a resource for contemporary concerns.[90] Contributors include John Barclay, Beverly Gaventa, Douglas Campbell, Philip Ziegler, Lisa Bowens, and more, while some of the topics are the poor, gender, prayer, protest, peacemaking, and dying well.

Ethics and Identity

Of perennial interest to Pauline studies is the question of ethics: life in Christ. We have already noted David Horrell's contribution to the overarching themes of unity and diversity guided by Christlike, or cruciform, love. Proponents of the NPP have produced a collection of essays on Paul and the Christian life.[91] Sampley offers a full-blown Pauline ethic that finds in baptism and the Lord's Supper the major "lodestars" that guide believers in life as they, enlivened by the Spirit, anticipate the parousia.[92]

Studies in moral formation and ecclesiology have expanded the notion of ethics to include believers' peculiar, or "alter-cultural," corporate existence in the ancient (and contemporary) world.[93] A new development in this regard has been a focus on identity formation in the Pauline communities, generally using some form of social-scientific approach to identity. We may single out recent interest in Corinth as a test case: Stephen Chester addresses the Corinthians' initial (incomplete) and necessary ongoing conversion, while Brian Tucker argues that Paul proposes a new, common identity in Christ that also permits the continuation (yet transformation) of existing cultural and ethnic

---

90. Presian R. Burroughs, ed., *Practicing with Paul: Reflections on Paul and the Practices of Ministry in Honor of Susan G. Eastman* (Eugene, OR: Cascade, 2018).

91. Scot McKnight and Joseph B. Modica, eds., *The Apostle Paul and the Christian Life: Ethical and Missional Implications of the New Perspective* (Grand Rapids: Baker Academic, 2016). For a different approach, see the work of Jesuit scholars Daniel J. Harrington and James F. Keenan, *Paul and Virtue Ethics: Building Bridges between New Testament Studies and Moral Theology* (Lanham, MD: Rowman & Littlefield, 2010).

92. Sampley, *Walking in Love*.

93. See, among others, James Thompson's books mentioned below.

identities.[94] Similar concerns emerge, focusing on race and ethnicity, in the work of Love Sechrest.[95] Somewhat differently, and more broadly, Erin Heim uses metaphor theory to consider the cultural meaning of adoption for Paul and his communities.[96]

Specific moral issues that bear mentioning briefly are gender and sexuality, economic justice, peace and reconciliation, and ecology.

Cynthia Long Westfall argues that Paul often subverts cultural norms for both genders and for their mutual relationship.[97] In *Remember the Poor*, Bruce Longenecker contends that Paul had a general concern for the poor (beyond the collection for Jerusalem) and expected that concern to be expressed in his communities.[98] Jeremy Gabrielson, one of Longenecker's doctoral students, argues persuasively that nonviolence and peacemaking were central to Paul's identity, gospel, and communities.[99] Similarly, Juan Manuel Granados Rojas develops a Pauline theology of reconciliation.[100]

Those concerned about ecology have begun to enlist Paul as a contributor to the conversation. *Greening Paul*, for instance, is an interdisciplinary work that explores various perspectives on Paul and ecology, naming Romans 8 and Colossians 1 as the Pauline ecotheological "mantra" texts.[101] As one of three contributors, Horrell seeks to enlarge christologically motivated regard for the other to include the *nonhuman* other. Within the field of ecotheology more generally, there is also attention to Pauline texts, and there is

---

94. Stephen J. Chester, *Conversion in Corinth: Perspectives on Conversion in Paul's Theology and the Corinthian Church* (London: T&T Clark, 2003); J. Brian Tucker, *You Belong to Christ: Paul and the Formation of Social Identity in 1 Corinthians 1–4* (Eugene, OR: Pickwick, 2010); Tucker, *Remain in Your Calling: Paul and the Continuation of Social Identities in 1 Corinthians* (Eugene, OR: Pickwick, 2011).

95. Love L. Sechrest, *A Former Jew: Paul and the Politics of Race*, LNTS 410 (London: T&T Clark, 2009).

96. Erin M. Heim, *Adoption in Galatians and Romans*, BIS 153 (Boston: Brill, 2017).

97. Cynthia Long Westfall, *Paul and Gender: Reclaiming the Apostle's Vision for Men and Women in Christ* (Grand Rapids: Baker Academic, 2016).

98. Bruce W. Longenecker, *Remember the Poor: Paul, Poverty, and the Greco-Roman World* (Grand Rapids: Eerdmans, 2010). See also Viateur Habarurema, *Christian Generosity according to 2 Corinthians 8–9: Its Exegesis, Reception, and Interpretation Today in Dialogue with the Prosperity Gospel in Sub-Saharan Africa* (Carlisle, UK: Langham Partnership, 2017). For justice more generally, see A. Katherine Grieb, "'So That in Him We Might Become the Righteousness of God' (2 Cor 5:21): Some Theological Reflections on the Church Becoming Justice," *Ex Auditu* 22 (2006): 58–80; Michael J. Gorman, *Becoming the Gospel: Paul, Participation, and Mission* (Grand Rapids: Eerdmans, 2015), 212–96.

99. Jeremy Gabrielson, *Paul's Non-Violent Gospel: The Theological Politics of Peace in Paul's Life and Letters* (Eugene, OR: Pickwick, 2014).

100. Juan Manuel Granados Rojas, *La Teología de la Reconciliación en las Cartas de San Pablo* (Estella, Navarra, Spain: Editorial Verbo Divino, 2016).

101. David G. Horrell, Cherryl Hunt, and Christopher Southgate, *Greening Paul: Rereading the Apostle in a Time of Ecological Crisis* (Waco: Baylor University Press, 2010).

likewise increasing attention from some Pauline scholars to broader biblical-theological efforts in creation care.[102]

Suffering and Persecution

Related to the general field of life in Christ is the corollary reality of suffering and persecution. The exegetical and theological work of Ann Jervis on suffering, *At the Heart of the Gospel*, has become a touchstone for discussions of the topic in Paul.[103] Jervis finds several sorts of suffering in Paul's letters: that which is specific to believers; that of nonbelievers; and that of shared humanity, tied to the suffering of creation. She also shows the links between suffering and hope.

As Pauline studies becomes increasingly global, the human and Christian experience of suffering has been interpreted globally, too. Siu Fung Wu, writing out of his experiences in East Asia, focuses on suffering and hope in Romans. Furthermore, he has edited a collection of essays on suffering in Paul with contributors from five countries on three continents.[104] The theological significance of persecution in Paul's communities has also been explored by, among others, John Anthony Dunne.[105] In all these studies, suffering is closely linked to participation in Christ.[106]

Spirituality

The field of spirituality as a discipline of academic theology has given birth to studies that both exposit and engage Paul's own spirituality. Contemporary interest in Paul as a spiritual person, even a mystic, can perhaps be traced back to Albert Schweitzer's work.[107] Although historical investigations and

---

102. For the former, see, e.g., Felipe de Jesús Legarreta-Castillo, *The Figure of Adam in Romans 5 and 1 Corinthians 15: The New Creation and Its Ethical and Social Reconfiguration* (Minneapolis: Fortress, 2014); for the latter, see, e.g., Douglas J. Moo and Jonathan A. Moo, *Creation Care: A Biblical Theology of the Natural World* (Grand Rapids: Zondervan, 2018).

103. L. Ann Jervis, *At the Heart of the Gospel: Suffering in the Earliest Christian Message* (Grand Rapids: Eerdmans, 2007).

104. Siu Fung Wu, *Suffering in Romans* (Eugene, OR: Pickwick, 2015); Wu, ed., *Suffering in Paul: Perspectives and Implications* (Eugene, OR: Pickwick, 2018). See also Bruce T. Clark, *Completing Christ's Afflictions: Christ, Paul, and the Reconciliation of All Things*, WUNT 2/383 (Tübingen: Mohr Siebeck, 2015).

105. John Anthony Dunne, *Persecution and Participation in Galatians*, WUNT 2/454 (Tübingen: Mohr Siebeck, 2017).

106. This is the particularly insightful focus of Wesley Thomas Davey, *Suffering as Participation with Christ in the Pauline Corpus* (Lanham, MD: Lexington Books/Fortress Academic, 2019).

107. Albert Schweitzer, *The Mysticism of Paul the Apostle*, trans. William Montgomery (London: Black; New York: Holt, 1931).

analyses of Paul's spirituality in its own right continue,[108] these are also often blended with theological interest in Paul's spirituality for today.

Of particular importance has been the theme of dying and rising with Christ, which is sometimes described as (resurrectional) cruciformity, or Christoformity, and sometimes (especially among Roman Catholics) as participation in the paschal mystery.[109] Craig Keener's recent work on the mind—its corruption and renewal in Christ by the Spirit—fills a lacuna in Pauline studies, displaying careful historical research blended with theological and pastoral concern.[110]

Missional/Pastoral Paul

Paul was, of course, a missionary, and studies of him as such continue.[111] The still-developing field of missional hermeneutics, however, engages Paul for shaping contemporary Christian mission. The exegetical groundwork for this sort of approach is laid in Michael Barram's *Mission and Moral Reflection in Paul*.[112] Two further examples of it in practice are Andy Johnson's commentary on 1–2 Thessalonians and my own monograph *Becoming the Gospel*.[113] From the majority world, Paul as worldwide missionary within an interfaith, intercultural context remains significant.[114]

Paul was also a pastor, a shepherd, to the communities he founded. His theology was forged in these experiences. James Thompson has written a trilogy on Paul as pastor, preacher, and moral guide, with sometimes explicit and sometimes implicit connections to contemporary pastoral ministry.[115] Various

---

108. See, e.g., Nils Aksel Røsæg, "The Spirituality of Paul: An Active Life," *Studies in Spirituality* 14 (2004): 49–92; Litwa, *We Are Being Transformed*.

109. See especially Gorman, *Cruciformity*; Rodney Reeves, *Spirituality according to Paul: Imitating the Apostle of Christ* (Downers Grove, IL: InterVarsity, 2011); Frank J. Matera, *The Spirituality of Saint Paul: A Call to Imitation* (New York: Paulist Press, 2017). For "resurrectional" cruciformity, see Gorman, *Participating in Christ*.

110. Craig S. Keener, *The Mind of the Spirit: Paul's Approach to Transformed Thinking* (Grand Rapids: Baker Academic, 2016).

111. E.g., Peter Bolt and Mark Thompson, eds., *The Gospel to the Nations: Perspectives on Paul's Mission* (Downers Grove, IL: InterVarsity, 2000); Trevor J. Burke and Brian S. Rosner, eds., *Paul as Missionary: Identity, Activity, Theology, and Practice*, LNTS 420 (London: T&T Clark, 2011).

112. Michael Barram, *Mission and Moral Reflection in Paul*, StBibLit 75 (New York: Peter Lang, 2006).

113. Andy Johnson, *1–2 Thessalonians*, THNTC (Grand Rapids: Eerdmans, 2016).

114. See, e.g., Subhro Sekhar Sircar, *Paul's Theology of Mission to the Nations in Romans*, Biblical Hermeneutics Rediscovered 8 (New Delhi, India: Christian World Imprints, 2017).

115. James W. Thompson, *Preaching Like Paul: Homiletical Wisdom for Today* (Louisville: Westminster John Knox, 2001); Thompson, *Pastoral Ministry according to Paul: A Biblical Vision* (Grand Rapids: Baker Academic, 2006); Thompson, *Moral Formation according to Paul: The Context and Coherence of Pauline Ethics* (Grand Rapids: Baker Academic, 2011).

aspects of Paul's pastoral ministry in concrete locations, with some connections to contemporary ministry, are explored in a collection of essays called *Paul as Pastor*. Focused more directly on ministry today, yet grounded in Paul's first-century context, is Scot McKnight's *Pastor Paul*.[116]

Reflections: Looking Back and Looking Ahead

This chapter has examined recent work in Pauline theology with a twofold emphasis: (1) various perspectives that have emerged or developed in new directions; and (2) perennial topics that have been addressed in fresh ways. In addition, the chapter briefly considered contributions to Pauline theology as a whole. Throughout the essay, I have drawn attention to contributions from interpreters in the majority world. Given the limitations of space and the enormous amount of scholarly activity devoted to Paul, the chapter could not consider certain other significant aspects of the field, such as the ongoing production of commentaries (both the more historical-critical and the more theological) and the ever-increasing focus on reception history.

Perhaps the most significant development in the recent study of Paul has been the proliferation of approaches. We looked at representative contributions from nine basic perspectives: traditional, new, narrative, apocalyptic, participationist, political, Paul-within-Judaism, Wrightian, and social-science. Each of these approaches understands Paul as a first-century Jew whose theology emerged in that ancient context. Although there is overlap among the various perspectives, each represents a particular way of understanding the basic framework and focus of Pauline theology. Much work within these various perspectives constitutes an explicit or implicit attempt to synthesize the theology of Paul found in his various letters.

It would be impossible, however, to synthesize the many recent studies of particular aspects of Pauline theology. Yet this chapter did note that attention to the dimension of "relationship" (e.g., Christ to God; believers to their culture) is one noteworthy aspect of recent scholarship. In addition, a number of interpreters have worked to bridge the gap between biblical studies and other theological subdisciplines, including systematic theology, ethics, and practical theology.

Although I am no prophet, here are a few brief observations about the future of Pauline theology.

First, scholars will continue to situate all aspects of Paul's theology in the context(s) of Second Temple Judaism, even as they disagree about Paul's

---

116. Brian S. Rosner, Andrew S. Malone, and Trevor J. Burke, eds., *Paul as Pastor* (London: Bloomsbury T&T Clark, 2018); Scot McKnight, *Pastor Paul: Nurturing a Culture of Christoformity in the Church* (Grand Rapids: Brazos, 2019).

precise place in that setting. At the same time, they will not (or at least should not) box Paul in to preexisting thought structures and practices. Rather, they will also expect to find, and therefore explore, his creativity: the reconfiguration of his beliefs and behaviors in Christ.

Second, interpreters will continue to search for appropriate ways to integrate and synthesize the various dimensions of Paul's theology. Some will especially insist on recognizing development and contextualization in his thinking, but this will not take away from attempts to interpret the corpus as a whole. This effort will include bringing the various scholarly perspectives into even more conversation with one another—additional attempts, in Pauline fashion, at reconciliation. Furthermore, as the authorship of the disputed letters continues to be reevaluated, the understanding of Pauline theology will likely expand to include at least 2 Thessalonians, Colossians, and Ephesians.

Third, the relationship between Pauline theology and both systematic and practical theology will continue to grow and flourish, despite the objections of some interpreters of Paul. The wall between biblical studies and theology is in the process of being dismantled.[117]

Finally, Pauline studies will become an increasingly global activity, with theologically, culturally, and politically contextualized interpretations of Paul's theology continuing to enrich the interpretation of the apostle. His words have prodded and provoked for nearly two thousand years—and will continue to do so.[118]

---

117. See now, for example, Douglas A. Campbell, *Pauline Dogmatics: The Triumph of God's Love* (Grand Rapids: Eerdmans, 2019).

118. I am grateful to Ron Witherup and Andy Johnson for conversation about this chapter, and to Michelle Rader for her proofreading.

11

New Testament Eschatologies

PATRICK MITCHEL

Introduction

Eschatology is one of the most complex, contested, and theologically significant domains within NT studies. As such, it is at once both fascinating and challenging. On the one hand, it is fascinating in that eschatology forms the very fabric of NT thought into which themes such as Christology, pneumatology, somatology, ethics, ecclesiology, mission, and salvation are stitched. As we shall see, it is perhaps one of the most valuable contributions of modern scholarship that—to switch metaphors—eschatology is now widely accepted to constitute the core framework for Jesus's teaching on the kingdom of God in the Synoptics as well as, in distinct ways, that of Paul, John, and other authors of the NT. Gone are the days of eschatology being tacked on to the end of systems of Christian doctrine, equated with little more than the narrow concerns of personal destiny after death.[1] The main aim of this chapter

---

1. Commenting on Jerry L. Walls, ed., *The Oxford Handbook of Eschatology* (Oxford: Oxford University Press, 2008), missiologist Rian Venter notes that "clearly, in the house of eschatology, it is not business as usual." Traditional "end of the world" issues are present; however, alongside these chapters is extensive discussion of the plurality of eschatological views among various theological and confessional traditions and engagement with the eschatology of other world religions. Of particular note is a culturally engaged final section of eleven chapters on everything from eschatology and modernity to politics, personal identity, cosmology, epistemology, near-death experiences, fine art, and pop culture. Rian Venter, "Trends in Contemporary Christian Eschatological Reflection," *Missionalia* 43, no. 1 (2015): 106.

is to sketch the developments behind that trend within the restless ebb and flow of NT eschatological scholarship. The first edition of *The Face of New Testament Studies* did not include a distinct chapter on eschatology, so this chapter will review its story within modern scholarship before focusing on selected examples of contemporary research. In the process, significant theological and hermeneutical questions will emerge.

On the other hand, the study of NT eschatology can, for a number of reasons, also be a challenging, if not an overwhelming, enterprise. One reason is its sheer scope. We have already alluded to the considerable diversity of eschatological imagination within the NT itself. To this multiplicity can be added a host of adjectival descriptors such as personal eschatology, cosmic eschatology, thoroughgoing or consistent eschatology, realized eschatology, inaugurated eschatology, consummated eschatology, apocalyptic eschatology, and eco-eschatology, not to mention various millenarian schemes and varieties of dispensational theologies.

Linked to this, second, is the considerable hermeneutical challenge of understanding and interpreting the wide range of eschatological imagery within biblical texts. This issue has a number of dimensions that can be unpacked by a series of questions. What is the distinctive character and content of the eschatologies of the historical Jesus, of Paul, of Luke-Acts, of John, of Hebrews, and of other NT authors? Are they internally consistent? When they are put together, is it possible to reconstruct a coherent picture of something called "New Testament eschatology"? What does such a picture communicate about the content of Christian hope: the parousia of Jesus Christ, heaven, judgment, the future of the body, the new creation, and the people of God?

A third challenge follows any reconstruction of NT eschatology—namely, how was it understood and received in the communities to whom it was addressed? Intrinsic to this question are the historical origins of Christian eschatological imagery, particularly its relationship to Jewish apocalypticism.[2]

---

2. The term *apocalypse* is often defined using a description developed by the Apocalypse Group of the Society of Biblical Literature Genres Project back in the late 1970s. It states that "'apocalypse' is a genre of revelatory literature with a narrative framework, in which a revelation is mediated by an otherworldly being to a human recipient, disclosing a transcendent reality which is both temporal, insofar as it envisages eschatological salvation, and spatial, insofar as it involves another, supernatural world" (John J. Collins, *Apocalypse: The Morphology of a Genre*, Semeia 14 [Atlanta: Scholars Press, 1979], 9). While this captures well the form and content of apocalyptic literature, it does not address motive. Thus, the following was later added: "[An apocalypse is] intended to interpret present, earthly circumstances in light of the supernatural world and of the future, and to influence both the understanding and the behavior of the audience by means of divine authority" (Adela Yarbro Collins, introduction to *Early Christian Apocalypticism: Genre, Social Setting*, ed. Adela Yarbro Collins, Semeia 36 [Decatur, GA: Scholars Press, 1986], 6). This expansion captures well the dynamic interplay of future

Fourth, and perhaps most challenging of all, is how a NT eschatology relates to the "concreteness" of our modern world. In other words, how does that *future* hope impact Christian life in the *present*? As we shall discuss below, answers to this final question shape considerable debate within academic as well as popular theology. Are eschatological hopes within the NT an intrinsic component of Christian doctrine that should be taught and believed today? Or is to do so naively "literalistic"? Is the NT's eschatological language better understood as symbolic of religious truth to be interiorized by the believer (Friedrich Schleiermacher)? Or does it provide a figurative framework, detached from history, for an existential leap of faith to create meaning in the present (Rudolf Bultmann)? Or do the Gospels indeed accurately capture something of Jesus the fearsome apocalyptic Jewish prophet, who, like any human, had the capacity for self-delusion and died without seeing the arrival of his hoped-for eschatological kingdom of God (Albert Schweitzer)?

Similarly, if Paul expected the imminent return of Christ within his lifetime (1 Thess. 4:15, 17; 1 Cor. 15:52) but was mistaken, does this mean that Jörg Frey's argument is valid? "Paul's expectations," Frey writes, "are far from being a firm basis of any Christian doctrine of what is to come; they must be interpreted in historical terms as a time-related expression of his own religious viewpoints, as a perspective that had to be corrected at least when Paul—and all others of the first Christian generation (cf. Mk 9:1; John 21:22–23)—had died before the end of the world."[3] This means for Frey that "it has been in the field of eschatology that traditional views of Christian doctrine have had to face their most severe crisis."[4] If a pressing task of eschatological hermeneutics is to consider how ideas within an ancient world view "can be of theological relevance or even be meaningful for Christian life within the modern or postmodern world view," then "any naïve transmission of NT concepts into the present—as often practiced in traditional and conservative Christian circles or, especially in evangelical preaching—has to face massive problems."[5]

Frey's comments are a reminder that, when it comes to eschatology, scholarship, no less than "popular" Christianity, faces questions of the constitution of reality itself: of God's existence and his gracious action in the world; of some sort of radical *discontinuity* between this world and a world to come; of the

---

and present characteristics within much of the NT. In this sense, apocalyptic can be seen as a subgenre of a broader eschatological literature.

3. Jörg Frey, "New Testament Eschatology—an Introduction: Classical Issues, Disputed Themes and Current Perspectives," in *Eschatology of the New Testament and Some Related Documents*, ed. Jan G. van der Watt, WUNT 2/315 (Tübingen: Mohr Siebeck, 2011), 5.

4. Frey, "New Testament Eschatology," 5.

5. Frey, "New Testament Eschatology," 8.

essentially eschatological "grammar" of Christianity; and of epistemic issues that cannot be divorced from the business of biblical exegesis. We shall return to questions of eschatology's place in the modern world at various points in this chapter. The next section will trace the story of this recovery of the central place of eschatology in NT studies. It will be followed by brief discussion of selected significant voices in contemporary eschatology. A concluding section will consider future challenges in NT eschatology.

Twentieth-Century Eschatology: From Margin to Center

Various frameworks exist for categorizing interpretative approaches to NT eschatology.[6] One particularly memorable one is used by N. T. Wright, picking up on an image originally used by T. W. Manson[7] and later by Norman Perrin,[8] in arguing that critical Jesus research in the 1990s could be divided in two camps: those that generally followed the *Wredestrasse* and those that generally followed the *Schweitzerstrasse*. While each *Strasse* had become a complex *Autobahn* with even some attempts to build junctions between them, "the distinction between them remains illuminating. . . . Do we know rather little about Jesus, with the gospels offering us a largely misleading portrait (Wrede)? Or was Jesus an apocalyptic Jewish prophet, with the gospels

---

6. In an earlier survey of the field, Scot McKnight proposed a heuristically useful threefold framework for categorizing interpreters of the Gospels: literal (Weiss and Schweitzer, followed in various ways by E. P. Sanders, D. C. Allison, and McKnight himself); myth and metaphor (scholars with distinct emphases such as R. Bultmann, C. H. Dodd, G. B. Caird, and N. T. Wright); and inauthentic (heirs of W. Wrede like M. Borg). Scot McKnight, "Jesus of Nazareth," in *The Face of New Testament Studies: A Survey of Recent Research*, ed. Scot McKnight and Grant R. Osborne (Grand Rapids: Baker Academic, 2004), 162–70. Alternatively, J. Richard Fountain identifies five broad paradigms for understanding NT apocalyptic eschatology: (1) apocalyptic as unimportant in classic liberalism (e.g., H. S. Reimarus, F. C. Baur, H. J. Holzman, D. E. Strauss, A. Ritschl); (2) apocalyptic as central (J. Weiss and A. Schweitzer, followed in quite different directions by W. Bousset and R. Bultmann); (3) apocalyptic as reinterpretation of the OT by the church (represented in varied ways by E. Käsemann, C. H. Dodd, N. Perrin, and M. Borg and other members of the Jesus Seminar); (4) apocalyptic as metaphor for renewal (G. B. Caird and N. T. Wright); (5) apocalyptic as central for Jesus and the Church (J. C. Beker, Dale Allison). See J. Richard Fountain, *Eschatological Relationships and Jesus in Ben F. Meyer, N. T. Wright and Progressive Dispensationalism* (Eugene, OR: Wipf & Stock, 2018), 42–56.

7. T. W. Manson, "The Life of Jesus: Some Tendencies in Present-Day Research," in *The Background of the New Testament and Its Eschatology*, ed. W. D. Davies and David Daube (Cambridge: Cambridge University Press, 1964), 216. Manson called the *Wredestrasse* "the road to nowhere."

8. Norman Perrin, "The *Wredestrasse* Becomes the *Hauptstrasse*: Reflection on the Reprinting of the Dodd *Festschrift*," *JR* 46 (April 1966): 297–98. Perrin, in contrast to Manson, proposed that "the *Wredestrasse* has become the *Hauptstrasse*, and it is leading us to new and exciting country."

reflecting, within their own contexts, a good deal about his proclamation of the kingdom (Schweitzer)?"[9]

Wright sees the *Wredestrasse* as the option that dominated the century as reflected in Bultmann through to the Jesus Seminar scholars like Robert Funk, Burton Mack, John Dominic Crossan, and Marcus Borg. His own work, to which we shall return below, he locates firmly in line with Schweitzer in his attempt to recover appreciation for the eschatological diversity and depth of Second Temple Judaism and how the Synoptic Gospels are to be read as effectively trustworthy historical documents in that context. I mention these different frameworks for two reasons. First, to illustrate the complexity of the subject. There is no obvious way to categorize a rather bewildering array of eschatological scholarship. Second, despite this, complexity can be better appreciated via some sort of organizing structure. In what follows we will mention many of these scholars but will use as simple an interpretive approach as possible. Since eschatology fundamentally revolves around the dynamic between present and future, we will organize discussion around how different approaches interpret this tension.

Weiss and Schweitzer: "Resurrection" and "Burial" of Eschatology

Eschatology barely existed as a significant and distinct exegetical category until the arrival of the "consequent eschatology" of Johannes Weiss, articulated in an explosive little sixty-seven-page book published in 1892.[10] Weiss was son-in-law of Albrecht Ritschl, the classic voice of a nineteenth-century German Lutheran liberalism in which the kingdom of God was typically an inward, spiritual, and already present reality, largely detached from contemporary Judaism and its apocalyptic eschatological hopes. Its motive was to demonstrate that the essential nature of Christian thought is focused on this world and current religious experience rather than some vague future realm. In utter contrast, Weiss followed an exegetical path that led him to believe in "the completely apocalyptic and eschatological character of Jesus' idea of the Kingdom."[11] Jesus's task was to proclaim the imminent kingdom, not establish it. When the mission of the Twelve failed to persuade many of the impending arrival of kingdom, Jesus decided to atone for the people's guilt by his own death. He hoped to return, after death, in messianic glory, revealed at last to be the Danielic Son of Man at the coming of the kingdom.

---

9. N. T. Wright, *Jesus and the Victory of God*, vol. 2 of *Christian Origins and the Question of God* (London: SPCK, 1996), 21.

10. Johannes Weiss, *Jesus' Proclamation of the Kingdom of God*, trans. and ed. R. H. Hiers and D. L. Holland (Philadelphia: Fortress, 1971).

11. Weiss, *Jesus' Proclamation*, 56.

This reconstruction differs only very slightly from how it was later developed and popularized by the remarkable Schweitzer in what remains the most significant book ever published in Jesus studies.[12] His rejection of the illusion that a moderate modern Jesus could be detached from his historical context continues to hang over all Christian eschatological debate. We may think we have Jesus neatly defined as "one of us," but Schweitzer's words of warning echo down the decades: "But He does not stay; He passes by our time and returns to his own."[13] For Schweitzer, Jesus's entire life and thought are shaped by eschatological thought, leading to his heroic, yet doomed, attempt to force the hand of history through his own human agency. Schweitzer's Jesus journeys to Jerusalem to die, giving his life as an atonement to facilitate the kingdom's coming. Eschatology is, in effect, buried with Jesus; it is only Jesus the human whose valiant world-renouncing actions continue to speak radically within our age. The future was meant to revolutionize the present but failed to do so. Ironically, Weiss and Schweitzer's reconstruction results in a truncated ethical version of Christianity not unlike the liberalism they were reacting against.

The next three scholars also wrestled with the eschatological tension between present and future. All, in different ways, stressed the significance of the present over the future.

Karl Barth: The Future in the Present

Particularly after World War I and the cataclysmic blow it represented to belief in human progressivism, German liberal scholarship largely gave up the quest for a historical Jesus. As the century progressed, new theologians like Karl Barth and Emil Brunner asked fresh questions that widened out the eschatological discussion. Barth's opposition to any form of anthropocentric theology led to his well-known claim in his 1922 Romans commentary that if "Christianity be not altogether thoroughgoing eschatology, there remains in it no relationship whatsoever with Christ."[14] Eschatology in this early Barthian sense becomes an existential and abstract type of shorthand for the "infinite qualitative distinction"

---

12. Albert Schweitzer, *The Quest for the Historical Jesus*, trans. W. Montgomery (London: A&C Black, 1910); first published as *Von Reimarus zu Wrede* (Tübingen: Mohr Siebeck, 1906). The second edition was published in 1913 as *Geschichte der Leben-Jesu-Forschung*; 9th ed. (Tübingen: Mohr Siebeck, 1984). The reception of the book's 1910 ET with its famous title is well considered by Francis Watson, "Eschatology and the Twentieth Century: On the Reception of Schweitzer in English," in *Eschatology: The Sixth Durham-Tübingen Research Symposium; Eschatology in Old Testament, Ancient Judaism and Early Christianity*, ed. Hans-Joachim Eckstein et al. (Tübingen: Mohr Siebeck, 2011), 331–47.

13. Schweitzer, *Quest for the Historical Jesus*, 397.

14. Karl Barth, *The Epistle to the Romans*, trans. E. C. Hoskyns (London: Oxford University Press, 1968), 314.

between God and man rather than for a belief in any specific event or end point within history. Later, in his *Church Dogmatics*, Barth moved beyond the sharp existentialist contrast between time and eternity to a more fully defined christological eschatology. If God is known only in Christ, this means that the eschaton is the "re-velation" (un-veiling or parousia) of what God from all eternity has decided to do in Christ. In terms of each person's eternal future, it is therefore not so much a new beginning after death, but life as it has already been redeemed through God's saving judgment in Christ. It is doubtful whether Barth's scheme left much room, if any, for a future transformative eschatology, and his *Church Dogmatics* remained unfinished. What is striking is his insistence on the significance of this earthly life, as a life that one day we will see from the standpoint of God's eternity. Barth's emphasis resonates with the subsequent appreciation for the nonlinear "now and not yet" character of NT eschatology discussed earlier. His emphasis on this life, even if seen from the perspective of God's future, also had implications for social ethics in the "now." Our task is to follow God's will for society as well as for our own lives.[15]

Rudolf Bultmann: Eschatology Detemporalized

Bultmann's program of demythologization was an outworking of his uncompromising commitment to the Weiss-Schweitzer notion of the otherness of Jesus's eschatological vision. The kingdom of God is a thoroughly eschatological concept.[16] Within his existentialist framework, eschatology becomes shorthand for all that is particularly Christian. Like Barth, he believed it is in the proclamation of the kerygma that we are faced with an eschatological decision in which eternity breaks into our present, freeing us from our inauthentic past. "Every instant has the possibility of being an eschatological instant and in Christian faith this possibility is realised."[17] In this sense eschatology is reduced to a general abstract principle of value within the here and now. "The story of Christ's descent into hell and of his ascension into heaven is done with. We can no longer look for the return of the Son of Man on the clouds of heaven or hope that the faithful will meet him in the air (1 Thess 4. 15ff)."[18] To make it relevant, the narrative needs to be

---

15. Brian Hebblethwaite argues that Barth, despite acute awareness of the ambiguity of the relationship between faith and politics, remained politically radical. His sympathy for Christian socialism was a logical implication of his eschatology. Brian Hebblethwaite, *The Christian Hope*, rev. ed. (Oxford: Oxford University Press, 2010), 142–43.

16. Rudolf Bultmann, *Theology of the New Testament*, vol. 1 (London: SCM, 1952), 4–11.

17. Rudolf Bultmann, *History and Eschatology: The Gifford Lectures, 1955* (Edinburgh: University Press, 1957), 154.

18. Rudolf Bultmann, "New Testament and Eschatology," in *Kerygma and Myth: A Theological Debate*, ed. Hand Werner Bartsch, ed. and trans. Reginald H. Fuller (New York: Harper & Row, 1961), 5.

demythologized. By this Bultmann meant a radical process by which future-oriented or apocalyptic events are relentlessly interpreted within a present horizon—the call for authentic decision. In this scheme, the Gospel of John's strong emphasis on present-oriented eschatology (e.g., eternal life experienced in the now [John 5:24]) reflects the NT's most advanced eschatological awareness. Eschatology is detemporalized; the future has been swallowed up in the present.

C. H. Dodd: The Kingdom Now

If Bultmann accepted that much NT eschatological language was meant literally but needed to be demythologized, his British counterpart, Charles Harold Dodd, challenged the idea that Jesus was a prophet of a future eschatological kingdom at all. His program of "realized eschatology" outlined in his 1935 *The Parables of the Kingdom*, like Bultmann's but for very different reasons, also stressed the present nature of the imminent kingdom.[19] Contrary to Weiss-Schweitzer's thoroughgoing framework, Dodd sought to harmonize the future and present aspects of Jesus's teaching about the kingdom. A key achievement was to show how the parables confronted listeners with the reality of the kingdom of God in the present in the person of Jesus; *now* was the time of both judgment and salvation. "This world has become the scene of a divine drama, in which the eternal issues are laid bare. It is the hour of decision. It is realized eschatology."[20] While this kingdom is not merely earthbound, neither is it a future reality to be consummated;[21] it represents the challenge of eternity within time. Those who respond with faith have eternal life now. In this light, the kingdom of God in the Synoptics parallels the realized eschatology within the less apocalyptic Gospel of John and also Paul. If Dodd's conception of time and eternity was overly Platonic and his realized eschatology failed to carry the day, he did pave the way for subsequent NT eschatologies that sought to hold the present inaugurated kingdom alongside a future consummation in a more holistic tension.

Kümmel, Cullmann, and Others: Inaugurated Eschatology

This development was represented in the work of Werner Georg Kümmel in Germany and Oscar Cullmann in Switzerland. Focusing first on

---

19. C. H. Dodd, *The Parables of the Kingdom* (London: The Religious Book Club, 1935).
20. Dodd, *Parables of the Kingdom*, 198.
21. Dodd concluded that "we have, it appears, no warrant in the teaching of Jesus for affirming that the long cycles of history will lead inevitably to a millennial 'Kingdom Come' on earth." Dodd, *Parables of the Kingdom*, 209.

Jesus[22] but later extending analysis to Paul and John, Kümmel argued that a dynamic synthesis of present and future eschatology best represented the thought of the NT. "On the basis of the belief in the resurrection of the crucified One, and on the basis of the experience of the gift of the Spirit, the primitive community extended this claim of Jesus to say that the promised bearer of salvation of the end-time already now as the heavenly Lord rules his eschatological community; in it are assembled those who, in faith in the Lord who is even now presently at work, are already experiencing together the reality of the final salvation that is promised to them."[23] Cullmann's *heilsgeschichtliche* theology confronted Bultmann's deeschatologizing and dehistoricizing of the NT as well as the consequent eschatology of Weiss-Schweitzer by arguing that NT eschatology reflects a tension between "already fulfilled" and "not yet consummated" aspects that exist within a redemptive-historical framework.[24] This tension reflects the "innermost character" of the NT message.[25] The Christian faith is determinedly historical, awaiting that which has not yet happened in the light of that which has. The future is really future. New events are yet to happen: the parousia, the resurrection, and the new creation.[26] Eschatology is not an existential, abstract concept; it talks of events still to unfold within a temporal framework. Space precludes further discussion, but this integration of the present reality of the kingdom (Dodd) and a future expectation awaiting consummation (Weiss-Schweitzer) was also reflected in various ways in scholars like Joachim Jeremias,[27] Günther Bornkamm,[28] G. E. Ladd,[29] and George R. Beasley-Murray.[30]

---

22. W. G. Kümmel, *Promise and Fulfilment: The Eschatological Message of Jesus*, trans. Dorothea M. Barton (London: SCM, 1957).

23. W. G. Kümmel, *The Theology of the New Testament according to Its Major Witnesses: Jesus-Paul-John*, trans. John E. Steely (London: SCM, 1976), 330–31.

24. Two works stand out: Oscar Cullmann, *Christ and Time: The Primitive Christian Conception of Time and History*, trans. Floyd V. Filson (London: SCM, 1951); Cullmann, *Salvation in History*, trans. Sidney G. Sowers (London: SCM, 1967).

25. Cullmann, *Christ and Time*, 3.

26. Cullmann, *Salvation in History*, 177. It is in this perspective that Cullmann developed his famous illustration of D-Day and VE-Day for the first and second comings of Jesus.

27. J. Jeremias, *The Parables of Jesus*, 3rd rev. ed. (London: SCM, 2003).

28. G. Bornkamm, *Jesus of Nazareth*, trans. Irene and Fraser McLuskey with James M. Robinson (New York: Harper & Row, 1960). Originally published as *Jesus von Nazareth* (Stuttgart: Kohlhammer, 1956). With Bornkamm the emphasis was decidedly on a present realized scheme of a kingdom of God as a timeless transcendent reality largely shorn of Jewish particularity.

29. G. E. Ladd, *The Gospel of the Kingdom: Scriptural Studies in the Kingdom of God* (London: Paternoster, 1959); Ladd, *A Theology of the New Testament* (Grand Rapids: Eerdmans, 1974); Ladd, *The Presence of the Future: The Eschatology of Biblical Realism* (Grand Rapids: Eerdmans, 1974).

30. George R. Beasley-Murray, *Jesus and the Kingdom of God* (Grand Rapids: Eerdmans, 1986).

Jürgen Moltmann: The Future Determines the Present

These developments within NT studies overlapped with the recovery of the significance of the future within German systematic theology, particularly in the work of Wolfhart Pannenberg[31] and Jürgen Moltmann.[32] Their work had major implications for developments in eschatology in general. Since systematics takes us outside our remit, we will comment only briefly on Moltmann.[33] In doing so, we take seriously Richard Bauckham's statement that "all theological eschatology of the early twenty-first century must be in at least implicit dialogue with Moltmann."[34] Moltmann's seminal work on eschatology, *The Theology of Hope*, was published in German in 1964.[35] Written within a context of social upheaval, it was also a conscious reaction against both Bultmann's individualism and neo-pietism and Barth's effective lack of teleology.[36] Moltmann's agenda, particularly given theology's

---

31. For specific discussion of eschatology within his three-volume theology, see Wolfhart Pannenberg, *Systematic Theology*, vol. 2, trans. Geoffrey W. Bromiley (Grand Rapids: Eerdmans, 1998), 527–646.

32. Other German theologians like Johann-Baptist Metz and Gerhard Sauter made significant contributions to theologies of hope regarding the future of the world that developed from the 1960s on.

33. For a helpful survey see Stephen Williams, "Thirty Years of Hope: A Generation of Writing on Eschatology," in *"The Reader Must Understand": Eschatology in Bible and Theology*, ed. K. E. Brower and M. W. Elliott (Leicester, UK: Apollos, 1997), 243–62.

34. Richard Bauckham, "Conclusion: Emerging Issues in Eschatology in the Twenty-First Century," in Walls, *Oxford Handbook of Eschatology*, 671. Bauckham is Moltmann's most influential English-speaking interpreter.

35. Jürgen Moltmann, *The Theology of Hope: On the Ground and the Implications of a Christian Eschatology*, trans. James Leitch (New York: Harper & Row, 1967; first published as *Theologie der Hoffnung: Untersuchungen zur Begründung und zu den Konsequenzen einer christlichen Eschatologie* [Munich: Chr. Kaiser, 1964]); Moltmann's subsequent output has been prolific. His most significant works related to eschatology are *The Crucified God: The Cross as the Foundation and Criticism of Christian Theology*, trans. R. A. Wilson and J. Bowden (London, SCM, 1974; first published as *Der gekreuzigte Gott* [Munich: Chr. Kaiser, 1972]); *The Church in the Power of the Spirit: A Contribution to Messianic Ecclesiology*, trans. M. Kohl (London: SCM, 1977; first published as *Kirche in der Kraft des Geistes* [Munich: Chr. Kaiser, 1975]); *The Future of Creation*, trans. M. Kohl (London: SCM, 1979; first published as *Zukunft der Schöpfung: Gesammelte Aufsätze* [Munich: Chr. Kaiser, 1977]); *God in Creation: An Ecological Doctrine of Creation*, trans. M. Kohl (London: SCM, 1985; first published as *Gott in der Schöpfung: Ökologische Schöpfungslehre* [Munich: Kaiser, 1985]); *History and the Triune God: Contributions to Trinitarian Theology*, trans. J. Bowden (London: SCM, 1992; first published as *In der Geschichte des dreieinigen Gottes: Beiträge zur trinitarischen Theologie* [Munich: Kaiser, 1991]); *The Coming of God: Christian Eschatology*, trans. M. Kohl (Minneapolis: Fortress, 1996; first published as *Das Kommen Gottes: Christliche Eschatologie* [Gütersloh: Kaiser, 1995]).

36. Moltmann, *Theology of Hope*, 39. For Moltmann, eschatology in both Bultmann and Barth remained too much an abstract idea of a transcendental eternity detached from history moving toward a final end. Even in Barth's *Church Dogmatics*, the future remains merely an unveiling of what God has already done in Christ. Another significant dialogue was with the

marginalization of eschatology throughout most of the twentieth century, was nothing short of revolutionary.

Whereas Weiss-Schweitzer, Bultmann, and Dodd had, in different ways, concluded that future eschatology was a *problem* to be overcome in making Christianity credible in the modern world, Moltmann set out to argue precisely the opposite.[37] Famously, he claimed, "From first to last, and not merely in the epilogue, Christianity is eschatology, is hope, forward looking and forward moving, and therefore also revolutionizing and transforming the present. The eschatological is not one element of Christianity, but it is the medium of Christian faith as such, the key in which everything in it is set, the glow that suffuses everything here in the dawn of an expected new day."[38] This is a complex and far-reaching agenda of eschatological recovery, built on the premise that future hope defines all authentically Christian theology.[39] The resurrection is the ground of Christian hope, yet the resurrection follows the cross: the cross stands as testimony to God's solidarity with the godlessness of the world (*The Crucified God*). The dialectic between the cross and resurrection is being resolved by the Spirit, who is transforming present darkness toward a future glorious kingdom (*The Church in the Power of the Spirit*).

This represents a "*Novum*" in history—something transcendentally new, effected by God. The resurrection opens up the possibility of a future that will embrace the new creation of all things and thus fosters hope, especially for the marginalized. In this sense "the future exceeds the present and the past."[40] Because of the resurrection "the future of the new creation sheds its luster into the present of the old world."[41] This is only the barest of sketches of a voluminous output. Before moving on we need only note in agreement with Bauckham that after Moltmann, the proposition "that the resurrection of the crucified Christ provides in some sense a model, as well

---

Marxist Ernst Bloch; through this conversation Moltmann came to see how the Bible and church had rich resources for articulating hope *in this world* dependent not on immanent hopes of human history but on God's transcendent action in the resurrection of Jesus Christ.

37. Richard Bauckham, "Moltmann's Theology of Hope Revisited," *SJT* 42, no. 2 (1989): 199–214.

38. Moltmann, *Theology of Hope*, 16.

39. For largely positive critique see Richard Bauckham, *The Theology of Jürgen Moltmann* (Edinburgh: T&T Clark, 1995). For a less sympathetic assessment see, Tim Chester, *Mission and the Coming of God: Eschatology, the Trinity and Mission in the Theology of Jürgen Moltmann and Contemporary Evangelicalism* (Milton Keynes, UK: Paternoster, 2006). See also Lanier Burns, "The Doctrine of the Future in Jürgen Moltmann," in *Eschatology: Biblical, Historical and Practical Approaches: A Volume in Honor of Craig R. Blaising*, ed. D. Jeffrey Bingham and Glenn R. Kreider (Grand Rapids: Kregel, 2016).

40. Moltmann, *Coming of God*, 26.

41. Moltmann, *Coming of God*, 28.

as a promise, of what the future general resurrection and the new creation of all things might mean has been widely accepted and developed in recent theology."[42]

Norman Perrin and Marcus Borg: The Present Eclipses the Future

This being said, the older tensions between the Jesus of William Wrede and Weiss-Schweitzer continue to play out in some strands of modern scholarship. In the English-speaking world Norman Perrin concluded that an apocalyptic future coming of the Son of Man was not authentic to Jesus, who "gave neither specific form to his future expectation (beyond the general one of vindication and implied judgement), nor did he express it in terms of a specific time element."[43] In talking about "present and future," Jesus was emphasizing not the temporal but the experiential. Thus Perrin reinterprets the kingdom of God as a "tensive symbol" used "to evoke the myth of God acting as king."[44] Of real significance is that the kingdom of God is a "true myth, i.e., as a narrative means of demonstrating 'the inner meaning of the universe and of human life.'"[45] A very similar emphasis was later developed in the non-eschatological Jesus of Borg[46] and others at the Jesus Seminar. Writing personally at a popular level shortly before his death in 2015, Borg described his "postcritical" understanding of Christianity as expressing truth in metaphorical and symbolic language. A future-dominated eschatology seriously distorts a Christian understanding of salvation.[47] Eschatological language in the NT (kingdom of God in the Synoptics and being "in Christ" in Paul) is about transformation into new life here and now.[48] A bigger gulf between the eschatologies of Perrin and Borg and that of Moltmann is hard to conceive. It is questionable whether the former's attempts to "rescue"

---

42. Bauckham, "Conclusion," 672.
43. Norman Perrin, *Rediscovering the Teaching of Jesus* (London: SCM, 1967), 204.
44. Norman Perrin, *Jesus and the Language of the Kingdom: Symbol and Metaphor in New Testament Interpretation* (Philadelphia: Fortress, 1976), 196.
45. Perrin, *Jesus and the Language of the Kingdom*, 23.
46. For example, see Marcus J. Borg, *Jesus in Contemporary Scholarship* (Harrisburg, PA: Trinity Press International, 1994); Borg, *Jesus: Uncovering the Life, Teachings, and Relevance of a Religious Revolutionary* (San Francisco: HarperSanFrancisco, 2006); Borg, *Convictions: How I Learned What Matters Most* (New York: HarperOne, 2014); Marcus J. Borg and N. T. Wright, *The Meaning of Jesus: Two Visions* (San Francisco: HarperSanFrancisco, 1999); Marcus J. Borg, Dale Allison, John Dominic Crossan, and Stephan J. Patterson, *The Apocalyptic Jesus: A Debate* (Santa Rosa, CA: Polebridge Press, 2001).
47. According to Borg, such future-dominated hope turns Christianity into a religion of requirements and rewards; creates a contractual understanding of the Christian life; makes Christianity a religion of self-preservation; fosters individualism; divides people between "saved" and "unsaved"; and leads to a neglect of justice in this life. *Convictions*, 63–65.
48. Borg, *Convictions*, 62.

Christianity from eschatology leaves behind anything recognizably Christian, theologically or historically.

Contemporary Eschatologies

More recent studies in NT eschatology are rooted within the critical traditions described above. Five broad themes can be discerned. First is an ongoing tension between predominantly present or future-oriented eschatologies. Second, notwithstanding discussion on Perrin and Borg above, mirroring developments within the "Third Quest" for the historical Jesus, contemporary eschatological debate has generally moved beyond depoliticized, individualized, and unapocalyptic emphases of earlier scholarship. Third, the most interesting and compelling work being done today is by a diverse range of scholars who take seriously the religious, political, and social world of Jesus and Paul and locate their understanding of the future within that Jewish context.[49] Fourth, in the post-Moltmann era, contemporary eschatology has become more closely related to social ethics, particularly, for example, around the ecological crisis and the future sustainability of this world.[50] Fifth, a significant influence is the recovery of narrative theology and how NT eschatologies are best interpreted within a coherent biblical metanarrative.[51] Overall, we might say that the *Schweitzerstrasse* is most-traveled these days. What follows is a brief guide to a hopefully representative sample of types of traffic negotiating its twists and turns. We will begin with, and give most space to, the juggernaut that is N. T. Wright.[52]

---

49. In this context, even Ladd's influential definition of the kingdom of God as "primarily the dynamic reign or kingly rule of God, and derivatively, the sphere in which the rule is experienced" is conceptually abstract and overly detached from its Jewish context. Ladd, *Theology of the New Testament*, 109.

50. For example, see Richard Bauckham, *The Bible and Ecology: Rediscovering the Community of Creation* (Waco: Baylor University Press, 2010); Douglas J. Moo, "Nature in the New Creation: New Testament Eschatology and the Environment," *JETS* 49 (2006): 449–88; Keith Innes, "Towards an Ecological Eschatology: Continuity and Discontinuity," *EQ* 81, no. 2 (2009): 126–44.

51. This premise is foundational to the work of scholars like E. P. Sanders, N. T. Wright, and J. Richard Middleton. A recent and significant work on this theme, arguing that the Jewish metanarrative of exile and restoration is key to interpreting NT theology, is Timo Eskola, *A Narrative Theology of the New Testament: Exploring the Metanarrative of Exile and Restoration*, WUNT 350 (Tübingen: Mohr Siebeck, 2015), discussed below.

52. Since his *Jesus and the Victory of God* (1996), Wright has continued to produce works related to eschatological themes in Jesus and Paul. Some of the most significant are *What Saint Paul Really Said* (Oxford: Lion, 1997); *The Challenge of Jesus* (London: SPCK, 1999); "Romans," in *The New Interpreter's Bible*, vol. 10 (Nashville: Abingdon, 2002), 393–770; *The Resurrection of the Son of God* (London: SPCK, 2003); *Paul: Fresh Perspectives* (London: SPCK, 2005); *Surprised by Hope* (London: SPCK, 2007); *Justification: God's Plan and Paul's Vision* (London:

N. T. Wright: Eschatology through the Lens of Historical Realism

Wright's eschatology is central to his mammoth project of historical reconstruction of the beliefs of Jesus, Paul, and the first Christians, articulated in most detail within his *Christian Origins and the Question of God* but present within most of his work. As with some other proposals emerging from Wright's fertile mind, his eschatological synthesis is storied, imaginative, and controversial. When *Jesus and the Victory of God (JVG)* first came out, some reviewers thought that Wright had effectively abandoned belief in the second coming and moved toward a fully preterist position.[53] There was reason for this, not least Wright's reaction against what he judged to be popular Christianity's Platonized eschatology—that is, his consistent polemic against heaven being the goal of eschatological hope, conjoining a strong emphasis on realized eschatology in the line of Dodd and G. B. Caird with a historically realist assessment of Jesus as a sociopolitical Jewish Messiah who came to understand himself as the embodiment of an Israel in exile awaiting YHWH's return to his elect people. That return took the form of Jesus reading Israel's Scriptures and coming to the risky faith-filled conclusion that he was the true Israelite in whom God acts and is uniquely present.[54] Consequently, and in true Schweitzer-like style, this Messiah acts courageously in himself to confront evil in and through his sin-atoning and representative death. His coming simultaneously enacts divine judgment on Israel's rejection of her true king and brings his gospel of the kingdom come. Jesus's announcement of judgment is nowhere more graphically pictured than in the Olivet Discourse (Matt. 24–25; Mark 13; Luke 21). Wright's historical realist reading of Daniel 7:13 and Jewish apocalyptic language insists that Mark 13 be read

---

SPCK, 2009); *Pauline Perspectives (Collected Essays, 1978–2013)* (London: SPCK, 2013); *Paul and the Faithfulness of God* (London: SPCK, 2013); *Paul and His Recent Interpreters* (London: SPCK, 2015); *The Day the Revolution Began: Reconsidering the Meaning of Jesus' Crucifixion* (London: SPCK, 2016).

53. For early discussion see Craig Blomberg, "Eschatology and the Church: Some New Testament Perspectives," in *Themelios* 23, no. 3 (June 1998): 3–26, esp. 15–18; Steve Walton, "Exit the Second Coming? N. T. Wright's *Jesus and the Victory of God*," *Anvil* 16, no. 4 (1999): 281–91; Carey C. Newman, ed., *Jesus and the Restoration of Israel: A Critical Assessment of N. T. Wright's "Jesus and the Victory of God"* (Downers Grove, IL: InterVarsity Press, 1999); Robert Stein, "N. T. Wright's *Jesus and the Victory of God*: A Review Article," *JETS* 44, no. 2 (June 2001): 207–18. An influential earlier partial preterist interpretation of the Olivet Discourse was that of R. T. France, most fully articulated in his *Matthew*, NICNT (Grand Rapids: Eerdmans, 2007).

54. It is worth noting how Wright's strong this-worldly historicism emphasizes Jesus's Jewish humanity and works "up" from "below" toward a higher Christology. Wright has been criticized for his apparently "low" Christology. (I remember being present when D. A. Carson did so in debate. Wright replied that he felt that "an accusation of Arianism came whistling past my nose.") The point of mentioning this is that such critique shares the same root as some later resistance to his apparently overly realized eschatology.

as eschatological imagery of the vindication of the Son of Man *within* history (namely the fall of Jerusalem in 70 CE) and not as a literal description of Jesus's second coming in the clouds with power and glory.⁵⁵

It has been over twenty years since the publication of *JVG*, and while there have been some clarifications and significant additions over the years (not least the massive *Resurrection of the Son of God* [*RSG*] and *Paul and the Faithfulness of God* [*PFG*]), Wright's overall framework has not shifted substantially. In the 2018 Gifford Lectures, for example, he broadly rearticulates the narrative above in dialogue with Caird⁵⁶ and familiar opponents representing differing forms of dualism—whether an Enlightenment split between past and present, an Epicurean separation of heaven and earth, or a dehistoricized Bultmannianism.⁵⁷ What has developed since *JVG* is a sustained articulation of an inaugurated "already and not yet" eschatology—within which some of his own more contested proposals are located.⁵⁸ Jesus is an eschatological

---

55. Wright, *JVG*, 80–82, 96–97, 207–9. J. D. G. Dunn describes Wright's eschatology here as containing apocalyptic features that are "simply cosmic sound effects." They tell us nothing about whether Jesus expected anything beyond the destruction of the temple in 70 CE (J. D. G. Dunn, *Jesus Remembered* [Grand Rapids: Eerdmans, 2003], 479). Other criticism of Wright's historically realized interpretation includes that of Edward Adams, who contends such texts do have a future catastrophe in view. While not necessarily literal descriptions of the end of the world, they function to evoke imagination of the unknowable (Edward Adams, *The Stars Will Fall from Heaven: "Cosmic Catastrophe" in the New Testament and Its World*, LNTS 347 [London: T&T Clark, 2007]). Alternatively, a radical version of realized eschatology that builds on Wright is that of Andrew Perriman, *The Coming of the Son of Man: New Testament Eschatology for an Emerging Church* (Milton Keynes, UK: Paternoster, 2005). Perriman heads back toward Dodd in arguing that the NT imagines three eschatological horizons: the coming of the Son of Man announced by Jesus, the parousia of the Lord, and the hope of a new creation. The first two horizons *have already occurred*: the suffering of the Son of Man, linked with 70 CE, and the parousia, linked with the fall of the Roman Empire, which vindicated the suffering people of God and revealed Christ as Lord. Thus for Perriman the "central action of New Testament eschatology" has therefore *already* unfolded *within* history (225). The church now exists in "the age that has come."

56. For the full series of eight lectures see "2018 Lecture Series: NT Wright," website of the University of Aberdeen, https://www.abdn.ac.uk/sdhp/events/gifford-lectures/2018-lecture-series-n-t-wright-1089.php. I am referencing lecture 4, "The End of the World? Eschatology and Apocalyptic in Historical Perspective," https://www.youtube.com/watch?v=DHubt-njRlM&feature=youtu.be. The engagement is with G. B. Caird, *The Language and Imagery of the Bible* (London: Duckworth, 1980), and Caird's definitions of eschatology and apocalyptic.

57. Wright, "End of the World?," Gifford Lecture 4.

58. Arguably *JVG*'s emphasis on the Olivet Discourse's single referent being 70 CE gave a confusing impression of the destruction of the temple as the climax of God's judgment. See Wright's specific rejection of full preterism in *Surprised by Hope*, 139. Wright's wariness of any eschatology with an "other-worldly" flavor has also led some to claim that he marginalizes the place of heaven within Christian hope—a charge that Wright rejects. See Markus Bockmuehl, "Did St. Paul Go to Heaven When He Died?," in *Jesus, Paul and the People of God: A Theological Dialogue with N. T. Wright*, ed. Nicholas Perrin and Richard Hays (London: SPCK, 2011), 211–34. Similarly, Nicholas Perrin, in a deeply appreciative review, comments that *JVG* neglected, out of a reaction against dehistoricized pietism, Jesus's eschatological summons

and apocalyptic prophet in and through whom the kingdom comes. *This world has been changed as a result and, because of Jesus's resurrection, will be fully transformed in the future.* Thus for Paul "this hope both *had been fulfilled* through Jesus, in his kingdom-establishing death and resurrection, and the life-transforming spirit, and *would yet be fulfilled* in the second coming of Jesus and in the work of the same spirit to raise all of the Messiah's people from the dead."[59] The nature of that transformation is holistic; it embraces the spiritual, political, and social within a renewed creation. A consistent Wrightian theme is that the emphatically "earthy" nature of that future hope has social implications for the praxis of Christian ethics in the "here and now."[60]

What has also become more evident is how, in dramatic contrast to the atomistic methodology of those like the Jesus Seminar, Wright sees an essential storied coherence within diverse strands of NT eschatology as a whole. Paul's eschatology as presented in *PFG* follows the broad contours of the Synoptics' eschatologies presented within *JVG* with the added significance of the Spirit within Pauline eschatological hope.[61] Similarly, in the Gifford lectures Wright argues that Paul, the Synoptics, John, and other NT authors all, in distinct ways, articulate a recognizably consistent eschatological hope in light of the story of Jesus Christ. In contrast to Frey's comment about Paul's mistaken hopes discussed above, Wright, in summarizing Paul, contends that "the belief in a now and not yet inaugurated kingdom through the exaltation of the human being Jesus, Israel's messiah, was not then a piece of clever apologetic invented in the late first century let alone the mid-twentieth century. It was part of the earliest apostolic gospel itself."[62] In regard to the Gospels, "John has his own ways of saying the same thing, but it is the same thing [as the

---

to individuals to enter the kingdom of God in the present and so secure future hope—a criticism Wright accepts (Nicholas Perrin, "Jesus' Eschatology and Kingdom Ethics," in Perrin and Hays, *Jesus, Paul and the People of God*, 113). Another highly contested eschatological theme is Wright's "reworked" notion of the people of God, a topic that takes up the 268 pages of chap. 10 ("The People of God, Freshly Reworked") in *PFG* plus another 140 pages in chap. 11 ("God's Future for the World, Freshly Imagined"). Questions are raised by Wright's understanding of Israel and Jesus within the eschatological work of God. Has ethnic Israel failed in its elective calling to be God's means of redemption? Does Jesus fulfill Israel's calling in his faithful self-giving life and death, effectively "becoming Israel" in the process? Do all who have faith in Jesus then become, in effect, members of Israel (the church)? Does this mean that in Paul terms like "Jew" and "Israel" are so radically reworked as to no longer refer to actual Jews and actual Israel? For critical questioning of Wright's answers to these questions, see, for example, Michael G. Vanlaningham, "An Evaluation of N. T. Wright's View of Israel in Romans 11," *BSac* 170 (April–June 2013): 179–93.

59. Wright, *PFG*, 1258–59.
60. For example, see Wright, *Surprised by Hope*, chaps. 12–15; Wright, *PFG*, 1095–1128.
61. See Wright, *PFG*, 1061–95.
62. Wright, "The End of the World?," Gifford Lecture 4.

Synoptics]. The gospels do not contain apocalyptic; in the first-century sense they are apocalyptic. They are describing how the revelation, the unveiling, the visible coming of God took place."[63] This is where Wright departs from Weiss-Schweitzer. There is no hint, he argues, in the NT of the first Christians wrestling with the failure of eschatological hopes. Rather, there is a pervasive inaugurated eschatology that has come retrospectively to understand the death, resurrection, and vindication of Jesus Christ. This is expressed in apocalyptic language, which is "biblical language to convey the meaning of the one-off event; meaning which came through its *unique* and *disruptive* role *within* the narrative of creation and covenant."[64]

Brant Pitre: Jesus the Prophet of Eschatological Tribulation

Wright forms one of the main dialogue partners in Brant Pitre's significant 2005 work on NT eschatology.[65] In it the author has two overall objectives: to identify the development and content of the concept of eschatological tribulation in late Second Temple Judaism and to determine if the historical Jesus spoke of or acted on the basis of his own expectation of a period of eschatological tribulation, and if so, how he did.[66] Schweitzer's ghost looms large here, and Pitre is consciously walking in its shadow. If Jesus's expectation of a final messianic tribulation formed the heart of Schweitzer's consequent eschatology, Pitre sets out to explore what that expectation may have looked like in light of detailed historical and exegetical study. In doing so he distances himself from scholars like E. P. Sanders and others who disconnect the notion of an eschatological tribulation from the life and teaching of Jesus and from those who question the authenticity of the eschatological prophecies in the Olivet Discourse.[67]

Pitre differs sharply from Wright's view that the "end" of the Babylonian exile is to be interpreted in political and metaphorical terms.[68] Rather, Pitre

---

63. Wright, "The End of the World?," Gifford Lecture 4.
64. Wright, "The End of the World?," Gifford Lecture 4. In this lecture Wright specifically responds to criticism by Jörg Frey that Wright's grand narrative interpretation of Paul effectively neutralizes Paul's apocalypticism and distances the apostle from Jesus. Jörg Frey, "Demythologizing Apocalyptic? On N. T. Wright's Paul, Apocalyptic Interpretation, and the Constraints of Construction," in *God and the Faithfulness of Paul: A Critical Examination of the Pauline Theology of N. T. Wright*, ed. Christoph Heilig, J. Thomas Hewitt, and Michael F. Bird, WUNT 2/413 (Tübingen: Mohr Siebeck, 2016), 489–532.
65. Brant Pitre, *Jesus, the Tribulation, and the End of Exile: Restoration Eschatology and the Origin of the Atonement*, WUNT 2/204 (Tübingen: Mohr Siebeck, 2005). Other dialogue partners for whom the coming of a new age of salvation is linked in some way to a time of tribulation include Albert Schweitzer, C. H. Dodd, J. Jeremias, Ben F. Meyer, Dale Allison, James D. G. Dunn, and C. Marvin Pate and Doug Kennard.
66. Pitre, *Jesus, the Tribulation, and the End of Exile*, 3.
67. E. P. Sanders, *Jesus and Judaism* (Philadelphia: Fortress, 1985).
68. Pitre, *Jesus, the Tribulation, and the End of Exile*, 31–40.

argues it should be understood within a literal horizon in line with what the OT prophets foretold—namely, *"the ingathering of all twelve tribes of Israel to Zion from among the Gentiles."*[69] For example, the "many" of Mark 10:45 are the Jews of the exile, and "ransom" refers to his death, which will inaugurate the final great tribulation.[70] Pitre summarizes his most significant conclusion as this: *"Jesus, speaking of himself as both Son of Man and Messiah, deliberately took the sufferings of the tribulation upon himself in order to atone the sins of Israel, sins which had led them into exile. Because he saw this tribulation as nothing less than an eschatological Passover, he sought to inaugurate it in both word and deed, thereby, to bring about the End of the Exile and the restoration of the twelve tribes in a New Exodus."*[71] This portrait of Jesus's self-understanding and the significance of the tribulation and end of exile in it is a striking one that will continue to be debated within studies in eschatology and the historical Jesus.

Timo Eskola: Exile and Restoration as the Framing Story of the NT

Themes of metanarrative, exile, and restoration are also taken up in Timo Eskola's ambitious 2015 study, which explores whether Jesus's eschatological identity as a rebuilder of the temple announcing judgment on Israel was intrinsic to his teaching. Eskola, though, widens the conversation to engage with how Paul's narrative theology, as well as that of John, Hebrews, 1 Peter, James, and Revelation, relates to that of Jesus.[72] Rather than "real" history hiding behind allegedly corrupted texts (Wrede), history, he argues, comes to us in the form of narratives, and so "a proper understanding of New Testament theology depends on a proper reading of narratives."[73] He specifically locates his research in the wake of Wright's expansion of his interpretive framework in *JVG* to Paul,[74] and he takes as a starting point that Jesus's self-understanding was that of a messianic vocation to effect the end of exile and reform Israel's worship by building an eschatological temple. His thesis is that the theme of exile and restoration forms a metanarrative within the Bible that gives explanatory power for the construction of NT soteriology. "Reading the prophets taught both Jesus and the first apostles that reconciliation comes through atonement. The Suffering Servant must give his sacrifice

---

69. Pitre, *Jesus, the Tribulation, and the End of Exile*, 40.
70. Pitre, *Jesus, the Tribulation, and the End of Exile*, 384–454.
71. Pitre, *Jesus, the Tribulation, and the End of Exile*, 505–6 (italics original).
72. Eskola, *Narrative Theology*, 13. Eskola builds on the earlier work of Sanders (*Jesus and Judaism*, 1985), which emphasized the importance of exile in Second Temple Judaism, as well as on Ben F. Meyer, *The Aims of Jesus* (London: SCM, 1979).
73. Eskola, *Narrative Theology*, 8.
74. Eskola, *Narrative Theology*, 11.

in order to bring peace to Israel. Jesus's resurrection, then, becomes the end time enthronement where God is King and starts his jubilee, the year of mercy and release for those in slavery. Only after that can the triumphant events of eschatology take place and the Heavenly King return in his power."[75]

This soteriology is inseparable from the resurrection Christology of Jesus's followers. For believers the exile has ended; Jesus is the exalted eschatological Savior, the enthroned Son of David ruling a new kingdom in which the temple has been rebuilt in the form of renewed believers.[76] For Paul this "new community is Christ's temple where the Holy Spirit has returned."[77] Eskola concludes that restoration eschatology permeates Paul's soteriology[78] and provides a key for fresh thinking about Paul's relationship with the law and other issues within the New Perspective. While elements of his reconstruction will undoubtedly be debated, such a reading offers a far more satisfying and persuasive account of NT eschatology than older twentieth-century interpretations that often de-Judaized, dehistoricized, and de-eschatologized the text, driving a wedge between Jesus and the rest of the NT in the process.

James D. G. Dunn: Metaphorical Eschatology

Since the turn of the millennium the prolific James D. G. Dunn has completed his massive, three-volume *Christianity in the Making*,[79] and no analysis of NT scholarship on eschatology can overlook his contribution.[80] Dunn tends to display more historical caution than Wright.[81] Within Jesus's teaching on

---

75. Eskola, *Narrative Theology*, 418.
76. Eskola, *Narrative Theology*, 387.
77. Eskola, *Narrative Theology*, 419.
78. Eskola argues that Paul follows most themes of Jesus's mission: (1) the fulfilment of time, (2) gospel, (3) tribulation, (4) suffering, (5) substitutional sacrifice, (6) resurrection from the dead, (7) enthronement on the throne of glory, (8) realization of restoration, (9) gathering the tribes and mission to the nations, (10) parousia, (11) last judgment, and (12) the final restoration of Eden. *Narrative Theology*, 424.
79. James D. G. Dunn, *Jesus Remembered*, vol. 1 of *Christianity in the Making* (Grand Rapids: Eerdmans, 2003); Dunn, *Beginning from Jerusalem*, vol. 2 of *Christianity in the Making* (Grand Rapids: Eerdmans, 2009); Dunn, *Neither Jew nor Greek: A Contested Identity*, vol. 3 of *Christianity in the Making* (Grand Rapids: Eerdmans, 2015). Much of the material in Dunn, *A New Perspective on Jesus: What the Quest for the Historical Jesus Missed*, Acadia Studies in Bible and Theology (Grand Rapids: Baker Academic, 2005), is covered in more detail in *Jesus Remembered*, so discussion here will focus on the larger work.
80. *Jesus Remembered* contains a masterful discussion of two centuries of historical-Jesus studies. See chap. 3, "The (Re)-Awakening of Historical Awareness"; chap. 4, "The Flight from Dogma"; and chap. 5, "The Flight from History."
81. This is the case in both eschatology and Christology. For an example of Dunn's historically restrained Christology see J. D. G. Dunn, *Did the First Christians Worship Jesus?* (London: SPCK, 2010).

the kingdom of God—and in Paul[82] and the other authors of the NT[83]—Dunn proposes a now "standard" inaugurated eschatology that embraces both present and future strands that are firmly rooted in Jesus himself. He rejects attempts to promote one strand at the expense of the other, whether it is Dodd, Käsemann,[84] or the Jesus Seminar overemphasizing the present or Weiss, Schweitzer, Sanders, Dale Allison,[85] and Bart Ehrman[86] doing the same with the future.[87] Yet he also resists those who see the Jesus tradition through some grand unifying metanarrative—even radically divergent versions like those of Crossan[88] and Wright.[89]

When it comes to answering his own question, "What kind of 'end' does the Jesus tradition envisage?," Dunn remains circumspect. He accepts some sort of synthesis between the present and future, highlighting the Spirit as the "first instalment" of the kingdom whose full inheritance is yet to come.[90] Yet he also states that such "now and not yet" eschatologies struggle to account for Jesus's expectation of an *imminent* unfolding of final events that were not realized. This suggests (1) "putting it bluntly, Jesus was proved wrong by the course of events" and (2) "nor is this a conclusion I would wish to resist on my part."[91] Yet he adds this significant rider: within Jewish prophetic/apocalyptic tradition there was some recognition that partial fulfillment of hope did not invalidate that hope. Hope by definition is indeterminate and often "mistaken" because it looks forward into an unknowable future. More significantly, Jewish hope is

82. For example, commenting on 2 Thessalonians, Dunn concludes that "in all this, it is worth repeating, Paul's teaching was consistent with Jesus' own teaching on the coming of the kingdom: imminent, but with an interval prior to its full coming." Dunn, *Beginning from Jerusalem*, 719.

83. Summarizing Peter's legacy, Dunn writes that "the expectation of Christ's return as setting in train final judgement is clear in several passages. . . . The lively hope of an imminent 'end of all things' (4.7) is as clear as in the Synoptic tradition and in Paul, still retained even a full generation after Jesus' own mission." Dunn, *Beginning from Jerusalem*, 1161.

84. E. Käsemann, *New Testament Questions for Today* (London: SCM, 1969), 82–107.

85. See, for example, Dale Allison, "A Plea for a Thoroughgoing Eschatology," *JBL* 113, no. 4 (1994): 651–66; Allison, "The Eschatology of Jesus," in *The Encyclopedia of Apocalypticism*, ed. John J. Collins, vol. 1, *The Origins of Apocalypticism in Judaism and Christianity* (New York: Continuum, 1998), 267–302.

86. Bart D. Ehrman, *Jesus: Apocalyptic Prophet of the New Millennium* (Oxford: Oxford University Press, 1999).

87. Dunn, *Jesus Remembered*, 466.

88. J. D. Crossan, *The Birth of Christianity* (San Francisco: Harper, 1998).

89. Dunn identifies three significant problems with Wright's narrative of exile and restoration: (1) an exaggerated importance of the theme of return of exile within Palestinian Judaism; (2) the diversity of Jewish expectations among Jesus's contemporaries; (3) Wright's inability to demonstrate that the narrative of exile was a controlling factor in Jesus's own teaching. *Jesus Remembered*, 470–77.

90. Dunn, *Jesus Remembered*, 479. For more detailed discussion see J. D. G. Dunn, *Jesus and the Spirit*, vol. 2, *Pneumatology* (Grand Rapids: Eerdmans, 1998), 133–41.

91. Dunn, *Jesus Remembered*, 479–80.

centered not on hope itself or on a timetable of events but in God. Thus Dunn speculates whether the indeterminate nature of Jewish hope, shaped by image and symbol, is one reason why the supposed "delay" of the parousia was not a major issue for the early Christians.[92] Rather, they could live with an intrinsically "unordered narrative" characterized by metaphorical and mythical language (rather than imposing an ordered narrative like Wright's). Such language is pictorial and allusive, but can nonetheless denote that which is *beyond* history.

Dunn therefore resists Wright's confident application of apocalyptic language in the Olivet Discourse to a single referent (70 CE). A better question, Dunn suggests, is not, What does this *mean*? but, What does this *evoke*? Eschatological language is that which applies more to the heart than to the head.[93] Dunn's arguments are well made. His conclusions, particularly on Jesus being mistaken, will seem to many to be overly negative. Similarly, such caution extends to arguing that the phrase "the resurrection of Jesus" is a metaphor that says something *"which could not otherwise be said"* and arguing that to see it in literal terms is to "abandon" the metaphor.[94] Many will see it otherwise; to insist on resurrection as metaphor does not preserve its explanatory power but risks draining it of significance—however much Dunn affirms its essentially eschatological character.[95]

J. Richard Middleton: *The Case for Holistic Eschatology*

A well-received recent account of biblical eschatology, written for a broad audience but underpinned by substantial scholarship, is that of J. Richard Middleton in his book *A New Heaven and a New Earth: Reclaiming Biblical Eschatology*.[96] The "reclaiming" in question is the telos of eschatology as that

---

92. Dunn, *Jesus Remembered*, 482. How this suggestion fits conceptually with his earlier agreement with the idea that Jesus was mistaken requires clarification. Dunn's argument here is close to but not the same as that of Scot McKnight, *A New Vision for Israel: A New Vision for Israel* (Grand Rapids: Eerdmans, 1999), 128–39. McKnight resists saying that Jesus was mistaken but says that "we ought to admit that his knowledge of the future was limited in the same way that the Hebrew prophets' visions were limited to events of their respective generations" (138).

93. Dunn, *Jesus Remembered*, 486.

94. Dunn, *Jesus Remembered*, 878 (italics original). Dunn explicitly affirms the resurrection of Jesus but argues that as a metaphor it is not so much a criterion of faith as a paradigm of hope (479).

95. Dunn expands on the significance of the resurrection in vol. 2 of *Christianity in the Making*. However exactly understood, it was "probably seen as ushering in the new age, the end time which had long been seen as the climax of God's purpose in creation and for Israel in particular. . . . The end-time harvest had begun to be reaped. The final denouement could not be long delayed. . . . This is what is meant when the term 'eschatological' is used to describe the first community and its message. At the beginning it carried all the overtones of final expectation in process of being realized, with full consummation imminent." Dunn, *Beginning from Jerusalem*, 213–14.

96. J. Richard Middleton, *A New Heaven and a New Earth: Reclaiming Biblical Eschatology* (Grand Rapids: Baker Academic, 2014).

of a new heaven and a new earth rather than an often confused and dualistic notion of heaven as an atemporal and immaterial realm.[97] Middleton's work is a fine articulation of modern eschatological themes mentioned earlier: biblical hope as the climax of a unfolding narrative,[98] a coherent unity within distinct NT eschatologies interpreted within their Jewish context, and a dynamic interaction between future hope and present ethics.[99] Influenced by Ladd and with strong echoes of Wright, Middleton aims "to clarify how New Testament eschatology, rather than being a speculative add-on to the Bible, actually coheres with, and is the logical outworking of, the consistently holistic theology of the entirety of Scripture."[100] In this task he succeeds admirably. Whether all will be convinced by his synthesis of diverse biblical hopes remains open to question.[101]

Richard Bauckham: The Centrality of Eschatology

Few scholars have made as significant contribution to the study of eschatology as Christian historian Richard Bauckham. In an outstanding career characterized by remarkable theological and biblical breadth,[102] he has published widely on subjects with strong eschatological themes such as John's Gospel,[103] historical-Jesus studies,[104] apocalyptic literature[105] and particularly the book

---

97. An exceptionally useful appendix, "What Happened to the New Earth?," surveys historically how development of hope in an otherworldly heaven came to dominate Christian eschatology. Major turning points discussed include Augustine's Neoplatonism, the impact of millennialism, the rise of dispensational rapture theology, and the recovery of holistic eschatology during the twentieth century and onward. Middleton, *New Heaven and a New Earth*, 283–312.

98. Middleton, *New Heaven and a New Earth*, 37–175, comprising part 1, "From Creation to Eschaton"; part 2, "Holistic Salvation in the Old Testament"; and part 3, "The New Testament's Vision of Cosmic Renewal."

99. Middleton, *New Heaven and a New Earth*, part 5, "The Ethics of the Kingdom," 241–82.

100. Middleton, *New Heaven and a New Earth*, 15.

101. See, for example, Brian C. Dennert, review of Middleton, *New Creation*, in *BBR* 25, no. 4 (2015): 590–91.

102. Space here allows reference only to works related to eschatology in the last twenty years or so. For a full list of books and articles see the website "Richard Bauckham: Biblical Scholar and Theologian," http://richardbauckham.co.uk/index.php?page=publications.

103. Richard Bauckham, *Gospel of Glory: Major Themes in Johannine Theology* (Grand Rapids: Baker Academic, 2015); Bauckham, "Dualism and Soteriology in Johannine Theology," in *Beyond Bultmann: Reckoning a New Testament Theology*, ed. Bruce W. Longenecker and Mikeal C. Parsons (Waco: Baylor University Press, 2014), 133–53; Bauckham, *The Testimony of the Beloved Disciple: Narrative, History, and Theology in the Gospel of John* (Grand Rapids: Baker Academic, 2007).

104. Richard Bauckham, "The Future of Jesus Christ," in *The Cambridge Companion to Jesus*, ed. M. Bockmuehl (Cambridge: Cambridge University Press, 2001), 265–80; Bauckham, "The Restoration of Israel in Luke-Acts," in *Restoration: Old Testament, Jewish and Christian Perspectives*, ed. J. M. Scott, JSJSup 72 (Leiden: Brill, 2001), 435–87; Bauckham, "Life, Death, and the Afterlife in Second Temple Judaism," in *Life in the Face of Death: The Resurrection Message of the New Testament*, ed. Richard Longenecker (Grand Rapids: Eerdmans, 1998), 80–95.

105. Richard Bauckham, "Non-canonical Apocalypses and Prophetic Works," in *The Oxford Handbook of Early Christian Apocrypha*, ed. Andrew Gregory and Christopher Tuckett

of Revelation,[106] the eschatology of Jürgen Moltmann,[107] and various themes related eschatological ethics[108] and eschatology in general.[109] Given such a prodigious and varied output and limited space, I am not even going to attempt to offer a synthesis of his work.[110] Rather, as a "way in" to a flavor of Bauckhamian concerns, we will engage with his own recent reflections on emerging issues in eschatology in the twenty-first century.[111]

Referring to his sevenfold categorization of Moltmann's eschatology,[112] Bauckham argues that "Christian eschatology in the twenty-first century that aims at faithfulness to the theological heart of the gospel and at relevance to

---

(Oxford: Oxford University Press, 2015), 115–37; Bauckham, "Apocalypses and Prophetic Works in Volume 1 of the New Pseudepigrapha," *Early Christianity* 5 (2014): 127–38; Bauckham, "Apocalypses," in *Justification and Variegated Nomism*, vol. 1, *The Complexities of Second Temple Judaism*, ed. D. A. Carson et al. (Tübingen: Mohr Siebeck, 2001), 135–87; Bauckham, *The Fate of the Dead: Studies on the Jewish and Christian Apocalypses* (Leiden: Brill, 1998).

106. Richard Bauckham, "Judgment in the Book of Revelation," in *The Book of Revelation: Currents in British Research on the Apocalypse*, ed. Garrick V. Allen et al., WUNT 2/411 (Tübingen: Mohr Siebeck, 2015), 55–79; Bauckham, "The Language of Warfare in the Book of Revelation," in *Compassionate Eschatology: The Future as Friend*, ed. Ted Grimsrud and Michael Hardin (Eugene, OR: Cascade, 2011), 28–41; Bauckham, *The Climax of Prophecy: Studies on the Book of Revelation* (Edinburgh: T&T Clark, 1993); Bauckham, *The Theology of the Book of Revelation* (Cambridge: Cambridge University Press, 1993).

107. Richard Bauckham, ed., *God Will Be All in All: The Eschatology of Jürgen Moltmann*, (Edinburgh: T&T Clark, 1999), esp. chap. I/1, "Eschatology in *The Coming of God*"; chap. IV/1, "The Millennium"; chap. V/1, "Time and Eternity." See also Bauckham, "Must Christian Eschatology Be Millenarian? A Response to Jürgen Moltmann" (Tyndale Christian Doctrine Lecture for 1997), in *"The Reader Must Understand": Eschatology in Bible and Theology*, ed. K. E. Brower and M. W. Elliott (Leicester: Apollos, 1997), 263–77; Bauckham, *The Theology of Jürgen Moltmann* (Edinburgh: T&T Clark, 1995).

108. Richard Bauckham, "God's Creation and Its Goal: A Christian Perspective," in *God's Creativity and Human Action: Christian and Muslim Perspectives*, ed. Lucinda Mosher and David Marshall (Washington, DC: Georgetown University Press, 2017), 51–62; Bauckham, "Ecological Hope in Crisis?," in *Creation Care and the Gospel: Reconsidering the Mission of the Church*, ed. Colin Bell and Robert S. White (Peabody, MA: Hendrickson, 2016), 43–52; Bauckham, "Ecological Hope in Crisis?," *Anvil* 30 (2014): 43–54; Bauckham, "The Story of the Earth according to Paul: Romans 8:18–23," *Review and Expositor* 108 (2011): 91–97.

109. Bauckham, "Conclusion"; Bauckham, "Eschatology," in *The Oxford Handbook of Systematic Theology*, ed. John Webster et al. (Oxford: Oxford University Press, 2007), 306–22; Bauckham, "The Year 2000 and the End of Secular Eschatology," in *Called to One Hope: Perspectives on the Life to Come*, ed. J. Colwell (Carlisle, UK: Paternoster, 2000), 240–51; Bauckham, "Eschatology," in *The Oxford Companion to Christian Thought*, ed. A. Hastings (Oxford: Oxford University Press, 2000), 206–9; Bauckham, "The Decline of Progress and the Prospects for Christian Hope," *Evangel* 17 (1999): 87–95; Bauckham, "Approaching the Millennium," *Anvil* 16 (1999): 255–67; Richard Bauckham and Trevor Hart, *Hope against Hope: Christian Eschatology in Contemporary Context* (London: Darton, Longman & Todd, 1999).

110. For a recent Festschrift see Daniel M. Gurtner et al., eds., *In the Fullness of Time: Essays on Christology, Creation, and Eschatology in Honor of Richard Bauckham* (Grand Rapids: Eerdmans, 2016).

111. Bauckham, "Conclusion."

112. The seven characteristics are (1) christological eschatology, (2) integrative eschatology, (3) redemptive eschatology, (4) processive eschatology, (5) theocentric eschatology, (6) contextual

the cultural contexts to which it speaks is likely to show these characteristics."[113] He focuses on the first two. First, Christian hope is founded on the eschatological future promised by God in the resurrection of the crucified Christ. The resurrection is "the basis for expecting from God what has not yet happened in a future still open to the new creation of all things"[114] and relates closely to questions of continuity and discontinuity between old and new creations. But an authentically Christian eschatology must also remember Moltmann's insistence that hope is in the resurrection of a *crucified* Messiah who died identified with the godless and godforsaken. From this perspective, a christologically shaped eschatology will demonstrate solidarity with "the guilty and the despairing, the impoverished and the terminally ill, all the wretched of the earth, and, not least the dead. It is usually the affluent and the secure who think they can do without eschatology."[115]

Second, echoing Moltmann and themes in Wright and Middleton among many others, Bauckham proposes an integrative eschatology that refuses to divide God's creation into the immortal and the perishable by offering a "holistic vision of redemption and transfiguration for the whole of God's creation."[116] Such holistic eschatology speaks into the ecological crisis facing humanity, particularly around the destiny of nonhuman creation—*Are we saved from it or with it?*—and will likely be a fruitful avenue for further eschatological thought.

This tiny snapshot of Bauckham's astonishing spectrum of eschatological writing, and the impact of Moltmann on it, points to how he, probably more than any other scholar alive today, has made an overwhelming case for the absolutely central place of eschatology in NT thought. Bauckham has a remarkable ability to zoom out from specialized historical and exegetical research to reflect critically on broad theological themes and their implications for Christian life and ethics. In the remainder of the chapter, for example, he explores how Christian eschatology confronts modern metanarratives of progress, whether now largely incredible Enlightenment hopes in a utopian future, more recent neoliberal ideology of free-market globalization,[117] messianic claims of con-

---

eschatology, and (7) politically and pastorally responsible eschatology. For more detailed analysis see Bauckham, "Eschatology in *The Coming of God*."

113. Bauckham, "Conclusion," 672.

114. Bauckham, "Conclusion," 672.

115. Bauckham, "Conclusion," 673.

116. He adds that "eschatological thought has all too often abstracted the soul from the body, the individual from human community, and human history from the rest of creation." Bauckham, "Conclusion," 673.

117. Bauckham notes that in its American version "the old idea of America as a messianic nation still justifies an imperialistic role that is portrayed as a mission to bring freedom to the rest of the world" (Bauckham, "Conclusion," 677). Trump's election in 2016, I suggest, changed the narrative to a different form of messianism; an internally focused nationalistic story that promises another myth of progress—to "make America great again."

temporary science as inevitably beneficial,[118] or postmodern questioning of rational progressivism and postmodernism's subsequent tendency toward a present-oriented hedonism.[119] The creative tension for contemporary Christian eschatology, then, is between expressing hope in the transcendent possibilities of God and yet simultaneously ensuring that that hope is grounded in the cross and resurrection of Jesus. Bauckham suggests that this is where the rich imagery of biblical eschatology comes into its own. Hope is essentially an imaginative exercise that transcends present realities and pictures a transformed future. Images and symbols speak of a transcendent future that has continuity with our present experience; otherwise, they would be incomprehensible. But neither can they be literally described or reduced to abstract concepts; to attempt to do so is to miss the point. This is the great failing of so much popular Christian eschatological discourse. The eschatological language of Scripture, rather, invites readers into an imaginative world that needs continually fresh exposition in engagement with contemporary culture.[120]

Reflections

This survey of the face of studies in NT eschatology has, given the complexity and size of the subject matter, been necessarily broad in scope. Hopefully a reasonably "in focus" picture has emerged, even if we've taken it at a distance rather than zooming in on specific features. Our "lens" has been the dynamic tension between the present and future in NT scholarship, and so we have deliberately not engaged with detailed debates around more traditional issues of biblical eschatology,[121] such as death; the intermediate state; the resurrection body; the return of Christ;[122] millennialism;[123] heaven, hell, and

---

118. A powerful example of this sort of confrontation emerges from Bauckham's questioning of the assumption that intelligence, abstracted from other qualities of personhood, is a supreme good: "The project of creating post-humans is yet another example of the modern attempt to make immanent reality what Christian eschatology expects from the transcendent power of God: in this case, glorified humanity of the exalted Christ and those who will be like him in resurrection." Bauckham, "Conclusion," 678.

119. Bauckham, "Conclusion," 673–80.

120. Bauckham, "Conclusion," 680–82. Bauckham offers suggestions on the use of the arts, such as story, music, dance, and visual arts. Film, I suggest, is another area that has rich possibility. For more extended discussion on eschatological imagery see Bauckham and Hart, *Hope against Hope*, 72–173.

121. For critically thoughtful theological and biblical exploration of traditional themes, see Anthony C. Thiselton, *Life after Death: A New Approach to Last Things* (Grand Rapids: Eerdmans, 2012).

122. For an intriguing analysis of the "problem" between the imminent eschatological language of the NT and the fact that nearly two millennia have passed since, see Christopher M. Hays et al., *When the Son of Man Didn't Come: A Constructive Proposal on the Delay of the Parousia* (Minneapolis: Fortress, 2016).

123. For eschatological developments within progressive dispensationalism see Bingham and Kreider, *Eschatology*; Craig R. Blaising and Darrell L. Bock, *Progressive Dispensationalism*

final judgment;[124] universalism;[125] and the ultimate Christian hope as being in the presence of the triune God himself rather than exactly "where" the new creation will be and "what" it will look like.[126] From our vantage point ten concluding observations can be made.

1. In the heyday of liberal nonapocalypticism, Ernst Troeltsch reportedly affirmed the statement that "today the office of eschatology is usually closed. It is closed because the ideas upon which it is founded have lost their roots."[127] Today it is Troeltsch's assumptions that have been uprooted. Eschatology's comeback is founded on the widely held conviction that the images and ideas of NT hope originate within the narrative Jewish thought world of the first Christians and Jesus himself.[128]

2. As our discussion of Wright, Pitre, Eskola, and Dunn has shown, how NT hopes relate to those of the OT is perhaps one of the most interesting and debated questions of modern eschatology.[129]

3. Particularly post-Moltmann, and reinforced by Bauckham, the renaissance of eschatology is characterized by a recognition that it represents the

---

(Grand Rapids: Bridgepoint Books, 1993). For a recent restatement of nondispensational premillennialism, see Craig R. Blomberg and Sung Wook Chung, eds., *A Case for Historic Premillennialism: An Alternative to "Left Behind" Eschatology* (Grand Rapids: Baker Academic, 2009).

124. *Hell*—what the NT means by it, who goes there and for how long—continues to be much debated. Edward Fudge's biblical and theological case for conditional immortality is in its third edition, complete with a forward by Richard Bauckham: *The Fire That Consumes: A Biblical and Historical Study of the Doctrine of Final Punishment*, 3rd ed. (Eugene, OR: Cascade, 2011). See also Christopher M. Date et al., eds., *Rethinking Hell: Readings in Evangelical Conditionalism* (Eugene, OR: Cascade, 2014), with contributions by many well-known NT scholars. For creative analysis see Ramon W. Baker, *Issuant Views of Hell in Contemporary Anglo-American Theology* (Stockholm, Sweden: Åbo Akademi University Press, 2014).

125. Historically, universalism has been a "minority report" in Christian tradition and particularly evangelicalism. The publication of the second edition of Robin Parry's (originally published under the pseudonymn Gregory MacDonald) proposal that it become a legitimate strand of evangelical thought is indicative of universalism's growing appeal. Gregory MacDonald, *The Evangelical Universalist*, 2nd ed. (Eugene, OR: Cascade, 2012). For a reply, see Derek Tidball, "Can Evangelicals Be Universalists?," *Evangelical Quarterly* 84 (2012): 19–32.

126. Thiselton has an extended discussion of this important theme in *Life after Death*, 185–215.

127. Ernst Troeltsch, *Glaubenslehre*, ed. Martha Troeltsch (Munich: Duncker & Humblot, 1925), 36, cited in Gerhard Sauter, "The Doctrine of Last Things," in Walls, *Oxford Handbook of Eschatology*, 253.

128. It is in this sense that Richard Hays argues that "the church needs apocalyptic eschatology to carry Israel's story forward." It is in Jesus Christ that the hopes of Israel find their fulfilment. Richard Hays, "'Why Do You Stand Looking Up toward Heaven?' New Testament Eschatology at the Turn of the Millennium," *Modern Theology* 16, no. 1 (2000): 125–26.

129. One "symptom" of this fact is a series of studies on the significance of the temple in Christian eschatology. See, for example, Desmond Alexander and Simon Gathercole, eds., *Heaven on Earth: The Temple in Biblical Theology* (Carlisle, UK: Paternoster, 2004); Gregory Beale, *The Temple and the Church's Mission: A Biblical Theology of the Dwelling Place of God* (Downers Grove, IL: InterVarsity Press, 2004); Nicholas Perrin, *Jesus the Temple* (London: SPCK, 2010).

spine of early Christian faith, giving the rest of the skeleton support, shape, and ability to function. Without it, the entire body collapses. Such eschatology is intrinsically particular; right across the NT it is relentlessly christological, focused on the person, resurrection, and enthronement of Jesus.

4. Linked to the last point, significant attention is being given in contemporary studies of eschatology to its relationship with the mission of the church. Within this trend is a critique of dualism and an emphasis on a holistic eschatology—both in terms of the resurrection body and the redemption of all creation.[130]

5. There are multiple reasons behind shifting answers in NT studies as to how present and future hopes relate to each other. One of the most significant is the imprecise nature of eschatological imagery itself. If considerable agreement now exists that present and future hope need to be held together in a dynamic tension, how that is done will very probably continue to be a source of creative dialogue.

6. Much attention in contemporary eschatology is rightly given to exploring the theological and ethical implications of future hope. I say "rightly" because NT eschatology right across its diverse expressions is overwhelmingly ethical at heart.[131]

7. Those emphasizing some form of grand eschatological narrative in the NT (e.g., Wright, Middleton, Eskola, Andrew Perriman) tend to see an essential unity among diverse NT eschatologies. Others cautious about all-embracing narratives remain more guarded (e.g., Dunn, Frey). "Big picture" eschatologies have also tended to struggle to adequately incorporate individual eschatology within their frameworks.[132]

8. Our discussion has very much been a Western one, focusing on the story and hermeneutical challenges of eschatology within Europe and America. Given the shift of the global church to the south, the future of NT studies in general and of eschatology in particular will undoubtedly look very different. Rian Venter has important insights here. New voices from Africa, Asia, and Latin America hold immense promise for doing theology in general and

---

130. For an important and critical response from a systematic perspective to some links being made between eschatology and the church's activity in this world, see Stephen N. Williams, *The Limits of Hope and the Logic of Love: Essays on Eschatology and Social Action* (Vancouver: Regent College Publishing, 2006). See also Chester, *Mission and the Coming of God*.

131. Richard Hays's classic work on ethics includes an excellent exploration of the relationship between Christian ethics and eschatology; see *The Moral Vision of the New Testament: A Contemporary Introduction to New Testament Ethics* (London: T&T Clark, 1996). See also Hermut Löhr, "The Role of Eschatology in New Testament Moral Thought: Some Introductory Observations," in van der Watt, *Eschatology of the New Testament*, 644–65.

132. For critical response to Wright on this issue, see Richard H. Bell, "Individual Eschatology," in Heilig, Hewitt, and Bird, *God and the Faithfulness of Paul*, 553–54.

eschatology in particular. "Global Christianity may bring fruitful corrections; it may highlight orientations which are not biblical but typical [sic] Western, and it may encourage a more fruitful attention to the Bible."[133]

9. If the story of modern eschatology tells us anything, it is of the significance of the interpreter's prior hermeneutical and philosophical assumptions. This issue lies close to the surface of all discussion of eschatology. In this vein, the late Paul Minear wrote, "If the end has actually been inaugurated, then historical time is capable of embracing simultaneously both the old age and the new. No methodology whose presuppositions on time are limited to the old age will be adequate to cope with the historicity of the new age or with the temporal collision between the two times."[134] These are frank words about an important but oft-overlooked factor in NT studies. Philip Ziegler adds his own comments about how the apocalyptic nature of the cross overshadows all study of the Scriptures. Any "thoroughly historicist theology will finally adjudge eschatological dogmatics to be a sustained and elaborate category error, or perhaps at best an extended exercise in 'strong poetry.' Either way, it is intellectually suspect."[135] Contrariwise, "a properly eschatological dogmatics will consider historicism to be an intellectually sophisticated mode of unbelief."[136] For Ziegler, all this raises the question, When it comes to interpreting NT eschatology, is it a case of *either/or* in terms of historicist versus eschatological theologies?[137]

10. Finally, a significant amount of discussion is moving "beyond" the NT to how hopes expressed within it challenge narratives in contemporary politics, culture, science, and technology.[138] No one has been more insightful or

---

133. Venter, "Trends in Contemporary Eschatological Reflection," 110. Venter gives an example of Katongole (2008) from Africa critiquing Western anxiety about the future of the individual. See Emmanuel Kantogole and Chris Rice, *Reconciling All Things: A Christian Vision for Justice, Peace and Healing*, Resources for Reconciliation (Downers Grove, IL: IVP Books, 2008).

134. Paul S. Minear, *God and the Historian: Breaking the Silence about God in Biblical Studies* (Nashville: Abingdon, 2002), 54–55, cited in Philip G. Ziegler, "Eschatological Dogmatics—to What End?," in van der Watt, *Eschatology of the New Testament*, 359.

135. Ziegler, "Eschatological Dogmatics," 359.

136. Ziegler, "Eschatological Dogmatics," 359.

137. Ziegler, "Eschatological Dogmatics," 359. He notes that the question framed in this way echoes Karl Barth: "Revelation is not a predicate of history, but history is a predicate of revelation." Barth, *Church Dogmatics* I/2, 58, cited in Ziegler, "Eschatological Dogmatics," 359.

138. A particular question here is, How can a biblical hope of a "physical" new creation be reconciled with the findings of modern science and cosmology that predict a "cosmic freeze" and the end of all life and matter in the universe? For example, see Robert John Russell, "Resurrection, Eschatology and the Challenge of Big Bang Cosmology," *Int* 70, no. 1 (2016): 48–60. See also Anna Case-Winters, "The End? Christian Eschatology and the End of the World," *Int* 70, no. 1 (2016): 61–74. Such questions prompted C. J. Steckel to propose relatively recently that "it is time to give eschatology a rest, a time out." Not only has postmodern critique eroded belief in future progressivism; the entropic nature of the cosmos described by modern

articulate here than Bauckham in expressing how NT eschatology confronts the twenty-first century's erosion of hope. No doubt this will continue to be an area for ongoing critical thought, particularly for scholars who see their work as serving the mission of the church.

---

science reinforces disbelief in progressivism. C. J. Steckel, "Confessions of a Post-Eschatologist," *Theology Today* 64 (2007): 144.

12

New Testament Ethics

Nijay K. Gupta

Introduction

In 1985, Wayne A. Meeks gave the presidential address at the annual meeting of the Society of Biblical Literature and divulged the problem that led to the inspiration for his paper, "Understanding Early Christian Ethics." He confessed, "In my first year of teaching, I offered a course called 'New Testament Ethics.' The students who enrolled were bright and interested, and they plunged with verve into our analysis of several difficult texts. Nevertheless, by the end of term it was clear to them as to me that none of us had a clear conception what New Testament ethics was. I have not repeated the experiment."[1] Meeks and his students were not alone. While "New Testament ethics" might sound like a straightforward subject, it is not, and Meeks went

---

1. Wayne A. Meeks, "Understanding Early Christian Ethics," *JBL* 10, no. 1 (1986): 3. In 1987, Abraham Malherbe gave an important paper to the Christian Scholars Conference (Pepperdine University) titled "New Testament Ethics and the Church Today." At that time Malherbe confidently pronounced, "A striking feature of NT scholarship is its comparative neglect of ethics. It is only very seldom that ethics receives any attention in books on NT theology, and equally rare that separate studies are devoted to it" (1). He went on to say (just over thirty years ago), "The study of ethics in the NT appears to be developing from an area of concentration in NT studies to a distinct subdiscipline in the field." He claimed then, though, that this burgeoning field lacks methodological strength, something I believe Malherbe would not have claimed today. Malherbe, "New Testament Ethics and the Church Today," *Restoration Quarterly* 55, no. 1 (2013): 15–23.

on in his lecture to recommend the abandonment of the phrase altogether.[2] Today there are hardly "schools of thought" under the heading of "New Testament ethics," and until recently there weren't really any scholars who specialized in this area. And yet now we can confidently say that there is a field called New Testament ethics. So what changed and why? First we will examine the birth and growth of the study of New Testament ethics in the twentieth century, and then we will consider currents in New Testament ethics today.

The Emergence of a Modern Discipline

To speak of the origins or emergence of the discipline of "New Testament ethics" (hereafter NTE) in the twentieth century should *not* imply that no books on NTE were written until recently. There have always been practice-oriented or value-focused studies related to Scripture. One could point to Charles A. A. Scott's *New Testament Ethics: An Introduction* (1930) or John Murray's *Principles of Conduct* (1957).[3] And it should not come as a surprise to learn that there has been a long history of study of, and steady interest in, the Sermon on the Mount, as we see with A. D. Lindsay's *The Moral Teaching of Jesus* (1937) or, more recently, Dale Allison's *The Sermon on the Mount: Inspiring the Moral Imagination* (1999) and Jonathan Pennington's *The Sermon on the Mount and Human Flourishing* (2017).[4]

When we look at how several of these books approach NTE, though, we see that they tend to focus on how particular commitments or practices from the NT relate to the modern world (subjects like marriage, war, and capital punishment). The general mentality has often been that one can or ought to refer to Scripture to inform how one navigates a particular ethical problem.[5]

---

2. His preference was to talk about "early Christian ethics" from a more concrete sociohistorical perspective.

3. Charles A. A. Scott, *New Testament Ethics: An Introduction* (Cambridge: Cambridge University Press, 1930); John Murray, *Principles of Conduct: Aspects of Biblical Ethics* (Grand Rapids: Eerdmans, 1957).

4. A. D. Lindsay, *The Moral Teaching of Jesus: An Examination of the Sermon on the Mount* (London: Hodder, 1937); Dale C. Allison Jr., *The Sermon on the Mount: Inspiring the Moral Imagination* (New York: Crossroad, 1999); Jonathan Pennington, *The Sermon on the Mount and Human Flourishing* (Grand Rapids: Baker Academic, 2017).

5. Two early and notable twentieth-century exceptions to this would be James Stalker, *The Ethic of Jesus according to the Synoptic Gospels* (New York: Hodder and Stoughton, 1909); Francis N. Davey and Edwyn C. Hoskyns, *Crucifixion-Resurrection: The Pattern of the Theology and Ethics of the New Testament*, ed. Gordon S. Wakefield (London: SPCK, 1981). It should be noted that Hoskyns and Davey intended to cowrite this book, but Hoskyns passed suddenly in 1937 and Davey in 1973. Wakefield brought their notes together to form this book. While we do get hints and glimpses of NT theological ethics according to Davey and Hoskyns, it is far more "theology" with little direct reflection on "ethics."

That has meant that the Bible has always had something to say about ethical issues, but it also could imply that only very *specific* portions of Scripture are relevant to these matters.

In a moment we will attend to works that inspired or catalyzed the development of the field of NTE, but we ought to consider reasons why such movements may have been forestalled or derailed. First, we can say with confidence that the study of the NT has largely been preoccupied with matters related to "belief" and "salvation." Put another way, Protestant scholarship has long emphasized research pertaining to *believing* and left questions and matters associated with *doing* underaddressed.[6]

A more particular obstacle has involved concerns raised in the past—especially in the early-middle twentieth century—that it is a mistake to use the word "ethics" (in German, *Ethik*) in relation to the intentions and perspectives of the NT writers. For someone like Albert Schweitzer, the moral teaching of Jesus offered not a universal ethic but an "interim ethic," only pertinent until the impending eschaton. Schweitzer claimed that Jesus presented no "Ethik" of the kingdom of God, "for in the Kingdom of God all natural relationships . . . are abolished. Temptation and sin no longer exist. . . . To serve, to humble oneself, to incur persecution and death, belong to the 'ethic of the interim' just as much as does penitence."[7] Martin Dibelius had a different concern with studying NTE. He argued that someone like Paul was so driven by an imminent anticipation of the parousia that he never actually intended to develop or transmit a moral code or ethos for his churches.[8] Dibelius dismissed the paraenetic sections of Paul's letters, for example, arguing that "they have nothing to do with the theoretical foundation of the ethics of the Apostle, and very little with other ideas peculiar to him."[9] Put another way, Dibelius saw Paul's moral commands as "traditional," borrowed and not essential to his theological ideas.

Perhaps a larger concern with the use of the term "ethics" was the assumption that this involved the application of a rigid system of rules, norms, and behaviors that one was expected to follow within a particular group. Rudolf Bultmann strongly resisted this idea. In his *Theology of the New Testament* he writes, "Jesus's proclamation of the will of God is not an ethic

---

6. See Stanley Hauerwas's essay "How 'Christian Ethics' Came to Be," in *The Hauerwas Reader*, ed. John Berkman and Michael G. Cartwright (Durham, NC: Duke University Press, 2001), 37–50.

7. Albert Schweitzer, *The Quest of the Historical Jesus*, trans. W. Montgomery (New York: A. and C. Black, 1910), 364; translated from *Von Reimarus zu Wrede: Eine Geschichte der Leben-Jesu-Forschung* (Tübingen: Mohr Siebeck, 1906).

8. See Martin Dibelius, *Urchristentum und Kultur* [Early Christianity and Culture] (Heidelberg: C. Winter, 1928).

9. Martin Dibelius, *From Tradition to Gospel*, trans. B. L. Woolf (London: Ivor Nicholson and Watson, 1934), 239.

of world-reform. Rather, it must be described as an eschatological ethic. For it does not envisage a future to be molded within this world by plans and sketches for the ordering of human life. It only directs man into the Now of his meeting with his neighbor. It is an ethic that, by demanding more than the law that regulates human society does and requiring of the individual the waiver of his own rights, makes the individual immediately responsible to God."[10] Bultmann resisted any attempt to systematize and/or extract an "Ethik" from the NT because one's relationship and response to God must happen *in the moment*, as it were—a hallmark concept of his existential approach to Scripture. Somewhat ironically, Bultmann was responsible in many ways for inspiring a fresh approach to NTE despite these criticisms, because he is credited primarily with the "indicative and imperative" approach to Paul, the notion that by faith the believer can respond to the divine call with obedience.[11] "The indicative calls forth the imperative. The indicative gives expression to the new self-understanding of the believer, for the statement, 'I am free from sin' is not a dogmatic one, but an existential one . . . the imperative reminds him that he is free from sin, provided that his will is renewed in obedience to the commandment of God."[12] Ernst Käsemann, like his teacher Bultmann, also rejected any attempt to synthesize a NTE artificially.[13] As with Bultmann, so with Käsemann behavior and the Christian life ought always to come back to the nature of a *relationship*. For Bultmann this was expressed in terms of responsiveness in the moment of decision; for Käsemann it was about true worship and true discipleship. Käsemann invested heavily in a theological perspective inspired by the biblical command to honor God and reject idols—all behavior is reflected in this commitment. In a posthumously published lecture transcription, Käsemann explained, "For the Christian there

---

10. Rudolf Bultmann, *Theology of the New Testament* (New York: Scribner, 1951–55), 1:19.

11. See Rudolf Bultmann, "Das Problem der Ethik bei Paulus," ZNW 23, no. 1 (1924): 123–40; reprinted in Brian S. Rosner, ed., *Understanding Paul's Ethics: Twentieth-Century Approaches* (Grand Rapids: Eerdmans, 1995).

12. Rudolf Bultmann, *Jesus Christ and Mythology* (New York: Scribner, 1958), 76–77, cited in David G. Horrell, *Solidarity and Difference: A Contemporary Reading of Paul's Ethics*, 2nd ed. (London: Bloomsbury T&T Clark, 2016), 11–12. An important early critic of the indicative/imperative formulation was Hans Windisch, "Das Problem des paulinischen Imperativs," ZNW 23 (1924): 271; cf. also Hans Weder, "Gesetz und Gnade," in *Ja und Nein: Christliche Theologie im Angesicht Israels*, ed. K. Wengst et al. (Neukirchen-Vluyn: Neukirchener Verlag, 1998), 171–73; Knut Backhaus, "Evangelium also Lebensraum: Christologie und Ethik bei Paulus," in *Paulinische Christologie: Exegetische Beiträge*, ed. Udo Schnelle and Thomas Söding (Göttingen: Vandenhoeck & Ruprecht, 2000), 9–14; Karl Kertelge, *Ethik im Neuen Testament* (Vienna: Herder, 1984).

13. One can easily see the influence of Bultmann on Käsemann's statement here: "Individual injunctions can . . . only serve as reminders that Christian behaviour is a matter of discovering the demand of the present moment and that God as Lord of the world wills to be acknowledged in man's interior life." Ernst Käsemann, "Worship and Everyday Life," in *New Testament Questions for Today*, trans. W. J. Montague (Philadelphia: Fortress, 1979), 189.

are absolutely no basic values if one takes the New Testament seriously." By this Käsemann simply meant that the Christian acted not in accordance with a formal handbook of rules, for that would be a form of spirit-less *nomism*. Rather, the believer responded to God himself in discipleship. Similarly, Dietrich Bonhoeffer urged that it is a mistake to establish an ethical framework by which Christianity operates, because to do so is to deny the primacy of divine revelation. Now, Bonhoeffer did go on to publish a book on ethics, but his stated aim was for it to be "a critique of all ethics simply as ethics."[14]

Perhaps no NT scholar has been so negative about the enterprise of NTE as Jack T. Sanders.[15] In his *Ethics in the New Testament*, Sanders affirms Henry Cadbury's famous warning about "the peril of modernizing Jesus."[16] According to Cadbury, students of the Jesus presented in the NT ought to recognize that nowhere do we find Jesus talking about civil rights or even how society should be operated in general.[17] Sanders also takes seriously Schweitzer's emphasis that one can easily fall into the trap of screening out imminent eschatology in an attempt to examine "ethics" all by itself. This would be a catastrophic mistake and would strip Jesus out of his time and effectively destroy his core message about the kingdom of God.[18]

In more recent work on NTE, we see the same cautions and hesitations raised in response to the use of the term "ethics," but there is demonstrably more willingness to give it a general meaning in regard to the behavior that ought to correspond to the grace and calling of God in Jesus Christ. Stephen Barton, for example, commenting on the NT epistles and the question of "ethics," warns that these documents offer nothing like a "compendium of systematic reflection on the good" but that there is much to examine when it comes to "the implications of conversion and baptism."[19]

As already noted, these concerns did have an effect on the development of NTE, but emerge it still did. It is futile to trace the origins of the discipline of NTE back to a certain person or work. NTE apparently emerged organically, or at least without intentional cooperation from a particular group. Here we can note nine key works that supported the shaping of NTE.

14. Dietrich Bonhoeffer, *Ethics*, trans. Reinhard Kraus, Charles C. West, and Douglas W. Stott (2005; repr., Minneapolis: Fortress, 2015; originally written in German between 1940 and 1943 and published in 1949 by Christian Kaiser Verlag; first ET, London: SCM, 1955), 1.
15. Jack T. Sanders, *Ethics in the New Testament: Change and Development* (Philadelphia: Fortress, 1975; London: SCM, 1986).
16. See Henry J. Cadbury, *The Peril of Modernizing Jesus* (New York: Macmillan, 1937), cited in Sanders, *Ethics in the New Testament*, 1.
17. Cadbury, *Peril of Modernizing Jesus*, 86–119.
18. Sanders, *Ethics in the New Testament*, 29.
19. Stephen C. Barton, "The Epistles and Christian Ethics," in *The Cambridge Companion to Christian Ethics*, ed. Robin Gill (Cambridge: Cambridge University Press, 2001), 63–73, 63.

C. H. Dodd: *Gospel and Law*

To begin, let's turn the clock back to 1946: C. H. Dodd gave the Bampton Lectures at Columbia University and published his papers the next year under the title *Gospel and Law: The Relation of Faith and Ethics in Early Christianity*.[20] Dodd noted that it would be impossible and irresponsible *not* to consider what effects the religious commitments of the early Christians would have had on their lives. He observes that the early Christians were clearly influenced by their Jewish heritage in their values, behaviors, and practices. But these Christians also believed they were driven by an eschatological urgency. Dodd turned much of his interest in the subject of ethics to the principles and motives that inspired and drove the early Christian movements.

Dodd gave focused attention to the Pauline imagery of the "law of Christ" (Gal. 6:2); he presumed this phrase referred to the notion of transformation in Christ. He offered this explanation in relation to NTE:

> The law of Christ works by setting up a process within us which is itself ethical activity. His precepts stir the imagination, arouse the conscience, challenge thought, and give an impetus to the will, issuing in action. In so far as we respond, holding the commandments steadily in view, reflecting upon them, and yet treating them not merely as objects for contemplation, but as spurs to action, there gradually comes to be built up in us a certain outlook on life, a bias of mind, a standard of moral judgment. The precepts cannot be directly transferred from the written page to action. They must become, through reflection and through effort, increasingly a part of our total outlook upon life, of the total bias of our minds. Then they will find expression in action appropriate to the changing situations in which we find ourselves.[21]

This statement encapsulates well the way scholars at this time began to take an interest in the *effects*, so to speak, of NT theology, moving from faith to commitment and action. To have a respected scholar of Dodd's stature give serious attention to this matter certainly opened up a pathway for others to follow.

Victor Furnish: *Theology and Ethics in Paul*

Nearly two decades later Victor Furnish penned his *Theology and Ethics in Paul*, a book I consider to be the fountainhead for the study of NTE.[22]

---

20. C. H. Dodd, *The Gospel and the Law of Christ* (New York: Green, 1947).
21. Dodd, *Gospel and the Law of Christ*, 77.
22. V. P. Furnish, *Theology and Ethics in Paul* (Nashville: Abingdon, 1968; repr., Louisville: Westminster John Knox, 2009).

As Furnish explains in his work, his objective was to establish "the essential character and structure of the Pauline ethic."[23] He argued that Pauline interpreters had focused on Paul's theological concepts without really grappling with the notion that the apostle was deeply interested in Christian behavior. Furnish began with the matter of sources—that is, what influenced Paul's ethics? Unsurprisingly, Furnish pointed to two key places, the OT and early Christian traditions. Yet when it came to the former, Furnish was quick to point out that Paul did not cite or refer to OT commands casuistically; thus Paul did not treat the OT as a manual of ethics.[24] A significant contribution Furnish made to the "sources" question relates to the famous Judaism-Hellenism tension, a juxtaposition that Furnish challenged: "A one-sided decision about Paul's background, whether in favor of his Jewish or Greek heritage, is bound to result in a one-sided interpretation of his ethic. This ethic can be brought into sharper focus when it is acknowledged that Paul was a Jew of the Diaspora—of the Hellenistic world."[25] Furnish underscored that ultimately Paul was most influenced in his ethics by the Christ event, and this served as the main "source" and inspiration for his ethical instruction.

Furnish also gave attention to what he called the "logic" of Paul's ethics, which he explained as a compound of theological, eschatological, and christological convictions. He held that for Paul the eschatological aspect was most weighty, a "heuristic key" to Paul's thought and teaching.[26] The gospel Paul preached was about the liberative power of God, freeing enslaved humanity and opening up the possibility of new life. Thus the decision to obey the truth of the gospel of Christ becomes an act of allegiance to the power and authority of Christ: "The total claim which Christ's lordship lays upon the believer is a basic and pervasive element of Pauline thought."[27] In terms of Christology, the believer's union with and dependence on Christ facilitates this change of lordship from sin to righteousness. From this vantage point, Furnish argued, Paul's ethic was more about obedience than determining what is "right" and "wrong." The Spirit guides the believer, and the faith community nurtures and comes alongside.[28] Furnish's lasting contributions to NTE involve his attention to eschatology and ethics and also to the divine-relation dynamic—the new social orientation that humans have with God and also with one another in Christ and the Spirit.

23. Furnish, *Theology and Ethics in Paul*, 8.
24. Furnish, *Theology and Ethics in Paul*, 33–34.
25. Furnish, *Theology and Ethics in Paul*, 50.
26. Furnish, *Theology and Ethics in Paul*, 114.
27. Furnish, *Theology and Ethics in Paul*, 169.
28. Furnish, *Theology and Ethics in Paul*, 231–33.

Rudolf Schnackenburg: The Moral Teaching of the NT

Around the same time that Furnish was working on his study of Pauline ethics, German priest and scholar Rudolf Schnackenburg was writing his *Die sittliche Botschaft des Neuen Testaments*, published in English in 1962 as *The Moral Teaching of the New Testament*.[29] While Furnish focused narrowly on Paul, Schnackenburg took a much broader interest in early Christian ethics, spending significant time on the ethics of Jesus and the kingdom of God; he included as well sections on Paul, John, James, and also the Catholic Epistles and Revelation. For Schnackenburg, the place to begin with the early Christian ethic was Jesus (as narrated in the Gospels). While one could focus on themes such as the fatherly love of God, the salvation of souls, or discipleship, Schnackenburg argued that the foundation is clearly "the proclamation of the reign of God."[30] When it comes to the ethical imperative of the NT, Schnackenburg was insistent that NTE is not about merely parroting the commands within the NT, but maintaining faithfulness to the eschatological call to alertness and discernment. Schnackenburg states of the NT writers that "the task which they performed then for their communities is still ours to fulfill in our own times: with equal ardour in the faith, equal moral earnestness and above all equal eschatological vigilance, to proclaim the gospel of Jesus."[31]

So influential has Schnackenburg's work been (in German scholarship especially) that in 1989 a Festschrift was written in his honor with the title *Neues Testament und Ethik* (*The New Testament and Ethics*) with nearly thirty contributors, amounting to almost six hundred pages. What this reflects is Schnackenburg's inimitable ability to examine the subject of NTE diachronically from Jesus to the end of the first century, and synchronically in the work of individual writers.

Allen Verhey: The Great Reversal

We turn now to the much shorter, but recognizably impactful, work of Allen Verhey called *The Great Reversal*, published in 1984. Verhey, a theological ethicist, desired to go beyond the examination of specific ethical commands in the NT to consider the unique worldview of Jesus and the NT writers. What he called the "great reversal" was the way in which the NT writers subverted and overturned the conventions and values of their time, not just in paraenesis but in the expression of their beliefs and in their whole

---

29. Rudolf Schnackenburg, *The Moral Teaching of the New Testament*, trans. J. Holland-Smith and W. J. O'Hara (London: Burns & Oates, 1962).
30. Schnackenburg, *Moral Teaching of the New Testament*, 13; see also 13–25.
31. Schnackenburg, *Moral Teaching of the New Testament*, 388.

lives.³² Verhey urged that the kingdom of God for the early Christians called into question the present order's "conventional rules of prestige and protocol." The early Christians were committed to a "transformation of values" that sought to undermine the popular estimations of superiority and violence.³³ Much like Furnish, Verhey explained that NTE is not found in rules but in countercultural perspectives, values, and principles.

Wolfgang Schrage: The Ethics of the NT

German biblical scholar Wolfgang Schrage dedicated significant time and energy to NTE, especially in his 1982 work *Ethik des Neuen Testaments* (ET: *The Ethics of the New Testament* [1988])).³⁴ Like Schnackenburg, Schrage was also concerned with "how life was lived in the earliest Christian communities."³⁵ Schrage considered the early Christian ethic to be dynamic and somewhat organic. It operated in accordance with a dialectic of "freedom and restraint."³⁶ Also in line with Furnish and Schnackenburg, Schrage's ethic of the NT was thoroughly christological, centered on "God's saving act in Jesus Christ."³⁷ Schrage largely rejected Bultmann's existential approach to ethics and focused NTE on divine lordship and human obedience via participation in Christ. Ethics is not a duty per se for Schrage, but a reality established by a new life in Christ.³⁸ Schrage interpreted the concept of participation via the notion of sacramental theology, where "a sacrament is nothing other than the present reality of the Christ event."³⁹

Unsurprisingly, eschatology plays an important role as well in Schrage's work on NTE. The systems and patterns of worldly power and authority are fading, and believers anticipate the consummation in their thought and life: "The perspective of the ultimate makes all else penultimate at best."⁴⁰ In the present time, love is the highest standard, the heart of the Pauline ethic. Schrage also dwelt on the importance of embodiedness and life in relationship

---

32. See Allen Verhey, *The Great Reversal: Ethics and the New Testament* (Grand Rapids: Eerdmans, 1984), 15.
33. Verhey, *Great Reversal*, 22.
34. W. Schrage, *The Ethics of the New Testament*, trans. David E. Green (Philadelphia: Fortress, 1988). Other key works from Schrage on NTE include "Zur Frage nach der Einheit und Mitte neutestamentlicher Ethik," in *Die Mitte des Neuen Testaments*, ed. Eduard Schweizer, Urlich Luz, and Hans Weder (Gottingen: Vandenhoeck & Ruprecht, 1983), 238–53; Schrage, *Kreuzestheologie und Ethik im Neuen Testament* (Gottingen: Vandenhoeck & Ruprecht, 2004).
35. Schrage, *Ethics of the New Testament*, 1.
36. Schrage, *Ethics of the New Testament*, 10.
37. Schrage, *Ethics of the New Testament*, 8.
38. See Schrage, *Ethics of the New Testament*, 172.
39. Schrage, *Ethics of the New Testament*, 174.
40. Schrage, *Ethics of the New Testament*, 182.

with others. Unlike Bultmann, Schrage believed that the Greek word σῶμα (*sōma*) in the NT referred to the *physical* body, not just the person. Thus, "because the body is the primary place where Christ exercises dominion in the reality of the present world, it is here or nowhere that Christians encounter their Lord."[41]

J. Paul Sampley: Walking between the Times

Another key contribution in the development of the study of NTE is J. Paul Sampley's *Walking between the Times* (1991).[42] As the title suggests, Sampley was interested in eschatology, not particularly the apocalyptic and cosmic eschatology of Furnish, but more generally what it means to live between the death/resurrection of Jesus and his return: "Paul is concerned with how believers behave, or walk, between these two times."[43] Sampley took special interest in the nature of Christian discernment in this in-between time. The Christ event threw off slavery to sin, according to Paul, but believers are still able to be tempted and deceived. That is, "[Paul] thinks of sin as if it were a power stalking about looking for a beachhead . . . from which to launch a campaign to take over someone's life."[44] What is necessary is not commitment to particular ethical rules, but rather an active and attentive responsiveness to God.[45]

Sampley's most important contribution to the study of NTE is his application of Paul's ethical logic to moral reasoning today. He acknowledges that many ethical decisions are focused on the self (*Will this cause me to sin?*), but Paul had a special concern for how a decision impacts the community—*is this beneficial to others?* It is no surprise, then, that Sampley underscored the centrality of love in Paul (like Schrage), that ethos that involves "acting in careful consideration for the well-being of others."[46]

Richard Hays: The Moral Vision of the New Testament

Perhaps no modern English work on NTE has become more popularly used than Richard B. Hays's *Moral Vision of the New Testament*. What makes Hays's work unique is the way he tackles the subject of NTE from

---

41. Schrage, *Ethics of the New Testament*, 219.
42. J. Paul Sampley, *Walking between the Times: Paul's Moral Reasoning* (Minneapolis: Fortress, 1991).
43. Sampley, *Walking between the Times*, v.
44. Sampley, *Walking between the Times*, 13.
45. See Sampley, *Walking between the Times*, 104.
46. Sampley, *Walking between the Times*, 62. See too now Sampley's capstone work, which sums up his career of study, *Walking in Love* (Minneapolis: Fortress, 2017).

a panoramic perspective, including not only historical study of the NT but extensive hermeneutical analysis including comparison with perspectives from modern ethicists and lengthy discussions of select modern ethical concerns.

Hays approaches the topic of NTE using the metaphor of a lens with three "focal images": eschatology, the cross, and the new community in Christ. Eschatology relates to the temporal context of NTE and the hope of new creation in Christ. When it comes to Christology, Hays underscores the image of the cross as the master paradigm for discipleship, such that "[it] becomes the ruling metaphor for Christian obedience."[47] For the third focal image, Hays chose the faith community, reasoning that the goal of the gospel is the formation of God-centered, Spirit-led social bodies that "prefigure and embody the reconciliation and healing of the world."[48]

Along with these focal images, Hays discusses warrants, norms, and sources of NTE. He gives attention to the transformative union with Christ and the call to obedience as the believer is freed by Christ and then turns to him in allegiance. Hays also points to the role of the Holy Spirit to inspire and empower transformation towards holiness and righteousness in Christ.

Where Hays goes beyond earlier works on NTE is in his theological-hermeneutical chapters. In line with his earlier works, Hays describes the engagement of reader and text as an act of imagination. Here metaphors play a major part in reshaping perception and changing one's whole value system—a conversion of the imagination, as it were.[49]

Brian Rosner: Understanding Paul's Ethics

Brian Rosner wrote his doctoral dissertation on the subject of ethics and Scripture in 1 Corinthians.[50] He also published an important collection of essays on NTE called *Understanding Paul's Ethics*, showcasing key contributions of scholars such as Bultmann, Edwin Judge, and Gerd Theissen.[51] Rosner made his own contribution to the topic by reflecting on seven key questions that relate to the discipline of NTE: origin, context, social dimension, shape, logic, foundations, and relevance. Rosner succeeded at the close of the twentieth century at analyzing the work that had been done in the previous half-century, and he organized and framed it in terms of these categories. What

---

47. Richard B. Hays, *Moral Vision of the New Testament: A Contemporary Introduction to New Testament Ethics* (San Francisco: HarperSanFrancisco, 1996), 31.

48. Hays, *Moral Vision of the New Testament*, 32.

49. See Hays, *Moral Vision of the New Testament*, 300–301.

50. Brian S. Rosner, *Paul, Scripture, and Ethics: A Study of 1 Corinthian 5–7* (Leiden: Brill, 1994).

51. Brian S. Rosner, *Understanding Paul's Ethics: Twentieth Century Approaches* (Grand Rapids: Eerdmans).

we learn from this exercise is that a scholar or community is often addressing only one or two of these categories or dimensions and that rarely do we find discussions that consider all or most of them.

Dictionary of Scripture and Ethics

Our goal in this section has been to reflect on the development of the discipline of NTE in the twentieth century, and then to turn to key conversations and the "state" of NTE today. However, when we talk about the birth of a discipline, one indicator that the "baby" of NTE had been born was the publication of the well-received reference work *Dictionary of Scripture and Ethics* (*DSE*; 2011), edited by Joel Green, Jacqueline Lapsley, Rebekah Miles, and Allen Verhey. One distinctive feature of this volume is the inclusion of contributions from not only biblical scholars (e.g., Richard Burridge, Furnish, Michael Gorman, Rosner, and Willard Swartley) but also theologians and ethicists (e.g., Ellen Charry, David Gushee, Christine Pohl, Wyndy Corbin Reuschling, Ronald Sider, and Glen Stassen) and well over two hundred essay contributors overall.

In the introduction to the volume, Green observes how he and other scholars have lamented, throughout the years, how biblical studies and Christian ethics have rarely intermingled in the academy. Green uses the image of a "labyrinth" to portray the way students, pastors, and scholars conceive of the subject of "Scripture and ethics." This dictionary, in an interdisciplinary way, aims to offer expert guidance through this maze.[52] *DSE* is also prefaced by three leading essays: "Ethics in Scripture" (Allen Verhey), "Scripture in Ethics: A History" (Charles H. Cosgrove), and "Scripture in Ethics: Methodological Issues" (Bruce C. Birch).[53]

Currents in NTE Today (2000–2017)

While it is possible to talk today of a certain discipline called NTE, it is far from homogeneous and centralized. Few scholars writing in this field would label themselves as NT ethicists, and fewer still devote their whole research agenda to NTE. Rather, we see a handful of scholars regularly participating in the discussion today and many more making observations and presenting thoughts from various perspectives as their own interests intersect with NTE. One way we might consider the "currents" of the discussion of NTE

---

52. Joel B. Green, introduction to *Dictionary of Scripture and Ethics*, ed. Joel B. Green, Jacqueline E. Lapsley, Rebekah Miles, and Allen Verhey (Grand Rapids: Baker Academic, 2011), 2.
53. *DSE*, 5–12, 13–26, 27–34.

today would be to focus on individuals, or perhaps particular NT books. But one can get a better overall understanding of the shape and "flow" of NTE by looking at three productive areas of interest: methods and approaches, sociohistorical context, and ethical themes.

Methods and Approaches

As should be rather clear from the above discussion of the development of NTE in the twentieth century, much concern has been directed toward more sophisticated methodology. What tools, approaches, and methods are most responsible in and conducive to analyzing the NT with respect to ethics? We have already noted Rosner's approach to this subject as it relates to Paul in his *Understanding Paul's Ethics*. Ruben Zimmerman has made several important contributions in the area of what he calls "implicit ethics," the idea that the NT does not present a rulebook of ethics or systematic presentation of norms, but rather offers a moral world through stories or concepts that impel one toward action.[54] Crucial to Zimmerman's analysis of implicit ethics is the role of the community in fostering these norms and ethics.[55] Zimmermann and like-minded colleagues have applied this implicit ethics mind-set and approach to texts such as the Johannine writings, finding (where others have often denied) deep interest in moral wisdom and behavioral formation.[56]

One will notice that much of the reflection of NTE in the twentieth century concentrated on Paul and other NT epistles, not least because of the presence of explicit paraenesis in those letters. Comparatively, the Gospels and Acts suffered major neglect for many years. What we have seen in the last few decades—parallel with and certainly connected to the prominence of narrative criticism in NT studies—is methodological reflection on how *stories* can invest in and communicate morality. Dan O. Via offered in 1985 insight pertaining to Mark on how one can identify a constructive Christian ethic developed in the narrative.[57] More recently Burridge offered his own treatment of how a genre-aware approach to ethics in the Gospels ought to

---

54. See Ruben Zimmermann, "The 'Implicit Ethics' of New Testament Writings: A Draft on a New Methodology for Analyzing New Testament Ethics," *Neot* 43, no. 2 (2009): 403.
55. Zimmermann, "'Implicit Ethics' of New Testament Writings," 403.
56. See Jan G. van der Watt and Ruben Zimmermann, eds., *Rethinking the Ethics of John: "Implicit Ethics" in the Johannine Writings* (Tübingen: Mohr Siebeck, 2012); see too Sherri Brown and Christopher W. Skinner, *Johannine Ethics: The Moral World of the Gospels and Epistles of John* (Minneapolis: Fortress, 2017).
57. Dan O. Via, *The Ethics of Mark's Gospel: In the Middle of Time* (Philadelphia: Fortress, 1985); see especially the introductory discussion, "An Approach to New Testament Ethics and Narrative" (pp. 3–23).

take seriously the morally formative elements of Jesus's portrayed *actions*, and not just his *words*.[58]

A rather robust ongoing conversation has involved applied moral hermeneutics of the NT—that is, how to move from the ancient text of Scripture to "life today" in theology and ethics. This is not a "new" subject, of course, but in the last two decades there has been significant and renewed attention to this matter. Part of this resurgence has come from fresh intersection with philosophical hermeneutics, and part of it has been generated by urgent (ecological, anthropological, political, etc.) ethical questions of our time. William Webb's "Redemptive-Movement Hermeneutic" has received both exuberant praise and incisive criticism.[59] Webb also contributed to a multiple-perspectives discussion called *Four Views on Moving beyond the Bible to Theology*.[60] N. T. Wright, too, has inspired the theological and ethical imagination of many with his "five-act-play" approach to trajectory hermeneutics.[61]

Another development related to methodology and NTE involves interest in "virtue ethics" and the employment of "missional hermeneutics." As for the former, interest in virtue ethics has been around for many ages, but as of late NT scholars have found the category of virtue to fit the implicit ethical dynamic of the NT writers and their ethos closely. Virtues involve "habituated dispositions involving both an affective desire for the good and the skill to both discern and act accordingly."[62] Tradition and the life of the community are crucial for nurturing virtues, and when it comes to the NT the relevant character qualities are oriented toward the way of Jesus.[63]

---

58. Richard Burridge, *Imitating Jesus: An Inclusive Approach to NTE* (Grand Rapids: Eerdmans, 2007).

59. See William J. Webb, *Slaves, Women and Homosexuals: Exploring the Hermeneutics of Cultural Analysis* (Downers Grove, IL: InterVarsity, 2001).

60. Gary T. Meadors, ed., *Four Views on Moving beyond the Bible to Theology* (Grand Rapids: Zondervan, 2009); see too the discussion among I. H. Marshall, Kevin Vanhoozer, and Stanley Porter in *Beyond the Bible: Moving from Scripture to Theology* (Grand Rapids: Baker Academic, 2004); cf. also Hays, *Moral Vision of the New Testament*.

61. N. T. Wright, *The Last Word* (New York: HarperCollins, 2005); for a condensed version of Wright's approach, see N. T. Wright, "How Can the Bible Be Authoritative?," NTWrightPage, http://ntwrightpage.com/2016/07/12/how-can-the-bible-be-authoritative/. Also see the methodologically self-reflective work of theologians Glenn Stassen and David Gushee, *Kingdom Ethics: Following Jesus in Contemporary Context*, 2nd ed. (Grand Rapids: Eerdmans, 2016).

62. DSE, 814.

63. See Daniel Harrington and James F. Keegan, *Jesus and Virtue Ethics* (Lanham, MD: Rowman & Littlefield, 2005); Harrington and Keegan, *Paul and Virtue Ethics* (Lanham, MD: Rowman & Littlefield, 2010); Robert L. Brawley, ed., *Character Ethics and the New Testament: Moral Dimensions of Scripture* (Louisville: Westminster John Knox, 2007); cf. also N. T. Wright, *After You Believe: Why Christian Character Matters* (New York: HarperOne 2010); cf. Pennington, *Sermon on the Mount and Human Flourishing*.

What is "missional hermeneutics"? It approaches the Bible with the assumption that God has a mission to carry out in the world and the church is a missionary community participating in that divine operation.[64] For many involved in the conversation on missional hermeneutics and missional theology, one of the core concepts is that the Bible exists for believers not simply to convey doctrine but also to form lives and communities for redemptive mission in the world.[65] This has inspired how scholars think about justice and redemptive activity as part of "gospel-ing" the world.

In terms of NTE and hermeneutics, we can also direct attention to certain explicit "commitment" or "perspective" readings of Scripture, which have had a consciously ethical thrust, such as liberation hermeneutics, African American criticism, feminist criticism, postcolonial interpretation, and agrarian readings of Scripture.[66] Needless to say, this has pointed in the direction of acknowledging that the reader does not simply "discover" ethics in the biblical text, but is bound up with the formation of ethical meaning in the act of reading itself.

Sociohistorical Context

As observed above, several scholars have approached NTE with intentionality when it comes to appropriate and fruitful methodology. Another "way" into the discussion of NTE has been via a close examination of the ancient sociohistorical context. What is especially interesting here is that several scholars who have come to the NT with a historian's eye have not always intended to contribute to NTE but eventually did so because the world of the earliest Christians came alive to them in such a way that their behavior—both in relation to and distinct from their current neighbors and predecessors—was noteworthy. Perhaps no scholar has done more foundational work in this area than Meeks with his three important volumes *The First Urban Christians: The*

---

64. See Michael J. Gorman, *Becoming the Gospel: Paul, Participation, and Mission* (Grand Rapids: Eerdmans, 2015); see also Michael W. Goheen, *A Light to the Nations: The Missional Church and the Biblical Story* (Grand Rapids: Baker Academic, 2011); Goheen, ed., *Reading the Bible Missionally* (Grand Rapids: Eerdmans, 2016).

65. See Dean Flemming, *Recovering the Full Mission of God: A Biblical Perspective on Being, Doing, and Telling* (Downers Grove, IL: InterVarsity, 2013); see, too, relevant chapters of Jon C. Laansma, Grant Osborne, and Ray van Neste, *New Testament Theology in Light of the Church's Mission* (Eugene, OR: Cascade, 2011); Stanley E. Porter and Cynthia Long Westfall, eds. *Christian Mission: Old Testament Foundations and New Testament Developments* (Eugene, OR: Pickwick, 2011).

66. See chap. 3, by Dennis R. Edwards, in this volume; Joel Green, *Hearing the New Testament: Strategies for Interpretation*, 2nd ed. (Grand Rapids: Eerdmans, 2010); cf. also Michael J. Gorman, *Scripture and Its Interpretation: An Ecumenical, Global Introduction to the Bible* (Grand Rapids: Baker Academic, 2017).

Social World of the Apostle Paul (1983), *The Moral World of the First Christians* (1986), and *The Origins of Christian Morality: The First Two Centuries* (1993).[67] When we look at Meeks's overall contribution to the subject of early Christian ethics, we can see that he desired to examine the topic with an interest in the roles played by social and political factors.[68] Inspired by Meeks's works and other NT studies interested in the social world of early Christianity, important work in NTE has developed in the twenty-first century related to areas such as economics, politics, religion, and philosophy. We will briefly treat each of these areas in turn.

In recent years there has been increased interest in the economy of the Roman Empire during the NT era and the matter of wealth and poverty at that time.[69] This investigation has opened up questions about how the NT writers (and first-century Christians) handled money and reflected on the poor. Some, like Bruce Longenecker, have made the case that "care for the poor" was of deep concern to the apostle Paul, a conviction he passed on to the churches under his care.[70]

For centuries biblical scholars have engaged in comparative religious and cultural studies, but only more recently has this matter focused on comparison of norms and community lifestyle. One might point out the important work of Edwin Judge titled *Social Distinctives of the Christians in the First Century*.[71] Again, more recently Larry Hurtado has addressed the unique

---

67. Wayne Meeks, *The First Urban Christians: The Social World of the Apostle Paul* (New Haven: Yale University Press, 1983); Meeks, *The Moral World of the First Christians* (Philadelphia: Westminster, 1986); Meeks, *The Origins of Christian Morality: The First Two Centuries* (New Haven: Yale University Press, 1993).

68. See, similarly, Wolfgang Stegemann, "The Contextual Ethics of Jesus," in *The Social Setting of Jesus and the Gospels*, ed. Wolfgang Stegemann, Bruce Malina, and Gerd Theissen (Minneapolis: Fortress, 2002), 45–61.

69. See, e.g., Justin Meggitt, *Paul, Poverty, and Survival* (Edinburgh: T&T Clark, 1998); Steven J. Friesen, "Poverty in Pauline Studies: Beyond the So-Called New Consensus," *JSNT* 26 (2004): 323–61; Bruce W. Longenecker and Kelly D. Liebengood, *Engaging Economics: New Testament Scenarios and Early Christian Reception* (Grand Rapids: Eerdmans, 2009); Thomas R. Blanton IV and Raymond Pickett, eds., *Paul and Economics: A Handbook* (Minneapolis: Fortress, 2017).

70. See Bruce W. Longenecker, *Remember the Poor: Paul, Poverty, and the Greco-Roman World* (Grand Rapids: Eerdmans, 2010). An interesting comparative study can also be found in Eyal Regev, "Wealth and Sectarianism: Comparing Qumranic and Early Christian Social Approaches," in *Echoes from the Caves: Qumran and the New Testament*, ed. F. Garcia Martinez (Leiden: Brill, 2009), 211–29; more recently, Helen Rhee, *Loving the Poor, Saving the Rich: Wealth, Poverty, and Early Christian Formation* (Grand Rapids: Baker Academic, 2012); Gary A. Anderson, *Charity: The Place of the Poor in the Biblical Tradition* (New Haven: Yale University Press, 2013); David J. Armitage, *Theories of Poverty in the World of the New Testament* (Tübingen: Mohr Siebeck, 2016).

71. Edwin A. Judge, *Social Distinctives of the Christians in the First Century*, ed. David M. Scholer (Grand Rapids: Baker Academic, 2008).

social and normative character of the earliest Christians in his *Destroyer of the Gods: Early Christian Distinctiveness in the Roman World*.[72] As the title of the book makes clear, Hurtado finds the early Christians unusual in a variety of ways, some of them relating to ethical behavior, including their strict sexual ethics, and their opposition to common cultural practices such as infant exposure and the violent, deadly, and degrading gladiatorial games.[73]

Again, interrelated to all these above matters we can also (for heuristic reasons) isolate how ethical issues are addressed via the political milieu of the Greco-Roman world.[74] Suffice it to say here that one of the hottest topics in NT studies as of late is Roman imperial ideology and propaganda and to what degree early Christians subverted, parodied, ignored, or supported it.[75] Much inspiration has come from John Howard Yoder's *The Politics of Jesus*, where Yoder argued that Jesus is portrayed in the Gospels as a "model of radical political action."[76] At the forefront of the current discussion of politics, macroethics, and early Christianity are scholars like Wright, John Dominic Crossan, Richard Horsley, and Warren Carter.[77] Much of this work has developed in view of the obvious tensions in the world today over the dominance of political "superpowers" and the formative influence of political ideology when it comes to the shaping of cultural values.[78] It seems that scholars, especially many of those trained as historians, have continued to recognize the power that empires have had throughout history in the shaping

---

72. Larry W. Hurtado, *Destroyer of the Gods: Early Christian Distinctiveness in the Roman World* (Waco: Baylor University Press, 2016); cf. Jan Willem van Henten and Joseph Verheyden, eds., *Early Christian Ethics in Interaction with Jewish and Greco-Roman Contexts* (Leiden: Brill, 2013), esp. George J. Brooke, "Some Issues behind the Ethics in the Qumran Scrolls and Their Implications for New Testament Ethics," 83–106, and Thomas H. Tobin, "The Importance of Hellenistic Judaism for the Study of Paul's Ethics," 147–66. In regard to early Christianity and early Judaism, see Gordon Zerbe, *Non-Retaliation in Early Jewish and New Testament Ethics* (Sheffield: Sheffield Academic, 1993).

73. See, e.g., J. T. Fitzgerald, "Orphans in Mediterranean Antiquity and Early Christianity," *Acta Theologica Supplement* 23 (2016): 29–48; P. Lampe, "Social Welfare in the Greco-Roman World as a Background for Early Christian Practice," *Acta Theologica Supplement* 23 (2016): 1–28.

74. See chap. 1, by Greg Carey, in this volume.

75. For a "rear-view mirror" discussion, see Scot McKnight and Joseph Modica, eds., *Jesus Is Lord, Caesar Is Not: Evaluating Empire in New Testament Studies* (Downers Grove, IL: IVP Academic, 2013).

76. John H. Yoder, *The Politics of Jesus* (Grand Rapids: Eerdmans, 1972), 2.

77. See Wes Howard-Brook and Anthony Gwyther, *Unveiling Empire: Reading Revelation Then and Now* (Maryknoll, NY: Orbis, 1999); J. Nelson Kraybill, *Apocalypse and Allegiance: Worship, Politics, and Devotion in the Book of Revelation* (Grand Rapids: Brazos, 2010); see too David A. deSilva, *Unholy Allegiances: Heeding Revelation's Warning* (Peabody, MA: Hendrickson, 2013). On Acts, see C. Kavin Rowe, *World Upside Down: Reading Acts in the Graeco-Roman Age* (Oxford: Oxford University Press, 2011).

78. See Richard A. Horsley, ed., *In the Shadow of Empire: Reclaiming the Bible as a History of Faithful Resistance* (Louisville: Westminster John Knox, 2008).

of peoples and ideas—for good or ill—such that even if these seem to lie in the "background" of the NT world, they are certainly doing much more than serving as a "backdrop"; there is nowhere in the NT where its life and thought is not touched in some way by empire, including in moral formation (in all the many ways early Christians challenged, accepted, and participated in imperial ideology).[79]

As of late, there has also been a surge of interest in how the early Christians related to and were like and unlike the philosophers of their time, and of course most philosophers took a deep interest in the subject of "the good life." Insofar as the early Christians were "bookish" and passionate about their central beliefs (in addition to their religious practices), no doubt those beliefs would have been treated by many pagans *as* a philosophy. We are seeing now a proliferation of studies that compare and contrast NT writers and the various ancient philosophies (especially Stoicism) on a variety of topics including the good, the structure of the home and society, questions about suffering and bravery, gender, race, war and peace, and so forth.

What we are seeing with all these sociohistorical studies is the way that NT scholars are trying to piece together the social world of the earliest Christians and understand their life, culture, norms, commitments, relationships, politics, and religion as a whole and in relation to society.[80] This, of course, cannot help but raise "ethical" questions about the cultural values these early Christians shared with their non-Christian neighbors, but certainly also about where they proved to be distinctive and countercultural.

Particular Ethical Themes

Examining the matter of ethics via social history and the history of ideas has caused us to step back and look at macroethics—and there is much discussion right now at that level. But equally well we can demonstrate that there is steady interest in narrowing the view to look at very specific ethical themes, virtues, and commitments in the NT. Now more than in any time in academic history we are seeing emphasis on the theme of (social) justice.[81] Related to

---

79. See Peter Oakes, ed., *Rome in the Bible and the Early Church* (Grand Rapids: Baker Academic, 2002).

80. See C. Kavin Rowe, *One True Life: The Stoics and Early Christians as Rival Traditions* (New Haven: Yale University Press, 2016); Abraham J. Malherbe, *Light from the Gentiles: Hellenistic Philosophy and Early Christianity*, ed. Carl R. Holloday et al. (Boston: Brill, 2015); F. W. Horn, U. Volp, R. Zimmerman, and Esther Verwold, eds., *Ethische Normen des frühen Christentums: Gut-Leben-Leib-Tugend* (Tübingen: Mohr Siebeck, 2013); John T. Fitzgerald, *Passions and Moral Progress in Greco-Roman Thought* (New York: Routledge, 2008); T. Engberg-Pedersen, *Paul and the Stoics* (Edinburgh: T&T Clark, 2000).

81. Cynthia Long Westfall and Bryan Dyer, eds., *The Bible and Social Justice* (Eugene, OR: Pickwick, 2015); Matthew Coomber, ed., *Bible and Justice* (London: Equinox, 2010); N. T.

this are reflection and discussion on crime and punishment, on equity and fairness,[82] and the perennially controversial topic of war/conflict and peace.[83] Other important themes of interest have been humility[84] and love.[85] Again, one cannot help but observe a dynamic where (almost certainly) scholars and communities are observing ethical problems in our own society today (discrimination, gun violence, etc.)[86] and asking questions about the NT and the early Christians in their time and place. The topics themselves are an insightful window into the concerns and questions that seem to be addressing persons and communities in our own troubled times.

Reflections

This essay has erred on the side of providing a very broad look at the development of the study of NTE and the nature of currents and conversations today. We have not been able to look in detail at past and present academic work. But what we are seeing is rather clear—in the last thirty years, NTE has indeed emerged as a subject in its own right, perhaps signaled in small part by various groups in SBL and other academic societies dedicated to "biblical ethics." In the past, what apparently counted as "ethics" was any modern

---

Wright, *Evil and the Justice of God* (Downers Grove, IL: InterVarsity, 2006). Not unrelated to this is concern regarding economic justice. See, e.g., T. M. Garrett, "The Message to the Merchants in James 4:13–17 and Its Relevance for Today," *JTI* 10, no. 2 (2016): 299–315.

82. Christopher D. Marshall, *Beyond Retribution: A New Testament Vision for Justice, Crime, and Punishment* (Grand Rapids: Eerdmans, 2002).

83. William M. Swartley, *Covenant of Peace: The Missing Peace in New Testament Theology and Ethics* (Grand Rapids: Eerdmans, 2006); Swartley, *The Love of Enemy and Non-Retaliation in the New Testament* (Louisville: Westminster John Knox, 1992).

84. Reinhard Feldmeier, *Power, Service, Humility: A New Testament Ethic* (Waco: Baylor University Press, 2014); cf. Craig E. Hill, *Status, Ambition, and the Way of Jesus* (Grand Rapids: Eerdmans, 2016).

85. Thomas Söding, *Das Liebesgebot bei Paulus: Die Mahnung zur Agape im Rahmen der paulinischen Ethik*, NTAbh N. F. 26 (Münster: Aschendorff, 1992); Francis J. Moloney, *Love in the Gospel of John* (Grand Rapids: Baker Academic, 2013); M. Ebner et al., eds., *Liebe* (Neukirchen-Vluyn: Neukirchener Verlag, 2015); Oda Wischmeyer, *Liebe als Agape: Das frühchristliche konzept und der moderne Diskurs* (Tübingen: Mohr Siebeck, 2015); Sampley, *Walking in Love*; see relevant sections from Gorman, *Becoming the Gospel*; Horrell, *Solidarity and Difference*.

86. Note how *JBL* published in 2017 an article by Bernadette Brooten titled "Research on the New Testament and Early Christian Literature May Assist the Churches in Setting Ethical Priorities" (*JBL* 136, no. 1 [2017]: 229–36), where Brooten broaches the controversial topic of racism and violence and #BlackLivesMatter in modern America . It is quite remarkable for the leading American biblical studies journal to publish an article that closes with a statement like this: "The lives of black persons of all genders will only matter to all once non-black persons make it so" (236). I mention this not as either praise for or criticism of Brooten or *JBL*, but as an indicator that the "academy" cannot help but be affected today by ethical subjects of public concern.

interest in "what the Bible has to say about _____." Fill in the blank with any number of modern ethical concerns (abortion, divorce, war, etc.). Answers were all too often binary and/or entailed sweeping judgments.

What changed and why, such that we are in a place now where NTE is growing in attention and interest? Many, like Furnish, successfully argued that one cannot really isolate the "theology" of the NT writers from the socially and ethically formative purposes of their discourses. Paul's letters, especially, are primarily pastoral and paraenetic documents. We ought not to forget, though, those voices, like Bultmann, that have warned against forcing the NT into certain prefabricated ethical frameworks or systems. Such concerns have necessitated important conversations about method. Thus we have seen more precision with interpretive tools and more self-awareness regarding personal and cultural biases and the power of our presuppositions. Furthermore, as we have had clearer and larger windows into social life in the ancient world, we are able to piece the world of the NT together now in such a vivid way that the social and political lives of the earliest Christians have generated all kinds of new conversations about how these men and women were like and unlike their neighbors in both small and great ways.

What does the future hold for NTE? A few texts, especially in the Pauline letters, have received the lion's share of attention on this subject. I imagine we will see more focused studies on the Gospels, Acts, the Catholic Epistles, and Revelation. Interdisciplinary work will also continue to contribute to NTE, offering insight from such fields as philosophy, global theology, social anthropology, and the social sciences. There is also room for further exploration of topics such as a comparison of ethics in the OT and NT, moral transformation as a result of the endowment of the Holy Spirit, and ethical themes that relate to modern public discourse, such as honesty and integrity, and diplomacy, and charity.

PART 4

New Testament Texts

13

The Gospel of Matthew

RODNEY REEVES

Introduction

Summing up thirty-five years of Matthean scholarship, Graham Stanton anticipated the direction studies in Matthew's Gospel would take after 1980.[1] Stanton mentions the following:

1. Attempts to "expound systematically the evangelist's thought"
2. An "urgent need for several full-scale commentaries on the gospel"[2]
3. Efforts to situate Matthew's community more definitively in its relationship to first-century Judaism
4. The application of social sciences and narrative criticism to Matthew[3]

---

1. Graham N. Stanton, "The Origin and Purpose of Matthew's Gospel: Matthean Scholarship from 1945 to 1980," ANRW, part 2, *Principat*, 25.3:1889–1951. This was later reprinted under the same title in *Studies in Matthew and Early Christianity*, ed. Markus Bockmuehl and David Lincicum (Tübingen: Mohr Siebeck, 2013), 9–76. The latter publication will be cited in following notes.
2. Several commentaries have been published: Carson (EBC, 1984), Schnackenburg (1985–87; ET, 2002), Luz (1985–2002; Hermeneia, 2001–7), Bruner (1987–90), Davies and Allison (ICC, 1988–97), Harrington (SP, 1991), Morris (PNTC, 1992), Blomberg (NAC, 1992), Hagner (WBC, 1993–95), Hare (Interpretation, 1993), Senior (1997), Keener (1999), Garland (2001), Carter (2003), Wilkins (NIVAC, 2004), Nolland (NIGTC, 2005), Witherington (SHBC, 2006), Hauerwas (BTC, 2006), France (NICNT, 2007), Turner (BECNT, 2008), Talbert (PCNT, 2010), Osborne (ZECNT, 2010), Doriani (REC, 2011), Evans (NCBC, 2012), Allen (FBP, 2013), J. Brown (TTC, 2015), Quarles (EGGNT, 2017), Reeves (SGBC, 2017).
3. Stanton, "Origin and Purpose of Matthew's Gospel," 67–68.

Stanton ended his prediction with this observation: "Matthean scholarship between 1945 and 1980 has been dominated by the development of redaction criticism. In future years this method will need to be refined if it is to continue to be fruitful."[4] That redaction criticism had run its course—no longer able to carry alone the freight of scholarly interests—became apparent to many over the next two decades: some questioned the foundation (two-document hypothesis), others attributed Matthean modifications of Mark and Q to style (not theology), and others in addition found theological significance writ large in the *whole* Gospel (material shared by Matthew, Mark, and Q reveals theological intent as much as Matthean modifications).[5] Recognizing Matthew as the creative author of the entire Gospel, scholars turned to composition criticism[6] to overcome the limitations of redaction criticism,[7] and to social-scientific methods to determine the *Sitz im Leben* of Matthew's Gospel.[8]

Determining the social location of Matthew's community—whether Jewish Christian or Christian Judaism—dominated Matthean studies during the 1990s.[9] Did Matthew and his community consider themselves a sect within Judaism (*intra muros*), one of several groups of "formative Judaism" competing for influence against the Pharisees and their interpretation of the law post-70 CE?[10] Or does Matthew's Gospel mark one of the first signs of the "parting of the ways"? Were they either *extra muros*, kicked out of "their synagogues" as heretics (victims of the *birkat ha-minim*)?[11] Did they depart

---

4. Stanton, "Origin and Purpose of Matthew's Gospel," 68.

5. See Donald Senior, *What Are They Saying about Matthew?*, rev. ed., WATSA (New York: Paulist Press, 1996), 1–3.

6. H. Benedict Green claimed redaction criticism had reached a dead end unless it moved "into composition criticism: the units of added material must be examined first as literary texts in themselves, and secondly in their relation to the total composition that is the Gospel. Where this priority is not observed redaction criticism has a tendency to fall back on the two methods which preceded it: [source and form criticism]" (*Matthew, Poet of the Beatitudes*, JSNTSup 203 [Sheffield: Sheffield Academic, 2001], 20). In defense of redaction criticism, see Gerd Häfner, "Das Matthäus-Evangelium und seine Quellen," in *The Gospel of Matthew at the Crossroads of Early Christianity*, ed. Donald Senior (Leuven: Peeters, 2011), 25–71.

7. See Graham N. Stanton, "Redaction Criticism: The End of an Era?," in *A Gospel for a New People: Studies in Matthew* (Louisville: Westminster John Knox, 1992), 23–53.

8. See Graham N. Stanton's summary, "Matthew's Gospel and the Damascus Document in Sociological Perspective," in *Gospel for a New People*, 85–107; Dennis C. Duling, *A Marginal Scribe: Studies in the Gospel of Matthew in Social-Scientific Perspective* (Eugene, OR: Cascade, 2012), 36–61.

9. Donald A. Hagner, "Matthew: Christian Judaism or Jewish Christianity?," in *The Face of New Testament Studies: A Survey of Recent Research*, ed. Scot McKnight and Grant R. Osborne (Grand Rapids: Baker Academic, 2004), 263–82.

10. J. A. Overman, *Matthew's Gospel and Formative Judaism: The Social World of the Matthean Community* (Minneapolis: Fortress, 1990).

11. G. D. Kilpatrick, *The Origins of the Gospel according to St. Matthew* (Oxford: Oxford University Press, 1946), 106–23—even though he still cast Matthew's opposition "within Judaism."

willingly due to their Christology[12] or their mission to gentiles?[13] Or were they about to be *extra muros* due to Matthew's Gospel, where he encourages a christologically focused, law-observant mission to the gentiles?[14] Nearly every issue (Matthew's Christology, his use of the OT, his view of discipleship) was pressed into service of the *intra/extra muros* debate—a trend that has continued during the last twenty-five years of Matthean scholarship.[15]

The World within the Text

The so-called antitheses in the Sermon on the Mount (Matt. 5:21–48) could be seen as a microcosm of Matthew's entire Gospel, where various incongruities and apparent "contradictions" are common; for example, if the scribes and Pharisees are hypocrites and blind guides, why listen to what they say (23:2–3, 16)? If gentiles and tax collectors should be welcomed into Matthew's community, what does it mean to treat an unrepentant brother like a gentile and a tax collector (18:17; 21:31; 28:19)? If the "sons of the kingdom" are good seed, why are they cast into "outer darkness" on the judgment day (8:12; 13:38)?[16] It's no wonder scholars come to different conclusions about Matthew's Christology, his use of the OT, or his ideas about discipleship.[17]

Matthew's Christology

Since most scholars contend that Matthew's Gospel was written by a Jew for Jews, tracing the influence of Jewish literature (both the OT and extracanonical writings) in the evangelist's presentation of Jesus as the Christ continues to be a significant area of research, perhaps even indicating Matthew's purpose. For example, according to David Kupp, the impetus for Matthew's divine-presence Christology was the controversy that erupted during the "parting of the ways" with Judaism. Matthew did not set out to produce an Immanuel Christology

---

12. Stanton, *Gospel for a New People*, 169–91.
13. See Eung Chun Park, *The Mission Discourse in Matthew's Interpretation*, WUNT 2/81 (Tübingen: Mohr Siebeck, 1995).
14. Anthony J. Saldarini, *Matthew's Christian-Jewish Community* (Chicago: University of Chicago Press, 1994).
15. See also Daniel M. Gurtner, "The Gospel of Matthew from Stanton to Present: A Survey of Some Recent Developments," in *Jesus, Matthew's Gospel and Early Christianity: Studies in Memory of Graham N. Stanton*, ed. Daniel M. Gurtner, Joel Willitts, and Richard A. Burridge (London: T&T Clark, 2011), 23–38.
16. See Dale C. Allison Jr., "Deconstructing Matthew," in *Studies in Matthew: Interpretation Past and Present* (Grand Rapids: Baker Academic, 2005), 237–49.
17. According to Edwin K. Broadhead, since Matthew's Gospel is a "living tradition," it shouldn't surprise us that he preserves dissonant voices in his narrative. *The Gospel of Matthew on the Landscape of Antiquity* (Tübingen: Mohr Siebeck, 2017), 13–24.

per se. Rather, in light of the post-70 CE trauma that threw Judaism into a crisis of social identity, Matthew presented Jesus as the "centripetal" force of God's presence for his community—a new temple drawing worshipers to the "I am with you" God of Israel.[18] And since Matthew's Gospel isn't a static text issued for one community at a particular time, it "may reflect both *intra muros* and *extra muros* moments" during the crisis.[19] A. D. A. Moses argues that Matthew relied on a Moses-Sinai typology (radiant face, bright garments, divine voice) informed by the theophany at Mount Sinai and the "Son of Man" figure of Daniel 7:13–14 in order to present the transfiguration as a sign and prolepsis of the "coming of God" in Christ. In this way, Matthew presents the transfiguration as superior to the "coming of God" Sinai event in order to counter Jews who pitted Jesus against Moses and to exalt Peter over Paul (who also claimed apostolic authority via a similar experience in 2 Cor. 3–4) in the ongoing controversy between Jewish and gentile Christianity.[20]

Since Jesus first appears in Matthew's Gospel as the "son of David" (1:1), several scholars find correlations between Jewish traditions about a Davidic Messiah and Matthew's unique Christology—especially his portrayal of a therapeutic "son of David." Since Davidic messianism didn't include the expectation of a healer, why did Matthew make the correlation—especially since the "Son of David" title appears most often in healing stories in his Gospel?[21] According to Lidija Novakovic, the idea of a "son of David" healer didn't derive from the Solomonic exorcists traditions or the Moses-like prophet performing signs. Rather, since there is some evidence in Jewish literature that linked Davidic promises to the expectation of the forgiveness of sins (Pss. Sol. 17–18), Matthew presented Jesus as the Davidic Savior (1:20–21) through his healing ministry (chaps. 8–9) and crucifixion.[22] Using Richard Hays's method of determining intertextuality, Young S. Chae argues that Matthew relied on the Davidic Shepherd tradition (Mic. 2–5; Zech. 9–14; Ezek. 34–37) modified

---

18. See also Blaine Charette, *Restoring Presence: The Spirit in Matthew's Gospel*, JPTSup 18 (Sheffield: Sheffield Academic, 2000).

19. David D. Kupp, *Matthew's Emmanuel: Divine Presence and God's People in the First Gospel*, SNTSMS 90 (Cambridge: Cambridge University Press, 1996), 223. Concerning the idea that Matthew's Christology was significantly influenced by the alienation of his community, see Camille Focant, "La christologie de Matthieu à la croisée des chemins," in Senior, *Matthew at the Crossroads*, 73–97.

20. A. D. A. Moses, *Matthew's Transfiguration Story and Jewish-Christian Controversy*, JSNTSup 122 (Sheffield: Sheffield Academic, 1996).

21. Walter T. Wilson reads the miracle stories in Matt. 8–9 through the lens of disability studies, noticing how Matthew emphasized the importance of boundary crossing in the healing ministry of Jesus. *Healing in the Gospel of Matthew: Reflections on Method and Ministry* (Minneapolis: Fortress, 2014).

22. Lidija Novakovic, *Messiah, the Healer of the Sick: A Study of Jesus as the Son of David in the Gospel of Matthew*, WUNT 2/170 (Tübingen: Mohr Siebeck, 2003).

by Second Temple literature (1 En. 85–90; Pss. Sol. 17–18; Qumran texts). He finds three kinds of allusions in Matthew's Gospel: (1) texts involving sheep/ shepherd images, (2) texts that emphasize the "therapeutic Son of David," and (3) "the Ezekielian pattern" of the eschatological Davidic Shepherd in Matthew's vision of the restoration of Israel (restoration of YHWH as Shepherd, establishment of the new leader/Davidic Shepherd-King, eschatological regathering of Israel as the sheep of God's pasture). Countering the notion that a therapeutic son of David derived from the Solomon-as-exorcist Jewish legends or the Greek divine-man tradition, Matthew drew primarily from the shepherd image in Ezekiel 34, creating a "two Shepherds schema": both the eschatological (judgment [Matt. 25]) and Davidic (restoration [Matt. 10]) Shepherd of Israel and the whole world.[23]

Embracing the geopolitical significance of Matthew's Davidic messianism, Joel Willitts explores the Shepherd-King motif in the OT, Psalms of Solomon 17, and the Qumran literature as a context for Jesus's mission to recover the "lost sheep" of Israel—the remnant of the ten lost tribes of Israel. "The mission of Jesus as construed by Matthew centres on the restoration of Israel as a nation-state and relates to the future reconstitution of the twelve-tribe league of political Israel within the ideal Land."[24] Furthermore, Matthew believed his community was the true remnant of Israel, and (like Qumran) believed that those who refused to join their messianic community (both Jews and gentiles) would be judged on the last day. Attempting to broaden the focus on the Davidic Shepherd motif in the first Gospel, Wayne Baxter also sees Matthew's Shepherd Christology in Jewish national terms, locating Matthew's community in a socioreligious context that challenges the binary intramural/extramural debate. Matthew demonstrates how Jesus "saved his people from their sins" by fulfilling the Davidic Shepherd of Ezekiel 34 through miracles of healing, by condemning the religious leadership, and by eventually overcoming the Roman rulers at his parousia. Consequently, Matthew is keen on showing how Jesus not only refused to abandon the mission to restore Israel but also held up the law as the means of moral renewal for the gentiles as well. Therefore, Baxter locates Matthew's community in Judaism while maintaining an "open-ethnic" mission to the gentiles, whose obedience to the law would have fostered table fellowship between Jews and gentiles.[25]

23. Young S. Chae, *Jesus as the Eschatological Davidic Shepherd: Studies in the Old Testament, Second Temple Judaism, and in the Gospel of Matthew*, WUNT 2/216 (Tübingen: Mohr Siebeck, 2006).
24. Joel Willitts, *Matthew's Messianic Shepherd-King in Search of "the Lost Sheep of the House of Israel,"* BZNW 147 (Berlin: de Gruyter, 2007), 31.
25. Wayne Baxter, *Israel's Only Shepherd: Matthew's Shepherd Motif and His Social Setting*, LNTS 457 (London: Bloomsbury T&T Clark, 2012).

But could the "son of David" refer to Solomon? How early and widespread was the "Solomon-as-Exorcist" tradition in Judaism? According to Jiří Dvořáček, implicit references to the tradition in the Wisdom of Solomon and the Dead Sea Scrolls and explicit references in Josephus, the Testament of Solomon, Gnostic literature, and Aramaic and Greek Magical texts (bowls and papyri) reveal that the Jewish tradition of Solomon as an exorcist was prominent in Matthew's day. But does exorcism belong to the therapeutic Davidic motif, since exorcisms were not the same as healings? In some Jewish texts, episodes of exorcism and healing are blended together—even though Solomon himself is never pictured as a healer. Nevertheless, Dvořáček makes a case for seeing how the tradition informed Matthew's presentation of Jesus as the "son of David" when the evangelist conflated the therapeutic-Son-of-David and the exorcist-Solomon traditions, which is why Jesus claimed, "Someone greater than Solomon is here."[26]

Daniel Zacharias, however, takes a different tack when considering the son of David typology in Matthew. From the first verse of the Gospel (likely functioning as a title for the entire book according to Zacharias), Matthew relies on Davidic typology throughout the Gospel, typology that reaches a climax when Jesus quotes the Davidic lament (Ps. 22) on the cross. Furthermore, Matthew presents Jesus as an antitype of David (welcoming the blind in the temple)—a correspondence that is especially evident in Jesus's burial and resurrection. "The lack of typology in this instance actually serves to highlight the uniqueness of Jesus."[27] So Matthew deconstructs the Davidic typology, casting Jesus not as a militant leader who would bring about geopolitical restoration of Israel (Pss. Sol. 17 and DSS), but as a healing shepherd and humble king, using David's own words from the Psalms to confirm the evangelist's portrayal of Jesus as the last "Son of David."

Since Matthew relied so heavily on the OT, it's not surprising that scholars find other typologies in the first Gospel. Keying on annotations in the genealogy of Jesus in Matthew's Gospel ("and his brothers" and references to women), Jason Hood explains how the genealogy functions as a compressed version of the story of Israel, thereby serving Matthew's Christology. Since Judah was prophesied to rule over his brothers and since both Judah and Jeconiah were heroes who sacrificed themselves to redeem Israel, Matthew used this micronarrative within the story of Israel to portray Jesus as the messianic redeemer destined to rule over his brothers. Furthermore, Matthew signals his intention to highlight praiseworthy gentiles in the Gospel

---

26. Jiří Dvořáček, *The Son of David in Matthew's Gospel in the Light of the Solomon as Exorcist Tradition*, WUNT 2/415 (Tübingen: Mohr Siebeck, 2016).

27. H. Daniel Zacharias, *Matthew's Presentation of the Son of David: Davidic Tradition and Typology in the Gospel of Matthew* (London: Bloomsbury T&T Clark, 2016), 19.

by including four gentile women in Jesus's family tree, revealing how Jesus fulfilled Israel's vocation to bring the nations to God.[28] According to Alistair Wilson, Matthew presents Jesus as "the Prophet" and "Wisdom" of God, who brings eschatological judgment informed only by the OT (not extra-canonical apocalypses). Matthew cites apocalyptic imagery from the OT "as figurative expressions used to describe events which may belong to the realm of historical experience."[29] Therefore, as prophet and sage delivering the judgment of God against Israel and all humanity, Jesus (1) performed symbolic acts against the temple (clearing, healing, cursing fig tree), (2) told parables and proclaimed woes against Jewish leaders, (3) predicted the destruction of the temple, and (4) predicted the eschatological judgment of Israel and all nations at his parousia.

Regarding the temple, according to Daniel Gurtner, the torn veil at the death of Jesus not only symbolized God's judgment against the temple's leadership but also was a messianic sign of the promise of God's eschatological presence. According to Matthew's "Emmanuel Christology," the torn veil represents the accessibility to God for all people via the death of Christ. Furthermore, since the temple symbolized the cosmos (with the veil representing the heavenly firmament), the torn veil pictures the opening of heaven, the outpouring of divine secrets to be revealed during the messianic age, and God dwelling among his people for the restoration of Israel (Ezek. 37).[30] Leroy Huizenga sees temple imagery blending with Isaac typology throughout Matthew's Gospel. Matthew relied on a model reader (operating with a Jewish encyclopedia) to hear allusions to an Isaac typology informed by traditions surrounding the Akedah (Gen. 22), heard in the divine voice at Jesus's baptism and transfiguration, and revealed by Jesus as the "willing son of sacrifice," who is the new temple where "the Lord provides."[31] According to Catherine Hamilton, the episode of Pilate washing his hands and the people's response ("His blood be on us and our children!") is the climax of the theme of innocent blood that runs throughout Matthew's Gospel. Hamilton draws on innocent blood traditions in Judaism to understand Matthew's purpose: to explain both the end of exile through defilement and destruction, and the restoration of Israel through cleansing and new creation via the death of Jesus. Consequently, Hamilton

---

28. Jason B. Hood, *The Messiah, His Brothers, and the Nations (Matthew 1.1–17)* (London: T&T Clark, 2011).

29. Alistair I. Wilson, *When Will These Things Happen? A Study of Jesus as Judge in Matthew 21–25* (Milton Keynes, UK: Paternoster Press, 2004), 22.

30. Daniel M. Gurtner, *The Torn Veil: Matthew's Exposition of the Death of Jesus*, SNTSMS 139 (Cambridge: Cambridge University Press, 2007).

31. Leroy A. Huizenga, *The New Isaac: Tradition and Intertextuality in the Gospel of Matthew* (Leiden: Brill, 2012).

challenges the false dichotomy of the intramural/extramural readings of Matthew 27:25.[32]

In his study of one of Matthew's favorite words (*proskyneō*), Joshua Leim argues that the evangelist ascribed to Jesus *theologoumena* (divine ascription) reserved for the God of Israel. Tracing the Gospel's narrative-christological pattern in "worship"-language episodes, Leim shows how Matthew binds together the identity of Father and Son while affirming "the unity-in-distinction" between YHWH and Jesus: "The Son is the filial repetition of the Father, his immanent presence among his people."[33] Consequently, "not to know the Son is not to know the Father."[34] Using the incarnation as a model for heaven and earth (two realms revealed in one person), Patrick Schreiner argues for the spatial significance of the kingdom in light of Matthew's Christology. We conceive of space in three ways: physical (what it is), ideological (meaning we assign to it), and imaginative (what it should be). "*Theologically*, Jesus' mission is the reordering of the earth with his body as the nucleus. In *metaphysical* terms, the spatial aspect of the kingdom is localized in the human body, and human bodies create 'imagined' kingdom spaces by social living."[35] Therefore, in Matthew's narrative world, Schreiner sees chapter 12 as the turning point in the reclamation of earth for heaven's purpose as revealed in human bodies—especially the Beelzebul controversy, where Jesus reveals that "something greater" than the "Lord of the earth" (Beelzebul) is present *spatially*.

Matthew's Use of the OT

The long-standing questions regarding how Matthew interpreted the OT and what text form he used for citations[36] and to what extent intertextuality reveals the influence of the OT on Matthew, have continued to attract the attention of some Matthean scholars over the last twenty-five years. For example, according to Benedict Green, Matthew did not rely on Q as a source for the Beatitudes. Rather, he used several OT texts to compose the poetry, a pattern evident by the way Matthew reworked the Septuagint (LXX) for his

---

32. Catherine Sider Hamilton, *The Death of Jesus in Matthew: Innocent Blood and the End of Exile* (New York: Cambridge University Press, 2017).
33. Joshua E. Leim, *Matthew's Theological Grammar: The Father and the Son*, WUNT 2/402 (Tübingen: Mohr Siebeck, 2015), 243.
34. Leim, *Matthew's Theological Grammar*, 243.
35. Patrick Schreiner, *The Body of Jesus: A Spatial Analysis of the Kingdom in Matthew*, LNTS 555 (London: Bloomsbury T&T Clark, 2016), 14 (italics original).
36. Robert H. Gundry, *The Use of the Old Testament in St. Matthew's Gospel* (Leiden: Brill, 1967); Krister Stendahl, *The School of St. Matthew and Its Use of the Old Testament* (Ramsey, NJ: Sigler, 1990).

purposes; for example, when combining several texts throughout the Gospel, Matthew tends to give "the result a clear rhythmic structure"[37]—a preference for quatrains. In other words, where scholars see the hand of a redactor of Q, Green attributes the compositional work to Matthew as author—the "versifier" of the OT. When it comes to direct OT citations in Matthew's Gospel, Maarten Menken maintains that the text form of Matthew's quotations derives neither from the LXX nor from the Hebrew text. Although some variations can be attributed to the way Matthew edited his sources (Mark and Q), many of the fulfillment quotations diverge from the LXX, even though they seem to be based on it. Since these variations are consistently different from the way Matthew edited Mark and Q, Menken posits that Matthew didn't revise the LXX on his own, nor did he occasionally translate the Hebrew Scriptures. Rather, Matthew used a revised version of the LXX that was circulating at his time.[38]

Lena Lybæk claims that Matthew used the Jesus tradition (Q and Mark) in the same way he referenced the Hebrew Scriptures, revealing a normative function for all three sources. Furthermore, by placing the Jesus story in the context of Scripture, Matthew rewrites the Gospel as authoritative for his theological purposes (revealed in Matt. 11–13): presenting Jesus as the "coming one," the "more than" character prefigured in Elijah, Solomon, and Jonah, and the revealer/concealer of Isaiah. Since "Matthew continually adds the story of Jesus to Scripture,"[39] revealing its normative and formative function for Matthew, his Gospel does not necessarily reflect the social context of the Matthean community—for example, the polemic against the scribes and the Pharisees. Rather, Matthew's emphatic criticism, partly preserved by the Jesus tradition, derives from his reading of the OT. According to Michael Theophilos, perhaps Jesus's invective against the scribes and Pharisees in Matthew 23 was informed by warnings in Deuteronomy of God's curse on the disobedient. Therefore, Jesus's prediction regarding the destruction of the temple in Matthew 24 would be the fulfillment of God's punishment.

---

37. H. Benedict Green, *Matthew, Poet of the Beatitudes*, JSNTSup 203 (Sheffield: Sheffield Academic, 2001), 50.

38. Maarten J. J. Menken, *Matthew's Bible: The Old Testament Text of the Evangelist* (Leuven: Leuven University Press, 2004).

39. Lena Lybæk, *New and Old in Matthew 11–13: Normativity in the Development of Three Theological Themes*, FRLANT 198 (Göttingen: Vandenhoeck & Ruprecht, 2002), 248. See also Anne M. O'Leary, *Matthew's Judaization of Mark: Examined in the Context of the Use of Sources in Graeco-Roman Antiquity*, LNTS 323 (Leiden: T&T Clark, 2006). In the same way that ancient writers of Greco-Roman literature produced works of "creative imitation," Matthew rearranged the macrostructure of Mark to reflect Jewish symbolic numbers (fives, sevens, and twelves), inserting OT quotations, allusions, and echoes, not only to "Judaize" Mark to "legitimize" Jesus as the Christ but also to "Christianize" the Hebrew Scriptures for the Matthean community, presenting Jesus as the "new Torah."

Using Daniel's prediction regarding the abomination of desolation—applied to Israel's enemy during the Maccabean revolt—as a commentary for the destruction of the Jewish temple, Matthew offers an ironic twist to the prophecy: Israel is the enemy that God uses against Israel to punish his people. Therefore, suggestively, Theophilos posits a twofold, two-stage fulfillment of the coming of the Son of Man: stage one for Israel (ministry of Jesus) and for the nations (preaching the gospel to gentiles post-Matt. 28:20); stage two for Israel (destruction of temple) and for the nations (the second coming of Christ).[40] Brandon Crowe takes a different approach, arguing that Matthew applied to Jesus Deuteronomy's emphasis on Israel's responsibility to obey the God of Israel as their Father, thereby revealing that Jesus fulfilled Scripture as the "obedient son." Matthew's purpose was to show how Jesus succeeded where Israel failed: in the temptation of Christ (direct references to Deut. 6 and 8), in the Sermon on the Mount (several references to Deuteronomy, to blessings and curses [also in Matt. 23], and to God as Father [seventeen times] and disciples as obedient "sons" who reflect their Father's righteous character), and in reference to the "disobedient son" (Deut. 21:18–21) in Matthew 11:16–19.[41]

Given Matthew's portrait of Jesus as the "suffering servant," it's astonishing that when he quoted Isaiah 42:1–4 (Matt. 12:18–21), he omitted the line that best supports his purpose: "He will not grow faint or be crushed" (Isa. 42:4). Furthermore, the Isaiah quote doesn't appear to relate to the surrounding context. So, why would Matthew use it? Showing how Matthew's usage reflects the fluidity and variety of text forms of Isaiah 42:1–4 in Second Temple Jewish literature (appearing often as a "nonaligned" text), Richard Beaton maintains that the evangelist offers a "bi-referential" reading of the text: on a literary level, the citation validates Jesus's withdrawal; on a theological level, the extraneous material added by Matthew reveals his christological purpose to present Jesus as the Spirit-endowed servant who brings justice to the nations. This explains why Matthew omitted Isaiah 42:4a, since "humility" of the servant was not the primary focus of his Christology.[42] Using Hays's methodology for tracing intertextuality, Charlene Moss infers that Matthew was significantly influenced by Zechariah—not only in the passion narrative (eighteen references), where one would expect Zechariah 9–14 to play a prominent role, but also in the infancy narratives (three references) and Galilean

---

40. Michael P. Theophilos, *The Abomination of Desolation in Matthew 24.15* (London: Bloomsbury T&T Clark, 2012).

41. Brandon D. Crowe, *The Obedient Son: Deuteronomy and Christology in the Gospel of Matthew* (Berlin: de Gruyter, 2012).

42. Richard Beaton, *Isaiah's Christ in Matthew's Gospel*, SNTSMS 123 (Cambridge: Cambridge University Press, 2004).

ministry of Jesus (three references), echoing texts from Zechariah 1–8. These "allusive echoes" may not represent "Matthew's conscious choice" to import Zechariah material, but may well reflect what Moss calls Matthew's "biblical consciousness" in portraying Jesus as the healing "shepherd king" who cares for his flock until the end, when he is struck down and establishes a new covenant in his blood.[43] According to Nicholas Piotrowski, Matthew fused together two themes (Davidic Messiah and the end of exile) derived from several prophets (Isaiah, Micah, Hosea, and Jeremiah) in order to convince his model reader (operating with a Jewish encyclopedia) that those who reject Jesus as God's eschatological king continue to endure exile. Nevertheless, Matthew's community should "positively locate themselves on the redemptive-historical calendar as Yahweh's covenantal end-of-exile people."[44]

Matthew's View of Discipleship

"So often the First Evangelist, while addressing christological issues with his right hand, is at the same time delivering teaching on discipleship with his left."[45] Indeed, in certain episodes (like the "stilling of the storm"; Matt. 8:23–27), it's often difficult to distinguish whether Matthew's emphasis is christological or ecclesiological. Therefore, Matthew's view of discipleship has continued to spark interest among scholars, who either rely on narrative criticism to study certain characters in the Gospel that may reflect Matthew's purpose—a reading strategy for his implied reader—or who employ social-scientific methods to uncover the social dynamics of Matthew's narrative world, especially since marginalized people play a significant role in the first Gospel. Therefore, some scholars wonder whether different characters within Matthew's Gospel function like a window into Matthew's community. Does Matthew's ecclesiology reveal a polemical edge that reflects the social world of Matthew's community? Pushing against the tendency to interpret the implied reader as "transparent" of the Matthean community, Jeannine Brown uses a "three-tiered" model to establish the function of the disciples-as-character in the first Gospel. In the "textual" world, the disciples tend to misunderstand Jesus's authority and mission, thereby functioning as a "negative foil" to the implied reader. Brown is reluctant to use Matthew's

---

43. Charlene McAfee Moss, *The Zechariah Tradition and the Gospel of Matthew*, BZNW 156 (Berlin: de Gruyter, 2008). See also Clay Alan Ham, *The Coming King and the Rejected Shepherd: Matthew's Reading of Zechariah's Messianic Hope* (Sheffield: Sheffield Phoenix Press, 2005).

44. Nicholas G. Piotrowski, *Matthew's New David at the End of Exile: A Socio-Rhetorical Study of Scriptural Quotations*, NovTSup 170 (Leiden: Brill, 2016), 243.

45. W. D. Davies and Dale C. Allison Jr., *The Gospel according to Saint Matthew*, ICC (Edinburgh: T&T Clark, 1991), 2:512–13.

characterizations of the Twelve as a reflection of the "concrete" world of the Matthean community since the Gospels functioned like *bioi*[46] for a general readership. Finally, the disciples function in Matthew's "symbolic" world as part of the construct of ideal discipleship: the negative examples of the Twelve, coupled with Jesus's teaching and his exemplary life, provide a holistic vision of discipleship for the implied reader.[47]

According to J. R. C. Cousland, the crowds provide insight into Matthew's view of discipleship. They function as a literary character who at times is favorably disposed to Jesus and his ministry and at other times is not. Matthew's "ambivalent" depiction mirrors the way the Jewish people are often characterized in the Hebrew Scriptures: vulnerable sheep who are abused by evil shepherds and a stiff-necked people who stone the prophets sent to them. Matthew uses this common topos to depict the Jewish people of his time, who are equally conflicted about the gospel. The crowds function, therefore, as the "transparent" character of the Jewish people—distinct from the religious leaders—who may still respond the same way to Jesus, offered by Matthew as an encouragement to his *extra muros* community to continue the gospel mission to the "lost sheep" of the house of Israel—a "re-judaization" of the gospel.[48] Talvikki Mattila expands the focus to include several groups in Matthew's Gospel. After a character study of the twelve disciples, the crowds, and women in Matthew, Mattila infers that, even though women are not named as disciples, they fulfill an exemplary role as faithful followers of Jesus. Coming from the margins, they represent the true virtues of the kingdom: service, humility, suffering, and healing—deconstructing the hierarchy of patriarchy.[49]

Robert Gundry goes the opposite direction, narrowing his focus on one character, Simon Peter. Due to Jesus's repeated warnings about false disciples, Gundry sizes up Matthew's portrayal of Peter and concludes that Peter, just like Judas Iscariot, fits the bill. Whereas other scholars argue for Peter's rehabilitation, Gundry sees Matthew's redaction of Mark as evidence that he

---

46. For discussion of the term *bios* (pl. *bioi*), see chap. 5.

47. Jeannine K. Brown, *The Disciples in Narrative Perspective: The Portrayal and Function of the Matthean Disciples* (Atlanta: SBL Press, 2002).

48. J. R. C. Cousland, *The Crowds in the Gospel of Matthew*, NovTSup 102 (Leiden: Brill, 2002).

49. Talvikki Mattila, *Citizens of the Kingdom: Followers in Matthew from a Feminist Perspective* (Göttingen: Vandenhoeck & Ruprecht, 2002). See also Baby Parambi, *The Discipleship of the Women in the Gospel according to Matthew: An Exegetical Theological Study of Matt 27:51b–56, 57–61 and 28:1–10* (Rome: Editrice Pontifica Università Gregoriana, 2003); Stuart L. Love, *Jesus and Marginal Women: The Gospel of Matthew in Social-Scientific Perspective* (Cambridge: James Clarke, 2010). According to Love, women appear as marginal characters in Matthew's Gospel (not disciples or Jewish leaders), but find their place among the crowds, where they are revealed as faithful followers of Jesus versus the "little faith" of the twelve. The same is true, therefore, for the Matthean community.

intended for readers to judge Peter as a false disciple. The fact that later Gospel writers (Luke and John) softened Matthew's depiction of Peter as a false disciple has clouded our reading of Matthew; for example, "upon this rock" (Matt. 16:18) refers not to Peter but to Jesus's words, echoing his teaching from the Sermon on the Mount (7:24). If Matthew's Gospel was written for Christians living in Antioch in the 60s CE, then his portrayal of Peter as a waffling disciple confirms Paul's caricature of Peter during the Antioch incident (Gal. 2:11–14). Peter serves, therefore, as a pastoral warning for Matthew's readers: If someone like Peter can fall from grace, how much more can you?[50]

In light of a post-70 CE Jewish context, Margaret Hannan argues that Matthew wrote his Gospel to "ensure the survival of the Jewish faith despite the destruction of its temple and the loss of its related political institutions."[51] Matthew frames the importance of the kingdom by relying on certain literary markers (*inclusios*, doublets, and formulas or the grouping of certain episodes thematically—e.g., the way characters "come to" Jesus), guiding the implied reader to embrace the way of Jesus (the long-awaited Messiah), which brings the sovereign rule of God to earth at the present time—censuring injustice, empowering the marginalized, establishing Jesus's new fictive family, challenging social and economic norms via an alternative community. "Thus, Matthew uses the term [*hē basileia tōn ouranōn*, "the kingdom of the heavens"] to refer to God's past and present activity, as sovereign ruler, and not to the eschatological event, when God's rule over creation is fully established."[52] The first Gospel functions, then, like a "manual of instruction on the nature and demands of God's sovereign rule" for the Matthean community.[53] But why does Matthew prefer the plural, "kingdom of the heavens"? According to Jonathan Pennington, "kingdom of heaven(s)" doesn't function as a circumlocution for "kingdom of God" since Matthew used both expressions. Rather, Matthew intended to highlight the difference between human and divine rule to show how the rule of God in heaven comes to earth through Jesus Christ—both earthly (visible) and spiritual (invisible) rule. The plural form didn't derive from Semitic morphology (Hebrew and Aramaic words for heaven are dual/plural nouns). Matthew developed a distinct usage—singular and plural—to unpack the rich literary background of heaven/earth language in Jewish literature (especially the dualistic worldview of apocalyptic literature), emphasizing the universality of God's dominion. In Matthew's

---

50. Robert H. Gundry, *Peter: False Disciple and Apostate according to Saint Matthew* (Grand Rapids: Eerdmans, 2015).
51. Margaret Hannan, *The Nature and Demands of the Sovereign Rule of God in the Gospel of Matthew*, LNTS 308 (London: T&T Clark, 2006), 10.
52. Hannan, *Nature and Demands of the Sovereign Rule of God*, 34.
53. Hannan, *Nature and Demands of the Sovereign Rule of God*, 230.

Gospel, then, the singular form, "the kingdom of heaven," refers to the visible realm of God's rule (heaven and earth). The plural form, "the kingdom of the heavens," refers to the invisible realm of God's reign. Thus Matthew's community should see themselves as "heavenly people," opposing worldly empires (even breaking with Judaism) by living the radical ways of Christ's kingdom on earth, awaiting the final *eschaton*.[54]

But what did Matthew expect of his community in the meantime? Did he expect them to carry on the mission to Israel or not? According to Wesley Olmstead, Matthew intended for his readers to infer that the judgment of God for rejecting Jesus as the Messiah cannot be restricted to the religious leaders—despite his withering criticism of the Jewish leadership. Although Matthew casts the people in a sympathetic light, Olmstead believes Matthew's trilogy of parables (two sons, vineyard, wedding feast) was intended as a warning to all Israel because of the people's role in rejecting God's son, the Messiah. And yet the evangelist doesn't look on the people of Israel as a lost cause, especially the marginalized. Rather, just as Jesus looked on the masses with compassion, Matthew's Gospel was supposed to encourage the Matthean community (the new "nation") not only to continue the messianic mission to recover the "lost sheep" but also to extend the Abrahamic blessing of God to all nations—a "gentile subplot" that runs throughout the First Gospel.[55] But some argue that the two missions in Matthew's Gospel, first to Israel (10:6) and then to the nations (28:19–20), represent a progression in Matthew's narrative purpose.[56] So did Jesus establish the *ekklēsia* to replace Israel's privileged position in the covenant (due to their rejection of Jesus as the Messiah), or does the church represent an expansion of the covenant promise?

Matthias Konradt believes the answer depends on how Matthew portrays the people's reaction to Jesus as a "therapeutic" version of the Davidic Shepherd-King motif: by distinguishing the crowd's reaction from that of the Jewish leaders, by setting Jesus's teaching and "therapeutic activity within the theme of conflict"[57] with the religious leaders, by highlighting the hypocrisy of the scribes and Pharisees, and by casting the people of Jerusalem as culpable (distinguished from "all Israel") for Jesus's death—with the parable trilogy

---

54. Jonathan T. Pennington, *Heaven and Earth in the Gospel of Matthew*, NovTSup 126 (Leiden: Brill, 2007).

55. Wesley G. Olmstead, *Matthew's Trilogy of Parables: The Nation, the Nations and the Reader in Matthew 21:28–22:14*, SNTSMS 127 (Cambridge: Cambridge University Press, 2003).

56. Ulrich Luz, *Matthew 8–20*, trans. James E. Crouch, Hermeneia (Minneapolis: Fortress, 2011), 2:72–75.

57. Matthias Konradt, *Israel, Church, and the Gentiles in the Gospel of Matthew*, trans. Kathleen Ess (Waco: Baylor University Press, 2014), 136; in German, *Israel, Kirche und die Völker im Matthäusevangelium* (Tübingen: Mohr Siebeck, 2007).

(Matt. 21:28–22:14) and the prediction of the destruction of the temple confirming the same. The transfer language of Matthew 21:43 refers to Jesus's disciples (not to the gentiles), who are empowered to bring about God's reign on earth through the teaching of Jesus, who fulfilled the Law and the Prophets. "The disciples, however, are neither the shepherds of *Israel* alone nor the light for the *nations* as the holy remnant of *Israel* or in the place of *Israel*. Rather, the disciples—and this includes those disciples gained from the Gentiles—are charged to be the light of the *world*, for all other people, whether they are Jews or Gentiles."[58] According to Anders Runesson, Matthew never intended for his Gospel to be anything more than a call to Israel to obey the whole law.[59] For only those who truly obey God are saved from divine wrath on the last day. According to Matthew, then, it is Jesus's interpretation of the law that is determinative for righteousness. Since the evangelist presents Jesus as the "sent one" who rightly interprets the law of God, Torah obedience, according to Jesus, results in salvation for those who have ears to hear. This means, of course, that only Jews and proselytes can be saved. Stories of gentiles seeking Jesus are included by Matthew only to encourage Israel to repent as the day of judgment draws near. We also find out as Matthew's story unfolds that the Pharisees are the primary target of Jesus's judgment against "this generation" because they don't obey the law. That's why Jesus blames them for the upcoming destruction of the temple—the sign of God's wrath.

Convinced that Matthew was "trained in the conventional educational manner as found in the *progymnasmata*,"[60] and therefore knew the rhetoric of praise and blame, Jerome Neyrey argues that Matthew composed his Gospel with a different missional focus: to subvert the social norms of honor and shame for his community. When Matthew's readers learn to praise Jesus for his divinely orchestrated birth, countercultural life, and noble death, "Jesus socializes would-be disciples to a new set of expectations about what is honorable and shameful"[61]—they embrace the cross as loss of honor and learn to honor the "shamed," knowing that God rewards those who praise him. But Louise Lawrence questions the reductionist tendencies of the honor/shame model when it is applied to Matthew's Gospel. Relying on Mikhail Bakhtin's ideas about diverse social voices revealed in dialogic interaction, Lawrence challenges the honor/shame dichotomy: the presumption of "anti-introspection"

---

58. Konradt, *Israel, Church, and the Gentiles*, 349–50 (italics original).
59. Anders Runesson, *Divine Wrath and Salvation in Matthew: The Narrative World of the First Gospel* (Minneapolis: Fortress, 2016).
60. Jerome H. Neyrey, *Honor and Shame in the Gospel of Matthew* (Louisville: Westminster John Knox, 1998), 4. *Progymnasmata* are preliminary rhetorical exercises; for futher discussion see chap. 15 in this volume, under "Luke the Literary Artist."
61. Neyrey, *Honor and Shame in the Gospel of Matthew*, 227.

in the pursuit of honor (Lawrence finds several examples in Matthew where introspection plays a key role in social relationships—e.g., Pilate's doubts about the guilt of Jesus), assuming an agonistic context that fostered only honor precedence (seeking honor in public) and not honor virtue (inner sense of honor coming from God despite social threats), and the gender divisions embedded in the quest for honor precedence (in Matthew's world, women embody honor virtue).[62]

Finally, Warren Carter explores how Matthew's Gospel functioned as a counternarrative ("work of resistance") against the dominant Roman imperial power.[63] Matthew wrote his Gospel to encourage an alternative community of disciples to challenge the Roman way of life—economically (taxes), politically (Roman sovereignty), and socially (promoting an egalitarian community).[64]

The World behind the Text

To what extent does the polemical thrust of the narrative reveal the social situation behind Matthew's Gospel? According to David Sim, Matthew wrote his Gospel for a Jewish sect in Antioch fighting a war on two fronts: (1) by preserving the newly won James/Petrine law-observant gospel, the Matthean community opposed the remnants of Paul's law-free gospel in Antioch, and (2) by affirming a law-observant mission of faith in Christ to Jews (and gentiles who submitted to circumcision), the Matthean community battled the post-70 CE transplanted Pharisees over true obedience to the law. As a sect within Judaism, Matthew's community no longer gathered with fellow Jews in the synagogue and, facing increased isolation,[65] needed a Gospel to help define their identity.[66] Paul Foster, however, maintains that Matthew's Gospel

---

62. Louise Joy Lawrence, *An Ethnography of the Gospel of Matthew: A Critical Assessment of the Use of the Honour and Shame Model in New Testament Studies*, WUNT 2/165 (Tübingen: Mohr Siebeck, 2003).

63. Warren Carter, *Matthew and Empire: Initial Explorations* (Harrisburg, PA: Trinity Press International, 2001).

64. See also the collection of essays *The Gospel of Matthew in Its Roman Imperial Context*, ed. John Riches and David C. Sim (London: T&T Clark, 2005).

65. Alienation also contributed to their interest in apocalyptic eschatology, highlighted by Matthew. See David C. Sim, *Apocalyptic Eschatology in the Gospel of Matthew*, SNTSMS 88 (Cambridge: Cambridge University Press, 1996); Robert Charles Brandon calls Matthew "the Apocalyptic Scribe"; see *Satanic Conflict and the Plot of Matthew*, StBibLit 89 (New York: Peter Lang, 2006), 85–89.

66. David C. Sim, *The Gospel of Matthew and Christian Judaism: The History and Social Setting of the Matthean Community* (Edinburgh: T&T Clark, 1998). According to Charles E. Carlston and Craig A. Evans, the war on two fronts was the rejudaizing of the church and the threat of assimilating to gentile culture. See *From Synagogue to Ecclesia: Matthew's Community at the Crossroads* (Tübingen: Mohr Siebeck, 2014). On the thesis that Matthew rejected gentile

was written for a community that originated in Judaism but had experienced a "major breach" with the synagogue, revealed by the way Jesus read the Torah in the Sermon on the Mount. "The composition of the antitheses (Matt. 5:21–48) reflects both the social circumstances of the community as well as the creative manner in which Matthew presents his understanding of Jesus in order to address the pastoral needs of his community. To this end, he portrays Jesus not only as the supreme interpreter of Torah, but rather, as the ultimate source of authority within the community."[67] Having been ostracized by the synagogue, the group needed to go beyond the mission to Israel (Matt. 10) and begin converting gentiles (28:19–20), which led to significant issues for some more conservative Jewish members regarding righteousness according to the law.

If Matthew's Gospel provides a window into his community, then how he used "Christian" sources[68] may reveal several stages of social history behind the Gospel. Kenneth Newport infers that (1) Matthew 23 does not derive from Q; (2) Matthew 23 was not a Matthean creation; but rather (3) Matthew took a lengthy source (Matt. 23:2–31) that belonged to a different *Sitz im Leben* (an *intra muros* context prior to 70 CE, similar to the Sermon on the Mount) and appended an eschatological judgment against the religious leaders (vv. 32–39).[69] Andrew Doole goes even further, challenging the thesis that Matthew was primarily beholden to Q and used Mark only when necessary. Matthew wasn't a "Q Christian" who recently came into possession of Mark's Gospel. Rather, Matthew relied on Mark as *the* authoritative account of Christ and decided to supplement the narrative with Q material to produce a "new edition of Mark."[70] Wim Weren finds three layers of literary development that correspond

---

culture but still held out hope for the salvation of gentiles, see Anders Runesson, "Judging Gentiles in the Gospel of Matthew: Between 'Othering' and Inclusion," in Gurtner, Willitts, and Burridge, *Jesus, Matthew's Gospel and Early Christianity*, 138–51.

67. Paul Foster, *Community, Law and Mission in Matthew's Gospel* (Tübingen: Mohr Siebeck, 2004), 142. See also John Yueh-Han Yieh, *One Teacher: Jesus' Teaching Role in Matthew's Gospel Report*, BZNW 124 (Berlin: de Gruyter, 2004); Jesus as "the only teacher" had a fourfold social effect on the community: polemic (versus the synagogue), apologetic (new people of God with mission to gentiles), didactic (twelve as models of discipleship), and pastoral (caring for the least).

68. According to Alan Garrow, "Christian" sources for Matthew's Gospel included the Didache. Since similarities between Matthew and the Didache occur within the first layers of the tradition, Garrow infers Matthew used an early version of the Didache. See Alan J. P. Garrow, *The Gospel of Matthew's Dependence on the Didache*, JSNTSup 254 (London: T&T Clark, 2004).

69. Kenneth G. C. Newport, *The Sources and Sitz im Leben of Matthew 23*, JSNTSup 117 (Sheffield: Sheffield Academic, 1995).

70. Andrew Doole, *What Was Mark for Matthew? An Examination of Matthew's Relationship and Attitude to His Primary Source* (Tübingen: Mohr Siebeck, 2013), 79. Alan Kirk challenges the "sub-literary" status of Q as a random collection of sayings—contra James

to three phases of social history. Prior to 70 CE, Christian Jews considered themselves full members of the multiform Jewish community (Jewish material unparalleled in Mark and Q). During the second phase (ca. 70–80), they became a minority group within the Jewish community in conflict with the Pharisees (material redacted from Mark and Q—e.g., increased disputes with the Pharisees). "In the third phase (ca. 80–90), the Christian Jews gradually detached themselves from the Jewish community and came into contact with a broad multicultural network of Christian communities"[71] (final redaction that reflects an *extra muros* context—e.g., warnings against "false prophets").

According to Boris Repschinski, the way Matthew redacted Mark's version of the controversy stories reveals a pattern: (1) heightened conflict between Jesus and Jewish leadership (e.g., Jesus calls them "evil"), (2) the scribes and the Pharisees identified as his primary opponents, (3) the crowds characterized as generally supportive of Jesus during the contest, (4) Jesus presented as more faithful to the law than his opponents were. Repschinski reads the major characters as transparent of the challenges Matthew's community faced in a post-70-CE context. "Thus the Matthean claim to leadership within Judaism does not just seek to displace the Pharisees from their position of prominence. It seeks to introduce a form of Judaism that is radically different from that of its opponents"[72]—a difference that centers on righteousness via the law according to Jesus as the Messiah. Similarly, Glenna Jackson argues that Matthew redacted Mark's version of Jesus's encounter with the Canaanite woman to reinforce Jewish law, elevate women, and demonstrate

---

D. G. Dunn, who sees an unstructured Q used by Matthew (who relied on Mark for structure) (Dunn, "How Did Matthew Go about Composing His Gospel?," in Gurtner, Willitts, and Burridge, *Jesus, Matthew's Gospel and Early Christianity*, 39–58). According to Kirk, since manuscripts were used by scribes (the text brokers of cultural tradition) as repositories to guard what had already been memorized through oral recitation, the interdependence of oral and written texts reveals a "source-utilization" process that explains how Matthew used Q and Mark—two written sources that were memorized by Matthew (Alan Kirk, *Q in Matthew: Ancient Media, Memory, and Early Scribal Transmission of the Jesus Tradition*, LNTS 564 [New York: Bloomsbury T&T Clark, 2016]). Duling sees Matthew as a "marginal scribe" (once belonging to the "structurally marginalized" in Judea, perhaps even the Pharisees), who functioned as a text broker for his culturally determined (Jewish), ideologically marginalized (Christ-believing) community (Duling, *A Marginal Scribe: Studies in the Gospel of Matthew in Social-Scientific Perspective* [Eugene, OR: Cascade, 2012]). According to Aaron M. Gale, Matthew's Gospel presumes not only scribal literacy for the author/redactor/editor but also a "learned community" of readers who would appreciate the Gospel's literary techniques. Gale, *Redefining Ancient Borders: The Jewish Scribal Framework of Matthew's Gospel* (London: T&T Clark, 2005).

71. Wim J. C. Weren, *Studies in Matthew's Gospel: Literary Design, Intertextuality, and Social Setting* (Leiden: Brill, 2014), 9.

72. Boris Repschinski, *The Controversy Stories in the Gospel of Matthew: Their Redaction, Form and Relevance for the Relationship between the Matthean Community and Formative Judaism* (Göttingen: Vandenhoeck & Ruprecht, 2000), 346.

requirements of gentile inclusion—a paradigm for female proselytism in the Matthean community. The persistence of a gentile woman (much like Ruth, who appears in Matthew's version of Jesus's genealogy) is championed by Matthew since converts to Judaism were the ones who initiated proceedings for membership—something required by Matthew's community as well, since the story of Ruth functioned as a rabbinic formula for testing a prospective proselyte. Therefore, this story reveals Matthew's thoroughly *intra muros* context: gentiles must become Jews to join the community.[73] Anthony Ewherido, however, argues that Matthew's version of the parables in Matthew 13 reveals the "*corpus mixtum*" of the church—for example, the sower's field is a mixed body (formative Judaism) that reflects the challenges of discipleship for Matthew's *extra muros* community.[74]

The World in Front of the Text

Considering the extent to which biases and presuppositions influence the way we read Matthew has attracted the attention of a few scholars. Elaine Wainwright offers an "engendered reading" of Matthew's Gospel by highlighting the feminine voices in the narrative in order to challenge the conventional, male-dominant readings of the Gospel. For example, she finds the confession of the Canaanite Woman to be as important to Matthew's narrative as Peter's. But an emerging "patri/kyriarchal church determined to maintain its androcentric power base" favored the Petrine episode in order to "subjugate" the voices of those seeking a more inclusive "household"—voices that still linger in the text.[75] In a significant collection of essays, several scholars have offered a feminist reading of Matthew's Gospel—for example, Matthew's Wisdom Christology in light of the feminine metaphor of "Lady Wisdom";[76] challenging the presumption (and the biases that come with it) that the hemorrhaging

---

73. Glenna S. Jackson, *"Have Mercy on Me:" The Story of the Canaanite Woman in Matthew 15:21–18*, JSNT 228 (Sheffield: Sheffield Academic, 2002).

74. Anthony O. Ewherido, *Matthew's Gospel and Judaism in the Late First Century CE: The Evidence from Matthew's Chapter on Parables (13:1–52)*, StBibLit 91 (New York: Peter Lang, 2006). According to Petri Luomanen, there isn't enough direct evidence in Matthew's Gospel to infer a *"corpus mixtum"*; see *Entering the Kingdom of Heaven: A Study on the Structure of Matthew's View of Salvation*, WUNT 2/101 (Tübingen: Mohr Siebeck, 1998), 265–66.

75. Elaine M. Wainwright, *Shall We Look for Another? A Feminist Rereading of the Matthean Jesus* (Maryknoll, NY: Orbis, 1998), 100.

76. Celia Deutsch, "Jesus as Wisdom: A Feminist Reading of Matthew's Wisdom Christology," in *A Feminist Companion to Matthew*, ed. Amy-Jill Levine with Marianne Blickenstaff (Sheffield: Sheffield Academic, 2001), 88–113.

woman was menstruating;[77] and highlighting the role of several women in Matthew's Gospel, both as characters in the Gospel[78] and as characters in its parables.[79] Additionally, besides Carter, a few scholars have offered post-colonial readings of Matthew's Gospel.[80]

Reflections

Even though I began our survey with Stanton's prediction regarding the future of Matthean studies, I am reluctant to offer any opinions about the direction of Matthean scholarship beyond current trajectories: (1) since Jesus is the main subject of Matthew's Gospel, explorations in his Christology will continue to take center stage; (2) due to more nuanced studies of Matthew's community (e.g., what do we mean by the terms "Jewish" and "Christian"?),[81] the strict dichotomy of an *extra/intra muros* context will no longer prove helpful; and (3) scholars will continue to take an eclectic approach, combining several methods to mine the riches of the First Gospel.

A canonical approach that relies on Matthew to flesh out the NT Christology of the Synoptic Gospels[82] should always bring to light the uniqueness of Matthew's view of Christ. Although one might want to minimize the distinctive features of the Matthean Christ in the pursuit of a coherent Christology, the incongruities within Matthew's own portrait of Christ will continue to puzzle scholars, warning us: "Not so fast. That doesn't quite fit." Of course, what makes Matthew's Christology so intriguing is his reliance on the OT, whether by direct citation, typologies, allusions, or echoes. And I suspect there's more to be discovered here—determining to what extent the OT influenced Matthew's view of Christ. But it's the Jewish tradition surrounding these texts, as well as the various text forms of Matthew's "Bible," that will require more nuanced portrayals of Matthew's Christology. Furthermore (due to my particular interest), I wonder whether Matthew's

---

77. Amy-Jill Levine, "Discharging Responsibility: Matthean Jesus, Biblical Law, and Hemorrhaging Woman," in Levine and Blickenstaff, *Feminist Companion to Matthew*, 70–87.

78. Gail R. O'Day, "Surprised by Faith: Jesus and the Canaanite Woman," in Levine and Blickenstaff, *Feminist Companion to Matthew*, 114–25.

79. Marie-Eloise Rosenblatt, "Got into the Party after All: Women's Issues and the Five Foolish Virgins," in Levine and Blickenstaff, *Feminist Companion to Matthew*, 171–95.

80. See Fernando F. Segovia, "Postcolonial Criticism and the Gospel of Matthew," in *Methods for Matthew*, ed. Mark Allan Powell (Cambridge: Cambridge University Press, 2009), 216–28.

81. Christopher Tuckett, "Matthew: The Social and Historical Context—Jewish Christian and/or Gentile?," in Senior, *Matthew at the Crossroads*, 99–129.

82. Simon Gathercole, *The Preexistent Son: Recovering the Christologies of Matthew, Mark, and Luke* (Grand Rapids: Eerdmans, 2006).

Christology might have as much to do with his view of discipleship as it does with any attempt to offer a polemical response to other Jewish or Christian communities. In other words (as we've discovered in Pauline studies), it's difficult to separate his Christology from his ecclesiology. For Matthew, who Jesus is reveals who his disciples are. Lordship and discipleship are symbiotic. Therefore, further study of Matthew's view of discipleship[83] and spirituality[84] may prove as helpful in sorting out his christological purpose as is any supposed social context.

Although social science methods have helped bring the *Sitz im Leben* of Matthew into sharper focus than what redaction-critical studies could reveal, situating Matthew's community in relation to Judaism seems to be more complex than the either/or categories of *intra/extra muros* would allow. It's because Matthew's view of "all things Jewish" (whether the law, the Pharisees, or the temple) has blurred the lines of Jewish and Christian identity. To be sure, Matthew belongs to the Jewish matrix of literature that seeks to argue for Israel's true identity (whether Josephus, Philo, OT apocrypha, Pseudepigrapha, or DSS). But the diversity within Second Temple Judaism as well as emerging Christianity makes it far more difficult to determine where Matthew's Gospel fits in the "parting of the ways." Terms like "Jewish" and "Christian" (whether adjectives or nouns) seem out of place in light of the ambiguity of identity in Matthew's narrative world. Furthermore, treating Matthew's Gospel like one of Paul's letters leads to "mirror reading" of the text, where certain characters are supposed to reflect the social situation of Matthew's community—something assumed more than proven. When it comes to the historical context of Matthew's community, we tend to find what we're looking for.

That's why the current trend in Matthean studies, using several methods to serve our scholarly interests, will continue in the near future. We used to spend much time refining procedures of a particular methodology in order to yield the best results, whatever they may be. There was a certain confidence in the method itself (most recently, literary criticism and social-scientific methods), as if developing and applying a rigorous methodology would serve our purpose. That's why (I think) predictions about the future of Matthean studies used to highlight new methods in research. But Matthean scholarship over the

---

83. See Michael J. Wilkins, *Discipleship in the Ancient World and Matthew's Gospel*, 2nd ed. (Grand Rapids: Baker, 1995); after considering the classical and Hellenistic, OT, and intertestamental background of the term *mathētēs* (disciple), Wilkins studies Matthew's use of the term—especially as it relates to Peter's role as an exemplar in the First Gospel.

84. Nijay Gupta, "The Spirituality of Faith in the Gospel of Matthew," in *Matthew and Mark across Perspectives: Essays in Honour of Stephen C. Barton and William R. Telford*, ed. Kristian A. Bendoraitis and Nijay Gupta, LNTS 538 (London: Bloomsbury T&T Clark, 2016), 108–24.

last twenty-five years has taken a more "hybrid" approach, combining several methods to pursue a particular topic.[85] It's the area of interest that drives our study (not the method), and we'll use whatever tool to get the job done. To use a golfing analogy, we used to have to play the fairways with woods or low irons. These days most use a hybrid club to approach the green.

---

85. To illustrate, at first I tried to divide the discussion of this essay according to method (redaction, literary, social-scientific, ideological), but I soon gave up.

14

The Gospel of Mark

JIN YOUNG CHOI

Introduction

This chapter lays out the current state of Markan studies. It classifies interpretive approaches into four representative paradigms: historical criticism, literary criticism, social criticism, and ideological criticism.[1] Historical criticism, which dominated from the mid-nineteenth century through the mid-1970s and still prevails in Western Markan scholarship, is usually author oriented. It seeks to find meaning intended in the text by Mark. I shall start with the predominant theme of the so-called messianic secret[2] and move on to discuss historical reconstruction of the context in which Mark's theology was produced. Studies of Mark's literary forms and patterns in the wider cultural background are also included under this heading.

Second, as advanced through the 1980s to 1990s, literary criticism in Markan studies is basically *text* oriented, but there are multiple ways of finding meaning in the text. This section first treats a formalist approach known as

---

1. I appropriate Fernando F. Segovia's four umbrella models of interpretation, found in "'And They Began to Speak in Other Tongues': Competing Modes of Discourse in Contemporary Biblical Criticism," in *Reading from This Place*, vol. 1, *Social Location and Biblical Interpretation in the United States*, ed. Fernando F. Segovia and Mary Ann Tolbert (Minneapolis: Fortress, 1995), 1–32.

2. William Wrede, *The Messianic Secret*, trans. J. C. G. Greig (Cambridge, MA: J. Clarke, 1971; first published 1901).

narrative criticism and then examines a few works that unearth multiple textures and ideologies in Mark's narrative. While the treatment of textures and ideologies necessarily explores historical realities behind conflicting textures in the narrative, this section lastly presents a poststructuralist and reader-oriented move in literary criticism.

Third, we will look at social criticism in a separate section; this approach engages historical reconstruction but at the same time recognizes not only the ideological nature of the literary text but also the interpreter's position. These interpretations, developed in the 1980s to 1990s, include sociopolitical, sociolinguistic, and sociorhetorical approaches. Meaning is located in the history of early Christians in the narrative form and its social dimension, but some of these interpreters highlight the praxis of the reading community.

Lastly, ideological criticism emphasizes readers' social locations, suggesting that meaning is found in front of the readers. As the most recent emerging discourse of interpretation in Markan studies, this paradigm can be represented by feminist criticism, liberation hermeneutics, and postcolonial criticism. In relation to the current state of Markan studies, this review is inevitably confined and the choice of resources admittedly eclectic and subjective. Nonetheless, the contribution of this chapter may be to broaden Markan scholarship by involving the voices of previously marginalized interpreters and simultaneously engaging with more traditional readings.

Historical Criticism

The "Messianic Secret"

Older scholarship regarded Mark as the earliest narrative of Jesus and the original source for the historical Jesus. Based on the secrecy text, historical-Jesus scholarship argued that Jesus revealed his identity deliberately as his messianic consciousness developed so the disciples would come to a deeper understanding of his identity. William Wrede, conversely, argued the messianic secret does not prove Jesus's messianic consciousness, but reflects the early Christians' experience of Jesus as the Messiah after Easter. Such realization resulted in Mark's creation of the theological idea that the secret of Jesus's messiahship is revealed only after his resurrection.[3]

Yet a problem with the messianic secret arises when Mark describes that the secret is not always kept even before the resurrection. Wrede admits that there is another group of materials in which the secret is precluded, and he

---

3. Wrede, *Messianic Secret*, 236.

attributes those accounts to tradition.[4] Critics attempted to resolve such inconsistencies. Whereas Ulrich Luz distinguishes the injunction to silence related to the healing miracles from the true messianic secret that is pertinent to Jesus's identity, Heikki Räisänen breaks the theme down into four subthemes: (1) the injunction of silence given to the demons and the disciples, (2) the secret healings, (3) the parable theory, and (4) the disciples' lack of understanding.[5]

Other scholars argue that the texts related to secrecy do not necessarily constitute the unified theme of "the *messianic* secret."[6] Rather than focusing on Mark's christological concern, David F. Watson maintains that Mark intended to counter the conventional honor-shame code.[7] For Kelly R. Iverson, however, Watson contradicts his own argument when he ignores conflicting textual evidences such as Jesus's manifestation of "his power via public display."[8] Iverson's narrative-performance criticism leads him to argue that the secrecy motif includes seemingly unrelated subthemes in the text but that the audience, hearing the repeated motif, experiences the effect of "revelatory disclosure."[9] Adam Winn improves the weakness of Watson's argument by contending that Mark co-opts the imperial motif of "resisting public honor," as practiced by emperors, and thus exhibits Jesus as the true world ruler for the audience in Rome.[10]

While Watson and Winn shift the traditional emphasis on the christological significance of the secrecy to considerations of Greco-Roman cultural codes and imperial politics, respectively, it was Wrede who turned the course of historical criticism from the quest for the historical Jesus in the nineteenth century to the studies of Mark's own time and theology in the twentieth century's historical scholarship. Furthermore, Wrede's literary approach to the secrecy anticipated redaction criticism, pioneered with respect to Mark by Willi Marxsen.

Historical Reconstruction and Mark's Theology

Redaction criticism in the 1960s regarded the author of Mark as a collector, transmitter, or editor of inherited traditions. For Marxsen, however,

---

4. Wrede, *Messianic Secret*, 125–29.
5. Ulrich Luz, "The Secrecy Motif and the Marcan Christology," in *The Messianic Secret*, ed. C. M. Tuckett (Philadelphia: Fortress, 1983), 75–96; Heikki Räisänen, "The 'Messianic Secret' in Mark's Gospel," in Tuckett, *Messianic Secret*, 132–33.
6. Kelly R. Iverson, "Whereas the Gospel Is Preached," in *Mark as Story: Retrospect and Prospect*, ed. Kelly R. Iverson and Christopher W. Skinner (Atlanta: SBL Press, 2011), 186.
7. David F. Watson, *Honor among Christians: The Cultural Key to the Messianic Secret* (Minneapolis: Fortress, 2010); cf. Bruce Malina, *The New Testament World: Insights from Cultural Anthropology*, 3rd ed. (Louisville: Westminster John Knox, 2001), 125.
8. Iverson, "Whereas the Gospel Is Preached," 188.
9. Iverson, "Whereas the Gospel Is Preached," 189, 203.
10. Adam Winn, "Resisting Honor: The Markan Secrecy Motif and Roman Political Ideology," *JBL* 133, no. 3 (2014): 599–600.

Mark is a Galilean "gospel" and Galilee is "not primarily of historical but rather of theological significance as the locale of the imminent Parousia."[11] Since Marxsen argued for the need to "inquire into the situation of the community" in which the Gospel was written, redaction critics have attempted to reconstruct the historical situation of Mark's community.[12] With further emphasis on Mark as an imaginative theologian, Norman Perrin points out that Christology, discipleship, and historical situation constitute the dominant concerns of Markan scholarship.[13] Such theological constructions are assumed to be Mark's response to particular historical circumstances.

Theodore J. Weeden represents one of these positions. Mark's adversaries advocate a *theios-anēr* theology—the theology of glory under the influence of Hellenistic ideas of "divine man."[14] Mark refutes the divine-man Christology with a theology of the cross based on the suffering Son of Man. The disciples fail to understand the true identity of Jesus because of their obstinate allegiance to a false Christology. Werner Kelber also reconstructs Mark as opposing the Jerusalem theology—a theology of power, in contrast to his theology of the cross.[15] The negative portrayal of the disciples reflects the Jewish-Christian community of Jerusalem, which awaited the parousia of Jesus the Son of Man before the fall of Jerusalem in 70 CE.

As an alternative interpretation, Ernest Best suggests that Mark's community faced persecution. Then Jesus's miracles are viewed as his care for the ongoing Christian community's journey rather than representing an erroneous Christology, and the figure of the disciples encourages persecuted Christians, teaching them true discipleship.[16]

---

11. Willi Marxsen, *Mark the Evangelist: Studies on Redaction History of the Gospel*, trans. J. Boyce et al. (Nashville: Abingdon, 1969; first published 1956), 92.

12. Marxsen, *Mark the Evangelist*, 24–29. For an argument about the composition of Mark's Gospel in Rome, see Martin Hengel, *Studies in Mark* (Philadelphia: Fortress, 1985), 28–29. More scholars suggest Palestine or Syria as the place of the writing (Howard Kee, *The Community of the New Age: Studies in Mark's Gospel* [Macon, GA: Mercer University Press, 1983]). For parallels between Mark and Qumran documents in light of Jewish apocalypticism, see Joel Marcus, *The Mystery of the Kingdom of God* (Atlanta: Scholars Press, 1986).

13. Dennis C. Duling and Norman Perrin, *The New Testament: Proclamation and Parenesis, Myth and History*, 3rd ed. (Fort Worth: Harcourt Brace, 1994), 332. Some scholars add Mark's eschatology to the list of master themes; see Adam Winn, *The Purpose of Mark's Gospel: An Early Christian Response to Roman Imperial Propaganda* (Tübingen: Mohr Siebeck, 2008), 150–52.

14. Theodore J. Weeden, *Mark: Traditions in Conflict* (Philadelphia: Fortress, 1971). For a discussion of a royal, Davidic Christology, see Frank J. Matera, *What Are They Saying about Mark?*, WATSA (New York: Paulist Press, 1987), 32–32. Cf. Marie Noon Sabin, *Reopening the Word: Reading Mark as Theology in the Context of Early Judaism* (New York: Oxford University Press, 2002).

15. Werner H. Kelber, *The Kingdom in Mark: A New Place and a New Time* (Philadelphia: Fortress, 1974).

16. Ernest Best, *Disciples and Discipleship: Studies in Gospel according to Mark* (Edinburgh: T&T Clark, 1986), 130.

The attempts to piece together Mark's community along with the theological constructions prevailed in the 1970s, and particularly *theios-anēr* Christology revived in the 1990s.[17] However, historical criticism has been challenged because such reconstructions, while seemingly objective, often reflect subjective theological representations of the interpreter.[18] Some of the recent historical studies pay attention to the political context of the Roman Empire rather than the Mediterranean cultural milieu and understand the Gospel as an intentional response to the imperial power and theology.[19] Such a counterimperial stance is also employed in most sociopolitical interpretations and in some postcolonial studies.

Genre and Rhetoric

Rather than reconstructing Mark's context and theology, other scholars have focused on the Gospel's literary form and attempted to relate the Gospel to Greco-Roman literary genres such as biography, epic, myth, tragedy, comedy, and romance. For example, "aretalogy," a form of biography of an extraordinary divine figure, is often regarded as a literary prototype of Mark.[20] Whitney T. Shiner demonstrates that Jesus's disciples function rhetorically in Mark's Gospel. She explores how Greek philosophical biographies, as well as Jewish wisdom teaching of Sirach, use flawed disciples to highlight their philosophical heroes as authoritative figures and the founders of communities.[21] While some scholars question the existence of such a genre and view the biographical hypothesis as an artificial scholarly construction,[22] studies of the Gospel's links with ancient literary genres continue.[23]

---

17. Edwin K. Broadhead, *Teaching with Authority: Miracles and Christology in the Gospel of Mark* (Sheffield: JSOT Press, 1992).

18. George Aichele, *Jesus Framed* (New York: Routledge, 1996), 2.

19. Winn, *Purpose of Mark's Gospel*. Winn's anti-imperial reading locates "Mark's response to Roman imperial power in the city of Rome" (Adam Winn, "Tyrant or Servant? Roman Political Ideology and Mark 10.42–45," *JSNT* 36, no. 4 [2014]: 329). Cf. Craig A. Evans, "The Beginning of the Good News and the Fulfillment of Scripture in the Gospel of Mark," in *Hearing the Old Testament in the New Testament*, ed. Stanley E. Porter (Grand Rapids: Eerdmans, 2006), 83–103.

20. Kee, *Community of the New Age*, 17.

21. Whitney Taylor Shiner, *Follow Me! Disciples in Markan Rhetoric*, SBLDS 145 (Atlanta: Scholars Press, 1995), 32–34, 186–91.

22. W. R. Telford, *The Theology of the Gospel of Mark*, NTT (Cambridge: Cambridge University Press, 1999), 97–98; Richard A. Burridge, *What Are the Gospels? A Comparison with Graeco-Roman Biography*, 2nd ed. (Grand Rapids: Eerdmans, 2004), 16–18. Burridge's work is considered a breakthrough in the field in the use of genre theory.

23. Dennis R. MacDonald, *The Homeric Epics and the Gospel of Mark* (New Haven: Yale University Press, 2000); Justin Marc Smith, *Why Bios? On the Relationship between Gospel Genre and Implied Audience* (New York: Bloomsbury T&T Clark, 2015).

Instead of searching for connections between the Gospel and Greco-Roman genres, others observe rhetorical patterns or exercises such as *chreia*.[24] Such a rhetorical analysis applies to Mark's narrative or the characters' speeches. Michael Strickland and David M. Young examine the discourses of Jesus in the context of Greco-Roman rhetoric. Their main questions revolve around "how first-century audiences would have heard the discourses of Jesus, and what they would have understood them to be 'about.'"[25]

As demonstrated above, a multitude of studies focus on the audience of Mark, employing theories of performance, orality, and speech act.[26] If rhetorical criticism is concerned with the text's effect on the audience, this authorial audience is part of historical reconstruction and thus such rhetorical criticism often serves historical ends. However, rhetorical approaches can be employed in both literary criticism and sociopolitical criticism. When a rhetorical analysis concentrates on the aesthetic or literary properties inherent in the discourse of the Gospel, this mode of literary analysis often merges with so-called New Criticism.[27]

Literary Criticism

Narrative Criticism and Character Studies

Narrative criticism, influenced by both New Criticism and narratology in secular literary studies, fully developed from the 1980s into the mid-1990s in Gospel studies. The narratological study of David M. Rhoads, Joanna

---

24. The *chreia* was a rhetorical exercise taught in an intermediate level of education using the rhetorical handbooks called the *progymnasmata*. The *chreia* is a brief anecdote about a famous person and includes the person's speech, action, or both. Some scholars argue that the *chreia* is the prevalent form in Mark's story in which Jesus is engaged in controversies or in exchanges of challenge and riposte. Vernon Robbins, *Jesus the Teacher: A Socio-Rhetorical Interpretation of Mark* (Minneapolis: Fortress, 1992); Jerome H. Neyrey, "Questions, *Chreiai*, and Challenges to Honor: The Interface of Rhetoric and Culture in Mark's Gospel," *CBQ* 60, no. 4 (1998): 657–81.

25. Michael Strickland and David M. Young, *The Rhetoric of Jesus in the Gospel of Mark* (Minneapolis: Fortress, 2017), xix.

26. Werner Kelber, *The Oral and Written Gospel: The Hermeneutics of Speaking and Writing in the Synoptic Tradition, Mark, Paul and Q* (Philadelphia: Fortress, 1983); Mary Ann Beavis, *Mark's Audience: The Literary and Social Setting of Mark 4:11–12* (Sheffield: Sheffield Academic, 1989); Whitney Shiner, *Proclaiming the Gospel: First-Century Performance of Mark* (Harrisburg, PA: Trinity Press International, 2003); Bridget Gilfillan Upton, *Hearing Mark's Endings: Listening to Ancient Popular Texts through Speech Act Theory* (Leiden: Brill, 2006); Richard A. Horsley, Jonathan A. Draper, and John M. Foley, *Performing the Gospel: Orality, Memory, and Mark* (Minneapolis: Fortress, 2006).

27. New Criticism is characterized by its exclusive interest in "the text in itself"; see C. Clifton Black, "Rhetorical Criticism," in *Hearing the New Testament: Strategies for Interpretation*, ed. Joel B. Green, 2nd ed. (Grand Rapids: Eerdmans, 2010), 171.

Dewey, and Donald Michie is regarded as a significant milestone in this development.[28] Narrative critics often appeal to Seymour Chatman's distinction between story and discourse.[29] If story consists of elements such as setting, events, characters, and plot, then discourse is how the story is told using rhetorical devices. The implied author presents Mark's story to the implied reader, who is expected to understand the story.[30]

Mary Ann Tolbert argues that the levels of the implied author-reader and the narrator-narratee are merged into one level in Mark's Gospel. The implied reader is informed about who Jesus is by the narrator from the beginning (1:1).[31] On the level of the characters of the story, Jesus as the private narrator of parables shares a significant amount of omniscience with the implied author and the narrator. This alliance of the implied author, the narrator, and Jesus creates a sturdy framework for the reader's evaluation of the speech and action of the characters in the narrative.

Recent narrative studies focus on characters or characterization in Mark's Gospel.[32] Grouping Markan characters into the disciples, Jewish leaders, and minor characters,[33] all of whom interact, Elizabeth Struthers Malbon argues that the disciples, particularly the women followers at the empty tomb, are merely fallible learners, not those who ultimately fail. The disciples, therefore, serve as "realistic and encouraging models" of discipleship for hearers/readers.[34]

In an earlier volume, Malbon addresses discipleship based on a structuralist analysis of the text. She suggests that "the way" (*ho hodos*) is the final

---

28. David M. Rhoads, Joanna Dewey, and Donald Michie, *Mark as Story: An Introduction to the Narrative of a Gospel*, 3rd ed. (Philadelphia: Fortress, 2012; previous editions published 1982, 1999).

29. Elizabeth Struthers Malbon, "Characters in Mark's Story: Changing Perspectives on the Narrative Process," in Iverson and Skinner, *Mark as Story*, 45. Seymour Chatman, *Story and Discourse: Narrative Structure in Fiction and Film* (Ithaca, NY: Cornell University Press, 1978).

30. Elizabeth Struthers Malbon, "Narrative Criticism: How Does the Story Mean?," in *Mark and Method*, ed. Janice Capel Anderson and Stephen D. Moore (Minneapolis: Fortress, 2008), 32–33.

31. Mary Ann Tolbert, *Sowing the Gospel: Mark's World in Literary-Historical Perspectives* (Minneapolis: Fortress, 1996; first published 1989), 93–103.

32. Jack Dean Kingsbury, *Conflict in Mark: Jesus, Authorities, Disciples* (Minneapolis: Fortress, 1989); Elizabeth Struthers Malbon, *Between Author and Audience in Mark: Narration, Characterization, Interpretation* (Sheffield: Sheffield Phoenix, 2009); Cornelis Bennema, *A Theory of Character in New Testament Narrative* (Minneapolis: Fortress, 2014), 114–32.

33. Joel F. Williams, *Other Followers of Jesus: Minor Characters as Major Figures in Mark's Gospel* (Sheffield: JSOT Press, 1994); Kelly R. Iverson, *Gentiles in the Gospel of Mark* (New York: T&T Clark, 2007).

34. Elizabeth Struthers Malbon, *In the Company of Jesus: Characters in Mark's Gospel* (Louisville: Westminster John Knox, 2000), xii. For Malbon, Williams, and Iverson, the portrayals of the disciples are not necessarily negative.

mediation of the fundamental opposition—the opposition of order and chaos.[35] Despite the recognition of the mixed portrayals of the disciples, many narrative-critical studies emphasize resolution of conflicts within the text and seek internal narrative logic and coherent meaning through a consistent interpretation. Tolbert understands the task of the reader as filling in the narrative "gap" in the story and making sense of the whole.[36] However, some scholars oppose such a structuralist view by acknowledging multiple levels of discourses or plurality of meanings in the narrative.

Multiple Textures and Ideologies in the Narrative

Using literary criticism, John Riches argues that conflicting ideologies—that is, forensic myth and cosmological myth—are embedded in Mark's narrative.[37] From the view of the cosmological mythology, the disciples' failure is caused by Satan, and Jesus struggles with this satanic power. However, from the forensic mythological perspective, their failure is caused by moral temptation; then, Jesus struggles to restore the hearts of people to the divine will through his teaching and healing.[38] Similarly, Burton Mack argues that there were diverse configurations of the Jesus movement that produced different kinds of myths. Mark integrated these multiple traditions into a single narrative of the obedient martyr, which Mack calls a "myth of innocence."[39]

While Mack's study shows different layers of traditions behind the narrative and thus is diachronic, Vernon K. Robbins explains such tensions in the narrative by exploring multiple levels of discourses such as the inner texture, intertexture, social and cultural texture, and ideological texture. His social-rhetorical criticism is essentially synchronic as it incorporates a multidiscourse analysis and a social-scientific method, which explores the social system and cultural values in the Mediterranean world of the first century.[40]

What is common in these studies is the use of literary approaches, but they do not assume that Mark's narrative and textual meaning are unified. In addition, they see the Gospel not only as a literary artifact but also as a

---

35. Elizabeth Struthers Malbon, *Narrative Space and Mythic Meaning in Mark* (San Francisco: Harper & Row, 1986), 68–71.

36. Tolbert, *Sowing the Gospel*, 3, 7.

37. John K. Riches, *Conflicting Mythologies: Identity Formation in the Gospels of Mark and Matthew* (Edinburgh: T&T Clark, 2000).

38. Riches, *Conflicting Mythologies*, 145–79.

39. Burton Mack, *A Myth of Innocence: Mark and Christian Origins* (Minneapolis: Fortress, 1988).

40. Vernon K. Robbins, *The Tapestry of Early Christian Discourse: Rhetoric, Society and Ideology* (London: Routledge, 1996); cf. David Rhoads, *Reading Mark, Engaging the Gospel* (Minneapolis: Fortress, 2004).

distinct "ideological discourse that originated in a particular real-life context" beyond the narrated world.[41] However, their literary or rhetorical approaches that count on historical or social-scientific methods could be viewed as scientistic and objectivist.[42]

Both formalist and social-scientific approaches to literary criticism demonstrate a structuralist tendency or deal with the social structures and cultural grammar of the Mediterranean as fixed and universally applicable. In contrast, poststructuralist interpretation, still employing narrative criticism or narratology, resists seeing "the narrative-critical construal of character" as unified and coherent. Even when readers identify themselves with certain characters, readers and their subjectivities are "constructed narratively."[43] Poststructuralist approaches to literary criticism of the Gospel include deconstruction and reader-response criticism, which highlight multiple meanings in the text and the role of the reader.

Reader-Response and Deconstructive Criticism

While Robert Fowler's reader-response criticism follows narrative criticism's distinction between story and discourse, he argues that the discourse of Mark's Gospel exhibits uncertainty, mystery, and doubt through the rhetoric of indirection, which often set story and discourse at odds.[44] For example, he argues that the "perennial puzzle such as the messianic secret" is not that which is found in the story but that which is "encountered in the reading of the story."[45] Thus the primary goal of the Gospel is not to convey information to the reader but to bring the reader into the "experience" of reading the Gospel. Fowler tends to privilege the critic's reading process and limit the ordinary reader's experience of reading to the story level.

41. P. Merenlahti and R. Hakola, "Reconceiving Narrative Criticism," in *Characterization in the Gospels: Reconceiving Narrative Criticism*, ed. David Rhoads and Kari Syreeni (Sheffield: Sheffield Academic, 1999), 17.
42. Elisabeth Schüssler Fiorenza, "Challenging the Rhetorical Half-Turn: Feminist and Rhetorical Biblical Criticism," in *Rhetoric and Ethic: The Politics of Biblical Studies* (Minneapolis: Fortress, 1999), 83–102.
43. Scott S. Elliott, *Reconfiguring Mark's Jesus: Narrative Criticism after Poststructuralism* (Sheffield: Sheffield Phoenix, 2011), cited in Stephen D. Moore, "Biblical Narrative Analysis from the New Criticism to the New Narratology," in *The Oxford Handbook of Biblical Narrative*, ed. Danna Nolan Fewell (New York: Oxford University Press, 2016), 40–41; also see Stephen D. Moore, "Why There Are No Humans or Animals in the Gospel of Mark," in Iverson and Skinner, *Mark as Story*, 78.
44. Robert M. Fowler, *Let the Reader Understand: Reader-Response Criticism and the Gospel of Mark* (Harrisburg, PA: Trinity Press International, 2001), 20.
45. Fowler, *Let the Reader Understand*, 174–75. Fowler sees the messianic secret as irony. Also see Jerry Camery-Hoggatt, *Irony in Mark's Gospel: Text and Subtext* (New York: Cambridge University Press, 1992).

George Aichele argues that critics often take the position of the insider when they interpret the text, and he suggests "reading from outside."[46] Since those insiders know the secret of the kingdom, they are the alleged legal owners of the text and thus genuine disciples (4:11–12). However, Aichele contends that no one can be the legitimate insider of the text because it suggests that the values of outside and inside are relative (2:17; 8:35).[47] Aichele accepts the ultimate failure of reading because the text is always incomplete and even expresses reading as violence done to the text because the text resists interpretation.[48] However, his postmodern idea of a "text without meaning, without ideology" is challenged when the text is considered to be a cultural and ideological product.[49]

In contrast, for Stephen D. Moore, the text is not completely innocent. He adapts deconstructive strategies of reading from the "early" writings of Jacques Derrida, whose primary goal is to destabilize binary oppositions.[50] In dealing with the issue of insider/outsider, Moore's political and ethical deconstructive reading leads him to focus on the central ethnic opposition of gentile/Jew and, consequently, that of Christian/Jew in Mark. Moore considers the centurion's words to oscillate irreconcilably between crypto-Christian christological confession and derision by a gentile of a Jew (15:39).[51]

Whereas critics who employ reader-response or deconstructive methods highlight indeterminacy and undermine the insider/outsider binary in the text, others argue that poststructuralists' argument about the autonomy of literary text is elitist and modernist, as they often ignore the history of colonialism, which must become an integral part of the postmodern.[52] Therefore, certain alternative interpretations stress the social locations of both implied and present readers, underscoring politics of the Roman Empire and/or of the present imperial context. Sociopolitical and cultural interpretations go beyond a pure literary approach by presupposing that meaning is produced when a reader situated in a particular sociohistorical circumstance engages with the text.

46. Aichele, *Jesus Framed*, 2.
47. Aichele, *Jesus Framed*, 3, 85.
48. Aichele, *Jesus Framed*, 33.
49. Aichele, *Jesus Framed*, 5.
50. Stephen D. Moore, "Deconstructive Criticism: Turning Mark Inside-Out," in Anderson and Moore, *Mark and Method*, 95–110. For Moore, it is the parables that "unexpectedly begin to threaten *everyone* with exclusion in Mark." Moore, "Deconstructive Criticism," 101; Moore, *Mark and Luke in Poststructuralist Perspectives: Jesus Begins to Write* (New Haven: Yale University Press, 1992), 23–24.
51. Moore, "Deconstructive Criticism," 106–8.
52. Tat-siong Benny Liew, *Politics of Parousia: Reading Mark Inter(con)textually* (Leiden: Brill, 1999), 7–16.

Social Criticism

Sociopolitial Interpretations

Richard A. Horsley reads Mark from a sociopolitical perspective as narrative rather than theology, which he views as a scholarly construct.[53] Like poststructuralist critics, Horsley argues that Mark's story is "full not only of ambiguity, but of incongruity and double meaning" because of the metaphor, irony, and paradox used in the story.[54] Yet in Mark's historical presentation "built upon narrative forms in Israelite cultural tradition,"[55] the prominent plot is "Jesus' renewal of Israel in Galilean villages" in opposition to economic exploitation by Roman rulers and Judean elites, and discipleship is a subplot.[56]

Herman C. Waetjen argues that the Roman-occupied Palestine where Jesus conducted his ministry and the Roman-occupied Syria where the text originated merge in the Gospel.[57] Nevertheless, for Waetjen, the Gospel is not a biography or documentary record of the past, but an aesthetic literary creation. The depiction of disciples is ideological, not historical. Thus the Gospel authenticates itself in the process of reading and the attendant production of meaning.[58]

Similarly, Ched Myers maintains that Mark employs apocalyptic discourse to subvert the dominant cultural codes of both Rome and Jews.[59] While the good news of Jesus the Messiah challenges Roman propaganda, Mark advocates the ending of the temple's exploitative economy and building of an egalitarian community.[60] Discipleship inaugurates the new world by involving costly political engagement that Myers calls "nonviolent revolution."[61] The negative portrait of the disciples functions to "reduce the distance between the reader and these characters."[62] Thus, introducing a "center-periphery" model, Myers brings social locations of both the present reader and the authorial reader to the fore.

These sociopolitical interpretations of Mark's Gospel share common elements. First, they are not preoccupied with the quest for Jesus's identity or

---

53. Richard A. Horsley, *Hearing the Whole Story: The Politics of Plot in Mark's Gospel* (Louisville: Westminster John Knox, 2001), x.
54. Horsley, *Hearing the Whole Story*, 17.
55. Horsley, *Hearing the Whole Story*, 23.
56. Horsley, *Hearing the Whole Story*, xiv, 91.
57. Herman C. Waetjen, *A Reordering of Power: A Socio-Political Reading of Mark's Gospel* (Minneapolis: Fortress, 1989), 4.
58. Waetjen, *A Reordering of Power*, 2, 17.
59. Ched Myers, *Binding the Strong Man: A Political Reading of Mark's Story of Jesus* (Maryknoll, NY: Orbis, 1992), 416.
60. Myers, *Binding the Strong Man*, 166–67.
61. Myers, *Binding the Strong Man*, 416, 438.
62. Myers, *Binding the Strong Man*, 106.

Christology but instead highlight the disciples' political praxis, which brings the kingdom of God into the present. Second, these interpretations, unlike traditional historical criticism, go beyond historical reconstruction, paying attention to the ideological nature of the Gospel narrative as cultural production or oral performance. Last, these critics attend not only to the sociohistorical site of the Gospel writing but also to social locations of the present readers.

Sociolinguistic and Rhetorical Interventions

Brian K. Blount also examines the sociohistorical setting of the Gospel of Mark utilizing a sociolinguistic model, yet in the context of the African American church and society.[63] What language conveys is meaning *potential*, not meaning itself, and this potential was and is accessed contextually.[64] Hence, to understand the meaning potential of the kingdom of God—the most significant sign in Mark—Blount investigates Mark's cultural context, in which a believing community in northern Palestine and southern Syria faced conflicts and persecution during the war in 66–70 CE. In this context, Jesus's kingdom preaching is understood as an apocalyptic intervention—an apocalyptic "pocket of resistance." Then, discipleship means to "follow the mission plan he laid out as *the* tactical way to participate in God's strategic kingdom design" through the ministry of preaching.[65] Blount's apocalyptic and iconoclastic interpretation of the kingdom message has a direct impact on his own context—the black church's struggle to exorcise demonic forces like racism and sexism in American culture.[66]

Paying attention to the sociopolitical location and rhetorical situation of Mark's story, Elisabeth Schüssler Fiorenza argues that the Galilean Jesus movement as an inner-Jewish renewal movement with its inclusive vision and praxis presents an alternative option to the dominant patriarchal structures. While it is a gentile woman who joined the Jesus movement at an early stage (7:24–30), the Galilean women disciples were decisive for the extension and continuation of the movement to gentiles "as examples of suffering discipleship" as well as "the apostolic eye-witnesses" of the Jesus event (14:3–9; 15:47; 16:1–8).[67] Schüssler Fiorenza's feminist reconstruction of the Jesus movement is accompanied by a "rhetoric of inquiry," which applies not only to androcentric

---

63. Brian K. Blount, *Go Preach! Mark's Kingdom Message and the Black Church Today* (Maryknoll, NY: Orbis, 1998).
64. Blount, *Go Preach!*, 35; cf. Brian K. Blount, *Cultural Interpretation: Reorienting New Testament Criticism* (Minneapolis: Fortress, 1995).
65. Blount, *Go Preach!*, 7.
66. Blount, *Go Preach!*, 10–12.
67. Elisabeth Schüssler Fiorenza, *In Memory of Her: A Feminist Theological Reconstruction of Christian Origins* (New York: Crossroad, 1994; first published 1983), 136–38, 321.

texts but also to sociopolitical interests of scholarship "that undergirds its self-understandings as value-detached, objectivist science."[68] As her feminist critical-rhetorical approach views "the Bible and biblical interpretation as a site of struggle over authority, values and meanings,"[69] it opens up pathways for feminist and liberation interpretations.

Ideological Criticism

Feminist Criticism

Feminist criticism brings the gender issue to the forefront in the matter of Markan discipleship. While some feminist critics attempt to recover the history of women disciples' critical role in Jesus's movement, others seek to construct the character of women in Mark's narrative as ideal or potential disciples.[70] However, while exploring mainly women characters, these feminist interpretations seek to restore the ideal woman and thereby assume a univeral woman's experience.

Hisako Kinukawa interprets women characters in Mark's stories in light of her social location in Japan, in which a divisive honor-shame framework is valued along with the patriarchal social structure. While elucidating the reciprocal relationship between women and Jesus, Kinukawa maintains that discipleship means "taking on shame" and life-giving praxis, which necessitates suffering as the outcome of following Jesus in a patriarchal society.[71]

For Raquel Annette St. Clair, however, Kinukawa's "taking on shame" and positing the necessity of suffering for discipleship may be dangerous considering African American women's experience of suffering, shame, and surrogacy.[72] Similar to Kinukawa, St. Clair maintains that suffering is a consequence (inevitability) of discipleship, not a condition (divine necessity).[73] She finds a correspondent relationship between pain/suffering and honor/shame

---

68. Schüssler Fiorenza, *Rhetoric and Ethic*, 85.
69. Schüssler Fiorenza, *Rhetoric and Ethic*, 45.
70. Winsome Munro, "Women Disciples in Mark?," *CBQ* 44, no. 2 (1982): 232; Mary Ann Beavis, "Women as Models of Faith in Mark," *BTB* 18 (1988): 3–9; Marla Jean Selvidge, *Woman, Cult, and Miracle Recital: A Redactional Critical Investigation on Mark 5:24–34* (Lewisburg, PA: Bucknell University Press, 1990), 107; Joan L. Mitchell, *Beyond Fear and Silence: A Feminist-Literary Reading of Mark* (New York: Continuum, 2001); Susan Miller, *Women in Mark's Gospel* (New York: T&T Clark, 2004), 259; Joanna Dewey, "Women in the Gospel of Mark," *WW* 26 (2006): 22–29.
71. Hisako Kinukawa, *Women and Jesus in Mark: A Japanese Feminist Perspective* (New York: Orbis, 1994), 98–102.
72. Raquel Annette St. Clair, *Call and Consequences: A Womanist Reading of Mark* (Minneapolis: Fortress, 2008), 96.
73. St. Clair, *Call and Consequences*, 67–68.

in that both pain and honor are the consequences of discipleship, while suffering and surrogacy are considered shameful.[74] In this way, St. Clair provides a corrective to the traditional African American affirmations of Jesus as the divine cosufferer and of the cross as self-denial and promotes the womanist values of wholeness and honor.

Employing feminist reader-response criticism, Janice Capel Anderson focuses on the "gender ideologies—the social and symbolic constructions of gender"—of both Mark and his interpreters.[75] Malestream interpretations view Herodia as a depraved mother based on male fear of females possessing power, and they view the daughter and her dance either as innocent or as erotic (6:14–29). Anderson argues that these views represent "male constructions of female gender" as Other. Anderson not only analyzes the androcentric gender constructions of female characters in the text and culture but also interprets the female or feminized imagery of John's head on a platter and Christ's eucharistic body as the source of life: "They are sources of food who bleed and feed just as women bleed and feed."[76]

Although many feminist critics either promote the role of women in the Jesus movement or characterize women as ideal disciples, such interpretations, which reinforce gender opposition, impose the ideal on all women and exclude those who do not fit into gender stereotypes.[77] Additionally, the ideal portrait of women disciples may reinforce the suffering of women who have already suffered. As in Kinukawa's and St. Clair's interpretations, discipleship and suffering are interpreted differently, according to their social locations and experiences. Anderson's reader-response reading demonstrates that gender both shapes and is constructed in interpretation. Feminist scholarship pays more attention than before to this gender construction as intersecting with race/ethnicity, class, religion, and other identity factors.

Liberation Hermeneutics

Critical feminist interpretation is concerned with liberation of women and men, but Western feminist interpretation has often failed to relate patriarchy to colonialism. Liberation hermeneutics was originally produced in the Latin American context, in which the poor (e.g., the Catholic Christian base

---

74. St. Clair, *Call and Consequences*, 28.
75. Janice Capel Anderson, "Feminist Criticism: Dancing Daughter," in Anderson and Moore, *Mark and Method*, 125.
76. Anderson, "Feminist Criticism," 140.
77. See Manuel Villalobos Mendoza's queer interpretation of Mark's passion narrative, which disrupts the normative gender roles and highlights ambiguity produced by gender, racial, cultural, and ethnic otherness. Mendoza, *Abject Bodies in the Gospel of Mark* (Sheffield: Sheffield Phoenix, 2012).

communities) took the Bible from the conquerors into their own hands and began to read it out of their own sufferings and struggles. The most critical hermeneutical principle is God's preferential option for the oppressed.

Elsa Tamez reads the Gospel of Mark considering three contexts that share the same situation of armed conflict: of Jesus, of Mark, and of the present reader in Colombia.[78] Following Jesus in times of war and internal armed conflict inevitably causes silence and fear. Jesus's pursuit of secrecy and his followers' self-imposed silence can be viewed as a survival strategy, which was not unfamiliar to the Roman audience. Tamez's interpretation shows how this Latin American life-context can function as a lens to read Mark in the life context of the early Christians.

Byung-Mu Ahn reads the Gospel of Mark as a social biography of *ochlos* in the 1970s Korean context in which *minjung* (the "masses") suffered from political oppression and social injustice. Ahn argues that Mark was the first author to use the term *ochlos* in the NT, and *ochlos* is not merely the background of narratives or the audience of Jesus. Rather, *ochlos-minjung* transmitted the Jesus tradition through rumors so that minjung's witness to the Jesus event could be preserved in the narrative tradition.[79] Jesus sided with the suffering minjung on the front line of the advent of God's kingdom, and this brought a new hope to minjung. Ahn's minjung hermeneutics has recently been appropriated in various other contexts, such as transnational minjung and the black masses in the United States.[80]

The Dalits, derogatively called the "untouchables," are victims of the Indian caste system. Dalit hermeneutics has developed since the 1980s and, like other libration hermeneutics, starts with a contextual analysis of oppressive experiences particularly caused by poverty, caste, and gender discrimination.[81] Dalit interpretation aims to give voice to the collective struggles of the Dalits and articulate the vision of liberation. Dalit consciousness or Dalit ethos is indispensible for Dalit liberation hermeneutics. Using the heuristic category of "Dalithos," Peniel Jesudason Rufus Rajkumar interprets Mark's story of the

---

78. Elsa Tamez, "The Conflict in Mark: A Reading from the Armed Conflict in Colombia," in *Mark*, ed. Nicole W. Duran, Teresa Okure, and Daniel M. Patte, Texts @ Contexts (Minneapolis: Fortress, 2010).

79. Volkner Küster, "Jesus and the Minjung Revisited: The Legacy of Ahn Byung-Mu (1922–96)," *BibInt* 19 (2011): 1–18; Jin-Ho Kim and Yung Suk Kim, eds., *Reading Minjung Theology in the Twenty-First Century: Selected Writings by Ahn Byung-Mu and Modern Critical Responses* (Eugene, OR: Pickwick, 2013), 27–48, 49–64.

80. Kim and Kim, *Reading Minjung Theology in the Twenty-First Century*; Jin Young Choi, *Postcolonial Discipleship of Embodiment: An Asian and Asian American Feminist Reading of the Gospel of Mark* (New York: Palgrave Macmillan, 2015), 97–106.

81. Monica Jyotsna Melanchthon, "Dalits, Bible, and Method," in *Voices from the Margin: Interpreting the Bible in the Third World*, ed. R. S. Sugirtharajah, 25th anniversary ed. (Maryknoll, NY: Orbis, 2016), 115–28.

Gerasene Demoniac.[82] Jesus's exorcism demonstrates liberation from alienation and from self-destructive images of the Dalits, and it critiques collusion with casteism. From a Dalit feminist perspective and her autobiographical experience, Surekha Nelavala reads Mark 7:24–30 within the casteistic context. She parallels the Syrophoenician woman with the "trickster" figure deployed by James C. Scott as a form of resistance, as well as with the Dalit woman who is unclean by her caste and birth.[83]

Although the political energy found in liberation hermeneutics seems to have decreased, indigenous communities in Africa, Asia, and Latin America still struggle for liberation. Postcolonial criticism also emphasizes sociopolitical struggles for liberation, but it is often conducted by interpreters from the margin, including those with diasporic or pluralistic identities, in the metropolitan center.

Postcolonial Criticism

Tat-siong Benny Liew develops an inter(con)textual reading focusing on both the sociopolitical and apocalyptic dimensions of Mark's Gospel.[84] He considers the Gospel, as apocalyptic literature, to have been produced within the (con)text of Roman colonization but also believes the Gospel constructs colonial subjects through the discourse of parousia. In Liew's subject construction, Mark mimics Roman colonial ideology, particularly in terms of authority, agency, and gender. Mark's colonial replication culminates in presenting Jesus's absolute authority, especially in the parousia, with the result that human beings, including the disciples and particularly women, have no agency but are only objects who are saved or destroyed by God's violent intervention.[85]

In contrast to Liew's emphasis on "more cultural replication than resistance,"[86] Simon Samuel argues that the superscript of Mark's Gospel (1:1) shows a minority community's simultaneous assimilation and abrogation of both the imperial ideology and the Jewish dominant nationalist discourses.[87]

---

82. Melanchthon, "Dalits, Bible, and Method," 125; see Peniel Jesudason Rufus Rajkumar, "A Dalithos Reading of a Markan Exorcism: Mark 5:1–20," *ExpTim* 118, no. 9 (2007): 428–35.
83. Surekha Nelavala, "Smart Syrophoenician Woman: A Dalit Feminist Reading of Mark 7:24–31," *ExpTim* 118, no. 2 (2006): 64–69. James C. Scott, *Domination and the Arts of Resistance: Hidden Scripts* (New Haven: Yale University Press, 1990), 162–66.
84. Liew, *Politics of Parousia*.
85. Liew, *Politics of Parousia*, 123.
86. Tat-siong Benny Liew, "Re-Mark-able Masculinities? Jesus, the Son of Man, or the (Sad) Sum of Manhood," in *New Testament Masculinities*, ed. Janice Capel Anderson and Stephen Moore (Atlanta: SBL Press, 2003), 94.
87. Simon Samuel, *A Postcolonial Reading of Mark's Story of Jesus*, LNTS 340 (New York: T&T Clark, 2007).

Ultimately, such political ambivalence and cultural hybridity decenter the dominant discourses. Samuel's interpretation is concerned mainly with the role of Jesus as the Son of Humanity, who both exerts his power and suffers, in Mark's mimetic design.[88] Seong Hee Kim also employs the concept of hybridity but applies it to Mark's marginal characters—subaltern women—from Korean women's postcolonial experience.[89] Such subaltern women are hybrid subjects living in the "third space," or "the transitional time between two empires."[90] There these women create an alternative life, as seen in the poor widow's act of radically choosing God's empire by returning everything she got from Caesar to Caesar.[91]

In my own postcolonial feminist interpretation, the subject that disrupts the presence of the empire is the mystery of Jesus's body (broken, crucified, and absent) and of Jesus, who engages with the subjects—those who are invisible, placeless, and voiceless (Mark 6–7).[92] I argue that the mystery cannot be mastered by knowledge about Jesus's identity or a messianic secret but is a haunting cultural memory of colonized subjects.[93] Thus discipleship means a particular form of "understanding"—that is, embodying the mystery. Related to this study, emerging interests lie in interpreting Mark using such cultural studies as psychoanalysis, trauma studies, and affective theory.[94]

Postcolonial readings all attend to the unrepresented past or subaltern history that inevitably involves colonial subjects in the imperial-colonial context of Mark. In addition, postcolonial interpretations construct either colonial subjects, who are devoid of agency, or the agency of subalterns, who resist the empire, while being conscious of their own construction of the text.[95] For

---

88. Samuel, *Postcolonial Reading of Mark's Story of Jesus*, 103.

89. Seong Hee Kim, *Mark, Women and Empire: A Korean Postcolonial Perspective* (Sheffield: Sheffield Phoenix, 2010).

90. Kim, *Mark, Women and Empire*, 73–77, 131.

91. Kim, *Mark, Women and Empire*, 92–96. David Joy also engages Mark's Gospel as an anticolonial narrative from a subordinated social group, specifically represented by subaltern women. David Joy, *Mark and Its Subalterns: A Hermeneutical Paradigm for a Postcolonial Context* (London: Equinox, 2008).

92. Choi, *Postcolonial Discipleship of Embodiment*. Chapters 5–7 provide interpretations of Mark 6:45–52; 7:24–30; and 7:31–37, focusing on the themes of Jesus's "phantasmic," "consumed," and "passive" body, respectively.

93. Choi, *Postcolonial Discipleship of Embodiment*, 63–84.

94. Abraham Smith, "Cultural Studies: Making Mark," in Anderson and Moore, *Mark and Method*, 181–209; Maia Kotrosits and Hal Taussig, *Re-reading the Gospel of Mark amidst Loss and Trauma* (New York: Palgrave Macmillan, 2013); Tat-siong Benny Liew, "Haunting Silence: Trauma, Failed Orality, and Mark's Messianic Secret," in *Psychoanalytic Mediations between Marxist and Postcolonial Readings of the Bible*, ed. Tat-siong Benny Liew and Erin Runions (Atlanta: SBL Press, 2016), 99–128.

95. For more postcolonial studies, see Stephen D. Moore, *Empire and Apocalypse: Postcolonialism and the New Testament* (Sheffield: Sheffield Phoenix, 2006); Laura Donaldson, "Gospel Hauntings: The Postcolonial Demons of New Testament Criticism," in *Postcolonial Biblical*

this reason, postcolonial criticism, along with other ideological criticisms, often faces arguments that such a perspectival interpretation is subjective and partial.

Reflections

I have outlined Markan scholarship according to four paradigms of interpretation. The Gospel of Mark, though the shortest canonical Gospel, has received concentrated scholarly attention, and thus this essay cannot be exhaustive. Moreover, those four approaches are not "mutually exclusive" but "subject to creative interaction."[96] For instance, the themes of secrecy and silence recur in various models of interpretation regarding Jesus's messianic consciousness or identity, rhetorical purposes, honor-shame codes, survival strategy in war situations, or the agency of the subjects engaging Jesus's mystery. While sociocultural interpretations often utilize both historical and literary criticisms, rhetorical approaches are employed in all types of interpretative models. Especially for ideological criticism, interpreters are not limited to a particular method but may involve historical, literary, imperial-critical, and cultural methods according to the interpreter's perspective and agenda.

Despite the intersecting nature of different interpretive paradigms, such a mapping shows how historical criticism as both a model and a method of interpretation has been pervasive throughout modern interpretation of Mark but is losing traction. At the same time, we can detect a noticeable shift in the demographics of criticism, as well as a shift of interpretive framework. New voices from the margins, such as racial/ethnic and sexual minorities, and voices from the global south have joined in Markan scholarship.

Finally, although I avoided organizing this essay according to themes, Markan scholars continue to give attention to recurrent themes of, and different approaches to, Jesus Christ's person and ministry, along with discipleship in Mark. However, scholars also bring fresh ideas pertaining to nontraditional topics in relation to interpreting the Gospel (such as performativity, memory, haunting, trauma, abjection, and nonhumans such as demons and animals). Those new faces and themes may be striking for some readers of the Gospel. Yet, just as Mark's story ends with fear, wonder, or the mixture of both, Mark invites the reader to an open ending—to a new phase of Markan studies.

Criticism: Interdisciplinary Intersections, ed. Stephen D. Moore and Fernando F. Segovia (New York: T&T Clark, 2007), 97–113; Malebogo Kgalemang, "A Postcolonial Feminist Reading of Mark 14–16," in *Postcolonial Perspectives in African Biblical Scholarship*, ed. Musa W. Dube, Andrew Mbuvi, and Dora Mbuwayesango (Atlanta: SBL Press, 2012); Hans Leander, *Discourses of Empire: The Gospel of Mark from a Postcolonial Perspective* (Atlanta: SBL Press, 2013).

96. Segovia, "And They Began to Speak," 5.

15

The Gospel of Luke

Drew J. Strait

Introduction

Henry J. Cadbury once wrote that "Luke's work is not entirely spun out of his own brain . . . as the spider-web is spun out of the spider." Rather, according to Cadbury, Luke's Gospel is spun out of real, lived events set in motion through the life of Jesus—or what Luke calls "the things fulfilled among us" (1:1).[1] The theological ramifications of these historical events, catalyzed by the missional impulse of early Christianity—and crystallized in the written word by Luke—have captivated the imagination of both historians and theologians. To be sure, the volume of secondary literature on Luke's Gospel in the past fifty years is unwieldy, which is why we are indebted to François Bovon for masterfully overviewing this material from 1950 to 2005 in *Luke the Theologian*.[2] I won't mince words: if you are a serious student of Luke's Gospel, then you should stop what you are doing now and buy, read, and take extensive notes on Bovon's gift to us all. Then you can proceed to what I have to offer here. Admittedly, overviewing recent scholarship is an exercise in subjectivity. Even so, I have tried to choose what I deem legitimately

---

1. Henry J. Cadbury, *The Making of Luke-Acts* (Peabody, MA: Hendrickson, 1958), 22.
2. François Bovon, *Luke the Theologian: Fifty-Five Years of Research (1950–2005)* (Waco: Baylor University Press, 2006).

new or growing trends that have rippled through Lukan studies since the publication of Bovon's compendium. In what follows I attend to three topics: (1) literary approaches to Luke's Gospel, specifically as they relate to Luke's Christology and literary characterization; (2) imperial-critical and postcolonial readings of Luke's Gospel; and (3) new optics from historically marginalized interpreters.

Luke the Literary Artist

Luke wrote the early Jesus movement into history by drawing on the *topoi* and persuasive strategies of the Greco-Roman world. With the Septuagint in one hand and perhaps Homer or the preliminary rhetorical exercises (*progymnasmata*) in the other, Luke narrates the expansion of the gospel from Jerusalem to Rome.[3] Whereas questions of historicity and sources pervaded Lukan scholarship in past generations, the past three decades have seen a resurgence of interest in Luke as narrative.[4] Underlying this shift is a conviction that Luke's theology is not encrusted in the atomizing effects of the redaction-critical school but, rather, "is intricately and irreversibly bound up with the story he tells."[5] Two recent literary trends stand out. First, since Cadbury's groundbreaking hyphen (Luke-Acts), the unity of Luke's two-volume work has been more or less assumed by most scholars.[6] Strikingly, this consensus has recently been problematized by the dearth of evidence that Luke *and* Acts were interpreted together in the second century CE.[7] New insights from reception history are here to stay; these debates should not go unnoticed. Second, narrative criticism remains a tacit force in the field. Where this discipline has developed is in its utility for interpreting the Christology of Luke's Gospel and characterization of Jesus and various other protagonists. To these latter two points I now turn.

---

3. On the genre of Luke-Acts, see Sean A. Adams, "The Genre of Luke and Acts: The State of the Question," in *Issues in Luke-Acts*, ed. Sean A. Adams and Michael Pahl (Piscataway, NJ: Gorgias Press, 2012), 97–120. On Luke and the rhetorical handbooks, see Mikeal Parsons, *Luke: Storyteller, Interpreter, Evangelist* (Peabody, MA: Hendrickson, 2007), 15–52.

4. So Bovon: "Many of these books have abandoned redaction criticism for a literary approach" (*Luke the Theologian*, 563). The question of Luke's sources has not gone completely out of fashion. In fact, a recent volume of essays focuses on Luke's authorial strategies of "rewriting" traditions, including Mark *and* Matthew. See the essays in Mogens Müller and Jesper Tang Nielsen, eds., *Luke's Literary Creativity* (London: Bloomsbury T&T Clark, 2016).

5. Beverly Gaventa, "Toward a Theology of Acts: Reading and Rereading," *Int* 42, no. 2 (1988): 150.

6. See Henry Cadbury, "Lexical Notes on Luke-Acts: I," *JBL* 44 (1925): 214–27.

7. See the essays in Andrew Gregory and C. Kavin Rowe, eds., *Rethinking the Unity and Reception of Luke and Acts* (Columbia: University of South Caroline Press, 2010).

Characterization in Luke's Gospel

The prologue to Luke's Gospel gives away *what* Luke is writing—namely, a narrative account (*diegesis*) of the things fulfilled in the life of Jesus (1:1–4).[8] Since the work of Cadbury, much energy has been expended on understanding Luke's literary methods.[9] In reaction to the surgical studies of the redaction- and form-critical schools, Robert Tannehill's two-volume *The Narrative Unity of Luke-Acts* set a new trajectory and appreciation for the thematic coherence of Luke's two-volume work.[10] More recently, the trend toward narrative criticism has shifted gears to focus more on Luke's characterization of various agents within his narrative.[11] The brief survey that follows will illustrate the diverse ways this methodology has been employed.

Mikeal Parsons takes a highly creative approach to characterization, investigating the impact of ancient Greek, Roman, and Jewish physiognomy on characterization in Luke-Acts. By physiognomy, Parsons means the ancient practice of interpreting one's inner character by judging outer physical characteristics.[12] After a survey of physiognomy in antiquity, Parsons investigates Luke's characterization of four agents' physical features (the bent woman [Luke 13], Zacchaeus [Luke 19], the lame man [Acts 3–4], and the Ethiopian eunuch [Acts 8]). Parsons concludes that, in Luke's portrayal of these characters, "no one is excluded from the eschatological community on the basis of his or her looks."[13] One advantage of Parsons's study is that he thoroughly grounds his angle on characterization within Hellenistic literary culture.

Drawing on contemporary literary theory, Michal Beth Dinkler explores the role of silence in Luke's Gospel—what she calls "Luke's narrative

---

8. On Luke's narrative poetics in its Hellenistic environment, the work of David Moessner remains crucial. See the expanded and updated essays in *Luke the Historian of Israel's Legacy, Theologian of Israel's 'Christ': A New Reading of the 'Gospel of Acts' of Luke* (Berlin: de Gruyter, 2016).

9. Henry J. Cadbury, *The Style and Literary Method of Luke* (Cambridge: Harvard University Press, 1920).

10. Robert C. Tannehill, *The Narrative Unity of Luke-Acts: A Literary Interpretation*, vol. 1 (Philadelphia: Fortress, 1986); Tannehill, *The Narrative Unity of Luke-Acts: A Literary Interpretation*, vol. 2 (Philadelphia: Fortress, 1990).

11. Especially foundational were David B. Gowler, *Host, Guest, Enemy, and Friend: Portraits of the Pharisees in Luke and Acts* (New York: Peter Lang, 1991); John A. Darr, *On Character Building: The Reader and the Rhetoric of Characterization in Luke-Acts* (Louisville: Westminster John Knox, 1992); Darr, *Herod the Fox: Audience Criticism and Lukan Characterization in Luke-Acts* (Sheffield: Sheffield Academic, 1998).

12. Mikeal Parsons, *Body and Character in Luke and Acts: The Subversion of Physiognomy in Early Christianity* (Grand Rapids: Baker Academic, 2006), 12.

13. Parsons, *Body and Character*, 82. See also Parsons's doctoral student Chad Hartsock, who employs a similar methodology in *Sight and Blindness in Luke-Acts: The Use of Physical Features in Characterization* (Leiden: Brill, 2008).

soundscape."[14] Dinkler fills a significant research gap, showing that narratorial and character communication through silence is a type of speech that is multivalent, contextually determined, and rhetorically powerful.[15] As a component of Luke's persuasion strategies, the Lukan narrator employs silence to "shape the reader/hearer into an ideal witness to his message."[16] By silence, Dinkler means the narrator's capacity to construct meaning through the anonymity of characters, literary gaps, delays, open endings, and internal monologue (the last relates specifically to parables).[17] In my mind, the most interesting part of Dinkler's study is her interpretation of Jesus's silence in the passion narrative. Dinkler asks, "What does it mean that he does not take up the weapons of words he has so powerfully wielded thus far in the narrative?"[18] Jesus's silence, for Dinkler, is an invitation for disciples "to remember his words and be his witnesses."[19] Dinkler has established herself as the leading bridge builder between literary theory and Lukan studies—a point that is especially evident in her most recent article on the state of the field of characterization and Luke's Emmaus pericope.[20]

Frank Dicken employs narrative criticism to make sense of the historical conundrum that is Luke's presentation of the Herodian dynasty. Historians have long noted that Luke commits anachronism when he uses the name "Herod" for Herod Antipas, who incarcerated John the Baptist (Luke 3:19–20), *and* Agrippa I, who is eaten by worms and dies (Acts 12:20–23). Dicken doesn't see this anachronism as an inconsistency but, rather, as a literary device where Luke conflates three *different* rulers into *one* "composite character."[21] Dicken situates the role of composite characters in the Septuagint (LXX) and Greco-Roman literature, and he profiles the Herodian family in the writings of Josephus. Key to Dicken's study is the "cosmic conflict" in the temptation narrative, where Satan is portrayed as holding authority over the kingdoms of the world (i.e., the Roman Empire [Luke 4:5–6]).[22] This cosmic antagonism is embodied in Luke's characterization of the Herodian family, who impede John the Baptist's, Jesus's, and the Apostles' efforts to "preach

---

14. Michal Beth Dinkler, *Silent Statements: Narrative Representations of Speech and Silence in the Gospel of Luke* (Berlin: Walter de Gruyter, 2013), 2.
15. Dinkler, *Silent Statements*, 5, 10–13.
16. Dinkler, *Silent Statements*, 3.
17. Dinkler, *Silent Statements*, 148, 180.
18. Dinkler, *Silent Statements*, 201.
19. Dinkler, *Silent Statements*, 202.
20. Michal Beth Dinkler, "Building Character on the Road to Emmaus: Lukan Characterization in Contemporary Literary Perspective," *JBL* 136, no. 3 (2017): 687–706.
21. Frank Dicken, *Herod as a Composite Character in Luke-Acts* (Tübingen: Mohr Siebeck, 2014), 1–3.
22. Dicken, *Herod as a Composite Character*, 140–45.

the good news to the end of the earth."[23] Although not explicitly a work of political theology, Dicken provides much for future studies to mull over regarding Luke's attitude toward Rome.

The trend toward characterization does not show any signs of slowing down. This is evident in the recent edited volume *Characters and Characterization in Luke-Acts* (ed. Frank Dicken and Julia Snyder).[24] The volume focuses on reader-response approaches, the utility of characterization for understanding social relations and ethics, and various approaches to Acts. As the editors acknowledge, "some of the most famous" characters in the NT surface in Luke's Gospel. This point in fact will continue to inspire future studies in a field that is increasingly theoretically sophisticated.

The Christology of Luke's Gospel

The primary subject of Luke's Gospel is Jesus. But Luke's Christology reflects a spectrum of angles on Jesus's divinity, power, humiliation, and exaltation, "making it difficult to posit a convincing single emphasis that distinguishes the work."[25] To be sure, Douglas Buckwalter's 1996 monograph catalogs eighteen thematic lenses through which scholars have sought to interpret Luke's Christology.[26] Recent scholarship still employs methodologies similar to those of these older studies but has moved the discussion forward through new intertextual and literary insights into Luke's representation(s) of Jesus.

The entry point to recent trends on Luke's Christology is C. Kavin Rowe's study of the christological title Lord (*kyrios*) in Luke's Gospel.[27] Strikingly, until Rowe's monograph, a sustained investigation of Luke's use of *kyrios* in the history of interpretation had "not really been explored."[28] Rowe employs a narrative methodology to show that Luke's use of *kyrios* evokes ambiguity and can be applied to the God of Israel and Jesus. By treating the narrative whole, Rowe is able to make a sophisticated case for a high Christology, wherein Jesus and God are understood together as *kyrios*.[29] One disadvantage of Rowe's study is that he does not address the robust use of *kyrios* in Luke's second

---

23. Dicken, *Herod as a Composite Character*, 7.
24. Frank Dicken and Julia Snyder, eds., *Characters and Characterization in Luke-Acts* (London: Bloomsbury T&T Clark, 2016).
25. Larry Hurtado, "Christology in Acts: Jesus in Early Christian Belief and Practice," in Adams and Pahl, *Issues in Luke-Acts*, 220.
26. Douglas Buckwalter, *The Character and Purpose of Luke's Christology* (Cambridge: Cambridge University Press, 1996), 3–24.
27. C. Kavin Rowe, *Early Narrative Christology: The Lord in the Gospel of Luke* (Berlin: de Gruyter, 2006).
28. Rowe, *Early Narrative Christology*, 2.
29. Rowe, *Early Narrative Christology*, 218.

volume.[30] As Bovon warns, "When we approach Christology, the distinction between the gospel and Acts is hardly justifiable. The Christ of Acts cannot be dissociated from the Jesus of the Gospel, at least if we place ourselves in the Lukan perspective."[31]

Joshua Jipp draws on neglected intertexts to make sense of Jesus's claim in the Emmaus pericope: "Thus it is written, that the Messiah is to suffer" (Luke 24:46). Jipp observes that scholars have struggled to find where this messianic emphasis on suffering is "written," including in Second Temple Jewish sources. Whereas many scholars point to the Isaianic servant of Isaiah 53, Jipp contends that the Davidic psalms provide the proper christological template for Luke's "paradoxical combination of kingship and righteous suffering."[32] Jipp draws on Psalms 22, 31, 38, and 69 to animate Luke's emphases on royal suffering in the passion narrative; it is worth noting that Jipp extends his argument into an investigation of the apostolic speeches of Acts.[33] Jipp's exegesis provides an exemplar for penetrating the ways Luke weaves the Scriptures of Israel into his presentation of Jesus.

Two recent monographs focus on Luke's Christology from different angles, but both employ narrative methods. In contrast to Hans Conzelmann, whose redaction-critical methods led him to assert that Luke does not present Jesus as divine, Nina Henrichs-Tarsenkova argues through a nuanced approach to characterization and identity construction in the ancient Mediterranean that Luke "indirectly characterizes Jesus (together with Yahweh) as the one God of Israel."[34] Henrichs-Tarsenkova's exegetical analysis of Luke's Gospel focuses only on the infancy narrative; however, her extended contextualization of Richard Bauckham's idea of "divine identity" within Jewish and Greco-Roman identity/characterization patterns is a significant contribution.[35] Ultimately, Henrichs-Tarsenkova's study charts a path forward that avoids the high-versus-low christological dichotomy, opting for what she calls "Luke's divine Christology."[36]

---

30. However, see the excursus on *kyrios* in Acts 2:36. Rowe, *Early Narrative Christology*, 189–96.

31. Bovon, *Luke the Theologian*, 134.

32. Joshua W. Jipp, "Luke's Scriptural Suffering Messiah: A Search for Precedent, a Search for Identity," *CBQ* 72, no. 2 (2010): 259. See also David P. Moessner's approach to the suffering messiah through the lens of Hellenistic narrative poetics in "Reading Luke's Gospel as Ancient Hellenistic Narrative: Luke's Narrative Plan of Israel's Suffering Messiah as God's Saving 'Plan' for the World," in *Reading Luke: Interpretation, Reflection, Formation*, ed. Craig G. Bartholomew, Joel B. Green, and Anthony C. Thiselton (Grand Rapids: Zondervan, 2005), 125–56.

33. Jipp, "Luke's Scriptural Suffering Messiah," 266–73.

34. Nina Henrichs-Tarsenkova, *Luke's Christology of Divine Identity* (London: Bloomsbury T&T Clark, 2016), 194.

35. Henrichs-Tarsenkova, *Luke's Christology of Divine Identity*, 64–88.

36. Henrichs-Tarsenkova, *Luke's Christology of Divine Identity*, 195.

It is well known that Davidic motifs underlie Luke's Christology.[37] Sarah Harris employs narrative criticism and intertextuality to show that Luke's Christology is influenced by imagery of the Davidic Shepherd-King in the LXX.[38] This Davidic shepherd imagery is woven into Luke's message of universal salvation in that it provides "another style of leadership"—one other than that of the religious leaders and Caesar Augustus—a leadership that operates on radical inclusion, searching for the lost and feeding and eating with the sheep.[39] Harris's study should be commended for its deft theological interpretation and relevance for this moment in history.

Jocelyn McWhirter's *Rejected Prophets: Jesus and His Witnesses in Luke-Acts* attempts to make sense of the Jewish rejection of Jesus and gentile inclusion through the lens of the rejected prophet in the Hebrew Bible. McWhirter suggests that rejected prophets like Hosea, Zephaniah, Zechariah, Isaiah, Jeremiah, and Ezekiel "set a precedent for Gentile inclusion, Jewish rejection, and condemnation of the temple."[40] Through a close reading of Luke's presentation of Jesus, McWhirter shows how this tripartite pattern reassures Luke's audience that Jesus's rejection is a part of God's plan.[41] The relationship between Christology and the people of God is further taken up in Jens Schröter's *From Jesus to the New Testament*. Schröter explores two lines of Lukan Christology that he terms "Davidic" (rooted in Luke 1:32–35) and "Prophetic" (rooted in 2:30–35).[42] Luke's Davidic Christology, Schröter contends, is expanded from Gabriel's birth announcement to incorporate gentiles through Jesus's resurrection, the giving of the Spirit on "all flesh," and universal mission.[43] Luke's prophetic Christology, however, understands Israel's rejection of Jesus (4:16–30) as a part of God's plan to include gentiles in the people of God. So it is not that "salvation passes over from Israel to the church but that Gentiles are *brought into* the history of God with Israel."[44] Schröter offers an important corrective to those who think Luke rejects the Jews.[45] For our purposes, what is striking is that Schröter finds in

---

37. See especially Mark Strauss, *The Davidic Messiah in Luke-Acts* (Sheffield: Sheffield Academic, 1995).

38. Sarah Harris, *The Davidic Shepherd King in the Lukan Narrative* (London: Bloomsbury T&T Clark, 2016), 19–36.

39. Harris, *Davidic Shepherd King*, 156.

40. Jocelyn McWhirter, *Rejected Prophets: Jesus and His Witnesses in Luke-Acts* (Minneapolis: Fortress, 2013), 4.

41. McWhirter, *Rejected Prophets*, 123.

42. Jens Schröter, *From Jesus to the New Testament: Early Christian Theology and the Origin of the New Testament Canon*, trans. Wayne Coppins (Waco: Baylor University Press, 2013), 230.

43. Schröter, *From Jesus to the New Testament*, 230–37.

44. Schröter, *From Jesus to the New Testament*, 244.

45. So Hans Conzelmann, *Acts of the Apostles*, trans. J. Limburg, A. T. Kraabel, and D. H. Juel (Philadelphia: Fortress, 1987), 227.

Luke's Christology a hermeneutical key for understanding the incorporation of gentiles into the people of God.

Imperial-Critical Readings of Luke's Gospel

Luke's attitude toward imperial Rome has been an area of industrious activity over the past two decades. If a "storm center" still exists in Lukan scholarship, then Luke's attitude toward Rome comprises the eye of the storm.[46] To be sure, until the early 2000s, Luke was understood as the most pro-Roman document in the NT, a scholarly consensus that held significant sway in one way or another for three centuries.[47] Underlying this view was Luke's purported positive presentation of Roman rulers and officials and presentation of Paul's innocence (*dikaios*) in Roman custody.[48] Additionally, although Luke is the only author in the NT to acknowledge a Roman emperor by name (Augustus [Luke 2:1], Tiberius [3:1], and Claudius [Acts 11:28; 18:2]), nowhere does he explicitly acknowledge or criticize the emperor cult.[49] These observations led a number of scholars—including scholarly giants such as Cadbury, Conzelmann, and F. F. Bruce—to suggest that Luke wrote a political apology on behalf of the church (*apologia pro ecclesia*) to show Rome that the church was a politically innocuous movement.[50] In recent years this consensus has been called into question, resulting in what Raymond Pickett calls a "paradigm shift."[51] In what follows I overview recent imperial-critical trends and approaches to Luke's Gospel.

Why a Paradigm Shift?

Before reviewing some of the secondary sources, it is worth stopping to ask: Why a paradigm shift toward an imperial-critical reading of Luke's Gospel

---

46. W. C. van Unnik, "Luke-Acts, A Storm Center in Contemporary Scholarship," in *Studies in Luke-Acts*, ed. Leander Keck and J. Louis Martyn (Philadelphia: Fortress, 1966), 15–32.

47. So C. A. Heumann, "Dissertatio de Theophilo: Cui Lucas Historiam Sacram Inscripsit," *BHPT* classis IV (Bremen, Germany, 1720): 483–505.

48. For an overview of apologetic approaches, see especially Alexandru Neagoe, *The Trial of the Gospel: An Apologetic Reading of Luke's Trial Narratives*, SNTSMS 116 (Cambridge: Cambridge University Press, 2002), 4–22.

49. But see C. Kavin Rowe, "Luke-Acts and the Imperial Cult: A Way through the Conundrum?," *JSNT* 27, no. 3 (2005): 279–300.

50. Cadbury, *Making of Luke-Acts*, 308–15; Hans Conzelmann, *The Theology of St. Luke* (London: Faber, 1960), 137–49; Ernst Haenchen, *The Acts of the Apostles: A Commentary*, trans. Bernard Noble et al. (Oxford: Basil Blackwell, 1971), 106; and F. F. Bruce, *The Book of Acts* (Grand Rapids: Eerdmans, 1988), 8–13.

51. Raymond Picket, "Luke and Empire: An Introduction," in *Luke-Acts and Empire: Essays in Honor of Robert L. Brawley*, ed. David Rhoads, David Esterline, and Jae Won Lee (Eugene, OR: Pickwick, 2011), 1.

now? After all, if the brilliance of Cadbury didn't see criticism of Rome, then why should we? Two observations warrant consideration. First, until the publication of Simon Price's 1984 monograph on emperor worship, titled *Rituals and Power*, classicists had heretofore caricatured the Roman imperial cults as a form of crude political superstition imposed from above by the ruling power.[52] Price's thesis ruptured this consensus, showing that the divine honors conferred on Hellenistic/Roman warrior kings were a veritable form of religious expression set up from below by subjects in response to the king's overwhelming concentration of supraregional power. In other words, subjects absorbed the king's image and power into the "symbolic system" of their local traditional gods, thereby giving the king "honors like the gods" (*isotheoi timai*).[53] Price's thesis forced NT scholars to acknowledge the integration of politics and religion in antiquity and to take more seriously the cultic conflicts and competing allegiances that could arise between Jesus worship and emperor worship.

The second reason for this paradigm shift is a deeper appreciation for the asymmetrical relationship of power between imperial authority and subordinate subjects through postcolonial criticism. Postcolonial critics have done much to animate the imperial-metanarrative in the world behind the text, including the role of imperial domination, hegemonic stressors, and especially nonbinary strategies of resistance called "hybridity," wherein subjects contest imperial power in the "third space" between assimilation and violent resistance.[54] When evaluating Luke's attitude toward Rome, then, interpreters should strive to (1) hold in tension—or attempt to make sense of!—the positive *and* negative portrayals of Rome in Luke's Gospel and (2) discern Luke's strategies of resistance *and* objects of resistance—that is, the cultic and/or hegemonic stressors that Luke's persuasion strategies seek to criticize.[55]

Historical and Literary Approaches to Luke and Empire

The first major reassessment of Luke's attitude toward Rome after the so-called paradigm shift in NT scholarship is Steve Walton's 2002 essay "The

---

52. Simon Price, *Rituals and Power: The Roman Imperial Cult in Asia Minor* (Cambridge: Cambridge University Press, 1984), 11–15, 224–25. For those in need of a primer on ruler worship as it relates to early Judaism/Christianity, I know of no better diachronic discussion than what Hans-Josef Klauck offers in *The Religious Context of Early Christianity: A Guide to Graeco-Roman Religions*, trans. Brian McNeil (Minneapolis: Fortress, 2003), 250–330.

53. Price, *Rituals and Power*, 247–48, but see also 29–30.

54. On hybridity, see Homi K. Bhabha, *The Location of Culture* (New York: Routledge, 1994), 37. On the imperial metanarrative, see Leo G. Perdue and Warren Carter, *Israel and Empire: A Postcolonial History of Israel and Early Judaism*, ed. Coleman Baker (New York: Bloomsbury T&T Clark, 2015), 30–32.

55. Here I draw on Anathea Portier-Young's language of conditions for resistance, objects of resistance, and strategies of resistance in *Apocalypse against Empire: Theologies of Resistance in Early Judaism* (Grand Rapids: Eerdmans, 2011), 11.

State They Were In: Luke's View of the Roman Empire."[56] Walton critiques five previous perspectives on Luke's view of the Roman Empire—from the political to the apolitical—concluding that Luke falls at "both ends of the political spectrum," which, according to Walton, provides a strategy for early Christians to remain at a "critical distance" to the empire.[57] Walton's essay moves beyond political apologetic approaches by acknowledging friction between Lukan christological titles and the royal epithets conferred on emperors (e.g., Lord and Savior [Luke 2:11] and King [19:38]), and he observes that Luke throws shade in various hues on *some* Roman officials in his second volume (see Sosthenes [Acts 18:17], Lysias [23:27], Felix [24:26–27], and Festus [25:25]).[58]

Following on the heels of Walton, Gary Gilbert more subversively argues that Luke co-opts Roman political propaganda to "critique Rome and its claims to universal authority and dominion."[59] Drawing on inscriptional and literary evidence, Gilbert shows how Augustus was eulogized as a savior and bringer of peace, which creates a polemically charged background for Luke's synchronism of Jesus's birth with the Augustan census (Luke 2:1).[60] For Gilbert, then, it is Jesus who is the true bringer of peace (1:79) and Savior of the inhabited world (2:11).[61] Gilbert also reads the ascension of Jesus (Luke 24:50; Acts 1:9–11) in light of Roman political propaganda surrounding the emperor's apotheosis rituals, wherein the emperor's soul was thought to posthumously ascend into heaven.[62] Taken together, Luke co-opts Roman propaganda to legitimate the Christian movement and its message that Christ is the true universal ruler over the nations.

---

56. Steve Walton, "The State They Were In: Luke's View of the Roman Empire," in *Rome in the Bible and the Early Church*, ed. Peter Oakes (Grand Rapids: Baker Academic, 2002), 1–41.

57. Walton, "State They Were In," 40–41.

58. See Walton, "State They Were In," 26–28; Steve Walton, "Trying Paul or Trying Rome? Judges and the Accused in the Roman Trials of Paul in Acts," in Rhoads, Esterline, and Lee, *Luke-Acts and Empire*, 122–41.

59. Gary Gilbert, "Roman Propaganda and Christian Identity in the Worldview of Luke-Acts," in *Contextualizing Acts: Lukan Narrative and Greco-Roman Discourse*, ed. Todd C. Penner and Caroline Vander Stichele (Atlanta: Scholars Press, 2003), 255.

60. Gilbert, "Roman Propaganda and Christian Identity," 237–42.

61. On Luke's political synchronisms, see also Christian Blumenthal, "Augustus' Erlass und Gottes Macht: Überlegungen zur Charakterisierung der Augustusfigur und ihrer erzählstrategischen Funktion in der lukanischen Erzählung," *NTS* 57 (2010): 1–30; Richard Hays, "The Liberation of Israel in Luke-Acts: Intertextual Narration as Countercultural Practice," in *Reading the Bible Intertextually*, ed. Richard B. Hays, Stefan Alkier, and Leroy A. Huizenga (Waco: Baylor University Press, 2009), 113–18.

62. Gilbert, "Roman Propaganda and Christian Identity," 242–47. More cautiously, see James Buchanan Wallace, "Viewing Jesus's Ascension in Luke-Acts through Greco-Roman Traditions," in *Ascent into Heaven in Luke-Acts*, ed. David K. Bryan and David W. Pao (Minneapolis: Fortress, 2016), 83–110.

Craig A. Evans uses a tactic similar to Gilbert's with the specific aim of illuminating the political dimensions of Luke-Acts. For Evans, "in the ancient world politics and religion were inextricably intertwined."[63] Though Evans doesn't acknowledge it explicitly, his thesis reflects post–Simon Price thinking by treating politics and religion as an integrated sphere in the world behind the text so as to show "that Jesus was perceived as king and rival to Caesar himself."[64] Particularly profitable is Evans's discussion of benefaction, where he draws on a rich tapestry of inscriptional and Greco-Roman and Jewish literary evidence that eulogizes Hellenistic and Roman rulers with the royal title "benefactor" (*euergetēs*).[65] Evans observes that Luke is the only author in the NT to employ *euergetēs*, and that he does so in direct association with gentile rulers (Luke 22:25–26). Evans's essay lacks the theological interpretation due to this passage but rightly alludes to the polemical potential of Jesus's critique of gentile euergetism. Moreover, Evans shows the merits of taking seriously the epigraphic record and Jewish sources that reflect on gentile royal ideology; this emphasis would only be strengthened by more attention to Hellenistic treatises on kingship.

Taking a more cautious approach, Dean Pinter explores Luke's attitude toward Rome by comparing Luke's writings with those of the historian T. Flavius Josephus (b. 37–95/96 CE). Pinter draws on John M. G. Barclay's work to show how Josephus "snarls sweetly" at imperial Rome—that is to say, Josephus rhetorically obscures his criticism of Rome to avoid retaliation.[66] But Pinter does not believe that Luke wrote under the same circumstances as Josephus or that Rome was "a police state with secret agents ready to intercept written communications."[67] This claim leads Pinter to question the existence of coded language in Luke's Gospel, including a "competitive relationship" between Jesus and the emperor cult through overlapping royal titles.[68] Underlying Pinter's approach is a problematic assertion that "if indeed Luke is free to write as he chooses, then it is surprising that he does not use this freedom to

---

63. Craig A. Evans, "King Jesus and His Ambassadors: Empire and Luke-Acts," in *Empire in the New Testament*, ed. Stanley Porter and Cynthia Long Westfall (Eugene, OR: Pickwick, 2011), 120–37.

64. See Price, *Rituals and Power*, 15–22.

65. Evans, "King Jesus and His Ambassadors," 125–30. For further discussion on euergetism in Luke's Gospel, see Jonathan Marshall, *Jesus, Patrons, and Benefactors* (Tübingen: Mohr Siebeck, 2009).

66. Dean Pinter, "The Gospel of Luke and the Roman Empire," in *Jesus Is Lord, Caesar Is Not: Evaluating Empire in New Testament Studies*, ed. Scot McKnight and Joseph B. Modica (Downers Grove, IL: IVP Academic, 2013), 109. See John M. G. Barclay, "Snarling Sweetly: Josephus on Images and Idolatry," in *Idolatry: False Worship in the Bible, Early Judaism and Christianity*, ed. Stephen C. Barton (New York: T&T Clark, 2007), 73–87.

67. Pinter, "Gospel of Luke," 109.

68. Pinter, "Gospel of Luke," 110.

make any direct comments *against* the empire."[69] But here Pinter overlooks the art of safe criticism in antiquity, wherein dissident voices figured their criticism allusively; this strategy of hidden criticism was especially important in the aftermath of Augustus's rise to power, when the scope of treason laws was intensified to include "written libel" (Tacitus, *Annales* 1.72).[70] Still, Pinter's comparative methodology deserves consideration by future studies, and he is certainly correct to push back against reducing Luke's polemical aims to a Jesus-versus-Caesar polemical dichotomy. Indeed, for Pinter, Luke's resistance strategies are broader, including a critique of the demonic realm, power, and the multiple hierarchies that existed in Rome's socially stratified society.[71]

Three recent studies have revisited Luke's presentation of Roman rulers and soldiery as a heuristic for understanding the role of Roman power in Luke's narrative. The first study is by Kazuhiko Yamazaki-Ransom, titled *The Roman Empire in Luke's Narrative*. Yamazaki-Ransom takes an innovative approach by examining Jewish portrayals of gentile rulers in the OT and Second Temple literature with the aim of understanding the triangular relationship between God, the people of God, and Roman provincial governors and the Herodian dynasty in Luke's narrative. Yamazaki-Ransom concludes that Luke's characterizations of eight rulers—with the exception of Sergius Paulus—are negative.[72] Luke's attitude toward Rome is negative, he says, because of rulers' "failure to acknowledge God's sovereignty and Christ's lordship."[73] Yamazaki-Ransom's study is commendable in that he draws on Second Temple Jewish literature to support his thesis, a point of entry that even he acknowledges "will be a fruitful field for future scholarship."[74] The absence of any sustained analysis of Luke's positive presentation of centurions, however, will leave some scholars wanting more (see Luke 7:1–10; 23:47; Acts 10:1–48; 27:1–44).

The next two studies portray Luke's attitude toward Rome in a more amicable light. Laurie Brink focuses on Luke's characterization of soldiers through comparative analysis with an impressive array of Greek and Roman literary characterizations of soldiers. For Brink, Luke subverts negative stereotypes

69. Pinter, "Gospel of Luke," 109–10.
70. See Frederick Ahl, "The Art of Safe Criticism in Greece and Rome," *AJP* 105, no. 2 (1984): 174–208. On secret police, see Ramsay MacMullen, *Enemies of the Roman Order: Treason, Unrest, and Alienation in the Empire* (Cambridge: Harvard University Press, 1966), 164–65; Christopher J. Fuhrmann, *Policing the Roman Empire: Soldiers, Administration, and Public Order* (Oxford: Oxford University Press, 2012), 143.
71. Pinter, "Gospel of Luke," 113.
72. Kazuhiko Yamazaki-Ransom, *The Roman Empire in Luke's Narrative*, LNTS 404 (New York: T&T Clark, 2010), 201.
73. Yamazaki-Ransom, *Roman Empire in Luke's Narrative*, 202.
74. Yamazaki-Ransom, *Roman Empire in Luke's Narrative*, 203.

of Roman soldiers as violent and brutish in order to show that even enemies of God's people do not fall outside the ambit of God's salvation. Brink ultimately concludes that Roman soldiers function as a "parabolic exemplum of a good disciple" and reflect "the author's optimistic expectation of imperial benevolence."[75] But how would the active reader in antiquity understand such irony? Brink insinuates that it would promote "a positive view of the empire."[76] But is it also possible that such irony could be received negatively, especially in a world of double innuendo where eulogistic characterization of political authority could evoke reflection on one's living antithesis?[77] And from another angle, in positively portraying notoriously corrupt soldiery, is it possible that Luke intends to evoke an ironic caricature of Roman power in the sense that God's "supra-imperial" kingdom overrides the soldiers' hearts and their control of subjects to ultimately advance the church's mission?[78] In other words, Roman soldiers are ultimately God's—not Rome's—subordinates. Along similar methodological lines, Joshua Yoder investigates Luke's presentation of Roman governors (Pontus Pilate, Sergius Paulus, Gallio, Felix, and Festus) in Luke-Acts using "narrative-rhetorical criticism."[79] Yoder provides a remarkable overview of Roman governors in Jewish and Greco-Roman sources as comparanda with governors in Luke-Acts. Yoder acknowledges the "ambiguity" and lack of "clear point of view in every case" but ultimately concludes that Luke espouses "a fundamentally positive attitude toward the Roman system."[80]

Resistance from the Subaltern

Taking a different methodological tactic, Eric Barreto draws on insights from postcolonial theory to animate Luke's negotiation of imperial Rome through the optics of the powerless (or what some call the "subaltern").[81] Specifically, Barreto draws on the idea of ambivalence and hybridity to show how colonized communities could embody "a posture that seemingly sanctions the identity imposed by the colonizer while simultaneously undermining

---

75. Laurie Brink, *Soldiers in Luke-Acts: Engaging, Contradicting, and Transcending Stereotypes* (Tübingen: Mohr Siebeck, 2014), 56.

76. Brink, *Soldiers in Luke-Acts*, 175.

77. See Drew J. Strait, *Hidden Criticism of the Angry Tyrant in Early Judaism and the Acts of the Apostles* (Minneapolis: Lexington/Fortress Press Academic, forthcoming).

78. I borrow this descriptor from Karl Galinsky, "The Cult of the Roman Emperor: Uniter or Divider?," in *Rome and Religion: A Cross-Disciplinary Dialogue on the Imperial Cult*, ed. Jeffrey Brodd and Jonathan L. Reed (Atlanta: SBL Press, 2011), 222.

79. Joshua Yoder, *Representatives of Roman Rule: Roman Provincial Governors in Luke-Acts* (Berlin: de Gruyter, 2014).

80. Yoder, *Representatives of Roman Rule*, 40, 336.

81. See Gayatri Spivak, "Can the Subaltern Speak?," in *Marxism and the Interpretation of Culture*, ed. C. Nelson and L. Grossberg (Urbana: University of Illinois Press, 1988), 271–314.

this very same identity."[82] The advantage of Barreto's methodology is that it penetrates the multidimensional methods that subordinates used to resist imperial power—how they could resist "in ways that the empire [would] not recognize as betrayal."[83] But how does Luke craft these strategies of resistance in his narrative? To start, Barreto suggests that Luke's political synchronisms are not mere chronological markers (Luke 2:1–2; 3:1–2).[84] Rather, "they are symbolic points of resistance," whereby the power invested in John the Baptist and Jesus presents a contrast "between the servants of God and the imperial forces that fear them."[85] This subtle polemical contrast, for Barreto, comes into sharper focus in the temptation scenes, where Satan offers Jesus authority over "the kingdoms of the world" (4:5; although note that the Greek word here translated "world" is *oikoumenē*, which can also be translated "empire").[86] Barreto sees venom in Luke's innuendo: Rome's imperial apparatus lies under the authority of the devil (4:6).[87]

Barreto then proceeds to make sense of Luke's positive portrayal of tax collectors and Roman soldiers (3:12–14; 7:1–10). Barreto asks why Luke does not call them, as agents of Israel's colonial occupation, to repentance or, more aggressively, why he does not call them to new vocational identities. Here Barreto argues that Luke is not making an accommodation to Rome by portraying Caesar's agents positively; rather, through hybrid identities, these enemies of Israel are challenged to bear fruits worthy of repentance through a different understanding of power and wealth and thereby to transform the empire from the inside out. In attending to subordinates' hybrid identities, Barreto's analysis pushes interpreters beyond binary pro-/anti-imperial readings, toward a more sophisticated appreciation for early Christianity's negotiation of imperial power and hegemony and toward alternatives to Rome's attempts at universalizing ethnic homogeneity.

Also offering a critique of binary readings of Luke's political posture is Amanda Miller's methodologically sophisticated study of three status re-

---

82. Eric D. Barreto, "Crafting Colonial Identities: Hybridity and the Roman Empire in Luke-Acts," in *An Introduction to Empire in the New Testament*, ed. Adam Winn (Atlanta: SBL Press, 2016), 108. Yong-Sung Ahn employs postcolonial theory to investigate the role of Rome in Jesus's death; see *The Reign of God and Rome in Luke's Passion Narrative: An East Asian Global Perspective* (Leiden: Brill, 2006).
83. Barreto, "Crafting Colonial Identities," 107.
84. Barreto, "Crafting Colonial Identities," 111.
85. Barreto, "Crafting Colonial Identities," 111–12.
86. Barbara Rossing argues that *oikoumenē* in Luke-Acts should be translated "empire" rather than "whole inhabited world." See "Turning Empire (οἰκουμένη) Upside Down: A Response," in *Reading Acts in the Discourses of Masculinity and Politics*, ed. Eric D. Barreto, Matthew L. Skinner, and Steve Walton (London: Bloomsbury T&T Clark, 2017), 148–55. Luke employs the word in Luke 2:1; 4:5; 21:25; Acts 11:28; 17:6, 31; 19:27; 24:5.
87. Barreto, "Crafting Colonial Identities," 113.

versal texts in Luke's Gospel (Mary's Magnificat [1:46–55], Jesus's sermon at Nazareth [4:16–30], and the rich man and Lazarus [16:19–31]). Miller's study draws on James C. Scott's popular theory of "hidden transcripts," where the powerless disguise their dissent "offstage" through various tactics of predominantly oral forms of foot dragging (encoded songs of resistance, anonymous mass defiance, gossip, etc.).[88] Miller argues that Luke's status reversal texts are infused with hidden transcripts that contest power relations without inviting "retaliation from the elites in control of the situation."[89] This methodological angle allows Miller to explain the lack of explicit critique of Rome in Luke's Gospel, which is "neither entirely resistant nor entirely complicit and conciliatory."[90] One question for future studies will be the relationship between the oral nature of hidden transcripts and discursive resistance. As Miller herself observes, the "hidden transcript is practically impossible to recover, as it is by definition hidden, seldom written down."[91] One answer to this historical conundrum is to investigate more judiciously the ways that early Jewish and Greco-Roman discursive resistance may have influenced Luke's hand, especially with regard to rhetorical strategies of anti-imperial innuendo under repression of speech. This methodological approach, I contend in my own book, provides a profitable optic through which to understand strategies of resistance among literary sophisticates like Luke who are clearly influenced by Hellenistic literary culture.[92]

New Optics from Historically Marginalized Interpreters

The production of meaning in the world in front of the text is a contested space in biblical studies. Although postmodern biblical interpretation is not new in the past decade, it has grown in presence and substance as interpreters wrestle with how readers map meaning onto texts of antiquity. The influence of an interpreter's social location and the polyvalence of a text are common methodological idioms among postmodern interpreters. The significance of social location is brilliantly illustrated in a recent case study by Mark Allan

---

88. Amanda C. Miller, *Rumors of Resistance: Status Reversals and Hidden Transcripts in the Gospel of Luke* (Minneapolis: Fortress, 2014), 44–51. For a similar method applied to Mary's Magnificat, see Warren Carter, "Singing in the Reign: Performing Luke's Songs and Negotiating the Roman Empire (Luke 1–2)," in Rhoads, Esterline, and Lee, *Luke-Acts and Empire*, 23–43.
89. Miller, *Rumors of Resistance*, 253.
90. Miller, *Rumors of Resistance*, 255.
91. Miller, *Rumors of Resistance*, 51. For Scott's comments on the preference for and advantages of oral resistance among the powerless, see James C. Scott, *Domination and the Arts of Resistance: Hidden Transcripts* (New Haven: Yale University Press, 1990), 160.
92. See Strait, *Hidden Criticism of the Angry Tyrant*.

Powell on Luke's parable of the prodigal son (Luke 15:11–32).[93] Powell traveled to three separate cultural groups—Americans, Russians, and Tanzanians—to lecture on the prodigal son to seminarians and asked each group to retell the story from memory. Notably, each group retold the prodigal's spiral into poverty through a different lens. For the Americans, the prodigal spent everything (influenced by capitalism); for the Russians, the prodigal experienced a famine (influenced by the nine-hundred-day famine after Germany occupied St. Petersburg in 1941); for the Tanzanians, however, the prodigal's neighbors failed to provide him hospitality (influenced by v. 16: "and no one gave him anything"). All three answers are viable interpretations of Luke 15:13–16, but each interpretive community refracts the story through their shared cultural experiences, thereby producing different meanings.

Powell's study shows us why our hermeneutical lenses matter and the riches that a multicultural lens can bring to a text. What, then, should students of Luke's Gospel do with the history of interpretation that is dominated by the voices of privileged white men—myself included? This question is one, I believe, that will receive more critical attention in the coming years, especially as social movements like #BlackLivesMatter and #MeToo animate the racial and gender disparities in our society—which are also embedded in the academy. The movement toward raising up (and listening to!) the voices of marginalized interpreters of Luke's Gospel has made some slow progress in the past decade. But the emphasis here is on *some*. Here I wish to briefly overview recent contributions by African American/womanist, Latinx, and feminist interpreters.

Among African American interpreters, the work of Brian Blount stands out as pioneering. Blount is a NT scholar—not a theologian in the strict sense—who has brought antebellum slave narratives into conversation with NT ethics. In *Then the Whisper Put On Flesh*, Blount draws on Luke's emphasis on "social and political reversal" to elucidate how slaves read the Bible through a lens of liberation to resist their masters' oppressive readings of Scripture.[94] More recently, Blount edited a single-volume commentary on the NT by African American scholars, titled *True to Our Native Land: An African American New Testament Commentary*. The commentary on Luke, by Stephanie Buckhanon Crowder, interprets Luke's Gospel in conversation with a number of key black intellectuals and events in the struggle for civil rights. Crowder's optics encompass both the oppressed and oppressors, wherein Jesus came "not just to offer compassion to those who are wounded

---

93. Mark Allan Powell, *What Do They Hear? Bridging the Gap between Pulpit and Pew* (Nashville: Abingdon, 2007), 11–28.

94. Brian K. Blount, *Then the Whisper Put On Flesh: New Testament Ethics in an African American Context* (Nashville: Abingdon, 2001), 79.

but to speak to the evil of those who wound."[95] Crowder's more holistic reading of Luke's Gospel reflects the tenets of womanist interpretation, where a "hermeneutic of wholeness" is sought in response to black women's experience of "racism, sexism, and classism."[96] Bridgett Green brings this hermeneutic of intersectionality to bear on Jesus's blessing of children in Luke 18:15–17. Green shows that, in allowing children to come to him, Jesus confronts the disciples' privilege, which empowers the marginalized *and* confronts power dynamics that undermine the "equity and dignity of all people."[97]

Latinx interpreters of Luke's Gospel have a veritable feast of theology in the work of Justo González. In the past decade, González has published a theological commentary on Luke's Gospel and, more recently, a theology of Luke's Gospel, titled *The Story Luke Tells: Luke's Unique Witness to the Gospel*.[98] González also contributed an essay on reading Luke through the lens of liberation theology in *Methods for Luke* (ed. Joel Green).[99] Central to González's theological interpretation is an emphasis on the subversive pattern of "great reversal" for the marginalized in Luke's Gospel and the priority of praxis over methodology for Latinx interpreters.[100]

Gender-critical approaches to Luke's Gospel operate on shifting grounds. Luke mentions women by name more than any other Gospel (but named men outnumber named women thirteen to one).[101] The presence of women has inspired some to see Luke as a medium through which to resist toxic manifestations of misogyny and androcentrism.[102] However, recent feminist scholars, largely influenced by Elisabeth Schüssler Fiorenza's more holistic critique of "kyriarchal structures," have drawn more negative conclusions, such that Luke "threatens any attempt made by women . . . to find a voice

---

95. Stephanie Buckhanon Crowder, "Luke," in *True to Our Native Land: An African American New Testament Commentary*, ed. Brian K. Blount et al. (Minneapolis: Fortress, 2007), 158.

96. Raquel St. Clair, "Womanist Biblical Interpretation," in Blount et al., *True to Our Native Land*, 54–55.

97. Bridgett A. Green, "'Nobody's Free Until Everybody's Free': Exploring Gender and Class Injustice in a Story about Children (Luke 18:15–17)," in *Womanist Interpretations of the Bible: Expanding the Discourse*, ed. Gay L. Byron and Vanessa Lovelace (Atlanta: SBL Press, 2016), 307.

98. Justo L. González, *Luke* (Louisville: Westminster John Knox, 2010); González, *The Story Luke Tells: Luke's Unique Witness to the Gospel* (Grand Rapids: Eerdmans, 2015).

99. Justo L. González, "A Latino Perspective," in *Methods for Luke*, ed. Joel Green (Cambridge: Cambridge University Press, 2010), 113–43.

100. González, *Story Luke Tells*, 113–18, 127.

101. Jane D. Schaberg and Sharon H. Ringe, "Gospel of Luke," in *Women's Bible Commentary: Twentieth-Anniversary Edition*, ed. C. A. Newsom, S. H. Ringe, and J. E. Lapsley (Louisville: Westminster John Knox, 2012), 499.

102. So F. Scott Spencer, *Salty Wives, Spirited Mothers, and Savvy Widows: Capable Women of Purpose and Persistence in Luke's Gospel* (Grand Rapids: Eerdmans, 2012).

in either society or the church."[103] The diversity of readings among feminist interpreters can be felt throughout the essays in *A Feminist Companion to Luke*—a tension that Turid Karlsen Seim recently brought to bear on the story of the widow's mites (Luke 21:1–4). While acknowledging the negative characterization of the widow's silence, Seim aims to move her actions to the center of the story, whereby the poor widow serves as a paradigm of "prophetic justice" for Jesus's followers when she exposes the "system that exploits her."[104] More recently, Brittany Wilson has shifted our optics on gender in Luke's Gospel by drawing on masculinity studies to show that Luke's characterization of men does not conform to Greco-Roman standards of manliness. In Luke's Gospel, both Zechariah (through the loss of voice) and Jesus (through crucifixion) are emasculated; this results in an "unmanning of men" that reorients male identity around God's power rather than manliness in the Greco-Roman machismo sense.[105]

Reflections

As a work of Hellenistic history and theology, Luke's Gospel demands multiple reading strategies to penetrate its "theocentric" message incarnated in Jesus of Nazareth.[106] The turn toward narrative criticism in the past thirty years has produced much fruit in the areas of Christology and characterization. But should these literary approaches eclipse historical methods? Here I again turn to Bovon, who warns that while these literary methods are valuable, "from a historical and theological point of view it is an error to neglect the question of the material, sources, and traditions that biblical authors use."[107] Assuming a nugget of truth in Bovon's words, how can future studies hold in tension historical and literary methods, all the while not falling prey to compartmentalizing the final form of Luke's Gospel?

On Luke's attitude toward imperial Rome, where are we since Walton's 2002 essay? One thing is certain: the *apologia pro ecclesia* approach no longer meets the quorum needed for it to be called a "scholarly consensus." The new trends that have emerged reflect (1) a deeper appreciation for the

---

103. Amy-Jill Levine, introduction to *A Feminist Companion to Luke*, ed. Amy-Jill Levine (London: Sheffield Academic, 2002), 1. See Elisabeth Schüssler Fiorenza, *In Memory of Her: A Feminist Theological Reconstruction of Christian Origins* (New York: Crossroad, 1983).
104. Turid Karlsen Heim, "Feminist Criticism," in Green, *Methods for Luke*, 64, 73.
105. Brittany E. Wilson, *Unmanly Men: Refigurations of Masculinity in Luke-Acts* (Oxford: Oxford University Press, 2015), 257.
106. Joel Green, *The Theology of the Gospel of Luke* (Cambridge: Cambridge University Press, 1995), 22–23.
107. Bovon, *Luke the Theologian*, 563.

emperor cult as a competing allegiance to Christ the king, (2) a more nuanced understanding of Luke's negotiation of imperial hegemony/domination in power relations, and (3) a clarion call to hold in tension Luke's positive *and* negative literary representations of Rome.[108] The result is a sharper focus on the contrasting narratives of early Christianity and Roman colonial power. Future studies will profit from further situating Luke's historiographical aims within literary strategies of Hellenistic discursive resistance, with the aim of better understanding how Luke straddles a rhetorically crafted narrow ridge of subversion but not insurrection (*stasis*), criticism but not frank speech, regard but not acquiescence, redefinition but not nationalism, and peace but not violent coercion.

Finally, the pervasive danger in our interpretation(s) of Luke's Gospel is the gravitational pull toward reading in a homogeneous echo chamber—or what Willie James Jennings calls the "segregationist habits of mind."[109] These tribal reading habits, no doubt, are entrenched in NT studies, no less in the study of Luke's Gospel. How do majority interpreters foster new patterns of reading that inculcate a posture of intentional listening to the voices of marginalized interpreters? And how do minority voices—especially those who find themselves in the discipline of theology—find a place at the table in the sea of whiteness that is Lukan studies? Surely in the answer to these questions lies a hermeneutical key that could unlock a more multidimensional optic through which to grasp the scope and challenge of Luke's emphasis on universal salvation, inclusive table fellowship, status inversion, and mission to the ends of the earth.

---

108. On this tension, see especially C. Kavin Rowe's emphasis on the "pendulum effect" in *World Upside Down: Readings Acts in the Graeco-Roman Age* (Oxford: Oxford University Press, 2011), 55. An appreciation for these imperial-critical dynamics in Luke's Gospel can be felt in the excellent discussions in John T. Carroll, *Luke: A Commentary* (Louisville: Westminster John Knox), 398–404, and the introduction by Karl Allen Kuhn, *The Kingdom according to Luke and Acts: A Social, Literary, and Theological Introduction* (Grand Rapids: Baker Academic, 2015); see also pp. 223–28.

109. Willie James Jennings, "The Change We Need: Race and Ethnicity in Theological Education," *Theological Education* 49, no. 1 (2014): 42.

16

The Gospel of John

ALICIA D. MYERS

Introduction

Recent studies on the Gospel of John vary considerably in their approaches, though the dominance of literary or narrative readings can hardly be overlooked, especially in North American circles.¹ Synchronic studies of the Fourth Gospel have proliferated in the last thirty-plus years of scholarship, largely in the wake of R. Alan Culpepper's monumental work *Anatomy of the Fourth Gospel*.² Diachronic reconstructions and historical concerns have not, however, disappeared, despite some predictions that they might do so.³ Reading

---

1. For more comprehensive summaries of research see Tom Thatcher, ed., *What We Have Heard from the Beginning: The Past, Present, and Future of Johannine Studies* (Waco: Baylor University Press, 2007); Tom Thatcher and Stephen D. Moore, eds., *Anatomies of Narrative Criticism: The Past, Present, and Futures of the Fourth Gospel as Literature*, RBS 55 (Atlanta: SBL, 2008); Francis J. Moloney, "Recent Johannine Studies, Part One: Commentaries," *ExpTim* 123, no. 7 (2012): 313–22; Moloney, "Recent Johannine Studies, Part Two: Monographs," *ExpTim* 123, no. 9 (2012): 417–28; Tom Thatcher and Catrin H. Williams, eds., *Engaging with C. H. Dodd: Sixty Years of Tradition and Interpretation on the Gospel of John* (Cambridge: Cambridge University Press, 2013). See also Marianne Meye Thompson, *John: A Commentary*, NTL (Louisville: Westminster John Knox, 2015).

2. R. Alan Culpepper, *Anatomy of the Fourth Gospel: A Study in Literary Design* (Philadelphia: Fortress, 1983).

3. Robert Kysar, *John: The Maverick Gospel*, 3rd ed. (Louisville: Westminster John Knox, 2007), 159–64; Paul N. Anderson, Felix Just, and Tom Thatcher, eds., *John, Jesus, and History*, vols. 1–3, SBLSymS 44 and ECIL 2, 18 (Atlanta: SBL, 2007, 2009, 2016).

the Gospel as a unified, or at least coherent, document—even if scholars acknowledge a complicated composition process—has opened the door to new readings and analyses. The ways in which these synchronic readings converse with more diachronic approaches have been consistent topics of reflection and debate. Many Johannine scholars argue for a complementary relationship between these approaches, even as others see a persistent divide.[4]

The overview of current research on the Gospel of John offered here will proceed in three main parts. The first will outline the primarily synchronic readings of John, and the second those that are primarily diachronic. While such a division is convenient for the purpose of this summary, too stark a division between these groups is a false one, as the previous paragraph indicates. The third section of this overview will explore in more detail some perennial topics in the study of the Gospel, as well as some approaches from traditionally marginalized voices and perspectives, many of which have come to greater prominence in large part because of the literary swing in Johannine circles.

Anatomy Lessons: Reading John's Gospel as Story

From the mid-twentieth century onward the study of John's Gospel was dominated by theories of composition, the development of traditions, and the author, redactors, or community responsible.[5] Some of the most prominent works include those by Raymond Brown, J. Louis Martyn, and Robert Fortna, as well as Culpepper's dissertation monograph.[6] Yet, even as this work continued, a new wave of scholarship began implementing techniques from literary studies.[7] Although such studies had their beginnings in the Gospel of Mark, they were quickly picked up in the work of Johannine scholars,

---

4. E.g., Thatcher and Moore, *Anatomies of Narrative Criticism*.

5. In this period, the work of Rudolf Bultmann dominated the field of Johannine studies (*Das Evangelium des Johannes* [Göttingen: Vandenhoeck & Ruprecht, 1941]). For a more complete overview, see Tom Thatcher, "Anatomies of the Fourth Gospel: Past, Present, and Future Probes," in Thatcher and Moore, *Anatomies of Narrative Criticism*, 1–35.

6. Raymond Brown, *Community of the Beloved Disciple: The Life, Love, and Hates of an Individual Church in New Testament Times* (New York: Paulist Press, 1979); J. Louis Martyn, *History and Theology in the Fourth Gospel*, 3rd ed. (Nashville: Abingdon, 2003; first published 1968); Robert T. Fortna, *The Fourth Gospel and Its Predecessor: From Narrative Source to Present Gospel* (Philadelphia: Fortress, 1980); R. Alan Culpepper, *The Johannine School: An Evaluation of the Johannine-School Hypothesis Based on an Investigation of the Nature of Ancient Schools*, SBLDS 26 (Missoula, MT: Scholars Press, 1975).

7. Of particular importance is David Rhoads, Joanna Dewey, and Donald Michie, *Mark as Story: An Introduction to the Narrative of a Gospel*, 3rd ed. (Minneapolis: Fortress, 2012; first published 1982). For a more general introduction to narrative criticism, see James L. Resseguie, *Narrative Criticism of the New Testament: An Introduction* (Grand Rapids: Baker Academic, 2005).

chief among them Culpepper's *Anatomy of the Fourth Gospel*. Appearing in 1983, Culpepper's work used theories from literary critics, such as Seymour Chatman, to approach the Gospel of John as a coherent and intentional narrative.[8] The "anatomy" Culpepper laid bare was not layers of tradition, but rather seven pieces that made up the narrative unity of the Gospel's final form: the narrator, point of view, narrative time, plot, characters, implicit commentary, and implied reader. Although Culpepper's work was, in his own words "exploratory and experimental," it quickly found traction among other interpreters who saw promise in his method and room for its improvement.[9]

As we approach forty years since the publication of Culpepper's work, narrative and literary studies dominate the field of Johannine scholarship, although they do not entirely dispense with historical concerns. Rather than denying the composition history of the Gospel, many of these scholars are skeptical of academic ability to identify and parse such layers, preferring instead to deal with the text "as it exists" rather than constructing a possible text that one cannot *prove* ever existed.[10] A complete list of narrative studies on the Gospel of John is not possible in this short chapter. I will, therefore, highlight only a few areas that have garnered significant interest from scholars in recent years. Most of these studies develop one of the seven "anatomical" areas explored by Culpepper, arguing for greater clarity of terminology or supplying greater depth of study.[11]

Point of View and Irony

One of the areas of interest includes the various points of view expressed in the Gospel. Most obvious is the contrast between the point of view of the narrator (often aligned with that of the "implied author"), those of various characters in the Gospel, and those of the Gospel audience ("implied reader"). By repeatedly providing the audience of the Gospel with clarifying asides not available to characters in the text, the narrator creates a dualism that separates

---

8. Seymour Chatman, *Story and Discourse: Narrative Structure in Fiction and Film* (Ithaca, NY: Cornell University Press, 1978); Culpepper, *Anatomy of the Fourth Gospel*, 6–11. While his "theoretical model" depends on Chatman's work, Culpepper uses work from a variety of literary theorists (Thatcher, "Anatomies of the Fourth Gospel," 18–27).

9. R. Alan Culpepper, "Pursuing the Elusive," in Thatcher, *What We Have Heard*, 113; Thatcher and Moore, *Anatomies of Narrative Criticism*.

10. Marinus de Jonge, "The Gospel and the Epistles of John Read against the Background of the History of the Johannine Communities," in Thatcher, *What We Have Heard*, 127–48.

11. These seven areas are: narrator, point of view, narrative time, plot, characters, implicit commentary, and implied reader. The recent collection edited by Douglas Estes and Ruth Sheridan includes many of these topics, although they are not always identified by the same terms, along with others that have emerged in the literary studies beyond Culpepper's early work. *How John Works: Storytelling in the Fourth Gospel*, RBS 86 (Atlanta: SBL Press, 2016).

the characters and the audience, an irony that draws the audience to the "narrator's ideological point of view."[12] James Resseguie, for example, explores five points of view in John: "spatial, temporal, psychological, phraseological, and ideological."[13] Resseguie argues these five aspects work together to show "the way [John's] story is told," impacting the settings, the relationship between the audience and narrative events, the ways characters are presented, and the overall persuasive goal of the narrative, or its "ideological point of view." For Resseguie, this final point of view is the most important. It is nothing less than the "paradox" laid out in the Gospel prologue that "Jesus's otherworldliness can only be seen in his flesh" (1:14).[14] While some characters and audience members are drawn in to this paradox for belief, others are hopelessly alienated by it.

Imagery, Symbolism, and Metaphor

The imagery used throughout the Fourth Gospel has led other scholars to delve more deeply into its use of symbolism, figurative language, and metaphor. Dorothy Lee, Craig Koester, Jan G. van der Watt, and Ruben Zimmermann are just a few of the scholars who have explored these elements of the Gospel, noting how the layers of figurative language and imagery weave networks of meaning throughout John's story.[15] Lee notes that John's Gospel encourages symbolic exploration with its frequent use of double meanings and repeated motifs from daily life (e.g., water, bread, light/darkness, birth), from Israel's Scriptures and other Jewish contexts (e.g., Jewish festivals, Moses, Abraham, manna), and from its Roman imperial context (e.g., "Savior of the world" [John 4:42]).[16] By wandering into and attempting to navigate the

---

12. Culpepper, *Anatomy of the Fourth Gospel*, 164. Significant works on John's use of irony include Paul D. Duke, *Irony in the Fourth Gospel* (Atlanta: John Knox, 1985); Gail R. O'Day, *Revelation in the Fourth Gospel: Narrative Mode and Theological Claim* (Philadelphia: Fortress, 1986); Jeffrey Lloyd Staley, *The Print's First Kiss: A Rhetorical Investigation of the Implied Reader in the Fourth Gospel*, SBLDS 82 (Atlanta: Scholars Press, 1988); Adele Reinhartz, *The Word in the World: The Cosmological Tale in the Fourth Gospel*, SBLMS 45 (Atlanta: Scholars Press, 1992).

13. James Resseguie, "Point of View," in Estes and Sheridan, *How John Works*, 81–82.

14. Resseguie, "Point of View," 96.

15. Dorothy A. Lee, *The Symbolic Narratives of the Fourth Gospel: The Interplay of Form and Meaning*, JSNTSup 95 (Sheffield: Sheffield Academic, 1994); Lee, "Imagery," in Estes and Sheridan, *How John Works*, 151–69; Craig R. Koester, *Symbolism in the Fourth Gospel: Meaning, Mystery, Community*, 2nd ed. (Minneapolis: Fortress, 2003; first published 1995); Jan G. van der Watt, *Family of the King: Dynamics of Metaphor in the Gospel according to John*, BIS 47 (Leiden: Brill, 2000); Ruben Zimmermann, "Metaphoric Networks as Hermeneutic Keys in the Gospel of John: Using the Example of the Mission Imagery," in *Repetitions and Variations in the Fourth Gospel: Style, Text, Interpretation*, ed. Gilbert van Belle, Michael Labahn, and Petrus Maritz, BETL 223 (Leuven: Peeters, 2009), 381–402.

16. These categories are adapted from Lee, "Imagery," 152.

webs of Johannine imagery, the Gospel audience forms new and greater understandings of Jesus. Rather than employing these metaphors and symbols one at a time, the Gospel layers these images on top of each other so that it is impossible to extract just one from many others. For this reason, scholars note it is often difficult to progress in a linear fashion through the Gospel of John as one reaches backward and forward to connect images, symbols, and metaphors to interpret the narrative.[17] Indeed, Lee suggests that audience members can be transformed through this process when they use their imagination to interpret the complex symbols, senses, and metaphors of the Gospel.[18]

Ancient Comparative Literature: Genre and Rhetoric

The literary analysis of John's Gospel has also encouraged some scholars to examine its relationship to other ancient literary genres and writing techniques, or rhetoric.[19] Harold Attridge argues that the Gospel of John adjusts the gospel genre received, "bending" historical and biographical aspects with novelistic and dramatic features to tell another story of Jesus. Far from a unique invention, the Gospel's bending of genres is a common feature of Greco-Roman literature in the first century, including Jewish literature.[20] Jo-Ann Brant and George Parsenios explore the connections between John and drama, in particular, including Jesus's repeated one-on-one encounters with other characters, the chorus-like aspects of the group characters, and rhetorical patterns in Jesus's speeches.[21] For Parsenios, John occupies a space "between narrative and drama," blending biographical features with formal elements of drama, where the narrator disappears behind the scene to allow the main characters to speak and occupy the stage alone.[22]

17. Zimmermann calls collections of terms in the Gospel of John "clusters." Ruben Zimmerman, "Imagery in John: Opening Up Paths into the Tangled Thicket of John's Figurative World," in *Imagery in the Gospel of John: Texts, Forms, Themes, and Theology of Johannine Figurative Language*, ed. Jörg Frey et al., WUNT 200 (Tübingen: Mohr Siebeck, 2007), 31.
18. Lee, "Imagery," 167–69.
19. Kasper Bro Larsen, "Introduction: The Gospel of John as Genre Mosaic," in *The Gospel of John as Genre Mosaic*, ed. Kasper Bro Larsen, SANt 3 (Göttingen: Vandenhoeck & Ruprecht, 2015), 13–24; Alicia D. Myers, "Rhetoric," in Estes and Sheridan, *How John Works*, 187–203; Ruth Sheridan, "Persuasion," in Estes and Sheridan, *How John Works*, 204–23.
20. Harold Attridge, "The Gospel of John: Genre Matters?," in Larsen, *Gospel of John as Genre Mosaic*, 27–45; Harold Attridge, "Genre," in Estes and Sheridan, *How John Works*, 7–22.
21. Jo-Ann A. Brant, *Dialogue and Drama: Elements of Greek Tragedy in the Fourth Gospel* (Peabody, MA: Hendrickson, 2004); Brant, *John*, PCNT (Grand Rapids: Baker Academic, 2011); George L. Parsenios, *Departure and Consolation: The Johannine Farewell Discourses in Light of Greco-Roman Literature*, NovTSup 117 (Leiden: Brill, 2005).
22. George Parsenios, "The Silent Spaces between Narrative and Drama: *Mimesis* and *Diegesis* in the Fourth Gospel," in Larsen, *Gospel of John as Genre Mosaic*, 85–97.

Yet while Brant and Parsenios agree on the dramatic features in John's Gospel, they determine different rhetorical aims for the Gospel as a whole. Brant argues the Gospel is primarily epideictic, reinforcing the audience's belief in Jesus's identity as "the Christ, the Son of God" (John 20:31). In this way, Brant agrees with Jerome Neyrey, who finds contrasting elements of encomium (praise) and vituperation (blame) for Jesus throughout the Gospel.[23] Parsenios, however, focuses on juridical features in John's narrative, leading him to interpret the Gospel as the investigation of Jesus by various characters, leading up to his trial before Pilate.[24] For Parsenios, the combination of dramatic and juridical elements resonates with other dramas from the ancient world, such as Aeschylus's *Eumenides*, which narrates Orestes's trial before Athena. Kasper Bro Larsen takes yet a different path, noting similarities between Jesus's conversations with characters and the "recognition scenes" that appear in ancient literature.[25] Other scholars have investigated Jesus's discourses in light of riddles, suggesting that Jesus's double meanings and contradictions act as pedagogical devices for the audience.[26] Overall, most Johannine scholars are unwilling to limit John's Gospel to a single genre, but rather find resonances between it and several types of ancient literature. While the overview here highlights Greco-Roman literary comparisons, Brant and others have noted connections to Jewish literature as well, not least because the Gospel regularly appeals to the OT.[27]

Characters, Characterization, and Ethics

Perhaps no area of narrative study on John has garnered as much attention in recent years as that of character and characterization. As with the

---

23. Brant, *John*, 11–12; Jerome H. Neyrey, *The Gospel of John in Cultural and Rhetorical Perspective* (Grand Rapids: Eerdmans, 2009), 3–28.

24. George Parsenios, *Rhetoric and Drama in the Johannine Lawsuit Motif*, WUNT 258 (Tübingen: Mohr Siebeck, 2010); Andrew T. Lincoln, *Truth on Trial: The Lawsuit Motif in the Fourth Gospel* (Peabody, MA: Hendrickson, 2000); Per Jarle Bekken, *The Lawsuit Motif in John's Gospel from New Perspectives: Jesus Christ, Crucified Criminal and Emperor of the World*, NovTSup 158 (Leiden: Brill, 2015).

25. Kasper Bro Larsen, *Recognizing the Stranger: Recognition Scenes in the Gospel of John*, BIS 93 (Leiden: Brill, 2008); Meredith J. C. Warren, *My Flesh Is Meat Indeed: A Nonsacramental Reading of John 6:51–58* (Minneapolis: Fortress, 2015).

26. Tom Thatcher, *The Riddles of Jesus in John: A Study in Tradition and Folklore*, SBLMS 53 (Atlanta: SBL, 2000); Paul N. Anderson, *The Riddles of the Fourth Gospel: An Introduction to John* (Minneapolis: Fortress, 2011); Attridge, "Genre," 18–22; Jason S. Sturdevant, *The Adaptable Jesus of the Fourth Gospel: The Pedagogy of the Logos*, NovTSup 162 (Leiden: Brill, 2015), esp. 47–93.

27. Jo-Ann A. Brant, "John and Jewish Novels," in Larsen, *Gospel of John as Genre Mosaic*, 157–68; Lincoln, *Truth on Trial*, 36–56; Bekken, *Lawsuit Motif in John's Gospel*; Peder Borgen, *The Gospel of John: More Light from Philo, Paul and Archaeology: The Scriptures, Tradition, Settings, Meaning*, NovTSup 154 (Leiden: Brill, 2014).

discussions on genre above, these studies note the Gospel's focus on its protagonist, Jesus, and his episodic exchanges with individual characters and character groups. These features make character studies attractive for scholars exploring John's Christology, views of ancient Judaism, understanding of "belief" and the disciples, and so on.[28] Larger narrative studies have devoted chapters to the discussion of John's characters and his methods of characterization, but more recently individual studies and collections have emerged that are entirely devoted to the topic.[29] These studies use a variety of methods, some continuing Culpepper's tradition of relying primarily on contemporary literary criticism, others prioritizing ancient models and techniques, and yet others offering a combination of these approaches. Although past scholarship described John's characters as flat, typological representatives, current scholarship argues for a greater awareness of Johannine ambiguity, even for some of the characters or groups traditionally interpreted in the most negative of terms. Susan Hylen notes the ambiguity within John's depiction of the Jews, who are often singled out as Jesus's "opponents" par excellence in the Gospel. Hylen argues that, rather than wholly hostile, the Jews are of conflicted and even "contradictory" character in their relationship to Jesus (e.g., 7:14–52), thus inviting John's audience to reconsider its own understandings of Jesus and of people or groups they might deem his opponents.[30]

Driven especially by the work of van der Watt and Zimmermann, discussions of John's characters have encouraged scholars to reevaluate the longstanding position that John's Gospel lacks ethics. These scholars argue that, instead of offering ethical imperatives in the manner of the Synoptics (e.g., Matthew's Sermon on the Mount), John offers an ethics that is "implicit," coming through emphases on the "works of God" and love, as well as in the

---

28. Ruben Zimmermann reviews recent research in "Figurenanalyse im Johannesevangelium: Ein Beitrag zu Sinn und Wahrheit narratologischer Exegese," *ZNW* 105 (2014): 20–53.

29. E.g., Judith Hartenstein, *Charackterisierung im Dialog: Maria Magdalena, Petrus, und die Mutter Jesu im Johannesevangelium*, NTOA 64 (Göttingen: Vandenhoeck & Ruprecht, 2007); Cornelis Bennema, *Encountering Jesus: Character Studies in the Gospel of John*, 2nd ed. (Minneapolis: Fortress, 2014; first published 2009); Alicia D. Myers, *Characterizing Jesus: A Rhetorical Analysis on the Fourth Gospel's Use of Scripture in Its Presentation of Jesus*, LNTS 458 (London: Bloomsbury T&T Clark, 2012); Steve A. Hunt, D. Francois Tolmie, and Ruben Zimmermann, eds., *Character Studies in the Fourth Gospel: Narrative Approaches to Seventy Figures in John*, WUNT 314 (Tübingen: Mohr Siebeck, 2013); Christopher W. Skinner, ed., *Characters and Characterization in the Gospel of John*, LNTS 461 (London: Bloomsbury T&T Clark, 2013); Skinner, "Characterization," in Estes and Sheridan, *How John Works*, 115–32; Mark W. G. Stibbe, "Protagonist," in Estes and Sheridan, *How John Works*, 133–50.

30. Susan Hylen, *Imperfect Believers: Ambiguous Characters in the Gospel of John* (Louisville: Westminster John Knox, 2009), 118. See also Alicia D. Myers, "Just Opponents? Ambiguity, Empathy, and the Jews in the Gospel of John," in *Johannine Ethics: The Moral World of the Gospel and Epistles of John*, ed. Sherri Brown and Christopher W. Skinner (Minneapolis: Fortress, 2017), 195–212.

depiction of characters' behaviors.³¹ The new collection edited by Christopher Skinner and Sherri Brown, for example, contains individual character studies that focus on the implicit ethical formation that can result from John's characterizations.³² These scholars note that although perhaps not an explicitly "ethical" work in the traditional sense, John's Gospel has nevertheless impacted the ethics of various individuals and groups throughout Christian history. For some readers, this leads to an emphasis on John's "love" command (13:34–35).³³ However, Adele Reinhartz and Ruth Sheridan add significant nuance, noting the importance of resisting some of the potentially negative aspects of John's ethics, particularly toward Jews and other nonbelievers.³⁴ Reinhartz also cautions against focusing too much on ethics in John's Gospel, reminding readers that this Gospel is most concerned with Christology and not the validation of ancient or contemporary norms.³⁵

John and History: Deciphering Layers and Debating Contexts

In spite of their adamant emphasis on the "final form" of the Gospel, the vast majority of narrative and literary critics of John value its historical contexts. Indeed, most of these scholars acknowledge a complicated and drawn-out composition history for the Gospel, but they find it to be unrecoverable with any degree of certainty. Thus it is simply the context of the "final form" that holds paramount sway—that is, the late first century CE. It is this point of controversy that most frustrates traditional historical-critical scholars of John. John Ashton will act as our example. In a particularly honest assessment of his narrative-oriented colleagues, Ashton regards the dismissal of tradition and redaction-critical methods as naive and unsophisticated, not least because it belies the very constructed nature of the "final form" of the Greek text being explored. The text, he reminds narratologists, is "the result of thousands of tiny decisions on the part of [the] editors" between thousands of manuscripts

---

31. Jan G. van der Watt and Ruben Zimmermann, eds., *Rethinking the Ethics of John: "Implicit Ethics" in the Johannine Writings*, WUNT 291 (Tübingen: Mohr Siebeck, 2012); Karl Weyer-Menkhoff, *Die Ethik des Johannesevangeliums im sprachlichen Feld des Handelns*, Kontexte und Normen neutestamentlicher Ethik, WUNT 2/359 (Tübingen: Mohr Siebeck, 2014); Lindsey M. Trozzo, *Exploring Johannine Ethics: A Rhetorical Approach to Moral Efficacy in the Fourth Gospel Narrative*, WUNT 2/449 (Tübingen: Mohr Siebeck, 2017).

32. Brown and Skinner, *Johannine Ethics*.

33. E.g., Francis J. Moloney, *Love in the Gospel of John: An Exegetical, Theological, and Literary Study* (Grand Rapids: Baker Academic, 2013).

34. Adele Reinhartz, *Befriending the Beloved Disciple: A Jewish Reading of the Gospel of John* (London: Continuum, 2001); Sheridan, "Persuasion," 221–23.

35. Adele Reinhartz, "The Lyin' King? Deception and Christology in the Gospel of John," in Brown and Skinner, *Johannine Ethics*, 117–34, esp. 134.

that contain variants in almost every verse of John.[36] One need only compare the various versions of the Nestle-Aland to see his point. For Ashton, narrative and literary critics ignore a valuable, indeed indispensable, history of the text by glossing over its complicated construction. Such disregard not only ignores recoverable layers of editing, and therefore insight into the development of the Johannine tradition, but also elides the remaining seams (*aporias*) in the Gospel, preferring to regard these editorial marks as stylistic or rhetorical features rather than as breaks in the Gospel (e.g., John 14:31).[37]

It should be noted, however, that rather than ignoring these seams completely, many (dare I say, most) narrative critics have more or less accepted the development proposed by Martyn and Brown, whose theories of the Johannine community have dominated Johannine scholarship over the past fifty years, even if narrative critics do not participate in dividing layers within the text.[38] Focusing on the unique *aposynagōgos* passages in John ("out of the synagogue" [9:22; 12:42; 16:2]), along with the harsh polemic against the Jews (e.g., John 8), Martyn and Brown proposed a history of expulsion of Johannine believers from Jewish synagogues as they gradually developed higher and higher Christologies. Brown argued that the controversy continued beyond the Gospel into the Epistles, as believers debated various topics such as inspiration by the Spirit, the continued relevance of Jesus, and eschatology.[39] Although not arguing for specific textual divisions, and even questioning aspects of this "two-level drama," Johannine scholars still often perceive conflict (usually christological) as a key component of the Gospel's composition. Rather than existing during Jesus's lifetime, this conflict arises later in the life of the Johannine community as it works to define itself within, alongside, or outside local Jewish communities and other early Christian groups.

One of the main benefits of Martyn's and Brown's readings was an explanation for John's harsh polemic toward the Jews. Rather than a straightforwardly "anti-Jewish" Gospel, John is the product of an intra-Jewish debate. John's Gospel is not a general rejection of Jews by early "Christians" but rather a localized, sectarian debate. This move also locates the historical background of John away from predominantly Hellenistic and Gnostic contexts to Jewish ones, rescuing John's Gospel from accusations of syncretism and, therefore,

---

36. John Ashton, "Second Thoughts," in Thatcher, *What We Have Heard*, 8.

37. Ashton, "Second Thoughts," 2–9. See also Ashton, *Understanding the Fourth Gospel*, 2nd ed. (Oxford: Oxford University Press, 2007), 11–22; Ashton, *The Gospel of John and Christian Origins* (Minneapolis: Fortress, 2014), 119–32.

38. Synagogue expulsion is an undercurrent in much of R. Alan Culpepper's work and regularly recurs in narrative readings. Even if they do not postulate a formal synagogue break, Johannine scholars often argue for christological conflicts behind the Gospel (Thatcher, "Anatomies of the Fourth Gospel," 6–8).

39. Brown, *Community of the Beloved Disciple*, 93–144.

tying the Gospel more closely to the historical Jesus. It is this vein of scholarship that inspired the members of the Society of Biblical Literature's John, Jesus, and History Group to investigate John's Gospel for more glimpses of the historical Jesus, pushing back against the tide of scholarship that excluded John from such traditionally prized turf. For Paul Anderson, John's Gospel is an independent witness to early Jesus traditions that were later developed with specific, Johannine concerns in mind, even though they may have influenced the authors of Luke and Matthew (and contrasted sharply with Mark).[40] Tom Thatcher also argues for independence, though his approach focuses on the role of memory in the preservation and cultivation of Jesus traditions in John's Gospel.[41] At the same time, however, Frans Neirynck has encouraged other scholars back toward reading evidence of John's dependence on various Synoptic Gospels.[42] There is, therefore, a growing number of arguments for potential interactions between John and other Gospels, even among those who emphasize John's strong editorial hand in shaping shared traditions.[43]

More robust composition theories have also been put forward. Jean Zumstein and Andreas Dettwiler have developed a theory of "re-reading" (*relecture*) within the Gospel, arguing that odd breaks and repetitions are a result of the community's reworking of traditional material and then preserving the revisions alongside earlier texts. Klaus Scholtissek builds on Zumstein and Dettwiler's work but suggests that the work could be from one author rather than a community as a process of "re-writing" (*réécriture*).[44] In more recent years, however, the most thorough reconstruction of the composition process

40. See Paul Anderson, "Why This Study Is Needed and Why It Is Needed Now," in *John, Jesus, and History*, vol. 1, *Critical Apraisals of Critical Views*, ed. Paul N. Anderson, Felix Just, and Tom Thatcher; SBLSymS 44 (Atlanta: SBL Press, 2007), 13–74; as well as Anderson, *The Fourth Gospel and the Quest for Jesus: Modern Foundations Reconsidered*, LNTS 321 (London: T&T Clark, 2006); Anderson, "The Community That Raymond Brown Left Behind: Reflections on the Johannine Dialectical Situation," in *Communities in Dispute: Current Scholarship on the Johannine Epistles*, ed. R. Alan Culpepper and Paul N. Anderson, ECIL 13 (Atlanta: SBL Press, 2014), 47–94.

41. Tom Thatcher, *Why John Wrote a Gospel: Jesus, Memory, History* (Louisville: Westminster John Knox, 2006); Richard Horsley and Tom Thatcher, *John, Jesus, and the Renewal of Israel* (Grand Rapids: Eerdmans, 2013).

42. Frans Neirynck, "John 4:46–51: Signs, Source, and/or Synoptic Gospels," *ETL* 60 (1984): 367–75; Frans van Segbroeck and C. M. Tuckett, eds., *The Four Gospels 1992: Festschrift Frans Neirynck*, 3 vols., BETL 100 (Leuven: Peeters, 1992); D. Moody Smith, *John among the Gospels*, 2nd ed. (Columbia: University of South Carolina Press, 2001; first published 1992).

43. E.g., Thatcher and Williams, *Engaging with C. H. Dodd*; Wendy E. S. North, *A Journey round John: Tradition, Interpretation and Context in the Fourth Gospel*, LNTS 534 (London: Bloomsbury T&T Clark, 2015), 179–92, 207–19; James W. Barker, *John's Use of Matthew* (Minneapolis: Fortress, 2015).

44. Jean Zumstein, *La Mémoire revisitée: Etudes johanniques*, MdB 71 (Geneva: Labor et Fides, 2017); Zumstein, "Intratextuality and Intertextuality in the Gospel of John," trans. Mike Gray, in Thatcher and Moore, *Anatomies of Narrative Criticism*, 121–35. Scholtissek's more

of the Gospel and Epistles of John is in Urban von Wahlde's three-volume commentary.⁴⁵ Relying heavily on Brown, von Wahlde establishes criteria for the division of the Johannine material into compositional layers. He finds evidence for three editions of the Gospel, maintaining that its final form postdates 1 John, which he suggests clarifies aspects of the earlier Gospel editions. These clarifications, he argues, were then incorporated into the final edition of the Gospel to create a more uniform Johannine theology.⁴⁶ The consistent criticism leveled against these types of reconstructions is that they do not adequately enumerate their criteria for dividing layers other than commenting on "clear" breaks or ideological inconsistencies in the text. Von Wahlde's thoroughness is, in part, a response to such criticisms.

Additional pushback in recent decades has emerged against Brown's and Martyn's emphases on the Johannine community. The aspect of Martyn's theory that has endured the most forceful critique is its reliance on the debated use of the Birkat Ha-Minim ("cursing of the heretics") in local synagogues by the end of the first century.⁴⁷ Even as recent scholars have renewed arguments in favor of its employment, Reinhartz maintains that John's Gospel records only one side of the story of division.⁴⁸ As a result, its own biases should be acknowledged, rather than read as a transparent window to the world behind the text. Other scholars, however, question Brown's reconstruction by positing a single, christological debate in Johannine circles rather than a twofold division, first from Jewish groups and then within the Johannine community. Udo Schnelle, for example, argues that 2–3 John are the first Johannine writings, acting as short, punctuated responses to a developing docetic tide. First John, and then the Gospel, are fuller theological arguments to combat these anti-incarnational teachings.⁴⁹ Still others, led by Richard Bauckham, argue that no Gospel should be read as though confined or purposed for a single, early Christian community. Bauckham suggests that the core of John's Gospel

---

recent work focuses on the potential for *relecture* for interpreting 1 John. See Klaus Scholtissek, "Die relecture des Johannesevangeliums im ersten Johannesbrief," *BK* 59 (2004): 152–65.

45. Urban von Wahlde, *A Commentary on the Gospel and Letters of John*, 3 vols., ECC (Grand Rapids: Eerdmans, 2010).

46. von Wahlde, *Commentary*, vol. 1; von Wahlde, "Raymond Brown's View of the Crisis of 1 John: In the Light of Some Peculiar Features of the Johannine Gospel," in Culpepper and Anderson, *Communities in Dispute*, 19–45.

47. E.g., Reinhartz, *Befriending the Beloved Disciple*, 39–40.

48. Joel Marcus, "*Birkat Ha-Minim* Revisited," *NTS* 55 (2009): 523–51. Cf. Reinhartz, *Befriending the Beloved Disciple*, 40–53; Reinhartz, "Incarnation and Covenant: The Fourth Gospel through the Lens of Trauma Theory," *Int* 69 (2015): 35–48.

49. Udo Schnelle, *Antidocetic Christology in the Gospel of John: An Investigation of the Place of the Fourth Gospel in the Johannine School*, trans. Linda M. Maloney (Minneapolis: Fortress, 1992); Georg Strecker, *Theology of the New Testament*, ed. Friedrich Wilhelm Horn, trans. M. Eugene Boring (Berlin: de Gruyter, 2000), 419–515.

is in the eyewitness of the beloved disciple (who is not John son of Zebedee) and that the Gospel was meant to be heard in a variety of early Christian communities.[50] For this reason, Bauckham finds John's Gospel useful for historical reconstructions of Jesus traditions (as "eyewitness" testimony) even though it is not helpful for reconstructing a Johannine community. Indeed, for him there is no purely "Johannine community" to reconstruct.[51]

Perennial Topics and Emerging Horizons

The above overview has already touched on some of the enduring topics in Johannine studies, including especially John's troubled history with regard to its presentation of the Jews (*hoi Ioudaioi*).[52] The study of these topics has been influenced by the influx of narrative-critical studies and postmodernism, particularly the awareness of the reality that ideologies impact all interpretations. Nevertheless, as with other studies described above, such awareness does not necessarily cause scholars to divorce their study of John from historical contexts. Instead, it opens up avenues for new contexts, both ancient and modern, for interpreters to read the Gospel. In what follows, I divide these final topics into two categories for ease of review: studies based on primarily Jewish contexts and those focused on Roman imperial and postcolonial contexts. Although these categories are discrete here, they necessarily overlap in practice.

Jewish Contexts

John's complex relationship with, and presentation of, Jews and Judaism persists as a significant topic for Johannine scholars. Interpreters often debate whether John can be classified as "anti-Jewish," given its ancient contexts and its use in Christian history.[53] John's often polemical presentations of the Jews in the Gospel are made even more complicated by their frequent

---

50. Richard Bauckham, ed., *The Gospels for All Christians: Rethinking the Gospel Audiences* (Grand Rapids: Eerdmans, 1998), esp. 9–48, 147–71; Bauckham, *The Testimony of the Beloved Disciple: Narrative, History, and Theology in the Gospel of John* (Grand Rapids: Baker Academic, 2007), 73–123.

51. Edward W. Klink III, *The Sheep of the Fold: The Audience and Origin of the Gospel of John*, SNTSMS 141 (Cambridge: Cambridge University Press, 2007); Jonathan Bernier, *Aposynagōgos and the Historical Jesus in John: Rethinking the Historicity of the Johannine Expulsion Passages*, BIS 122 (Leiden: Brill, 2013); David A. Lamb, *Text, Context, and the Johannine Community: A Sociolinguistic Analysis of the Johannine Writings*, LNTS 477 (London: Bloomsbury T&T Clark, 2015).

52. On the translation of *hoi Ioudaioi* see Myers, "Just Opponents?," 195.

53. Reinhartz, *Befriending the Beloved Disciple*; Lars Kierspel, *The Jews and the World in the Fourth Gospel: Parallelism, Function, and Context*, WUNT 2/220 (Tübingen: Mohr

incorporation of OT and Second Temple elements. John's Gospel values the OT, the Jewish liturgical calendar, and Jewish practices, even if it interprets them in radically Christocentric ways (e.g., 5:39–47; 10:30 [cf. Deut. 6:5]). In her recent study, Ruth Sheridan explores how the Gospel uses Scripture to cast the Jews as negative characters.[54] Other scholars explore patterns and methods of quotation, as well as larger intertextual connections that provide depth to the Gospel's incorporation of these elements. Areas of interest include how memory contributes to John's use of traditions and how John's rhetoric may be compared to ancient rhetorical practices used by Jewish and non-Jewish authors.[55]

In addition to using OT traditions, John's Gospel also has interesting overlaps with material in the Dead Sea Scrolls (DSS). Initially the scrolls were considered a potential treasure trove of insights into the Johannine movement. Some more recent studies, however, have downplayed direct connections. Areas of overlap do remain, however, even if they also exist between John and the first-century world more generally. As James Charlesworth explains, this observation means that one now need not resort to Hellenistic texts to find similarities to Johannine thought.[56] John is at home in a Jewish milieu. Indeed, so close are some of these connections that Charlesworth and others claim that John may have emerged from an Essene-type Judaism, if not Qumran itself.[57] Current interest has also turned to examine John's relationship to apocalyptic aspects of Judaism, at least in part because of the overlap between Qumranite and Johannine dualisms. Building on the suggestions from Ashton, Catrin Williams, Christopher Rowland, and others explore the possibility that, although John is not an apocalypse, it retains apocalyptic elements.[58] Like other Jewish apocalyptic texts, for example, John is also primarily focused on revelation. Moreover, this Gospel is traditionally linked to Revelation as part of the Johannine corpus.

Siebeck, 2006); R. Alan Culpepper and Paul N. Anderson, eds., *John and Judaism: A Contested Relationship in Context*, RBS 87 (Atlanta: SBL Press, 2017).

54. Ruth Sheridan, *Retelling Scripture: "The Jews" and the Scriptural Citations in John 1:19–12:15*, BIS 110 (Leiden: Brill, 2012). See also Jaime Clark-Soles, *Scripture Cannot Be Broken: The Social Function of the Use of Scripture in the Fourth Gospel*, 2nd ed. (Leiden: Brill, 2003).

55. Alicia D. Myers and Bruce G. Schuchard, eds., *Abiding Words: Perspectives on the Use of the Old Testament in the Gospel of John*, RBS 81 (Atlanta: SBL Press, 2015); Richard B. Hays, *Echoes of Scripture in the Gospels* (Waco: Baylor University Press, 2016).

56. James Charlesworth, "The Fourth Evangelist and the Dead Sea Scrolls: Assessing Trends over Nearly Sixty Years," in *John, Qumran, and the Dead Sea Scrolls: Sixty Years of Discovery and Debate*, ed. Mary L. Coloe and Tom Thatcher, EJIL 32 (Atlanta: SBL, 2011), 164.

57. Charlesworth, "Fourth Evangelist," 165–72.

58. Ashton, *Understanding the Fourth Gospel*, 305–29; Catrin H. Williams and Christopher Rowland, eds., *John's Gospel and Intimations of Apocalyptic* (London: Bloomsbury T&T Clark, 2014).

Imperial and Anti-imperial Readings

Led primarily by the work of Warren Carter, scholars are also examining what it means for John's Gospel to have been written in the midst of the Roman Empire. Often this results in anti-imperial readings that note how the Gospel promotes Jesus as "Savior of the world" (rather than Caesar [John 4:42]) and shows the impotence and ignorance of Rome's representative, Pilate (John 18–19).[59] These studies dovetail well with postcolonial approaches that likewise challenge so-called normative, or imperial, readings of John. R. S. Sugirtharajah explains that "postcolonialism was never conceived as a grand theory, but as creative literature and as a resistance discourse emerging in the former colonies of the Western empires." This literature has subsequently been taken up, especially alongside feminism and globalization, "to analyze the diverse strategies by which the colonizers constructed images of the colonized" and "to study how the colonized themselves made use of and went beyond many of those strategies in order to articulate their identity, self-worth, and empowerment."[60]

Following this route, a number of recent studies explore and deconstruct various normative principles in the text. Colleen Conway and Lee, for example, have led the charge of analyzing the Gospel's use of gender. Conway especially focuses on the lens of Greco-Roman understandings of masculinity and femininity for understanding characters in John.[61] Although Conway argues that John's Jesus conforms to the "hegemonic masculinity" of the Roman Empire, Jason Ripley and I both nuance this reading, nevertheless maintaining John's indebtedness to ancient masculine assumptions.[62] Conway's and Lee's work has also encouraged scholars to explore the Gospel's use of and assumptions concerning bodies, including "disabled" bodies.[63] The function of

---

59. Warren Carter, *John and Empire: Initial Explorations* (London: T&T Clark, 2008); Tom Thatcher, *Greater Than Caesar: Christology and Empire in the Fourth Gospel* (Minneapolis: Fortress, 2009); Thomas Rasimus, ed., *The Legacy of John: Second-Century Reception of the Fourth Gospel*, NovTSup 132 (Leiden: Brill, 2010).

60. R. S. Sugirtharajah, "Charting the Aftermath: A Review of Postcolonial Criticism," in *The Postcolonial Biblical Reader*, ed. R. S. Sugirtharajah (Malden, MA: Blackwell, 2006), 7. Fernando Segovia traces postcolonial works in Johannine circles in "Johannine Studies and the Geopolitical: Reflections upon Absence and Interruption," in Thatcher, ed., *What We Have Heard*, 281–306.

61. Colleen M. Conway, *Behold the Man: Jesus and Greco-Roman Masculinity* (New York: Oxford University Press, 2008); Dorothy Lee, *Flesh and Glory: Symbol, Gender, and Theology in the Gospel of John* (New York: Crossroad, 2002).

62. Conway, *Behold the Man*, 157; Alicia D. Myers, "Gender, Rhetoric and Recognition: Characterizing Jesus and (Re)defining Masculinity in the Gospel of John," *JSNT* 38 (2015): 191–218; Jason Ripley, "'Behold the Man'? Subverting Imperial Masculinity in the Gospel of John," *JBRec* 2 (2015): 219–39.

63. Jaime Clark-Soles, "John, First–Third John, and Revelation," in *The Bible and Disability: A Commentary*, ed. Sarah J. Melcher, Mikael C. Parsons, and Amos Yong (Waco: Baylor University Press, 2017), 333–60.

bodies in John is particularly significant because of the Gospel's emphasis on the spirit. Indeed, as mentioned above, John is often interpreted as combating docetic trends. Gitte Buch-Hansen and Christina Pettersen push back against such readings, Buch-Hansen by means of Stoic influences on the Gospel and Petterson by suggesting that John should be read on its own terms, apart from later Gnostic fears.[64] As a result, she argues that the Gospel communicates the presence of Christ, and indeed stands in the place of Christ's body, as the vehicle of revelation for the Gospel audience.

Reflections

The overview of studies on John offered here could be easily multiplied, but I have attempted to give a representative sampling of some of the most consistent topics of interest and methodological trends in recent years. In narrative-critical circles, plot, space, time, metaphor, and discourse analysis occupy scholars, who have been invigorated by the literary turn in Johannine studies.[65] Nevertheless, the focus on narrative elements and coherence in John is not without critique. Stephen Moore notes that many narrative critics are not well versed in literary theory. As a result, he argues, scholars domesticate (or, perhaps in Johannine circles, "anatomize") theory by tying it down in repeatable methodologies due to preoccupations with historicity and often unarticulated ecclesiological and professional commitments.[66] Other scholars, however, argue that narrative critics do not pay enough attention to history, opening the way for more individualized (and ahistoricized) readings.[67] While some scholars see such detachment as liberative, others are alarmed. Unwilling to detach John from its historical contexts and complicated composition history, these scholars remain interested in more traditionally historical-critical investigations.

The continued debates over the history of the Gospel of John and over the history it may or may not contain concerning Jesus or a "Johannine community" demonstrate that despite predictions to the contrary, historical-critical approaches are alive and well among Johannine interpreters. Indeed,

---

64. Gitte Buch-Hansen, *"It Is the Spirit That Gives Life": A Stoic Understanding of Pneuma in John's Gospel*, BZNW 173 (Berlin: de Gruyter, 2010); Christina Petterson, *From Tomb to Text: The Body of Jesus in the Book of John* (London: Bloomsbury T&T Clark, 2016). See also Warren, *My Flesh Is Meat Indeed*.

65. E.g., Estes and Sheridan, *How John Works*; Beth M. Stovell, *Mapping Metaphorical Discourse in the Fourth Gospel: John's Eternal King*, LBS 5 (Leiden: Brill, 2012); Adesola Joan Akala, *The Son-Father Relationship and Christological Symbolism in the Gospel of John*, LNTS 505 (London: Bloomsbury T&T Clark, 2014).

66. Stephen Moore, "Afterword: Things Not Written in This Book," in Moore and Thatcher, *Anatomies of Narrative Criticism*, 253–58.

67. Thatcher, "Anatomies of the Fourth Gospel," 28.

scholars continue debating and deciphering layers within the text in hopes of delineating the development (and reception) of the Gospel and the communities who constructed it, be they specifically Johannine or not. This does not mean, however, that such approaches have not been affected by the rise of narrative and literary studies in John, especially their postmodern insights on the inescapable role ideologies have in interpretation. Reflecting this tension, Reinhartz writes, "My own position on the fate of historical criticism is somewhat conflicted."[68] As someone inspired by narrative studies, she is also motivated by the historical people and groups behind John's story, but whether one can access them, and if so, how much, is highly contested. Nevertheless, she can agree that John's Gospel is a product of history, meaning that it too is motivated by, constructed by, preserved by, and influencing historical persons. There are, therefore, insights to be made when contexts are explored, even though ideological assessments will always color the interpretations offered.

Thus this overview of research ends in a manner similar to how it began: by noting the inescapable connection between literary and historical-critical studies of the Gospel of John. Profiting from the energy of exploring the Gospel as a coherent story, narrative critics also benefit from the resistance their readings encounter from historical critics, who continue to remind them of the importance of the history that is inherent in and to the Gospel text, even when the very idea of "history" is a topic of debate.[69] The friction and collaboration between these groups of scholars have sparked the continuing growth of Johannine studies in other, previously unforeseen ways. Remembering that the Gospel is a story inspired, written, and preserved by real people reminds contemporary readers of their own contexts and embodiment as well. Along these lines, Conway has noted how studying the Gospel as literature pushed her to grapple with its historical contexts, its relationship to history, and the idea of "history" itself, suggesting maybe John's Gospel has more of a "postmodern" outlook than interpreters often imagine.[70] Rather than forfeiting historical exploration, therefore, current Johannine scholars more often debate how John, as religious literature, relates to history. Reinhartz, for one, suggests that scholars bring "humility, imagination, and good humor" to the task.[71]

---

68. Adele Reinhartz, "Building Skyscrapers on Toothpicks: The Literary-Critical Challenge to Historical Criticism," in Thatcher and Moore, *Anatomies of Narrative Criticism*, 69.

69. Colleen Conway, "New Historicism and the Historical Jesus in John: Friends or Foes?," in Anderson, Just, and Thatcher, *John, Jesus, and History*, 1:199–215; see also Claire Clivaz, "'Asleep by Grief' (Luke 22:45): Reading from the Body at the Crossroads of Narratology and New Historicism," *The Bible and Critical Theory* 2, no. 3 (2015): 29.1–29.15.

70. Conway, "New Historicism," 210; Colleen Conway, "There and Back Again: Johannine History on the Other Side of Literary Criticism," in Thatcher and Moore, *Anatomies of Narrative Criticism*, 89–91.

71. Reinhartz, "Building Skyscrapers," 70.

17

The Acts of the Apostles

JOSHUA W. JIPP

Introduction

Scholarship on Acts is difficult to summarize and synthesize by means of only a few discrete topics. Many excellent studies are not discussed in this chapter, and it is with regret that I have passed over some important topics related to genre and historiography, literary characterization, questions related to historicity, and some significant new commentaries. Still, the four topics I have chosen do reflect well where a significant amount of recent research has been invested in Acts within the past twenty years: (1) Acts and Judaism, (2) Acts and Greco-Roman religion and culture, (3) masculinity and ethnic reasoning, and (4) the portrait of God.

Acts and Judaism

One of the persistent questions that has dominated scholarship on Acts is its relationship to Judaism. Does Acts represent a form of gentile Christianity that has displaced Judaism, such that the former now takes the place of Israel? Is the gentile mission rooted in Israel's rejection of the gospel (e.g., Acts 13:46; 18:6; 28:26–28) and, as such, disconnected from its Jewish origins? Many— though their positions of course require further nuance—have indeed seen Acts as representative of a Christian text that makes a clean break between

"Judaism" and (gentile) "Christianity," with the former portrayed by Luke in a negative light.[1] Jacob Jervell's well-known work on Acts almost systematically sought to overturn this view, stressing a greater continuity between God's ongoing election of Israel and the inclusion of gentile believers into the people of God. Jervell argued that, instead of gentile Christianity replacing Israel as the people of God, Acts depicts a remarkable amount of Jewish belief in the gospel and that it makes better sense to speak of a "division" in the people of God rather than rejection or replacement.[2]

While many of the details of Jervell's arguments remain controversial, the past twenty years or so of scholarship has, in my view, lent strong support to a more positive relationship, and one that stresses greater ecclesiological continuity between Judaism and the people of God in the Acts of the Apostles.[3] Some have argued, for example, that Christianity's origins as narrated by Acts are rooted in Israel's prophetic promises for the restoration of Israel.[4] Simon David Butticaz argues that Acts does precisely this by showing how the origins of the church, in Acts 1–7, reenacts momentous patterns from Israel's history.[5] Thus Luke describes Judas's apostasy within the framework of the reconstitution of the twelve apostles as the eschatological continuation of Israel (Acts 1:15–26), the outpouring of the Spirit is narrated within the prophetic promises and Israel's regathering at Zion (2:1–21), and the speeches in Acts 3–5 declare that the resurrection of the Messiah is the royal enthronement of the Davidic king, which thereby continues the stories of Abraham and Moses (e.g., 3:18–26).[6] Butticaz does not see Stephen's speech as a rejection of Judaism but, rather, as an articulation of Israel's history that

---

1. E.g., Jack T. Sanders, *The Jews in Luke-Acts* (Philadelphia: Fortress, 1987); Lawrence M. Wills, "The Depiction of the Jews in Acts," *JBL* 110 (1991): 631–54; Ernst Haenchen, *The Acts of the Apostles: A Commentary* (Philadelphia: Westminster, 1971). A helpful orientation toward the history of scholarship on this point can be found in Joseph B. Tyson, *Luke, Judaism, and the Scholars: Critical Approaches to Luke-Acts* (Columbia: University of South Carolina Press, 1999). Of course, not all recent scholarship has emphasized a positive relationship between Acts and Judaism. See here especially Shelly Matthews, *Perfect Martyr: The Stoning of Stephen and the Construction of Christian Identity* (Oxford: Oxford University Press, 2012).

2. See here especially Jacob Jervell, *Luke and the People of God: A New Look at Luke-Acts* (Minneapolis: Augsburg, 1972); Jacob Jervell, *Die Apostelgeschichte*, KEK 3 (Göttingen: Vandenhoeck & Ruprecht, 1998).

3. There have certainly been earlier works continuing Jervell's trajectory of Acts as taking a more positive approach to Israel. See, for example, Robert L. Brawley, *Luke-Acts and the Jews: Conflict, Apology, and Conciliation*, SBLMS 33 (Atlanta: Scholars Press, 1987).

4. See here also Alan J. Thompson, *The Acts of the Risen Lord Jesus: Luke's Account of God's Unfolding Plan*, NSBT 27 (Downers Grove, IL: InterVarsity Press, 2011).

5. Simon David Butticaz, *L'Identité de l'église dans les Actes des Apôtres de la restauration d'Israël à la conquête universelle*, BZNW 174 (Berlin: de Gruyter, 2011).

6. There are similarities between the argument of Butticaz and the thesis of David W. Pao, *Acts and the Isaianic New Exodus* (Grand Rapids: Baker Academic, 2002), 111–46.

emphasizes continuity between God's prior revelation to his people outside the land of Israel and the current move of the gospel outside the land of Israel. Paul's final encounter with the Jews in Rome simultaneously emphasizes the Christian movement's salvation-historical continuity with Israel even as Israel itself increasingly rejects the gospel message (28:16–31).

Jens Schröter argues that the question of continuity is best approached through examining the relationship "between Christology and the conception of the people of God in Luke."[7] Schröter examines both the "Davidic" and "Prophetic" streams of Lukan Christology. Luke's vision of Jesus as the Davidic Messiah is from the very beginning universally oriented, as it pertains to both Israel and the nations (Luke 1:32–35; 24:44–49; Acts 13:17–38; 26:6–8, 22–23). Schröter summarizes: "The new definition of the people of God is thus a direct consequence of Lukan Christology and is already anchored in the designation of Jesus as the one begotten by God. It is part of the universally oriented salvation plan of God, which is grounded in the writings of Israel, takes concrete form in the announcement of the Son of God and Davidide, and is realized in history since his birth."[8] In a similar vein, Schröter notes that Luke's prophetic Christology is consistently oriented toward the salvation of both Israel and the gentiles (e.g., Luke 2:30–35; 4:16–30).[9] Thus God's provision of salvation fulfills the promises God made *to Israel*, and thus it makes no sense to speak of Luke's vision of the people of God having no room for Israel within it![10] Israel is not disinherited or rejected, even if there is something of a current "hardening" of Israel occurring within God's plan for salvation.

Susan Wendel's monograph is noteworthy here for her examination of how the writings of Luke-Acts and Justin portray believers in the Messiah as the people of God. She argues that Luke portrays the apostles as prophetic interpreters of Israel's Scriptures; there is, thereby, a strong sense of continuity between these sacred Scriptures and the events described in Acts.[11] One might say that Acts is the continuation of Israel's biblical history. Whereas Justin sees a contrast and clear-cut distinction between "Christians" and "Jews," Acts

---

7. Jens Schröter, "Salvation for the Gentiles and Israel: On the Relationship between Christology and the People of God in Luke," in *From Jesus to the New Testament: Early Christian Theology and the Origin of the New Testament Canon*, trans. Wayne Coppins, Baylor–Mohr Siebeck Studies in Early Christianity (Waco: Baylor University Press, 2013), 230.

8. Schröter, "Salvation for the Gentiles and Israel," 236–37.

9. While Schröter focuses on the interpretation of Israel's Scriptures as seen in the speeches of Acts, a similar argument for Luke's vision of the people of God being rooted in both a prophetic Christology and a Davidic-messianic Christology is advanced in Luke Timothy Johnson, *Septuagintal Midrash in the Speeches of Acts* (Milwaukee: Marquette University Press, 2002).

10. Schröter, "Salvation for the Gentiles and Israel," 243.

11. Susan Wendel, *Scriptural Interpretation and Community Self-Definition in Luke-Acts and the Writings of Justin Martyr*, NovTSup 139 (Leiden: Brill, 2011).

portrays *some Jews* as rejecting the gospel message. In Acts, then, there is no universal and global judgment on or rejection of the Jewish people. Wendel demonstrates that whereas Justin sees Christ-believers as the recipients of the promises God made *to Israel*, Acts is clear that "only Christ-believing Jews [are] heirs" to the divine promises made for Israel (see especially Acts 3:22–26).[12] Thus, Luke does not erase or deny the significance of Israel *even as* he portrays both Christ-believing Jews *and* gentile believers as composing the people of God.

Representing a largely complementary approach with those who emphasize a more positive relationship between the ecclesiological vision of Acts and Judaism are those scholars who have emphasized how Luke's primary protagonists are Torah observant. Isaac Oliver sets his work against those who presume Acts is representative of a form of gentile Christianity that is unacquainted and unconcerned with Judaism.[13] Oliver make the bold and surprising claim that Luke's impressive and deep knowledge of Torah observance and halakah demonstrates the likelihood that the author of Luke-Acts was both born and raised as a Torah-observant Jew.[14] Oliver argues that there is nothing within Luke-Acts that would justify speaking of the abrogation of the pentateuchal food laws.[15] For example, Peter's vision from heaven ultimately focuses not on food but on persons; in other words, God's declaration concerns the cleansing and purification of people, rather than justifying dispensing with the food laws.

Furthermore, Oliver argues that the context for the apostolic decree in Acts 15 is to be found in Leviticus 17–18, and thereby one purpose of the decree is to encourage gentile believers to properly respect Jewish observance of the food laws when Jewish and gentile believers share meals. Luke's recounting the circumcisions of both John the Baptist and Jesus would be quite odd, argues Oliver, had Luke not expected Jewish believers in Jesus to follow the same practice. Further, gentile believers are discouraged from undergoing circumcision precisely because gentile converts obviously cannot fulfill the command for *eighth-day* circumcision (see Luke 2:20–23; Acts 7:8). This supports the Lukan James's implication that Paul does not teach diaspora Jews to cease circumcising their children (Acts 21:20–21).[16]

Matthew Thiessen, likewise, notes that the eighth-day circumcisions of John, Jesus, and Isaac indicate that Luke "consistently stresses [circumcision's]

12. Wendel, *Scriptural Interpretation and Community Self-Definition*, 214.
13. Isaac W. Oliver, *Torah Praxis after 70 CE: Reading Matthew and Luke-Acts as Jewish Texts*, WUNT 2/355 (Tübingen: Mohr Siebeck, 2013).
14. Oliver, *Torah Praxis after 70 CE*, 447–48.
15. For this paragraph, see Oliver, *Torah Praxis after 70 CE*, 320–98.
16. Oliver, *Torah Praxis after 70 CE*, 401–38.

rightful timing [and] does not denigrate circumcision."[17] Thus Luke insists on the necessity of Jewish believers circumcising their children and rejects the same need for gentile believers. Like Oliver, Thiessen emphasizes that the point of Peter's vision centers on God cleansing the gentiles by means of God's Spirit; it does not imply the rejection of the observance of food laws for Jewish believers. Thus "Jews continue to be Jews. Gentiles continue to be Gentiles. The ethnic ties linking Abraham and his descendants remain intact and significant for Luke. Gentiles may now belong on the pure side of the pure/impure binary, but Luke continues to distinguish them from Jews."[18]

An increasing appreciation for Luke's more positive assessment of Judaism has also resulted in a reevaluation of the portrait of Paul in Acts, often with a more open assessment of the relationship between the Paul of Acts and the so-called historical Paul (or perhaps better, epistolary Paul).[19] I have emphasized, for example, the way in which the Paul of Acts bears remarkable similarities to what is foregrounded by Pauline scholars working with the "Paul within Judaism approach."[20] The Paul of Acts, for example, is emphatic that he observes the Torah and is loyal to his Jewish heritage in every way. He is a Jew of the Pharisaic sect who is zealous for the God of Israel (21:20–26; 22:1–3; 23:1, 5; 26:4–5) and believes all that is written in the Law and the Prophets (24:14–15; 26:22–23). He stands trial for the "hope of Israel," which is the "promise our twelve tribes hope to attain" (26:6–7; cf. 28:20). He circumcises Timothy (16:1–5). He gives alms when he visits Jerusalem (24:17–24). Paul carries out his mission by first proclaiming the gospel in the Jewish synagogues (9:19–29; 13:4–5, 42–43; 14:1; 16:12–13). Paul's defense speeches in Acts 22–28 are remarkably emphatic in their depiction of Paul as one who is loyal to historical Judaism, strictly obeys the Torah, and has as his mission the proclamation of the hope of Israel.[21]

Oliver covers some of the same ground in his essay "The 'Historical Paul' and the Paul of Acts" as he draws attention to four examples in which Paul's

---

17. Matthew Thiessen, *Contesting Conversion: Genealogy, Circumcision, and Identity in Ancient Judaism and Christianity* (Oxford: Oxford University Press, 2011), 122.

18. Thiessen, *Contesting Conversion*, 139–40.

19. The classic essay emphasizing the difference and incompatibility between the Paul of Acts and the historical Paul is Philipp Vielhauer, "On the 'Paulinism' of Acts," in *Studies in Luke-Acts*, ed. Leander E. Keck and J. Louis Martyn (Mifflintown, PA: Sigler Press, 1966), 33–50.

20. Joshua W. Jipp, "What Are the Implications of the Ethnic Identity of Paul's Interlocutor? Continuing the Conversation," in *The So-Called Jew in Paul's Letter to the Romans*, ed. Rafael Rodriguez and Matthew Thiessen (Minneapolis: Fortress, 2016), 183–203; see especially 192–96. See here also the valuable essay by Reidar Hvalvik, "Paul as a Jewish Believer—according to the Book of Acts," in *Jewish Believers in Jesus: The Early Centuries*, ed. Oskar Skarsaune and Reidar Hvalvik (Grand Rapids: Baker Academic, 2007), 121–51.

21. This was argued forcefully by Jervell, who saw these trial narratives functioning as a defense of Paul's loyalty to the Jewish people. See Jervell, *Luke and the People of God*, 153–83.

positive affirmations about Torah and Judaism in Romans have significant parallels in Acts.[22] More specifically, both texts affirm God's election of Israel and its privileged status; both affirm the Torah as holy and good; both portray Paul as one who continues to live as a Jew; and both affirm an ultimate salvation for ethnic Israel after a period of hardening and ignorance. Oliver concludes that both Romans and Acts demonstrate "that many Jewish followers of Jesus continued to remain loyal to their Jewish heritage, both before and after 70 CE: that the relationship between the Jesus movement and Judaism remained a perennial concern for many followers of Jesus who continued to long for Israel's restoration."[23]

In fact, an entire edited volume has been recently devoted to reexamining the Paul of Acts in light of Judaism.[24] In it, Richard B. Hays examines the intertextual engagement with the Scriptures of Israel in Paul and in Acts and suggests there is an overlapping "profile of a certain set of theological themes and convictions shared by Paul's letters and the author of Acts."[25] Butticaz argues that Luke works hard "to *translate narratively* the major axes of Paul's argumentation in Romans 9–11," even if "the Pauline hope for the salvation of all Israel is reduced to a bare minimum in Luke."[26] The editors' conclusion to their volume also works well to summarize the broad trend examined here. They conclude by noting that the days of seeing Acts as marginalizing and denigrating Judaism as a religion of the past that has now been superseded by the universal gospel of Paul and Christianity are over. Instead, the book of Acts should be seen as a "promoter rather than archiver of Israel's history and heritage in the Messiah Jesus."[27]

Acts and Greco-Roman Religion and Culture

If there has been a growing trend in seeing a more positive relationship between Acts and Judaism, can the same be said for how Acts portrays and

---

22. Isaac W. Oliver, "The 'Historical Paul' and the Paul of Acts: Which Is More Jewish?," in *Paul the Jew: Rereading the Apostle as a Figure of Second Temple Judaism*, ed. Gabriele Boccaccini and Carlos A. Segovia (Minneapolis: Fortress, 2016), 51–80.

23. Oliver, "'Historical Paul' and the Paul of Acts," 71.

24. David P. Moessner, Daniel Marguerat, Mikeal C. Parsons, and Michael Wolter, eds., *Paul and the Heritage of Israel: Paul's Claim upon Israel's Legacy in Luke and Acts in the Light of the Pauline Letters* (London: Bloomsbury T&T Clark, 2012).

25. Richard B. Hays, "The Paulinism of Acts, Intertextually Reconsidered," in Moessner et al., *Paul and the Heritage of Israel*, 44.

26. Simon Butticaz, "'Has God Rejected His People?' (Romans 11.1): The Salvation of Israel in Acts; Narrative Claim of a Pauline Legacy," in Moessner et al., *Paul and the Heritage of Israel*, 163–64.

27. See the heading in the conclusion to Moessner et al., *Paul and the Heritage of Israel*, 321.

interacts with non-Jewish peoples? Is the relationship between the early Christian movement in Acts and Greco-Roman religion and culture one of direct conflict? Alternatively, does the Christian movement represent something truly new, distinctive, and innovative, or should it be seen as bearing many of the hallmarks of ancient Mediterranean religions?

C. Kavin Rowe has written a remarkably penetrating analysis of the encounter between the early Christian movement (as seen in Acts) and paganism.[28] Rowe's recent scholarship represents many scholars who see this relationship as one of critique and conflict and who emphasize early Christian distinctiveness.[29] The title of Rowe's book comes from the accusation made against the early Christians that they worship another king instead of Caesar and that they have turned the world upside down (Acts 17:6–7). There is truth in the accusation, for the protagonists of Acts do indeed give singular allegiance to Jesus the King, and yet they have no interest in a political coup against Rome but, rather, are aiming toward the creation of a new culture and way of life that is directly antithetical to Greco-Roman religion and culture.[30] The older view that Acts presents the Roman Empire in a positive light as means of political apologetic is probably no longer tenable. And many, in addition to Rowe, have noted that Acts does not portray the Roman imperial authorities positively.[31]

Rowe examines in historical and exegetical detail four scenes in Acts centering on Paul's collision with Greco-Roman religious beliefs and practice (Lystra in Acts 14; Philippi in Acts 16; Athens in Acts 17; and Ephesus in Acts 19). Rowe describes Christianity as a "new culture" that arises out of the "clash between the exclusivity of the Christian God and the wider mode

---

28. C. Kavin Rowe, *World Upside Down: Reading Acts in the Graeco-Roman Age* (Oxford: Oxford University Press, 2011). I will focus primarily on chaps. 2 and 4.

29. Generally supportive, then, of Rowe's overall thesis is Larry W. Hurtado, *Destroyer of the Gods: Early Christian Distinctiveness in the Roman World* (Waco: Baylor University Press, 2016). While Hurtado's book is not primarily about Acts, he emphasizes ways in which early Christianity was distinctive, different, and in conflict with other religious values characterizing Greco-Roman religion and culture.

30. Rowe's argument thereby has significant consequences for how one thinks of the relationship between Christianity in Acts and the Roman Empire. See here especially Matthew Skinner, "Who Speaks for (or against) Rome? Acts in Relation to Empire," in *Reading Acts in the Discourses of Masculinity and Politics*, ed. Eric D. Barreto, Matthew L. Skinner, and Steve Walton, LNTS 559 (London: Bloomsbury T&T Clark, 2017), 107–25. See also the argument that Christianity's discourse in Acts works within the discourses of imperial ideology and thereby reinscribes exploitation and domination within itself, an argument offered by Christian Petterson, *Acts of Empire: The Acts of the Apostles and Imperial Ideology*, Sino-Christian Studies Supplement Series 4 (Chung Li, Taiwan: Chung Yuan Christian University Press, 2012).

31. In addition to Rowe, *World Upside Down*, chap. 3, see Kazuhiko Yamazaki-Ransom, *The Roman Empire in Luke's Narrative*, LNTS 404 (London: T&T Clark, 2010).

of pagan religiousness."³² Acts intends to portray the deep incompatibility and incommensurability between the gospel of Jesus Christ and the common ways of pagan life.³³ Thus whenever Paul and the gospel go into non-Jewish territory, the result is conflict and disruption, for the gospel profoundly destabilizes pagan religion. Rowe summarizes: the complete incommensurability between Christianity and paganism "rests ultimately in the theological affirmation of the break between God and the cosmos. For to affirm that God has 'created heaven and earth' is, in Luke's narrative, simultaneously to name the entire complex of religiousness as idolatry and, thus, to assign to such religiousness the character of ignorance. Pagan religion . . . does not know God."³⁴

As a result, Rowe argues forcefully that one cannot engage in "translation" between paganism and Christianity, for they are two competing grammars.³⁵ In particular, Rowe, in an important article, argues that readings of Acts 17 that "argue for a deep theological *Anknüpfungspunkt* between pagan philosophical thinking and Paul's proclamation" are entirely wrong, *even though*, as he acknowledges, this "long history of reading Acts 17 . . . constitutes a relatively stable and coherent hermeneutical tradition."³⁶ Again, Rowe emphasizes the misguided history of *the* interpretation of Acts 17:22–31: "Given the power and longevity of this way of thinking, it is really no less remarkable that this is not what Acts 17 actually argues." By "this way of thinking" Rowe refers to the view that Paul's sermon is "a paean of the Greek intellectual or spiritual achievement."³⁷ Paul's sermon is, rather, "the presentation of an alternative pattern of life."³⁸ Thus Paul's message ("Christianity") and Stoicism are entirely incongruent and even incommensurable; instead, the speech provides evidence for "the conflict and confrontation that occurs when irreducibly particular patterns of life offer irreducibly different ways of being."³⁹ Rowe has expanded this argument with a full-length monograph comparing early Christianity (including

---

32. Rowe, *World Upside Down*, 18.

33. See here also the work of Christoph W. Stenschke, *Luke's Portrait of Gentiles prior to Their Coming to Faith*, WUNT 2/108 (Tübingen: Mohr Siebeck, 1999). Stenschke argues that Luke consistently critiques the religiosity of gentiles, their bondage to sin, and their spiritual ignorance and failure.

34. Rowe, *World Upside Down*, 50.

35. I have engaged Rowe on this point, with both some level of agreement and critique, in a forthcoming essay: Joshua W. Jipp, "Does Paul Translate the Gospel in Acts 17:22–31? A Critical Engagement with C. Kavin Rowe's *One True Life*," *PRS* 45, no. 4 (2018): 361–76.

36. C. Kavin Rowe, "The Grammar of Life: The Areopagus Speech and Pagan Tradition," *NTS* 57, no. 1 (2011): 34.

37. For both quotes, see Rowe, "Grammar of Life," 35.

38. Rowe, "Grammar of Life," 35.

39. Rowe, "Grammar of Life," 49–50.

Luke-Acts) and Stoicism, and he argues that at every point of significance Stoicism and Christianity are rival traditions that offer visions of life that are incompatible and *incommensurable*.[40] One cannot, then, be both a Stoic and a Christian, for these traditions require two entirely different kinds of lives, and, as Rowe has said, we only have a single life to live. Since Christianity and Stoicism are both *traditions*, in the thick sense of the term, *comparison can only be carried out*, for Rowe, as "an exploration in the conflict of traditions."[41]

Others, however, have seen the relationship between the early Christian movement in Acts and Greco-Roman religion and culture as something a bit less adversarial. For example, though I am largely in agreement with Rowe's interpretation of Paul's Areopagus speech, I have argued that the sermon emphasizes *both* the conflict between Paul's gospel and gentile religion *and* the exaltation of "the Christian movement as comprising the best features of Greco-Roman philosophical sensibilities and therefore as a superior philosophy."[42] Rowe argues that something like "translation" is impossible, but he has not successfully accounted for the ways in which Paul's speech draws on some of the best features of Hellenistic philosophy, especially Stoic traditions, as a means of exalting the Christian movement as a legitimate, even superior philosophy. The obvious overlap between Paul's speech and Stoic philosophy, then, is not accidental or incidental to Paul's sermon, and all scholars recognize that the topics of monotheism, the critique of temples and sacrifices, the deity's providential arrangement of the seasons, and the unity of humankind resonate quite clearly with Stoic philosophy. Paul works within the cultural and religious logic of Stoicism and presents the Hellenistic philosophers as capable of rightly responding to Paul's God even out of their own philosophical commitments.

Hans-Josef Klauck has written a very helpful account of paganism in the Acts of the Apostles, and he suggests that Luke simultaneously shows overlap and distancing tactics when describing his protagonists. For example, Luke is careful to show that the powerful deeds of the apostles are not magic but are the result of the superior power of the singular God at work within them and that the apostles "reject any cult of persons."[43] Luke's audience, according to Klauck, is engaged in a "difficult balancing act which is continually

---

40. C. Kavin Rowe, *One True Life: The Stoics and Early Christians as Rival Traditions* (New Haven: Yale University Press, 2016).

41. Rowe, *One True Life*, 205.

42. Joshua W. Jipp, "Paul's Areopagus Speech of Acts 17:16–34 as *Both* Critique *and* Propaganda," *JBL* 131 (2012): 568.

43. Hans-Josef Klauck, *Magic and Paganism in Early Christianity: The World of the Acts of the Apostles*, trans. Brian McNeil (Edinburgh: T&T Clark, 2000), 120.

demanded between seeking contact and offering contradiction, between the search for common elements and the endeavor to identify boundaries, i.e., between inculturation and evangelization."[44]

If this is accurate, then we can simultaneously embrace Rowe's emphasis on critique, conflict, and cultural destabilization while also recognizing that Luke draws on a plethora of Greco-Roman cultural scripts in his articulation of the gospel.[45] In addition to the well-known example of Paul's appropriation of Stoic philosophy in his proclamation in Athens (Acts 17:16–34),[46] an abundance of scholarship has shown Luke's adaptation of the gospel to Greco-Roman cultural patterns and traditions. I think, for example, of Luke's literary prefaces and their similarities to Hellenistic historiography (Luke 1:1–4; Acts 1:1–2),[47] the table of nations in Acts 2:5–11 as mimicking Rome's rule over the known world,[48] the transformation of the traditions of Jesus's crucifixion into a tradition of noble death (Luke 23; cf. Acts 4:27–30; 5:29–31),[49] the way Luke admirably praises the early Christians for *philanthrōpia* and the successful resolution of conflict,[50] the shaping of Jesus's resurrection appearance in the literary guise of a divine visitation (Luke 24:13–35; cf. Acts 28:1–10),[51] the use of philosophical friendship language to exalt the Jerusalem church's common life (Acts 2:41–47; 4:32–35),[52] God's validation of the Christian movement as exemplified in the apostle's prison escapes (5:19–20; 12:1–17; 16:25–34),[53] the depiction of the apostles as engaging in powerful declamations that discuss

---

44. Klauck, *Magic and Paganism in Early Christianity*, 121.

45. See here the important work of Luke Timothy Johnson, *Among the Gentiles: Greco-Roman Religion and Christianity*, AYBRL (New Haven: Yale University Press, 2009), which draws attention to some of the deep similarities between ancient pagans and Christians in terms of religious impulses, convictions, and practices. I am drawing and adapting briefly here from my "Does Paul Translate the Gospel in Acts 17:22–31?"

46. On Acts 17:22–31 as best explained by "the nexus of traditions crystallized around the figure of Epimenides in the second century C.E.," see Clare K. Rothschild, *Paul in Athens: The Popular Religious Context of Acts 17*, WUNT 341 (Tübingen: Mohr Siebeck, 2014).

47. See here the important work of David Paul Moessner, *Luke the Historian of Israel's Legacy, Theologian of Israel's 'Christ': A New Reading of the 'Gospel Acts' of Luke*, BZNW 182 (Berlin: de Gruyter, 2016).

48. Gary Gilbert, "The List of Nations in Acts 2: Roman Propaganda and the Roman Response," *JBL* 121 (2002): 497–529.

49. Greg Sterling, "*Mors Philosophi*: The Death of Jesus in Luke," *HTR* 94 (2001): 383–402.

50. Todd Penner, *In Praise of Christian Origins: Stephen and the Hellenists in Lukan Apologetic Historiography* (London: T&T Clark, 2004).

51. Joshua W. Jipp, *Divine Visitations and Hospitality to Strangers in Luke-Acts: An Interpretation of the Malta Episode in Acts 28:1–10*, NovTSup 153 (Leiden: Brill, 2012). See also Rick Strelan, "Recognizing the Gods (Acts 14.8–10)," *NTS* 46 (2000): 488–503.

52. Gregory E. Sterling, "'Athletes of Virtue': An Analysis of the Summaries in Acts (2:41–47; 4:32–35; 5:12–16)," *JBL* 113 (1994): 679–96.

53. John B. Weaver, *Plots of Epiphany: Prison-Escape in Acts of the Apostles*, BZNW 131 (Berlin: de Gruyter, 2004).

topics related to virtue, piety, and ethnicity,[54] Paul's sea voyage that draws on other Greco-Roman accounts of sea journeys and thereby makes the claim that the Mediterranean Sea is the cultural territory of the apostles (27:1–44),[55] and the depiction of the Christian movement's power and success as validated through victorious healings and exorcisms in turf wars against its competitors (8:14–25; 13:5–12; 19:11–20; 28:3–6).[56] One strand in recent scholarship on Acts, then, emphasizes the early Christian movement's intense conflict with and critique of Greco-Roman religiosity, while others have made abundant contributions emphasizing that the early Christian discourse in Acts draws on Greco-Roman religious scripts, themes, and philosophy in such a way as to both critique Greco-Roman religion and show cultural convergences between it and Christianity.

Acts, Masculinity, and Ethnic Reasoning

While traditional questions in scholarship on Acts such as "Acts and Judaism" and "Acts and the Greco-Roman world" show no signs of abating, newer methods and questions related to how Acts constructs and articulates social identities represent a significant recent trend. While feminist studies on Acts are by no means new,[57] more recent analysis has turned to the gendered nature of Acts and how it constructs male identity and masculinity.[58] One cannot, of course, underestimate the influence of Michel Foucault's three-volume *The History of Sexuality* and his argument that representations of sexuality and gender are deeply related to power, status, and systems of control.[59] Thus, analysis of masculinity is often coupled with a move toward analyzing

---

54. See here Laura S. Nasrallah, *Christian Responses to Roman Art and Architecture: The Second Century Church amid the Spaces of Empire* (Cambridge: Cambridge University Press, 2010), 87–118; Todd Penner, "Civilizing Discourse: Acts, Declamation, and the Rhetoric of the Polis," in *Contextualizing Acts: Lukan Narrative and Greco-Roman Discourse*, ed. Todd Penner and Caroline Vander Stichele, SBLSymS 20 (Atlanta: SBL Press, 2003), 65–104.

55. Loveday Alexander, "'In Journeyings Often': Voyaging in the Acts of the Apostles and in Greek Romance," in *Acts in Its Ancient Literary Context: A Classicist Looks at the Acts of the Apostles*, LNTS 298 (London: T&T Clark, 2005), 69–96.

56. See Lee M. Jefferson, *Christ the Miracle Worker in Early Christian Art* (Minneapolis: Fortress, 2014).

57. See, for example, Margaret Aymer, "Acts of the Apostles," in *Women's Bible Commentary*, ed. Carol A. Newsom, Sharon H. Ringe, and Jacqueline E. Lapsley, 3rd ed. (Louisville: Westminster John Knox, 2012), 536–46; Turid Karlsen Seim, *The Double Message: Patterns of Gender in Luke-Acts* (Nashville: Abingdon, 1994).

58. See the methodological comments of Caroline Vander Stichele, "Gender and Genre: Acts in/of Interpretation," in Penner and Vander Stichele, *Contextualizing Acts*, 311–29.

59. Michel Foucault, *The History of Sexuality*, 3 vols., trans. R. Hurley (New York: Pantheon, 1978–88). Also important here is Judith Butler, *Gender Trouble: Feminism and the Subversion of Identity* (New York: Routledge, 1990).

how gender is situated more broadly within Acts' ideological and rhetorical agenda.[60] For example, Caroline Vander Stichele and Todd Penner note that while women play an important role in Acts, "Luke chooses to focus on public male characters [and] it is these men who embody all the virtues of the Christian narrative Luke is creating, and the women are used to enhance that image whenever appropriate." Thus women need to be analyzed within Luke's broader ideological and sociopolitical understandings of masculinity. For example, the role that women play in dispensing hospitality in Acts does point to their formative role in early Christianity, but given Luke's identity as an "elite male" who is indebted to "an *imperial poetics*," these women are "hospitable, but mostly marginal participants."[61]

The majority of Lukan scholarship on masculinity, in fact, is broadly sympathetic to a similar view—namely, that Luke portrays his characters as embodying the Roman virtues of masculinity, primarily those of self-mastery and powerful declamations.[62] Colleen Conway's introductory paragraph to her chapter on masculinity in Luke-Acts states this clearly: "With Luke-Acts, we enter a narrative world that is completely at home within the masculine power structures of the Roman Empire. Almost anywhere we turn in this world, we find those elements that were necessary for the construction of the ideal man in the Roman world. The heroes that we encounter in this world—Jesus, Stephen, Peter, Paul—are portrayed as educated, articulate, reasonable, self-controlled, pious men, fully capable of holding their own in the upper echelons of the masculine world of the Roman Empire."[63]

Two recent studies, however, challenge the largely dominant view that Acts mimics imperial, elite masculine values in its depiction of its primary characters. Bonnie J. Flessen explores how Acts characterizes Cornelius positively, as one who is submissive, pious, and a giver of alms.[64] But Cornelius

---

60. See here Christina Petterson, "The Language of Gender in Acts," in Barreto, Skinner, and Walton, *Reading Acts in the Discourses of Masculinity and Politics*, 3–16.

61. See throughout Caroline Vander Stichele and Todd Penner, "'All the World's a Stage': The Rhetoric of Gender in Acts," in *Luke and His Readers: Festschrift A. Denaux*, ed. R. Bieringer, G. van Belle, and J. Verheyden (Leuven: Leuven University Press, 2005), 373–96.

62. Mary Rose D'Angelo, "The ANHR Question in Luke-Acts: Imperial Masculinity and the Deployment of Women in the Early Second Century," in *A Feminist Companion to Luke*, ed. Amy-Jill Levine (London: Sheffield Academic, 2002), 44–69. It has also been argued that Stephen is an embodiment of the Roman ideal of masculine self-mastery. See, for example, Abraham Smith, "'Full of Spirit and Wisdom': Luke's Portrait of Stephen (Acts 6:1–8:1a) as a Man of Self-Mastery," in *Asceticism and the New Testament*, ed. L. E. Vaage and Vincent L. Wimbush (New York: Routledge, 1999), 97–114.

63. Colleen M. Conway, *Behold the Man: Jesus and Greco-Roman Masculinity* (New York: Oxford University Press, 2008), 127.

64. Bonnie J. Flessen, *An Exemplary Man: Cornelius and Characterization in Acts 10* (Eugene, OR: Pickwick, 2011).

is a *Roman centurion* who is submissive to *Israel's God* and to Peter, a Judean. As a military leader, Cornelius does not exert authority over or brutally subjugate his Judean subjects. In fact, he and the other male protagonists in Acts are not powerful, manly men, for they are not exemplars of self-mastery but are controlled and led throughout by the Holy Spirit. Thus, for Flessen, the vision of masculinity propagated by Acts is one that disrupts and, in some ways, even subverts Roman imperial conceptions of manly men. While not a study of masculinity, Laurie Brink's study of the characterization of centurions in Luke-Acts supplements Flessen's argument nicely. Brink argues that Luke both employs and transforms recognizable stereotypes of Roman soldiers. Like Flessen, Brink notes that throughout Luke-Acts one finds Roman centurions portrayed as embodying faith, love, piety and fear of God, and humane kindness.[65]

Brittany Wilson's *Unmanly Men* argues against the dominant trend that Luke-Acts mimics and reproduces elite, Roman masculine values. She argues, instead, that God's act in Jesus "ultimately transforms prevalent ways of viewing the world, *including conceptions of masculinity.*"[66] Wilson examines Luke's characterizations of Zechariah, Jesus, Paul, and the Ethiopian Eunuch to demonstrate that they "do not easily align with elite masculine categories, for Luke claims that God has upended many preconceived categories by dying on a cross."[67] To give one example, Wilson notes that Luke repeatedly refers to the man in Acts 8:26–40 as a "eunuch" (five references).[68] Eunuchs were considered to be effeminate, unmanly men and sometimes even sexual monstrosities since they disrupted a male-female binary. Yet even though this character transgresses gender norms, Luke portrays him as a model convert: he seeks to worship the Judean God in Jerusalem, is reading Isaiah 53, seeks guidance from Philip, and receives Christian baptism. Luke's version of Christianity, then, is not deeply wed to procreative power and does not conform to elite Roman masculine norms.

The past twenty years has also seen in a rise in studies examining the ethnic reasoning at work in Acts. By ethnic reasoning, I refer to what Denise Kimber Buell has called "culturally available understandings of human difference, which we can analyze in terms of our modern concepts of 'ethnicity,' 'race,' and 'religion.'"[69] I have already mentioned the role of the Ethiopian eunuch

---

65. Laurie Brink, *Soldiers in Luke-Acts: Engaging, Contradicting, and Transcending Stereotypes*, WUNT 2/362 (Tübingen: Mohr Siebeck, 2014).
66. Brittany E. Wilson, *Unmanly Men: Refigurations of Masculinity in Luke-Acts* (New York: Oxford University Press, 2015), 4.
67. Wilson, *Unmanly Men*, 9.
68. Wilson, *Unmanly Men*, 113–49.
69. Denise Kimber Buell, *Why This New Race? Ethnic Reasoning in Early Christianity* (New York: Columbia University Press, 2005), 2.

with respect to masculinity, but it is no surprise that those studying ethnic reasoning in Acts also highlight the *Ethiopian* eunuch as a black individual. Gay Byron, for example, has noted the variety of negative stereotypes of blackness, associated with Egyptians and Ethiopians, in ancient literature; and while early Christianity reproduced some problematic discursive ethnic readings, Acts' story of the Ethiopian eunuch establishes him "as a model of virtue and employs subtle clues within the story to demonstrate to [Luke's] audience that Christianity can extend to every nation—*even* Ethiopia."[70]

One of the most innovative contributions here comes from Eric Barreto's examination of ethnic reasoning in Acts 16.[71] Barreto's study is marked by an impressive methodological investigation of ethnicity that is attuned both to the ancient world and to contemporary studies of race and ethnicity. He argues that one's definition of these social concepts needs to take into account both the flexible nature of ethnicity and group members' perception that ethnicity is fixed and immutable. Barreto tackles the difficult episode of Paul's circumcision of Timothy in Acts 16:1–5 and notes that Timothy is portrayed as neither Greek nor Jewish but is instead in between. This fits with Luke's broader agenda, where he neither eliminates ethnicity nor seeks to create a new one (e.g., a "third race"); instead, Luke portrays the early Christian movement as a flexible, hybrid movement that incorporates all ethnicities and races. In Barreto's words, "Ethnic difference ultimately was not an obstacle but an opportunity, a resource in theological reflection on the expansion of the followers of Jesus" in the different cities and regions in the Mediterranean.[72] Laura S. Nasrallah also argues that the author of Acts engages in ethnic reasoning by portraying the distinct ethnic Christian communities as "unified by common (divine) origins, kinship, and worship."[73] The author of Acts does this in a way that is remarkably similar to Hadrian's Panhellenion. Thereby, given that ancient conceptions of ethnicity are deeply connected to one's civic identity, Acts' author "uses the story of Paul travelling between cities in order to provide a foundation myth of Christianity."[74]

Willie James Jennings's *The Christian Imagination: Theology and the Origins of Race* argues that Christianity has a diseased and racist social imagination that stems from its underestimation of God's election of Israel. Christianity's "scandal of particularity" has been traded for a universalizing

---

70. Gay L. Byron, *Symbolic Blackness and Ethnic Difference in Early Christian Literature* (New York: Routledge, 2002), 115.
71. Eric D. Barreto, *Ethnic Negotiations: The Function of Race and Ethnicity in Acts 16*, WUNT 2/276 (Tübingen: Mohr Siebeck, 2010).
72. Barreto, *Ethnic Negotiations*, 184.
73. Nasrallah, *Christian Responses to Roman Art and Architecture*, 89.
74. Nasrallah, *Christian Responses to Roman Art and Architecture*, 90.

discourse that lacks "patterns of communion" whereby it can understand and enter into a relationship with "the cultural inner logics of peoples."[75] Jennings has also written a noteworthy theological commentary on Acts that extends many of his theological reflections on race and ethnicity. Jennings warns against reading Acts 1 as a support for a nationalist vision "that interprets peoples on a plain of group sameness, each seeking self-determination, control of their land and resources, and desiring full membership and participation in the global economy."[76] Acts tells a story of revolution whereby Jewish identity is not destroyed, and yet the "space of Israel is expanding by the Spirit" through the inclusion of gentiles whose conversion to the God of Israel means that "they are on their way to communion with Jews while remaining Gentiles. This is the most terrifying aspect of interruption: love."[77] A short quote cannot do justice to Jennings's reading of Acts, for his reading has significant implications for understanding the theological ramifications of Acts' vision for race and ethnicity, the significance of God's election of Israel, and valuing the cultural logics of others.[78] I have found Jennings's *The Christian Imagination* to hold great promise for thinking about race and ethnicity alongside Acts and have argued that Acts portrays a frequent overturning and rejection of negative ethnic stereotyping and employs the sociocultural practice of "ritualized friendship" as a means of describing how the early Christians were able to conceptualize becoming part of one family and yet retaining their ethnic identities.

Acts and the Divine

One final trend is a resurgence in works devoted to the portrayal of God, the continued acts of the risen and enthroned Christ, and the theological texture and implications of Acts. I have argued, for example, that Acts is from beginning to end a narrative construal of God and God's activity.[79] Characters respond to and reject divine activity, Israel's Scriptures are evoked to give witness to God's acts, the Spirit enables characters to prophesy regarding God's plan, characters respond with praise when God's activity is discerned, and

---

75. Willie James Jennings, *The Christian Imagination: Theology and the Origins of Race* (New Haven: Yale University Press, 2010), 154.
76. Willie James Jennings, *Acts* (Louisville: Westminster John Knox, 2017), 21.
77. Jennings, *Acts*, 8.
78. See Joshua W. Jipp, "Hospitable Barbarians: Luke's Ethnic Reasoning in Acts 28:1–10," *JTS* 68 (2017): 23–45.
79. Portions of this section have been reproduced and revised from Joshua W. Jipp, "The Beginnings of a Theology of Luke-Acts: Divine Activity and Human Response," *JTI* 8 (2014): 23–43.

God's plan is expressed through language such as "the will/purpose of God" and other words expressing divine necessity. Despite the primacy of God as the subject matter of Acts, Daniel Marguerat has shown that the narrator rarely *directly* refers to God doing something, and never does God appear directly and obviously.[80] Rather, identifying, naming, and interpreting God's work in the world is usually left to the characters, who are responsible to discern God's activity through various media; thus a variety of studies have been devoted to examining *how* characters discern the work of God—for example, through dreams, visions, prophecies, and the interpretation of Scripture.[81] Scott Shauf has written an important work comparing the role of the divine in Acts with contemporary works of historiography and shows the similarities and differences between Acts and other works of Jewish historiography in regard to God's work. He notes that one finds in Acts a remarkable emphasis on God's Spirit and "an intensity of divine presence and action unparalleled in extant ancient historiography, and unparalleled in its intense focus on such a small group of people."[82]

Perhaps the most significant way in which Acts portrays God acting in the world is through the resurrected and enthroned Messiah. One of the most helpful studies here is Matthew Sleeman's examination of "the earthly implications of an absent-but-active ascending Christ" who orders both geographical and narrative space in the book of Acts.[83] Much could be said about Matthew Sleeman's study, but most important is the way in which he has shown how Christ's ascension and heavenly location exert a central influence on Acts beyond the traditional ascension texts. A variety of important studies on Acts have recently appeared that address the importance of the Messiah's resurrection, ascension, and enthronement.[84]

---

80. Daniel Marguerat, *The First Christian Historian: Writing the "Acts of the Apostles,"* trans. Ken McKinney, Gregory J. Laughery, and Richard Bauckham, SNTSMS 121 (Cambridge: Cambridge University Press, 2002), 86–92.

81. See, for example, John B. F. Miller, *Convinced That God Had Called Us: Dreams, Visions, and the Perception of God's Will in the Book of Acts*, BIS (Leiden: Brill, 2006); Ling Cheng, *The Characterisation of God in Acts: The Indirect Portrayal of an Invisible Character*, Paternoster Biblical Monographs (Milton Keynes, UK: Paternoster, 2011); Michael A. Salmeier, *Restoring the Kingdom: The Role of God as the "Ordainer of Times and Seasons" in the Acts of the Apostles*, Princeton Theological Monographs (Eugene, OR: Pickwick, 2011).

82. Scott Shauf, *The Divine in Acts and in Ancient Historiography* (Minneapolis: Fortress, 2015), 264.

83. Matthew Sleeman, *Geography and the Ascension Narrative in Acts*, SNTSMS 146 (Cambridge: Cambridge University Press, 2009), 49.

84. For example, Thompson, *Acts of the Risen Lord Jesus*; Lidija Novakovic, *Raised from the Dead according to Scripture: The Role of Israel's Scripture in the Early Christian Interpretations of Jesus' Resurrection*, Jewish and Christian Texts in Contexts and Related Studies Series (London: Bloomsbury T&T Clark, 2012), 197–215; David K. Bryan and David W. Pao, eds., *Ascent into Heaven in Luke-Acts: New Explorations of Luke's Narrative Hinge* (Minneapolis: Fortress, 2016).

Though intended for a more accessible audience, Matthew Skinner's *Intrusive God, Disruptive Gospel* presents a thorough reading of Acts that is deeply attentive to Acts' portrait of God and divine activity, activity that is often surprising, confusing, and disruptive. Skinner notes that the surprising and disruptive "theological vision of Acts" has the power to "enliven the expectations we have about God and how God might connect to our lives [thereby working to make us] more creative, more imaginative, and more perceptive, and even sometimes more suspicious in our outlook on where and how we might look for or encounter God."[85] Luke Timothy Johnson's *Prophetic Jesus, Prophetic Church* also sets forth a literary examination of Luke-Acts that offers a theologically engaged call to the church to take Luke-Acts seriously as a means of recovering its prophetic vision. Both Jesus and the apostles, in Johnson's view, are prophetic characters who challenge Acts' audience to continue the prophetic vision of Luke-Acts in "being led by the spirit, sharing possessions, engaging in an itinerant mission, exercising servant leadership, [and] bearing powerful witness before religious and state authorities."[86]

Reflections

Ending my discussion of Acts here is in some ways arbitrary, since many other significant works of research could be discussed. I have, however, tried to give a substantive overview of what I find to be some of the most interesting and important recent works on Acts. I conclude with two reflections. First, it is no surprise that new research on Acts has been stimulated by means of new questions and methods. For example, scholarship on gender and masculinity in Acts is, in part, the result of the rise of new methods and questions that have centered on how discourse and ideology are related to power and control. Luke's ethnic reasoning has taken an important role in studies on Acts no doubt due to concerns related to Christian supersessionism and questions pertaining to the racialized nature of biblical interpretations. I have nothing profound to say here except that this continues to remind us that there is an inextricable relationship between all our readings or exegesis of Acts and the hermeneutical frameworks we bring to or use in our readings. Thus evaluations of our interpretations of Acts should not be divorced from our evaluations of the methods we use.

85. Matthew L. Skinner, *Intrusive God, Disruptive Gospel: Encountering the Divine in the Book of Acts* (Grand Rapids: Brazos, 2015), xiii–xiv.
86. Luke Timothy Johnson, *Prophetic Jesus, Prophetic Church: The Challenge of Luke-Acts to Contemporary Christians* (Grand Rapids: Eerdmans, 2011), 5.

Second, discerning purposes and agendas in a narrative text like Acts is no simple task and is easily susceptible to reductionism. Grasping at one strand of Acts may provide some significant insight into the purposes of Acts, but it is all too easy to ignore evidence that does not easily fit one's construal. For example, recent studies of Acts have tended to emphasize a positive depiction of Judaism in Acts. But can these construals of Acts also make good sense of the accusations brought against Stephen (6:11–15) and Paul (21:15–21)? Was there something culturally and religiously disruptive about the apostles that led to charges they were apostate? Similarly, can one simultaneously account for ways in which Luke's male characters conform to elite Roman ideals *and* on occasions disrupt them? Can one provide a reading of Acts that demonstrates how the early Christians destabilize and critique pagan religiosity while still recognizing Luke's abundant positive use of pagan cultural and religious scripts to communicate the gospel? An ability to hold together and do justice to aspects of Acts that may seem contradictory may act as a boon for further robust and nonreductionist readings of Acts.

18

Paul and Romans

Scot McKnight

Introduction

To read Romans is to read Paul, and that means Pauline mission and theology—both abstract and lived—are Romans, and Romans is those and even more. To read Romans is also to read the history of Christian, especially Protestant, theology. One cannot think of Augustine, Luther, Calvin, Tyndale, Wesley, Edwards, or Barth without thinking of Romans, and every major NT theologian today writes (in effect) a theology of Paul. That is, beginning with Barth's NT scholar counterpart, Rudolf Bultmann, we cannot think of any of the following scholars without thinking of Romans: Ernst Käsemann, W. D. Davies, C. E. B. Cranfield, E. P. Sanders, J. Christiaan Beker, James D. G. Dunn, Douglas J. Moo, Peter Stuhlmacher, N. T. Wright, J. Louis Martyn, Leander E. Keck, Robert Jewett, Douglas A. Campbell, John M. G. Barclay, Richard N. Longenecker, and Beverly Roberts Gaventa. And that's just the beginning of a patchy list! Dunn, in his magisterial theology of Paul, openly states that the place to begin this dialogue is Romans.[1] As he puts it, "In short, Romans is still far removed from a dogmatic or systematic treatise on theology, but it nevertheless is the most sustained and reflective statement of Paul's own theology by Paul himself."[2]

---

1. James D. G. Dunn, *The Theology of Paul the Apostle* (Grand Rapids: Eerdmans, 1998), 19–26; hereafter *TPA*.
2. Dunn, *TPA*, 25.

To read Romans is to read Pauline theology, a discipline that transcends Romans but cannot get by without the letter as the structural core. It will be to our advantage then to sort out some major presentations of Paul in the current landscape, though Michael J. Gorman's chapter in this volume provides a much more complete sketch.[3] I have outlined some of the major themes because of the role they will play in my sketch of Romans scholarship. Following that we will sample—one can do no more than that with the pile of books and essays on Romans on offer—representative studies on Romans. The literature on Romans boggles the mind, as the letter continues to fascinate professors, pastors, philosophers, and politicians.[4] A recent set of books expanded scholarship as it sought the influence of Romans in history and culture.[5]

Paul after E. P. Sanders

A decisive moment, if not the decisive moment, in modern readings of Romans came in 1977. E. P. Sanders's famous study of Paul in the context of Palestinian Judaism and over against the traditional Lutheran (and somewhat Reformed) reading of Romans ignited a firestorm of studies about Paul, polemically challenged older studies of Paul, and created the opportunity for rereading Romans. James D. G. Dunn, in a variety of publications, gave the post-Sanders reading of Paul the name "new perspective," which rhetorically entailed an

---

3. See chap. 10 in this volume.

4. For recent studies of the history of interpretation of Romans, see Mark Reasoner, *Romans in Full Circle: A History of Interpretation* (Louisville: Westminster John Knox, 2005); Jeffrey P. Greenman and Timothy Larsen, eds., *Reading Romans through the Centuries: From the Early Church to Karl Barth* (Grand Rapids: Brazos, 2005); Magnus Zetterholm, *Approaches to Paul: A Student's Guide to Recent Scholarship* (Minneapolis: Fortress, 2009); Benjamin L. White, *Remembering Paul: Ancient and Modern Contests over the Image of the Apostle* (New York: Oxford University Press, 2014); Patrick Gray, *Paul as a Problem in History and Culture: The Apostle and His Critics through the Centuries* (Grand Rapids: Baker Academic, 2016).

5. The series title is Romans through History and Culture, and the volumes include K. K. Yeo, ed., *Navigating Romans through Cultures: Challenging Readings by Charting a New Course* (New York: T&T Clark, 2004); Kathy L. Gaca and L. L. Welborn, eds., *Early Patristic Readings of Romans* (New York: T&T Clark, 2006); Daniel Patte and Vasile Mihoc, eds., *Greek Patristic and Eastern Orthodox Interpretations of Romans* (London: Bloomsbury T&T Clark, 2013); Daniel Patte and Eugene TeSelle, eds., *Engaging Augustine on Romans: Self, Context, and Theology in Interpretation* (Harrisburg, PA: Trinity Press International, 2003); William S. Campbell, Peter S. Hawkins, and Brenda Deen Schildgen, eds., *Medieval Readings of Romans* (New York: T&T Clark, 2007); Kathy Ehrensperger and R. Ward Holder, eds., *Reformation Readings of Romans* (London: T&T Clark, 2008); David Odell-Scott, ed., *Reading Romans with Contemporary Philosophers and Theologians* (New York: T&T Clark, 2007); Cristina Grenholm and Daniel Patte, eds., *Reading Israel in Romans: Legitimacy and Plausibility of Divergent Interpretations* (Harrisburg, PA: Trinity Press International, 2000); Patte and Grenholm, eds., *Modern Interpretations of Romans: Tracking Their Hermeneutical/Theological Trajectory* (London: Bloomsbury T&T Clark, 2013).

"old" perspective and led to Dunn's magisterial commentary on Romans.[6] Sanders did not spawn only the "new" perspective but also the apocalyptic, the participationist, and the Paul-within-Judaism approaches, and he had his impact on all mediating and even political approaches to Paul. Since Gorman's essay in this volume maps this discussion, a brief word on a few of the recent approaches is needed to set up what is to be said about Romans scholarship.

The "old," or perhaps more sensitively the "Reformation," perspective emerges out of an Augustinian anthropology (humans are created good but are corrupted and even depraved through Adam's sin and are incapable of pleasing God) that forms into a soteriological reading of Paul (divine grace, not works; salvation by faith, not by works; redemption accomplished by Christ; and notions like double imputation—our sin to Christ, Christ's righteousness to believers), and much of that reading of Paul is based on Romans with some Galatians. Inherent to this view is a correlation: humans infected by such a sin nature seek to establish themselves before God on the basis of their works. This is where Sanders entered the discussion. This view of humanity—works driven—emerged from a reading of Judaism that was not accurate, and he sought to rectify Judaism and then reread Paul with a new view of Judaism. Judaism was now defined not as a works-righteousness religion but as a grace-based religion, which he named "covenantal nomism."[7] Which is to say, one did not obey the law (nomism) to *enter* the covenant (obedience earning salvation) but instead, on the basis of grace and God's covenantal favor (Gen. 12; 15), one obeyed the Torah in order to *maintain* one's covenant standing.[8] Put differently, Sanders redefined what the "old" perspective was actually doing, and it perhaps needs to be emphasized that what he says is not trivial information about history but what gives rise to many treatments of soteriology in the Protestant tradition:[9]

> The principal element is the theory that works *earn* salvation; that one's fate is determined by *weighing* fulfillments against transgressions. Maintaining this view necessarily involves *denying* or getting around in some other way *the grace of God in the election.* . . . A third aspect of Weber's view, which is also tied

---

6. James D. G. Dunn, *Romans*, 2 vols., WBC 38 (Waco: Thomas Nelson, 1988); Dunn, *The New Perspective on Paul*, rev. ed. (Grand Rapids: Eerdmans, 2008).

7. Sanders has responded to his critics: see E. P. Sanders, *Comparing Judaism and Christianity: Common Judaism, Paul, and the Inner and the Outer in Ancient Religion* (Minneapolis: Fortress, 2016), 51–83. See also Sanders, *Judaism: Practice and Belief, 63 BCE–66 CE* (Minneapolis: Fortress, 2016), 430–51.

8. John Barclay presses Sanders's view of grace beyond its priority: see John M. G. Barclay, *Paul and the Gift* (Grand Rapids: Eerdmans, 2015), 151–58.

9. One has to ask aloud if the "covenant of works" that shapes much Reformed theology could ever have come into articulation had its view of Judaism not been shaped by works righteousness.

to the theory of salvation by works, is that of establishment of merit and the possibility of a *transfer of merit* at the final judgment. The fourth element has to do with the attitude supposedly reflected in Rabbinic literature: *uncertainty of salvation* mixed with the self-righteous feeling of accomplishment. This too depends on the view that a man is saved by works. He will either be uncertain that he has done enough or proud of having been so righteous. Besides these main elements of Weber's soteriology, his view that God was *inaccessible* has also been maintained to the present day.[10]

This is how Sanders defines what is now called the "old" perspective, and Sanders boldly declares that he is out "to destroy the view of Rabbinic Judaism which is still prevalent in much, perhaps most, New Testament scholarship."[11] Sanders named names, including the Reformers.[12] The fundamental implication of Sanders's 1977 work was that scholars could no longer assume the traditional theory that Judaism was pockmarked by works righteousness and that therefore Christianity's fundamental difference was that it was a religion of grace.[13]

The "new" perspective—the term used today for Dunn and N. T. Wright especially—cannot be summarized in a way that maps neatly onto either Dunn or Wright[14] because they differ with each other in important ways.[15] I offer the following summary:

1. The stage of Pauline theology is Israel's story and the one true God's work in Israel to bless the entire created order, and this stage differs from, even if it shares some commonalities with, the Augustinian anthropology and soteriological readings of the "old" perspective.

---

10. E. P. Sanders, *Paul and Palestinian Judaism: A Comparison of Patterns of Religion*, Reprint ed. (Philadelphia: Fortress, 2017), 54.

11. Sanders, *Paul and Palestinian Judaism*, xii.

12. Now rescuing the Reformers from stereotypes, in part begun by Sanders and continued in others, is Stephen J. Chester, *Reading Paul with the Reformers: Reconciling Old and New Perspectives* (Grand Rapids: Eerdmans, 2017).

13. That old perspective, and Sanders's counter to it, are challenged now from another angle in Barclay, *Paul and the Gift*.

14. Dunn, *Romans*; Dunn, *New Perspective on Paul*; Dunn, *TPA*; Dunn, *Beginning from Jerusalem*, vol. 2 of *Christianity in the Making* (Grand Rapids: Eerdmans, 2009); N. T. Wright, "The Letter to the Romans," in *The New Interpreter's Bible*, vol. 10, ed. Leander E. Keck (Nashville: Abingdon, 2002), 393–770; N. T. Wright, *Paul and the Faithfulness of God*, 2 vols., part 4 of *Christian Origins and the Question of God* (Minneapolis: Fortress, 2013); N. T. Wright, *Pauline Perspectives: Essays on Paul, 1978–2013* (Minneapolis: Fortress, 2013); N. T. Wright, *Paul and His Recent Interpreters* (Fortress, 2015).

15. For a full examination of Wright's Paul project, see Christoph Heilig, J. Thomas Hewitt, and Michael F. Bird, eds., *God and the Faithfulness of Paul: A Critical Examination of the Pauline Theology of N. T. Wright* WUNT 2/413 (Tübingen: Mohr Siebeck, 2016). For Dunn's own response, see "An Insider's Perspective on Wright's Version of the New Perspective on Paul," in Heilig, Hewitt, and Bird, *God and the Faithfulness of Paul*, 347–58.

2. Judaism is covenantal nomism, and Israel's God has one singular plan for the redemption of all creation. So covenant with Israel is God's one plan.
3. Among the problems resolved in Christ are the sin problem, Israel's failure to bless the nations, Israel's failure to be obedient, and Israel's privilege usurping its mission.
4. Works of the law are about social boundaries between Jews and gentiles, even as they are also are perceived to be a commitment to the whole torah of Moses.
5. The covenant of God with Abraham comes to its fulfillment in Jesus as Messiah. New creation then begins with a new exodus, but new creation remains Israel-shaped.
6. The Christology of Pauline theology is an incarnation of the Messiah that includes life, death, resurrection, and exaltation as the complete means of redemption for those who believe in him.
7. Its ethic is Christocentric but also pneuma-centric and ecclesio-centric: one follows Christ in the power of the Spirit in fellowship with other believers.

In summary, then, Jews *and* gentiles are very much to the front of the messianic plan. The heart of God's work in the world is the church, which is both a fulfillment of the land promise and a concrete visible fellowship of people from all sorts (Jew, gentile, slave, free, male, female, barbarian, Scythian). Hence the church becomes the location of God's redemption in the world. Thus in comparison to other approaches to Paul, in this approach his theology is grounded less in anthropology and more in historiography, ecclesiology, and Christology. The problem is to be found in Israel's story in search of fulfillment, and this story's fulfillment entails soteriology through Christ in the power of the Spirit.

Alongside this new perspective and growing in new ways out of the revolution of Sanders is the apocalyptic approach to Paul.[16] Before getting to him,

---

16. Ernst Käsemann, *Commentary on Romans* (Grand Rapids: Eerdmans, 1980); J. Christiaan Beker, *Paul the Apostle: The Triumph of God in Life and Thought* (Philadelphia: Fortress, 1980); J. Louis Martyn, "The Apocalyptic Gospel in Galatians," *Int* 54, no. 3 (2000): 246–66; Martinus C. de Boer, *The Defeat of Death: Apocalyptic Eschatology in 1 Corinthians 15 and Romans 5*, LNTS 22 (Sheffield: Sheffield Academic, 1988); Douglas A. Campbell, *The Quest for Paul's Gospel* (London: T&T Clark, 2005); Campbell, *The Deliverance of God: An Apocalyptic Rereading of Justification in Paul* (Grand Rapids: Eerdmans, 2013); Beverly Roberts Gaventa, *When in Romans: An Invitation to Linger with the Gospel according to Paul* (Grand Rapids: Baker Academic, 2016); Ben C. Blackwell, John K. Goodrich, and Jason Maston, eds., *Paul and the Apocalyptic Imagination* (Minneapolis: Fortress, 2016); Susan Grove Eastman, *Paul and the Person: Reframing Paul's Anthropology* (Grand Rapids: Eerdmans, 2017).

though, note that the term *apocalyptic* is contested in meaning. A recent attempt to find common ground concludes that apocalyptic operates on three intersecting axes: the time-space axes of eschatology (e.g., two ages) and revelation (spatial/vertical) as well as epistemology.[17] This conclusion is that there are two fundamental views, then: an emphasis on eschatological invasion or on unveiled fulfillment, one emphasizing discontinuity and newness and the other continuity with newness. What is this apocalyptic Paul all about?[18]

Nuances aside, Paul's perspective begins with an apocalyptic invasion that shatters all previous categories. First, God in Christ unconditionally delivers or redeems all. Everything becomes new. Second, the apocalypse of God in Christ retrospectively characterizes all that came before so that the problem is understood anew in terms of the solution in Christ—that is, the death and resurrection and ascension. That problem is the flesh-indwelling hostile powers of Sin and Death that enslave humanity.[19] The law exacerbates this slavery, which also makes humans incapable of knowing the problem or solution apart from a divine revelation through the Spirit. Third, God's grace or benevolence prompts the Father to send the Son to participate in the human (Adamic) condition in order to slay the Adamic condition by atoning for it, but the Son's death is overcome by the Son's resurrection in order to bring in the new condition: the new age with new life in Christ. The Son's resurrection leads to the Son's exaltation as the eternal Son of God. Fourth, the Spirit incorporates humans into Christ. Humans must first die and then are raised to new life in Christ through the Spirit (in baptism), and through this humans in Christ receive a new ontology. Thus redemption in Christ is framed as liberation from slavery into a new communal identity[20] and a new family, the community of the Spirit in Christ.

The participationist approach, brought to one of its cleanest expositions in the various works of Gorman, is beginning to influence Romans scholarship. Note the one-sentence summary that explains the participationist view:

> Paul preached, and then explained in various pastoral, community-forming letters, a narrative, apocalyptic, theopolitical gospel of God's shocking faithfulness and grace, (1) in continuity with the story of Israel and (2) in distinction to the imperial gospel of Rome (and analogous powers), that was centered on God's crucified and exalted Messiah Jesus, whose incarnation, life, and death

---

17. Ben C. Blackwell, John K. Goodrich, and Jason Maston, "Paul and the Apocalyptic Imagination: An Introduction," in *Paul and the Apocalyptic Imagination* (Minneapolis: Fortress, 2016), 3–21.
18. Campbell, *Deliverance of God*, 72–73.
19. Uppercase terms abound in apocalyptic Paul scholarship—and for good reason.
20. Especially Eastman, *Paul and the Person*.

by crucifixion were validated and vindicated by God in his resurrection and exaltation as Lord, which inaugurated the new age or new creation, in which all members of this diverse but consistently covenantally dysfunctional human race who respond in self-abandoning and self-committing faith thereby participate in Christ's death and resurrection and are (1) justified, or restored to right covenant relations with God and with others, and adopted into God's family; (2) incorporated into a particular manifestation of Christ the Lord's body on earth, the church, which is an alternative community to the status-quo human communities committed to and governed by Caesar (and analogous rulers) and by values contrary to the gospel; and (3) infused both individually and corporately by the Spirit of God's Son so that they may lead "bifocal" lives, focused both back on Christ's first coming and ahead to his second, consisting of Christlike, cruciform (1) faith(fullness) and (2) hope toward God and (3) love toward both neighbors and enemies (a love marked by peaceableness and hospitality), thereby bearing witness in word and deed to the one true God and the Lordship of Christ, and participating by the power of the Holy Spirit in God's mission of reconciliation and restorative justice in Christ, even at the risk of suffering and death, all in joyful anticipation of (1) the return of Christ, (2) the resurrection of the dead to eternal life, and (3) the renewal of the entire creation.[21]

One can read Gorman's one-sentence summary and hear echoes of what is best in the old, new, and apocalyptic approaches; one can hear new themes (participation in particular); one can see a soteriological orientation to Paul that is new without neglecting the salvation-historical, the ecclesiological, or the ethical; and one can simply take a big breath upon finishing, only to start all over and wonder if it might be cut into more manageable sections (which it can be!).

Much more could be said, and again I refer the reader to the fuller sketch of Gorman in this volume, but Romans scholarship to date itself has been influenced mostly by the above approaches. Others deserve mention briefly, including Garwood Anderson's suggestion that the "new" perspective prevailed in Paul's early years but shifted toward an "old" perspective in Paul's later writings.[22] Always and forever someone will find more politics in Paul than the tradition has found, and one who has made a singular contribution

---

21. Michael J. Gorman, *Apostle of the Crucified Lord: A Theological Introduction to Paul and His Letters*, 2nd ed. (Grand Rapids: Eerdmans, 2016), 183. For Gorman's formative books, see *Cruciformity: Paul's Narrative Spirituality of the Cross* (Grand Rapids: Eerdmans, 2001); *Inhabiting the Cruciform God: Kenosis, Justification, and Theosis in Paul's Narrative Soteriology* (Grand Rapids: Eerdmans, 2009); *Becoming the Gospel: Paul, Participation, and Mission* (Grand Rapids: Eerdmans, 2015).

22. Garwood P. Anderson, *Paul's New Perspective: Charting a Soteriological Journey* (Downers Grove, IL: IVP Academic, 2016).

here is Neil Elliott, who examines empire, justice, mercy, "piety," and virtue in their Roman context with vigor and insight.[23] Many today find plenty of anti-imperialism in Paul's letters and at the heart of his mission churches.[24] Running throughout every interpretation of Paul are Pauline readings of his Jewish Scriptures, and such approaches to Paul make singular approaches simplistic. If some emphasize an almost arbitrary usage of the Bible, others, especially now Francis Watson, argue that Paul has a singular hermeneutic that knows itself in the reading of the Pentateuch and the Prophets.[25] It is not simplistic to ask if Paul arrived at this hermeneutic by reading the Pentateuch or if he knew how to read because of the revelation of Christ,[26] but a bit more of that below. A sensitive liberationist approach, from an African American perspective, is seen in Thomas Hoyt Jr.'s contribution to *True to Our Native Land*, where a soteriological and ecclesiological reading comes into balance with an eye toward social justice, racial reconciliation, and the gospel as an agent of redemption.[27] A special place must be reserved as well for what some call "Paul within Judaism," while others speak here of post-supersessionism and others of a post–new perspective approach to Paul. The voice that powered this to the fore is Mark Nanos, who made his imprint on Romans and Pauline scholarship before earning his PhD when he published his study of Romans.[28] Others have shaped this conversation, including Pamela Eisenbaum,[29] but in general, scholars think the audience of Romans was a synagogue-participating group. The Weak are said to be non-Jesus-as-Messiah folks while the Strong are composed of both Jewish and gentile believers, and the book itself then becomes not so much a denigration of Judaism as a form of Judaism for the gentile world. Themes from Nanos's work will appear in specific sections about Romans below.

23. Neil Elliott, *The Arrogance of Nations: Reading Romans in the Shadow of Empire* (Minneapolis: Fortress, 2008).

24. Richard A. Horsley, ed., *Paul and the Roman Imperial Order* (Harrisburg, PA: Trinity Press International, 2004).

25. Francis Watson, *Paul and the Hermeneutics of Faith* (New York: T&T Clark, 2004); Preston M. Sprinkle, *Paul and Judaism Revisited: A Study of Divine and Human Agency in Salvation* (Downers Grove, IL: IVP Academic, 2013).

26. For now, Richard B. Hays, *The Faith of Jesus Christ: The Narrative Substructure of Galatians 3:1–4:11*, 2nd ed. (Grand Rapids: Eerdmans, 2002); Hays, *Echoes of Scripture in the Gospels* (Waco: Baylor University Press, 2016); Hays, *The Conversion of the Imagination: Paul as Interpreter of Israel's Scripture* (Grand Rapids: Eerdmans, 2005).

27. Thomas Hoyt Jr., "Romans," in *True to Our Native Land: An African American New Testament Commentary*, ed. Brian K. Blount et al. (Minneapolis: Fortress, 2007), 249–75.

28. Mark D. Nanos, *The Mystery of Romans: The Jewish Context of Paul's Letters* (Minneapolis: Fortress, 1996); Nanos, *Reading Romans within Judaism: Collected Essays of Mark D. Nanos* (Eugene, OR: Cascade, 2018).

29. Pamela Eisenbaum, *Paul Was Not a Christian: The Original Message of a Misunderstood Apostle* (New York: HarperOne, 2010).

Reading Romans Today

Commentaries have been the lifeblood of preachers and professors from at least the third century. If preaching is lectionary based or Bible generated, then commentaries will remain a staple diet. Each generation produces commentaries reflecting and for that generation. One hour with Chrysostom or Augustine, and even less so with Aquinas or Luther or Calvin, makes one aware of how deeply different approaches, subjects, questions, and at times even basic message are.

Commentaries

In our generation we are served by too many bulky and at times nearly inaccessible (to the student and to the pastor) commentaries on Romans. Even the accessible writers turn Romans into a thousand-page book. The most accessible commentaries today are by Leander E. Keck, Paul Achtemeier, A. Katherine Grieb, Craig Keener, Sarah Lancaster, Robert Jewett (his shorter commentary), Stanley Porter, and Michael Bird.[30] In our scheme above, Keck and Lancaster lean apocalyptic; Lancaster appropriates much of Jewett's work; Grieb offers a more narrative, political, and somewhat apocalyptic study; Jewett has a social and mission- and empire-shaped reading of Romans; Porter is simultaneously theological, linguistic, and literary-rhetorical; and Achtemeier and Keener and Bird do their best to be eclectic: here a little old, there a little new, and over here a bit of apocalyptic. What divides commentaries on Romans the most will be discussed below, but for now I put it this way: either the letter is read as a soteriological or even a last-testament letter with less emphasis on Romans 12–16, or it is read more ecclesiologically and contextually with more emphasis on those last chapters, particularly the sections on the Strong and Weak in chapters 14–15. Of the above, Jewett stands out as the most ecclesiological of the readings.

Middle-level commentaries, readable mostly for pastors and exegesis students in seminaries or colleges, include Wright, A. Hultgren, Joseph A. Fitzmyer, Stuhlmacher, Moo, and Colin Kruse.[31] Apart from Wright and

---

30. Leander E. Keck, *Romans*, ANTC (Nashville: Abingdon, 2005); Paul J. Achtemeier, *Romans*, Interpretation (Atlanta: John Knox, 1986); A. Katherine Grieb, *The Story of Romans: A Narrative Defense of God's Righteousness* (Louisville: Westminster John Knox, 2002); Craig S. Keener, *Romans*, New Covenant Commentary (Eugene, OR: Wipf & Stock, 2009); Sarah Heaner Lancaster, *Romans*, Belief: A Theological Commentary on the Bible (Louisville: Westminster John Knox, 2015); Robert Jewett, *Romans: A Short Commentary* (Minneapolis: Fortress, 2013); Stanley E. Porter, *The Letter to the Romans: A Linguistic and Literary Commentary* (Sheffield: Sheffield Phoenix, 2015); Michael F. Bird, *Romans*, SGBC (Grand Rapids: Zondervan, 2016).

31. Wright, "Romans"; Arland J. Hultgren, *Paul's Letter to the Romans: A Commentary* (Grand Rapids: Eerdmans, 2011); J. A. Fitzmyer, *Romans*, AYB 33 (New Haven: Yale University

Fitzmyer, these commentaries represent Lutheran or Reformed approaches, but each one is a full discussion of all major issues; Wright is a defining voice in the new perspective and Fitzmyer's is Roman Catholic, with plenty of opportunity to be more historically oriented. Each of these is soteriological in approach.

Three academic commentaries shape the modern discussion in their own ways:[32] Dunn's pioneering new perspective orientation, where he worked out his understanding of Judaism and "works of the law" and elective privilege for Israel; Jewett's twenty-seven-year-long examination of the Greco-Roman and Jewish contexts, which led to a socially sensitive approach to Paul's missionary plans to go on to Spain with a strong ecclesiological shaping to the whole of Romans; and Richard Longenecker's eleven-hundred-page commentary and almost-five-hundred-page introduction. Longenecker is eclectic but focuses on the gospel message of Paul preached to the gentiles in his mission, the importance of Rome for Paul's further mission to Spain, and the tension between the Weak and Strong. What is distinctive to Longenecker, and what appears increasingly in scholarship today, is that he finds Romans 1–4 and 9–11 to be aimed at a mixed audience, while Romans 5–8 becomes the clearest expression of the Pauline message for the gentile mission, and 12:1–15:13 becomes its application.

Context of Romans

There are two major studies on the context of Romans, each emphasizing Romans 12–16 more than many, and they stand out as pioneering methodologically and historically. Peter Lampe's study of the archaeological, prosopographical, and literary evidence of Rome maps not only where the earliest Christians (or Jesus-followers, or messianists) lived but where they formed churches.[33] Peter Oakes has examined with extreme care the archaeological evidence of Pompeii and transferred it with historical nuance to Rome to outline who would have been in a household if we are

---

Press, 2007); Peter Stuhlmacher, *Paul's Letter to the Romans: A Commentary* (Louisville: Westminster John Knox, 1994); Douglas J. Moo, *The Epistle to the Romans*, 2nd ed., NICNT (Grand Rapids: Eerdmans, 2018); Colin G. Kruse, *Paul's Letter to the Romans*, PNTC (Grand Rapids: Eerdmans, 2012).

32. Dunn, *Romans*; Robert Jewett, *Romans: A Commentary*, Hermeneia (Minneapolis: Fortress, 2007); Richard N. Longenecker, *Introducing Romans: Critical Issues in Paul's Most Famous Letter* (Grand Rapids: Eerdmans, 2011); Richard N. Longenecker, *The Epistle to the Romans*, NIGTC (Grand Rapids: Eerdmans, 2016).

33. Peter Lampe, *From Paul to Valentinus: Christians at Rome in the First Two Centuries*, ed. Marshall D. Johnson, trans. Michael Steinhauser (Minneapolis: Fortress, 2003). See also Harry J. Leon, *The Jews of Ancient Rome*, rev. ed. (Peabody, MA: Hendrickson, 1995); Peter Oakes, ed., *Rome in the Bible and the Early Church* (Grand Rapids: Baker Academic, 2002).

talking about house churches. In addition, Oakes takes us into such a house church to hear how various house members would have heard the letter Paul wrote to Rome.[34] These two books are required for all readings of Romans, whether soteriological or ecclesiological. In addition two student-oriented books help usher Romans into its world: Ben Blackwell, John Goodrich, and Jason Maston collect a variety of authors probing various sections in Romans in light of their historical context,[35] and Neil Elliott and Mark Reasoner sort out major topics in Pauline studies in the context of nonliterary sources.[36]

Selected Theological Topics

Anyone perusing the bookshelves of an academic theological library knows the stacks go on for shelves and shelves about Romans. A professor of mine once showed me his library, and he had six feet of commentaries on Romans. I venture to sample, albeit far too briefly, a few recent monographs or thematic studies of Romans.

A major voice in Pauline studies is Francis Watson,[37] whose published dissertation asserted a far more particularistic and therefore theologically not-as-useful theology shaped for a particular social setting, but whose dissertation has been modified. Along with that modification Watson now advances a "beyond the new perspective" approach to Paul and, in so doing, ventures into yet another mediating position on Pauline theology. It is perhaps best to outline what distinguishes his new approach: he affirms covenantal nomism as an irreducible feature of the Judaism with which Paul has direct polemics, but covenantal nomism for him is not a covenant theme of grace but of law; divine agency is more prominent in Pauline theology than in the Judaism Paul contests; he contends "works of the law" are the law of Moses, and, as such,[38] it is characteristic of Judaism, but it is not (as Dunn has argued) about boundary markers; Paul's strategy is to separate the Christians of Rome from

---

34. Peter Oakes, *Reading Romans in Pompeii: Paul's Letter at Ground Level* (Minneapolis: Fortress, 2009).

35. Ben C. Blackwell, John K. Goodrich, and Jason Maston, eds., *Reading Romans in Context: Paul and Second Temple Judaism* (Grand Rapids: Zondervan, 2015).

36. Neil Elliott and Mark Reasoner, eds., *Documents and Images for the Study of Paul* (Minneapolis: Fortress, 2010).

37. His published dissertation under the same title has been revised in Francis Watson, *Paul, Judaism, and the Gentiles: Beyond the New Perspective*, 2nd ed. (Grand Rapids: Eerdmans, 2007); Watson, *Paul and the Hermeneutics of Faith*.

38. We cannot enter here into a summary of Watson, *Paul and the Hermeneutics of Faith*. That book, which distances Watson even more from his previous approach, explores how Paul resolves the tension of the Pentateuch over law and promise. See also Sprinkle, *Paul and Judaism Revisited*.

Judaism instead of forming an inclusive community of the one people of God. Watson makes a bold step against most scholarship today when he says Paul's view of "Judaism" is "Pharisaism." Yet Watson remains convinced of the social particularities of the Pauline message and of the believers at Rome, focused as they are on the Weak (Jewish) and Strong (Pauline, gentile). Paul is not so much a theologian as he is a missional agent. Thus Paul's theology as such is a legitimating apparatus for the separability of the gentile Christians from Judaism. Law, in an anti-Lutheran move, is what marks Judaism, while what marks a Pauline church community is faith.

In his study of social identity, Philip F. Esler contends that Paul's communication with the Romans serves to solidify social identity as part of the church, or the Christ community, by framing it as superior to all other identities on offer in Rome.[39] In so doing, Esler shows he cares deeply about historical context in Rome, by which he means Claudius and Nero and social, ethnic tensions and categories and the strong-and-weak issues—not just the theological or soteriological themes of the letter. It is their identity in Christ that is to reshape their imagination and practices and transcend their ethnic diversities.

One of the major approaches today is the apocalyptic approach. I used Douglas A. Campbell above, but I turn now to a significant collection of essays edited by Gaventa.[40] What are the primary proposals as detailed in her volume? First, the primary word is *apocalyptic*, but this term is not defined by Jewish apocalypses so much as it is almost equivalent to a cosmic, universalist redemption that has now invaded the world in Christ (the old age is shattered by the new age). Apocalyptic is associated closely with soteriology, especially cosmic soteriology, in this reading. God's acting in history is heavily emphasized; the divine action is at the core of the apocalyptic Paul. It is all played on the cosmic stage in grand categories—almost abstractions. In fact, one of the major players—Martinus de Boer—sees Paul as a mythologizer; that is, he mythologizes cosmic redemption and its major actors. Here are de Boer's words:

> *Paul*, I have argued, has introduced the cosmological understanding of sin and death into the Jewish Adam traditions—and he has done so to show that the Law, instead of being the solution for sin and thus death as in 2 Baruch and 4 Ezra, only solidified the hold of Sin and thus Death on human beings: Alas, the Law has nothing to do with obtaining the requisite righteousness, nor with justification, nor, then, with (eternal) life. Nothing.

---

39. Philip Francis Esler, *Conflict and Identity in Romans* (Minneapolis: Augsburg, 2003).
40. Beverly Roberts Gaventa, ed., *Apocalyptic Paul: Cosmos and Anthropos in Romans 5–8* (Waco: Baylor University Press, 2013).

> In Christ, God himself has entered the human cosmos, and God's powerful Grace, in contrast to the weak and ineffectual Law, is more than equal to the task of putting an end to the reigns of Sin and Death.[41]

Second, theological terms are turned into cosmic powers in uppercase letters: Sin, Law, Flesh, Grace, Love, Redemption. One might ask if these are personifications, agents, or mythologizations. But what they are in apocalyptic thinking are actors on the cosmic stage—and everyone is dressed up in the line of Adam's clothes or the line of Christ's. The world is the stage of a cosmic soteriological battle now won by Christ in his death and resurrection. The redemptive invasion of God in this world, then, is the unfurling of New Creation in Love and Grace and Forgiveness against the evil empires of Sin and Death and Law and Guilt.

Third, in Gaventa's volume one encounters humans as agents in this moral cosmic battle, but the battle has shifted from the days of yore, when it was so individualistic, to cosmic proportions. Adam is the key figure, not Abraham; Law and Sin and Flesh are the categories, not the torah of Moses; the alternatives are Christ versus Adam and Life versus Death. In addition to Gaventa's role as editor, she has contributed an early sketch of some major theological themes that will appear in her full commentary on Romans in the New Testament Library series. Her book *When in Romans* focuses on major themes, including God and worship and salvation and ethics and identity and church, but she enfolds each in the universal and cosmic redemption of God in Christ.[42]

Multiauthor volumes do not always approach a subject with such a singular voice, though sometimes the difficulty is in the subject or text chosen. Todd Still, editor of *God and Israel: Providence and Purpose in Romans 9–11*, brings together diverse studies on three chapters in Romans that are as difficult to tidy up as anything in the whole Bible.[43] In fact, J. Ross Wagner refers to these chapters as a "torturous argument,"[44] while someone like Wright offers a clever chiastic reading of the chapters that forces our attention to 10:5–13, especially the confession with the lips and belief in the heart of 10:9.[45] Still's volume is not univocal: Wagner focuses on the utter reliability of the love of God for Israel as a portal into the chapters and the claims of Paul, while

---

41. Martinus de Boer, "Paul's Mythologizing Program in Romans 5–8," in Gaventa, *Apocalyptic Paul*, 18, 20.
42. Gaventa, *When in Romans*.
43. Todd D. Still, ed., *God and Israel: Providence and Purpose in Romans 9–11* (Waco: Baylor University Press, 2017).
44. J. Ross Wagner, "'Enemies' Yet 'Beloved' Still: Election and the Love of God in Romans 9–11," in Still, *God and Israel*, 95.
45. Wright, *PFG*, 1156–259.

Simon Gathercole seeks to show that even if God is preeminent and in spite of the *Sonderweg* claim of redemption for some today, Christology remains central to the whole of these three chapters in Romans.[46] Jonathan Linebaugh addresses the issue of history and how to read it apocalyptically in his essay in *God and Israel*, arguing, among other things, that "Paul knows the future because he knows the present and the past." That is, "the hermeneutical direction is not, in the first instance, from Israel's story to Israel's Christ; it is, rather, from Israel's Christ to Israel's story."[47]

When it comes to selected theological topics, pride of place goes here to perhaps the most profound study of Paul since the work of Sanders: John Barclay's study of grace.[48] His phenomenology of grace/gift—rooted in both anthropology and the ancient sources (Greek, Roman, Jewish) and expounding with aplomb the rich and varied and at times badly mistaken tradition of grace in the history of Christian theology—finds six "perfections" of grace: (1) superabundance, (2) singularity, (3) priority, (4) incongruity, (5) efficacy, and (6) noncircularity. Barclay, so it seems, has turned over every stone and thereby done the same to the classic Judaism-and-works versus Christianity-and-grace hermeneutic; the Augustinian, Lutheran, and Calvinist tension with the Arminian and Anabaptist frameworks; and the tension between the old and new and apocalyptic approaches. He has also set on a new footing much that comes into play in the theology of Paul and therefore in systematic theology.

Sin in the Pauline letters seems to be more than the violation of a command and seems to take on systemic force. Christian theology's doctrines of original sin and guilt are but one example of theological attempts to come to terms with lowercase sins and uppercase Sin as a tyrant. Matthew Croasmun's recently published dissertation, *The Emergence of Sin*, puts forward a series of proposals providing innovative solutions to all the above and more.[49] Is Paul's use of sin as an agent (Rom. 6:6, 12, 14; 7:8) the act of an individual sinner? Is it mythological? Is it personification? Is it systemic? Or is it cosmic? Such are the questions Croasmun probes. He concludes that the phenomenon of sins becoming Sin (individual actions becoming systemic agency) is best explained through emergence theory—that is, how higher-order properties emerge into complexities (Sin) that are based on both the original (sins) and

---

46. Simon Gathercole, "Locating Christ and Israel in Romans 9–11," in Still, *God and Israel*, 115–39.

47. Jonathan Linebaugh, "Not the End: The History and Hope of the Unfailing Word in Romans 9–11," in Still, *God and Israel*, 141–63, here 144, 161.

48. Barclay, *Paul and the Gift*.

49. Matthew Croasmun, *The Emergence of Sin: The Cosmic Tyrant in Romans* (New York: Oxford University Press, 2017).

more complex. The core to Croasmun's explanation of emergence theory itself is the dialectical relationship of supervenience and downward causation. Supervenience is not as intuitively clear as downward causation: the former refers to a causal basis of higher properties from which they emerge, while the latter contends that what emerges works back almost in cyclical fashion on the supervenience base, making it more of what it is. They feed on and form each other. Thus human agents sin, and from these sins Sin emerges, and Sin as an agent works back on humans to precipitate more sin and sinning. Sin is ontologically dependent for its existence on human sinning.

Croasmun's study enters into the intermingling of persons in our society and leads me to mention the recent study of Susan Eastman.[50] She contends that humans in Pauline theology/anthropology are a *we* before they are an *I*, that we are embedded and embodied. She ties this to Christ-incarnation theology to contend that all humans through Christ are images of God. The Western sense of freedom is dealt a death blow as Eastman argues over and over that we are selves-in-relation and that—to tie into Croasmun—sin then is systemic and socially mediated before it is personal. Eastman's work, too, tied into the participatory theology of Gorman. Croasmun and Eastman, then, challenge the historic Augustinian-based theory of original sin and guilt, and they are joined by the recent monograph by Miryam T. Brand, a study about the source of sin in Jewish writings.[51] Brand's book challenges Eastman's contention of a more one-way relation of evil and personal sin by showing that Jewish sources, shaped significantly by genre, see sin's source both in the person and in external forces (demonic). Consistent in Judaism, but at odds with Romans, in my view, is the notion of law as a means of conquering sin and evil. Thus positing Adam and Eve as the source of sin is rare in Second Temple literature of Judaism and is almost entirely dated past the destruction of the temple.

Christian theologians tend to assume meanings of words until someone says, "Time to give this term a new investigation!" Barclay's decades-long work in Paul led to a reformulation of grace, and I suspect the published dissertation of Haley Goranson Jacob will lead to fresh studies of what *glory* means in Pauline theology.[52] While most think *glory* in Romans 8:18 or 8:21 and 8:29 describes the effulgence of personal salvation in the eschaton (i.e., heaven), transformation into holiness or love, or even transcending suffering

---

50. Eastman, *Paul and the Person*.

51. Miryam T. Brand, *Evil Within and Without: The Source of Sin and Its Nature as Portrayed in Second Temple Literature*, Journal of Ancient Judaism Supplements 9 (Göttingen: Vandenhoeck & Ruprecht, 2013).

52. Haley Goranson Jacob, *Conformed to the Image of His Son: Reconsidering Paul's Theology of Glory in Romans* (Downers Grove, IL: IVP Academic, 2018).

with Christ or restoration to the presence of God, Jacob contends that *glory* here refers to vocation, to the divinely inscribed mission for Adam and Eve in Genesis 1 and Psalm 8. Humans are delivered from death for life, and that life is to become all God meant it to be for us when he created the cosmos. Thus *glory* refers to vocational participation by the new family, the church, in the Son of God's exalted position and rule over all creation.

The Romans Debate

There is a book all Romans scholars know, and it is called *The Romans Debate*.[53] What is that debate? After all, one might say that about two dozen topics. In brief, one could say it has to do with how integrated Romans 1–8 or 1–11 is with Romans 12–16. Is Romans 1–8 (or 1–11) theology, abstract and unhitched from anything particular about the Roman house churches mentioned in Romans 16? Or is Romans 1–8 (or 1–11) deeply connected to 12–16, so much so that one has to read the situation of those latter chapters into the theology of the earlier chapters? Many editions of this "Romans debate" have been published, the first one in 1977 and subsequent revised and expanded editions in 1991, 2003, 2006, and 2011.[54]

This particular "Romans debate"[55] got its impetus from Günther Bornkamm's contention that Romans was contextless and was Paul's last will and testament, which was part of a discussion about the reliability of Romans 16's names (T. W. Manson) and whether there was an apostolic foundation in the churches in Rome (G. Klein), and Jacob Jervell then said the letter was actually sent to Jerusalem, and the suggestion was made that the Romans 16 names were added later. All this generated discussion of the importance of Romans 14–15 (Strong and Weak; R. J. Karris) and the Jewish community in Rome (W. Wiefel), and this led Karl P. Donfried to his collection and to his own methodological chapter, a chapter that still provides light on all the discussions.

More studies on the situation of the church in Rome have been completed more or less in the work of Lampe mentioned above; studies on the rhetoric, genre, and structural flow of Romans follow, and then more recent studies take center stage. Donfried collects an essay from each of four distinct viewpoints: from Dunn, an argument for the new perspective; from Lloyd Gaston, a discussion of the issue of supersessionism; from J. C. Beker, his

---

53. Karl P. Donfried, ed., *The Romans Debate* (Minneapolis: Augsburg, 1977).

54. Karl P. Donfried, ed., *The Romans Debate*, rev. and expanded ed. (Peabody, MA: Hendrickson, 1991, 2003, 2006). Donfried, ed., *The Romans Debate*, rev. and expanded ed. (Grand Rapids: Baker Academic, 2011).

55. What follows is an inadequate, quick sketch of what is found in Donfried.

well-known examination of God's faithfulness to Israel; and then a classic "old" perspective from Stuhlmacher.[56] *The Romans Debate* was published in 1991, but Romans scholarship did not stop, nor was the debate settled. So Jerry Sumney has collected noteworthy essays in Romans scholarship in more recent discussions, including the development of more diverse voices: Sylvia C. Keesmaat's essay on political anti-empire reading of Romans, Grieb's essay on the righteousness of God, Rodrigo J. Morales's important essay on how Scripture is used in Romans, Elizabeth Johnson's much-discussed essay on God's faithfulness to Israel, and Caroline Johnson Hodge's discussion of the role of Israel.[57]

A. Andrew Das has been such a large part of this Romans debate discussion that he has produced four erudite volumes about Pauline theology in recent conversation as he disputes especially the new perspective in favor of the old with his own nuances; but he has especially focused on discussing the relationship of Jewish and gentile believers in Rome and whether the audience is Jewish (no) or gentile Judaizing believers (yes).[58] One must avoid simplifications, but the Romans-debate concerns tend to create tension between more abstract, soteriological readings of Romans and more particularistic, ecclesial, contextual readings. Which leads into a recent intense debate among Romans scholars, and that will be followed with yet one more probing of the contextual nature of Romans.

Rhetoric and Gentile Audience

A discussion has arisen about the audience of Romans, and some have argued fiercely for an entirely gentile audience. Basing their argument in part on the explicit identification of a gentile audience in Romans 1:5 and 11:13 and 15:15–16, this group of scholars contends that the entire audience is gentiles and that the Jewish-sounding bits are actually addressed to Judaizing

---

56. James D. G. Dunn, "The New Perspective on Paul," in Donfried, *Romans Debate*, 245–50; Lloyd Gaston, "Israel's Misstep in the Eyes of Paul," in Donfried, *Romans Debate*, 309–26; J. C. Beker, "The Faithfulness of God and the Priority of Israel in Paul's Letter to the Romans," in Donfried, *Romans Debate*, 327–32; Peter Stuhlmacher, "The Theme of Romans," in Donfried, *Romans Debate*, 333–46.

57. Jerry L. Sumney, *Reading Paul's Letter to the Romans* (Atlanta: SBL Press, 2012). See in this volume, Keesmaat, "Reading Romans in the Capital of the Empire," 47–64; Grieb, "The Righteousness of God in Romans," 65–78; Morales, "'Promised through His Prophets in the Holy Scriptures': The Role of Scripture in the Letter to the Romans," 109–124; Johnson, "God's Covenant Faithfulness to Israel," 157–68; Johnson Hodge, "'A Light to the Nations': The Role of Israel in Romans 9–11," 169–86.

58. A. Andrew Das, *Paul and the Jews* (Peabody, MA: Hendrickson, 2004); Das, *Paul, the Law, and the Covenant* (Peabody, MA: Hendrickson, 2001); Das, *Solving the Romans Debate* (Minneapolis: Fortress, 2006); Das, *Paul and the Stories of Israel: Grand Thematic Narratives in Galatians* (Minneapolis: Fortress, 2016).

gentiles—that is, gentiles who convert to Judaism and Torah observance and who may well be exerting pressure for more to join their team. The scholarship here is formidable (and I will not lightly dismiss it, as some have done).[59] This has to do with, in part, how to define what the Torah and halakic bits in Romans 14 are about, how to read Romans 1:18–32 as tied to Romans 2, and whether the "judge" of Romans 2:1 is a Jew or a Judaizing gentile. It has been customary to equate the judge of 2:1 with the "so-called Jew" of 2:1. Stanley Stowers masterfully examines the speech-in-character rhetoric of Romans 2:1–16, 2:17–29, 3:1–9, and 3:27–4:2 as well as Romans 7, though his follow-through in the rest of Romans is not as suggestive. Stowers resisted seeing the actual audience of Romans 16 with the intended audience of Romans itself, and he has focused his work on the theme of self-mastery in Romans. Stowers unleashed a reevaluation of Romans.

This kind of attention to rhetoric was picked up by Runar Thorsteinsson, whose interest in rhetoric and epistles led to the conclusion that the interlocutor in Romans will always be the same person who is embodied in the audience of the letter. That interlocutor, he argues, is a gentile throughout the letter. When Romans then addresses entirely a gentile audience, the entire letter is turned inside out and against the tradition of the church, which has seen Jews prominent in the letter, or at least Christian Jews.[60]

Audience

Our final topic has to do with the audience, and we can drop for here the issue of the greetings in Romans 16[61] because this scholarship believes the audience of Romans 16 maps onto the intended audience of the letter itself. Three moments of scholarship can be mentioned.[62] We go back in time to 1971, when Paul Minear argued that the entire letter was addressed in various bits to five

---

59. I list here only the major voices, but the volume edited by Rafael Rodríguez and Matthew Thiessen below is a good place to start: Stanley K. Stowers, *A Rereading of Romans: Justice, Jews, and Gentiles* (New Haven: Yale University Press, 1994); Runar Thorsteinsson, *Paul's Interlocutor in Romans 2: Function and Identity in the Context of Ancient Epistolography*, ConBNT 40 (Stockholm: Almqvist & Wiksell, 2003); Joshua D. Garroway, *Paul's Gentile-Jews: Neither Jew nor Gentile, but Both* (New York: Palgrave Macmillan, 2012); Rafael Rodríguez, *If You Call Yourself a Jew: Reappraising Paul's Letter to the Romans* (Eugene, OR: Cascade, 2014); Gabriele Boccaccini and Carlos A. Segovia, eds., *Paul the Jew: Rereading the Apostle as a Figure of Second Temple Judaism* (Minneapolis: Fortress, 2016); Rafael Rodríguez and Matthew Thiessen, eds., *The So-Called Jew in Paul's Letter to the Romans* (Minneapolis: Fortress, 2016); Matthew Thiessen, *Paul and the Gentile Problem* (New York: Oxford University Press, 2016).

60. Thorsteinsson, *Paul's Interlocutor in Romans 2*.

61. On which see Jewett, *Romans: A Commentary*, 949–74.

62. Two others who have examined the whole of Romans with the audience of Romans 14–15 in mind are Esler, *Conflict and Identity in Romans*; Watson, *Paul, Judaism, and the Gentiles*.

different groups in Rome:[63] (1) the Weak who condemned the Strong, (2) the Strong who despised the Weak, (3) doubters (cf. 14:23), (4) the Weak who did not condemn the Strong, and (5) the Strong who did not despise the Weak. It is unfortunate that the insight of Minear has been ignored, because some think he overspecified his audience—since if groups 1 and 2 are admitted entry, then the others are commonsensical—while others dismiss his study because they aren't sure passages can be assigned. The problem is that this is the audience of Paul as he himself describes it, and it ought to play more of a role.

Which it did for A. J. M. Wedderburn.[64] The issue behind the writing of Romans, however complex it might be and however many subthemes one wants to chase (like the Spanish mission or Claudius's edict and Nero's economics and taxation, not to ignore Paul's imminent trip to Jerusalem), is a divided church, and it is divided along mostly ethnic lines but established on the basis of agreeing to the Pauline mission. To call some "Strong" is to agree with that mission; to call someone "Weak" is to reject it. Paul wants the Strong to embrace the faithfulness of Israel's God and the reliability of God's will revealed in the Scriptures, while he doesn't think the way forward is Torah observance for gentile believers.

If I may, I refer to a forthcoming study of mine titled *Reading Romans Backward*, in which I argue that Paul's letter is entirely shaped by the tension between the Weak (mostly Jewish, but believers who think Torah observance remains for all of God's people) and the Strong (mostly gentile and Pauline mission to the core, and those who think Torah observance is not for gentiles and is adiaphora for Jewish believers). The Weak are Jewish believers who are in the stream of God's election and need to be affirmed in their election but who have questions about the faithfulness of God to that election and who need to embrace the surprising moves of God throughout Israel's history. The Weak know the Torah, practice the Torah, but in the person of The Judge sit in judgment on gentiles, especially the Strong in the Christian community in Rome, even though they (the Weak) have no status or privilege or power. Furthermore, the Weak are tempted to resist paying taxes to Rome on the basis of the Jewish zealotry tradition. In addition, the Weak—in the face of the Judge—need to apply "faith in Christ" more radically to themselves. In doing so, they will discover that they are a new example of the "remnant" of Israel. And they need to see that the sufficiency of faith means that gentile believers in Christ are siblings and that Torah observance is not the way of transformation for either themselves or for the Strong in Rome.

---

63. Paul S. Minear, *The Obedience of Faith: The Purposes of Paul in the Epistle to the Romans*, SBT 2.19 (London: SCM, 1971).

64. A. J. M. Wedderburn, *The Reasons for Romans* (Minneapolis: Fortress, 1991).

The Strong are predominantly gentiles who believe in Jesus as Messiah or king, who do not observe Torah as the will of God for them, and who have condescending and despising attitudes probably toward Jews but especially towards Jewish believers in Jesus; all of this is wrapped up in the superior status of the Strong in Rome. Paul and Jewish believers who embrace the nonnecessity of Torah observance are at least at times among the Strong in their theological convictions about Torah observance as the way of Christoformity. But the Strong are taking advantage of their superior social status to denigrate the Torah and holiness as the quest of the Christians in Rome, and so they are coercing the Weak into table fellowship over nonkosher food. The Strong then are as known for their position on observance of Torah and for their status as they are for ethnicity.

I seek to show that once we get Romans 12–16 in hand, we can see that Romans 1–8 and 9–11 are typical arguments used by Paul in his gentile mission, with Romans 1–4 parallel in substantive ways with 9:1–11:10 and Romans 5–8 more in line with Romans 11:11–36. I argue that Romans 1–4 is addressed entirely—or almost entirely—to the Weak argument for elective privilege and that the soteriological reading fails to appreciate what is happening in Romans 1:18–32, given how well that passage is tied to Romans 2 and given the heavy emphasis on questions in Romans 3–4. The theory for how to find peace in the empire, which is core to Romans 12–15 especially, is the baptismal life of the indwelling Spirit.[65]

Reflections

Scholarship on Romans presses the traveler to consider several directions at once—like a European roundabout. Wondering which road to take, many simply drive in circles until they acquire some confidence about direction. One must decide on the overall perspective on Paul's theology—old, new, apocalyptic, participationist, or some eclectic combination of them. One must choose whether to read soteriologically or ecclesiologically—that is, is this letter addressed specifically to the Strong and Weak issues in Rome, or is this a more general theological letter with some applications to the situation in Rome? One must decide whether the letter is addressed to a mixed audience of Jewish and gentile believers or to an exclusively gentile audience.

Some stimulating studies emerge from considerations of rhetoric, and here one thinks of Stowers's seminal contribution as well as those studies concentrating on a gentile Christian audience. Apocalyptic readings of Romans, especially that of Campbell, have established a deeper concentration on

---

65. Scot McKnight, *Reading Romans Backward* (Waco: Baylor University Press, forthcoming).

themes of liberation, and I expect apocalyptic readings will gain in strength in the coming decade. Those new perspective studies that avoid the stronger sense of supersessionism, while also emphasizing reconciliation of Jewish and gentile believers, can become a paradigm for integrating differences but also for churches to become more gospel shaped by becoming more reconciled. As an American I pray that the privileged and dominant white voice can learn the ethical pragmatics of Romans 14–15 as it surrenders and learns to share power with minority voices. Feminist and African American as well as African, Latino, and Asian voices are beginning to be heard more and more in Romans studies, and we expect Romans scholarship to shift, advance, and take on new shapes in the decade ahead as these voices gain a hearing and Anglo voices become less privileged.

19

The Epistle to the Hebrews

David M. Moffitt

Introduction

The first two decades of this century have witnessed a rising tide of interest in the Epistle to the Hebrews. Hebrews continues to be, as George Guthrie opined fifteen years ago, a Cinderella at the ball.[1]

Given Guthrie's earlier essay, I survey selected publications dating from 2003 onward.[2] Hebrews has featured in several scholarly conferences and seminars.[3] A few collections of essays old and new have appeared,[4] and numerous jour-

---

1. George H. Guthrie, "Hebrews in Its First-Century Contexts: Recent Research," in *The Face of New Testament Studies: A Survey of Recent Research*, ed. Scot McKnight and Grant R. Osborne (Grand Rapids: Baker Academic, 2004), 414–43. Guthrie borrows and develops the metaphor from J. C. McCullough, "Hebrews in Recent Scholarship," *IBS* 16 (1994): 66.

2. For another superb overview of work done prior to this point see Daniel J. Harrington, *What are They Saying about the Letter to the Hebrews?*, WATSA (New York: Paulist, 2005).

3. E.g., Rainer Kampling, ed., *Ausharren in der Verheissung: Studien zum Hebräerbrief*, Stuttgarter Bibelstudien 204 (Stuttgart: Katholisches Bibelwerk, 2004); Gabriella Gelardini, ed., *Hebrews: Contemporary Methods—New Insights*, BIS 75 (Leiden: Brill, 2005); Richard Bauckham et al., eds., *A Cloud of Witnesses: The Theology of Hebrews in Its Ancient Contexts*, LNTS 387 (London: T&T Clark, 2008); Richard Bauckham et al., eds., *The Epistle to the Hebrews and Christian Theology* (Grand Rapids: Eerdmans, 2009); Dirk J. Human and Gert Jacobus Steyn, eds., *Psalms and Hebrews: Studies in Reception*, LHBOTS 527 (London: T&T Clark, 2010); Jon C. Laansma and Daniel J. Treier, eds., *Christology, Hermeneutics, and Hebrews: Profiles from the History of Interpretation*, LNTS 423 (London: Bloomsbury T&T Clark, 2012); Gabriella Gelardini and Harold W. Attridge, eds., *Hebrews in Contexts*, AJEC 91 (Leiden: Brill, 2016); Régis Burnet, Didier Luciani, and Geert Van Oyen, eds., *The Epistle to the Hebrews: Writing at the Borders*, CBET 85 (Leuven: Peeters, 2016).

4. E.g., Knut Backhaus, *Der sprechende Gott: Gesammelte Studien zum Hebräerbrief*, WUNT 240 (Tübingen: Mohr Siebeck, 2009); Harold W. Attridge, *Essays on John and Hebrews*, WUNT 264 (Tübingen: Mohr Siebeck, 2010).

nal articles have been published. Here, however, I focus primarily on recently published monographs.[5] Space limitations prohibit critical engagement with the volumes discussed. Instead, I summarize their major arguments in order to help interested readers assay the landscape and to guide them on what recent books and scholars might be most germane to their interests. The following categories set the parameters of this survey: (1) issues broadly relating to the historical context of Hebrews (e.g., audience, genre, provenance, cultural and theological assumptions), (2) textual and hermeneutical discussions related to Hebrews' use of the OT, and (3) reflections on current trends.

Questions of Historical Background: The Contexts of Hebrews

The author of Hebrews addressed a congregation who confessed central beliefs about Jesus (particularly his identity as Divine Son, Messiah, and heavenly high priest). But questions of provenance remain under debate. When was the letter written, who wrote it, and to whom was it written? Additionally, what are the genre and purpose of Hebrews, and what might be the most helpful contextual background issues for interpreting the epistle and/or the identity of the original audience?

A wide variety of commentaries,[6] as well as a few volumes dealing with introductory matters and current issues in Hebrews, have been published.[7]

---

5. Well over thirty monographs, many of them revised doctoral dissertations, have appeared in the major academic series alone (e.g., BIS, BZNW, LNTS, NovTSup, WUNT and WUNT 2).

6. Martin Karrar, *Der Brief an die Hebräer*, ÖTK 20, no. 1–2 (Gütersloh: Gütersloher Verlagshaus, 2002–8); Edgar V. McKnight and Christopher Church, *Hebrews–James*, SHBC (Macon, GA: Smyth & Helwys, 2004); George Wesley Buchanan has revised his earlier commentary, *The Book of Hebrews: Its Challenge from Zion* (Eugene, OR: Wipf & Stock, 2006); Luke Timothy Johnson, *Hebrews: A Commentary*, NTL (Louisville: Westminster John Knox, 2006); Alan C. Mitchell, *Hebrews*, SP 13 (Collegeville, MN: Liturgical Press, 2007); Ben Witherington III, *Letters and Homilies for Jewish Christians: A Socio-Rhetorical Commentary on Hebrews, James and Jude* (Downers Grove, IL: IVP Academic, 2007); James W. Thompson, *Hebrews*, PCNT (Grand Rapids: Baker Academic, 2008); David L. Allen, *Hebrews*, NAC 35 (Nashville: Broadman & Holman, 2010); D. Stephen Long, *Hebrews*, Belief (Louisville: Westminster John Knox, 2011); Gareth Lee Cockerill, *The Epistle to the Hebrews*, NICNT (Grand Rapids: Eerdmans, 2012); Mary Ann Beavis and HyeRan Kim-Cragg, *Hebrews*, Wisdom Commentary 54 (Collegeville, MN: Liturgical Press, 2015); Thomas R. Schreiner, *Commentary on Hebrews*, BTCP (Nashville: Broadman & Holman, 2015); Mary Healy, *Hebrews*, CCSS (Grand Rapids: Baker Academic, 2016); Jean Massonnet, *L'Épître aux Hébreux*, Commentaire Biblique: Nouveau Testament (Paris: Cerf, 2016); James Swetnam, *Hebrews: An Interpretation*, SubBi 47 (Rome: Gregorian & Biblical Press, 2016); John W. Kleinig, *Hebrews*, ConcC (St. Louis: Concordia, 2017); Jon C. Laansma, *The Letter to the Hebrews: A Commentary for Preaching, Teaching and Bible Study* (Eugene, OR: Cascade, 2017). Given the publisher recalls of Peter O'Brien's commentary and monograph on Hebrews, I have not included them in this survey.

7. Kenneth L. Schenck, *Understanding the Book of Hebrews: The Story behind the Sermon* (Louisville: Westminster John Knox, 2003); Andrew T. Lincoln, *Hebrews: A Guide* (London:

With a few exceptions,[8] the authors of these volumes generally agree that we do not know who wrote Hebrews. A growing number argue for the plausibility of a date prior to the destruction of the Jerusalem temple in 70 CE.[9] Many think Rome remains the most likely destination,[10] though a few find Jerusalem more probable.[11] A handful of monographs, however, offer fresh perspectives and arguments on these issues.

New (and Renewed) Cases for Authorship

David L. Allen (not to be confused with David M. Allen, whose work features below) revives the ancient tradition of Luke as the author.[12] Ruth Hoppin continues to press for Priscilla.[13] More novel is the case laid out by Clare Rothschild that even though no author is named, Hebrews should be viewed as Pauline pseudepigraphon.[14]

The Genre of Hebrews: Ancient Sermon

Most scholars conclude that Hebrews was originally a homily delivered to a Jewish-Christian congregation in the context of worship. As is the case with many of the subsections in this survey, the studies here cannot be neatly split off from those in other subsections. The volumes discussed in this section, however, place special emphasis on Hebrews' sermonic character.

T&T Clark, 2006); Eric F. Mason and Kevin B. McCruden, *Reading the Epistle to the Hebrews: A Resource for Students*, SBLRBS 66 (Atlanta: SBL Press, 2011); David A. deSilva, *The Letter to the Hebrews in Social-Scientific Perspective* (Eugene, OR: Cascade, 2012).

8. Apollos is favored by Johnson (*Hebrews*, 42–44), Witherington (*Letters and Homilies*, 22–24), and Cockerill (*Epistle to the Hebrews*, 41).

9. For those who find a pre-70 CE date highly likely see, e.g., D. L. Allen, *Hebrews*, 74–78; Cockerill, *Epistle to the Hebrews*, 39–41; Healy, *Hebrews*, 22–23; Johnson, *Hebrews*, 39–40; Kleinig, *Hebrews*, 9; Massonnet, *L'Épître aux Hébreux*, 31; Schreiner, *Commentary on Hebrews*, 5–6; Witherington, *Letters and Homilies*, 27–30. On the other side, Schenck pushes for a later and more specific date during the years of Domitian's reign in 81–96 CE (*Understanding the Book of Hebrews*, 104). Pamela M. Eisenbaum argues for the likelihood of a second-century date in her essay "Locating Hebrews within the Literary Landscape of Christian Origins," in Gelardini, *Hebrews*, 213–37.

10. So Cockerill, *Epistle to the Hebrews*, 41; Laansma, *Letter to the Hebrews*, 8–9; Lincoln, *Hebrews*, 38–39; Schenck, *Understanding the Book of Hebrews*, 91; Witherington, *Letters and Homilies*, 28–33.

11. Carl Mosser gestures toward this conclusion in his essay "Rahab outside the Camp," in Bauckham, *Hebrews and Christian Theology*, 404.

12. David L. Allen, *The Lukan Authorship of Hebrews*, NACSBT (Nashville: Broadman & Holman, 2010).

13. See the rerelease of Ruth Hoppin, *Priscilla's Letter: Finding the Author of the Epistle to the Hebrews* (Ft. Bragg, CA: Lost Coast Press, 2009).

14. Clare K. Rothschild, *Hebrews as Pseudepigraphon: The History and Significance of the Pauline Attribution of Hebrews*, WUNT 235 (Tübingen: Mohr Siebeck, 2009).

Gabriella Gelardini offers an original account of the situation and the chiastic structure of Hebrews.[15] Based on comparisons with later rabbinic liturgy, she concludes that Hebrews is a synagogue sermon originally given on the Ninth of Av, the fast-day of remembrance for the destruction of the first and second Jewish temples. The author aims to comfort a congregation reeling from the loss of the temple by showing them that through Jesus, they have access to heavenly realities that far exceed those of the earthly cult.

Markus-Liborius Hermann argues that Hebrews seeks to persuade Jewish-Christians of their need to see how their identity now deviates and differs from that of the Hellenistic synagogue with which they share so much.[16] The homily draws on the exegetical methods and traditions of Hellenistic Judaism to reinterpret Scripture and scriptural categories in light of the Christ event. The author crafts his sermon to counter the pull of the ritual and liturgy of the synagogue. Jesus offers a better and more effective sacrifice, priestly service, and Day of Atonement to celebrate.

Jonathan Griffiths identifies Hebrews as a sermon structured around the exposition of OT texts.[17] The form and content of God's speech (*logos*) as well as the experience of the divine word (*hrēma*) come to the congregation partly by way of the scriptural exposition in the discourse. The sermon itself mediates divine speech to the audience. God meets with people by means of preaching, which passes on and effects an encounter with the divine word about salvation spoken in and by Jesus himself.

Hebrews' Structure

Cynthia Westfall examines Hebrews through the lens of discourse analysis.[18] She works methodically through the epistle, noting especially the author's clusters of hortatory subjunctive verbs ("let us" verbs) in Hebrews 4 (see vv. 1, 11–16) and 10 (see vv. 22–24). From these clusters she suggests a tripartite structure in the epistle that consists of three topics and corresponding hortatory themes—(1) Jesus is an apostle/messenger, so "let us" hold fast to the confession (1:1–4:16); (2) Jesus is a high priest, so "let us" draw near to God

---

15. Gabriella Gelardini, *"Verhärtet eure Herzen Nicht": Der Hebräer, eine Synagogenhomilie zu Tischa be-Aw*, BIS 83 (Leiden: Brill, 2006). For a summary of her argument in English, see Gabriella Gelardini, "Hebrews, an Ancient Synagogue Homily for Tisha be-Av: Its Function, Its Basis, Its Theological Interpretation," in Gelardini, *Hebrews: Contemporary Methods*, 107–27.

16. Markus-Liborius Hermann, *Die "hermeneutische Stunde" des Hebräerbriefs: Schriftauslegung in Spannungsfeldern*, Herders Biblische Studien 72 (Freiburg: Herder, 2014).

17. Jonathan I. Griffiths, *Hebrews and Divine Speech*, LNTS 507 (London: Bloomsbury T&T Clark, 2014).

18. Cynthia L. Westfall, *A Discourse Analysis of the Letter to the Hebrews: The Relationship between Form and Meaning*, LNTS 297 (London: T&T Clark, 2005).

(4:11–10:25); and (3) the audience are partners with Jesus, so "let us" move forward spiritually (10:19–13:16).

John Paul Heil takes a different approach arguing that a focus on linguistic features suggests the whole of Hebrews is organized chiastically.[19] He argues for three major units (A, 1:1–5:10; B, 5:11–9:28; A', 10:1–13:25), each of which contains eleven subunits that can themselves be shown to contain further chiastic relationships.

Hebrews' Situation

Jason Whitlark offers a fresh account of the purpose and situation of Hebrews, rereading large portions of the epistle as a call directed primarily to gentile Christians living in Rome under the rule of the emperors Titus and Domitian.[20]

Bryan Dyer examines Hebrews' emphasis on the topics of suffering and death, arguing that the original recipients faced these trials on account of their confession.[21] The author offers a theological account of suffering as divine discipline that intends to show that suffering is a sign of God's saving love. Jesus's death not only brings salvation for his people; it also provides evidence that death has been defeated and that God's people will receive what he has promised. Jesus is the chief example of endurance and obedience, and his life in spite of his death encourages the audience to persevere in the face of their suffering.

General Greco-Roman Backgrounds

Several monographs attend to the potential importance of aspects of the homily's Greco-Roman cultural milieu for understanding Hebrews. Patrick Gray examines Hebrews' assumptions regarding fear and fearlessness in light of Hellenistic moral philosophy, especially Plutarch, as these relate to suffering, death, and deities.[22] With this background, Hebrews' call for faith is

---

19. John Paul Heil, *Hebrews: Chiastic Structures and Audience Response*, CBQMS (Washington, DC: Catholic Biblical Association of America, 2010).

20. Jason A. Whitlark, *Resisting Empire: Rethinking the Purpose of the Letter to "the Hebrews,"* LNTS 484 (London: Bloomsbury T&T Clark, 2014). For additional, related discussions on the imperial context of Hebrews see the relevant essays in part 2 of Gelardini and Attridge, *Hebrews in Contexts*, as well as Ellen Bradshaw Aitken, "Life on the Frontier: The Transformation of Liminality in the Epistle to the Hebrews," in Burnet, Luciani, and Van Oyen, *Epistle to the Hebrews*, 205–28.

21. Bryan R. Dyer, *Suffering in the Face of Death: The Epistle to the Hebrews and Its Context of Situation*, LNTS 568 (London: Bloomsbury T&T Clark, 2017).

22. Patrick Gray, *Godly Fear: The Epistle to the Hebrews and Greco-Roman Critiques of Superstition*, AnBib 16 (Atlanta: SBL Press, 2003).

not a species of superstition, but a call grounded in Jesus's atoning death to find balance between an inappropriate fear of God and a refusal to believe in God. This balanced, godly fear (*eulabeia*) enables the believer to live in a way that pleases God.

Whitlark examines perseverance in Hebrews against the backdrop of reciprocity systems in the ancient Mediterranean world.[23] While benefaction was important for securing fidelity in human relationships, God's beneficence alone does not ensure human fidelity in Hebrews because humans cannot maintain their obligations. Only divine enablement—that is, an ongoing act of divine transformation of the human condition—can make human fidelity possible.

Kevin McCruden notes that in legal, documentary papyri in Egypt the verb meaning "to perfect" (*teleioun*) has to do with the definitive attestation (i.e., binding and publicly available confirmation) that a legally binding obligation (such as a business transaction or a loan) has been executed and its terms are valid and in force.[24] If Hebrews intends this meaning, Jesus's perfection entails the display and confirmation of his loving character evident in his suffering and death.

The Interplay of Platonic and Apocalyptic Ideas

The extent to which Hebrews reflects philosophical, especially Platonic, ideas and how these relate to the eschatological and apocalyptic elements of the text continues to be debated.

STUDIES EMPHASIZING HEBREWS' PLATONISM

According to Wilfried Eisele, Hebrews affirms a Platonic dualism between the realm of being and that of becoming.[25] The concrete spatial and temporal categories the author uses in relation to the heavenly realm are only metaphors. Because of Jesus's salvific death, the death of each believer enables that person's soul to leave the material realm and inherit the unshakable, immaterial kingdom where Jesus has already gone. Christ's second appearing (see 9:28) refers, then, not to his return at the end of history, but to the moment when one dies, escapes from the material body, and meets the exalted Jesus in the invisible, heavenly world.

---

23. Jason A. Whitlark, *Enabling Fidelity to God: Perseverance in Hebrews in Light of the Reciprocity Systems of the Ancient Mediterranean World*, Paternoster Biblical Monographs (Eugene, OR: Wipf & Stock, 2008).

24. Kevin B. McCruden, *Solidarity Perfected: Beneficent Christology in the Epistle to the Hebrews*, BZNW 159 (Berlin: de Gruyter, 2008).

25. Wilfried Eisele, *Ein unerschütterliches Reich: Die mittelplatonische Umformung des Parusiegedankens im Hebräerbrief*, BZNW 116 (Berlin: de Gruyter, 2003).

Kenneth Schenck argues that Hebrews represents a blend of philosophical and Jewish-eschatological elements.[26] The author correlates a two-age, apocalyptic eschatology with a dualism between the body/physical world and the spirit/heavenly realm. In the present age the human spirit is embodied in the physical realm. In the coming age, materiality will be destroyed and only the eternal heavenly realities will remain. Hebrews has wed apocalyptic notions of a transformed creation and a coming judgment with a Platonic dualism between the realms of body/material and soul/immaterial.

Stefan Svendsen suggests that Hebrews combines apocalyptic ideas with ideas from Philo of Alexandria.[27] The writer transforms Philo's approach to allegory, which draws on Platonic dualism, by combining it with a different metaphysics—that of Jewish apocalyptic dualism. Hebrews uses the form of Philonic allegory to undermine the practices of Judaism in order to persuade gentile Christians not to embrace Torah.[28]

Studies Emphasizing Jewish Eschatology and Apocalypticism

A number of recent publications challenge the notion that Hebrews envisions salvation in terms of the soul's escape from the material realm.[29] Others argue further that the epistle's dualism makes more sense when understood in terms of the kinds of cosmological and temporal commitments found in Jewish apocalyptic texts.

Scott Mackie argues that apocalyptic two-age eschatology drives the exhortation of Hebrews.[30] The author subordinates Platonic ideas to his eschatological commitments. The fullness of the eternal age is yet to come, but Jesus's death and exaltation mean that believers live in the "last days" (1:2). The dawning of the age to come explains the urgency of the author's exhortation. Final judgment is coming soon, but because Jesus now resides

---

26. Kenneth L. Schenck, *Cosmology and Eschatology in Hebrews: The Settings of the Sacrifice*, SNTSMS 143 (Cambridge: Cambridge University Press, 2007).

27. Stefan Nordgaard Svendsen, *Allegory Transformed: The Appropriation of Philonic Hermeneutics in the Letter to the Hebrews*, WUNT 2/269 (Tübingen: Mohr Siebeck, 2009).

28. A somewhat similar argument is advanced by A. J. M. Wedderburn in "Sawing Off the Branch: Theologizing Dangerously *ad Hebraeos*," *JTS* 56 (2005): 393–414. Wedderburn neither specifies who the audience is nor discusses allegory, but his view of the clash between Platonic and apocalyptic elements in Hebrews leads him to conclude that the author abandons Jewish sacrifice while still relying on sacrificial categories.

29. So, e.g., Edward Adams, "The Cosmology of Hebrews," in Bauckham et al., *Hebrews and Christian Theology*, 122–39; Jon C. Laansma, "The Cosmology of Hebrews," in Jonathan T. Pennington and Sean M. McDonough, eds., *Cosmology and New Testament Theology*, LNTS 355 (London: T&T Clark, 2008), 125–43; Philip Church, "Hebrews 1:10–12 and the Renewal of the Cosmos," *TynBul* 67 (2016): 269–86.

30. Scott D. Mackie, *Eschatology and Exhortation in the Epistle to the Hebrews*, WUNT 2/223 (Tübingen: Mohr Siebeck, 2007).

in the heavenly sanctuary, those to whom the author writes have direct access to God.[31]

Eric Mason examines Second Temple era texts, especially from Qumran, that contain priestly messianic traditions and notions about Melchizedek as an angelic figure.[32] The reflection on Melchizedek evident in these works provides a helpful analog for the priestly Christology of Hebrews. Of special interest are apocalyptically influenced texts (e.g., Aramaic Levi Document, Testament of Levi, Songs of the Sabbath Sacrifice, 11QMelchizedek) that envision a heavenly priesthood populated by angels and Melchizedek as one of the chief angelic priests. Such notions reflect the kinds of ideas that Hebrews assumes and invokes when portraying Jesus as the great heavenly high priest.[33]

Hebrews and the Heavenly Tabernacle

A handful of monographs look explicitly at the ways in which Jesus's sacrifice, his high-priestly ministry, and the concept of the heavenly tabernacle interrelate. Georg Gäbel locates Hebrews within the broad context of early Judaism.[34] Hebrews, he argues, consistently locates Jesus's priestly service and sacrificial offering in the sphere of the heavenly tabernacle. Jesus's exaltation marked his high-priestly investiture and his cultic acts of inaugurating the new covenant and approaching God to offer himself. Nevertheless, Jesus's heavenly work assumes his earthly obedience. His earthly work accomplishes all it was intended to do because Jesus serves in heaven.

In my own work I argue that Jesus's death inaugurates the new covenant and that his bodily resurrection marks the perfection/purification of his mortal humanity and the moment of his investiture as high priest.[35] The culmination of the process of his sacrifice occurred when, as high priest and offering, he ascended bodily into the heavenly holy of holies and presented

---

31. Mackie has gone on to argue in several articles for mystical elements in Hebrews. See especially Scott D. Mackie, "Heavenly Sanctuary Mysticism in the Epistle to the Hebrews," *JTS* 62 (2011): 77–117.

32. Eric F. Mason, *"You Are a Priest Forever": Second Temple Jewish Messianism and the Priestly Christology of the Epistle to the Hebrews*, STDJ 74 (Leiden: Brill, 2008).

33. Mason has published additional essays emphasizing the importance of Jewish apocalypticism in Hebrews. See, e.g., Eric F. Mason, "'Sit at My Right Hand': Enthronement and the Heavenly Sanctuary in Hebrews," in *A Teacher for All Generations: Essays in Honor of James C. VanderKam*, ed. Eric F. Mason et al., JSJSup 153 (Leiden: Brill, 2012), 2:901–16.

34. Georg Gäbel, *Die Kulttheologie des Hebräerbriefes: Eine exegetisch-religionsgeschichtliche Studie*, WUNT 2/212 (Tübingen: Mohr Siebeck, 2006).

35. David M. Moffitt, *Atonement and the Logic of Resurrection in the Epistle to the Hebrews*, NovTSup 141 (Leiden: Brill, 2011). See also my essay "Blood, Life, and Atonement: Reassessing Hebrews' Christological Appropriation of Yom Kippur," in *The Day of Atonement: Its Interpretation in Early Jewish and Christian Traditions*, ed. Thomas Heike and Tobias Nicklas, TBN 15 (Leiden: Brill, 2011), 211–24.

himself alive to the Father.³⁶ Sacrificial atonement—forgiveness of sin and ritual purification—has thereby become available even at the level of the human conscience. Jesus's ongoing intercession maintains the new covenant he inaugurated. Thus the author sees analogies between the Levitical high priest's drawing near to God's presence to offer sacrificial blood in the holy of holies on the Day of Atonement and the incarnate Son's death, resurrection, ascension, and perpetual intercession as high priest for his people in the holy of holies in the heavenly tabernacle.³⁷

Jody Barnard explores ways that apocalyptic mysticism informs Hebrews, noting that the mystical dimension of the epistle is often eclipsed by a scholarly focus on apocalyptic eschatology.³⁸ Jesus has entered the heavenly tabernacle in the presence of the angels and has there presented his offering to the Father. The author and audience practice a liturgy that intends to usher them into a mystical experience of these heavenly realities.³⁹

Jared Calaway argues that Hebrews draws on Jewish priestly conceptions that, like the Songs of the Sabbath Sacrifice, linked the celebration of Sabbath with access to the sanctuary where God dwells.⁴⁰ Both Hebrews and Songs envision their respective communities gaining access to the heavenly realities via liturgies linked with Sabbath, though in different ways. The Sabbath liturgy of Songs helps its community gain weekly access to worship in the heavenly tabernacle. Hebrews envisions Jesus's death as enabling ongoing access to the eternal Sabbath, which is the heavenly sanctuary/world to come. Hebrews, that is, has transformed Sabbath and sanctuary into enduring states coterminous with the heavenly realm.

Benjamin Ribbens proposes that Hebrews views the Levitical sacrifices in terms of sacramental, christological typology.⁴¹ Thus the earthly, Levitical sacrifices were effective because they proleptically accessed the heavenly tabernacle and the benefits of Jesus's sacrifice. The heavenly cult provides the pattern that legitimates the earthly cult and ensures the effectiveness of its

---

36. Interestingly, something like this interpretation of Hebrews appears to have been assumed by a number of early Christians. See David M. Moffitt, "Jesus' Heavenly Sacrifice in Early Christian Reception of Hebrews: A Survey," *JTS* 68 (2017): 46–71.

37. I argue more extensively for this notion in "Serving in the Tabernacle in Heaven: Sacred Space, Jesus's High-Priestly Sacrifice, and Hebrews' Analogical Theology," in Gelardini and Attridge, *Hebrews in Contexts*, 259–79.

38. Jody A. Barnard, *The Mysticism of Hebrews: Exploring the Role of Jewish Apocalyptic Mysticism in the Epistle to the Hebrews*, WUNT 2/331 (Tübingen: Mohr Siebeck, 2012).

39. Mackie has recently argued in several articles for similar conclusions. See, e.g., Mackie, "Heavenly Sanctuary Mysticism."

40. Jared C. Calaway, *The Sabbath and the Sanctuary: Access to God in the Letter to the Hebrews and Its Priestly Context*, WUNT 2/349 (Tübingen: Mohr Siebeck, 2013).

41. Benjamin J. Ribbens, *Levitical Sacrifice and Heavenly Cult in Hebrews*, BZNW 222 (Berlin: de Gruyter, 2016).

sacrifices. The earthly cult and ministry, therefore, were symbols that looked forward to Jesus and the salvation now made available by his once-for-all work.

Against the growing trend to emphasize the spatial reality of the heavenly tabernacle in Hebrews (either as heaven itself or as some kind of spatial reality located in the heavens), Philip Church argues that this language intends only to represent the fullness of God dwelling among humanity.[42] Jesus's death and exaltation allow access to this true dwelling. Hebrews' metaphorical heavenly-tabernacle language refers to the eschatological age and the heavenly world where God truly dwells fully among his people. Given this access, Church proposes a modified relapse theory for the epistle. The audience cannot leave Christianity to return to Judaism, since these were not yet distinct religions. They can, however, fail to see that their current ability to enter God's presence means that the old symbol (the earthly temple) should be abandoned.

Thematic Studies

Faith and Faithfulness in Hebrews

According to Matthew Marohl, faithfulness language functions as an identity marker in Hebrews.[43] Marohl suggests that members of the community have come to view their faith in Jesus in negative terms. The author creates a symbolic category, the *unfaithful* (a *them* or out-group). He has no real interest in identifying these outsiders. Rather, he presses the negative symbolism of the label in order to encourage the congregation to remain loyal to Jesus. The epistle intends to persuade its readers that they are the faithful and that faithfulness to their confession about Jesus is a positive marker of their identity.

Christopher Richardson explores the faithfulness of Jesus in Hebrews.[44] This aspect of Jesus's life marks one of the epistle's contributions to early Christology. In acting faithfully even to the point of death, Jesus is both the model of faithfulness for God's people and the means by which God's people obtain salvation. The encomiastic nature of Hebrews 11:1–12:3 offers the audience types of faithfulness by way of a renarration of Israel's history that anticipates and culminates in the perfect faith of Jesus himself. Thus Jesus's faithfulness brings the history of Israel to its climax.

---

42. Philip Church, *Hebrews and the Temple: Attitudes to the Temple in Second Temple Judaism and in Hebrews*, NovTSup 171 (Leiden: Brill, 2017).

43. Matthew J. Marohl, *Faithfulness and the Purpose of Hebrews: A Social Identity Approach*, Princeton Theological Monograph Series 82 (Eugene, OR: Pickwick, 2008).

44. Christopher A. Richardson, *Pioneer and Perfecter of Faith: Jesus' Faith as the Climax of Israel's History in the Epistle to the Hebrews*, WUNT 2/338 (Tübingen: Mohr Siebeck, 2012).

Matthew Easter argues that Hebrews contrasts two narratively shaped identities—that of *unfaith* (the default human story), which leads to death, and that of *faith* (a rewritten narrative), which leads to resurrection life and the enjoyment of the eternal inheritance.[45] Jesus's resurrection signifies that his story (the rewritten narrative) is the story one needs to participate in to gain life. Faith can therefore be seen in four dimensions. Because of Jesus's faithfulness (the christological dimension), others may follow his example (the ethical dimension) and receive resurrection like him (the eschatological dimension). Life is gained, then, by exercising faith in Jesus and by journeying with the community of faithful ones (the ecclesial dimension).

Hebrews' Critique of Judaism and the Mosaic Covenant

Many of the studies in this survey touch on Hebrews' relationship to elements of the Mosaic covenant. Some, however, directly address Hebrews' critical perspective on the Mosaic covenant and/or how that covenant and its law relate to the new covenant.

Barry Joslin examines Hebrews' engagement with the Mosaic law by arguing that the work of Christ allows the author to affirm both continuity and discontinuity between the Mosaic law and the new covenant.[46] Hebrews' appeal to Jeremiah 31 and the theme of the law's internalization means that much of what the law says still serves as a moral guide in the new covenant. The external aspects of sacrifice and purification in the old covenant are fulfilled and obsolete, but because of Jesus's work of forgiveness, the moral law can now be kept.

Engaging Hebrews' polemical statements about Jewish figures and institutions, Lloyd Kim argues that some aspects of Judaism are superseded in Hebrews, but that the author should not be labeled anti-Semitic.[47] The interplay of continuity and discontinuity with Judaism suggests an attempt to clarify the community's sectarian identity and defend its legitimacy. Hebrews is not, therefore, a rejection of the Jewish people. Rather, the author intends to sharpen distinctions between his community and other Jews. His Christocentric perspective on Jewish institutions such as the Levitical priesthood and sacrifice aims to legitimize the beliefs and practices of his community.

According to Michael Morrison, Hebrews seeks to persuade Jewish Christians being pressured to rely again on the old covenant sacrifices and priesthood

---

45. Matthew C. Easter, *The Faith and Faithfulness of Jesus in Hebrews*, SNTSMS 160 (Cambridge: Cambridge University Press, 2014).
46. Barry C. Joslin, *Hebrews, Christ, and the Law: The Theology of the Mosaic Law in Hebrews 7:1–10:18*, Paternoster Biblical Monographs (Milton Keynes, UK: Paternoster, 2008).
47. Lloyd Kim, *Polemic in the Book of Hebrews: Anti-Judaism, Anti-Semitism, Supersessionism?*, Princeton Theological Monograph Series 64 (Eugene, OR: Pickwick, 2006).

for their salvation that the old covenant has been comprehensively replaced by the new.[48] For Morrison, *covenant* implies a religious system (teachings/doctrines, communal identity, and obligations). Hebrews sets Christ and the new religious system of the new covenant against the religious system of the old in order to strengthen the community's commitment to Jesus.

Various Methodological and Thematic Studies

Martin Emmrich's study of the pneumatology of Hebrews notes some suggestive connections in Hebrews between Jesus's high-priestly ministry and the work of the Holy Spirit.[49] The eschatological presence of the Spirit, though not mentioned often in Hebrews, enables followers of Jesus to draw near to God, guides the community into fresh readings of their Scriptures, and warns them to continue faithfully toward God during their time of wandering.

R. J. McKelvey argues that Jesus's roles as pioneer and high priest must not be separated.[50] The dual roles hold the eschatological-temporal axis, sometimes viewed as the horizontal access of Hebrews theology, together with the vertical axis, wherein the congregation can go directly into God's heavenly presence. They can move forward in their pilgrimage spiritually, away from Judaism, and eschatologically, toward the goal of God's rest, because Jesus is both pioneer and high priest.

Amy Peeler explores Hebrews' development of a concept of God's family out of the divine relationship between God the Father and his Son.[51] Peeler notes that God's identity as Father stands at the core of the author's theology. Not only does the Father share his name with the Son; this paternal relationship drives the respect and obedience that the author calls Jesus's siblings to show. Further, Jesus provides the model for how God's fatherly instruction (*paideia*) perfects his children and leads them to their inheritance, even as his role as Son issues in his high priesthood, which frees them from enslavement to death.

Brian Small uses rhetorical criticism and literary theory to offer a synthetic account of how Hebrews characterizes Jesus.[52] By examining Hebrews' por-

---

48. Michael D. Morrison, *Who Needs a New Covenant? Rhetorical Function of the Covenant Motif in the Argument of Hebrews*, Princeton Theological Monograph Series 85 (Eugene, OR: Pickwick, 2008).

49. Martin Emmrich, *Pneumatological Concepts in the Epistle to the Hebrews: Amtscharisma, Prophet, and Guide of the Eschatological Exodus* (Lanham, MD: University Press of America, 2003).

50. R. J. McKelvey, *Pioneer and Priest: Jesus Christ in the Epistle to the Hebrews* (Eugene, OR: Pickwick, 2013).

51. Amy L. B. Peeler, *You Are My Son: The Family of God in the Epistle to the Hebrews*, LNTS 486 (London: Bloomsbury T&T Clark, 2014).

52. Brian C. Small, *The Characterization of Jesus in the Book of Hebrews*, BIS 128 (Leiden: Brill, 2014).

trayal of Jesus through the lens of various encomiastic *topoi*, Jesus's character emerges. Not only is Jesus depicted with divine and human characteristics, but the author also emphasizes his moral excellence. Jesus exemplifies virtue in his piety, obedience, perseverance, holiness, and humility. As divine Son, only Jesus can provide the privileges and benefits of salvation. His moral virtues, however, make him the chief example worthy of imitation for those who receive the benefits he offers.

Ole Jakob Filtvedt studies how Hebrews shapes the identity of its intended audience, particularly in light of the author's exhortation to go to Jesus outside the camp (13:13).[53] Hebrews puts the scriptural narrative of God's people, with its cultic rituals, at the core of the audience's identity while also calling them to turn from the old sacrifices and embrace the new things that have come in the Christ event. Only by becoming *outsiders* to so much of what shaped their Jewish identity in the past can they obtain the promises God always intended for his people. Hebrews' paradox lies in the fact that Jesus's death transforms and destabilizes the audience's old identity even as it makes available the true identity God always intended for his people.

Nicholas Moore revisits the motif of repetition in Hebrews.[54] Moore persuasively shows that the author views repetition positively or negatively depending on how, on the one hand, it derives from or promotes the Christ event and, on the other, how it opposes or conflicts with the salvation made available by Jesus's death. The Christ event cannot be repeated, but the worship of the community that confesses Jesus must be repeated. Hebrews, in other words, does not embrace a Platonic concept of repetition/plurality as a sign of imperfection. Rather, repetition is good or bad based on its relationship to Jesus's salvific work.

Hebrews' Use of the OT

The issue of Hebrews' curious use of the OT is a perennial topic of interest that runs like a scarlet thread through most of the studies surveyed above. Any number of them could easily be discussed in this subsection. The volumes engaged here, however, make this concern the heart of their projects.[55]

---

53. Ole Jakob Filtvedt, *The Identity of God's People and the Paradox of Hebrews*, WUNT 2/400 (Tübingen: Mohr Siebeck, 2015).

54. Nicholas J. Moore, *Repetition in Hebrews: Plurality and Singularity in the Letter to the Hebrews, Its Ancient Context, and the Early Church*, WUNT 2/388 (Tübingen: Mohr Siebeck, 2015).

55. George H. Guthrie's systematic study of Hebrews' use of the OT deserves mention here: George H. Guthrie, "Hebrews," in *Commentary on the New Testament Use of the Old Testament*, ed. G. K. Beale and D. A. Carson (Grand Rapids: Baker Academic, 2007), 919–95.

Hebrews, the LXX, and Jewish Exegesis

Radu Gheorghita argues that the Septuagint (LXX) played a distinct role in the theology and argumentation of Hebrews.[56] Not only does the author exploit nuances of the LXX; the eschatological and messianic concepts of Hebrews also derive from the LXX, not the Hebrew text. The theology of Habakkuk LXX even stands behind the way the author altered the text of Habakkuk 2:3–4 in Hebrews 10:37–38. Had the author used the Hebrew text tradition, Gheorghita concludes, the epistle would probably be "quite different from the one that we now possess."[57]

Susan Docherty offers a superb study on the ways in which Hebrews employs interpretive strategies common in early Jewish biblical exegesis.[58] She helpfully surveys two important fields of research directly relevant for understanding how the author of Hebrews handles Jewish Scripture: Jewish Midrash and LXX studies. Docherty makes a compelling case that the author of Hebrews shows great respect for the actual words of Scripture, as he knows them and largely interprets Scripture in line with the methods common to early Judaism. Any serious study of Hebrews' use of the OT will want to engage deeply with Docherty's volume.

Gert Steyn advances a detailed case that the author's *Vorlage*—the form of the Greek OT text he knew—is primarily Egyptian in character. While the author made stylistic changes when quoting, his citations suggest he knew a text that differs from the standard, eclectic editions of the LXX we use today.[59] Steyn's work contains numerous insights on the author's use of Scripture.

Georg Walser examines Hebrews' quotations of Jeremiah 31:33, Psalm 40:7b, and Genesis 47:31b.[60] He pays close attention to the textual and reception history of each of these citations, demonstrating that each of them circulated in different versions and with different interpretations. Walser shows that texts and their interpretive traditions were not always bound together. An interpreter could support a tradition/interpretation of a particular text that was based on a version of that text other than the one cited. Walser concludes that the author generally cites his texts accurately and may at times rely on interpretive traditions that depend on other versions of a given verse.

---

56. Radu Gheorghita, *The Role of the Septuagint in Hebrews: An Investigation of Its Influence with Special Consideration to the Use of Hab 2:3–4 in Heb 10:37–38*, WUNT 2/160 (Tübingen: Mohr Siebeck, 2003).

57. Gheorghita, *Role*, 227.

58. Susan E. Docherty, *The Use of the Old Testament in Hebrews: A Case Study in Early Jewish Bible Interpretation*, WUNT 2/260 (Tübingen: Mohr Siebeck, 2009).

59. Gert J. Steyn, *A Quest for the Assumed LXX* Vorlage *of the Explicit Quotations in Hebrews*, FRLANT 235 (Göttingen: Vandenhoeck & Ruprecht, 2011).

60. Georg A. Walser, *Old Testament Quotations in Hebrews: Studies in Their Textual and Contextual Background*, WUNT 2/356 (Tübingen: Mohr Siebeck, 2013).

The Role of Specific OT Figures and Texts

JOSHUA IN HEBREWS

Richard Ounsworth argues that Hebrews recognizes a genuine relationship—an ontological typology once hidden in Scripture but now revealed—between Joshua and Jesus.[61] The nature of the salvation that Jesus effects providentially shapes the story of Joshua. Nevertheless, Joshua did not bring ultimate salvation. There is a gap in the divine shaping of the story, one prepared for Jesus to fill by enabling God's people to enter his rest.

According to Bryan Whitfield, Hebrews' Christology draws not only on the Joshua of Numbers but also on Joshua the high priest in Zechariah, who enters the heavenly council and rebukes the accuser.[62] In Hebrews 3-4 the author looks especially at Joshua's faithfulness in his role as "pioneer" in Numbers 13-14, but his development of Jesus's high-priestly role, particularly in the heavenly realms, is informed by Zechariah 3. Whitfield's study pays particularly close attention to Second Temple and Rabbinic interpretations of Numbers 13-14 and Zechariah 3, showing ways in which Hebrews' interpretation is in dialogue with Joshua traditions, but also highlighting the author's unique link between the two OT Joshua figures and the ways these inform Hebrews' account of Jesus.

ZION AND SINAI IN HEBREWS

Kiwoong Son examines Hebrews' use of Zion imagery, arguing that the comparison and contrast between Sinai and Zion in Hebrews 12:18-24 is foreshadowed in Hebrews 1 and stands at the heart of the epistle's interpretation of Scripture.[63] For Son, the author's repeated conclusions that Jesus and the eternal, heavenly realm are better than so many Jewish figures and institutions culminates in the Sinai/Zion comparison.

Michael Kibbe argues that Hebrews' critical stance toward the Israelites' request for a mediator at Sinai depends on a reading of Deuteronomy's Horeb account. While the Israelites' claim to hear and obey in Exodus was acceptable to God, Deuteronomy knows they did not fear God enough to obey him and keep the covenant.[64] Israel's refusal to approach God at Sinai/Horeb is, from this standpoint, indicative of a bigger issue and leads to a

---

61. Richard Ounsworth, *Joshua Typology in the New Testament*, WUNT 2/328 (Tübingen: Mohr Siebeck, 2012).

62. Bryan J. Whitfield, *Joshua Traditions and the Argument of Hebrews 3 and 4*, BZNW 194 (Berlin: de Gruyter, 2013).

63. Kiwoong Son, *Zion Symbolism in Hebrews: Hebrews 12:18–24 as a Hermeneutical Key to the Epistle*, Paternoster Biblical Monographs (Milton Keynes, UK: Paternoster, 2005).

64. Michael Harrison Kibbe, *Godly Fear or Ungodly Failure? Hebrews 12 and the Sinai Theophanies*, BZNW 216 (Berlin: de Gruyter, 2016).

provisional covenant that did not allow the people to dwell in God's presence. Hebrews again calls God's people to come to the mountain, but this time they are summoned to Zion, the heavenly sanctuary, and ultimately to the world to come.

Hebrews' Use of Specific OT Texts

Sebastian Fuhrmann argues that Jeremiah 38:31–34 LXX (in English versions, 31:31–34), with its promise of a new *covenant* (*diathēkē*) in which God will no longer remember sins—that is, he will forgive them—serves as the key for understanding the meaning and role of Jesus's death in Hebrews.[65] Because the Greek word *diathēkē* most commonly meant "last will and testament," the use of this word in the LXX to render the Hebrew word for covenant (*berit*) allows the author to conceive of covenant in terms of a will. Hebrews finds in Jeremiah 38 LXX a divine promise about a new will coming into effect. Through the incarnation, Jesus's death is the event that brings the new covenant/will into effect. The idea that God would, under the terms of this new will, forgive sins then leads the author to further link Jesus's death with the Day of Atonement.

David M. Allen explores the importance of Deuteronomy for Hebrews' exhortation.[66] Taking his cue from recent scholarship on intertextuality, he identifies elements such as (1) Hebrews' citations of and allusions to Deuteronomy (esp. from Deut. 29 and 32), (2) the author's use of Deuteronomic motifs (e.g., the land, blessing/cursing imagery), and (3) similarities between the narrative situation of Israel in Deuteronomy and that of Hebrews' audience (e.g., poised on the edge of the promised inheritance). Allen demonstrates that Deuteronomy served as a pervasive intertext for Hebrews.

In a different vein, Jared Compton attempts to explain Hebrews as a straightforward exposition of Psalm 110.[67] Hebrews accurately expounds the original logic and intent of the psalmist. The author works with a narrative in which the fall means that humanity could return to paradise only by way of the promised Messiah's suffering and death. This narrative is "anticipated in the dual claims of Ps. 110.1 and Ps. 110.4."[68] Thus Psalm 110 "contained Hebrews *in nuce*."[69]

---

65. Sebastian Fuhrmann, *Vergeben und Vergessen: Christologie und Neuer Bund im Hebräerbrief*, WMANT 113 (Neukirchen-Vluyn: Neukirchener Verlag, 2007).
66. David M. Allen, *Deuteronomy and Exhortation in Hebrews: A Study in Narrative Re-Presentation*, WUNT 2/238 (Tübingen: Mohr Siebeck, 2008).
67. Jared Compton, *Psalm 110 and the Logic of Hebrews*, LNTS 537 (London: Bloomsbury T&T Clark, 2015).
68. Compton, *Psalm 110 and the Logic of Hebrews*, 166.
69. Compton, *Psalm 110 and the Logic of Hebrews*, 170.

Hermeneutics and God's Speech

Tomasz Lewicki locates Hebrews' recipients within a cultural context in which middle Platonic reflection on God's otherness and transcendence has caused a crisis of faith.[70] The author's focus on God's speech in Scripture and through his Son intends to reinvigorate their faith by stressing both their access to the living God and his ongoing revelation to them. Through the Spirit, the past words of God in Scripture to and through his Son admonish and encourage the community in the present.

Angela Rascher argues that the author's Christology determines his interpretation of the OT.[71] God's past speech in the OT provides the author with key texts, images, and ideas (e.g., Son, new covenant, heavenly sanctuary) to express the relationship between God's old promises and the now realized salvation. The freedom the author exercises in his interpretation of Scripture stems from the Christ event, which fills the old words spoken by God with new content (see Heb. 1:2).

Reflections

A variety of new and intriguing approaches are being applied to some of the old questions surrounding this enigmatic epistle. A few important trends are identifiable. First, a number of scholars suspect that Hebrews predates 70 CE and was originally intended as a sermon for a Jewish-Christian congregation familiar with the worship and liturgy of the Hellenistic-Jewish synagogue. Second, a great deal of attention in contemporary research touches in one way or another on two broad areas of research: (1) questions relating to the philosophical and cosmological assumptions of the author (Is he more in tune with Greco-Roman philosophical ideas or with Jewish creational and eschatological thinking?) and (2) questions relating to the author's use of the OT.

Apart from the discovery of new evidence, it is difficult to see how some of the central questions of Hebrews' dating, authorship, and provenance can be definitively answered. More fruitful, in my judgment, are those studies that examine this early Jewish-Christian homily through the lens of its engagement with Jewish Scripture, exegetical practices, and interpretive traditions. Real progress has been made in our understanding of the textual pluriformity of Hebrew and Greek texts of Jewish Scripture in the late Second Temple period. Studies such as those of Docherty and Walser caution not only against

---

70. Tomasz Lewicki, *"Weist nicht ab den Sprechenden!" Wort Gottes und Paraklese im Hebräerbrief*, Paderborner Theologische Studien 41 (Paderborn: Schöningh, 2004).

71. Angela Rascher, *Schriftauslegung und Christologie im Hebräerbrief*, BZNW 153 (Berlin: de Gruyter, 2007).

speaking about *the* LXX and *the* Hebrew text but also against assuming that the available LXX texts are all basically translations of the Masoretic Text. The realities of local manuscripts and textual pluriformity complicate simplistic conclusions about the form of the author's biblical citations. We cannot assume that the author freely changed his citations of Scripture where these differ from our editions of the LXX and/or the Masoretic Text. Moreover, this kind of careful work shows in fresh ways the extent to which Hebrews reads Scripture in light of Second Temple Jewish interpretive traditions and methods. The author did not engage Scripture in a cultural vacuum. He did not move directly from Jesus to the OT. His Christology, soteriology, cosmology, and eschatology were not fully preformed and then retroverted back onto Jewish Scripture. Rather, he lived at a time when early followers of Jesus not only read their Scriptures in light of their belief in Jesus's death, resurrection, and ascension but also filled out the content of those beliefs in light of their Scriptures.

Whenever Hebrews was written and wherever it was originally sent, the author assumes that those to whom he sends this homily are well versed in Jewish Scripture, understand Jewish interpretive strategies and traditions, and hold a worldview that shares much with those of apocalyptically minded Jews of the time. Hebrews' christological, soteriological, and eschatological reflection is shaped by exegetical engagement with Scripture that brings interpretive traditions, methods, and confession about Jesus into dialogue. Those studies (noted above) that argue that Hebrews simply expounds the original meaning of the OT and also those that conclude that Hebrews sees the OT only as meaningful insofar as Jesus fills it with new content are overly reductive, even historically implausible. Early Christian confession about Jesus did not emerge simply from reading Scripture, nor did it fall fully formed from heaven. Hebrews offers us an example of an early, Jewish follower of Jesus who works hard to interpret his Scriptures in light of Jesus and Jesus in light of his Scriptures.

20

The Epistle of James

Mariam Kamell Kovalishyn

Introduction

It is reasonable to assume that the Epistle of James will never reach the scholarly popularity of the Pauline epistles, but the field is flourishing nevertheless. An earlier survey of the field offered a chapter on the *person* of James but not one on the Epistle of James.[1] In the present volume, however, the epistle has merited its own chapter. This change might also indicate a broader shift in the field. The works of John Painter,[2] Patrick Hartin,[3] Bruce Chilton,[4] and Richard Bauckham,[5] several of which shaped the prior essay by Chilton on the person of James,[6] seem to have culminated the major interest in the historical person of James the Just. Most writing subsequent to *The Face of New Testament Studies* has assumed "James the Just" as the referent of James 1:1

---

1. Bruce Chilton, "James, Jesus' Brother," in *The Face of New Testament Studies*, ed. Scot McKnight and Grant R. Osborne (Grand Rapids: Baker Academic, 2004), 251–62.
2. John Painter, *Just James: The Brother of Jesus in History and Tradition* (Columbia: University of South Carolina Press, 1997).
3. Patrick J. Hartin, *James of Jerusalem: Heir to Jesus of Nazareth* (Collegeville, MN: Liturgical Press, 2004).
4. Bruce Chilton and Craig A. Evans, eds., *James the Just and Christian Origins*, NovTSup 98 (Leiden: Brill, 1999).
5. Richard Bauckham, *Jude and the Relatives of Jesus in the Early Church* (Edinburgh: T&T Clark, 1990); Bauckham, *James: Wisdom of James, Disciple of Jesus the Sage* (London: Routledge, 1999).
6. Chilton, "James, Jesus' Brother."

(whether as author or pseudepigraphic referent) and has focused instead on ways of reading the epistle.

The Epistle of James has gained in popularity in the last fifteen years. Dale Allison published his monumental commentary in the International Critical Commentary (ICC) series in 2013,[7] John Kloppenborg is writing a commentary on James that will take the place of Martin Dibelius's in the Hermeneia series, and many monographs have come out in recent years, signifying any number of dissertations completed on James. Its popularity, perhaps, stems from the fact that the epistle still provides a manageable field for students. Research has flourished recently in a few key areas, particularly in the epistle's place in the canon and its use of the OT and in recognition of the advanced rhetoric and theological depths of the epistle. We will look first at the current status of background issues such as authorship and dating, before moving to some of the key ongoing discussions.

Authorship, Date, and Canonical Questions

There is a fairly well-established understanding of the towering figure of James "the Just" in the early church as the one alluded to in James 1:1—and for this reason, the author could refer to himself simply as "James." Patrick Hartin has conveniently summarized the data relating to the figure of James, both from the NT texts themselves and from later Christian and non-Christian sources.[8] A Catholic, Hartin unsurprisingly opts for James as a "relative, clansman, or kinsman of Jesus," for "family ties to Jesus are not what counts. Instead it is the eschatological family that is important, where one carries out God's will."[9] Alan Saxby takes the family relationship in an unusual direction.[10] He argues that James was a central figure in an apocalyptic community of Judaism in Jerusalem influenced by John the Baptist before Jesus's ministry began. For this James, Jesus's death and resurrection became the focus of his movement, while the Galilean ministry was of minimal importance.[11] Saxby's book provides an intriguing theory, but it collapses under the weight of the silences to which it is indebted and does not sufficiently wrestle with the mass of scholarship exploring James's dependence on all of Jesus's teaching (see below).

---

7. Dale C. Allison Jr., *A Critical and Exegetical Commentary on the Epistle of James*, ICC (London: Bloomsbury T&T Clark, 2013).
8. Hartin, *James of Jerusalem*.
9. Hartin, *James of Jerusalem*, 33.
10. Alan Saxby, *James, Brother of Jesus, and the Jerusalem Church: A Radical Exploration of Christian Origins* (Eugene, OR: Wipf & Stock, 2015), 209–25.
11. Saxby, *James, Brother of Jesus*, 209.

The lessening of interest in the *character* of James does not mean, however, that the question of authorship is settled—dates for the epistle range from the late 40s to the 150s, leaving it one of the most contested NT documents. Currently, most datings center on the extremes of the range, and views of authorship range accordingly. Some of the key arguments concern the text's relation to Greek philosophy[12] and whether the brother of Jesus could have known Greek well enough to compose the epistle.[13] Other concerns regard the relationship of James to the Pauline tradition,[14] to the Jesus tradition (below), and to the writings of the early church and the canonization process. It is the last one that we shall explore here, as it has produced the greatest amount of recent discussion related to authorship.

Perhaps unsurprisingly, evangelicals tend to argue for earlier dates, but this view is often held loosely as a data point that cannot be conclusively confirmed. Scot McKnight tentatively summarizes, "The arguments against the traditional authorship are inconclusive; the arguments for traditional authorship are better but hardly compelling. . . . Traditional authorship is probably the best conclusion based on the evidence we have and the arguments that can be brought to the table."[15] Dan McCartney concurs that the best approach is to "begin with the document's own claims and then evaluate whether such claims fit the internal and external evidence."[16] He finds eight points of convergence that support authorship by James the brother of Jesus. While authorship by James seems probable, many agree there is no way to prove absolutely the position.

In 2007, David Nienhuis published his revised thesis in which he argues for a canonical reading of the Catholic Epistles, contending that James was composed

---

12. Cf. Matt Jackson-McCabe, *Logos and Law in the Letter of James: The Law of Nature, the Law of Moses, and the Law of Freedom* (Leiden: Brill, 2001); John S. Kloppenborg, "James 1:2–15 and Hellenistic Psychagogy," *NovT* 52 (2010), 37–71.

13. To which Scot McKnight concludes confidently, "Those who argue from language to non-traditional authorship are standing on weak foundations. There is sufficient evidence that James *could* have known and written in Greek, at least with the help of an amanuensis, to dislodge the simple argument that this Greek is too sophisticated for a brother of Jesus." Scot McKnight, *The Letter of James*, NICNT (Grand Rapids: Eerdmans, 2011), 34.

14. Cf. Margaret M. Mitchell, "The Letter of James as a Document of Paulinism?," in *Reading James with New Eyes: Methodological Reassessments of the Letter of James*, ed. Robert L. Webb and John S. Kloppenborg (London: T&T Clark, 2007), 75–98; Jacques Buchhold, "La Justification chez Jacques et chez Paul: Un exemple scripturaire de contextualisation," *Hokhma* 98 (2010): 35–56; E. Cuvillier, "'Jacques' et 'Paul' en débat: L'Épître de Jacques et la tradition Paulinienne (Jc 2:14–26//Ep 2:8–10, 2 Tm 1:9 et Tt 3:5.8b)," *NovT* 53 (2011): 273–91; Jane Heath, "The Righteous Gentile Interjects (James 2:18–19 and Romans 2:14–15)," *NovT* 55 (2013): 272–95; V. George Shillington, *James and Paul: The Politics of Identity at the Turn of the Ages* (Minneapolis: Fortress, 2015).

15. McKnight, *Letter of James*, 37.

16. Dan G. McCartney, *James*, BECNT (Grand Rapids: Baker Academic, 2009), 30–31.

last to function as a "cover letter" to the group.¹⁷ He surveys the reception history of each letter in the early church as well as the letters as a group, finding James weak on the early evidence. He takes seriously the similarity of themes and ideas between James and the other letters and theorizes that the Catholic Epistles were brought together to balance the Pauline corpus and that "James" was drafted as a "canon-conscious pseudepigraph" to bring them together.[18] "Like most of his contemporaries, our author revered Paul, yet he was quite aware that Paul's teaching was being used to support opinions deemed unorthodox by nascent Catholic theology. . . . Paul and James could speak in rather different, mutually corrective tones without implying they were inharmonious."[19] This argument is also apparent in Nienhuis's book coauthored with Robert Wall, which argues that "the theological deposit of the different CE [Catholic Epistles], when taken up and used as a canonical whole, articulates a more fluent and influential word that more effectively forms the Christian faith and witness of its readers than does their use as individual documents."[20] Based on this, Nienhuis and Wall posit a late, pseudepigraphic origin for the epistle.

The introduction to Allison's magisterial ICC commentary examines the relationship of James to other early Christian literature as well as James's absence from various early canon lists. He concludes that "although James presents itself as a letter from a Jerusalem authority to Jews in the diaspora, this is a literary fiction."[21] He asks, instead, why the epistle appears "Janus-faced, why it seems so Christian yet is so resolutely mute on peculiarly Christian themes, and why it contains so many passages that could be taken one way by a Christian and another by a non-Christian."[22] He concludes that the pseudepigrapher wrote to Jewish Christians still in the synagogue in an apologetic effort to reach non-Christian Jews. Similar to Nienhuis's view that the Catholic Epistles were to counter Paul, Allison's view is that "the text bears witness to a Greek-speaking Christian Judaism that opposed Paul, upheld the law, and regarded James as its hero."[23] Ironically, Margaret Mitchell has argued the opposite, that the letter of James actually stems from *within* the Pauline community, noting parallels to 1 Corinthians and Galatians.[24] Aside

---

17. David R. Nienhuis, *Not by Paul Alone: The Formation of the Catholic Epistle Collection and the Christian Canon* (Waco: Baylor University Press, 2007).

18. Nienhuis, *Not by Paul Alone*; chap. 3 is titled "Reading James as a Canon-Conscious Pseudepigraph," 163.

19. Nienhuis, *Not by Paul Alone*, 230.

20. David R. Nienhuis and Robert W. Wall, *Reading the Epistles of James, Peter, John, and Jude as Scripture: The Shaping of a Canonical Collection* (Grand Rapids: Eerdmans, 2013), 247.

21. Allison, *Epistle of James*, 38.

22. Allison, *Epistle of James*, 48.

23. Allison, *Epistle of James*, 49.

24. Mitchell, "Letter of James as a Document of Paulinism?"

from convincingly revealing that James and Paul are not as opposed as is often thought, her argument has not carried the field, but neither has Allison's.

Darian Lockett also argues for taking the Catholic Epistles as a group, but he argues that "reading the Catholic Epistles as a coherent collection need not automatically indicate a particular view of the composition history behind these letters."[25] In terms of authorship, therefore, he falls amid the "group of scholars [who conclude] there is no reason to deny the plausibility of the epistolary situation indicated by James 1.1."[26] Chris Stephens, meanwhile, has recently argued against Nienhuis's reading of the early reception history. He acknowledges that "there is still 'no indisputable evidence' for the existence, circulation, and canonical reception of James before the third century."[27] Nevertheless, he argues linguistic and papyrological evidence favors James having been written early in Palestine.

The bulk of arguments regarding authorship these days are also arguments regarding reception and canonization. Whether James is related to or opposed to the Pauline corpus, whether it originates from a coleader with Peter and John or was composed to introduce their letters, whether it influenced the language of the Didache, Hermas, and 1 Clement or was itself influenced by those letters—these are the questions in the authorship (and consequently dating, audience, and provenance) debates. The author identified in James 1:1 is assumed to be James, the brother of Jesus and leader of the Jerusalem church; the question now is whether the putative true author can be identified on other grounds.

James and the Jesus Tradition

James is indisputably related to the teaching of Jesus. The exact relationship, however, is in question, because James fails to cite Jesus's words precisely.[28] Without explicit citations, the relationship between the teaching of Jesus and the Epistle of James remains in dispute. Bauckham paved the way by exploring how Sirach uses Proverbs in a way that shows indebtedness without quotations.[29]

---

25. Darian Lockett, *An Introduction to the Catholic Epistles* (London: T&T Clark, 2012), 132.

26. Lockett, *Introduction to the Catholic Epistles*, 12. Such a view is expressed in, e.g., McCartney, *James*, 9; Peter H. Davids, *A Theology of James, Peter, and Jude: Biblical Theology of the New Testament* (Grand Rapids: Zondervan, 2014), 41, which concludes the letter was likely "written shortly after the death of James, the brother of Jesus, making use of sermons and sayings stemming from James"; Karen H. Jobes, *Letters to the Church: A Survey of Hebrews and the General Epistles* (Grand Rapids: Zondervan, 2011), 158–59.

27. Chris S. Stevens, "Does Neglect Mean Rejection? Canonical Reception History of James," *JETS* 60 (2017): 780.

28. The only likely exception is James 5:12.

29. Bauckham, *James*; Richard Bauckham, "The Wisdom of James and the Wisdom of Jesus," in *The Catholic Epistles and the Tradition*, ed. Jacques Schlosser (Leuven: Leuven University Press, 2004), 75–92.

Using Sirach, Bauckham is able to show how wisdom teachers would appropriate prior teaching, making it their own for their particular audience.

Kloppenborg followed Bauckham's earlier work, arguing, for instance, that "James [in 2:5] has paraphrased the Jesus saying [from Q 6,20b] in such a way that his addressees would recognize the ultimate source, but also so that it will serve the particulars of his argument."[30] Kloppenborg works with several Q examples to show how James appropriates the Jesus tradition. Peter Davids agrees in his recent work on the theology of James but pushes further in recognizing *thematic* dependence on the teaching of Jesus: "Whether the topic is wealth and poverty, speech and anger, or persecution, in James the teaching of Jesus appears to be foundational to James's thinking."[31] For both these authors, James's relationship to Jesus's teaching is not one of verbal quotation but reappropriation.

One interesting gap in this research is the question of whether the parables can be "heard" in the Epistle of James or whether James appropriated only didactic material. While some have suggested various potential parabolic reinterpretations, such as the parable of the sower in Luke 8 in James 1:21,[32] a recent master's thesis by Samuel Grottenberg applied the principles put forth by Bauckham, Kloppenborg, and Davids to test whether the parables listed in the NA[28] and UBS[5] cross-references have been reappropriated by James.[33] Taking in resonances of wording, theology, and context, in the end he concludes that "in the first two chapters of the Epistle of James, there are two 'probable' and three 'plausible' instances of appropriation," and he rules out two more instances.[34] Grottenberg moves the conversation beyond genre-similar appropriation, broadening the picture of James's dependence on Jesus's teaching.

Although resonances can be found throughout the Gospels, Christopher Morgan observes that nearly every part of James can be mapped onto the Sermon on the Mount in particular.[35] "James's message often comes across as an extension of the teachings of Jesus in the Sermon on the Mount or the

---

30. John S. Kloppenborg, "The Reception of the Jesus Traditions in James," in Schlosser, *Catholic Epistles and the Tradition*, 139; see also Kloppenborg, "The Emulation of the Jesus Tradition in the Letter of James," in Webb and Kloppenborg, *Reading James with New Eyes*, 121–50.

31. Davids, *Theology of James, Peter, and Jude*, 86.

32. Peter H. Davids, "James and Jesus," in *Jesus Tradition outside the Gospels*, ed. David Wenham (Sheffield: JSOT Press, 1984), 70.

33. Samuel P. Grottenberg, "Deparabolization in James: A Study in the Theological and Thematic Appropriation of the Synoptic Parables of Jesus in the Epistle of James" (MA Thesis: Regent College, 2018).

34. Grottenberg, "Deparabolization in James," 131. See chap. 5, pp. 126–31, for the cumulative summary and charts.

35. Christopher W. Morgan, *A Theology of James: Wisdom for Consistent Churches* (Phillipsburg, NJ: P&R Publishing, 2010), 31–37, includes two pages of parallels.

Sermon on the Plain (Matt. 5–7; Luke 6)."[36] He quotes Bruce Metzger stating that "Luther was right in applying the criterion 'whatever promotes Christ is apostolic' but wrong in not recognizing that the Epistle of James also 'promotes Christ' by its practical application of the Sermon on the Mount."[37] He concludes that "the influence of the teachings of Jesus on the Epistle of James is astounding! There is not one section of the Sermon on the Mount that James does not reflect, and there is not one section of James that does not reflect the teachings of Jesus."[38] This judgment should bring James into closer conversation with studies of other NT texts, particularly Gospels studies. Given its close relation to Jesus's teaching, James should not be an outlier in NT studies but an early example of the application of Jesus's teaching to the Christian community.

The closeness of the Epistle of James with Jesus's teaching became the basis for an entire symposium held at the University of Tilburg in 2007, examining the relationship between Matthew, James, and the Didache.[39] The conference volume does not make an argument concerning literary dependence, given the varied scholars involved. But they posit in the introduction that "Matthew and James share important features," agreements that "may be accounted for by theories of sources or traditions the authors used, or more generally their common Jewish-Christian background."[40] The volume explores the ways the writings describe ideal communities, deal with conflict within and without, and interpret torah and ritual. Karl-Wilhelm Niebuhr, meanwhile, recently used Matthew's and James's discussions and depictions of righteousness and justification to critique a faulty Lutheran understanding.[41] These sorts of studies continue to strengthen the relationship between Matthew in particular and James.[42]

---

36. Morgan, *Theology of James*, 32. This is not a rare conclusion, as Davids can also conclude that "there is a high degree of intertextuality between James and the Matthean form of the teaching of Jesus, and in particular, the Sermon on the Mount." Davids, *Theology of James, Peter, and Jude*, 43.

37. Bruce M. Metzger, *The Canon of the New Testament* (Oxford: Clarendon, 1987), 244, cited in Morgan, *Theology of James*, 32.

38. Morgan, *Theology of James*, 37. He also has three pages of parallels to Jesus's other teaching.

39. Huub van de Sandt and Jürgen K. Zangenberg, *Matthew, James, and Didache: Three Related Documents in Their Jewish and Christian Settings* (Atlanta: SBL, 2008).

40. Van de Sandt and Zangenberg, *Matthew, James, and Didache*, 1.

41. Karl-Wilhelm Niebuhr, "Gerechtigkeit und Rechtfertigung bei Matthäus und Jakobus: Eine Herausforderung für gegenwärtige lutherische Hermeneutik in globalen Kontexten," *Theologische Literaturzeitung* 140 (2015): 1329–48.

42. Cf. Patrick J. Hartin, *James and the "Q" Sayings of Jesus* (Sheffield: Sheffield Academic, 1991), which concluded James was closest to Q[Matt]; see also Alicia Batten, "The Jesus Tradition and the Letter of James," *RevExp* 108 (2011): 381–90, concerning the parallel between Q[Matt] 5:3 and James 2:5.

Taking common background in an unusual direction, Saxby (see above) hypothesizes that the so-called quote of Jesus in James 5:12 (of Matt. 5:34–37) may be the other way around. Because of his theory that James was a revolutionary leader in Jerusalem even before Jesus's ministry, he suggests that James 5:12 reveals where Jesus was influenced by and quoting *his* brother James.[43] This takes seriously James's own position as a wisdom teacher, but perhaps it opens the question whether *both* were influenced elsewhere.

James and the OT

Although James's relationship to the teaching of Jesus is apparent, equally obvious is his relationship to prior Jewish literature. Luke Timothy Johnson notes the epistle's heavy dependence on Leviticus 19, most obvious in chapter 2, where it quotes Leviticus 19:18, but prevalent throughout the epistle, particularly chapter 5.[44] Now Leviticus 19:12–18 (not just 19:18) is presumed as active in the text.

David deSilva includes the Apocrypha and Pseudepigrapha, showing how James worked with a broader scope of literature than "merely" the Protestant canonical OT.[45] He sees Sirach, 1 Enoch, and the Testament of Job as having strong resonances to the Epistle of James. Mindful of Samuel Sandmel's warning against parallelomania,[46] deSilva argues that Jesus, James, and Jude were distinctly *Jewish* and influenced by their heritage and literary environment. In contrast to Bauckham and Kloppenborg, who used Sirach to create a pattern, deSilva takes Sirach seriously as a source for the epistle's wisdom. And he agrees with prior arguments that see the Testament of Job as the source for James 5:11.[47] Noting the ambiguity of Testament of Job's origin, he argues that "the case for interrelationship becomes stronger given that neither the original Hebrew text, the Septuagint, nor the Targumim explains James's use of Job as an example of patient endurance so well as the *Testament*."[48]

---

43. Saxby, *James, Brother of Jesus*, 225–27.

44. Luke Timothy Johnson, "The Use of Leviticus 19 in the Letter of James," *JBL* 101 (1982): 391–401, republished as a chapter in Johnson, *Brother of Jesus, Friend of God* (Grand Rapids: Eerdmans, 2004), 123–35.

45. David A. deSilva, *The Jewish Teachers of Jesus, James, and Jude: What Earliest Christianity Learned from the Apocrypha and Pseudepigrapha* (Oxford: Oxford University Press, 2012).

46. DeSilva, *Jewish Teachers of Jesus, James, and Jude*, 11.

47. DeSilva, *Jewish Teachers of Jesus, James, and Jude*, 237–51; See, e.g., Cees Haas, "Job's Perseverance in the Testament of Job," in *Studies in the Testament of Job*, ed. Michael A. Knibb and Pieter W. van der Horst (Cambridge: Cambridge University Press, 1989), 117–54; Patrick Gray, "Points and Lines: Thematic Parallelism in the Letter of James and the *Testament of Job*," *NTS* 50 (2004): 406–24.

48. DeSilva, *Jewish Teachers of Jesus, James, and Jude*, 250.

Two recent works have focused on the named examples in James. Nicholas Ellis looks at the combined history of the narratives of Abraham and Job in the varied Jewish literature.[49] Faced with James's declaration that God is both *apeirastos* (not tempted) and *peirazei . . . oudena* (tempts no one) in 1:13—which seemingly contradicts the OT, where God does test and is put to the test by his people—and concerned about the ad hoc translations of *peirasmos* in chapter 1 ("trials" in 1:2–12 and "temptation" in 13 onward), Ellis examines the literature to see if there is a tradition within which James fits. He finds that the rewritten Bible blends the narratives of Job and Abraham in such a way that Abraham's testing is the result of a cosmic courtroom scene like that seen in Job 1 ("Jobraham"). The result is that God does not, indeed, test anyone, but he does *allow* testing of his people to prove their faithfulness.

Robert Foster, meanwhile, seeks to "explore how the author uses his named exemplars (Abraham, Rahab, Job, Elijah). For example, does the author use them just for his immediate purpose (e.g., in support of his argument or exhortation), or is there some deeper connection between them that may help to bind the composition together?"[50] While Abraham and Rahab have commonly been seen as examples of hospitality,[51] Foster argues that all four "share at least three qualities that are vital both to the life of faith of the individual but especially to that of their community"—namely, demonstrable commitment to God, the status of outsiders with regard to the "world" due to that commitment, and enduring significant trials by relying on God.[52] By reference to these, Foster argues that the named exemplars not only function in their particular setting in the epistle but also speak to the larger theme of wholehearted commitment to God in face of trials.

Continuing the exploration of the exemplars, I have an article with the *Journal of Biblical Literature* regarding James's use of Elijah.[53] Because the conclusion of the epistle is opaque and suggestions for the conclusion's start span from 5:7 to 5:19, I asked whether Elijah might provide a clue. Using intertextual reading, I argue that James intends his readers to remember the entire narrative of 1 Kings 17–18, framed by his reminder

---

49. Nicholas Ellis, *The Hermeneutics of Divine Testing: Cosmic Trials and Biblical Interpretation in the Epistle of James and Other Jewish Literature*, WUNT 2/396 (Tübingen: Mohr Siebeck, 2015).

50. Robert J. Foster, *The Significance of Exemplars for the Interpretation of the Book of James*, WUNT 2/376 (Tübingen: Mohr Siebeck, 2014), 5.

51. Most notably R. B. Ward, "The Works of Abraham: James 2:14–26," *HTR* 61 (1968): 283–90, but see more recently Andrew E. Arterbury, "Abraham's Hospitality among Jewish and Early Christian Writers," *PRS* 30, no. 3 (2003): 359–76.

52. Foster, *Significance of Exemplars*, 193.

53. Mariam Kamell Kovalishyn, "The Prayer of Elijah in James 5: An Example of Intertextuality," *JBL* 137, no. 4 (2018): 1029–47.

that Elijah prayed against and for rain. When the narrative is in play, the conclusion settles to 5:12–20, which depicts a single-minded community exercising faithfulness to God in all situations and seeking to restore those who wander. In contrast, Allison argues that 5:13–20 reflects a tradition seen in Jewish prayers that engage with Ezekiel 32–33.[54] Allison observes that in prayers echoing the Ezekiel chapters themes of healing are traditionally paired with images of those who wander.[55] In doing so, he forwards Dean Deppe's suggestion that the conclusion of James reflects an early church order of worship.[56]

These sorts of exercises need to continue. Foster leaves out "the prophets who spoke in the name of the Lord" (James 5:10), but the Epistle of James shows a heavy dependence on the prophetic literature, albeit again one of appropriation. And because James has been categorized as "wisdom" literature, the Deuteronomic and prophetic traditions in the epistle lack exploration.

Rhetoric and Structure

The rhetoric and structure of the epistle have long been a key place for research.[57] Alicia Batten begins her state of the field by discussing rhetoric and structure as the key for understanding current scholarship on the Epistle of James.[58] Dibelius's commentary set the terms for the discussion: he determined that the epistle was "structureless," 1:1 was the only mark of an "epistle," and the rhetoric was that of *paraenesis*, unconnected wisdom snippets.[59] The notion that there is no discernible structure has been soundly challenged by many commentators but particularly by Mark Taylor and George Guthrie, who find a wisdom orientation guiding the structure of the epistle.[60] Dibelius's description of paraenesis has also been revised by Leo Purdue[61] and John El-

---

54. Dale C. Allison Jr., "A Liturgical Tradition behind the Ending of James," *JSNT* 34 (2011): 3–18.

55. Allison, "Liturgical Tradition," 12.

56. Allison, "Liturgical Tradition," 13, 15, citing Dean B. Deppe, *The Sayings of Jesus in the Epistle of James* (Chelsea, MI: Bookcrafters, 1980), 135.

57. Useful resources that have come out regarding the Greek include A. K. M. Adam, *James: A Handbook on the Greek Text* (Waco: Baylor University Press, 2013); Chris A. Vlachos, *James*, B&H Exegetical Guide to the Greek New Testament (Nashville: B&H Academic, 2012).

58. Alicia Batten, *What Are They Saying about the Letter of James?*, WATSA (New York: Paulist Press, 2009), 5–27.

59. Martin Dibelius, *James*, trans. Michael A. Williams, Hermeneia (Philadelphia: Fortress, 1975), 2–3.

60. Mark E. Taylor and George H. Guthrie, "The Structure of James," *CBQ* 68, no. 4 (2006): 681–705.

61. Leo G. Perdue, "Paraenesis and the Epistle of James," *ZNW* 72 (1981): 241–56.

liott[62] and more recently by Duane Watson.[63] Watson's work in comparing sections of the epistle to classical Greco-Roman argumentation has made clear that James is argued far more competently than previously thought.

Comparisons of James's rhetoric to that of classical literature are fairly pervasive. Carol Poster works with "the genre of philosophical protreptic," whose generalized purpose "is to exhort the reader to strive toward the good, or the divine . . . [swaying] the will rather than arguing with the intellect."[64] Protreptic allows for the author of James to embody a modesty Poster sees in play through the epistle, a modesty that "actually enacts Jas' theological position."[65] In contrast to the arrogant, workless teachers whom James condemns, James humbly "restricts himself to three major points."[66] In refusing to engage in the status fights and rhetorical flourishes of his opponents, James enacts his teaching, putting his theology to work even in how he composes the letter—and uses a recognizable philosophical argumentation to do so.

Lauri Thurén also fights the notion that James can have excellent Greek and yet no rhetorical competence. She argues that "although some of the most typical expressions are absent, the *exordium* and the *peroration* can be identified," which are the crucial pieces for discerning "the rhetorical situation and the goal of the speech."[67] She argues that "in good rhetoric, the tactical moves must often not be too clearly identifiable," a risk taken in James.[68] She concludes, however, that if we de-rhetoricize the epistle, we can see that the "author seeks to demonstrate what the imperfection and inconsistency mean in practice. In all three parts of the *argumentatio* he attempts to prove that small deviations from a perfect way of life spring from grave sins, incorrect theology, and dangerous attitudes."[69]

Several works have followed in Watson's footsteps by examining a specific section of the epistle to determine its rhetorical import and method. Two

---

62. J. H. Elliott, "The Epistle of James in Rhetorical and Social Scientific Perspective: Holiness-Wholeness and Patterns of Replication," *BTB* 23 (1993): 71–81.

63. Duane F. Watson, "An Assessment of the Rhetoric and Rhetorical Analysis of the Letter of James," in Webb and Kloppenborg, *Reading James with New Eyes*, 99–120; see also Watson, "James 2 in Light of Greco-Roman Schemes of Argumentation," *NTS* 39 (1993): 94–121; Watson, "The Rhetoric of James 3:1–12 and a Classical Pattern of Argumentation," *NovT* 35 (1993): 48–64.

64. Carol Poster, "Words as Works: Philosophical Protreptic and the Epistle of James," in *Rhetorics in the New Millennium: Promise and Fulfillment*, ed. James D. Hester and J. David Hester (New York: T&T Clark, 2010), 236.

65. Poster, "Words as Works," 253.

66. Poster, "Words as Works," 253.

67. Lauri Thurén, "Risky Rhetoric in James," *NovT* 37 (1995): 275.

68. Thurén, "Risky Rhetoric in James," 283.

69. Thurén, "Risky Rhetoric in James," 281.

older articles by Gary Burge[70] and J. van der Westhuizen[71] reveal the continued focus on 2:14–26 as one of the key passages of interest in the epistle. Jean Aletti resumes this focus, and he aligns with Thurén in arguing that the quality of the Greek should point us to wonder whether "the development of its thought follows a Greek pattern as well."[72] He posits that in 2:14–26 James follows a common pattern called *chreia*, "whose ultimate purpose was ethical: to furnish criteria of action and comportment."[73] He maintains that this section of James is a response to Galatians 3 and Romans 4, but "the *chreia* allows James to discuss and criticize an opinion that refers to the Pauline letters" without having to name Paul explicitly, "combatting an erroneous opinion without polemicizing against the one (Paul) who is probably being used by those defending it to recommend it."[74] Thus, using Greek rhetoric, Aletti offers one more analysis of the James-Paul debate.

Luke Cheung agrees that the epistle shows far more coherence and structured argument than Dibelius allowed, but Cheung states that "the precise *nature* and *structure* of that overall unity is still a matter of constant dispute."[75] He concludes that "James shows characteristic features of both Hellenistic paraenesis and Jewish wisdom instruction, yet its contents owe more to the latter."[76] Cheung brings the discussion of rhetoric in line with those who would see the Hebrew Bible and Second Temple literature as the better context for the epistle. In so doing, he also deals with the eschatological elements of the text, which colors the nature of the paraenesis.[77]

Finally, more scholars lately are paying attention to the masculine and feminine language in James. James has a rare example of gender inclusion in 2:15 when he asks his audience to consider "a brother *or sister*" (*adelphos ē adelphē*). But looking more closely at Rahab *the prostitute*, Timothy

---

70. Gary M. Burge, "'And Threw Them Thus on Paper': Recovering the Poetic Form of James 2:14–26," *StudBT* 7 (1977): 31–45.

71. J. D. N. van der Westhuizen, "Stylistic Techniques and Their Function in James 2:14–26," *Neot* 25, no. 1 (1991): 89–107.

72. Jean Noël Aletti, "James 2,14–26: The Arrangement and Its Meaning," *Biblica* 95 (2014): 88–101.

73. Aletti, "James 2,14–26," 91.

74. Aletti, "James 2,14–26," 97. As I am not choosing to focus on the James-Paul debate, which has not been the focus of much independent scholarship in the last fifteen years (outside of commentaries), I also note the following article, which also uses rhetoric to examine the James-Paul contrast: John Painter, "The Power of Words: Rhetoric in James and Paul," in *The Missions of James, Peter, and Paul: Tensions in Early Christianity*, ed. Bruce Chilton and Craig Evans (Leiden: Brill, 2005), 235–73.

75. Luke L. Cheung, *The Genre, Composition and Hermeneutics of the Epistle of James* (Carlisle, UK: Paternoster, 2003), 272.

76. Cheung, *Genre, Composition and Hermeneutics*, 272.

77. For more on this, see also Todd C. Penner, *The Epistle of James and Eschatology: Rereading an Ancient Christian Letter*, JSNTSup 121 (Sheffield: Sheffield Academic, 1996).

Cargal draws out the contrasting language in the epistle regarding her obedience versus the audience's covenant adultery and double-mindedness (chap. 4).[78] William Baker pursues the gendered birth language in 1:14–21.[79] He draws out not just the contrasting birth narratives for death and life and how children act like their "parents"; he also addresses the thorny issue of how the "word" can be "innate" (*emphytos*) in 1:21: "The positive birth allegory of 1:18 [is] intended both to mirror and replace the negative allegory of 1:14–15. If so, then just as the child of the union between self-will and Desire carries the genetic makeup of Desire (and herself gives birth to death), so the child born from the union of God via the word of truth with those who submit to the gospel carries the DNA of the word of God."[80] All through Scripture God uses maternal imagery, and the Epistle of James is no different.

Theological Themes

The Epistle of James has had a hard time recovering from Luther's dismissal of it and Dibelius's assessment that it "has no 'theology.'"[81] Those verdicts, however, have lost ground in recent years, and there are now many studies into its theological themes. As noted above, Morgan has published an entire volume titled *A Theology of James*. Like many,[82] he concludes that James is concerned for a theology that *works* in the community, and thus the theology tends to be under the surface of the practical advice.[83] In Baylor's ethics series, Christian Reflection, an entire volume on James was recently published that includes a number of approaches to the theological themes seen in James, each aware of what Hartin called "Faith-in-Action: An Ethic of 'Perfection.'"[84]

---

78. Timothy B. Cargal, "When Is a Prostitute Not an Adulteress? The Language of Sexual Infidelity in the Rhetoric of the Letter of James," in *A Feminist Companion to the Catholic Epistles and Hebrews*, ed. Amy-Jill Levine (Cleveland: Pilgrim, 2004), 114–26.

79. William Baker, "Who's Your Daddy? Gendered Birth Images in the Soteriology of the Epistle of James (1:14–15, 18, 21)," *EQ* 79 (2007): 195–207.

80. Baker, "Who's Your Daddy?," 204.

81. Dibelius, *James*, 21.

82. E.g., Robert W. Wall, *Community of the Wise: The Letter of James* (Valley Forge, PA: Trinity Press International, 1997).

83. Morgan writes that James "advances a robust view of God that shapes not only our theology but also our very lives. Because of who God is, in faith we ask him for wisdom, live consistently, fight temptation, control our speech, take care of the marginalized, reject favoritism, meet the needs of the poor, humble ourselves, worship with genuineness, live in patience and hope, and become people of prayer and forgiveness." Morgan, *Theology of James*, 181.

84. Patrick Hartin, "Faith-in-Action: An Ethic of 'Perfection,'" in *The Letter of James*, ed. Robert B. Kruschwitz, Christian Reflection: A Series in Faith and Ethics (Waco: The Center for Christian Ethics, Baylor University, 2012), 20–28.

This ethic depends on God's work in redeeming his people through the "word of truth"; thus James ought not to be accused of "works-righteousness."[85]

Most now concur that the central theme of James is "purity" or "perfection." Cheung concludes that "James presents the values of a new order in terms of perfection for members of the eschatological twelve tribes of the diaspora. The pursuit of perfection, and its counterpart the eradication of doubleness, are made possible through God's work of redemption by the word of truth . . . and the heavenly wisdom."[86] This pursuit of perfection is lived out in relationship with the neighbor. Lockett likewise finds single-mindedness to be crucial. "Purity language articulates and constructs the reality of the audience with reference to how they should relate internally and to their surrounding culture. . . . The text's worldview and primary theme (perfection) cannot be understood without reference to purity language."[87] Lockett shows how the *kosmos* functions as the cause of double-mindedness, and when people act in accordance with the *kosmos*, they fail to live with one another as they ought as members of the kingdom of God.

Following a similar line of thinking, Margaret Aymer focuses on how the epistle depicts God: "James, in describing God's essence, focuses on God's singularity and God's immutability,"[88] in line with Jewish theology of the time. These traits undergird the community's relationship with God, who is seen as their father and benefactor, which means that one who belonged to the community "should live out one's role in accordance with the expected norms of the social order so that one could maintain one's honor and the honor of one's community."[89] The praxis of the community becomes one that stands against the ethics of empire. But "James's language about empire shows again how complicated James's relationship is with kyriarchy."[90] Hers is not a comfortable book, like that of Tamez, who critiques those of us who would domesticate the epistle.[91] Aymer does not allow for a simple reading of the epistle, but sees it as one that engages its context (and God) with varying degrees of critique and appropriation, one that still has resonance for believers living "in diaspora" today.

---

85. See Mariam J. Kamell, "God Gave Us Birth," in Kruschwitz, *Letter of James*, 11–19.
86. Cheung, *Genre, Composition and Hermeneutics*, 275.
87. Darian Lockett, *Purity and Worldview in the Epistle of James* (London: T&T Clark, 2008), 184.
88. Margaret Aymer, *James: Diaspora Rhetoric of a Friend of God* (Sheffield: Sheffield Phoenix, 2015), 36.
89. Aymer, *James*, 38.
90. Aymer, *James*, 64.
91. Elsa Tamez, *The Scandalous Message of James: Faith without Works Is Dead*, rev. ed. (New York: Crossroad, 2002), 1–6.

Wealth and poverty cannot be ignored in the epistle.[92] Like Tamez, Pedrito Maynard-Reid writes from a Latin American perspective.[93] He concludes, however, that "for [James] the rich are outside the sphere of salvation and faith."[94] Regarding the "poor" in 2:5, he argues strongly that these are the literal poor and only the literal poor.[95] Peter Davids, while not romanticizing the poor, sees the believers "pictured as at least identifying with the poor and perhaps as themselves being the oppressed poor. These poor are the righteous, believers, those waiting for the coming of the Lord."[96] Davids agrees with Maynard-Reid that the so-called rich are excluded from the community of faith: "James consistently describes the wealthier people within the Christian community negatively, while 'the rich' (outside the community) are roundly condemned."[97]

I concur that the explicit term *rich* refers to those outside the community but argue instead that they are outside the community because they identify themselves by their riches, and it is "humility" (*tapeinos*; cf. 1:9) that God seeks.[98] In 1:9–11, "James thus sets up his basic contrast: those of the less specific category, the humble, will be elevated, whereas the rich, the [*plousios*], will be humiliated. Because he avoids using the term 'poor' (*ptōchos*), James allows for the possibility that the 'humble' could include people with means, in contrast with those who are 'rich' (*plousios*), a group specifically demarked by their self-identification through their economic status, not through their status before God."[99] Everyone will be humbled; the question is whether the audience members will choose to humble themselves before God (4:1–10), or be forcibly humbled by God (5:1–6). Roland Deines

---

92. See, e.g., how often James is cited in Craig Blomberg, *Christians in an Age of Wealth: A Biblical Theology of Stewardship* (Grand Rapids: Zondervan, 2013), for a sense of how pervasive this theme is to the epistle. Craig L. Blomberg and Mariam J. Kamell conclude, "If our suggested structure of James is at all on target, then the theme of wealth and poverty, at the center of the chiasm of three key topics, emerges as this letter's most important issue." Blomberg and Kamell, *Exegetical Commentary on the New Testament James* (Grand Rapids: Zondervan, 2008), 254.

93. Pedrito U. Maynard-Reid, *Poverty and Wealth in James*, repr. ed. (Eugene, OR: Wipf & Stock, 2004).

94. Maynard-Reid, *Poverty and Wealth in James*, 63.

95. Maynard-Reid, *Poverty and Wealth in James*, 62; cf. Tamez, *Scandalous Message of James*, 25. Maynard-Reid says James "thought of piety as belonging *only* to the poor" and not "*more* to the poor." Maynard-Reid, *Poverty and Wealth in James*, 63.

96. Peter H. Davids, "The Test of Wealth," in Chilton and Evans, *Missions of James, Peter, and Paul*, 373.

97. Davids, "Test of Wealth," 379.

98. Mariam J. Kamell, "The Economics of Humility: The Rich and the Humble in James," in *Economic Dimensions of Early Christianity*, ed. Bruce W. Longenecker and Kelly Liebengood (Grand Rapids: Eerdmans, 2009), 157–75.

99. Kamell, "Economics of Humility," 167–68.

puts it even more strongly: "The conflict between God and Mammon has a soteriological as well as an ethical dimension: it concerns who is Lord in this life, to whom one owes obedience, and what the result will be in the end. The soteriological dimension will find its resolution at the day of judgment and the ethical is embodied in the question of to whom we pledge allegiance."[100] Hearing the resonance between Luke and James, Deines sees them as challenging their hearers to "display with their possessions that they love God and their neighbours."[101]

Nelson Morales examines the question of wealth and poverty through James's use of the OT. He notes that "every time [the topic of poverty and wealth] is present in the epistle, the OT also appears."[102] Morales complicates the issue by seeing three "fronts," "the poor, the rich, and those in between."[103] Using relevance theory (which "adds to the historical-critical and literary methods by emphasizing that the writer's meaning is more than what is explicitly communicated"[104]), he shows how James "interpretively metarepresents the OT and Jesus's words. . . . Different segments of his addressees derive different implicatures. James can use different illocutive forces at the same time. To the poor, he uses them to give them hope. To the wealthy Christians, he warns them. To those believers socially in between, in some passages he warns them; in others, he encourages them."[105] Morales finds that James's overarching purpose is for the audience to develop a genuine faith in practice of a "pure and undefiled religion."

Clearly, varied methodologies are being used to explore the theological themes of the epistle. It was not always apparent whether one ought to put a scholar's work into a section on "rhetoric" or "use of the OT" or "theological themes"! But it should be easy to see that the earlier charges against James having no theology have been disproven.

Reflections

The Epistle of James remains an active, if small, field. That said, one of the biggest holes is in getting scholars in other parts of the NT to engage scholar-

---

100. Roland Deines, "God or Mammon: The Danger of Wealth in the Jesus Tradition and in the Epistle of James," in *Anthropologie und Ethik im Frühjudentum und im Neuen Testament*, ed. Matthais Konradt and Esther Schläpfer (Tübingen: Mohr Siebeck, 2014), 327.

101. Deines, "God or Mammon," 378.

102. Nelson R. Morales, "Poor and Rich in James: A Relevance Theory Approach to James's Use of the Old Testament" (PhD diss., Trinity Evangelical Divinity School, 2015), 32, forthcoming in the BBR Supplement Series.

103. Morales, "Poor and Rich in James," 328.

104. Morales, "Poor and Rich in James," 330.

105. Morales, "Poor and Rich in James," 331.

ship on James. Gospels scholars or Pauline scholars may well be overwhelmed by their literature, but to continue to ignore James (and the other General Epistles) is to perpetuate a lopsided reading of the NT and ignores that those shaping the canon felt all the varied voices were important. Questions about the nature of "grace," of "faith," of the Christian life, of the NT use of the OT, all have immediate resonance in the Epistle of James, and reading it may help bring needed balance.

James's use of the OT can be studied much further. How James uses the prophetic literature has not been given sufficient study. Further exploration of the exemplars (particularly Job and the prophets) in James could continue to help expand our understanding of his use of the terms for endurance (*hypomonē, makrothymeō*). Similarly, further study into James's relationship to the teaching of Jesus could continue to expand our sense of the "Christian" nature of this text that so rarely alludes to Jesus. As noted above, if James was indebted to Jesus's parables for the shape of his teaching, then it reveals a wider dependence on the *whole* of Jesus's teaching. This may also help us appreciate James's creative reappropriation of all his sources, broadening the general appreciation for the epistle's structure and rhetorical skill. Textually, whether James is more indebted to Hebrew or Greek thought, language, and structure could help continue to reveal the influences of his thought and possibly help with provenance.

Several theological themes could continue to be developed. James's use of nature is profound and flows through his examples (e.g., 1:17–18; 3:3–12; 4:13–17; 5:7–9). While his view of nature seems positive, or at least a counter to humanity's duplicity,[106] his view of humanity's natural desires is wholly negative. The use of creation imagery could also help with the vexing question of whether 1:18 refers to original creation or new birth—a question also dependent on whether the background is Stoic or Jewish thought. Questions of gender could be further explored. Aymer finds James traditional in terms of gender roles, but his gender-inclusive language in 2:15 and his pairing of Rahab with Abraham, not to mention his use of maternal birth imagery in 1:18, might well point to an equalizing of the sexes. Likewise, the question of his anthropology could be further explored.[107]

Two further areas are gaining momentum. A number of works, including Bauckham's *James*, which uses Kierkegaard as his foil, have explored a history of interpretation, and this should continue. Aymer examines how the epistle

---

106. See, e.g., Alicia J. Batten, "The Urban and the Agrarian in the Letter of James," *JECH* 3 (2013): 4–20, for one approach to this question.

107. Mariam Kamell Kovalishyn, "Life as Image Bearers in the New Creation: The Anthropology of James," in *Anthropology and New Testament Theology*, ed. Jason Maston and Benjamin Reynolds (London: Bloomsbury T&T Clark, 2018), 177–88.

influenced the thinking of the great emancipationist Frederick Douglass.[108] David Gowler produced a thorough exercise in history of interpretation in his *James through the Centuries*.[109] Allison ends his introduction with the reception of James and concludes that James's "most important and far-reaching" impact has been Alcoholics Anonymous, for the epistle was "of key importance to the founders of A. A., . . . so popular among early members of A. A. that some wanted their fellowship to be called 'The James Club.'"[110] For all that we hear of James's irrelevance, it is refreshing to read works like these and realize that the faithful witness of James has been ongoing.

And James has been gaining traction globally. Unsurprisingly, liberation theologians appreciated its message of God's favor to the poor. But as the Western world learns to listen to scholars and leaders around the world, we ought to hear more from how people read the text within their own contexts. Zondervan's *Africa Bible Commentary* is a good start, but more opportunities should be made to hear global and minority voices.[111] At the 2018 annual meeting of the Society of Biblical Literature, in Denver, the James, Peter, and Jude Study Group sought papers from around the world on those epistles, but such an effort is limited to those who can afford to come. Without ongoing effort to develop and provide opportunities for minority scholars, James risks continuing to be "intercepted" by those who would hear it well.[112]

---

108. Margaret Aymer, *First Pure, Then Peaceable: Frederick Douglass, Darkness and the Epistle of James* (London: T&T Clark, 2008).

109. David B. Gowler, *James through the Centuries* (Chichester, West Sussex, UK: Wiley Blackwell, 2014).

110. Allison, *Epistle of James*, 109.

111. Solomon Andria, "James," in *Africa Bible Commentary*, ed. Tokunboh Adeyemo (Grand Rapids: Zondervan, 2006), 1509–16.

112. Tamez, *Scandalous Message of James*, chap. 1, uses the word *scandalous* in the title to point to how, historically, attempts have been made to "intercept" and "tame" the message of James, particularly its hope for the poor and oppressed.

21

The Petrine Letters

ABSON JOSEPH

Introduction

The current state of scholarship on the Petrine letters owes much to a resurgence of interest in these letters between 1986 and 2006.[1] Three articles published between 2004 and 2006 provided a timely opportunity to look back at the progress made in the study of the letters bearing the name of the apostle Peter. Eugene Boring used John Elliott's 1976 article as a starting point to highlight the key aspects of the scholarly discussion up to 2004.[2] Robert Webb's assessment of the scholarship on the Petrine letters appeared that same year. In his survey, Webb focused primarily on the conversations that occurred on, and contributions made to, the literary and sociohistorical contexts of 1 Peter. He also briefly discussed developments in the study of 2 Peter.[3] Mark Dubis has offered an in-depth discussion on many issues in 1 Peter: authorship, date and historical setting, recipients and provenance,

---

1. See Abson Prédestin Joseph, *A Narratological Reading of 1 Peter*, LNTS 440 (London: Bloomsbury T&T Clark, 2012), 1–25.
2. Eugene Boring, "First Peter in Recent Study," *WW* 24, no. 4 (2004): 358–67. See also John H. Elliott, "The Rehabilitation of an Exegetical Step-Child: 1 Peter in Recent Research," *JBL* 95 (1976): 243–54.
3. Robert L. Webb, "The Petrine Epistles: Recent Development and Trends," in *The Face of New Testament Studies*, ed. Grant R. Osborne and Scot McKnight (Grand Rapids: Baker Academic, 2004), 373–90.

unity, genre and structure, and sources behind the text.[4] These publications coincided with the creation of a consultation sponsored by the Society of Biblical Literature (SBL) and titled "Methodological Reassessments of the Letters of the James, Peter, and Jude." The consultation provided a space for scholars to discuss fresh perspectives and approaches to the study of these letters. Seminal papers discussed among this working group were compiled and published in two volumes.[5] The meetings of the SBL consultation in 2006 and 2007 that focused on 1 and 2 Peter, respectively, represent a microcosm of a renewed and growing interest in the Petrine letters, as is evidenced by the number of monographs, commentaries, and scholarly articles appearing during that period and since.[6]

Methodological Considerations and Current Approaches

From a methodological standpoint, recent scholarship has focused on proposing new ways of reading the Petrine letters. There exist continuity and discontinuity in that sociological readings continue to play an important role, but sociohistorical concerns and conversations have also made way for nuanced and/or new approaches.[7]

Sociological Readings and Perspectives

Torrey Seland developed a methodology that combines social theory and diaspora Jewish literature, focusing particularly on the works of Philo of Alexandria, to perform a "Philonic" reading of some sections and aspects of 1 Peter.[8] Seland seeks to advance the scholarly conversation on the identity

---

[4]. Mark Dubis, "Research on 1 Peter: A Survey of Scholarly Literature Since 1985," *CBR* 4, no. 2 (2006): 199–239.

[5]. Robert L. Webb and Betsy Bauman-Martin, eds., *Reading First Peter with New Eyes: Methodological Reassessments of the Letter of First Peter*, LNTS 364 (London: T&T Clark, 2007); Robert L. Webb and Duane F. Watson, eds., *Reading Second Peter with New Eyes: Methodological Reassessments of the Letter of Second Peter*, LNTS 382 (London: T&T Clark, 2010).

[6]. Recent surveys on the scholarship on the Petrine Letters, particularly on 1 Peter, include Theo K. Heckel, "Neuere Literatur zum Ersten Petrusbrief," in *Theologische Literaturzeitung* 139 (2014): 522–30; Friedrich Wilhelm Horn, "Christen in der Diaspora: Zum Kirchenverständnis des 1. Petrusbriefs," *Kerygma und Dogma* 63 (2017): 3–17. See also John F. Evans, *A Guide to Biblical Commentaries and Reference Works* (Grand Rapids: Zondervan, 2016), 408–19.

[7]. Joseph, *Narratological Reading of 1 Peter*, 62–67.

[8]. Torrey Seland, *Strangers in the Light: Philonic Perspectives on Christian Identity in 1 Peter*, BIS 76 (Leiden: Brill, 2005). Cf. Paul Bony, *La Première Épître de Pierre: Chrétiens en diaspora*, Lire la Bible 137 (Paris: Editions du Cerf, 2004); Thorsten Klein, *Bewährung in Anfechtung: Der Jakobusbrief und der erste Petrusbrief als christliche Diaspora-Briefe* (Tübingen: A. Francke, 2011).

and social reality of the epistle's original readers.[9] He builds on previous studies on the controlling metaphor of 1 Peter to provide a better understanding of the concepts of *paroikos* and *parepidēmos*, which the author uses to describe the audience.[10] Seland arranges his argument not from the standpoint of the social situation of the readers but from the author's perception of their situation.[11] He argues that the author of 1 Peter considers his readers "as living a life influenced by social circumstances very much comparable to those experienced in the Diaspora by proselytes to Judaism."[12] Seland draws on the acculturation/assimilation research associated with social psychology and modern communication research and relies on the work of Milton M. Gordon in social studies and John Barclay in biblical studies to shape the lens through which he reads the author's description of the situation of the audience.[13]

David Horrell engages the Balch-Elliott debate to demonstrate how the scholarly discussion and current approaches to this debate have failed to solve the impasse.[14] David L. Balch proposes that the letter urges readers to comform and assimilate, whereas John Elliott argues that the letter was written to encourage readers to resist the pressures of the surrounding culture.[15] Horrell draws on the works of James C. Scott and Fernando Segovia, among

---

9. E.g., John H. Elliott, *A Home for the Homeless: A Sociological Exegesis of 1 Peter, Its Situation and Strategy* (London: SCM, 1981); Elliott, *A Home for the Homeless: A Social-Scientific Criticism of 1 Peter, Its Situation and Strategy* (Eugene, OR: Wipf & Stock, 2005); David Balch, "Hellenization/Acculturation in 1 Peter," in *Perspectives on First Peter*, ed. Charles H. Talbert, NABPRSS 9 (Macon, GA: Mercer University Press, 1986); Miroslav Volf, "Soft Difference: Theological Reflections on the Relation between Church and Culture in 1 Peter," *Ex Auditu* 10 (1994): 15–30; Stephen R. Bechtler, *Following in His Steps: Suffering, Community, and Christology in 1 Peter*, SBLDS 162 (Atlanta: Scholars Press, 1998).

10. See Troy W. Martin, *Metaphor and Composition in 1 Peter*, SBLDS 131 (Atlanta: Scholars Press, 1992); Reinhard Feldmeier, *Die Christen als Fremde: Die Metapher der Fremde in der antiken Welt, im Urchristentum und im 1. Petrusbrief*, WUNT 64 (Tübingen: Mohr Siebeck, 1992); Paul J. Achtemeier, *1 Peter*, Hermeneia (Minneapolis: Fortress, 1996).

11. Seland, *Strangers in the Light*, 39–40.

12. Seland, *Strangers in the Light*, 2.

13. Seland, *Strangers in the Light*, 147–65. Cf. Milton M. Gordon, *Assimilation in American Life: The Role of Race, Religion and National Origins* (New York: Oxford University Press, 1964); John M. G. Barclay, "Paul among Diaspora Jews: Anomaly or Apostate?," *JSNT* 60 (1993): 89–120; John M. G. Barclay, *Jesus in the Mediterranean Diaspora: From Alexander to Trajan (332 BCE—117 CE)* (Edinburgh: T&T Clark, 1996).

14. David G. Horrell, "Between Conformity and Resistance: Beyond the Balch-Elliott Debate towards a Post-Colonial Reading of 1 Peter," in Webb and Bauman-Martin, *Reading First Peter with New Eyes*, 111–43, reprinted in David G. Horrell, *Becoming Christian: Essays on 1 Peter and the Making of Christian Identity*, LNTS 394 (London: Bloomsbury T&T Clark, 2013), 211–38.

15. John H. Elliott, "1 Peter, Its Situation and Strategy: A Discussion with David Balch," in *Perspectives on First Peter*, ed. Charles H. Talbert, NABPRSS 9 (Macon, GA: Mercer University Press, 1986); Balch, "Hellenization/Acculturation in 1 Peter."

others, to construct a postcolonial reading of 1 Peter.[16] He proposes that postcolonialism "invites us to read 1 Peter as literary product of a colonial/imperial situation, with our ears especially attuned to the ways in which this letter constructs the identity of the people to whom it is addressed and offers one particular way of negotiating existence in the empire, between conformity and resistance."[17] Briefly surveying the text of the letter, he concludes that the author is encouraging his audience to embody polite resistance.[18]

Paul Holloway endeavors to move the conversation beyond mere agreement on the presence of conflict between 1 Peter's original readers and their non-Christian neighbors. Convinced that it is possible to be more specific about the nature of the conflict, he presents the case that the readers of 1 Peter were victims of social prejudice and that the letter was written to address the fears and various outcomes of this prejudice and instruct them on how to cope.[19] He appropriates insights gained from social psychology and provides evidence of anti-Christian prejudice at work in the early Roman Empire and in 1 Peter to substantiate his claim.[20] He surveys ancient theories and practices of consolation in Greco-Roman and early Jewish traditions as well as modern strategies for coping with prejudice to suggest that 1 Peter can be considered as a letter of consolation.[21]

Travis B. Williams draws on the work of David Horrell and Paul Holloway, among others, to diagnose the social strategy of 1 Peter.[22] He aims to challenge the modern consensus vis-à-vis the meaning and function of good works in 1 Peter and to provide a fresh perspective on the letter.[23] Like Horrell and Holloway, he acknowledges the contributions and shortcomings of the current sociological approaches to 1 Peter. He combines Horrell's postcolonial criticism and Holloway's social psychology to provide a more adequate and

---

16. See James C. Scott, *Weapons of the Weak: Everyday Forms of Peasant Resistance* (New Haven: Yale University Press, 1985); Scott, *Domination and the Arts of Resistance: Hidden Transcripts* (New Haven: Yale University Press, 1990); Fernando F. Segovia, "Biblical Criticism and Postcolonial Studies: Toward a Postcolonial Optic," in *The Postcolonial Bible*, ed. R. S. Sugirtharajah (Sheffield: Sheffield Academic, 1998), 49–65; Stephen D. Moore and Fernando F. Segovia, eds., *Postcolonial Biblical Criticism: Interdisciplinary Intersections* (London: T&T Clark, 2005).

17. Horrell, "Between Conformity and Resistance," 123.

18. Horrell, "Between Conformity and Resistance," 141–43.

19. Paul A. Holloway, *Coping with Prejudice: 1 Peter in Social-Psychological Perspective*, WUNT 244 (Tübingen: Mohr Siebeck, 2009).

20. Holloway, *Coping with Prejudice*, 40–73.

21. Holloway, *Coping with Prejudice*, 76–136.

22. Travis B. Williams, *Good Works in 1 Peter: Negotiating Social Conflict and Christian Identity in the Greco-Roman World*, WUNT 337 (Tübingen: Mohr Siebeck, 2014). Williams employs a similar methodology in an earlier work, where he focuses on the concept of persecution. See Williams, *Persecution in 1 Peter: Differentiating and Contextualizing Early Christian Suffering*, NovTSup 145 (Leiden: Brill, 2012).

23. Williams, *Good Works in 1 Peter*, 275.

nuanced picture of the social strategy of the author.[24] Williams is concerned with demonstrating the various emotional or psychological ways that targets of prejudice adapt to stigma-related stressors and how this adaptation influences their performance of good works.[25]

James C. Miller combines social identity theory and narrative methodology to address the issue of collective identity in 2 Peter.[26] He argues that 2 Peter "functions in significant part as an instrument of communal-identity formation. In other words, this document portrays a symbolic narrative world and attempts to persuade its auditors to locate themselves in it."[27] Miller's analysis of identity formation in 2 Peter rests on three key premises—namely, collective identity is the perception of similarities and differences, is perceived as persisting through time, and is a social process.[28] From a narrative standpoint, 2 Peter depicts a broad story of divine activity within which stories of human actors, characterized in moral terms, find their place.[29]

Political readings of texts are part of the larger category of sociological methodological perspectives. However, they take their point of departure from the oppressive realities that surround and may have affected the text and/or the reader. Recently, scholars studying the Petrine letters have become more interested in postcolonial reading as an interpretive lens.[30] To apply political perspectives to a text involves nuance, and an adequate discussion is beyond our scope here.[31] This type of methodology, more than others, is affected by issues such as who is doing the reading and what location she or he is reading from. Therefore, not all postcolonial readings are equal.

Betsy Bauman-Martin draws from the work of Musa Dube and Edward Said to engage in a postcolonial reading of 1 Peter.[32] Postcolonial analysis focuses on

---

24. Williams, *Good Works in 1 Peter*, 23–24.
25. Williams, *Good Works in 1 Peter*, 34.
26. James C. Miller, "The Sociological Category of 'Collective Identity' and Its Implications for Understanding Second Peter," in Webb and Watson, *Reading Second Peter with New Eyes*, 147–77. Cf. Philip F. Esler, *Conflict and Identity in Romans: The Social Setting of Paul's Letter* (Minneapolis: Fortress, 2003).
27. Miller, "Sociological Category of 'Collective Identity,'" 148.
28. Miller, "Sociological Category of 'Collective Identity,'" 149–50.
29. Miller, "Sociological Category of 'Collective Identity,'" 167–77.
30. E.g., Amy-Jill Levine with Maria Mayo Robbins, eds., *A Feminist Companion to the Catholic Epistles and Hebrews* (Cleveland: Pilgrim Press, 2004); Cary Reeder, "1 Peter 3:1–6: Biblical Authority and Battered Wives," *BBR* 25 (2015): 519–39; Elisabeth Schüssler Fiorenza, "1 Peter," in *A Postcolonial Commentary on the New Testament Writings*, ed. Fernando F. Segovia and R. S. Sugirtharajah (Sheffield: Sheffield Academic, 2007), 380–403.
31. Cf. Betsy Bauman-Martin, "Speaking Jewish: Postcolonial Aliens and Strangers in First Peter," in Webb and Baumann-Martin, *Reading First Peter with New Eyes*, 144–77, esp. 149n19; Horrell, "Between Conformity and Resistance," 124n51; Jennifer G. Bird, *Abuse, Power, and Fearful Obedience: Reconsidering 1 Peter's Command to Wives*, LNTS 442 (London: T&T Clark, 2011), 14.
32. Bauman-Martin, "Speaking Jewish," 144–45. See further Edward W. Said, *Orientalism* (New York: Random House, 1978); Musa Dube, *Postcolonial Feminist Interpretation of the Bible* (Atlanta: Chalice, 2000).

how victims of imperialism produce literature that arises out of their experience.[33] The methodology Bauman-Martin proposes consists of examining "the ways in which the borrowing of the language of chosenness and other identity markers of Judaism operate both as a means of resistance and ideological imperialism in 1 Peter."[34] She demonstrates the presence of supersessionist elements within 1 Peter and argues that the christological concepts present in the letter serve as evidence that 1 Peter cannot be legitimately identified as a "Jewish: text. The author's appropriation of diaspora language and his use of other metaphors related to Israel are an "imitation of imperialist domination and an attempt to create a universal, absolute identity for his marginalized readers."[35]

Jennifer Bird approaches her reading of 1 Peter from a feminist, postcolonial, and materialist perspective.[36] While building her methodology on the foundation of the scholarship that has preceded her, Bird is acutely aware of and challenges the influence of Eurocentric, white, "malestream" scholarship. She challenges the practice of having a handful of men speaking for all women and men and warns against women scholars internalizing the very worldview that has oppressed them.[37] She discusses the key aspects of each of the three elements of her methodology and demonstrates how they intersect in shaping the lens with which she reads 1 Peter. She lists seven specific dynamics that she looks for in a text.[38] She applies the methodology by looking at the narratological and rhetorical implications of the text that precedes the *Haustafel* section in 1 Peter, paying special attention to some of the religious and sociopolitical aspects of the text.[39] She then discusses the *Haustafel* of 1 Peter in light of those aspects, primarily to demonstrate how women/wives are constructed in the letter.[40]

Literary Readings and Perspectives

Recent scholarship in the Petrine letters also has become more interested in applying fresh literary perspectives to 1–2 Peter, such as classical rhetorical criticism, sociorhetorical criticism, and narrative criticism.

Rhetorical Readings and Sociorhetorical Interpretation

Troy W. Martin echoes John H. Elliott's famous statement that 1 Peter is an "exegetical step-child" as he calls for applying classical rhetorical criticism to

33. Bauman-Martin, "Speaking Jewish," 160.
34. Bauman-Martin, "Speaking Jewish," 146.
35. Bauman-Martin, "Speaking Jewish," 156–73.
36. Bird, *Abuse, Power and Fearful Obedience*, 37–60.
37. Bird, *Abuse, Power and Fearful Obedience*, 38–39.
38. Bird, *Abuse, Power and Fearful Obedience*, 59.
39. Bird, *Abuse, Power and Fearful Obedience*, 64–85.
40. Bird, *Abuse, Power and Fearful Obedience*, 37–60.

1 Peter.⁴¹ Martin identifies 1 Peter's lack of distinctive doctrinal sections and abundance of paraenetic materials as the reasons for the dearth of rhetorical approaches to the letter.⁴² Martin surveys examples of rhetorical criticism applied to Pauline letters and uses them as a springboard to discuss the application to 1 Peter.⁴³ He highlights the shortcomings of Barth Campbell's and Lauri Thurén's attempts to classify 1 Peter as either deliberative or epideictic and advises against assigning any of the species of rhetoric to the epistle.⁴⁴ Instead, one should allow each of the species to shed light on the paraenetic function of the letter. He proposes that 1 Peter is "perhaps a pre-trial letter advising conduct that will enable the recipients to obtain a favourable judgment in both the divine and human judicial settings mentioned in the letter."⁴⁵ Further, Martin discusses the arrangement and the invention of the rhetoric of 1 Peter, taking great care to highlight what has been learned from Pauline studies and applying to 1 Peter only what has proven to work.⁴⁶

Robert L. Webb combines intertextuality and apocalyptic discourse in applying sociorhetorical methodology to 1 Peter. He focuses on two key pericopes, 1 Peter 1:3–12 and 3:18–22, which contain clusters of apocalyptic *topoi*. Webb is concerned with demonstrating "how within the apocalyptic discourse the author uses a variety of intertextual resources to advance his rhetorical purpose."⁴⁷ He appropriates the work of Vernon K. Robbins on sociorhetorical interpretation and applies one of the six "rhetorelects" (six modes of discourse: wisdom, miracle, prophetic, precreation, priestly, and apocalyptic)—namely, the apocalyptic rhetorelect—in his study of 1 Peter.⁴⁸ According to Webb, applying a sociorhetorical perspective to 1 Peter reveals, among other things, the centrality of apocalyptic discourse to the rhetoric of the letter. Exploration of the intertexture discloses the author's dependence on a variety of oral, cultural, social, and historical

---

41. Elliott, "Rehabilitation of an Exegetical Step-Child," 243.

42. Troy W. Martin, "The Rehabilitation of a Rhetorical Step-Child: First Peter and Rhetorical Criticism," in Webb and Baumann-Martin, *Reading First Peter with New Eyes*, 41–71.

43. Martin, "Rehabilitation of a Rhetorical Step-Child," 44–46.

44. Martin, "Rehabilitation of a Rhetorical Step-Child," 46. See Barth L. Campbell, *Honor, Shame, and the Rhetoric of 1 Peter*, SBLDS 160 (Atlanta: Scholars Press, 1998); Lauri Thurén, *The Rhetorical Strategy of 1 Peter with Special Regard to Ambiguous Expressions* (Pargas, Finland: Åbo Academy Press, 1990).

45. Martin, "Rehabilitation of a Rhetorical Step-Child," 44.

46. Martin, "Rehabilitation of a Rhetorical Step-Child," 50–71.

47. Robert L. Webb, "Intertexture and Rhetorical Strategy in First Peter's Apocalyptic Discourse: A Study in Sociorhetorical Interpretation," in Webb and Bauman-Martin, *Reading First Peter with New Eyes*, 72–110.

48. Webb, "Intertexture and Rhetorical Strategy," 74. See Vernon K. Robbins, *Exploring the Texture of Texts: A Guide to Socio-Rhetorical Interpretation* (Valley Forge, PA: Trinity Press International, 1996); Robbins, "The Dialectical Nature of Early Christian Discourse," *Scriptura* 59 (1996): 353–62.

resources as well as his creativity in appropriating these resources for his own rhetorical purposes.[49]

Paul A. Himes brings together social-scientific criticism and lexical semantics in an effort to demonstrate that "1 Peter uses the concept of 'foreknowledge' as a word of comfort to offset his readers' status as socially-displaced strangers and thus emphasize their new-found social identity in Christ."[50] Himes focuses on the concepts of social displacement and social identity in 1 Peter 1:1–2:11 to demonstrate the centrality of the concept of "foreknowledge" in the development of 1 Peter's ecclesiology. He argues that *prognōsis and proginōskō* should be taken in a prescient or mantic sense. To substantiate his claims, Himes thoroughly investigates John Elliott's thesis and the responses to his argument;[51] he conducts a lexical semantic analysis of these words, studying every usage that occurs in Greek literature from 1 to 100 CE, and especially as they appear in the Septuagint (LXX).[52]

The application of classical rhetorical and sociorhetorical perspectives is also evident in the scholarship of 2 Peter. Terrance Callan, Dennis D. Sylva, and Duane F. Watson have all drawn from Robbins to construct their sociorhetorical reading of 2 Peter.[53]

Callan adopts Robbins's classification of early Christian discourse and builds on Robbins's concepts of texture and rhetorelects to discuss the rhetography and rhetology of the apocalyptic discourse of 2 Peter.[54] *Rhetography* describes the contexts and elaborations of a given discourse, and *rhetology* refers to the argumentation of the discourse.[55] Callan focuses on 2 Peter 1:16–2:10 and 3:1–13, explores how each type of discourse may be at work in these texts, and draws out the implications of each evident discourse for

49. Webb, "Intertexture and Rhetorical Strategy," 108–10.
50. Paul A. Himes, *Foreknowledge and Social Identity in 1 Peter* (Eugene, OR: Pickwick, 2014), 1–6.
51. Elliott, *Home for the Homeless*.
52. Himes, *Foreknowledge and Social Identity in 1 Peter*, 4–5.
53. Terrance Callan, "Rhetography and Rhetology of Apocalyptic Discourse in Second Peter," in Webb and Watson, *Reading Second Peter with New Eyes*, 59–90; Dennis D. Sylva, "A Unified Field Picture of Second Peter 1.3–15: Making Rhetorical Sense out of Individual Images," in Webb and Watson, *Reading Second Peter with New Eyes*, 91–118; Duane F. Watson, "Comparing Two Related Methods: Rhetorical Criticism and Socio-Rhetorical Interpretation Applied to Second Peter," in Webb and Watson, *Reading Second Peter with New Eyes*, 27–57. Given the overlap between these three proposals and space limitations, I will discuss only Callan's and Sylva's approaches. Watson's discussion is compelling, but to discuss it would be repetitive in the present context.
54. Callan, "Rhetography and Rhetology," 59–90. See Vernon K. Robbins, *The Tapestry of Early Christian Discourse: Rhetoric, Society, and Ideology* (London: Routledge, 1996); Robbins, *Exploring the Texture of Text*. Callan expands on this methodology and further demonstrates its application to 2 Peter in *Acknowledging the Divine Benefactor: The Second Letter of Peter* (Eugene, OR: Pickwick, 2014).
55. Callan, "Rhetography and Rhetology," 61–63.

understanding the message of the letter. He states, "Apocalyptic discourse sometimes functions as a further framework within which other kinds of discourse are used in support of it."[56] For Callan, applying a sociorhetorical perspective to 2 Peter helps to unify various approaches that are often pursued separately and helps the reader better understand the arguments of the text and how it makes these arguments. In this endeavor, to pursue rhetography and rhetology in tandem is a more fruitful enterprise than pursuing either one separately.[57] Further, this reading perspective is helpful because it focuses on "the ways a text awakens pictures in the imagination of the reader, develops them (or does not), and moves to other pictures."[58]

Sylva combines the concepts of rhetography (developed by Robbins) and conceptual-integration theory found in Gilles Fauconnier and Mark Turner to construct a more holistic approach to 2 Peter that takes seriously the corporate development of the visual components of 2 Peter 3:1–15.[59] He seeks to demonstrate that "individual images in 2 Pet. 1:3–15 are developed into a coherent larger picture of a journey in ways designed to inspire the reader to undertake the rigors of the moral life rather than sink into self-serving sensuality."[60] He elaborates on the elements of the methodology, discussing the nature and importance of such concepts as "mapping" (the process of connecting elements in different input spaces to each other), "generic space," "blended space," "composition," "completion," "elaboration," and "vital relations."[61] He then evaluates the images in 2 Peter 1:3–15 in light of that perspective.[62] For Sylva, the rhetographical study of knowledge in 2 Peter sheds light on the significance of "the letter's rhetorical impact and of the specific types of motivational power this rhetography brings to the exhortations to attend to the *epignōsis* that the recipients have been given and to grow in the *gnōsis* they are called to develop."[63]

Narratological Readings and Perspectives

In 2004, J. Ramsey Michaels published an article comparing Christ's passion as depicted in 1 Peter with the passion narratives in the Gospel of Mark

---

56. Callan, "Rhetography and Rhetology," 64.
57. Callan, "Rhetography and Rhetology," 88–90.
58. Callan, "Rhetography and Rhetology," 89.
59. Sylva, "Unified Field Picture of Second Peter 1.3–15." See also Gilles Fauconnier, *Mappings in Thought and Language* (Cambridge: Cambridge University Press, 1997); Gilles Fauconnier and Mark Turner, "Conceptual Integration Networks," *Cognitive Science* 22 (1998): 133–87; Gilles Fauconnier and Mark Turner, *The Way We Think: Conceptual Blending and the Mind's Hidden Complexities* (New York: Basic Books, 2002).
60. Sylva, "Unified Field Picture of Second Peter 1.3–15," 91.
61. Sylva, "Unified Field Picture of Second Peter 1.3–15," 95–96.
62. Sylva, "Unified Field Picture of Second Peter 1.3–15," 100–113.
63. Sylva, "Unified Field Picture of Second Peter 1.3–15," 115.

and in the Gospel of Peter.⁶⁴ Michaels believes that although 1 Peter is not a narrative per se, it can be thought of as a passion narrative because in it the author testifies to the sufferings of Christ.⁶⁵ The years that follow bear witness to a rise of interest in reading the Petrine letters from a narratological perspective.

Joel B. Green urges scholars to embrace narrative theology in their approach to the Petrine letters.⁶⁶ Green argues that the impetus to a narrative theology is warranted because (1) the bulk of Scripture comes to us in the form of narratives, (2) one finds in biblical texts the deliberate work of forming God's people by shaping their story, and (3) narrative and nonnarrative portions of Scripture all participate in a metanarrative.⁶⁷ As a result, though 1 and 2 Peter do not tell a story, "they manipulate the grand story of God's engagement with the world and his people for theological purposes."⁶⁸ For Green, the focus on narrative provides access to "the power of theology to shape a people's way of making sense of what they experience day by day.... Narrative representation is identity formation through theological intervention."⁶⁹ Green identifies a linear narrative in 2 Peter constituted of (1) Israel's past, (2) the Christ event, (3) the present, and (4) the eschatological judgment.⁷⁰ Similarly, the narrative of 1 Peter is set within a temporal map that includes primordial time, time of ignorance/emptiness, the end of the ages, liberation, time of alien life, and revelation of Jesus Christ. For Green, a narrative theology of 1–2 Peter provides us with the opportunity to shape our imagination and conception of the world.

J. de Wall Dryden's *Theology and Ethics in 1 Peter* helpfully offers a methodology that brings together sociorhetorical analysis and narratology.⁷¹ Dryden uses the work of W. T. Wilson on Colossians as a point of departure to argue that Greco-Roman paraenetic epistles like 1 Peter were not only confined to the use of typically "paraenetic elements" but also incorporated the use of narratives to accomplish exhortative goals.⁷² Dryden demonstrates how narrative plays an integral role in shaping theology and ethics and the impact of a narrative worldview on one's theology and ethics. He explores

---

64. J. Ramsey Michaels, "St. Peter's Passion: The Passion Narrative in 1 Peter," *WW* 24 (2004): 387–94.
65. Michaels, "St. Peter's Passion," 388.
66. Joel B. Green, "Narrating the Gospel in 1 and 2 Peter," *Int* 20 (2006): 262–77. See also Joel B. Green, *1 Peter*, THNTC (Grand Rapids: Eerdmans, 2007), 197–202.
67. Green, "Narrating the Gospel in 1 and 2 Peter," 266.
68. Green, "Narrating the Gospel in 1 and 2 Peter," 266.
69. Green, "Narrating the Gospel in 1 and 2 Peter," 267.
70. Green, "Narrating the Gospel in 1 and 2 Peter," 267.
71. J. de Wall Dryden, *Theology and Ethics in 1 Peter: Paraenetic Strategies for Christian Character Formation*, WUNT 209 (Tübingen: Mohr Siebeck, 2006).
72. Dryden, *Theology and Ethics in 1 Peter*, 7.

five paraenetic literary strategies—narrative worldview, conversion, social identity, moral instructions, and example—and discusses how they function in 1 Peter.[73] Dryden identifies two ways in which the narrative world is presupposed by 1 Peter: (1) the author refers to key elements of the story of salvation to evoke an entire worldview that is familiar to both the author and his audience, and (2) although 1 Peter is not a narrative, it is governed by a narrative substructure.[74] Dryden views the story of salvation as the organizing principle around which the author of 1 Peter builds his message. That story functions as integral paraenetic tool for moral formation and provides context for ethical instruction.[75]

Eugene Boring argues that 1 Peter "projects a narrative world composed of all the events it assumes to be real—compelling serious readers/hearers to examine their own understanding of reality, and indirectly inviting them to live their lives in the world projected by the letter."[76] Boring defines the terms that are crucial and relevant for the approach he is constructing—namely, *event*, *story*, *generic narrative*, *narrative world*, *story world*, and *letter*.[77] Boring enunciates several theses that guide the proposed methodology and maps the narrative world of 1 Peter, then identifies five areas in which narratology sheds lights on the study of this letter:[78]

1. It may provide an additional basis for rhetorical analysis.
2. It illumines the phenomenon of pseudepigraphy.
3. It allows us to see the distinctive way in which letters reflect the narrative mode of theological thought that pervades canonical Scriptures.
4. It lets us see paraenesis functioning as challenging us with an alternative vision of reality rather than a list of commands.
5. It illuminates 1 Peter's view of the way in which Christ speaks to the readers.[79]

In my own reading, I use Mieke Bal's three-layered distinction of narrative—*fabula*, story, and text—as a point of departure to formulate an approach to the

---

73. Dryden, *Theology and Ethics in 1 Peter*, 8–9.

74. Dryden, *Theology and Ethics in 1 Peter*, 66. See Joseph, *Narratological Reading of 1 Peter*, 23–24; Benjamin Sargent, "The Narrative Substructure of 1 Peter," *ExpTim* 124, no. 10 (2013): 485–90.

75. Dryden, *Theology and Ethics in 1 Peter*, 80–82; Joseph, *Narratological Reading of 1 Peter*, 24.

76. Eugene Boring, "Narrative Dynamics in First Peter: The Function of the Narrative World," in Webb and Baumann-Martin, *Reading First Peter with New Eyes*, 7–40.

77. Boring, "Narrative Dynamics in First Peter," 8–16.

78. Boring, "Narrative Dynamics in First Peter," 14–24.

79. Boring, "Narrative Dynamics in First Peter," 34–36.

study of 1 Peter that explores the letter's narrative substructure to illuminate the author's scriptural hermeneutic.[80] I argue that Peter's appropriation of the Hebrew Scriptures has "guided his christological understanding of God's actions on behalf of Israel."[81] I advance William Schutter's argument that 1 Peter 1:10–12 is the key to Peter's hermeneutics by showing that the characteristic elements of the author's hermeneutics are already at work in the letter's prescript (1:1–2).[82] I argue that election, suffering, steadfastness, and vindication are common to the experience of Israel, Jesus, and the audience of 1 Peter. They constitute the *fabula* of 1 Peter, the lens through which the author reads Scripture and encourages the audience to make sense of their situation.[83] This *fabula* guides the way he narrates the story of Israel, Jesus, and his audience. It is by means of this *fabula* that he gives theological significance to the sufferings of his audience and sketches for them the nature of faithful response.[84]

It is worthwhile to highlight four studies that are squarely located within the narrative methodological agenda but that, in order to bring fresh perspectives on a hermeneutical or intertextual issue in the text of 1 Peter, focus primarily on the appropriation of the narrative substructure.[85]

Kelly D. Liebengood embraces the presence of a narrative substructure in 1 Peter.[86] However, his focus is less on the development of a methodology and more on appropriating and demonstrating how "the eschatological programme of Zechariah 9–14, read through the lens of the Gospel, functions as the substructure for 1 Peter's eschatology and thus his theology of Christian suffering."[87]

Benjamin Sargent seeks to answer the question, "How does the apparent scriptural hermeneutic of 1.10–12 relate to the use of Scripture in the epistle?"[88]

---

80. Mieke Bal, *Narratology: Introduction to the Theory of Narrative*, 2nd ed. (Toronto: University of Toronto Press, 2009), 78–114; cited in Joseph, *Narratological Reading of 1 Peter*, 40–42.

81. Joseph, *Narratological Reading of 1 Peter*, 25.

82. William Schutter, *Hermeneutic and Composition in 1 Peter*, WUNT 2/30 (Tübingen: Mohr Siebeck, 1989), 109; cited in Joseph, *Narratological Reading of 1 Peter*, 55–62. For an evaluation, see Benjamin Sargent, *Written to Serve: The Use of Scripture in 1 Peter*, LNTS 547 (London: Bloomsbury T&T Clark, 2015), 14–15. Heckel, "Neuere Literatur zum Ersten Petrusbrief," 524–25.

83. Joseph, *Narratological Reading of 1 Peter*, 25, 50–54. See Patrick Egan, *Ecclesiology and the Scriptural Narrative of 1 Peter* (Eugene, OR: Pickwick, 2016), 12–13, 72–74.

84. Joseph, *Narratological Reading of 1 Peter*, 179.

85. Travis B. Williams has recently proposed a new approach toward intertextuality in 1 Peter: "Intertextuality and Methodological Bias: Prolegomena to the Evaluation of Source Materials in 1 Peter," *JSNT* 39 (2016): 169–87.

86. Kelly D. Liebengood, *The Eschatology of 1 Peter: Considering the Influence of Zechariah 9–14*, SNTSMS 157 (New York: Cambridge University Press, 2014).

87. Liebengood, *Eschatology of 1 Peter*, 8–22.

88. Sargent, *Written to Serve*, 3.

Sargent's aims, ultimately, to offer a new definition of 1 Peter's general approach to Scripture.[89] Sargent sets his work over against recent scholarship on 1 Peter. He argues that the theological narrative that is alluded to in 1 Peter is one of discontinuity; that is, there is no continuity between Israel and Peter's audience. Further, the author of 1 Peter views Scripture as having a single meaning. In other words, Scripture is oriented exclusively toward the audience that is to receive the epistle.[90]

Patrick T. Egan explores how the author of 1 Peter draws on Isaiah to address the concerns of his audience.[91] He argues, "Peter's use of the narrative [found in Isaiah] does not depict the church as in exile, but as the locus of the restoration of God's glorious presence among his people."[92] One can therefore map into 1 Peter the outline of Isaiah's story of redemption because they share similar movements.[93] The narrative of Isaiah, and most prominently Isaiah 40–66, depicts a suffering people who receive the good news of God's restored presence. First Peter takes up this narrative in order to address the church of Asia Minor with a story that meaningfully situates their suffering within an unfolding drama.[94]

Justin Langford draws from Charles Sanders Peirce, Stefan Alkier, and others to propose a semiotic approach to intertextuality that yields a better understanding of the relationship between Isaiah and 1 Peter.[95] Langford investigates the Isaianic signs that occur in 1 Peter and the world the letter establishes—the universe of discourse of 1 Peter—in order to ascertain "the structure and context in which the Isaianic signs within can operate."[96]

A similar approach is attested in the study of 2 Peter. For example, Ruth Anne Reese crafts a narrative approach to 2 Peter that focuses on the events, narrative voice, and time elements of narratology. She constructs her approach by drawing from the works of Bal, Seymour Chatman, Algirda J. Greimas, and others.[97] Of the three elements that make up a narrative—the object that

---

89. Sargent, *Written to Serve*, 2.

90. Sargent, *Written to Serve*, 19–21, 30, 33. For a more detailed evaluation, see Abson Joseph, review of Benjamin Sargent, *Written to Serve: The Use of Scripture in 1 Peter*, *RBL* (2017), http://www.bookreviews.org.

91. Egan, *Ecclesiology and the Scriptural Narrative of First Peter*, 3.

92. Egan, *Ecclesiology and the Scriptural Narrative of First Peter*, 12.

93. Egan, *Ecclesiology and the Scriptural Narrative of First Peter*, 74.

94. Egan, *Ecclesiology and the Scriptural Narrative of First Peter*, 2.

95. Justin Langford, *Defending Hope: Semiotics and Intertextuality in 1 Peter* (Eugene, OR: Wipf & Stock, 2013), xvi. See Stefan Alkier, "Intertextuality and the Semiotics of Biblical Texts," in *Reading the Bible Intertextually*, ed. Richard B. Hays, Stefan Alkier, and Leroy A. Huizenga (Waco: Baylor University Press, 2009), 3–21.

96. Langford, *Defending Hope*, 53.

97. Ruth Anne Reese, "Narrative Method and the Letter of Second Peter," in Webb and Watson, *Reading Second Peter with New Eyes*, 119–46.

is narrated, the act of composition, and the reception of the composition—Reese focuses on the first and uses that as a referent for narrative as a whole.[98] She defines narrative as "a perceived series of connected events that are caused or experienced by a character or characters and told by a narrator."[99] She also pays close attention to how events unfold in time as well as how characters act in, and are described within, time.[100] Reese discusses the narrative of 2 Peter and looks at the events associated with the readers, with God, and with the author, respectively, to demonstrate that events, point of view, and time are interrelated.[101] In sum, Reese explores how time is employed in the letter as a way to understand the author's message.[102]

One may note several smaller studies on intertextuality in 2 Peter—that is, the letter's use of Scripture or tradition.[103] These discussions either assume the presence of a narrative substructure or engage in a literary reading of 2 Peter, exploring the letter's relationship with Scripture and other Jewish or/and Hellenistic literature in order to shed light on the epistle's message.

Metaphorical and Conceptual Readings

Another literary approach to reading the Petrine letters that has been developed in fresh ways is the metaphorical and conceptual reading. I will address here three examples, one each from Bonnie Howe, Andrew Mbuvi, and Shively T. J. Smith.[104]

Howe demonstrates the link between metaphor and hermeneutics and constructs a methodology that uses cognitive metaphor principles to help us understand 1 Peter as a moral discourse.[105] Because reading and writing are both acts of the human mind, she appropriates tools from cognitive linguistics

---

98. Reese, "Narrative Method," 122. Reese draws from Paul Ricoeur, *Time and Narrative*, trans. Kathleen McLaughlin and David Pellauer (Chicago: University of Chicago Press, 1983), 1:46.

99. Reese, "Narrative Method," 122.

100. Reese, "Narrative Method," 125.

101. Reese, "Narrative Method," 127–45.

102. Reese, "Narrative Method," 125.

103. E.g., Scott Hafemann, "'Noah, the Preacher of (God's) Righteousness': The Argument from Scripture in 2 Peter 2:5 and 9," *CBQ* 76, no. 2 (2014): 306–20; Ryan P. Juza, "Echoes of Sodom and Gomorrah on the Day of the Lord: Intertextuality and Tradition in 2 Peter 3:7–13," *BBR* 24 (2014): 227–45; Nicholas R. Werse, "Second Temple Jewish Literary Traditions in 2 Peter," *CBQ* 78, no. 1 (2016): 111–30.

104. Williams's *Persecution in 1 Peter* could have been categorized here as well from a conceptual standpoint. However, his social-psychological approach and the nature of persecution itself makes that work a better fit for the heading "Sociological Readings and Perspectives" above.

105. Bonnie Howe, *Because You Bear This Name: Conceptual Metaphor and the Moral Meaning of 1 Peter*, BIS 81 (Leiden: Brill, 2006), 167–84.

to demonstrate how to engage the text adequately.[106] She states, "To read with understanding we must imaginatively put ourselves in the place of the original readership—and put the original author(s) in the place of Peter—not as a game but for the purpose of reading the text, for the purpose, that is, of entering the authorial audience."[107] She identifies seven major fields of metamoral metaphors in 1 Peter and proposes that it is these complex, blended spaces that provide the setting, the moral context, for Christian living where the letter's message takes shape.[108]

Mbuvi, seeking new understanding of the main themes of 1 Peter, investigates the metaphor of the temple in 1 Peter in light of the Second Temple Jewish framework of continuing exile and hope of restoration.[109] Mbuvi argues the temple imagery undergirds the entire epistle. It incorporates "the concepts of exile, judgment and restoration providing the cultic language by which 1 Peter addresses the concerns of identity and alienation with which his audience was struggling."[110]

The concept of diaspora is central to and undergirds Smith's work on 1 Peter.[111] According to Smith, her work is unique in that she approaches the concept of diaspora not from the typical tradition-history narrative perspective but provides "an appreciative reading of diaspora thinking present in the New Testament and other Second Temple Jewish writings."[112] She believes that much can be gained from a literary comparative analysis of diaspora as an ideological and social construction. She adopts an interdisciplinary approach and brings together several methodological perspectives to shed light on how biblical texts imagine and shape diaspora into a livable situation.[113]

Hermeneutical Conversations: The Message of the Petrine Letters

The study of the Petrine epistles is entirely a hermeneutical task, of course. Yet in the context of a conversation on the state of scholarship in the Petrine letters we can distinguish between works whose primary concern is methodological and those whose primary concern is interpreting the letters' message.

---

106. Howe, *Because You Bear This Name*, 168–73.
107. Howe, *Because You Bear This Name*, 181.
108. Howe, *Because You Bear This Name*, 185–232, 309.
109. Andrew M. Mbuvi, *Temple, Exile and Identity in 1 Peter*, LNTS 345 (London: T&T Clark, 2007).
110. Mbuvi, *Temple, Exile and Identity in 1 Peter*, 125.
111. Shively T. J. Smith, *Strangers to Family: Diaspora and 1 Peter's Invention of God's Household* (Waco: Baylor University Press, 2016).
112. Smith, *Strangers to Family*, 9.
113. Smith, *Strangers to Family*, 12–13.

Several recent commentaries have advanced our understanding of these letters' respective messages.

Commentaries on 1 Peter

Commentaries by Karen Jobes, Joel Green, and Reinhard Feldmier are the most significant treatments of 1 Peter.[114] Space here permits highlighting only key contributions from their interpretive approaches. In her commentary, Jobes presents a new theory on the historical background of 1 Peter, pays close attention to the LXX, and challenges scholarly opinion about the author's language aptitude (arguing that the author was a Semitic-speaking person for whom Greek was a second language).[115] Green's commentary extends and expands his narrative theology agenda, bringing into focus the theological message of the text as well as the theology's implications for today's readers. He challenges the twenty-first-century reader to approach 1 Peter as a letter "written to us."[116] Feldmeier focuses on a theological interpretation of the concept of "foreignness." He states, "The foreignness of the Christians is not in its essence derived from protests against society, but from correspondence to God and belonging to his new society."[117]

Commentaries on 2 Peter

Most recent commentaries on 2 Peter are combined either with a commentary on 1 Peter, with one on Jude, or with both. At times this happens out of convenience. At other times it signals acknowledgment of the literary, theological, and other relationships between 2 Peter and Jude. Scholars vary in their approach to the relationship between 2 Peter and Jude. This discussion is beyond the scope of this chapter.[118] The works highlighted below suggest the state of the scholarship as it relates to published commentaries on 2 Peter as part of the Petrine corpus.[119]

---

114. Karen H. Jobes, *1 Peter*, BECNT (Grand Rapids: Baker Academic, 2005); Green, *1 Peter*; Reinhard Feldmeier, *The First Letter of Peter: A Commentary on the Greek Text* (Waco: Baylor University Press, 2008). The commentary by Jacques Schlosser is also worth mentioning in this category. Schlosser, *La Première Épître de Pierre*, Commentaire Biblique: Nouveau Testament 21 (Paris: Cerf, 2011).
115. Jobes, *1 Peter*, xi.
116. Green, *1 Peter*, 12.
117. Feldmeier, *First Letter of Peter*, 14.
118. For a brief discussion, see Ruth Anne Reese, *2 Peter & Jude*, THNTC (Grand Rapids: Eerdmans, 2007), 1–15.
119. In addition to those highlighted below, see also Lewis R. Donelson, *1 and 2 Peter and Jude: A Commentary*, NTL (Louisville: Westminster John Knox, 2010); Daniel Keating, *First and Second Peter, Jude*, CCSS (Grand Rapids: Baker Academic, 2011); Duane Watson and Terrance Callan, *First and Second Peter*, PCNT (Grand Rapids: Baker Academic, 2012).

Peter H. Davids's commentary discusses both the differences between 1 and 2 Peter and the similarities between 2 Peter and Jude. He addresses the literary, narrative, and theological implications of the epistle, which he considers to be a farewell speech.[120] Reese engages the message of 2 Peter in such a way as to bring exegesis and theology together. She also advocates for a canonical reading of 1 and 2 Peter, because when read together 1 and 2 Peter "communicate a fuller theological understanding than either book could communicate on their own."[121] Gene L. Green interprets the message of 2 Peter by comparing it with Jude. He argues, "Peter's intertextual methodology transforms Jude's thought, making it his own to advance his own argument and offering us an example of *imitatio*."[122] G. Green's reading of 2 Peter is guided and framed by a rhetorical approach.

Some cultural, perspectival, and political readings, though limited in scope, provide insights on how diverse communities approach the Petrine letters. These include Larry George's interpretation of the Petrine letters from an African American perspective,[123] Irene Foulkes's feminist interpretation,[124] and Sicily Mbura Muriithi and Tokunboh Adeyemo's reading of 1 and 2 Peter, respectively, from an African perspective.[125]

Reflections

This chapter has offered evidence that interest in the study of the Petrine letters continues to rise. Recent scholarship has focused primarily on providing fresh ways of approaching these texts. The SBL consultations of 2006 and 2007 served as a turning point in Petrine scholarship in that they symbolized and captured the enthusiasm around the study of these letters and set the tone for the growth that followed. Since the current state of the scholarship

---

120. Peter H. Davids, *The Letters of 2 Peter and Jude*, PNTC (Grand Rapids: Eerdmans, 2006).

121. Reese, *2 Peter & Jude*, 121.

122. Gene L. Green, *Jude and 2 Peter*, BECNT (Grand Rapids: Baker Academic, 2008), 162–70. See also G. Green, "Second Peter's Use of Jude: *Imitatio* and the Sociology of Early Christianity," in Webb and Watson, *Reading Second Peter with New Eyes*, 1–25.

123. Larry George provided the interpretation of 1 and 2 Peter in *True to Our Native Land: An African American New Testament Commentary*, ed. Brian K. Blount et al. (Minneapolis: Fortress, 2007), 476–95.

124. See Irene Foulkes, "1 Peter: Survival Strategies for Harried Communities," in *Feminist Biblical Interpretation: A Compendium of Critical Commentary on the Books of the Bible and Related Literature*, ed. Luise Schottroff and Marie-Theres Wacker (Grand Rapids: Eerdmans, 2012), 878–85; Foulkes, "2 Peter: Guideposts for the Godly Life," in Schottroff and Wacker, *Feminist Biblical Interpretation*, 886.

125. See Tokunboh Adeyemo, ed., *Africa Bible Commentary* (Grand Rapids: Zondervan, 2006).

provides the springboard for future and further advances, the following comments are in order.

Overcoming Prejudice

The Petrine letters have enjoyed much attention in recent scholarship. One could argue that these texts have been successfully rehabilitated, yet they still suffer prejudice of some kind. David Horrell states, "First Peter remains, and is likely to always remain—for all sorts of theological and historical reasons—a relatively neglected corner of the NT canon, despite the best efforts of primo-petrophiles [scholars of 1 Peter] to rehabilitate it."[126] While methodologies that provide fresh perspectives abound, these need to be matched with a new posture toward the letters that takes seriously their place in the canon as theological and ecclesial documents in their own rights. Language has a way of perpetuating systems and (mis)conceptions. The time has come to move away from Elliott's 1976 description of the Petrine letters as marginal, which was true *then*, to appropriate and embrace fresh ways of describing and introducing the letters that acknowledge their theological richness, their strong influence in shaping the moral identity of readers, and the depth of their appropriation of and engagement with the Hebrew Scripture.

New Eyes: Conceptual and Teleological

Reading the Petrine letters with new eyes vis-à-vis a methodological reassessment is a worthy and successful endeavor. Scholarship on these letters can gain much by reassessing them from a conceptual and teleological perspective as well. Their theological richness and the purpose for which they were written make them all the more relevant today. How might 1–2 Peter shape our identity if we took their claims on our lives seriously? How might our interpretation of 1–2 Peter's message differ if we were to inhabit the narrative world created by these texts?

THE PETRINE LETTERS IN CANONICAL PERSPECTIVE

Irrespective of one's position on the preliminary issues that surround the authorship, date, and audience of the Petrine letters, their place in the canon and their association with the apostle Peter is of great importance. More can and needs to be done to pursue the implications of reading 1–2 Peter together. What theological threads run through both letters? What sources do they share? How are these sources being appropriated? How do these letters, read

---

126. Horrell, "Between Conformity and Resistance," 111.

together, inform what we know about God, Christ, the Holy Spirit, salvation, and redemption?

Toward a Postcolonial Ecclesiology

The Petrine letters are written to the church and for the church. It is worth noting that Christians from the majority world wrestle less with appropriating the message of these letters because they live through and can relate to some of the realities presupposed by the letters. Scholarship on the Petrine letters can benefit from listening closely to majority world and marginal voices and from observing the ways they engage the text.

22

The Epistles of John

Toan Do

Introduction

The Epistles of John have often been neglected or overlooked by scholars of Johannine literature.[1] The neglect is due in part to the puzzling canonical inclusion of 3 John (and also 2 John).[2] Attesting to this reality, Judith Lieu

---

1. See Jacques Schlosser, ed., *The Catholic Epistles and the Tradition*, BETL 176 (Leuven: Leuven University Press, 2004). The neglect of 2 and 3 John is evident in this 569-page study on the formation and development of the seven canonical Catholic Epistles. Every other letter, including 1 John, receives special attention, but 2 and 3 John are mentioned only in passing. See also R. Alan Culpepper and Paul N. Anderson, eds., *Communities in Dispute: Current Scholarship on the Johannine Epistles*, ECIL 13 (Atlanta: SBL Press, 2014). While this volume claims to be a collection of current studies on the Epistles of John, 90 percent of this 333-page volume is devoted to the relationship between the Gospel of John and 1 John or the Gospel and the Johannine communities in general. Cf. Marinus de Jonge, "The Gospel and the Epistles of John Read against the Background of the History of the Johannine Communities," in *What We Have Heard from the Beginning: The Past, Present and Future of Johannine Studies*, ed. Tom Thatcher (Waco: Baylor University Press, 2007), 127–44. Again, while it claims in the title to handle the relationship between the Gospel and the Epistles, the latter are mentioned only briefly.

2. When assessing NT letters based on their Christian characteristics as compared to, say, Aramaic or Hellenistic letters of their time, one can hardly categorize 3 John as one of the Catholic Letters. While God (*ho theos*) is mentioned in verses 6 and 11, neither "Jesus" nor "Christ" is used. Notably, *ho theos* ("god") was commonly found in Greco-Roman literature; hence the use of *ho theos* in 3 John can be deemed an appeal to the Christian God for Christian readers but simply to any "god" for non-Christians. This inference is well supported by Abraham J. Malherbe, *Light from the Gentiles: Hellenistic Philosophy and Early Christianity*, ed. Carl R. Holloday et al. (Leiden: Brill, 2015). All citations (including here) come from chap. 5,

validly commented (more than three decades ago in the introduction to her revised and published dissertation) on the lack of balanced attention to 2 and 3 John. When, Lieu argued, one carefully analyzes the questions about *how* 2 John and 3 John were received and *why* they were accepted into the NT canon, any results derived from this analysis ought to be considered plausible and tenable only on the basis of "examining 2 and 3 John in their own right and not, as is so often the case, in the shadow of, and along [the] lines determined by, the Gospel and First Epistle."[3] As is clear from Lieu's scholarly trajectory—a long career in which she would research these texts broadly and write a great deal about them—when she first articulated her hypothesis, she aimed only to study the Epistles of John. Then, twenty-two years later, Lieu expanded her initial observation and included 1 John in what she called the scholarly neglect of the Johannine epistles. In the preface to her commentary Lieu noted, "The Johannine Epistles have often been treated as footnotes to the Gospel, supplying supplementary resources for exposition of the latter's theology."[4] In a more recent study, Lieu's conviction that these letters have been neglected resonated loud and clear once again. Any scholarly study on the hypothetical audience of one or all of these Johannine epistles should "be addressed by treating the Epistles on their own, and specifically as letters, without reference to the Gospel—a position that is rarely adopted but surely defensible, at least on principle."[5] Any sympathetic reader of these epistles of John should share Lieu's dismay and may accordingly acknowledge that the history of scholarly studies on 1, 2, and 3 John has not advanced much beyond the shadow of the Gospel of John.

Among the diverse scholarly opinions, I prefer the position argued by Lieu, which I consider both tenable and prophetic. The aim of this essay is to further explain the hypothesis that the body of each individual Epistle of John ought to be treated not only as distinct from the Gospel but also as independent from the others.[6] This hypothesis is far from denying the dialectical

---

"The Inhospitality of Diotrephes," 69–82. The issue in 3 John, argues Malherbe, is neither theological nor christological, but "a purely personal issue" (80) between two individuals (the Elder vs. Diotrephes) or two groups of people (the Elder's delegate vs. those of the house church of Diotrephes). In fact, much of the content of this letter hardly seems to promote distinctly *Christian* concerns.

3. Judith Lieu, *The Second and Third Epistles of John* (Edinburgh: T&T Clark, 1986), 1.

4. Judith M. Lieu, *1, 2, and 3 John: A Commentary*, NTL (Louisville: Westminster John Knox, 2008), ix.

5. Judith M. Lieu, "The Audience of the Johannine Epistles," in Culpepper and Anderson, *Communities in Dispute*, 124.

6. Elsewhere I have examined this possibility at some length in Toan Do, *Rethinking the Death of Jesus: An Exegetical and Theological Study of* Hilasmos *and* Agapē *in 1 John 2:1–2 and 4:7–10*, CBET 73 (Leuven: Peeters, 2014), 1–26.

relationship among the Gospel and the three Johannine epistles.[7] Yet insofar as any relationship between and among written documents such as the Johannine writings is concerned, similarities complement dissimilarities and simultaneously intensify discrepancies.[8] It seems that to treat all three Epistles of John—as is the overwhelming tendency—as the offspring or aftermath of a peculiar Christian community born out of the Gospel is to run the risk of simply repeating the old and outdated idea of a *certain* Johannine "school," "circle," or "community." If we want to see scholarly interest in the Johannine epistles endure, we would do better to treat each one alone and distinctively.

Two trends are notable: (1) some scholars have formulated the concept of a single Johannine community without any basis in data outside the Johannine texts themselves; (2) others have discussed each epistle on the basis of the extant document and manuscript tradition. As a somewhat modified and hybrid model of reading the Epistles of John, this essay will proceed in the following three parts: The first part will survey recent scholarship on the epistles, which has largely been based on many versions of the assumption that these four documents hailed from the same roots in the so-called Johannine community. The second part will discuss how this assumption severely truncated scholarly advancement in the study of the epistles in the last two decades. The third part will discuss whether there should be a "continued" and "sustained" idea of Johannine history or whether the study of the Johannine letters ought to move in a different direction.

The Johannine Community Founded by the Beloved Disciple

The idea of a certain and peculiar Johannine school flourished between the 1960s and 1980s, as represented by, but not limited to, the works of Raymond E. Brown, Wayne A. Meeks, Oscar Cullmann, and R. Alan Culpepper.[9] Among these scholars, Brown holds the most consistent position in a volumi-

---

7. I shall return to this "dialectical" relationship in the last section of this essay.

8. See esp. Dale C. Allison Jr., "How to Marginalize the Traditional Criteria of Authenticity," in *Handbook for the Study of the Historical Jesus*, ed. Tom Holmén and Stanley E. Porter (Leiden: Brill, 2011), 3–30. Allison rightly argues that the more similarities between two ancient texts one attempts to show, the more dissimilarities the texts themselves present.

9. Raymond E. Brown, *The Gospel according to John*, AB 29 (New York: Doubleday, 1966), xxi–cxlvi; Brown, *The Epistles of John*, AB 30 (New York: Doubleday, 1982), 3–146; Wayne A. Meeks, "The Man from Heaven in Johannine Sectarianism," *JBL* 91 (1972): 44–72; Oscar Cullmann, *Der johanneische Kreis: Sein Platz im Spätjudentum, in der Jüngerschaft Jesu und im Urchristentum zum Ursprung des Johannesevangliums* (Tübingen: Mohr Siebeck, 1975); R. Alan Culpepper, *The Johannine School: An Evaluation of the Johannine-School Hypothesis Based on an Investigation of the Nature of Ancient Schools*, SBLDS 26 (Missoula, MT: Scholars Press, 1975).

nous number of publications concerning Johannine ecclesiology. Of particular significance is Brown's construction of the so-called community of the Beloved Disciple.[10] In this hypothesized and well-developed construct, Brown discerns four phases that symbolize the historical development of a single Johannine "history" and "church," which begins with the Beloved Disciple in the mid-50s (phase 1), then ends with the dissolution of this original community when it is fractured by the Gnostic secessionists in the second century (phase 4). Any modern student of the NT who reads Brown's breadth of scholarship cannot but get the impression that the audience or the implied readers of these four Johannine documents (i.e., the Gospel and 1, 2, and 3 John) must have experienced approximately, if not exactly, the sort of historical development mapped out by Brown's theory. Notably, Brown himself admits in *The Community of the Beloved Disciple* that "if sixty percent of my detective work is accepted, I shall be happy indeed."[11] Yet Brown's historical scheme must not be underestimated, and the impact of his hypothesis on the trajectory of this theory of Johannine history has reverberated ever since. Since this chapter mainly concerns itself with issues of the Epistles of John, much of the discussion on the Gospel can only be mentioned in passing.[12]

Essentially agreeing with Brown, John Painter frames the historical situation in 1 John based on "the evidence . . . that our knowledge of them [the opponents] must be reconstructed on the basis of the author's polemical statements against them."[13] Admitting that the task of reconstructing this hypothetical position has "to be done with caution,"[14] Painter speculates that the apparent schism of the Johannine community *at* and *during* the time of the composition of 1 John involved two groups. The first consists of those represented *at the beginning* by the Beloved Disciple, who had experienced conflict/dialogue and struggled with the synagogue while accompanying Jesus during his teaching (John 9:22, 34). The second group involves those represented by the *now* antichrists and deceivers (1 John 2:18, 22, 26; 2 John 7–8) who entered the community only after the first group's breach with Judaism. Because these opponents joined the community later than other members—after the group's Jewish-Christian era—they were largely gentiles who did not

---

10. Raymond E. Brown, *The Community of the Beloved Disciple: The Life, Loves, and Hates of an Individual Church in New Testament Times* (London: Geoffrey Chapman, 1979).

11. Brown, *Community of the Beloved Disciple*, 7. See also studies in Culpepper and Anderson, *Communities in Dispute*. For a summary of Brown's life and work by Francis J. Moloney, see Raymond E. Brown, *An Introduction to the Gospel of John: Edited, Updated, Introduced, and Concluded by Francis J. Moloney*, ABRL (New York: Doubleday, 2003).

12. For a survey of studies on the Gospel of John, see in this volume the chapter by Alicia D. Myers.

13. John Painter, "The 'Opponents' in 1 John," *NTS* 32 (1986): 49.

14. Painter, "'Opponents' in 1 John," 50, 66–67.

understand the Gospel tradition (3 John 5–6). They sharply collided with the author and the remainder of the author's community—those who ultimately confessed that Jesus is the Christ and the Son of God (1 John 2:22–23; 3:23; 4:15; 5:5, 10, 20) and that Jesus has come in the flesh (4:2, 9). As a result of such an intense impact, these opponents had to secede from the community (2:19–21).

One major issue in Painter's study of the opponents in 1 John is that because it was outside the scope of his project, Painter could not expound on the question of the authorship of the Johannine epistles. Yet this narrative frame eventually led Painter to develop the overall "historical prolegomena" for all three (1, 2, 3 John) in his commentary.[15] One of the bases for Painter's commentary is this clear distinction: while the implied audience of the Gospel is of Jewish background, the context of the Epistles is very much non-Jewish. Painter's distinction has been ignored by some scholars. I shall discuss this in the next section below.

Acknowledging influence from Brown's hypothesis, Urban C. von Wahlde launched an ambitious three-volume commentary on the Gospel and the Epistles of John.[16] According to von Wahlde's hypothetical trajectory, these four Johannine documents do not have the same author. The most complicated issue lies within his explanation of the authorship for the Gospel. Von Wahlde speculates that the text of the Gospel, as it exists today, has gone through three stages of composition. The materials of the second and third stages were added to the material of the first stage. The material of each stage represents a separate "edition" of the Gospel. By the same token, the hypothesized "extant" text of each edition of the Gospel (i.e., extant when the final version was being edited) was composed by a different author. Hence the final form of the Gospel consists of text written by three distinct authors.

What interests us in this chapter is the lapse of time between stages two and three, during which von Wahlde claims the Epistles of John were composed: 1 John around 70 CE and 2 and 3 John around 80 CE; he believes the same author penned all three letters.[17] Von Wahlde identifies this single author of

---

15. John Painter, *1, 2, and 3 John*, SP 18 (Collegeville, MN: Liturgical Press, 2002), 1–113, esp. 1, 51–57.

16. Urban C. von Wahlde, *The Gospel and Letters of John*, 3 vols., ECC (Grand Rapids: Eerdmans, 2010), see esp. 1:1–7, 55 and 3:1–15.

17. Von Wahlde, *Gospel and Letters of John*, 1:55. Let me comment on *only* one issue about the manuscript tradition for 1, 2, and 3 John. As acknowledged by von Wahlde himself, his commentary relies on the Greek manuscripts compiled by NA^{27} and UBS^4. For this, see his *Gospel and Letters of John*, 1:7–8; 2:1–2. Since his 2010 commentary, NA^{28} (2012) and UBS^5 (2014) has appeared. Related to these editions of the Greek text of the NT is the *Novum Testamentum Graecum Editio Critica Maior* (hence ECM) compiled and published by the Münster Institute for New Testament Textual Research. The first edition of this ECM for the First Letter of John appeared in 2003 and for 2 and 3 John was followed in 2005. Since NA^{27} was published, in which

the three Epistles as the "Elder." He even speculates that this Elder was "one of the younger disciples of Jesus," who "did live to an old age (a proposal based primarily on evidence in the Gospel and the Letters, not on external tradition)," and that this Elder died "at perhaps the age of 80."[18] However, the expression *ho presbyteros* (the elder) appears only at the beginning of 2 and 3 John—not in 1 John. While the seemingly self-assigned letterheads in both 2 John and 3 John refer to the author (or authors, if the two were written by different persons) as the Elder, this very designation says next to nothing about the real identity of the author(s) of each or all three epistles. Also ambiguous is the fact that the common term "elder" is used widely in the NT and for many disparate reasons.[19] Had the author of each epistle or all three wished to identify himself (or themselves), why did he (or they) not at least appeal to a name (e.g., John) as in the book of Revelation (1:1, 4, 9)?[20] But it seems that at the least this working scheme makes convenient and trouble free the hypothesis that there must have been a *certain* and *peculiar* Johannine history, during which the so-called Johannine Christians experienced some periods of expulsion (John 9:22, 34),[21] internal conflict and schism (1 John 2:18, 22, 26; 2 John 7–8), and final conflict over authority (2 John 9–10; 3 John 9–10).[22]

Marinus de Jonge's recent essay on the relationship between the Gospel and the Epistles of John merits brief attention, because he has raised awareness of the present trend toward giving priority to synchronic analysis of the Johannine writings, while also appropriately cautioning, "Exegetes can never limit themselves to synchronic analysis. I remain convinced that only literary analysis combined with historical criticism will lead to a full picture of the state of affairs."[23] His overall position follows the majority opinion—namely, that the Johannine epistles can hardly be historically constructed without reference to the shadowy figure of the Beloved Disciple of the Gospel of John.

---

the text for 1 John was based on about eighty-four manuscripts, many more manuscripts (about 150) for 1 John have been added to the list.

18. Von Wahlde, *Gospel and Letters of John*, 3:10.

19. To name only a few: Matt. 15:2; 16:21; 26:3, 47, 57; Mark 7:3, 5; 8:31; Luke 7:3; 9:22; John 8:9; Acts 4:5, 8, 23; Rom. 9:12; 1 Tim. 5:17, 19; Titus 1:5; James 5:14; 1 Pet. 5:1, 5; Rev. 4:4, 10; 5:5, 6, 8.

20. I deny any possible authorial relationship between Revelation and the Johannine writings. This issue has been dealt with by Elisabeth Schüssler Fiorenza in "The Quest for the Johannine School: The Apocalypse and the Fourth Gospel," *NTS* 23 (1997): 402–27; Adela Yarbro Collins, *Crisis and Catharsis: The Power of the Apocalypse* (Philadelphia: Westminster, 1984).

21. For a very informative discussion on the unproven theory of expulsion in the Gospel of John, see Adele Reinhartz, "Building Skyscrapers on Toothpicks: The Literary-Critical Challenge to Historical Criticism," in *Anatomies of Narrative Criticism: The Past, Present, and Futures of the Fourth Gospel as Literature*, ed. Tom Thatcher and Stephen D. Moore, RBS 55 (Atlanta: SBL, 2008), 55–76, esp. 72–76.

22. Von Wahlde, *Gospel and Letters of John*, 3:222, 243–44, 265, 282–84.

23. De Jonge, "Gospel and the Epistles of John," 144.

Nonetheless, his insistence on a balance of synchronic and historical analysis is salutary, and I will return in the last section of this chapter to the subject of combining methods.

Truncation of Johannine Studies on 1, 2, and 3 John

Lieu's work on 2 John and 3 John remains to date the only single volume dedicated to these letters.[24] Several one-volume studies on specific issues in 1 John, however, have appeared in the last two decades.[25] This section discusses representatives of the theory of the Johannine community, a theory that, according to Adele Reinhartz, is born out of "a scholarly construct, the product of a circular hermeneutical process: we assume its existence from the very fact that we have a Johannine Gospel [and Johannine epistles]."[26] Here, however, we will attend to the Epistles of John.

Working under the direction of Jean Zumstein and influenced by his position on the Gospel of John,[27] Horst Hahn sums up in his dissertation three main points in support of what he calls the tradition and new interpretation on the basis of which 1 John was composed. First, 1 John as a whole should be read and understood as the author's conscious renewal of and reflection on a current version of the theological tradition as found in the Gospel. Second, some members of the Christian community of 1 John have now found sharp conflict between their interpretation of the Johannine tradition and the earlier

---

24. Lieu, *Second and Third Epistles of John*. This statement excludes commentaries on the Johannine epistles.
25. To my knowledge only six studies on 1 John have appeared in the last two decades, all published dissertations: Hansjörg Schmid, *Gegner im 1. Johannesbrief? Zu Konstruktion und Selbstreferenz im johanneischen Sinnszstem*, BWANT 159 (Stuttgart: Kohlhammer, 2002); Terry Griffith, *Keep Yourselves from Idols: A New Look at 1 John*, JSNTSup 233 (London: Sheffield Academic, 2002); Horst Hahn, *Tradition und Neuinterpretation im ersten Johannesbrief* (Zürich: TVZ, 2009); Daniel R. Streett, *They Went Out from Us: The Identity of the Opponents in First John*, BZNW 177 (Berlin: de Gruyter, 2011); Matthew D. Jensen, *Affirming the Resurrection of the Incarnate Christ: A Reading of 1 John*, SNTSMS 151 (Cambridge: Cambridge University Press, 2012); Toan Do, *Rethinking the Death of Jesus*. Though not published in the last twenty years, Judith Lieu's short *Theology of the Johannine Epistles*, NTT (Cambridge: Cambridge University Press, 1991), remains valuable.
26. Reinhartz, "Building Skyscrapers from Toothpicks," 70. Added to Reinhartz's argument is a recent study by David A. Lamb, *Text, Context and the Johannine Community: Sociolinguistic Analysis of the Johannine Writings*, LNTS 423 (London: Bloomsbury T&T Clark, 2014). Lamb concludes "that the author [of the Gospel] had little or no personal knowledge of his intended readers and it [Lamb's argument] certainly does not support the idea of a closed community as its audience." Lamb believes that he has not "killed off the JComm completely" but has only "kept it in a modified form" (204).
27. Jean Zumstein, *Kreative Erinnerung, Relecture und Auslegung im Johannesevangelium* (Zürich: TVZ, 2004).

version found in the Gospel. Third, an amalgamation of the first and second points represents and reflects the actual historical situation of 1 John. Hahn argues that any inquiry into the historical milieu of the later Johannine community must stem from our understanding of the author's Christology and the opponents' divergence from it (as found particularly in 1 John 2:18–27).[28] As the title of Hahn's book indicates, in his opinion the First Letter of John not only continues the tradition of the Gospel but renews and reinterprets it for the sake of the remainder of the author's community. The main findings in this study, therefore, do not depend on taking for granted that the Gospel and 1 John must have hailed from one and the same Johannine community. One crucial issue left unexplored in Hahn's study is the possible identity of the opponents in 1 John, which takes us to the next representative.

Daniel R. Streett, in his study of 1 John, focuses on the author's statement that the opponents have left the community (2:19). In his first chapter (over one hundred pages), Streett surveys the entire history of interpretation and points out every possible option for the identity of the opponents of 1 John, beginning with some traces in the mere mentions[29] of the letter in second-century Christian writings and continuing through history until he had surveyed all major modern scholars who ever wrote on this epistle. Then Streett states his own position: "In contrast to these proposals, I suggested that the secessionists [as detected in 1 John 2:18–27; 4:1–6; 5:6–12; 2 John 7–9] are most easily understood as apostate Jews, who have not introduced a subtle Christological error, but rather have rejected the fundamental claim of the early Christian movement: that Jesus is the Messiah."[30]

While Streett's study is very well documented and informative, it is not free from historical and theological errors. We will consider two issues here: the apostate Jews and Jesus as the Messiah—both have to do with Streett's method of reading into, rather than out of, the text of 1 John. Painter, however, has warned scholars about the "non-Jewish context of the Epistles,

28. Hahn, *Tradition und Neuinterpretation*, 52–53. The summary from Hahn's German is mine.

29. There is neither clear nor direct evidence for either the whole of 1 John or any part of it through the first three quarters of the second century. Second and Third John appear only in mid-to-late third, or even early fourth, century. Streett thinks he may have found traces of similar expressions and allusions to theological statements that appear, for instance, in the following writings: Didache (ca. 90 to 120), the Epistle of Barnabas (ca. 130), the Second Letter to the Corinthians by Clement of Rome (ca. 150), the *Apologies* of Justin Martyr (ca. 150), the Epistle to Diognetus (ca. 125 to 225), and the *Epistle to the Philippians* by Polycarp (ca. 140). Moreover, no manuscripts for 1 John can be dated back to the second century. Streett, like other Johannine scholars of historical criticism, can only make inferences based on speculative allusions to Cerinthus and other second-century gnostics, whose identity and existence are, again, scholarly constructs. For further discussion on this issue, see Do, *Rethinking the Death of Jesus*, 1–26.

30. Streett, *Identity of the Opponents*, 110–11.

which make no mention of Jews, do not appeal to Jewish Scripture, and call on the readers (in 1 John) to guard against idols (5:21)."[31] Notwithstanding Streett's citation of several of Painter's works on the Johannine epistles, Streett disagrees and argues that the opponents in 1 John are the Jewish apostates.

Second, the statement "that Jesus is the Messiah" does not appear in 1 John, let alone 2 John and 3 John. Some key texts in 1 John are in order: (1) the author claims that the opponents have gone out "from us" (*ex hēmōn* presumably means leaving his group of Christians, or, to put it mildly, Christian community[32]) (1 John 2:19); (2) The author then asks a rhetorical question concerning the liar, implying that the liar is the one who says: "Jesus is not the Christ" (*Iēsous ouk estin ho christos*; 2:22). In other places, the author employs similar expressions as a double-title designation for Jesus as the Christ—namely, *Iēsous Christos* (cf. 2:1; 4:2; 5:6; 2 John 7). The essential issue in these mentions using this double-title designation is the very fact that nowhere in 1–3 John can either *Iēsous Christos* or simply *ho christos* be theologically and christologically equated with the Jewish concept and understanding of "Messiah" (*ho messias*). Although the term "Messiah" occurs several times in the Gospel,[33] nevertheless this double-title designation *Iēsous Christos* does not occur together with *ho messias*. Streett does not bother to explain how this Jewish concept of messiahship may be equivalent to or compatible with the Greek translation *christos* and how these two (*ho messias* and *ho christos*) may have played out in the context of 1 John. There is also the fact that the very expression *ho messias* never occurs in any of the Epistles of John. Streett simply takes for granted the very contested idea of Jewish-or-Samaritan Messiahship in the Gospel and attributes this to the First Letter of John.

This argument against the Jews as former Christians and apostates in 1 John also appears, though less forcefully, in the publications of Terry Griffith and Matthew D. Jensen.[34] Jensen looks at the word order and the syntax of

---

31. Painter, *1, 2, and 3 John*, 1.

32. By saying "Christian community," I am not ready to concede to the historical assumption that the author's group of Christians is one and the same as that of the Gospel. As we see in 3 John 9–10, a group of Christians can be a house church represented by Diotrephes and, say, his associates.

33. Cf. John 4:25–26, 29; 7:26–27, 31, 41–42; 9:22; 10:24; 11:27; 12:34; 20:31. This is not to mention that the Jewish concept of Messiah in the Gospel of John is also contested. Cf. Marinus de Jonge, "Jewish Expectations about the 'Messiah' according to the Fourth Gospel," *NTS* 19 (1973): 246–70. Others argue that the expectations of a Jewish Messiah in the Gospel were not unanimous but divergent. For example, Bruce W. Hall, *Samaritan Religion from John Hyrcanus to Baba Rabba: A Critical Examination of the Relevant Material in Contemporary Christian Literature, the Writings of Josephus, and the Mishnah*, SJ 3 (Sydney: Sydney University Press, 1987), 298–99, points out that the Samaritans were expecting the *Taheb* (the Returner).

34. Griffith, *Keep Yourselves from Idols*; Jensen, *Affirming the Resurrection of the Incarnate Christ*; also Matthew D. Jensen, "John Is No Exception: Identifying the Subject of εἰμί and Its Implications," *JBL* 135 (2016): 341–53.

the sentences in which a copula is expressed in 1 John. Specifically, Jensen calls attention to four instances from 1 John, as well as one from the Gospel of John: John 20:31; 1 John 2:22; 4:15; 5:1, 5—all of which have a similar construction. They each consist of an anarthrous *Iēsous*, a copula (i.e., a form of *eimi*, "to be"), and an arthrous *ho christos* and/or *ho huios tou theou* ("the Son of God"). For clarity's sake, here is the part of 1 John 2:22 concerning the denial: *ho arnoumenos hoti Iēsous ouk estin ho christos* ("the one who denies that Jesus is the Christ"). Appealing to other scholars,[35] Jensen argues that in these five instances "the articular noun [*ho christos* or *ho huios tou theou*] ought to be identified as the subject of εἰμί."[36] Hypothetically speaking, then, the denial in 1 John 2:22 would be read, "The Christ is not Jesus."

Following this logic, Jensen notes that "Jesus" should be the predicate noun simply because *Iēsous* is anarthrous and that "the Christ" must be the subject because *ho christos* is articular. Linking "the Christ" as the subject with his own hypothesis about the apostasy of Jews and former Christians in 1 John, Jensen wishes "to answer the Jewish question, Who is the Christ?"[37] Jensen answers his own question by asserting that the denial should be construed as the claim that the Christ is not Jesus. Accordingly, "this denial would not have meant anything to gentiles because they did not have the concept of 'Christ.' Therefore, this is a Jewish denial, which indicates that the opponents in First John were Jewish."[38] Needless to say, there is no such thing in any of the Epistles of John as a "Jewish question" to be answered; rather, this question is Jensen's own presumption. Furthermore, the very expression *ho christos*, which in Greek means "the anointed one," did not just belong to Jewish-Christian understanding but was also a word used in Greco-Roman writings.[39]

The argument based on Jewish apostasy appears to be fatally flawed when Jensen appeals to syntax so as to arrive at the conclusion that the denial of the Christ is linked with its Jewish roots.[40] For one thing, we have no way of reading either from or into the text of 1 John anywhere the hypothesis that the

---

35. Lane C. McGaughy, *Toward a Descriptive Analysis of* Einai *as a Linking Verb in New Testament Greek*, SBLDS 6 (Missoula, MT: Society of Biblical Literature for the Linguistics Seminar, 1972); D. A. Carson, "The Purpose of the Fourth Gospel: John 20:31 Reconsidered," *JBL* 106 (1987): 639–51; Carson, "Syntactical and Text-Critical Observations on John 20:30–31: One More Round on the Purpose of the Fourth Gospel," *JBL* 124 (2005): 693–714; Stanley E. Porter, *Idioms of the Greek New Testament*, 2nd ed. (Sheffield: JSOT Press, 1994).

36. Jensen, "Identifying the Subject of εἰμί," 347.

37. Jensen, "Identifying the Subject of εἰμί," 343.

38. Jensen, "Identifying the Subject of εἰμί," 350.

39. Cf. M. de Jonge, "The Use of the Word 'Anointed' in the Time of Jesus," *NovT* 8 (1966): 132–48.

40. The difficulty in identifying the apostates with Jewish background raises another serious problem in relation to Jewishness and/or Judaism. Matthew Thiessen argues that by the end of the first century, the uniformity of Judaism and/or Jewishness can no longer be held conclusively. Thiessen, *Paul and the Gentile Problem* (Oxford: Oxford University Press, 2016), 23–32.

subject "the Christ" implies a query from a Jewish background and that this question implies some form of identification of Jewish apostasy. The simple reason is that as a document or tractate, 1 John is an exhortation to believers in Jesus Christ (or simply an appeal to Christians) without any reference to Judaism. As Painter has noted (see above), there are no traces of Jewishness in any of the three Epistles of John.

Furthermore, Jensen's argument from syntax is flawed. While Jensen goes back over several decades of Johannine studies, he does not research far enough. In both "Identifying the Subject of εἰμί" and in *Affirming the Resurrection of the Incarnate Christ*, Jensen makes no mention of the important study of E. C. Colwell, who established the following rule for the definite predicate nominative in a sentence in which a copula is expressed: "A definite predicate nominative has the article when it follows the verb; it does not have the article when it precedes the verb."[41] Colwell has examined many instances in the NT (see, e.g., John 1:49; Matt. 23:8–10).[42] Based on Colwell's rule, Jensen's conclusions pertaining to 1 John 2:22—that "the Christ" is the subject because it is articular and that "Jesus" is the predicate nominative because it lacks the article—appears to be syntactically flawed.

In summary, these representative studies on 1 John in the last two decades have contributed little beyond the repetition of previous historical presumptions: (1) there must have been a Johannine history and community behind the writings of 1, 2, and 3 John; and (2) the implied audience or Christians of the epistles must have had origins in the Gospel of John. To balance this reading based on a hard-and-fast commitment to historical assumptions therefore, the following section considers a narrative approach to the texts of the Epistles of John.

Narrative as a Challenge to Historical Criticism

To be sure, as we noted earlier, citing de Jonge,[43] the recent trend has shown priority for synchronic reading of the Johannine epistles. What follows is an attempt to take up one issue that at least appears to be a perennial theme in 1 John, 2 John, and 3 John: the umbrella expression "antichrist" (1 John 2:18–28; 4:1–6; 2 John 7–8; 3 John 9–10).[44] As a response to the seemingly

---

41. E. C. Colwell, "A Definite Rule for the Use of the Article in the Greek New Testament," *JBL* 52 (1933): 13.

42. Colwell's rule has been tested and confirmed by Philip B. Harner: see Harner, "Qualitative Anarthrous Predicate Noun: Mark 15:39 and John 1:1," *JBL* 92 (1973): 75–87.

43. De Jonge, "Gospel and the Epistles of John," 144.

44. Third John does not mention the antichrist, but verses 9–10 have sometimes been linked with the aforesaid instances in 1 and 2 John. Cf. von Wahlde, *Gospel and Letters of John*, 3:278–84.

never-ending quest for some form of historical identification of the Christians and/or apostates within the early Christian movement, this section proposes to read the mentions of the antichrist based on the contexts of the individual Epistles without guessing their historical relationship with the Gospel—a proposal of *what* the texts say and *how* they are framed.

Commenting on her study of the letters of Ignatius, Lieu raises a question of boundaries in scholarly attempts to reconstruct various types of historiography of the early Christian movement *alongside* and/or *against* the Judaism and paganism contemporary with that movement. Lieu notes, "It [the early Christian movement] was a situation of weak or poorly defined boundaries, whether those were the boundaries between the Jewish and Christian Communities or, more probably, the internal boundaries within the Christian community which encompassed a broad range of possible belief and practice."[45] I would go further and suggest that in first- and second-century Greco-Roman environs, there were no clearly defined boundaries between Christianity, Judaism, and/or paganism.[46] Concerning the Johannine writings, this observation further points to this problematic question: Is it possible for scholars to reconstruct the so-called (Johannine) history from the confusion of these ill-defined boundaries?[47]

In his study of the opponents in 1 John, Hansjörg Schmid has proposed a promising and defensible direction.[48] Following Lieu's argument about the ill-defined boundaries of religious and nonreligious movements in first- and second-century Greco-Roman surroundings, Schmid seeks to offer a more plausible way of reading the epistolary authors' descriptions of *hoi antichristoi* (antichrists) and *hoi planoi* (deceivers). Schmid begins by noting the internal problem of the traditional and historical readings, which tend to focus on the polemical aspects of these terms, identifying and labeling these unidentified persons or this group of people with many unverifiable titles.[49] Schmid then proposes a nonpolemical reading of these texts.[50] He argues that

---

45. Judith Lieu, "History and Theology in Christian Views of Judaism," in *The Jews among Pagans and Christians in the Roman Empire*, ed. Judith Lieu, John North, and Tessa Rajak (London: Routledge, 1994), 93.

46. The conversation between Jesus and the Samarian woman in John 4:4–29 represents some unclear boundaries between the author's understanding of Jesus and the type of Judaism implied by the woman. Similarly, John 12:20–26 suggests that Greeks and Jews shared some commonality.

47. As the previous two sections showed, historical reconstructions of the Johannine history have led scholars in many disparate directions as they have tried to identify the author(s) of the Epistles and his (their) opponents.

48. Schmid, *Gegner im 1. Johannesbrief?*, 21–25.

49. Cf. Streett, *Identity of the Opponents*, 1–111; Jensen, *Affirming the Resurrection of the Incarnate Christ*, 113–17; Jensen, "Identifying the Subject of εἰμί," 347–53.

50. Hansjörg Schmid, "How to Read the First Epistle of John Non-Polemically," *Biblica* 85 (2004): 24–41.

since modern readers do not have direct access to the real, historical situations of these religious entities, the most probable reading of the Gospel of John and 1 John situates them within the framework of the early Christian religious movement (*das System urchristlicher Religiosität*).[51] As Schmid's proposal is compatible with Lieu's observation on ill-defined boundaries, any effort in looking for a precise and/or accurate form of a religious community is at the heart of the problem. Thus Schmid calls this working hypothesis *ein johanneischers Sinnsystem* (or a Johannine framework) under which the two documents were written. They share a system of meaning and have a dialectical relationship that is characteristically Johannine. But insofar as the term *Johannine* is used, it can only serve as a generic term without any specificity.[52]

Hence the terms *hoi antichristoi* ("antichrists") and *hoi planoi* ("deceivers") are best construed nonpolemically. To whomever the terms may have referred, they cannot be specifically reduced to any particular group. It is not possible to identify these persons with certainty as former Jewish Christians, gentiles, or pagans.[53] Furthermore, the expression "Johannine writings" in this framework does not guarantee any possibility that these writings must have represented the so-called Johannine history or community. Rather, as in the case of other books in the NT (e.g., Pauline letters, Lukan books, Markan Gospel, Matthean Gospel),[54] the Fourth Gospel and 1 John are linked together via an overall perspective called a Johannine theology. The theologies in these two books are closer to each other than to the theologies of other books (e.g., Gospel of Mark, Matthew, Pauline letters). This Johannine theology serves as one process of thought—among many others during and in the first- and second-century Greco-Roman environs—which gave rise to the Christian faith. In this regard, Fourth Gospel and/or 1 John were not formed through a distinct process in order to differentiate one group of Christians from another but, rather, were formed out of the necessity of the development of the Christian faith.[55]

---

51. Schmid, *Gegner im 1. Johannesbrief?*, 21. Translation is mine.

52. Just as Reinhartz noted earlier, so the generic *Johannine* does not presume that we have the Gospel of John per se. Reinhartz, "Building Skyscrapers from Toothpicks," 70.

53. Cf. Painter's article, which expresses a similar view of the term *opponent*. The term is politically and religiously neutral in connotation, and the authors of these letters have no intention of identifying this group more definitively than as "antichrists" or "deceivers." Thus rather than revealing to us something about who the opponents were in themselves, these terms remind us that opposition, dissidence, apostasy, departure, and so on are inherent in every socioreligious group throughout human history. Painter, "'Opponents' in 1 John," 48–71.

54. In narrative criticism, for example, the Markan Jesus must be treated autonomously and be kept distinct from the Jesus of the Gospels of Matthew, Luke, and John.

55. Schmid notes, "With this perspective it is possible to establish the statement which understands Johannine theology as a process of thought. Accordingly, that which gives rise to the Christian faith is also displayed in this process of thought. Standing in the center is not the

Schmid's proposal is certainly defensible, at least on principle. Although Schmid's study is on the opponents in 1 John, his proposal on the Johannine framework also extends to 2 and 3 John. In 2 John, for instance, the terms *hoi antichristoi* and *hoi planoi* are used in verse 7; yet the author does not identify who these people are. Nor does he identify himself except by the generic title "the Elder" (v. 1). In similar fashion, the author of 3 John begins with the title "the Elder" and indicates that the Elder wrote this letter to Gaius (v. 1). We do not know the answer to the question of boundaries and specificity— namely, whether or not this Elder of 3 John is the same as the Elder in 2 John and to what extent 2 John and 3 John are related to 1 John.[56] That the authors of these three Epistles have left many issues ambiguous and uncertain has purpose and meaning. In 2 John, for instance, the real identity of the "Elder," that of the "Elect Lady," and that of "the antichrist and deceiver" are not given. In 3 John, similarly, the locale of the sender (the Elder) and that of the addressee (Gaius) are entirely unknown. These account for the designation of these Epistles as "general" or "catholic."

Let us revisit again the centuries-old expression "Catholic Epistles." Although the Epistles of John are not completely independent from the Gospel of John, this corpus nomenclature lists 1 John, 2 John, and 3 John within the so-called "general" letters for the reason that they do not address any particular community or group of Christians.[57] Any effort to pin down some form of historical identity of any of these letters will find the burden of proof immense.

Reflections

Did the Johannine community and its history exist? It is convenient for scholars to speculate about many things concerning the history of the Epistles of John and then attribute them to the unidentifiable individuals of an implied audience and the unverifiable groups of the hypothetical opponents. In the end, our scholarly guesswork remains, as Reinhartz noted, "the product of a circular hermeneutical process"[58]—a scientific process that, as Robert Kysar

---

process of boundaries, but rather the necessity of the development of the Christian faith itself. Thus 1 John is here construed as an ethical unfolding of Johannine theology." Schmid, "*Gegner im 1. Johannesbrief?*, 22. Translation is mine.

56. Scholars such as Abraham J. Malherbe (cf. note 2 above) have wondered about the inclusion of 3 John in the canonical list, for the reason that the letter addresses a purely personal matter.

57. Cf. Jacques Schlosser, "Le Corpus des Épîtres catholiques," in *Catholic Epistles and the Tradition*, 3–41.

58. Reinhartz, "Building Skyscrapers from Toothpicks," 70.

said toward the end of his scholarly career, is "becoming more speculative."[59] Reading the first 110 pages of Streett's reconstruction of the opponents in 1 John, for instance, one feels that his scholarship on this epistle has begun and ended with a circular hermeneutical process. He terms *hoi antichristoi* the antichrists, then identifies the antichrists as Jewish apostates. Yet in the end, all we can justifiably conclude is that term simply refers to those people who formerly belonged to a group of Christians but no longer do.

One cannot simply deny the historical processes of ancient documents such as 1, 2, and 3 John, as they did not come out of a vacuum.[60] Yet one is better off with the question, To what end is our historical speculation moving? I propose that where history ends, narrative and semantic approaches begin. To read these Epistles of John more productively, therefore, is to look at their history from the perspectives of the narrative and semantics. Put differently, these Epistles of John *did* have a history with regard to their composition (1 John 1:1–4; 2:7–14; 2 John 1; 3 John 1), Christian backgrounds (1 John 2:18–27; 2 John 7–10), and social or personal disputes (3 John 9–10). Yet for us the more pressing and meaningful question is whether the narrative of these ancient epistles remains theologically significant for audiences and readers over time.

---

59. Robert Kysar, *Voyages with John: Charting the Fourth Gospel* (Waco: Baylor University Press, 2005), 145–46.

60. On this issue, see Francis J. Moloney, "Into Narrative and Beyond," in Thatcher, *What We Have Heard*, 195–210, esp. 200–201.

23

The Book of Revelation

Michael C. Thompson

Introduction

Over the past thirty years, research and publication on the book of Revelation has been moving rapidly, with books, monographs, and commentaries appearing constantly. Although the vast majority of this work is based on good and careful scholarship, advancing our understanding of the text and the world from which it emerged, the well-known observation by G. K. Chesterton remains true: "And though St. John the Evangelist saw many strange monsters in his vision, he saw no creature so wild as one of his own commentators."[1] This statement alone points to the ongoing need for biblical studies to continue in its quest to better understand the Apocalypse, so that John's voice might be heard as it was intended.

Keeping pace with the amount of scholarship devoted to Revelation can prove overwhelming. This chapter highlights the major areas of discussion and debate in recent interpretation. Hence, a number of issues and contributing voices will, out of necessity, be left to the side. To complement the content of this chapter, the reader is referred to the summary of Revelation's history of interpretation in Craig Koester's comprehensive commentary,[2] as well as Russell Morton's survey of recent research.[3]

---

1. G. K. Chesterton, *Orthodoxy* (New York: John Lane, 1990), 29.
2. Craig R. Koester, *Revelation: A New Translation with Introduction and Commentary* (New Haven: Yale University Press, 2014), 29–65. Cf. also Arthur Wainwright, *Mysterious Apocalypse: Interpreting the Book of Revelation* (Nashville: Abingdon, 1993).
3. Russell S. Morton, *Recent Research on Revelation* (Sheffield: Sheffield Phoenix, 2014).

Genre

At the heart of the interpretive issues surrounding Revelation is the question of genre. Scholars have long sought to identify the styles and influences of the text. Because of the nature of Revelation, evaluations of genre have a more significant impact on the process of interpreting it than on interpreting any other NT writing. Since genre "defines a set of expectations which guide our engagement with the texts,"[4] understanding the categories of composition is vital to the work of exegesis. John's use of metaphor and symbolism can be overwhelming to the reader, and knowing the text's genre can help reduce the complexity of background knowledge needed for the sake of clear communication.[5] It is widely accepted that Revelation is an apocalypse, though most scholars now agree that the book is a combination of genres.[6] At present, the two most significant advances of study on Revelation's genre are in the ongoing work to understand ancient apocalyptic literature and in the increasing realization that John's Apocalypse is "a text that overruns its boundaries to a high degree."[7] Although many subcategories of genre have been explored, the majority of modern scholars approach Revelation as a mixture of apocalypse, prophecy, and epistle.

Identifying Apocalypses

The book of Revelation is the first known writing to refer to itself as *apokalypsis*, and there is no clear historical evidence that this would have been understood as a reference to genre. Still, it is clear that this opening sentence is intended to function as a title, and the visionary narrative does exhibit a commonality with an identifiable Jewish literary tradition that had emerged in the late-exilic and postexilic period.[8] While early attempts to define the apocalyptic genre focused on its distinguishing features of style,[9] it was in the 1970s that scholarship sought a more formal definition. Emerging from the Society of Biblical Literature's study group on apocalypse, John J. Collins's

---

4. John Frow, *Genre*, 2nd ed. (London: Routledge, 2015), 113.
5. Frow, *Genre*, 113; cf. also Janet Martin Soskice, *Metaphor and Religious Language* (Oxford: Oxford University Press, 1985).
6. Cf. Dave Mathewson, "Revelation in Recent Genre Scholarship: Some Implications for Interpretation," *TJ* 13 (1992): 192–213.
7. Gregory L. Linton, "Reading the Apocalypse as Apocalypse: The Limits of Genre," in *The Reality of Apocalypse: Rhetoric and Politics in the Book of Revelation*, ed. David L. Barr (Atlanta: SBL Press, 2006), 10.
8. Stephen L. Cook, "Apocalyptic Prophecy," in *The Oxford Handbook of Apocalyptic Literature*, ed. John J. Collins (Oxford: Oxford University Press, 2014), 30–31.
9. One of the first and most significant contributors to this was D. S. Russell, *The Method and Message of Jewish Apocalyptic* (Philadelphia: Westminster, 1964). Certain aspects of his investigation remain remarkably relevant.

essay in *Apocalypse: The Morphology of a Genre* is a master paradigm of apocalyptic features, leading to the following foundational definition: "'Apocalypse' is a genre of revelatory literature with a narrative framework, in which a revelation is mediated by an otherworldly being to a human recipient, disclosing a transcendent reality which is both temporal insofar as it envisages eschatological salvation, and spatial insofar as it involves another, supernatural world."[10] This definition has proven to be the most widely accepted, though it has not been without challenge and critique.[11] The most oft-repeated criticism is that the definition does not address the function of apocalypse, which Collins claims was an intentional omission in order to push such discussion to the level of individual texts.[12]

In subsequent years of scholarship, a number of alternative approaches to defining apocalypse have been proposed,[13] yet Collins's 1979 definition remains the most influential. While the work of defining genre and identifying literary traits is necessary, locating Revelation's place among the apocalyptic writings remains challenging, especially in light of the realization that Revelation does not follow many of the conventions of common apocalyptic texts.[14] While knowing the genre of a particular text can certainly guide the process of communication, it would be misguided to expect any text to conform to our imputed categories of style.

Revelation as Apocalypse

When John used *apokalypsis* in the title of his work, it appears that he intended to connect his visionary narrative to a well-represented group of

---

10. John J. Collins, "Introduction: Towards the Morphology of a Genre," in *Apocalypse: The Morphology of a Genre*, ed. John J. Collins, Semeia 14 (Atlanta: SBL Press, 1979), 9.

11. The history of identifying and defining apocalyptic literature, most notably the work accomplished in 1979–89, has been recounted many times: John J. Collins, "What Is Apocalyptic Literature?," in Collins, *Oxford Handbook of Apocalyptic Literature*, 1–16; Adela Yarbro Collins, "Apocalypse Now: The State of Apocalyptic Studies near the End of the First Decade of the Twenty-First Century," *HTR* 104 (2011): 447–57; Lorenzo DiTommaso, "Apocalypses and Apocalypticism in Antiquity, Part One," *CBR* 5 (2007): 235–58.

12. J. Collins, "What Is Apocalyptic Literature?," 5.

13. A few significant attempts appear in the following sources: Christopher Rowland, *The Open Heaven: A Study of Apocalyptic in Judaism and Early Christianity* (London: SPCK, 1982), which does not consider common content in seeking to define the genre, instead searching for a definition based solely on literary form; David E. Aune, "The Apocalypse of John and the Problem of Genre," in *Early Christian Apocalypticism: Genre and Social Setting*, ed. Adela Yarbro Collins, Semeia 36 (Atlanta: SBL Press, 1986), which provides a very technical definition of apocalyptic; Grant R. Osborne, *The Hermeneutical Spiral: A Comprehensive Introduction to Biblical Interpretation*, rev. ed. (Downers Grove, IL: IVP Academic, 2007), 276, which offers a definition that seeks to combine those offered by J. Collins, Rowland, and Aune.

14. Linton, "Reading the Apocalypse as Apocalypse," 35.

writings that emerged from Second Temple Judaism.[15] Although clearly a product of the Christian movement, Revelation has more in common with Jewish apocalyptic literature than with later Christian apocalypses.[16] Most scholars see this connection as evidence of John's use of a common apocalyptic tradition.[17] Thus, although Revelation utilizes a number of genres, it is clear that the style of apocalypse is the primary vehicle for the text.[18] Having arrived at this conclusion, we can address the question of social function: What impact did John's Apocalypse intend to have on its audience?

As mentioned in many discussions on the topic, a text's genre is necessarily linked to its intended social function, and the specific goal of an apocalyptic work is to transform present reality through the experience of a larger, supernatural vision.[19] In other words, the nature of apocalyptic imagery is to pull the reader into an imaginative world in order to experience a fresh view of reality.[20] Apocalypse seeks to accomplish this type of communication by using symbolic language to connect various entities, establishing metaphor, and conveying a specific message. The challenge for the modern reader is to discover the common world of thought that would have allowed these images to have their intended impact, unveiling from a "mass of symbols" the dynamic, yet complicated, original context.[21]

Revelation as Prophecy

John refers to the content of his work as prophecy (1:3; 22:7, 10, 18, 19), and he speaks with a certain authority to the seven assemblies of Asia Minor,

---

15. Alexander Kulik, "Genre without a Name: Was There a Hebrew Term for 'Apocalypse'?," *JSJ* 40 (2009): 540–50.

16. David E. Aune, "The Apocalypse of John and Palestinian Jewish Apocalyptic," *Neot* 40, no. 1 (2006): 1–33. Cf. also J. Ramsey Michaels, *Interpreting the Book of Revelation* (London: T&T Clark, 1993), 30.

17. Richard Bauckham, *The Climax of Prophecy: Studies on the Book of Revelation* (Edinburgh: T&T Clark, 1993), 38–91.

18. Using the master paradigm first published by J. Collins (1979), David E. Aune offers a detailed inventory of Revelation's apocalyptic traits in *Revelation*, 3 vols., Word Biblical Commentary 52A–C (Grand Rapids: Zondervan, 1997–98), 1:lxxxii–lxxxviii.

19. David L. Barr, "Beyond Genre: The Expectations of Apocalypse," in *The Reality of Apocalypse: Rhetoric and Politics in the Book of Revelation*, ed. David L. Barr (Atlanta: SBL Press, 2006), 86. Cf. also David A. deSilva, *Seeing Things John's Way: The Rhetoric of the Book of Revelation* (Louisville: Westminster John Knox, 2009), 13; Leonard L. Thompson, *The Book of Revelation: Apocalypse and Empire* (Oxford: Oxford University Press, 1990), 32.

20. Christopher C. Rowland, "The Book of Revelation," in *The New Interpreter's Bible: New Testament Survey* (Nashville: Abingdon, 2005), 340–41.

21. Edmondo F. Lupieri, *A Commentary on the Apocalypse of John*, trans. Maria Poggi Johnson and Adam Kamesar (Grand Rapids: Eerdmans, 1999), 33. A helpful discussion about the methodology of interpreting Revelation's symbolism can be found in G. K. Beale, *The Book of Revelation* (Grand Rapids: Eerdmans, 1999), 50–69.

using the language of apocalypse to convey his message.[22] In an article published in 1957, G. E. Ladd suggested the category of "prophetic-apocalyptic" to describe the "eschatologically apocalyptic and ethically prophetic" nature of the teachings of Jesus.[23] This same approach has been adopted by a number of scholars in reading Revelation, though there remains a considerable variety in understanding the relationship between these two genre types. John himself provides no hint that he saw a distinction between the two.[24]

Beyond this self-designation, the message of Revelation does exhibit traits that would readily identify it as a work of prophecy. One of the most thorough investigations into these prophetic elements is found in the source-critical study by Frederick Mazzaferri,[25] who is so strongly convinced of the influence of a prophetic tradition that he outright dismisses the work as apocalyptic. More probably, however, Revelation reflects the work of one individual who participated in a circle of prophets who ministered among the early churches of Asia Minor, whose self-perception was that they stood in line with the traditions of prophecy in ancient Judaism.[26] Revelation is thus best understood as a "literary product of early Christian prophecy," using the imagery of apocalyptic language to convey its message.[27]

Revelation as Epistle

Following the extended heading, or prologue, the book of Revelation is presented in its own epistolary frame. A conventional letter greeting and salutation is given in 1:4–6, and John is instructed to write specific messages to the seven assemblies in 1:11. However, it is difficult to classify the work as a whole as an epistle per se.[28] Although Revelation does overlay the letter form on top of its prophetic-apocalyptic message, the question remains how formal (or essential) the reader should consider the epistolary aspects of the text to be.[29]

Revelation's unique use of the letter form does serve the interpreter in connecting the text to its original audience—namely, the seven specific assemblies

---

22. Richard Bauckham, *The Theology of the Book of Revelation* (Cambridge: Cambridge University Press, 1993), 6.
23. George Eldon Ladd, "Why Not Prophetic-Apocalyptic?," *JBL* 76 (1957): 192–200.
24. Adela Yarbro Collins, *The Apocalypse* (Collegeville, MN: Liturgical Press, 1979), 5.
25. Frederick David Mazzaferri, *The Genre of the Book of Revelation from a Source-Critical Perspective* (Berlin: de Gruyter, 1989), 379–84.
26. David E. Aune, "The Prophetic Circle of John of Patmos and the Exegesis of Revelation 22:16," *JBL* 37 (1989): 103–16.
27. Elisabeth Schüssler Fiorenza, *The Book of Revelation: Justice and Judgment*, 2nd ed. (Minneapolis: Fortress, 1998), 151.
28. Hans-Josef Klauck, *Ancient Letters in the New Testament: A Guide to Context and Exegesis* (Waco: Baylor University Press, 2006), 351.
29. Aune, *Revelation*, 1:lxxii.

to whom the book is addressed. The seven oracles given in chapters 2–3 identify specific issues within each community, to which the ensuing visionary narrative is given as a relevant prophetic message addressed to these particular situations.[30] John writes as one who is connected to these congregations, moving beyond the standard Greco-Roman letter-writing practice and offering a prophetic voice through his work.[31]

The issue of Revelation's genre is summarized quite well by J. Ramsey Michaels: "If a letter, it is like no other early Christian letter we possess. If an apocalypse, it is like no other apocalypse. If a prophecy, it is unique among prophecies."[32] To read Revelation effectively is to allow it to push against the limits of genre for the purpose of discovering what the original audience would have heard when presented with such a book.[33]

Social Setting

Along with genre, the social setting of Revelation has been shown to have had a profound impact on interpretation. It was common in past research to read Revelation as a document produced in the midst of intense and widespread imperial persecution of the church. Yet more recent study has challenged this viewpoint, demonstrating a much more complex social context for the seven assemblies. In particular, this approach has shown a lack of evidence for an empire-wide persecution of the church at the time of Revelation's composition.[34] Adela Yarbro Collins was among the early voices to contend that Revelation is a type of protest literature, reflecting a localized social pressure on the various Christian communities.[35] Such social pressure could come from a number of sources, and Leonard Thompson's study also explored these complexities, which included a number of *positive* elements of Roman rule for the church.[36]

In recent years NT scholarship as a whole has shown increasing interest in the dynamics of imperial rule on the early Christian movement.[37] This approach has also played a part in the detailed study of the Jewish and Christian

---

30. Koester, *Revelation*, 111.
31. Klauck, *Ancient Letters in the New Testament*, 352.
32. Michaels, *Interpreting the Book of Revelation*, 20.
33. Grant R. Osborne, "Genre Criticism—Sensus Literalis," *TJ* 4 (1983): 1–27; Barr, "Beyond Genre," 88.
34. Adela Yarbro Collins, *Crisis and Catharsis: The Power of the Apocalypse* (Philadelphia: Westminster, 1984), 70.
35. A. Collins, *Crisis and Catharsis*, 69–73.
36. Thompson, *Apocalypse and Empire*, 146–67.
37. Cf. Scot McKnight and Joseph B. Modica, eds., *Jesus Is Lord, Caesar Is Not: Evaluating Empire in New Testament Studies* (Downers Grove, IL: IVP Academic, 2013).

communities in Asia Minor, providing essential information for reading Revelation.[38] Those interpreters who come to the Apocalypse do so increasingly with the aim of placing the text within the "ordinary lives" of its first recipients, what Thompson refers to as "normal, not abnormal times."[39] Notable among this contextual research is Christopher Frilingos, who seeks to demonstrate how John's rhetorical strategies were bound to the context of Roman rule, and J. Nelson Kraybill, whose monograph explores the civic and economic realities of the seven assemblies.[40]

A significant piece of the social context in Roman Asia Minor is the role of the imperial cult.[41] One of the foundational studies into this phenomenon was published by S. R. F. Price,[42] who traced the emergence of ruler worship in Asia Minor as a practice transferred from Greek culture into Roman rule. Along similar lines, Steven Friesen has suggested that John utilizes the Roman mythology of empire, turning it back against itself to construct an opposing mythology.[43] Exploring the role of the imperial cult in the context of Revelation has been integrated into much recent research,[44] and the resulting work continues to yield important data for interpreting John's Apocalypse.

38. John M. G. Barclay, *Jews in the Mediterranean Diaspora: From Alexander to Trajan (323 BCE–117 CE)* (Berkeley: University of California Press, 1996); Philip A. Harland, *Associations, Synagogues, and Congregations: Claiming a Place in Ancient Mediterranean Society* (Minneapolis: Fortress, 2003); Colin J. Hemer, *The Letters to the Seven Churches of Asia in Their Local Setting* (Sheffield: Sheffield Academic, 1986); James S. Jeffers, *The Greco-Roman World of the New Testament Era: Exploring the Background of Early Christianity* (Downers Grove, IL: InterVarsity, 1999); Tessa Rajak, *The Jewish Dialogue with Greece and Rome: Studies in Cultural and Social Interaction* (Leiden: Brill, 2002); Paul R. Trebilco, *The Early Christians in Ephesus from Paul to Ignatius* (Grand Rapids: Eerdmans, 2004); Trebilco, *Jewish Communities in Asia Minor* (Cambridge: Cambridge University Press, 1991); Klaus Wengst, *Pax Romana and the Peace of Jesus Christ* (Philadelphia: Fortress, 1987). Additionally, although it is primarily focused on the Gospel of John, one can find excellent relevant information in Warren Carter, *John and Empire: Initial Explorations* (New York: T&T Clark, 2008).

39. Leonard L. Thompson, "Ordinary Lives: John and His First Readers," in *Reading the Book of Revelation: A Resource for Students*, ed. David L. Barr (Atlanta: SBL Press, 2003), 36.

40. Christopher A. Frilingos, *Spectacles of Empire: Monsters, Martyrs, and the Book of Revelation* (Philadelphia: University of Pennsylvania Press, 2004); J. Nelson Kraybill, *Imperial Cult and Commerce in John's Apocalypse* (Sheffield: Sheffield Academic, 1996).

41. Various perspectives have been offered regarding the "imperial cult," and the practice itself has proved quite difficult to define or describe since no single system of worship was ever established, nor was participation ever mandated for the citizenry. However, there is clear evidence of imperial cult practice, which is indeed reflected in the message of Revelation. For more information, see Mary Beard, John North, and Simon Price, *Religions of Rome*, vol. 1, *A History* (Cambridge: Cambridge University Press, 1998), 313–63.

42. S. R. F. Price, *Rituals of Power: The Roman Imperial Cult in Asia Minor* (Cambridge: Cambridge University Press, 1984).

43. Steven J. Friesen, *Imperial Cults and the Apocalypse of John: Reading Revelation from the Ruins* (Oxford: Oxford University Press, 2001), 208–9.

44. Other notable projects to this end include Wes Howard-Brook and Anthony Gwyther, *Unveiling Empire: Reading Revelation Then and Now* (Maryknoll, NY: Orbis, 1999), 101–18;

Recent readings of Revelation's historical context have also led to the publication of a number of commentaries, the most well-known being that of David Aune.[45] This major publication contains a very detailed historical-critical study, including constant interaction with the Jewish traditions of prophecy and apocalypse. Aune also utilizes source criticism, approaching Revelation as a composite text, searching for parallels and incorporations of Greco-Roman material into John's text. In 2014, Koester published another major commentary on Revelation.[46] With evidence of exhaustive research, this work explores the historical context of Revelation, while also considering the book's history of interpretation. Also, more than any other commentary to date, Koester provides extensive engagement with the effect that the social realities of Roman imperialism had on the seven assemblies, thus giving proper attention to "the world within the text of Revelation."[47]

Along with the Greco-Roman context, recent interpreters have also been attentive to the Jewish influences on Revelation, especially via the prophetic-apocalyptic tradition. One of the more prolific writers on the Apocalypse is Gregory K. Beale, who sees the book of Daniel as having unique influence on John's visionary narrative.[48] Beale later expanded his original approach in a monograph exploring John's apocalyptic use of the OT through textual analysis.[49] While there is merit in such detailed examination of the text, this approach can sometimes be constrained by a narrow reading of Revelation's social context. Several additional studies of the Jewish background of Revelation have also relied on textual dependence—that is, on a search for the echoes of one writer in another.[50]

Jörg Frey, "The Relevance of the Roman Imperial Cult for the Book of Revelation: Exegetical and Hermeneutical Reflections on the Relation between the Seven Letters and the Visionary Main Part of the Book," in *The New Testament and Early Christian Literature in Greco-Roman Context: Studies in Honor of David E. Aune*, ed. John Fotopoulos (Leiden: Brill, 2006), 231–55; Allen Brent, *The Imperial Cult and the Development of Church Order: Concepts and Images of Authority in Paganism and Early Christianity before the Age of Cyprian* (Leiden: Brill, 1999), 164–209; Bruce W. Winter, *Divine Honours for the Caesars: The First Christians' Responses* (Grand Rapids: Eerdmans, 2015).

45. Aune, *Revelation*.
46. Koester, *Revelation*.
47. Koester, *Revelation*, xiv.
48. Gregory K. Beale, *The Use of Daniel in Jewish Apocalyptic Literature and in the Revelation of St. John* (Lanham, MD: University Press of America, 1984).
49. G. K. Beale, *John's Use of the Old Testament in Revelation* (London: T&T Clark, 1998).
50. Jon Paulien, *Decoding Revelation's Trumpets: Literary Allusions and Interpretation of Revelation 8:7–12* (Berrien Springs, MI: Andrews University Press, 1988); Jean-Pierre Ruiz, *Ezekiel in the Apocalypse: The Transformation of Prophetic Language in Revelation 16,17–19,10* (Frankfurt am Main: Peter Lang, 1989); Jan Fekkes III, *Isaiah and Prophetic Traditions in the Book of Revelation: Visionary Antecedents and Their Development* (Sheffield: Sheffield Academic, 1994).

In 1999 Beale published his commentary on the Greek text of Revelation,[51] which contains valuable grammatical and textual insight. As for social setting, Beale adopts the more traditional reading of an imperial persecution on the church, either realized or expected. Following this, in 2002, Grant Osborne published his exegetical commentary,[52] exploring both historical background and intertextual information. Osborne also works to trace theological themes through Revelation and does well to provide the reader with various interpretive positions throughout his work. A similar approach is taken in more concise form by Ian Paul,[53] whose reading also shows a good balance between text structure and theological meaning. Finally, the commentary produced by Mitchell Reddish contains very good information on the historical context of the Apocalypse, maintaining balance between Hellenistic and Jewish influences on John's message.[54] Reddish offers what is certainly one of the most readable introductory commentaries on Revelation presently available.

Literary Readings

In recent years, scholarship on Revelation has been actively exploring the literary dynamics of the text. This type of approach tends to focus on an identifiable main plot, while considering the characters and symbols in relation to the overarching structure of the book. One of the leading voices in this methodology has been David Barr, who reads Revelation as "a complex story" that lies beyond the imagination of any one reader.[55] In his book-length study, Barr divides Revelation into three sections (three scrolls) and then explores the literary aspects of the narrative.[56] Other scholars have also taken up this same type of approach, including the narrative-critical work of James Resseguie, who is most helpful in discussing John's use of symbols and story.[57] A more specific study was completed by Barbara Rossing, who uses the historical context as a means of understanding John's use of metaphor.[58] As a result, Rossing can assert that John utilizes the ancient literary device of

---

51. Beale, *Book of Revelation*.
52. Grant R. Osborne, *Revelation* (Grand Rapids: Baker Academic, 2002).
53. Ian Paul, *Revelation* (Downers Grove, IL: IVP Academic, 2018).
54. Mitchell G. Reddish, *Revelation* (Macon, GA: Smyth & Helwys, 2001).
55. David L. Barr, "The Story John Told: Reading Revelation for Its Plot," in Barr, *Reading the Book of Revelation*, 13.
56. David L. Barr, *Tales of the End: A Narrative Commentary on the Book of Revelation*, 2nd ed. (Salem, MA: Polebridge, 2012).
57. James L. Resseguie, *The Revelation of John: A Narrative Commentary* (Grand Rapids: Baker Academic, 2009).
58. Barbara R. Rossing, *The Choice between Two Cities: Whore, Bride and Empire in the Apocalypse* (Harrisburg, PA: Trinity Press International, 1999).

two-city contrast to establish a political imagery. Such a reading thus impacts one's understanding of the structural elements of Revelation as well as of the rhetoric employed by John.[59]

The most comprehensive study of Revelation's rhetorical nature is provided by David deSilva.[60] He builds his approach on classical discussion of rhetoric drawn from the ancient world. One particular strength of deSilva's analysis is his integration of John's rhetorical devices with the historical setting and theological themes found in the apocalyptic text. Thus he finds the composition of Revelation as intended for moral persuasion, as John utilizes epideictic and deliberative rhetoric in order to move his audience toward particular goals.[61]

Theological Readings

Recent studies in Revelation have also focused on the theological significance of the text, building on the various historical and literary approaches. Perhaps the most well-known among these is Richard Bauckham's theological introduction to the book.[62] His reading is constructed on the theocentric nature of Revelation,[63] with the conclusion that John's prophetic voice reveals the nature of God in a way that continues to have dynamic implications for the church.[64] Bauckham also produced a collection of essays that explores Revelation's theological issues in greater detail, along with the book's structure and historical context.[65] Both of these works have proven quite valuable to research on the Apocalypse and remain remarkably relevant more than twenty-five years after their initial publication.

Although a handful of monographs and books engaging Revelation's theological message have been produced in recent scholarship,[66] two can be men-

---

59. A study on Revelation's literary structure was offered in Antoninus King Wai Siew, *The War between the Two Beasts and the Two Witnesses: A Chiastic Reading of Revelation 11:1–14:5* (London: T&T Clark, 2005). Although Siew's chiastic reading cannot be supported by the whole of Revelation, there are good aspects of his investigation into the book's structure.
60. DeSilva, *Seeing Things John's Way*, 16–25.
61. DeSilva, *Seeing Things John's Way*, 90–91.
62. Bauckham, *Theology of the Book of Revelation*.
63. Bauckham, *Theology of the Book of Revelation*, 23.
64. Bauckham, *Theology of the Book of Revelation*, 164.
65. Bauckham, *Climax of Prophecy*.
66. Laszlo Gallusz, *The Throne Motif in the Book of Revelation: Profiles from the History of Interpretation* (London: Bloomsbury T&T Clark, 2014); Loren L. Johns, *The Lamb Christology of the Apocalypse in John: An Investigation into Its Origin and Rhetorical Force* (Tübingen: Mohr Siebeck, 2003); Stephen Pattemore, *The People of God in the Apocalypse: Discourse, Structure and Exegesis* (Cambridge: Cambridge University Press, 2004); Rodney Lawrence Thomas, *Magical Motifs in the Book of Revelation* (London: T&T Clark, 2010).

tioned here. In 2010 a "theological commentary" on Revelation was published by Joseph Mangina.[67] The aim of the Brazos Theological Commentary series, in which this commentary was published, is to draw together the disciplines of biblical studies and systematic theology, and Mangina does this well. Although his is not a critical commentary on the text or its historical context, the work does offer theological reflection based on a responsible reading of Revelation. Then, in 2012, the papers of a conference focusing on the theology, politics, and intertextuality of Revelation were published as *Revelation and the Politics of Apocalyptic Interpretation*, where a number of accomplished scholars reflect theologically on the Apocalypse and apply its message for the world today.[68] A consistent theme of this volume is that Revelation's theological message is also a political vision, finding full expression in the ongoing witness of the church.

Reading Revelation from the Margins

Although these subcategories could rightfully be considered subsets of theological readings in general, it is important to highlight a handful of the specialized readings of the text. Some of these approaches represent minority viewpoints, and others speak from specific ideological positions. And while some of these studies may sometimes suffer from a tendency to unfairly superimpose a modern social and cultural understanding on the ancient context, the modern interpreter can often discover new insights by considering points of view that are not always represented in the mainstream.

Feminist Readings

Recent feminist readings of Revelation have challenged many of the cultural assumptions of John's language and use of metaphor, especially

---

67. Joseph L. Mangina, *Revelation*, BTC (Grand Rapids: Brazos, 2010).
68. Richard B. Hays and Stefan Alkier, eds., *Revelation and the Politics of Apocalyptic Interpretation* (Waco: Baylor University Press, 2012). The essays included in this important volume are Michael J. Gorman, "What Has the Spirit Been Saying? Theological and Hermeneutical Reflections on the Reception/Impact History of the Book of Revelation," 11–30; Steve Moyise, "Models for Intertextual Interpretation of Revelation," 31–46; Thomas Hieke, "The Reception of Daniel 7 in the Revelation of John," 47–68; Richard B. Hays, "Faithful Witness, Alpha and Omega: The Identity of Jesus in the Apocalypse of John," 69–84; Joseph L. Mangina, "God, Israel, and Ecclesia in the Apocalypse," 85–104; N. T. Wright, "Revelation and Christian Hope: Political Implications of the Revelation to John," 105–24; Stefan Alkier, "Witness or Warrior? How the Book of Revelation Can Help Christians Live Their Political Lives," 125–42; Tobias Nicklas, "The Apocalypse in the Framework of the Canon," 143–54; Marianne Meye Thompson, "Reading What Is Written in the Book of Life: Theological Interpretation of the Book of Revelation Today," 155–71.

his apocalyptic portrayal of women.[69] A recent collection of essays edited by Amy-Jill Levine focuses on the female imagery found in Revelation, although the contributors do well at engaging various aspects of the apocalyptic text overall.[70] Further, although the common theme centers on feminist concerns, the approaches exhibit methodological diversity in reading Revelation.

One of the primary benefits that has emerged from feminist readings of Revelation is the consideration of symbol and metaphor from an alternative perspective. That John would use this type of feminine imagery as a challenge to imperial Rome is intentional, and it appears to be based on standard *topoi* that can rhetorically undermine Roman social values.[71] Or perhaps the alternative reading points to a negative reality in the apocalyptic language, what Stephen Moore refers to as a "hypermasculinity," whereby John's vision of God and Christ are based on the characteristics of the emperor Domitian.[72]

Whereas many of the modern feminist readings of Revelation negatively critique John's language as being overly patriarchal, Elisabeth Schüssler Fiorenza offers a different approach,[73] seeking an alternative reading that will enable the Apocalypse to hold a liberating voice for its readers. Although she offers her own critique of John's feminine and masculine imagery, Schüssler Fiorenza pursues a reading of Revelation that identifies the alternative community of the church as the entity that can stand in opposition to imperial Rome, thereby challenging its accepted social order.[74] It is the same liberating voice that is put forward into our modern world as well.

Political Readings

When speaking about modern political approaches to Revelation, writers typically give attention to liberationist readings and those interpretations offered by minority cultures. In recent years both of these perspectives have been actively present in the reading of Revelation. The most widely recognized

---

69. Rossing, *Choice between Two Cities*; Jean K. Kim, "Uncovering Her Wickedness: An Inter(con)textual Reading of Revelation 17 from a Postcolonial Feminist Perspective," *JSNT* 73 (1999): 61–81; Tina Pippin, *Death and Desire: The Rhetoric of Gender in the Apocalypse of John* (Louisville: Westminster John Knox, 1992).

70. Amy-Jill Levine with Maria Mayo Robbins, eds., *A Feminist Companion to the Apocalypse of John* (London: T&T Clark, 2009).

71. Lynn R. Huber, *Like a Bride Adorned: Reading Metaphor in John's Apocalypse* (London: T&T Clark, 2007), 44.

72. Stephen D. Moore, "Hypermasculinity and Divinity," in Levine with Robbins, *Feminist Companion to the Apocalypse of John*, 180–204.

73. Schüssler Fiorenza, *Book of Revelation*.

74. Schüssler Fiorenza, *Book of Revelation*, 75.

liberationist voice on Revelation is Pablo Richard.[75] Richard does not read the apocalyptic language as otherworldly, but rather as metaphors of oppression that draw together images of economic, social, and political forces that prey on the poor.[76] Such negative imagery is thus contrasted with John's vision of heaven, which Richard reads as a state of justice for the oppressed.[77] Through this reading one can see how the message of Revelation has found a special place in the heart of many of the liberationist movements and is often held as a message of hope for the suffering.[78]

Another example of reading Revelation for the marginalized is found in David Sánchez,[79] who examines the construction of "counter-myths" as a means of the oppressed dealing with the realities of their oppression. He focuses mainly on how colonized people absorb the cultural attributes of their colonizers but then combine them with their own traditional cultural attributes to produce a new cultural identity as a means of resisting and subverting the power that has been pushed on them.[80] Thus John's ability to transform imperial mythology in his apocalyptic imagery is an example of offering a theology of hope for the oppressed.

An intercultural reading of Revelation is represented in a 2005 volume edited by David Rhoads,[81] in which nine authors explore various aspects of the apocalyptic message from their respective cultural and social vantage points. Because of the wide scope of interpretations offered by the contributors, it is quite difficult to summarize the book's main ideas. At times the reader might begin to wonder if the same primary text is being discussed, although such an experience does offer an important example of just how varied readings of Revelation can become.

Another perspective on Revelation's message is offered by Brian Blount,[82] who offers a reading based in African American culture. The main theological emphasis that emerges from Blount's study is that of nonviolent resistance, a posture against oppression that begins in John's own summons to the church.[83] Using the traditions of American black culture, Blount focuses

---

75. Pablo Richard, *Apocalypse: A People's Commentary on the Book of Revelation* (Maryknoll, NY: Orbis, 1995).
76. Richard, *Apocalypse*, 27.
77. Richard, *Apocalypse*, 173.
78. A brief summary of how liberationist readings have affected Western scholarship may be found in John-Pierre Ruiz, "Taking a Stand on the Sand of the Seashore," in Barr, *Reading the Book of Revelation*, 119–35.
79. David A. Sánchez, *From Patmos to the Barrio: Subverting Imperial Myths* (Minneapolis: Fortress, 2008).
80. Sánchez, *From Patmos to the Barrio*, 116.
81. David Rhoads, ed., *From Every People and Nation: The Book of Revelation in Intercultural Perspective* (Minneapolis: Fortress, 2005).
82. Blount, *Can I Get a Witness?*
83. Blount, *Can I Get a Witness?*, 39.

on the character of the Lamb, along with the role of the believers, who take a stand of active nonviolence against social and cultural oppression. His reading presents Revelation's challenge against the violent means of empire, a challenge that ought to be heard by all believers.[84] Additionally, a recent publication by Michael Battle[85] provides a good introduction to Revelation that incorporates theological perspectives of African liberationist movements as well as American black culture, again emphasizing a message of nonviolent resistance. He challenges readings of Revelation that are divisive and exclusive, suggesting a more diverse and incorporated approach that can represent the church as a whole.[86]

Reading Revelation for the Church

History has shown that one of the greatest challenges for interpreting Revelation involves achieving a responsible reading within the context of the church. Although John's message was intended to unveil theological truths to the assemblies of believers, it now lies (ironically) hidden from the average reader. Part of this is due to the nature of apocalypse, which is certainly a unique way of communicating that is intricately linked to its own time and space. Bridging the gap between academic exegesis and ecclesiastical understanding is a considerable task when one is dealing with Revelation, but it is a necessary endeavor when one is working with Scripture. Although sensational books, films, and sermons continue to be produced,[87] in the past twenty years scholarship seeking to reclaim a more responsible reading of Revelation among the church has surged.

One of the best introductory texts on Revelation is provided by Koester,[88] who is able to draw from his extensive research as well as his long experience teaching the text to numerous church groups. He writes in an engaging manner, enabling the reader to recognize the significance of John's message not only for today but throughout the history of the church. Koester does not approach Revelation as a vague, timeless truth, but rather demonstrates

---

84. Blount lends his perspective to his full-length commentary, in which he also engages the historical and theological aspects of Revelation in greater detail: Brian K. Blount, *Revelation* (Louisville: Westminster John Knox, 2009).

85. Michael Battle, *Heaven on Earth: God's Call to Community in the Book of Revelation* (Louisville: Westminster John Knox, 2017).

86. Battle, *Heaven on Earth*, 27.

87. An excellent response to such sensationalism, though focused on the *Left Behind* series of novels, is found in Barbara R. Rossing, *The Rapture Exposed: The Message of Hope in the Book of Revelation* (New York: Basic Books, 2005).

88. Craig R. Koester, *Revelation and the End of All Things*, 2nd ed. (Grand Rapids: Eerdmans, 2018).

the analogy between ancient and contemporary contexts. A more thematic survey was produced by Michael Gorman,[89] whose reading is firmly set in the context of the mission of the church. He recognizes the social and cultural challenge of John's message, which acts as a manifesto against the civil religions of imperial Rome through the worship and public witness given to the Lamb.[90]

The modern church would do well also to hear the challenging perspective of Kraybill,[91] who explores the social and political dimensions of worship as seen through the message of Revelation. Kraybill does well to capture the radical nature of John's message as it summons believers to a life of devotion in a world that operates with opposing values. Craig Keener's lay-oriented commentary also brings out Revelation's stark challenge to faithfulness against the world as he places modern America under his interpretive lens.[92] And, for those who wish to make sense of the nature of apocalyptic literature in their reading of Revelation, Paul Rainbow provides a readable resource on navigating this strange visionary world.[93]

A more recent commentary was produced by J. S. Duvall with the specific aim of equipping those who teach and preach Revelation as part of the life of the church.[94] Although Duvall does include brief exegesis of the text, the unique benefits of his effort are in keeping the message centered on its key points and in pointing to modern examples to which Revelation is applicable. Similarly, one could turn to the accessible commentary offered by N. T. Wright,[95] whose unique gift of speaking to the church allows him to bridge the gap between ancient and modern worlds. While not intended to be a traditional commentary, his *Revelation for Everyone* allows for the apocalyptic text to find its home in the life of the modern church. And finally, I should mention the brief introduction published by deSilva,[96] which effortlessly brings the reader into the imperial context of the seven assemblies of Revelation. His approach raises the question of what it would mean for a believer to adhere to John's message when facing the context of empire.

---

89. Michael J. Gorman, *Reading Revelation Responsibly: Uncivil Worship and Witness: Following the Lamb into the New Creation* (Eugene, OR: Cascade, 2011).
90. Gorman, *Reading Revelation Responsibly*, 55.
91. J. Nelson Kraybill, *Apocalypse and Allegiance: Worship, Politics, and Devotion in the Book of Revelation* (Grand Rapids: Brazos, 2010).
92. Craig S. Keener, *Revelation* (Grand Rapids: Zondervan, 2000).
93. Paul A. Rainbow, *The Pith of the Apocalypse: Essential Message and Principles for Interpretation* (Eugene, OR: Wipf & Stock, 2008).
94. J. Scott Duvall, *Revelation*, TTC (Grand Rapids: Baker Books, 2014).
95. N. T. Wright, *Revelation for Everyone* (Louisville: Westminster John Knox, 2011).
96. David A. deSilva, *Unholy Allegiances: Heeding Revelation's Warning* (Peabody, MA: Hendrickson, 2013).

Reflections

Over the past century academic interpretation of Revelation has been moving away from a futuristic approach to more contextual readings. In the latter half of the twentieth century scholars sought to understand the nature and nuances of apocalyptic thought and literature, which culminated in the debates over defining the genre that flourished in 1979–89. While explorations into the nature of apocalyptic literature continue, the emphasis has become less on definition and more on the social setting, seeking the impact these texts would have had on their intended audiences. For the most part the debates over a formal definition have subsided, and most interpreters working with Revelation are content to accept the description first published by John Collins in 1979. Among modern interpreters the book of Revelation is mostly viewed as a mixed genre, borrowing from an identifiable style of writing without being constrained to a set form. Interpreters taking this approach are increasingly interested in exploring the social impact of the text, and especially examining its rhetorical and literary aspects. Recent readings of Revelation have thus been dominated by the question of historical context, with the field of study presently continuing along these lines.

Of particular interest for reading Revelation's historical context is exploring the role of Roman imperialism in the setting of the text. Much work has already been done in this direction, and it appears that this approach will continue to yield exegetical insight. Revelation scholarship has greatly benefited from incorporating data from the field of Roman history to reconstruct a social and cultural context for first-century Asia Minor, and this trend is more than likely to continue to shape hermeneutical approaches to the book. As Revelation's interpreters continue to seek out the ordinary lives of the first recipients, we can expect a greater understanding of the world that John's apocalypse challenges.

Apocalyptic literature has been noted for its tendency to contain anti-imperial rhetoric, and this reality has also given shape to interpreting Revelation. When considering the historical context of Roman rule, one cannot easily ignore such a political perspective. At the heart of Revelation are the theological issues of worship and faithfulness, which alone make this a politically charged message. What is more, the increasing discovery and exploration of the Greco-Roman mythologies that lie behind so many of the symbols and images of Revelation also point to the political nature of the book. As interpreters continue to pursue a contextual reading of Revelation, we will continue to unveil more of John's sharp prophetic voice as it calls the people of God to a certain allegiance to the Lamb.

Additionally, although Revelation received some intercultural readings, more must be done so that minority voices in the worldwide church may be heard. While the same could be said for most of the work in hermeneutics, it is especially vital for a text as socially challenging as the Apocalypse. Many cultural readings of Revelation are simply not being heard by the larger church or by many in the academy, both of which would certainly benefit from hearing them. Those who write from a majority culture that stands on its militaristic, economic, and political power—as well as a dominance of Christian religious tradition—may be able to understand Revelation in a technical sense but will inevitably struggle to hear John's call to faithfulness in the midst of suffering in the same way the early church heard it. John's call to follow the Lamb quickly becomes a rather large obstacle for those whose culture is saturated with external power as the path to victory. To hear Revelation more clearly and accurately, interpreters must take into account these minority voices that can echo the prophetic nature of the text without becoming lost in political positioning.

Finally, we should note that most of Revelation's recent readings no longer rely on the categorizing of interpretations into groups (futurism, preterism, historicism, idealism). Not only have these categories proven unhelpful in exegeting the text; modern interpretations have also demonstrated that Revelation is much more fluid and dynamic than such classifications allow. The Apocalypse may continue to challenge and mystify its readers regardless of their particular engagement with the text. This remains, as Kathleen Norris described it, a "poet's book" that summons us to see this world from another perspective.[97] As modern readers our task is to take this mystifying book and allow its message to enlighten.[98] Thus the need to explore Revelation from every conceivable angle remains a priority as research moves forward.

---

97. Kathleen Norris, introduction to *Revelation* (New York: Grove, 1999), ix.
98. Rowland, "Book of Revelation," 339.

Contributors

Matthew W. Bates is associate professor of theology at Quincy University.

Michael F. Bird is academic dean and lecturer in theology at Ridley College in Melbourne, Australia.

David B. Capes is senior research scholar at Lanier Theological Library in Houston, Texas. He previously taught at Wheaton College and Houston Baptist University.

Greg Carey is assistant professor of New Testament at Portland Seminary.

Jin Young Choi is associate professor of New Testament and Christian origins at Colgate Rochester Crozer Divinity School.

Lynn H. Cohick is provost/dean and professor of New Testament at Denver Seminary.

Toan Do is research fellow and lecturer in biblical and early Christian studies at Australian Catholic University.

Dennis R. Edwards is associate professor of New Testament at Northern Seminary.

Rebekah Eklund is associate professor of theology at Loyola University Maryland.

Michael J. Gorman is Raymond E. Brown Professor of Biblical Studies and Theology at St. Mary's Seminary and University.

Nijay K. Gupta is associate professor of New Testament at Portland Seminary.

Dana M. Harris is associate professor of New Testament at Trinity Evangelical Divinity School.

Joshua W. Jipp is associate professor of New Testament at Trinity Evangelical Divinity School.

Abson Joseph is academic dean and professor of New Testament at Wesley Seminary, Indiana Wesleyan University.

Mariam Kamell Kovalishyn is assistant professor of New Testament at Regent College in Vancouver, British Columbia.

Scot McKnight is professor of New Testament at Northern Seminary.

Patrick Mitchel is senior lecturer in theology at the Irish Bible Institute in Dublin.

David M. Moffitt is senior lecturer in New Testament studies at the University of St. Andrews in St. Andrews, Scotland.

Alicia D. Myers is associate professor of New Testament and Greek at Campbell University Divinity School.

Wes Olmstead is Henry Hildebrand Professor of Biblical Studies at Briercrest College and Seminary.

Rodney Reeves is Redford Professor of Biblical Studies and dean of the Courts at Redford College of Theology and Ministry, Southwest Baptist University.

Drew J. Strait is assistant professor of New Testament and Christian origins at Anabaptist Mennonite Biblical Seminary.

Michael C. Thompson has taught biblical studies for fifteen years at various colleges, most recently as adjunct professor at Huntington University and Bethel College (IN). He currently pastors a church in Bellevue, Nebraska.

Scripture and Ancient Writings Index

Old Testament

Genesis
1 383
12 370
12:3 94
15 370
15:5 94
15:6 94
22 281
27:27 136
47:31b 402

Exodus
14–15 25
19–20 94

Leviticus
17–18 353
18:5 94
19 414
19:12–18 141
19:18 414

Numbers
13–14 403

Deuteronomy
6 284
6:5 346
8 284
21:18–21 284
22:4 89
27:26 94
29 404
30–32 94
32 404

1 Kings
17–18 415–16

Job
1 415
9 177
9:11 177

Psalms
2:7 181
8 383
22 280, 320
31 320
38 320
40:6–8 181
40:7b 402
69 320
110 404
110:1 169, 404
110:4 404

Proverbs
8 176

Isaiah
11:10 194
40–66 170n23, 437
40:3 25
42:1–4 284
42:4 284
42:4a 284
45:23 172
53 320, 362
53:4 101

Jeremiah
31 399
31:31–33 404
31:33 402

Ezekiel
1 170n23
32–33 416
34 279
34–37 278, 279
37 281

Daniel
7 167
7:1–8 12
7:13 170, 237–38
7:13–14 278

Joel
2:32 172

479

Micah

2–5 278

Habakkuk

2:3–4 402
2:4 92, 93, 100

Zechariah

1–8 284
3 403
9–14 278, 284, 436
14:5 172

New Testament

Matthew

1:1 278
1:20–21 278
4:23 117, 118
5–7 413
5:21–48 277, 291
5:34–37 414
8–9 278
8:12 277
8:17 101
8:23–27 285
9:35 117, 118
10 279, 291
10:6 288
10:17–18 20
11–13 283
11:16–19 284
12:11–12 89
12:14 89
12:18–21 284
13:38 277
16:18 287
16:24–27 21
18:17 277
21:24 132
21:28–22:14 289
21:31 277
21:43 289
23 283, 284, 291
23:2–3 277
23:2–31 291
23:8–10 454
23:16 277
23:37 176
24 20, 237, 283
24:9 20
24:14 117, 118
25 237, 279
26:13 117
28:8–10 53
28:19 277
28:19–20 288, 291
28:20 284

Mark

1:1 113, 114, 117, 312
1:2 118
1:1–3 112
1:11 181
1:14–15 112
2:17 306
4:11–12 306
6–7 313
6:14–29 310
6:47–52 177
6:48 177
7:24–30 308, 312
8:34–38 21
8:35 306
9:1 226
9:2–8 181
10:45 241
12:17 26
12:40 26
13 20, 237–38
13:9–11 32
14:3–9 308
15:47 308
16:1–8 308

Luke

1–2 176
1:1–4 317, 359
1:32–35 321, 352
1:46–55 329
1:79 324
2:1 322, 324
2:1–2 328
2:11 324
2:20–23 353
2:30–35 352
2:30–55 321
3:1 322

3:1–2 328
3:12–14 328
3:14 29
4:5 328
4:5–6 318
4:6 328
4:16–30 321, 329, 352
6 413
7:1–10 326, 328
8 412
9:23–26 21
13 317
13:31–32 25
14:7–11 24
15:11–32 330
15:13–16 330
16:19–31 329
18:15–17 331
19 317
19:10 176
19:38 324
20:47 26
21 20, 237
21:1–4 332
21:12–19 20
22:25–26 325
23 359
23:1–12 25
23:47 326
24:13–35 359
24:9–12 53
24:25–27 98
24:44–47 98
24:44–49 352
24:50 324

John

1:1–18 174, 176
1:14 337
1:49 454
2:22 98
4:42 337, 347
5:24 231
5:39–47 346
7:14–52 340
8 342
9:22 21, 342, 447, 449
9:34 447, 449
10:30 346
12:16 98

12:42 21, 342
13:34–35 341
14:9–10 146
14:31 342
15:18–19 30
15:18–25 21
16:2 21, 342
18–19 347
20:18 53
20:31 339, 453
21:18–19 20
21:22–23 226

Acts

1–7 351
1:1–2 359
1:9–11 324
1:15–26 351
2:1–21 351
2:5–11 359
2:23 29
2:36 162
2:38 174
2:41–47 359
3–4 317
3–5 351
3:13 29
3:18–26 351
3:19–20 318
3:22–26 353
4:10 29
4:27–30 359
4:32–35 359
5:19–20 359
5:29–31 359
6:11–15 367
7:8 353
7:52 29
8 317
8:26–40 362
9:14 174
9:19–29 354
9:21 174
9:23–24 29
10:1–48 326
10:36–43 115
10:39 29
11:1–3 185
11:2 194
11:26 9

11:28 322
12:1–17 359
12:20–23 318
13:4–5 354
13:17–38 352
13:27–29 29
13:32–35 181
13:42–43 354
13:46 350
13:50 29
14 356
14:1 354
14:2–6 29
15 353
16 356, 363
16–24 29
16:1–5 354, 363
16:11–12 29
16:12–13 354
16:25–34 359
17 356, 357
17:5 29
17:6 29, 194, 356
17:7 29
17:16–34 359
17:22–31 357
17:28 189
18:2 21–22, 322
18:6 350
18:12–17 17, 29
18:17 324
19 29, 356
19:23–41 29
20 29
20:19 29
21:15–21 367
21:17–26 29
21:20–21 353
21:20–26 354
21:21 186
21:39 183
22:1–3 354
22:3 183, 189
23:1 354
23:5 354
23:12 29
23:27 324
24:1–27 17
24:14–15 354
24:17–24 354

24:19 29
24:26–27 324
25:1–12 17
25:13–26:32 17
25:25 324
26:4–5 354
26:6–7 354
26:6–8 352
26:11 29
26:22–23 352, 354
26:28 9
27:1–44 326, 360
28:1–10 359
28:16–31 352
28:17 29
28:20 354
28:25–29 29
28:26–28 350
29:32 29

Romans

1–4 202, 377, 387
1–8 383, 387
1–11 383
1:2–4 98
1:5 384
1:8 174
1:13–3:20 202
1:17 92, 100
1:18–32 183, 385, 387
2 385, 387
2:1 385
2:1–11 190
2:1–16 385
2:16 194
2:17–29 385
3 387
3:1–9 385
3:7–8 186
3:20 185
3:21 186
3:27–4:2 385
3:30 183
4 184, 387, 418
4:15 185
4:23–25 183
5–8 202, 377, 387
5:20 185
6:1–14 185
6:3–4 174

6:6 381
6:12 381
6:14 381
7 385
7:4 185
7:7–25 191
7:8 381
8 219
8:2 185
8:3–4 204
8:18–25 191
8:18 382
8:21 382
8:29 382
8:37 194
8:38 194
9–11 195, 355, 377, 387
9:1–11:10 387
9:3–4 183
9:4–5 167
9:6 183
9:24–26 183
10:5–13 380
10:9–13 174
10:9 380
10:13 172
11:11–36 387
11:13 384
12–15 387
12–16 377, 383, 387
12:1–15:13 377
12:9–21 191
12:14 20
12:14–18 194
13–15 13
13:1–2 13
13:1–7 10, 27, 28
13:1–17 193
13:11–14 194
14 186, 385
14–15 383, 388
14:11 172
14:14 186
14:23 386
15:4 183
15:7–12 167
15:12 194
15:15–16 384
16 383, 385
16:7 20

16:10–11 193
16:23 193

1 Corinthians

1:2 174
1:3 174
1:18–2:5 183
1:18–2:8 190
2:6–8 28
2:8 10, 194
4:6 183
4:12 20
5:1–13 183
6:9 183
6:16 183
7:1–2 183
8:1–10 185
8:1–13 13, 24
8:4–6 183
8:6 168
9:1–19 190
9:9 186
9:19–23 188
9:20 184
9:20–21 185
10:1–22 13
10:7 183
10:8 183
10:11 183
10:14 183
10:14–22 174
10:25–30 185
10:32 185
11:17–34 174
12:2 183, 185
12:4–11 174
15:1–5 183
15:3–5 98
15:3–8 178
15:9 20
15:20–28 167
15:24 194
15:33 189
15:52 226
15:56 185
16:22 174

2 Corinthians

2:14 194
2:17 190

3–4 278
4:9 20
5:21 204
6:5 20
6:14–15 183
6:16 183
10:5 190, 191–92
11:22 183
11:23 20
11:23–26 20
11:24–26 186
11:26 20
12:10 20
12:21 183

Galatians

1:12 189
1:13 20
1:13–16 184
1:23 20
2:1–21 183
2:11–14 185, 287
2:12 185
2:15 183
2:19 185
2:20 185
3 418
3–4 184
3:1 183
3:10 185
3:13 184, 204
3:16 167
3:19–20 185
3:28 184, 185, 188
4:8–9 185
4:14 178
5:1–13 183
5:11 20, 186
5:19 183
6:2 24, 258
6:10 194
6:12 20
6:12–13 183
6:16 183

Ephesians

4:1 194
4:28 194
5:18–20 174
6:12 194

Philippians

1:7 20, 194
1:13–17 20
1:18 194
2:6–11 174, 178
2:9–11 179
2:10–11 172
3:1–11 183
3:2–4:1 13
3:4–8 184
3:5 183
3:6 20
4:8 191
4:11 191
4:22 193

Colossians

1 219
1:10 194
1:15–20 174
2:8 190
2:15 194
3:11 184, 185
3:16–17 174

1 Thessalonians

1:9 183, 185
2:1–12 190
2:12 194
2:14–16 20, 195
3:3–4 186
3:4 20
3:7 20, 186
3:11–13 174
3:13 172
4:3 183
4:5 185
4:15 226
4:17 226
5:15 194

1 Timothy

in toto 30, 38, 48, 50
5:11–15 50n66
5:17 449n19
5:18 88n13

Titus

1:5 449n19

Philemon

1 20
9 20
23 20

Hebrews

1:1–4:16 392
1:1–5:10 393
1:2 395, 405
3–4 403
4:1 392
4:11–16 392
4:11–10:25 392–93
5:5 181
5:11–9:28 393
9:28 394
10:1–13:25 393
10:5–7 181
10:19–13:16 393
10:22–24 392
10:37–38 402
10:38 100
11:1–12:3 398
12:18–24 403
13:13 401

James

1:1 407–8, 416
1:2–12 415
1:9–11 421
1:13 415
1:14–15 419
1:14–21 419
1:17–18 423
1:18 419
1:21 412, 419
2 414
2:5 412, 421
2:14–26 418
2:15 423
3:3–12 423
4:1–10 421
4:13–17 423
5 414
5:1–6 421
5:7–9 423
5:7–19 415
5:10 416
5:11 414
5:12 414, 415
5:12–20 416
5:13–20 416

1 Peter

1:1 10, 30
1:1–2 436
1:1–2:11 432
1:3–12 431
1:10–12 436
2:10 30
2:11 10, 12
2:11–12 30
2:12 31
2:13–3:7 31
2:13–17 30
2:18–20 31
2:18–3:8 30
3:14–22 31
3:18–22 431
4:12 30
4:14–16 31
4:16 9, 31
5:13 30

2 Peter

1:3–15 433
1:16–2:10 432
3:1–13 432
3:1–15 433
3:15–16 197

1 John

1:1–4 458
2:1 452
2:7–14 458
2:18 447, 449
2:18–27 451, 458
2:18–28 454
2:19 451
2:19–21 448
2:22 447, 449, 453, 454
2:22–23 448
2:26 447, 449
3:23 448
4:1–6 451, 454
4:2 448, 452
4:9 448

4:15 448, 453
5:1 453
5:5 448, 453
5:6 452
5:6–12 451
5:10 448
5:20 448
5:21 452

2 John

1 458
7 452
7–8 447, 449, 454
7–9 451
7–10 458
9–10 449

3 John

1 458
5–6 448
9–10 449, 454, 458

Revelation

1:1 449
1:3 462
1:4 449
1:4–6 463
1:9 21, 449
1:9–16 174
1:11 463
2–3 464
2:13 21
2:14 24, 32, 185
2:20 24, 32, 185
3:4 32
6:9–11 21
13 16–17
13:1–2 13
13:4 14
13:8–18 32
17–18 10
18:4 32
18:11–13 15
18:11–17 32
22:7 462
22:10 462
22:18 462
22:19 462

Deuterocanonical Works

1 Maccabees

in toto 165

2 Maccabees

in toto 165

4 Maccabees

4:26 186

Judith

in toto 165

Sirach

24 170n23, 176

Tobit

1 178

Old Testament Pseudepigrapha

1 Enoch

37–70 170
42 176
85–90 279

Jubilees

22:16 186

Letter of Aristeas

139 186

Martyrdom and Ascension of Isaiah

in toto 21, 31–33
4:2–8 22n54
4:2–19 32

Psalms of Solomon

17–18 278, 279, 280

Sibylline Oracles

3:67–74 22n54
4:119–24 22n54
4:138–39 22n54
5:361–96 22n54

Dead Sea Scrolls and Related Texts

CD 51, 52
CD A 11.13–14 89
1QS 52
1QSa 51, 52
1QSa I 11 52
4Q159 52
4Q270 53

Other Ancient Sources

Apocalypse of Peter

in toto 21, 31–33
23 32
27–29 32

Aristides

Apology of Aristides

2.1 12
15 185

Clement of Alexandria

Miscellanies

6.5.41 12

Clement of Rome

Second Letter to the Corinthians

in toto 451n29

Dio Cassius

History of Rome

57.10 15

Gregory of Nyssa

The Life of Moses

in toto 98

Irenaeus of Lyons

Against Heresies
3.11.8 114n69

Josephus

Jewish War
2.184–203 17
4.317 178

Against Apion
2.174 186

Antiquities of the Jews
18.265 17

Justin Martyr

First Apology
67 109, 115n88, 451n29

Philo of Alexandria

Moses
in toto 106n19

Pliny

Epistles
10.96–97 22–23

Polycarp

Epistle to the Philippians
in toto 451n29

Q

in toto 143, 151–52, 276, 282–83, 291–92
6,20b 412

Quintilian

Institutio
2.4.2 112n57
10.2.21 105n15

Sallust

Historiae
4.69.5 15

Seneca

On Clemency
1.24.1 15

Shepherd of Hermas

in toto 21, 32
4.2 31
6.7 31
22.7 31

Tacitus

Agricola
in toto 106n20
30.4 15n21

Annales
1.72 326
15.44 22

Historiae
4.69.17 16
5.5.1 186
5.5.2 186

Tertullian

On Baptism
1.17 49n61

Titus Livius

The History of Rome
in toto 18

Valerius Maximus

Memorable Deeds and Sayings
8.3 35n1

Virgil

Aeneid
in toto 18

Author Index

Achemeier, Paul, 376
Adeyemo, Tokunboh, 441
Agosto, Efrain, 77
Ahn, Byung-Mu, 311
Aichele, George, 306
Akyol, Mustafa, 157
Aletti, Jean-Noël, 212, 418
Alkier, Stefan, 437
Allan, Rutger J., 133
Allen, David L., 391
Allen, David M., 391, 404
Allison, Dale C., Jr., 141, 145–46, 148–51, 153, 158, 243, 254, 408, 410–11, 416, 424
Anderson, Garwood, 213, 374
Anderson, Janice Capel, 310
Anderson, Paul N., 343
Ashton, John, 341–42, 346
Aslan, Reza, 156–57
Attridge, Harold, 111, 338
Aubrey, Rachel, 135–36
Aune, David, 117, 466
Aymer, Margaret, 420, 423–24
Ayoub, Mahmoud, 157

Bailey, Kenneth, 147
Baker, William, 419
Bakhtin, Mikhail, 111, 289–90
Bal, Mieke, 435–36, 437
Balch, David L., 427
Barbaglio, Giuseppe, 212
Barbour, Robin, 140–41
Barclay, John M. G., 188, 193, 202, 206, 211, 213, 218, 325, 368, 381, 382, 427

Barnard, Jody, 397
Barr, David, 467
Barram, Michael, 221
Barreto, Eric, 327–28, 363
Barth, Karl, 203, 229–30, 233, 368
Barton, Stephen, 257
Bates, Matthew, 180, 216–17
Batten, Alicia, 416
Battle, Michael, 472
Bauckham, Richard, 107n30, 150, 153, 168–70, 172, 179, 215, 233–34, 245–50, 252, 320, 344–45, 407, 411–12, 414, 423, 468
Bauman-Martin, Betsy, 429–30
Baur, F. C., 166
Baxter, Wayne, 279
Beale, Gregory K., 85, 466–67
Beasley-Murray, George R., 232
Beaton, Richard, 284
Beker, J. Christiaan, 202, 368, 383–84
Best, Ernest, 300
Billings, J. Todd, 68
Birch, Bruce C., 264
Bird, Jennifer G., 78–79, 430
Bird, Michael, 376
Blackwell, Ben, 205, 378
Blomberg, Craig, 421n92
Blount, Brian K., 71–72, 308, 330, 471–72
Boakye, Andrew, 214
Bock, Darrell, 146, 159
Boer, Martinus de, 202–3, 379–80
Bond, Helen, 151–52
Bonhoeffer, Dietrich, 257
Borg, Marcus, 228, 235–36

487

Boring, Eugene, 425, 435
Bornkamm, Günther, 232, 383
Bourdieu, Pierre, 38–39
Bousset, Whilhelm, 161, 164, 167
Bovon, Francois, 315–16, 320, 332
Bowens, Lisa, 218
Boyarin, Daniel, 167
Boyd, Gregory, 148–49, 159
Brand, Miryam T., 382
Brant, Jo-Ann, 338–39
Brink, Laurie, 326–27, 362
Brooten, Bernadette, 42, 59
Brown, Jeannine, 285–86
Brown, Raymond, 335, 342, 344, 446–47
Brown, Sherri, 341
Bruce, F. F., 322
Brunner, Emil, 229
Buch-Hansen, Gitte, 348
Buckwalter, Douglas, 319
Buell, Denise Kimber, 362
Bultmann, Rudolf, 104, 114, 139, 147, 164, 226, 228, 230–34, 255–56, 261–63, 272, 368
Burge, Gary, 417–19
Burkett, Delbert, 154
Burns, Joshua Ezra, 183n3
Burridge, Richard, 103–11, 114, 118, 264–66
Burroughs, Presian, 218
Butticaz, Simon David, 351–52, 355
Byron, Gay L., 73, 363
Byrskog, Samuel, 150

Cadbury, Henry, 257, 315–17, 322–23
Caird, G. B., 237
Calaway, Jared, 397
Callahan, Allen Dwight, 72
Callan, Terrance, 432–33
Callow, Kathleen, 130
Campbell, Barth, 431
Campbell, Constantine R., 123–24, 126–29, 132–33, 204
Campbell, Douglas, 202–4, 218, 368, 379, 387
Capes, David, 108–9, 153, 215
Cargal, Timothy, 418–19
Carroll R., M. Daniel, 76–78
Carson, D. A., 67–69, 85
Carter, Warren, 269, 290, 294, 347
Casey, Maurice, 175
Chae, Young S., 278–79
Chancey, Mark, 19
Chandler, Paul-Gordon, 155

Charles, Ronald, 188
Charlesworth, James, 158, 346
Chatman, Seymour, 303, 336, 437
Chester, Stephen, 199, 218
Chesterton, G. K., 459
Cheung, Luke, 418, 420
Chilton, Bruce, 407
Church, Philip, 398
Clark, Elizabeth A., 47
Collins, Adela Yarbro, 109–13, 117, 153, 464
Collins, John J., 153, 166, 460–61, 474
Colwell, E. C., 454
Compton, Jared, 404
Cone, James, 71
Conrad, Carl W., 133–34
Conway, Colleen, 347, 349, 361
Conzelmann, Hans, 320, 322
Cooper, Kate, 48–50, 60
Cosgrove, Charles E., 264
Cousland, J. R. C., 286
Cranfield, C. E. B., 368
Crellin, Robert, 127
Crenshaw, Kimberlé Williams, 57
Croasmun, Matthew, 381–82
Crossan, John Dominic, 11, 87, 150, 228, 243, 269
Crossley, James, 154
Crowder, Stephanie Buckhanon, 330–31
Crowe, Brandon, 180, 284
Cuéllar, Gregory Lee, 79–80
Cullmann, Oscar, 231–32, 446
Culpepper, R. Alan, 334–36, 340, 446

Daly, Mary, 41
Das, A. Andrew, 199, 201, 384
Davids, Peter H., 412, 421, 441
Davies, J. P., 203
Davies, W. D., 368
Deines, Roland, 421–22
Deissmann, Adolf, 203–4
Derrida, Jacques, 306
deSilva, David, 2, 414, 468, 473
Despotis, Anthanasios, 205
Dettwiler, Andreas, 343
Dewey, Joanna, 302–3
Dibelius, Martin, 255, 408, 416–17, 418, 419
Dicken, Frank, 318–19
Dinkler, Michal Beth, 317–18
Docherty, Susan, 402, 405–6
Dodd, Charles Harold, 231–32, 234, 237, 243, 258

Donfried, Karl P., 383–84
Doole, Andrew, 291
Douglas, Kelly Brown, 154
Douglas, Mary, 87
Douglass, Fredrick, 424
Dryden, J. de Wall, 434–35
Dube, Musa, 429
Dubis, Mark, 425–26
DuBois, W. E. B., 72
Dunn, James, 145, 149–51, 159, 175, 199–200, 212–13, 242–44, 249, 250, 368–71, 377–78, 383
Dunne, John Anthony, 205, 220
Duvall, J. S., 473
Dvořáček, Jiří, 280
Dyer, Bryan, 393

Easter, Matthew, 399
Eastman, Susan, 202, 382
Eco, Umberto, 100–101
Eddy, Paul Rhodes, 148–49, 159
Egan, Patrick T., 437
Ehrensperger, Kathy, 207
Ehrman, Bart, 148, 177–79, 243
Eisele, Wilfried, 394
Eisenbaum, Pamela, 208, 375
Elliott, John, 416–17, 425, 427, 430–31, 432, 442
Elliott, Neil, 202, 206, 208, 212, 374–75, 378
Ellis, Nicholas, 415
Emmrich, Martin, 400
Engberg-Pedersen, Troels, 190–91
Eskola, Timo, 241–42, 249–50
Esler, Philip F., 379
Evans, Craig, 141, 152, 325
Eve, Eric, 146

Fanning, Buist, 121–28
Farrer, Austin, 151
Fauconnier, Gilles, 433
Fee, Gordon, 172, 215–16
Felder, Cain Hope, 70, 71
Feldmier, Reinhard, 440
Filtvedt, Ole Jakob, 401
Fiorenza, Elisabeth Schüssler, 41, 54n83, 56–57, 60, 76, 308–9, 331–32, 449n20, 470
Fitzmyer, Joseph A., 376–77
Flessen, Bonnie J., 361–62
Fletcher-Louis, Crispin, 170, 175
Fornara, Charles William, 112
Fortna, Robert, 335

Foster, Paul, 290–91
Foster, Robert, 415–16
Foucault, Michel, 360
Foulkes, Irene, 441
Fowl, Stephen, 66, 67, 68
Fowler, Robert, 305
Franke, William, 116
Fredriksen, Paula, 208
Frey, Jörg, 226–27
Freyne, Seán, 156
Friesen, Steven, 465
Fuhrmann, Sebastian, 404
Fukuyama, Francis, 11
Funk, Robert, 87, 228
Furnish, Victor, 258–62, 264, 272

Gäbel, Georg, 396
Gabrielson, Jeremy, 219
Gager, John, 208
García-Alfonso, Cristina, 77, 78
Gaston, Lloyd, 29–30, 207, 383
Gathercole, Simon, 176, 198, 381
Gaventa, Beverly, 202–3, 207, 218, 368, 379–80
Gelardini, Gabriella, 392
Georgi, Dieter, 206
Gerhardsson, Birger, 147–48
Gheorghita, Radu, 402
Gieschen, Charles, 165
Gilbert, Gary, 324–25
González, Justo, 77, 331
Goodacre, Mark, 143, 151–52, 160
Goodrich, John, 378
Gordon, Milton M., 427
Gorman, Michael J., 64, 205, 264, 369–70, 373–74, 382, 473
Goulder, Michael, 151
Gowler, David, 424
Grant, R. M., 96n31
Gray, Patrick, 187, 393
Green, Bridgett, 331
Green, Gene L., 441
Green, H. Benedict, 276n6, 282–83
Green, Joel, 65, 68, 70, 264, 331, 434, 440
Greggs, Tom, 82
Greimas, Algirda J., 87, 437
Grieb, Katherine A., 201, 376, 384
Griffith, Terry, 452
Griffiths, Jonathan, 392
Grossman, Maxine, 52–53
Grottenberg, Samuel, 412

Gundry, Robert, 116, 286–87
Gunkel, Hermann, 146
Gushee, David, 264
Guthrie, George, 389, 416

Hahn, Horst, 450–51
Halbwachs, Maurice, 147
Hamilton, Catherine, 281–82
Hannan, Margaret, 287
Harris, Sarah, 321
Hartin, Patrick, 407–8, 419
Hays, Richard B., 66–67, 87–89, 95, 177, 200–201, 204–5, 249n128, 262–63, 278, 284, 355
Heil, John Paul, 393
Heim, Erin, 219
Hengel, Martin, 114–15, 117–18, 164–65
Henrichs-Tarsenkova, Nina, 320
Hermann, Markus-Liborius, 392
Hill, Wesley, 216
Himes, Paul A., 432
Hodge, Caroline Johnson, 354
Holloway, Paul, 428–29
Holmén, Tom, 144–45, 159
Hood, Jason, 280
Hooker, Morna, 140–41, 204
Hoppin, Ruth, 391
Horbury, William, 165–66
Horrell, David, 210, 218–19, 427–29, 442
Horsley, Richard A., 10–11, 27, 156, 206, 269, 307
Howe, Bonnie, 438–39
Hoyt, Thomas, Jr., 375
Huizenga, Leroy, 281
Hultgren, Arland J., 376
Humphrey, Edith, 205
Hurtado, Larry, 152–53, 161–62, 168, 170, 172–75, 179, 215–16, 268–69, 356n29
Hylen, Susan, 39, 50, 58–59, 340

Ilan, Tal, 43
Iverson, Kelly R., 299

Jackson, Glenna, 292–93
Jacob, Haley Goranson, 382–83
Jennings, Willie James, 72, 333, 363–64
Jensen, Matthew D., 452–54
Jeremias, Joachim, 232
Jervell, Jacob, 351, 354n21, 383
Jervis, Ann, 220
Jewett, Robert, 368, 376

Jipp, Joshua, 167, 204, 214–15, 320
Jobes, Karen, 440
Johnson, Andy, 217, 221
Johnson, Elizabeth, 384
Johnson, Luke Timothy, 359n45, 366, 414
Jonge, Marinus de, 449–50, 454
Joslin, Barry, 399
Junior, Nyasha, 74–75

Kahl, Brigitte, 29
Kamell Kovalishyn, Mariam, 421
Kärkkäinen, Veli-Matti, 155
Karris, R. J., 383
Käsemann, Ernst, 202, 256–57, 368
Keck, Leander E., 368, 376
Keener, Craig S., 143, 149, 159, 221, 376, 473
Keesmaat, Sylvia, 206, 384
Keith, Chris, 140, 142–43, 146
Kelber, Werner, 300
Kibbe, Michael, 403–4
Kierkegaard, Søren, 423
Kim, Lloyd, 399
Kim, Seong Hee, 313
Kim, Seyoon, 206
Kim, Yung Suk, 207
King, Karen, 55
Kinukawa, Hisako, 309–10
Kirk, Alan, 148
Kirk, J. R. Daniel, 179–80, 214
Klauck, Hans-Josef, 358–59
Klein, G., 383
Kloppenborg, John, 408, 412, 414
Koester, Craig R., 337, 459, 466, 472–73
Kok, Jacobus, 205
Konradt, Matthias, 288
Kotrosits, Maia, 12
Kraemer, Ross, 43–44, 45–48, 49n63, 58n105, 60
Kraybill, J. Nelson, 465, 473
Kristeva, Julia, 99–100
Kruse, Colin, 376
Kümmel, Werner Georg, 231–32
Kupp, David, 277
Kysar, Robert, 457–58

Ladd, George Eldon, 232, 236n49, 245, 463
Lampe, Peter, 377, 383
Lancaster, Sarah, 376
Langford, Justin, 437
Lapsley, Jacqueline, 264

Author Index

Larsen, Kasper Bro, 111, 339
Leach, Edmund R., 87
Le Donne, Anthony, 140, 142–43, 148–49
Lee, Dorothy, 337–38, 347
Leim, Joshua, 282
Leithart, Peter, 217
Lévi-Strauss, Claude, 87
Levine, Amy-Jill, 44–45, 470
Levinsohn, Stephen H., 128–29
Lewicki, Tomasz, 405
Lewis, Brian, 70
Licona, Michael, 141n6, 143
Liebengood, Kelly D., 436
Lieu, Judith, 444–46, 450, 455–56
Liew, Tat-siong Benny, 312
Lindsay, A. D., 254
Linebaugh, Jonathan, 381
Litwa, David, 205
Lockett, Darian, 411, 420
Loke, Andrew Ter Ern, 170–71
Longenecker, Bruce, 200–201, 219, 268
Longenecker, Richard, 368, 377
Lopez, Davina C., 20
Lord, Albert, 147
Lovelace, Vanessa, 73
Luz, Ulrich, 299
Lybæk, Lena, 283

Macaskill, Grant, 204
MacDonald, Dennis, 111
MacDonald, Margaret Y., 45, 60
Mack, Burton, 228, 304
Mackie, Scott, 395
Malbon, Elizabeth Struthers, 303–4
Mangina, Joseph, 468–69
Manson, T. W., 227, 383
Marcus, Joel, 110, 115, 117
Marguerat, Daniel, 212, 365
Marohl, Matthew, 398
Martin, Clarice J., 71
Martin, Dale, 58
Martin, Troy W., 430–31
Martyn, J. Louis, 202–3, 335, 342, 344, 368
Marxsen, Willi, 299–300
Mason, Eric, 396
Maston, Jason, 378
Matera, Frank, 213
Matthews, Shelly, 36n4, 49
Mattila, Talvikki, 286
Maynard-Reid, Pedrito, 421

Mazzaferri, Frederick, 463
Mbuvi, Andrew, 438–39
McCartney, Dan, 409
McCruden, Kevin, 394
McGrath, James, 168
McGuire, Ann, 54
McIver, Robert, 149
McKay, Kenneth L., 122n10, 125
McKelvey, R. J., 400
McKnight, Scot, 28n70, 118, 158–59, 222, 227n6, 409
McWhirter, Jocelyn, 321
Meeks, Wayne, 210, 253–54, 267–68, 446
Menken, Maarten, 283
Merz, Annette, 143
Metzger, Bruce, 413
Meyer, Ben, 144–45
Meyers, Eric, 19
Michaels, J. Ramsey, 433–34, 464
Michie, Donald, 303
Middleton, J. Richard, 244–45, 247, 250
Míguez, Nestor, 244–45
Miles, Rebekah, 264
Miller, Amanda, 328–29
Miller, James C., 429
Miller, Neva F., 133
Minear, Paul, 251, 385–86
Mitchell, Margaret M., 50n65, 410–11
Modica, Joseph B., 28n70
Moltmann, Jürgen, 233–36, 246, 249–50
Moo, Douglas, 198, 368, 376
Moore, Nicholas, 401
Moore, Stephen D., 80, 306, 348, 470
Morales, Nelson, 422
Morales, Rodrigo J., 384
Morgan, Christopher, 412–13, 419
Morrison, Michael, 399–400
Morrison, Toni, 72
Morton, Russell, 459
Moses, A. D. A., 278
Moulton, James Hope, 132–33
Mournet, Terence, 148
Moxnes, Halvor, 154
Moyise, Steve, 86
Muriithi, Sicily Mbura, 441
Murray, John, 254
Myers, Ched, 25n62, 307

Nanos, Mark, 208, 375
Nasrallah, Laura S., 363

Neirynck, Frans, 343
Neyrey, Jerome, 339
Niebuhr, Karl-Wilhelm, 413
Nienhuis, David, 409–10
Nikolakopoulos, Konstantinos, 205
Norris, Kathleen, 475
Novakovic, Lidija, 278
Novenson, Matthew, 166, 214
Nthamburi, Zablon, 156

Oakes, Peter, 210, 377–78
O'Keefe, John J., 96–99, 102
Okure, Teresa, 155–58
Oliver, Isaac, 353–55
Olmstead, Wesley, 288
Osborne, Grant, 467
Osiek, Carolyn, 45, 60
Ounsworth, Richard, 403

Pagels, Elaine, 53–54
Painter, John, 407, 447, 451–52, 454, 456n53
Pannenberg, Wolfhart, 233
Parry, Milman, 147
Parsenios, George, 338–39
Parsons, Mikeal, 317
Patte, Daniel, 87
Paul, Ian, 467
Paul, Pathipati Victor, 205
Peirce, Charles Sanders, 437
Peeler, Amy L. B., 400
Penna, Romano, 212
Penner, Todd, 361
Pennington, Jonathan, 118, 133–34, 254, 287
Perriman, Andrew, 250
Perrin, Norman, 227, 235–36, 300
Pettersen, Christina, 348
Pickett, Raymond, 322
Pinter, Dean, 325–26
Piotrowski, Nicholas, 285
Piper, John, 199
Pitre, Brant, 146, 240–41, 249
Pohl, Christine, 264
Porter, Stanley E., 68, 121–23, 126–27, 129n60, 159, 376
Poster, Carol, 417
Powell, Mark Allan, 329–30
Powery, Emerson B., 71
Price, S. R. F., 323, 325, 465
Propp, Vladimir, 87
Purdue, Leo, 416–17

Rabens, Volker, 216
Rainbow, Craig, 473
Räisänen, Heikki, 299
Rajkumar, Peniel Jesudason Rufus, 311–12
Rascher, Angela, 405
Reasone, Mark, 378
Reddish, Mitchell, 467
Reed, Jeffrey, 129–30
Reese, Ruth Anne, 437–38, 441
Reid, Barbara E., 56, 63, 75–76, 78
Reinhartz, Adele, 341, 344, 349, 457–58
Renan, Ernest, 154
Reno, R. R., 96–99, 102
Repschinski, Boris, 292
Resseguie, James, 337, 467
Reuschling, Wyndy Corbin, 264
Rhoads, David M., 302–3, 471
Ribbens, Benjamin, 397–98
Richard, Pablo, 156, 471
Richardson, Christopher, 398
Riches, John, 110, 304
Ripley, Jason, 347
Ritschl, Albrecht, 228
Robbins, Vernon K., 304, 431, 433
Robertson, A. T., 133
Rodriguez, Luiz Rivera, 77
Rodríguez, Rafael, 142
Rojas, Juan Manuel Granados, 219
Rosner, Brian, 263–65
Rossing, Barbara, 467–68
Rothschild, Clare, 391
Rowe, C. Kavin, 176–77, 191, 319–20, 356–59
Rowland, Christopher, 346
Royalty, Robert M., 33n81
Ruether, Rosemary Radford, 41, 42
Ruiz, Jean-Pierre, 77
Runesson, Anders, 289
Runge, Steven, 128–32
Rutledge, Fleming, 214

Said, Edward, 429
Sampley, J. Paul, 201, 218, 262
Samuel, Hermann, 157
Samuel, Simon, 312–13
Sánchez, David, 471
Sanders, E. P., 199, 203–4, 240, 243, 368–71, 381
Sanders, Jack T., 257
Sandmel, Samuel, 414
Sargent, Benjamin, 436–37
Saritoprak, Zeki, 156–57

Sassure, Ferdinand de, 87
Saxby, Alan, 408, 414
Schenck, Kenneth, 395
Schleiermacher, Friedrich, 154, 226
Schmid, Hansjörg, 455–57
Schmidt, Karl Ludwig, 104, 110
Schnackenburg, Rudolf, 260
Schnelle, Udo, 212
Scholtissek, Klaus, 343
Schrage, Wolfgang, 261–62
Schreiner, Patrick, 282
Schreiner, Thomas R., 199–200
Schröter, Jens, 142–43, 321–22, 352
Schuller, Eileen, 51–52
Schultz, Celia, 37, 39n11, 40, 46
Schutter, William, 436
Schweitzer, Albert, 104, 203–4, 220, 226, 227–29, 231–32, 234–35, 237, 240, 243, 255, 257
Scott, Charles A. A., 254
Scott, James C., 24n59, 312, 329, 427–28
Sechrest, Love, 219
Segovia, Fernando F., 76–78, 80, 297n1
Seim, Turid Karlsen, 332
Seland, Torrey, 426–27
Shauf, Scott, 365
Sheridan, Ruth, 341, 346
Shiner, Whitney T., 301
Siddiqui, Mona, 156
Sider, Ronald, 264
Sim, David, 290
Skinner, Christopher, 341
Skinner, Matthew, 366
Sleeman, Matthew, 365
Small, Brian, 400–401
Smith, George Adam, 154
Smith, Justin, 108
Smith, Shanell T., 33n81
Smith, Shively T. J., 438–39
Snyder, H. Gregory, 54–55
Snyder, Julia, 319
Son, Kiwoong, 403
Southgate, Christopher, 219
Stalker, James, 254n5
Stanley, Christopher, 207
Stanton, Graham, 275–76, 294
Stassen, Glen, 264
St. Clair, Raquel, 73, 74, 309–10
Stendahl, Krister, 199
Steyn, Gert, 402
Stichele, Caroline Vander, 361

Still, David, 201
Still, Todd, 380
Stowers, Stanley, 208, 385
Strauss, David Friedrich, 154
Streett, Daniel R., 451–52, 458
Strickland, Michael, 302
Stuckenbruck, Loren, 141
Stuhlmacher, Peter, 368, 376, 384
Sugirtharajah, Rasiah S., 79–80, 154, 347
Svendsen, Stefan, 395
Swartley, Willard, 264
Sylva, Dennis D., 432–33

Tamez, Elsa, 311, 420, 421
Tannehill, Robert, 317
Taussig, Hal, 55
Taylor, Bernard A., 133
Taylor, Mark, 416
Thatcher, Tom, 343
Theissen, Gerd, 143, 154
Theophilos, Michael, 283–84
Thiessen, Matthew, 208, 353–54
Thiselton, Anthony C., 69–70
Thompson, James, 221
Thompson, Leonard, 464–65
Thorsteinsson, Runar, 385
Thurén, Lauri, 417, 418, 431
Tilling, Chris, 172–73, 179, 215–16
Tolbert, Mary Ann, 303–4
Treier, Daniel J., 68
Trible, Phyllis, 36, 41
Troeltsch, Ernst, 249
Tucker, Brian, 218–19
Turner, Mark, 433

van der Watt, Jan G., 337, 340–41
van der Westhuizen, J., 418
Vanhoozer, Kevin J., 65–66, 204
Venter, Rian, 224n1, 250
Verhey, Allen, 260–61, 264
Vermes, Geza, 141–42
Via, Dan O., 87, 265
Vines, Michael, 111
Von Wahlde, Urban C., 344, 448–49

Waetjen, Herman C., 307
Wagner, J. Ross, 380–81
Wainwright, Elaine, 293
Walker, Alice, 73–74
Wall, Robert, 410

Wallace, Daniel B., 131
Wallace, James Buchanan, 205
Walser, Georg, 402, 405–6
Walton, Steve, 323–24, 332
Wassen, Cecilia, 52
Watson, David F., 299
Watson, Duane, 417, 432
Watson, Francis, 90, 92–96, 99, 113–14, 117, 210–11, 375, 378–79
Webb, Robert, 159, 425, 431–32
Webb, William, 266
Wedderburn, A. J. M., 386
Weeden, Theodore J., 300
Weiss, Johannes, 228–29, 231–32, 234–35, 240, 243
Wendel, Susan, 352–53
Weren, Wim, 291–92
Westerholm, Stephen, 198, 202
Westfall, Cynthia Long, 219, 392
Whitfield, Bryan, 403
Whitlark, Jason, 393–94
Wiefel, W., 383
Wilkinson, Kate, 59
Williams, Catrin, 346
Williams, Travis B., 428–29
Willitts, Joel, 279
Wills, Lawrence, 110–11
Wilson, Alistair, 281
Wilson, Brittany, 332, 362
Wilson, W. T., 434
Wimbush, Vincent L., 71–72
Winn, Adam, 299
Wisdom, Matthew, 293–94
Witherington, Ben, III, 86, 200
Wolter, Michael, 205, 212–13
Woodley, Randy S., 79
Wrede, William, 227, 235, 298–99
Wright, N. T., 11, 90–92, 95–96, 99, 154, 169–71, 199–201, 203, 206, 209–10, 214, 227–28, 236–45, 247, 249–50, 266, 269, 368, 371, 376–77, 473
Wu, Siu Fung, 220

Yamazaki-Ransom, Kazuhiko, 326
Yoder, John Howard, 269
Yoder, Joshua, 327
Young, David, 302
Young, Frances M., 96–99, 102

Zacharias, Daniel, 280
Zerbe, Gordon, 206
Zetterholm, Magnus, 208
Ziegler, Philip, 202–3, 218, 251
Zimmerman, Ruben, 265, 337, 340–41
Zumstein, Jean, 343, 450

Select Subject Index

Adam, 163, 180, 370, 373, 379, 380, 382, 383

bios, 103–18, 286n46

characterization, 107, 285–86, 302–4, 317–19
Christology
   divine, 152–54, 171–73, 214–16
   of Luke, 319–22
   of Matthew, 277–82
   Pauline, 214–16
church, 13, 42, 267, 288, 372, 374
   in Acts, 21, 29, 351, 359
   early church, 108, 113, 140, 142, 145, 186, 187, 194, 322, 408, 409, 410, 411, 416, 463
   in 1 Peter, 347, 443
   in Matthew, 293
   modern church, 69, 71, 73, 158, 160, 250, 308, 366, 472–74
   Pauline churches, 27, 172, 179, 193, 210, 375, 377–78, 383, 385, 386
   and women, 45, 60
context, historical, 3–4

deponency, Greek, 132–36
diaspora, 30, 186, 189, 439
discipleship, 260, 285–90, 309
discourse analysis, 124, 129–32, 136, 348, 392

empire studies, 3, 9–34
eschatology, 224–52, 372–73, 395, 397, 406, 418, 436
   and ethics, 261–63
   in 1 Peter, 436

   in Mark, 113, 300
   in Paul, 188, 209
   Roman, 88
ethics, 218–20

faith/faithfulness in Hebrews, 398–99
First Jewish Revolt, 16–18, 34

gender, 36–37, 44–50, 55–58, 74–76, 219, 290–93, 309–10, 330–32, 360–62
grace, 257, 370, 373, 380–82, 423

habitus, 38–39, 58n105, 211
hermeneutics
   liberation, 310–12
   missional, 221–22, 266–67
   reader-response, 69–70, 305–6
historical monograph, Gospels as, 111–13
holiness, 52, 209, 263, 382, 387, 401
Holy Spirit, 68, 91, 188, 216–17, 242, 263, 272, 362, 374, 443

identity, divine, 168–71
imperial-critical readings / anti-imperial readings, 322–29, 347–448, 429–30
interpretation
   African American biblical, 70–73, 330–31, 471–72
   canonical, 294, 409–10
   feminist, 293–94, 309–10, 430, 469–70
   historical-critical, 298–302, 331–32
   Latinx biblical, 76–78, 331
   political, 470–71, 473

postcolonial biblical, 78–80, 312–14, 443
postmodern biblical, 63–66, 69–70, 81–82
social-scientific, 295, 432
sociological, 307–9, 426–29
womanist and feminist biblical, 73–76
intertextuality, 99–101, 282–85, 401–2, 437–38
Israel
ancient Israel, 12
and God, 172–77, 179, 209
mission of, 90–92, 279–81, 288–89
story of, 94–95, 112, 117–19, 169–70, 186–87, 209, 237, 239, 241, 284, 321, 350–53, 354–55, 371–72, 380–81, 398, 403, 404, 436

Jesus tradition, 146–48, 243, 283, 411–14
Johannine community, 446–50
Judaism, 350–55
justification, 24, 198, 199, 200, 201, 202, 205, 207, 217–18

kingdom of God, 141, 226, 228, 230, 231–32, 235, 255, 260–61

literary criticism, 302–5, 316, 430–31, 467–68
love, 180, 218, 262, 271, 340, 341, 364, 380
Christian, 191, 261, 362, 374, 422
God's, 211, 214, 260, 393

masculinity, 57, 332, 347, 360–64
memory, social, 146–49
messianic secret, 298–99
messianism, Jewish, 165–67
metaphor, 438–39
monotheism, Jewish, 153, 162, 168, 173–76, 209

narrative criticism / narratological readings, 302–5, 335–41, 433–37

Paul, 27–28, 183–89, 189–92
apocalyptic perspective on, 201–3, 372–73, 380
in Judaism, 208–9, 375

new perspective on, 199–200, 369–72
old perspective on, 198–99
participationist perspective on, 203–5, 373–74
political perspectives on, 206–8
social-science perspective on, 210–11
Pompeii, 3, 377–78

reader-response criticism, 69–70, 305–6, 310, 319
reception history, 4–5
rhetorical analysis, 4, 302, 416–19
Roman Empire, 9–34
Romans, the
persecution by, 21–23
propaganda, 18–20, 193, 269, 307, 324

Satan, 304, 318, 328
sin, 381–82
slavery, 15, 71–72, 81, 242, 262, 373
social identity theory, 379–80
Synoptic Gospels, 10, 25–27, 148–51, 176, 179, 228, 294, 343

testimony, eyewitness, 149–51
theological interpretation of Scripture, 4, 67–69, 468–69
theology of God, 364–66, 420

verbal aspect, Greek, 120–29

wealth and poverty, 421
wisdom
divine, 10, 56, 162, 165, 168, 170, 176
human, 265, 412, 414, 418, 431
Jesus as, 281, 293
Scripture and, 186, 301, 416
women, 78, 312, 313, 360–61, 430, 470
ancient, 35–60, 272
Jewish, 43–44
in Scripture, 286, 290–94, 303, 308–10, 360–61, 469–70